Programming
with Microsoft.
Visual Basic. 2.0/3.0
for Windows™

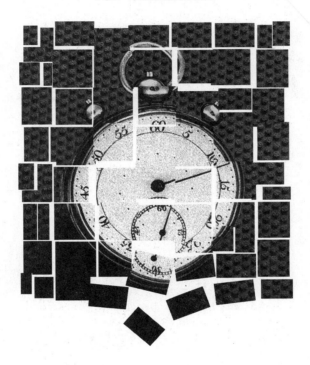

diane zak

college of dupage

Course
TECHNOLOGY

Course Technology, Inc. One Main Street, Cambridge, MA 02142

An International Thomson Publishing Company

Albany • Bonn • Boston • Cincinnati • London • Madrid • Melbourne • Mexico City
New York • Paris • San Francisco • Singapore • Tokyo • Toronto • Washington

Programming with Microsoft Visual Basic 2.0/3.0 for Windows is published by Course Technology, Inc.

Managing Editor	Mac Mendelsohn
Product Manager	Kim T. M. Crowley
Production Editor	Catherine Griffin
Text Designer	Kim Munsell
Cover Designer	John Gamache

© 1995 Course Technology, Inc.
A Division of International Thompson Publishing, Inc.

For more information contact:
Course Technology, Inc.
One Main Street
Cambridge, MA 02142

International Thompson Publishing Europe
Berkshire House 168-173
High Holborn
London WCIV 7AA
England

International Thompson Publishing GmbH
Konigswinterer Strasse 418
53227 Bonn
Germany

Thomas Nelson Australia
102 Dodds Street
South Melbourne, 3205
Victoria, Australia

International Thompson Publishing Asia
211 Henderson Road
#05-10 Henderson Building
Singapore 0315

Nelson Canada
1120 Birchmount Road
Scarborough, Ontario
Canada M1K 5G4

International Thompson Publishing Japan
Hirakawacho Kyowa Building, 3F
2-2-1 Hirakawacho
Chiyoda-ku, Tokyo 102
Japan

International Thompson Editores
Campos Eliseos 385, Piso 7
Col. Polsnvo
11560 Mexico D.F. Mexico

Trademarks
Course Technology and the open book logo are registered trademarks of Course Technology, Inc.

I(T)P The ITP logo is a trademark under license.

Microsoft and Visual Basic are registered trademarks of Microsoft Corporation and Windows is a trademark of Microsoft Corporation.

Some of the product names and company names used in this book have been used for identification purposes only, and may be trademarks or registered trademarks of their respective manufacturers and sellers.

Disclaimer
Course Technology, Inc. reserves the right to revise this publication and make changes from time to time in its content without notice.

ISBN 1-56527-284-6
Printed in the United States of America
10 9 8 7 6 5 4 3 2 1

Preface

Programming with Microsoft Visual Basic 2.0/3.0 for Windows is designed for a beginning programming course. This book uses Visual Basic, an object-oriented/event-driven language, to teach programming concepts. This book capitalizes on the energy and enthusiasm students naturally have for Windows-based applications and clearly teaches students how to take full advantage of Visual Basic's power. It assumes students have learned basic Windows skills and file management from *An Introduction to Microsoft Windows 3.1* or *A Guide to Microsoft Windows 3.1* by June Jamrich Parsons or from *an equivalent book.*

Organization and Coverage

Programming with Microsoft Visual Basic 2.0/3.0 for Windows contains an Overview, and ten tutorials that present hands-on instruction. In these tutorials students with no previous programming experience learn how to plan and create their own interactive Windows applications. Using this book, students will be able to do more advanced tasks sooner than they would using other introductory texts; a perusal of the table of contents affirms this. By the end of the book, students will have learned how to write If...Then...Else, Select Case, Do...While, Do...Until, and For...Next statements, as well as how to create and manipulate sequential access files, random access files, and arrays. Students will also learn how to create executable files and how to include multiple forms in a project.

Approach

Programming with Microsoft Visual Basic 2.0/3.0 for Windows distinguishes itself from other Windows textbooks because of its unique two-pronged approach. First, it motivates students by demonstrating why they need to learn the concepts and skills. This book teaches programming concepts using a task-driven, rather than a command-driven, approach. By working through the tutorials—which are each motivated by a realistic case—students learn how to use programming applications they are likely to encounter in the workplace. This is much more effective than memorizing a list of commands out of context. Second, the content, organization, and pedagogy of this book exploit the Windows environment. The material presented in the tutorials capitalizes on Visual Basic's power to perform complex programming tasks earlier and more easily than was possible under DOS.

Features

Programming with Microsoft Visual Basic 2.0/3.0 for Windows is an exceptional textbook also because it includes the following features:

- **"Read This Before You Begin" Page** This page is consistent with Course Technology's unequaled commitment to helping instructors introduce technology into the classroom. Technical considerations and assumptions about hardware, software, and default settings are listed in one place to help instructors save time and eliminate unnecessary aggravation.

- **Tutorial Cases** Each tutorial begins with a programming-related problem that students could reasonably expect to encounter in business, followed by a demonstration of an application that could be used to solve the problem. Showing the students the completed application before they learn how to create it is motivational and instructionally sound. By allowing the students to see the type of application they will be able to create after completing the tutorial, the student will be more motivated to learn because he or she can see how the programming concepts that they are about to learn can be used and, therefore, why the concepts are important to learn.

- **Lessons** Each tutorial is divided into three lessons—A, B, and C. Lesson A introduces the programming concepts that will be used in the completed application. In Lessons B and C, the student creates the application required to solve the problem specified in the Tutorial Case.

- **Step-by-Step Methodology** The unique Course Technology, Inc. methodology keeps students on track. They click or press keys always within the context of solving the problem posed in the Tutorial Case. The text constantly guides students, letting them know where they are in the process of solving the problem. The numerous illustrations include labels that direct students' attention to what they should look at on the screen.

- **TIPS** TIPS paragraphs anticipate the problems students are likely to encounter and helps them resolve these problems on their own. This feature facilitates independent learning and frees the instructor to focus on substantive conceptual issues rather than on common procedural errors.

- **Summaries** Following each lesson is a Summary, which recaps the programming concepts, commands, and controls covered in the lesson.

- **Questions and Exercises** Each lesson concludes with meaningful, conceptual Questions that test students' understanding of what they learned in the lesson. The Questions are followed by Exercises, which provide students with additional practice of the skills and concepts they learned in the lesson.

- **Discovery Exercises** Unlike DOS, the Windows environment allows students to learn by exploring and discovering what they can do. The Discovery Exercises are designated by the word "Discovery" in the margin. They encourage students to challenge and independently develop their own programming skills while exploring the capabilities of Visual Basic.

- **Debugging Techniques and Exercises** One of the most important programming skills a student can learn is the ability to correct problems in an existing application. The Debugging Techniques and Exercises at the end of each tutorial introduce various bug-detecting techniques and then provide an opportunity for students to apply the techniques to detect and correct errors in an existing application.

- **Glossary** A glossary of key programming terminology is included at the end of the book for easy reference.

Microsoft® Visual Basic® Programming System for Windows™

Microsoft® Visual Basic® Programming System for Windows™ is a Primer version of the software which is bundled free with each copy of this text. This programming system has all the functionality of the commercial version of Visual Basic excluding the MAKE.EXE capability (compiler), On-line Help, print capabilities, and the VB Icon Library. This version also has a one-form limit. The inclusion of this Primer allows students to take their learning home with them and further explore programming concepts and Visual Basic. However, to actually run and print their programs, students will need access to a computer with the full commercial version of Visual Basic 2.0/3.0 for Windows.

The CTI WinApps Setup Disk

The CTI WinApps Setup Disk, bundled with the Instructor's copy of this book, contains an innovative Student Disk generating program that is designed to save instructors time. Once this software is installed on a network, or a stand-alone workstation, students can double-click the "Make VisualBasic Programing Student Disk" icon in the CTI WinApps icon group. Double-clicking this icon transfers all the data files students need to complete the tutorials and exercises to a high-density disk in drive A or B. These files free students from tedious keystroking and allow them to concentrate on mastering the concept or task at hand. The overview provides complete step-by-step instructions for making the Student Disk.

Adopters of the text are granted the right to install the CTI WinApps icon group on any standalone computer or network used by students who have purchased this text.

For more information on the CTI WinApps Setup Disk, see the page in this book called "Read This Before You Begin."

The Supplements

- **Instructor's Manual** The Instructor's Manual is written by the author and is quality assurance tested. It includes:
  - Answers and solutions to all of the questions and exercises. Suggested solutions are also included for the Discovery Exercises.
  - A 3.5 inch disk containing solutions to all of the questions and exercises.
  - Tutorial Notes, which contain background information from the author about the Tutorial Case and the instructional progression of the tutorial.
  - Technical Notes, which include troubleshooting tips as well as information on how to customize the students' screens to closely emulate the screen shots in the book.
- **Microsoft® Visual Basic® 2.0 for Windows™ Working Model** This version of Visual Basic includes the On-line Help, the MAKE.EXE file (compiler), VB Icon Library, VBRUN200.DLL, and print features not available in the Microsoft® Visual Basic® Programming System for Windows™ Primer version which students receive free with the text. Adopters of the text are granted the rights to provide the Working Model to those students who are using the Primer to complete the tutorials and exercises in this text.
- **Test Bank** The Test Bank contains 50 questions per tutorial in true/false, multiple choice, and fill-in-the-blank formats, plus two essay questions. Each question has been quality assurance tested by students to achieve clarity and accuracy.
- **Electronic Test Bank** The Electronic Test Bank allows instructors to edit individual test questions, select questions individually or at random, and print out scrambled versions of the same test to any supported printer.

Acknowledgments

I would like to thank all of the people who helped make this book a reality, especially Ann Shaffer, my Development Editor, and Kim Crowley, Product Manager. You have been so kind, patient, understanding, helpful, and fun. I know I couldn't have made it without both of you.

Thanks also to Mac Mendelsohn, Managing Editor; Catherine Griffin, Production Editor; and the Quality Assurance testers—Scotty Powell, James Valente, Lyle Korytkowski, and Mikelle Eastley—managed by Jeff Goding. I am grateful to the many reviewers who provided invaluable comments on the manuscript, in particular: Jon E. Juarez, Dona Ana Branch Community College; Ronald Burgher, Metropolitan Community College; Mary Amundson-Miller, Greenville Technical College; and Dave Cooper of New River Community College, who was particularly helpful in revising Tutorial 7.

Finally, I would like to dedicate this book to my father, Henry.

Diane Zak

Contents

t u t o r i a l   2

DESIGNING APPLICATIONS *VB 69*

Creating an Order Screen

t u t o r i a l 3

STORING DATA IN VARIABLES *VB 128*

The Dots & Stripes Applications

t u t o r i a l   8

VARIABLE ARRAYS *VB 473*

The Personal Directory Application

Read This Before You Begin

To the Student

To use this book, you must have a Student Disk. Your instructor will either provide you with one or ask you to make your own by following the instructions in the section "Your Student Disk" in the Overview. See your instructor or technical person for further information. If you are going to work through this book using your own computer, you need a computer system running Microsoft Windows 3.1, Visual Basic (either Version 2.0 or 3.0), and a Student Disk. *You will not be able to complete the tutorials and exercises in this book using your own computer until you have a Student Disk.*

Microsoft® Visual Basic® Programming System for Windows™ is a Primer version of the software which is bundled free with each copy of this text. This programming system has all the functionality of the commercial version of Visual Basic excluding the MAKE.EXE capability (compiler), On-line Help, the VB Icon Library, and print capabilities. It also has a one-form limit. The system requirements for this Primer are as follows:

- Personal computer running Microsoft Windows 3.0 or later
- 2 MB of available memory
- One high-density disk drive and a hard disk with 1.2 MB available
- A mouse

To the Instructor

Making the Student Disk To complete the tutorials in this book, your students must have a copy of the Student Disk. To relieve you of having to make multiple Student Disks from a single master copy, we provide you with the CTI WinApps Setup Disk, which contains an automatic Student Disk generating program. Once you install the Setup Disk on a network or standalone workstation, students can easily make their own Student Disks by double-clicking the "Make VisualBasic Programing Student Disk" icon in the CTI WinApps group icon. Double-clicking this icon transfers all data files students will need to complete the tutorials and exercises to a high-density disk in drive A or B. If some of your students will use their own computers to complete the tutorials and exercises in this book, they must first obtain the Student Disk. The section called "Your Student Disk" in the Overview provides complete instructions on how to make the Student Disk.

Installing the CTI WinApps Setup Disk To install the CTI WinApps group icon from the Setup Disk, follow the instructions on the Setup Disk disk label and on the README file on the setup disk. By adopting this book, you are granted a license to install this software on any computer or computer network used by you or your students.

README File A README.TXT file located on the Setup Disk provides additional technical notes, troubleshooting advice, and tips for using the CTI WinApps software in your school's computer lab. You can view the README file using any word processor you choose.

System Requirements The minimum software and hardware requirements are as follows:
- Microsoft Windows Version 3.1 on a local hard drive or on a network drive
- A 286 (or higher) processor with a minimum of 2 MB RAM (4 MB RAM or more strongly recommended.)
- A mouse supported by Windows
- A printer that is supported by Windows 3.1
- A VGA 640 x 480 16-color display is recommended; an 800 x 600 or 1024 x 768 SVGA, VGA monochrome, or EGA display is also acceptable
- 1.5 MB of free hard disk space
- Student Workstations with at least 1 high-density disk drive
- If you wish to install the CTI WinApps Setup Disk on a network drive, your network must support Microsoft Windows.
- This book assumes Visual Basic is installed in the VB directory either on the workstation hard drive or on the network.

Microsoft® Visual Basic® 2.0 for Windows™ Working Model This version of Visual Basic is contained in the Instructor's Resource kit and includes the VB Icon Library, On-line Help, and the VBRUN200.DLL file not available in the Microsoft® Visual Basic® Programming System for Windows™ Primer version which students receive free with the text. Adopters of the text are granted the rights to provide the Working Model to those students who are using the Primer to complete the tutorials and exercises in this text. The system requirements for the Working Model are as follows:
- Personal computer running Microsoft Windows 3.0 or later
- 2 MB of available memory
- One high-density disk drive and a hard disk with 1.2 MB available
- A mouse

OVERVIEW
objectives

This overview contains basic definitions and background information, including:

- A brief description of Visual Basic
- A brief history of programming languages
- Your Student Disk
- A Visual Basic demonstration
- Using the tutorials effectively

An Overview of Visual Basic:

A History and a Demonstration

A Brief Description of Visual Basic

Although computers appear to be amazingly intelligent machines, they cannot yet think on their own. Computers still rely on human beings to give them directions. These directions are called programs, and the people who write the programs are called programmers.

Just as human beings communicate with each other through the use of languages such as English, Spanish, Hindi, or Chinese, programmers use a variety of special languages, called **programming languages**, to communicate with the computer. Some popular programming languages are COBOL (Common Business Oriented Language), Pascal, C, BASIC (Beginner's All-Purpose Symbolic Instruction Code), and Visual Basic. As its name implies, Visual Basic is more visually oriented than the other programming languages. In fact, you might think of Visual Basic as a sort of sign language. Visual Basic represents a new way to write computer programs.

A Brief History of Programming Languages

It is difficult to appreciate the Visual Basic language, and to understand its impact on the future of programming, without looking back at the programming languages that preceded it. Let's take a quick look at the forerunners to Visual Basic.

Machine Languages

Within a computer, all data is represented by microscopic electronic switches that can be either off or on. The off switch is designated by a 0, and the on switch is designated by a 1. Because computers can understand only these on and off switches, the first programmers had to write the program instructions using nothing but combinations of 0s and 1s. Instructions written in 0s and 1s are called **machine language** or **machine code**. The machine languages (each type of machine has its own language) represent the only way to communicate directly with the computer. Figure 1 shows a program written in a machine language.

```
0100
001101   100000   001101   110001
00101    10001    10000
01110
111001
111001   001   11000   001
11000
0011100
100010   00110
```

Figure 1: Machine language

As you can imagine, programming in machine language is very tedious and error-prone; it also requires highly trained programmers.

Assembly Languages

Slightly more advanced programming languages are called assembly languages. Figure 2 shows a program written in an assembly language.

The **assembly languages** simplify the programmer's job by allowing the programmer to use mnemonics in place of the 0s and 1s in the program. **Mnemonics** are memory aids—in this case, alphabetic abbreviations for instructions. For example, most assembly languages use the mnemonic ADD to represent an add operation, and the mnemonic MUL to represent a multiply operation. Programs written in an assembly language require an **assembler**, which is also a program, to convert the assembly instructions into machine code—the 0s and 1s the computer can understand. Although it is much easier to write programs in assembly language than in machine language, programming in assembly language still is tedious and requires highly trained individuals.

```
main proc pay
      mov ax, dseg
      mov ax, 0b00h
      add ax, dx
      mov al, bl
      mul bl, ax
      mov bl, 04h
```

Figure 2: Assembly language

High-Level Languages

High-level languages, which allow the programmer to use instructions that more closely resemble the English language, represent the next advance in programming languages. High-level languages require either an interpreter or a compiler to convert the English-like instructions into the 0s and 1s the computer can understand. Like assemblers, both interpreters and compilers are separate programs. An **interpreter** translates the high-level instructions into machine code, line by line as the program is running; a **compiler** translates the entire program into machine code before running the program. Like their predecessors, most high-level languages are procedure-oriented.

Procedure-Oriented High-Level Languages

In **procedure-oriented languages,** the emphasis of a program is on *how* to accomplish a task. The programmer must instruct the computer every step of the way, from the start of the task to its completion. The programmer determines and controls the order in which the computer should process the instructions. COBOL, BASIC, Pascal, and C are popular procedure-oriented languages.

Figure 3 shows a partial program written in BASIC. Notice how closely the instructions resemble the English language. Even if you do not know the BASIC language, it is easy to see that the program shown in Figure 3 tells the computer, step by step, *how* to compute and print an employee's net pay.

```
input "Enter Name";names$
input "Enter Hours";hours
input "Enter Rate";rate
gross = hours * rate
fwt = .2 * gross
socsec = .07 * gross
state = .06 * gross
net = gross - fwt - socsec - state
print names$, net
end
```

Figure 3: BASIC language—high-level, procedure-oriented

In all procedure-oriented programs, the order of the instructions is extremely important. For example, in the program shown in Figure 3, you could not put the instruction to print the net pay before the instruction to calculate the net pay and expect the computer to print the correct results. When writing programs in a procedure-oriented language, the programmer must determine not only the proper instructions to give the computer, but the correct sequence of those instructions as well.

Procedure-oriented high-level languages are a vast improvement over machine languages and assembly languages. Many of the high-level languages do not require a great amount of technical expertise; you do not need to be a professional programmer to write a program using these languages.

The Introduction of Windows

As you know, the Windows software provides an easy-to-use graphical interface, referred to as a **GUI**, with which a user can interact. This graphical interface is common to all applications written for the Windows environment. It is this standard interface that makes Windows applications so popular: once you learn one Windows application, it is very easy to learn another.

Although the standard interface found in all Windows applications makes the user's life much easier, it complicates the programmer's life a great deal. In the beginning, writing programs for the Windows environment was extremely tedious. Programmers found themselves spending countless hours writing instructions to create the buttons, scroll bars, dialog boxes, and menus needed in all Windows applications. Because the programmer has no control over which button the user will click in a Windows application, or which scroll bar the user will employ, the first Windows programmers had to write instructions that could handle any combination of actions the user might take. Tasks that used to take a few lines of program code now needed pages. Because programming Windows applications required a great amount of expertise, it appeared that the beginning of the Windows environment meant the end of the do-it-yourself, non-professional programmer. But then a new category of high-level languages emerged—the object-oriented/event-driven programming languages.

Object-Oriented/Event-Driven High-Level Languages

The object-oriented/event-driven languages simplified the task of programming applications for Windows. In **object-oriented/event-driven languages**, the emphasis of a program is on the *objects* included in the user interface (such as scroll bars and buttons) and the *events* that occur on those objects (such as scrolling and clicking).

Visual Basic is an object-oriented/event-driven programming language that is easy enough for a non-programmer to use, yet sophisticated enough to be used by professional programmers. (C++ and Smalltalk are also object-oriented/ event-driven programming languages.) With Visual Basic it takes just a few clicks of the mouse to include standard Windows objects such as buttons, list boxes, scroll bars, and icons in your Windows application. Once the objects are created, the programmer then concentrates on writing the specific instructions telling each object how to respond when clicked, double-clicked, scrolled, and so on. For example, Figure 4 shows the Visual Basic instructions that direct an object to end the program when the user clicks the object. (In this case the object is an Exit button.)

```
Sub CmdExit_Click ()
     End
End Sub
```

Figure 4: Visual Basic language—high-level, object-oriented/event-driven

Let's run a Visual Basic application so you can take a quick look at some of the objects you will learn how to create in the following tutorials. However, before you can run the application, you will need to make your Student Disk. The Student Disk will contain the practice files for both the demonstration and the tutorials. Because this book covers Visual Basic Version 2.0 and Visual Basic Version 3.0, the files for both versions of Visual Basic will be copied to your Student Disk. When working through the demonstration and the tutorials, you will use only the files appropriate for your version of Visual Basic.

Your Student Disk

To complete the tutorials and exercises in this book, you must have a Student Disk. The Student Disk contains all the practice files you need for the tutorials and the exercises. If your instructor or technical support person provides you with your Student Disk, you can skip this section and go to the section entitled "A Visual Basic Demonstration." If your instructor asks you to make your own Student Disk, you need to follow the steps in this section.

To make your Student Disk, you will need:

1 A blank, formatted, high-density 3.5 inch or 5.25 inch disk
2 A computer with Microsoft Windows 3.1 and the CTI WinApps group icon installed on it.

   If you are using your own computer, the CTI WinApps group icon will not be installed on it. Before you proceed, you must go to your school's computer lab and find a computer with the CTI WinApps group icon installed on it.

You need to be at your computer in order to create your Student Disk. You will create the disk by following the numbered steps shown in this section. Read each step carefully and completely before you try it. As you work, compare your screen with the figures to verify your results. Don't worry if your screen display differs slightly from the figures. The important parts of the screen display are labeled in each figure. Just be sure you have these parts on your screen. (The figures display the Version 3.0 screen. If you are using Version 2.0, you will notice that the differences between Version 2.0 and Version 3.0 are mostly minor. Any major differences will be noted in the figure.)

Tips boxes identify common problems and explain how to get back on track. You should complete the steps in the tips box *only* if you are having the problem described.

tips

▶ The exact steps you follow to launch Microsoft Windows 3.1 might vary depending on how your computer is set up. On many computer systems, type WIN, then press [Enter] to launch Windows. If you don't know how to lauch Windows, ask your instructor or your technical support person for assistance.

▶ If you do not know which version of Visual Basic you are using, ask your instructor or technical support person for assistance or look in the Program Manager for the Visual Basic icon, as shown in Figure 5.

To make your Visual Basic Student Disk:

1   Launch Windows and make sure the Program Manager window is open.

Keep in mind that, on occasion, the steps for Visual Basic Version 2.0 will be different from the steps for Version 3.0. This will be noted in the text, as shown in the next step. When you see this notation, follow only the instructions appropriate for your version of Visual Basic, then go to the next step.

2   *If you are using Version 2.0,* label your formatted disk "Visual Basic Student Disk Version 2.0."

   If you are using Version 3.0, label your formatted disk "Visual Basic Student Disk Version 3.0."

3   Place your Student Disk in drive A.

   If your computer has more than one disk drive, drive A is usually on top. If your Student Disk does not fit into drive A, then place it in drive B and substitute "drive B" anywhere you see "drive A" in the steps.

4   Look for an icon labeled "CTI WinApps" like the one in Figure 5 or a window labeled "CTI WinApps" like the one in Figure 6.

Visual Basic group icon

CTI WinApps group icon

version number

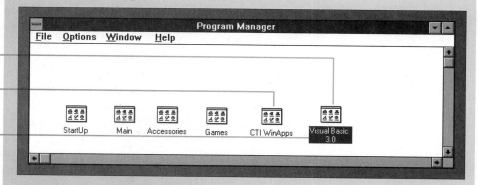

Figure 5: Program Manager window

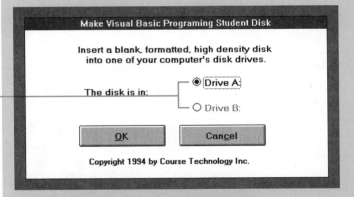

CTI WinApps group window

Figure 6: CTI WinApps group window

5   If you see an icon labeled "CTI WinApps," double-click it to open the CTI WinApps group window. If the CTI WinApps window is already open, go to Step 6.

6   Double-click the icon labeled "Make VisualBasic Programing Student Disk." The Make Visual Basic Programing Student Disk window opens. See Figure 7.

tips

If you cannot find anything labeled "CTI WinApps," the CTI software might not be installed on your computer. If you are in a computer lab, ask your technical support person for assistance.

If the Program Manager appears as an icon, double-click the icon to display the Program Manager window.

select the drive that contains your Student Disk

Figure 7: Make Visual Basic Programing Student Disk window

7   Make sure the drive that contains your formatted disk corresponds to the drive option button highlighted in the dialog box on your screen.

8   Click the **OK button** to copy the practice files to your formatted disk.

9   When the copying is complete, a message indicates the number of files copied to your disk. Click the **OK button**, then double-click the **Control menu box** on the CTI WinApps window. The CTI WinApps window closes.

Now the files you need to run the demonstration and to complete the Visual Basic tutorials and exercises are on your Student Disk.

A Visual Basic Demonstration

The Visual Basic application you are about to run will show you only some of the objects you will learn how to create in the tutorials. For now, it is not important for you to understand how these objects were created or why the objects perform the way they do. Those questions will be answered in the tutorials. Let's begin.

To run the Visual Basic application:

1　Make sure the Program Manager window is open and your Student Disk is in the appropriate drive.

2　Position the mouse pointer on File in the menu bar, then click **File** to open the File menu.

3　Position the mouse pointer on the Run... option in the File menu, then click **Run...** to choose that option. The Run dialog box appears. See Figure 8.

Browse button

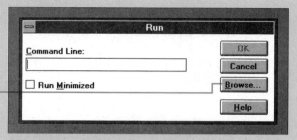

Figure 8: Run dialog box

4　Click the **Browse... button**. The Browse dialog box appears.

5　Click the **down arrow button in the Drives box**. From the list of available drives, click the drive containing your Student Disk. Then double-click **a:** (or **b:**) in the Directories list box.

6　Click **overview in the Directories list box**, then click the **OK button** to select the overview directory. See Figure 9.

your drive letter might be b:

choose the appropriate directory for your version of Visual Basic

drive letter containing your Student Disk

Figure 9: Browse dialog box

7 *If you are using Visual Basic Version 2.0,* click **ver2** in the Directories list box, then click the **OK button**. The over.exe filename appears in the File Name list box.

If you are using Visual Basic Version 3.0, click **ver3** in the Directories list box, then click the **OK button**. The over.exe filename appears in the File Name list box.

8 Click **over.exe** in the File Name list box, then click the **OK button** to close the Browse dialog box. The Run dialog box appears. The Command Line box should display the letter of the drive containing your Student Disk (either A: or B:), followed by the name of the directory in which the over.exe file is stored (either OVERVIEW\VER2 or OVERVIEW\VER3), followed by the name of the file you want to run (OVER.EXE). See Figure 10.

directory containing the file (yours might say VER2)

drive containing your Student Disk (yours might be B:)

filename to run

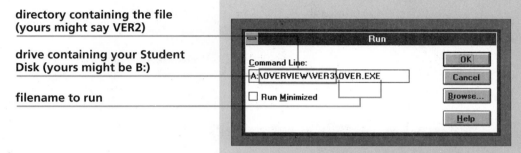

Figure 10: Run dialog box containing the filename

9 Click the **OK button**. The Monthly Payment screen appears. You can use this screen to compute a monthly payment on a car loan. See Figure 11.

scroll bar

Combo box

List box

command buttons

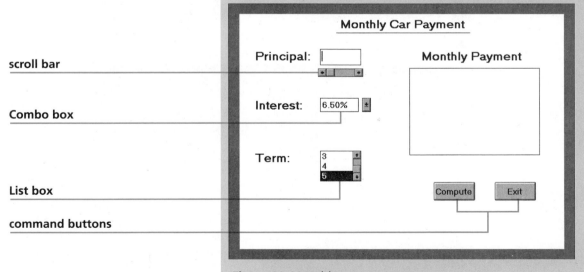

Figure 11: Monthly payment screen

Figure 11 identifies some of the different objects appearing on the screen. In the upper-left corner of the screen, for example, is a scroll bar. Immediately below the scroll bar is a Combo box, and immediately below the Combo box is a List box. You will also notice two Command buttons on the right side of the screen. Let's see what your monthly payment would be if you wanted to borrow $30,000 at 8% interest for five years.

To compute the monthly car payment:

1   Drag the scroll box all the way to the right in the scroll bar and release the mouse button. The number 30000 appears in the box above the scroll bar.

2   Click the **down arrow button in the Interest Combo box**, then click the **8.00%** interest rate. The 8.00% interest rate appears in the Combo box.

The five-year term is already selected in the term List box.

3   Click the **Compute button** to compute the monthly payment. Visual Basic computes and displays the monthly payment. See Figure 12.

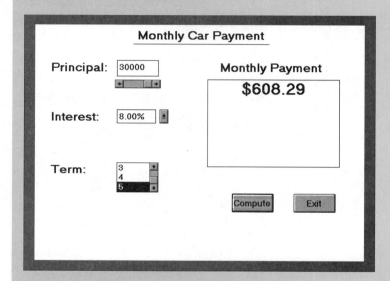

Figure 12: Computed monthly payment

When you click the Exit Command button, the demonstration will end.

4   Click the **Exit button**. The demonstration is now finished.

In the tutorials you will learn how to create Visual Basic applications that you can run directly from Windows, just as you did in the demonstration.

As you can see, programming languages have come a long way since the first machine languages. This brief history and demonstration should give you a better appreciation for the Visual Basic programming language you are about to learn.

Using the Tutorials Effectively

The tutorials in this book will help you learn about Microsoft Visual Basic Version 2.0/3.0. They are designed to be used at your computer. Begin by reading the text that explains the concepts. Then when you come to the numbered steps, follow the steps on your computer. Read each step carefully and completely before you try it. (Keep in mind that, on occasion, the steps for Visual Basic Version 2.0 will be different from the steps for Version 3.0. This will be noted in the text.)

As you work, compare your screen with the figures to verify your results. Don't worry if your screen display differs slightly from the figures. The important parts of the screen display are labeled in each figure. Just be sure you have these parts on your screen. (The figures display the Version 3.0 screen. If you are using Version 2.0, you will notice that the differences between Version 2.0 and Version 3.0 are mostly minor. Any major differences will be noted in the figures.)

Don't worry about making mistakes; that's part of the learning process. Tips boxes identify common problems and explain how to get back on track. You should complete the steps in the Tips box *only* if you are having the problem described.

Each tutorial is divided into three lessons. You might want to take a break between lessons. Following each lesson is a Summary section that lists the important elements of the lesson. After the Summary section are multiple-choice questions and exercises designed to review and reinforce that lesson's concepts. You should complete the end-of-lesson questions and exercises before going on to the next lesson.

Before you begin the tutorials, you should know how to use the menus, dialog boxes, Help facility, Program Manager, and File Manager in Microsoft Windows. Course Technology, Inc. publishes two excellent texts for learning Windows: *A Guide to Microsoft Windows 3.1* and *An Introduction to Microsoft Windows 3.1*.

Q U E S T I O N S

1. The set of directions given to a computer are called _____ .
   a. computerese
   b. commands
   c. instructions
   d. programs
   e. rules

2. Instructions written in 0s and 1s are called _____ .
   a. assembly language
   b. booleans
   c. computerese
   d. machine code
   e. mnemonics

3. The _____ languages allow the programmer to use mnemonics, which are alphabetic abbreviations for instructions.
    a. assembly
    b. high-level
    c. machine
    d. object
    e. procedure

4. The _____ languages allow the programmer to use instructions that more closely resemble the English language.
    a. assembly
    b. high-level
    c. machine
    d. object
    e. procedure

5. A(n) _____ translates high-level instructions into machine code, line by line as the program is running.
    a. assembler
    b. compiler
    c. interpreter
    d. program
    e. translator

6. A(n) _____ translates the entire high-level program into machine code before running the program.
    a. assembler
    b. compiler
    c. interpreter
    d. program
    e. translator

7. A(n) _____ converts assembly instructions into machine code.
    a. assembler
    b. compiler
    c. interpreter
    d. program
    e. translator

8. Visual Basic is a(n) _____ language.
    a. assembler
    b. mnemonic
    c. object-oriented/event-driven
    d. procedure-oriented

9. In procedure-oriented languages, the emphasis of a program is on how to accomplish a task.
    a. True
    b. False

10. In object-oriented languages, the emphasis of a program is on the objects included in the user interface and the events that occur on those objects.
    a. True
    b. False

TUTORIAL

1

An Introduction to Visual Basic

Creating a Copyright Screen

case ▶ **Interlocking Software Company**, a small firm specializing in custom programs, hires you as a programmer trainee. In that capacity you will learn to write Windows applications using the Visual Basic language, an object-oriented/event-driven programming language.

On your second day of work Chris Statton, the senior programmer at Interlocking Software, assigns you your first task: create a copyright screen. Chris explains that every custom application created at Interlocking Software must display a copyright screen when the application is launched. The copyright screen identifies the application's author and copyright year and includes the Interlocking Software Company logo. A sketch of the copyright screen is shown in Figure 1-1.

Figure 1-1: Sketch of the copyright screen

Although this first task is small, the copyright screen will give you an opportunity to learn the fundamentals of Visual Basic without having to worry about the design issues and programming concepts necessary for larger applications.

Previewing the Application

Before starting the first lesson, let's preview a completed copyright screen that was created using Visual Basic. You will run the completed application from the Windows Program Manager.

The exact steps you follow to launch Microsoft Windows 3.1 might vary depending on how your computer is set up. If you don't know how to launch Windows, ask your instructor or technical support person.

The instructions for creating your Visual Basic Student Disk are in the Overview section of this book.

To preview the completed copyright screen:

1 Launch Windows. Make sure the Program Manager window is open and your Visual Basic Student Disk is in the appropriate disk drive.

2 Position the mouse pointer on File in the menu bar, then click **File** to open the File menu. The File menu opens.

3 Position the mouse pointer on Run..., then click **Run...** to choose that option. The Run dialog box appears.

4 Click the **Browse... button**. The Browse dialog box appears.

5 Click the **down arrow button in the Drives box**. From the list of available drives, click the drive containing your Student Disk. Then double-click **a:** (or **b:**) in the Directories list box.

6 Double-click **tut1** in the Directories list box to open the tut1 directory.

7 *If you are using Visual Basic Version 2.0*, double-click **ver2** in the Directories list box to open the ver2 directory. The copyrght.exe filename appears in the File Name list box.

If you are using Visual Basic Version 3.0, double-click **ver3** in the Directories list box to open the ver3 directory. The copyrght.exe filename appears in the File Name list box.

8   Click **copyrght.exe** in the File Name list box, then click the **OK button.** The Run dialog box appears.

9   Click the **OK button** to run the application. The copyright screen appears. See Figure 1-2.

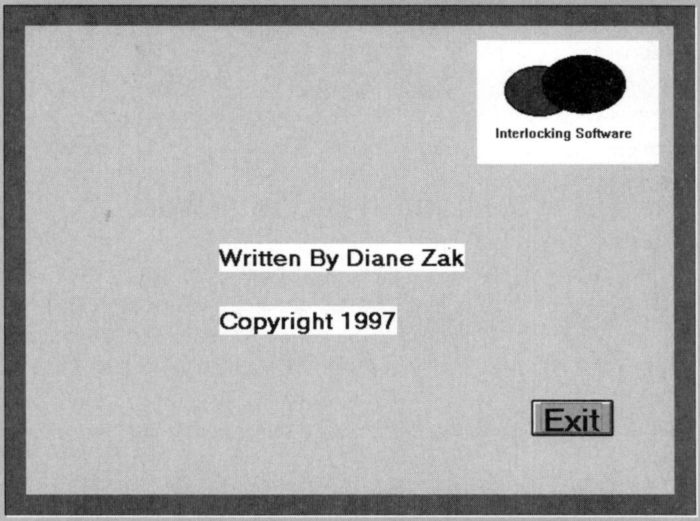

Figure 1-2: Copyright screen

10   Click the **Exit button.** The application ends.

Now you will create your own copyright screen.

Tutorial 1 is designed to get you comfortable with the Visual Basic environment. Beginning in Tutorial 2, you will learn techniques for planning and designing applications. You will also learn about the Visual Basic language. Remember, each tutorial contains three lessons. You should complete a lesson in full and do the end-of-lesson questions and exercises before going on to the next lesson.

In this lesson you will learn how to:

- Launch and exit Visual Basic
- Identify the components of the Visual Basic display
- Remove a file from a project
- Set the properties of an object
- Create, save, run, and stop a Visual Basic application
- Open both a new project and an existing project

Creating a New Project

Launching Visual Basic

Before you can begin creating your copyright screen, you must launch (or start) Visual Basic. You can launch Visual Basic from the Program Manager, the File Manager, or the MS-DOS prompt. In these tutorials you will launch Visual Basic from the Program Manager. Let's launch Visual Basic now.

tips

▶ If you don't have a group icon labeled either Visual Basic 2.0 or Visual Basic 3.0, ask your technical support person or instructor for help. It might be that Visual Basic has not yet been installed on the computer you are using.

Visual Basic group icon

version number

To launch Visual Basic from the Program Manager:

1   Launch Windows (if necessary) and make sure the Program Manager window is open. Also be sure your Student Disk is in the appropriate disk drive. Either the Visual Basic 2.0 group icon or the Visual Basic 3.0 group icon should be visible in the Program Manager window, as shown in Figure 1-3.

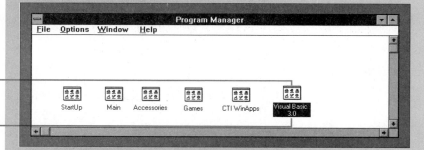

Figure 1-3: Program Manager window

To reduce some of the screen clutter, you will first instruct Microsoft Windows to minimize the Program Manager to an icon when you launch Visual Basic. You do that by activating the Minimize on Use option, located on the Program Manager's Options menu.

2 Click **Options in the Program Manager's menu bar** to open the Options menu. See Figure 1-4.

click to check this option ————

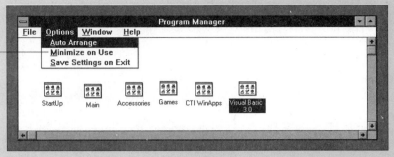

Figure 1-4: Options menu

3 If the Minimize on Use option is not checked, click **Minimize on Use** to check that option.

4 If the Options menu is still open, click **Options** again to close it.

The Program Manager will now be minimized to an icon as soon as you launch Visual Basic. In the next step, remember to follow only the instructions appropriate for your version of Visual Basic.

5 *If you are using Version 2.0,* double-click the **Visual Basic 2.0 group icon** in the Program Manager window. The Visual Basic group window opens. See Figure 1-5.

  If you are using Version 3.0, double-click the **Visual Basic 3.0 group icon** in the Program Manager window. The Visual Basic group window opens. See Figure 1-5.

not available in Version 2.0 ————

Microsoft Visual Basic icon ————

Version 2.0 icon says Visual Basic 2.0 (Version 2.0 window also contains an Introducing Visual Basic icon)

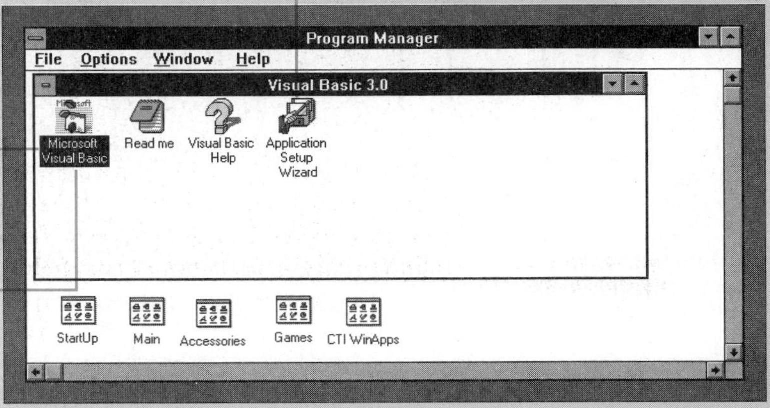

Figure 1-5: Visual Basic group window

6 Double-click the **Microsoft Visual Basic icon in the Visual Basic group window**. The Visual Basic copyright screen appears momentarily, and then the Visual Basic startup screen appears, as shown in Figure 1-6. Your screen might not look identical to Figure 1-6, but it should have all the parts labeled in the figure.

Project window

main window

Toolbox window

Form window

Properties window

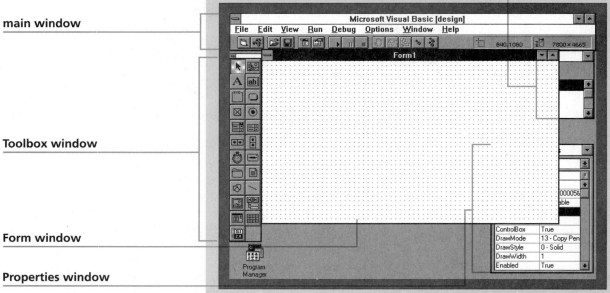

Figure 1-6: Visual Basic startup screen

tips

....

▶ If the toolbar does not appear on the screen, click View in the menu bar, then click Toolbar.

▶ If the Toolbox does not appear on the screen, click Window in the menu bar, then click Toolbox.

The Visual Basic Startup Screen

As Figure 1-6 shows, the Visual Basic startup screen contains five separate windows: the Visual Basic main window, the Toolbox window, the Form window, the Properties window, and the Project window. You can't see all of the Properties window and the Project window right now, because the Form window is overlapping them. You will learn how to display those windows in a little while. For now, let's take a closer look at Visual Basic's main window, Form window, and Toolbox window. (Remember that your screen will be different if you are using Version 2.0 or the professional developer's package of Visual Basic.)

The Main Window

The Visual Basic main window, at the top of the screen, contains the title bar, the menu bar, and the toolbar. Figure 1-7 shows these parts of the Visual Basic display.

title bar

indicates that Visual Basic is in design time

Control menu box

menu bar

toolbar

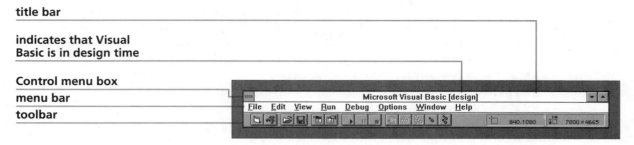

Figure 1-7: Visual Basic main window at the top of the screen

The title bar indicates that Microsoft Visual Basic is currently in **design time**, which means it is waiting for you to design your application. Below the Visual Basic title bar is the menu bar. The **menu bar** displays the commands you will use to build your application. Icons in the **toolbar**, located below the menu bar, provide quick access to the most commonly used menu commands.

The Form Window

A Visual Basic Form window, one of many objects you can create in Visual Basic, appears in the center of the screen, as shown in Figure 1-8.

Control menu box

default caption in title bar

Minimize button

Maximize button

form

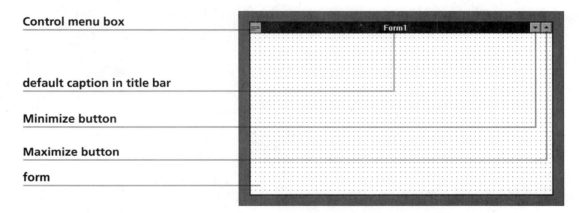

Figure 1-8: Visual Basic form window

A Visual Basic **Form window** is a window in which you design the user interface for your application. As you might recall, a **user interface** is what you see and interact with when running a Windows application. Notice that the Form window (or form) already contains its own Control menu box and title bar, as well as Minimize and Maximize buttons. Visual Basic assigns the default caption, Form1, to the first form. This caption appears in the form's title bar.

In these tutorials, you will learn how to customize a form by attaching other objects to it, such as buttons, boxes, and scroll bars. (Notice that a form is an object that can contain other objects.) During design time, Visual Basic displays dots in the form to assist you in aligning these objects. The dots disappear when you run the application.

The Toolbox Window

tips

....

▶ **Your Toolbox will differ from Figure 1-9 if you are using Version 2.0 or the professional developer's package of Visual Basic.**

On the left of the screen is the Toolbox window shown in Figure 1-9. The **Toolbox** contains the set of tools you use when designing a Visual Basic application. These tools allow you to place objects (also called **controls**) such as buttons, boxes, and scroll bars on the form.

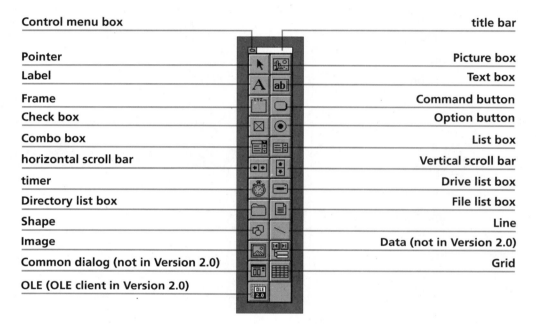

Control menu box — title bar

Pointer — Picture box
Label — Text box
Frame — Command button
Check box — Option button
Combo box — List box
horizontal scroll bar — Vertical scroll bar
timer — Drive list box
Directory list box — File list box
Shape — Line
Image — Data (not in Version 2.0)
Common dialog (not in Version 2.0) — Grid
OLE (OLE client in Version 2.0)

Figure 1-9: Toolbox window

Figure 1-10 describes the purpose of each of the tools in the Toolbox. Let's look at the Project window next.

The Project Window

An application can contain many files. The Project window lists the names of the files included in the application you are currently creating. (The terms project and application are used interchangeably in Visual Basic.) You can display the Project window by opening the Window menu and clicking Project. Let's display the Project window to see the names of the files included in this application.

Control	Purpose
Check box	Displays a box that is either checked (for Yes/True) or unchecked (for No/False); any number of check boxes can be checked at one time
Combo box	Combines and displays a Text box with a List box
Command button	Performs a command when clicked
Common dialog (Version 3.0)	Provides a standard set of dialog boxes for operations such as opening, saving, and printing files
Data (Version 3.0)	Allows you to display information from a database
Directory list box	Displays a list of directories from which the user can select
Drive list box	Displays a list of disk drives from which the user can select
File list box	Displays a list of filenames from which the user can select
Frame	Provides a visual and functional container for controls
Grid	Displays rows and columns, as in a spreadsheet
Horizontal scroll bar	Displays a horizontal scroll bar containing a range of values
Image	Displays a picture; simpler version of the Picture box control
Label	Displays text that the user cannot change
Line	Draws lines on a form
List box	Displays a list of choices from which a user can select
OLE (Version 3.0)	Allows object linking and embedding
OLE client (Version 2.0)	Allows object linking and embedding
Option button	Displays a button that can be either on or off; if the button is part of an option group, only one button can be on at any time
Picture box	Displays a picture
Pointer	Allows you to move and size forms and controls
Shape	Draws a circle, ellipse, square, or rectangle on a form
Text box	Accepts or displays text that the user can change
Timer	A clock that performs events at specified time intervals
Vertical scroll bar	Displays a vertical scroll bar containing a range of values

Figure 1-10: List of controls

To display the Project window:

1   *If you are using Visual Basic Version 2.0*, click **Window**, then click **Project**. The Project window appears on the screen, as shown in Figure 1-11.

   If you are using Visual Basic Version 3.0, click **Window**, then click **Project**. The Project window appears on the screen. Place the mouse pointer on the bottom border of the Project window until it becomes a double-headed arrow, then drag the border until the Project window matches the one shown in Figure 1-11, and then release the mouse button. (Remember, dragging means holding down the left mouse button while you move the mouse.)

Notice that the Project window title bar is now highlighted, which means the Project window is the currently selected window.

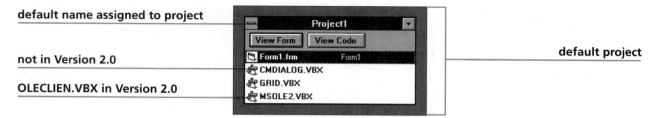

default name assigned to project

not in Version 2.0

OLECLIEN.VBX in Version 2.0

default project

Figure 1-11: Project window

Whenever you launch Visual Basic or whenever you create a new project, Visual Basic automatically creates a default project named Project1. (The name appears in the title bar of the Project window.) The default project contains the files shown in Figure 1-11. Although you can have only one Visual Basic project open at any time, that project can contain many different files. For example, notice that the default project for Version 3.0 includes four files: Form1.frm, CMDIALOG.VBX, GRID.VBX, and MSOLE2.VBX. (The default project for Version 2.0 contains three files: Form1.frm, GRID.VBX, and OLECLIEN.VBX.) Form1.frm is the default filename for the Form1 form on the screen; if you don't change the name of the form when you save it, this is the name Visual Basic will use to save the form on your Student Disk. The .frm extension identifies this file as a form file.

The .VBX files included in the default project provide tools in the Toolbox that allow you to create custom controls. For example, the MSOLE2.VBX file (OLECLIEN.VBX in Version 2.0) is represented, in the Toolbox, by the OLE tool, which allows your application to display and manipulate data from other Windows-based applications. The .VBX extension stands for "Visual Basic extension."

Notice that the Project window also contains two buttons labeled View Form and View Code. The View Form button displays the form associated with the selected file. Use this button to view the various forms included in a project, or to display a form you closed unintentionally. The View Code button displays the program instructions, called code, associated with the selected file.

Because you won't need the .VBX files for your copyright screen, you can remove those files from the project.

Removing a File from a Project Removing unnecessary files from a project allows Visual Basic to run the application more quickly. If you are using Version 3.0, you will need to remove three .VBX files; if you are using Version 2.0, you will need to remove two .VBX files. (If you are using the professional developer's version of Visual Basic, you will need to remove all of the .VBX files.) Removing a file from a project does not erase the file from the disk, so if you should need the .VBX files later on, you can always use the File menu's Add File... option to add the files to the project.

tips

• •

▶ **If you accidentally clicked the first icon in the Toolbar, a new form (Form2) appears in the project. To remove the Form2 form, click File, then click Remove File.**

▶ **If you accidentally removed the Form1.frm file from the Project window, click File in the menu bar, then click New Project, then click No to saving the current project. When the new project appears, display the Project window and remove the .VBX files.**

To remove the .VBX files from the Project1 project:

1   *If you are using Version 2.0,* go to step 2.

If you are using Version 3.0, click **CMDIALOG.VBX** in the Project window to select the CMDIALOG.VBX filename, then click **File** in the menu bar, and then click **Remove File**. Visual Basic removes the CMDIALOG.VBX file from the Project window. Visual Basic also removes the Common dialog tool from the Toolbox.

2   Click **GRID.VBX** in the Project window to select that file, then click **File**, and then click **Remove File**. Visual Basic removes the GRID.VBX file from the Project window. It also removes the Grid tool from the Toolbox.

3   *If you are using Version 2.0,* click **OLECLIEN.VBX** in the Project window to select that file, then click **File**, and then click **Remove File**. Visual Basic removes the .VBX file from the Project window. It also removes the OLE control from the Toolbox. See Figure 1-12.

If you are using Version 3.0, click **MSOLE2.VBX** in the Project window to select that file, then click **File**, and then click **Remove File**. Visual Basic removes the .VBX file from the Project window. It also removes the OLE control from the Toolbox. See Figure 1-12.

.VBX files were removed from the Project window

tools were removed from the bottom of the Toolbox

Version 3.0 only

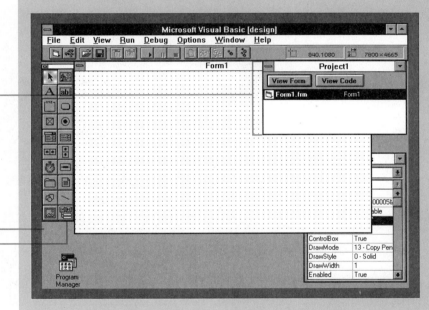

Figure 1-12: Current status of Project window and Toolbox

You will now size and drag the Project window to a new location on the screen.

4   Position the mouse pointer on the bottom border of the Project window until the mouse pointer becomes a double-headed arrow. Then drag the bottom border up, until it is positioned below the Form1.frm filename, and release the mouse button. You can look ahead to Figure 1-13 to see the result.

5   Position the mouse pointer on the Project window's title bar and drag the Project window to the lower-left corner of the screen. (Remember, dragging means holding the left mouse button down while you move the mouse.) You can look ahead to Figure 1-13 to see the result.

So far you have learned about four of the five Visual Basic windows: the main window, the Form window, the Toolbox window, and the Project window. The Properties window is next.

The Properties Window

Each object in Visual Basic has a set of characteristics, called properties, associated with it. These **properties**, listed in the **Properties window**, control the object's appearance and behavior. You can display the Properties window by clicking the Properties icon, which is the sixth icon from the left on the toolbar. You can also use the menu bar to display the Properties window. In that case, you would need to open the Window menu and click Properties. You can also display the Properties window by pressing [F4]. Before you can display the Properties window, however, you must select an object. In this case, you will select the form, which is the only object in the current application.

To display the Properties window:

1   Click the **form's title bar** to select the form. The form's title bar is now highlighted, indicating that it is the selected object.

2   Click the **Properties icon** 🔲 in the toolbar. The Properties window appears on the screen.

Let's arrange the screen so the Properties window does not overlap the Form window.

3   Position the mouse pointer on the Properties window's title bar and drag the Properties window to the upper-right corner of the screen.

4   Position the mouse pointer on the right border of the form until the pointer turns into a double-headed arrow, then drag the border to match Figure 1-13.

Object box

Settings box

Properties list

Properties window

Form window

Project window

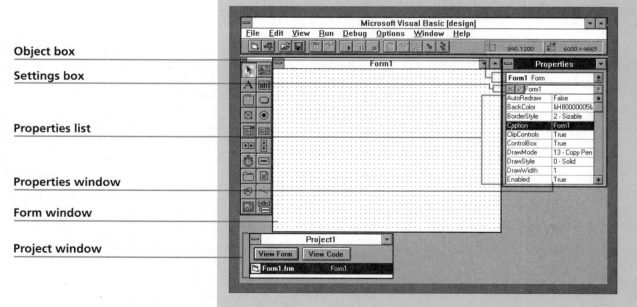

Figure 1-13: Screen arrangement of Project, Properties, and Form windows

As indicated in Figure 1-13, the Properties window includes an Object box, a Settings box, and a Properties list. The **Object box**, located immediately below the Properties window's title bar, displays the name of the selected object—in this case, the Form1 form. You can use the Object box to select an object in the user interface. You must select an object before you can either display or change the value of its properties. (You'll learn more about the Object box in Lesson B.)

The **Properties list** in the Properties window has two columns: The left column displays all the properties associated with the selected object (in this case, the form). The right column displays the current value, or setting, of each of those properties. For example, the current value of the Caption property is Form1.

tips

· · · · · · · · · · · · · · · · · · · ·

▶ If the Caption property is not highlighted, click Caption in the Properties window.

To view the properties in the Properties window:

1 Click the **down scroll arrow in the Properties window's vertical scroll bar** to scroll through the entire Properties list. As you scroll, notice the various properties associated with a form.

2 Drag the scroll box in the vertical scroll bar to the top to display the beginning of the Properties list once again.

Notice that the currently selected property in the Properties list is highlighted. In this case, the currently selected property is the Caption property.

The **Settings box**, located immediately above the Properties list, also shows the current setting, or value, of the selected property. You can change the setting for many of the listed properties by simply typing a new value into the Settings box. Some properties, however, have predefined settings. If a property has predefined settings, either the down arrow button on the right of the Settings box will appear darkened or the down arrow will be replaced by an ellipsis (...). When you click the darkened down arrow button in the Settings box, a drop-down list appears containing the valid predefined settings for that property; you then select the setting you want from that list. When you click the ellipsis in the Settings box, either a dialog box or a color palette will appear. You can then enter the information requested by the dialog box or choose a color from the color palette. You will get a chance to practice with both the darkened down arrow and the ellipsis as you change various properties throughout this lesson. Let's begin by changing the Caption property, which is the currently selected property.

Setting the Caption Property Programmers who create applications for the Windows environment need to be aware of the conventions used in Windows applications. For example, the name of the application usually appears in the application window's title bar. (Notice that "Microsoft Visual Basic" appears in the title bar of its window.) Because the form on the screen will become your application's window when the application is run, its title bar should display an appropriate name.

In Visual Basic the Caption property controls the text displayed in the form's title bar, as well as the text displayed below the form's icon when the form is minimized. As you've already seen, Visual Basic automatically assigns the default caption Form1 to the first form in a project. A better, more descriptive caption would be "Interlocking Software Company"—the name of the company responsible for the copyright screen application.

tips

If the Caption property is not selected, click Caption in the Properties list.

To set the Caption property of the selected form:

1   Verify that the Caption property is the currently selected property in the Properties window.

Notice that the down arrow button in the Settings box is grayed-out, which means this property does not have any predefined settings.

2   Type **Interlocking Software Company** and press **[Enter]**. The new caption appears in the Properties list, in the Settings box, and in the form's title bar. (Notice that you did not have to erase the old caption before entering the new caption.)

You will change the form's Name property next.

Setting the Name Property   Visual Basic automatically assigns a default name to every object it creates. For example, the default name for the first form in a project is Form1, the default name for the second form in a project is Form2, and so on. Because a project can contain many forms, it is a good practice to give each one a more meaningful name to help you keep track of the various objects in the application.

An object's name must begin with a letter and it must contain only letters, numbers, and the underscore character. You cannot use punctuation characters or spaces in an object's name, and the name cannot exceed 40 characters. One popular naming convention is to have the first three characters in the name represent the object's type (form, scroll bar, and so on), and the remainder of the name represent the object's purpose. For example, a more descriptive name for this form would be FrmCopyright. The "Frm" identifies the object as a form, and the "Copyright" reminds you of the form's purpose. Figure 1-14 contains a list of the three characters usually associated with each object.

Object	Three-Character Identifier
Check Box	Chk
Combo Box	Cbo
Command Button	Cmd
Common Dialog Box (Version 3.0)	Cdi
Data (Version 3.0)	Dat
Directory List Box	Dir
Drive List Box	Drv
File List Box	Fil
Form	Frm
Frame	Fra
Grid	Grd
Horizontal Scroll Bar	Hsb
Image	Img
Label	Lbl
Line	Lin
List Box	Lst
Menu	Mnu
Object Linking and Embedding	Ole
Option Button	Opt
Picture	Pic
Shape	Shp
Text Box	Txt
Timer	Tmr
Vertical Scroll Bar	Vsb

Figure 1-14: Objects and their three-character IDs for Name property

You assign a new name to a form by setting its Name property. Although you can type the entire name in uppercase letters, lowercase letters, or a combination of uppercase and lowercase letters, it is a common practice to capitalize just the first letter in the name and the first letter in the part of the name that identifies the purpose. For example, you will capitalize only the "F" in "Frm" and the "C" in "Copyright."

To set the Name property for the Form1 form, which is the currently selected object:

1   Scroll the Properties list until the Name property is visible. (You can also press the down arrow on your keyboard.) Then click the **Name** property to select it. The Name property is now highlighted.

Notice that the down arrow button in the Settings box is grayed-out. That means the Name property does not have any predefined settings, so you can simply type the new name into the Settings box.

2   Type **FrmCopyright** and press [**Enter**]. (Remember, you can't use spaces in the name.) The new name, FrmCopyright, is displayed in the Properties window. (If you are using Version 2.0, the Object box will say Form1 Form until you click the form.) See Figure 1-15.

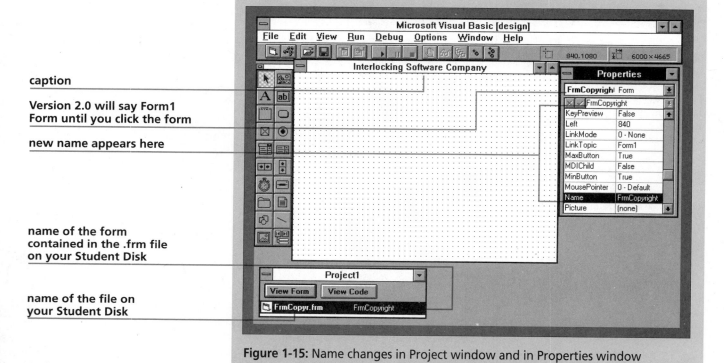

caption

Version 2.0 will say Form1
Form until you click the form

new name appears here

name of the form
contained in the .frm file
on your Student Disk

name of the file on
your Student Disk

Figure 1-15: Name changes in Project window and in Properties window

Visual Basic also makes two changes in the Project window: It replaces the default filename Form1.frm with FrmCopyr.frm and the default form name Form1 with FrmCopyright. FrmCopyr.frm is a filename, whereas FrmCopyright is the name of the form contained in the FrmCopyr.frm file. At this point you may be wondering why the filename (FrmCopyr) contains only the first eight characters of the form name (FrmCopyright). Recall that Visual Basic assumes you will want to call the file the same name as the form contained inside the file. However, because the disk operating system on your computer does not allow filenames to exceed eight characters, Visual Basic truncates the "ight" from the filename.

One important note: It is very easy to confuse the Name property with the Caption property. Recall that the form's Caption property controls the text displayed in the form's title bar and, when the form is minimized, the text displayed below the form's icon. The Name property, however, assigns a name to an object. When writing Visual Basic instructions, you use an object's name, not its caption, to refer to the object. In other words, the name is used by the programmer, whereas the caption is read by the user.

Now let's add some color to the copyright screen.

Setting the BackColor Property The BackColor property controls the background color of an object. Unlike the Caption and Name properties, the BackColor property has predefined settings.

To change the background color of an object:

1   The form is already selected, so you just need to scroll the Properties list until the BackColor property is visible.

2   Click **BackColor in the Properties list**. Notice the ellipsis (...) to the right of the Settings box.

3   Click the ... (ellipsis) in the Settings box. A color palette appears.

4   *If you have a color monitor*, click a **light yellow square**. The background color of the form changes to a light yellow.

   If you do not have a color monitor, click the ... (ellipsis) in the Settings box to close the color palette.

tips

....

► If you minimized the Properties window to an icon, double-click the icon to display the Properties window.

► If you accidentally clicked the Object box's arrow, simply click the same arrow to remove the incorrect drop-down list.

Now save what you have done so far.

Saving a Visual Basic Project

It is a good practice to save the current project every 10 or 15 minutes so you won't lose a lot of work if the computer loses power. When you save a project for the first time, Visual Basic asks you for a filename for the form and a filename for the project. The project file will contain the names of the files appearing in the Project window, along with their location on the disk. The project file also records information on how the windows are arranged and sized when you open the project.

You can now save the current form and the current project on your Student Disk. The easiest way to save the form and the project is to click the Save Project icon in the toolbar.

To save a Visual Basic project:

1   Click the **Save Project icon** 🔲 in the toolbar. The Save File As dialog box appears on the screen.

The dialog box prompts you for the name of the form file first. Notice that the name appearing in the File Name box (frmcopyr.frm) is the name you assigned to the form with the Name property, or at least the first eight characters of the form name. (Recall that your computer's operating system limits filenames to eight characters and a three character extension — .frm, in this case.) You can keep the name that Visual Basic offers in the File Name box or, if you prefer, you can change the name. In this case, to keep the files you create in these tutorials grouped together in a meaningful way, you will save this form file as T1A. The "T1A" indicates that the file was created or saved in Tutorial 1, Lesson A.

2   Type **t1a** in the File Name box. Do not press the Enter key yet, however. (Be sure to use the number one and not the lowercase letter "l.") Visual Basic will automatically add the .frm extension when it saves this file.

Now you need to save the file on drive A (or drive B) where your Student Disk is located.

3   Click the **down arrow button in the Drives box**, then click the letter of the drive containing your Student Disk, then double-click **a:** (or **b:**) in the Directories list box. The Directories list box displays the available directories on your Student Disk.

Each tutorial, as well as the overview, has its own directory. Overview is the name of the Overview's directory, tut1 is the directory for Tutorial 1, tut2 is the directory for Tutorial 2, and so on. See Figure 1-16.

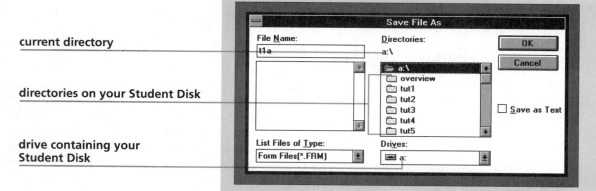

current directory

directories on your Student Disk

drive containing your
Student Disk

Figure 1-16: Save File As dialog box

You will save the files associated with Tutorial 1 in the tut1 directory.

4   Double-click **tut1** in the Directories list box to open the tut1 directory. The ver2 and ver3 directories now appear below the tut1 directory in the list box.

5   *If you are using Version 2.0,* double-click **ver2** in the Directories list box to open the ver2 directory. A:\tut1\ver2 (or b:\tut1\ver2) appears above the Directories list box. This tells Visual Basic to save the file in the tut1\ver2 directory on your Student Disk.

If you are using Version 3.0, double-click **ver3** in the Directories list box to open the ver3 directory. A:\tut1\ver3 (or b:\tut1\ver3) appears above the Directories list box. This tells Visual Basic to save the file in the tut1\ver3 directory on your Student Disk.

6   Click the **OK button** to save the form file on your Student Disk. Now that the file is saved, Visual Basic prompts you for the Project name.

Notice that the default project is named project1.mak. Visual Basic assigns the .mak extension to all project filenames. You should change the default project name, project1, to a more descriptive name. Here again, to keep the files grouped together in a meaningful way, you will call the project file the same name as the form file T1A. Visual Basic automatically adds the .mak extension when it saves a project file. (It is not necessary for the project file to have the same name as the form file.)

7   Type **t1a** in the File Name box. The directory and drive information is the same as for the form file, so you just need to click **OK**. Visual Basic saves the t1a.mak project file in the appropriate directory on your Student Disk.

Notice the changes in the Project window displayed in Figure 1-17.

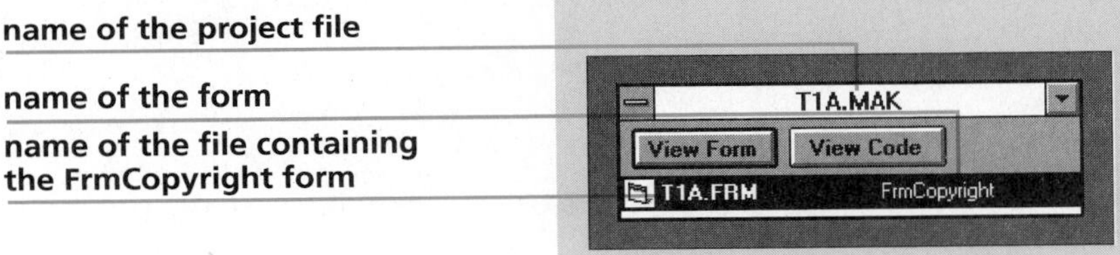

name of the project file

name of the form

name of the file containing the FrmCopyright form

Figure 1-17: Project window

The T1A.MAK project file contains the names of all files included in the project—in this case, only the T1A.FRM file. The name of the form contained in the T1A.FRM file is FrmCopyright. Think of the .MAK file as being a drawer in a filing cabinet, think of the .FRM file as being a folder in the drawer, and think of the form as being a piece of paper in that folder. See Figure 1-18.

Now that the form file and the project file are saved, you can run the project to see what you have accomplished so far.

Running and Stopping a Visual Basic Project

The only way you can tell if your application works is by running (executing) it. When you run the application, Visual Basic displays the user interface you created. You can run an application by clicking the Run icon or by pressing [F5]. You can also click Run in the menu bar, and then click Start to run an application.

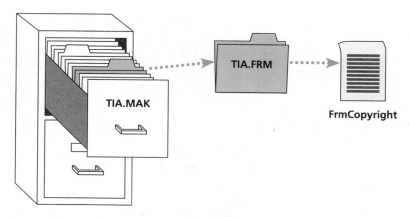

Figure 1-18: Project file, form file, and form

To run the copyright screen application:

1   Click the **Run icon** ▶ in the toolbar. Visual Basic enters run time, as shown in Visual Basic's title bar, and the user interface appears on the screen.

Notice that the user interface does not fill the entire screen, as you would like it to. You will need to stop the application and return to the design screen to fix this problem.

2   Click the **Stop icon** ■ in the toolbar to stop the execution of the program. (Or click **Run,** then click **End.**) Visual Basic leaves run time and returns to design time, as Visual Basic's title bar now shows.

You can make a form fill the entire screen by setting the form's WindowState property.

Setting the WindowState Property

The WindowState property determines the visual state of a form window during run time. The property has three valid settings: Normal, Minimized, and Maximized. The default setting is Normal. If you change the setting of this property to Minimized, Visual Basic will shrink the form to an icon when the application is run. Setting the value of this property to Maximized enlarges the form to its maximum size when the application is run. Because you want the form to fill the entire screen, you will set the value of the WindowState property to Maximized.

tips

▶ If you minimized the Properties window to an icon, double-click the icon to display the Properties window.

▶ If you accidentally clicked the Object box's arrow, simply click the same arrow to remove the incorrect drop-down list.

▶ If you clicked the Minimize button, double-click the Interlocking Software Company icon to display the form on the screen, then click the Restore button to restore the form to its standard size.

To set the value of the WindowState property, and then save and run the application:

1 Scroll the Properties list until the WindowState property is visible, then click the **WindowState** property in the Properties list. Notice the darkened down arrow to the right of the Settings box, indicating that this property has predefined settings.

2 Click the **down arrow button in the Settings box** to display the valid settings for this property, then click **2 - Maximized**.

3 Click the **Save Project icon** in the toolbar. Visual Basic saves the form and the project using the names you specified earlier.

4 Click the **Run icon** in the toolbar. The form now fills the entire screen.

Notice that you can't see the Stop icon or the menu bar when the form is maximized. You can, however, use the Restore button, located in the form's title bar, to restore the form to its standard size. You will then be able to see the Stop icon and the menu bar.

5 Click the **Restore button** (the button with the up and down triangles, located in the form's title bar) to restore the form to its standard size, then click the **Stop icon**.

Before finishing Lesson A, you will learn how to begin a new project and how to open an existing project. Both of these skills will help you complete the end-of-lesson exercises.

Opening a New Project

When you are finished with one project and want to begin another project, you simply click File, then click New Project. You can open a new project while a previous project is on the screen. When you open the new project, Visual Basic closes the previous project. Let's try opening a new project now.

To open a new project:

1 Click **File**, then click **New Project**. The T1A project is closed and a new project is opened. (If you did not save the current project first, Visual Basic displays a dialog box asking if you want to save the current project before a new project is opened. The dialog box contains three buttons: Yes, No, and Cancel. If you do want to save the current project, click Yes. If you do not want to save the current project, click No. If you don't want to open a new project, click Cancel.)

Now let's learn how to continue working on a project that was previously saved.

Opening an Existing Project

If you want to continue working on an existing project, you simply click the Open Project icon (or click File, then click Open Project...) and then tell Visual Basic which project you want to open. Let's open the T1A project.

tips

● ● ● ● ● ● ● ● ● ● ● ● ● ● ● ● ● ●

▶ If, instead of the Open Project dialog box, you see a dialog box that asks if you want to save the Form1 form, click the No button. This dialog box will not appear if you already saved the current form or if you have not made any changes to the current form. After you click the No button, the Open Project dialog box will appear.

To open an existing project:

1   Click the **Open Project icon** 🖻 in the Toolbar. The Open Project dialog box appears.

2   If necessary, click the **down arrow button in the Drives box,** then click the drive containing your Student Disk, then double-click either **a:** (or **b:**) in the Directories list box. A list of directories available on your Student Disk appears in the Directories list box.

3   If necessary, double-click **tut1** in the Directories list box to open the tut1 directory. The ver2 and ver3 directories now appear below the tut1 directory in the list box.

4   *If you are using Version 2.0*, double-click **ver2** in the Directories list box to open the ver2 directory. The File Name list box displays the names of the project files on your Student Disk. Recall that project filenames have a .MAK extension.

   If you are using Version 3.0, double-click **ver3** in the Directories list box to open the ver3 directory. The File Name list box displays the names of the project files on your Student Disk. Recall that project filenames have a .MAK extension.

5   Click **t1a.mak** in the File Name list box, then click the **OK button** to open the T1A project. The T1A Project window opens.

6   Click the **View Form button** in the Project window to display the form.

You can now exit Visual Basic. You will complete the copyright screen in the remaining two lessons.

Exiting Visual Basic

As in most Windows applications, you exit an application using either the Control menu box or the File menu.

To exit Visual Basic:

1   Double-click the Microsoft Visual Basic **Control menu box** in the upper-left corner of the screen (or click **File**, then click **Exit**).

2   Double-click the **Program Manager icon** to maximize it.

3   Double-click the **Visual Basic Control menu box** to close the Visual Basic group window. You can now exit Windows or choose another application.

S U M M A R Y

To launch Visual Basic:

- Launch Windows and make sure the Program Manager window is open.
- Place your Student Disk in the appropriate disk drive.
- Activate the Minimize on Use option (on the Program Manager's Options menu).
- Double-click either the Visual Basic 2.0 or the Visual Basic 3.0 group icon in the Program Manager window.
- Double-click the Microsoft Visual Basic (or Visual Basic 2.0) icon in the Visual Basic group window.

To display the Project window:

- Click Window, then click Project.

To remove a file from an open project:

- Display the Project window on the screen, then click the name of the file you want to remove from the project.
- Click File, then click Remove File.

To add a file to an open project:

- Click File, then click Add File....
- Select the Drive, Directory, and File Name of the file you want to add to the project.

To display the Properties window:

- Click the Properties icon in the toolbar [icon] (or click Window, then click Properties; you could also press [F4]).

To set the value of a property:

- Select the object whose property you want to set.
- Display the Properties window.
- Select the property whose value you want to set.

If the down arrow button in the Settings box is darkened:
- Click the down arrow button in the Settings box. A drop-down list appears.
- Click the desired value in the drop-down list.

If the down arrow button in the Settings box is replaced by ... (an ellipsis):
- Click the ... (ellipsis). Either a dialog box or a color palette will appear. Enter the information requested by the dialog box or choose a color from the color palette.

If the down arrow button in the Settings box is grayed-out:
- Enter the new value into the Settings box.

To save a Visual Basic form and project for the first time:

- Click the Save Project icon [icon] in the toolbar.
- Enter a filename for the form in the File Name box, then select the appropriate drive in the Drives box, and the appropriate directory in the Directories box.

■ Click the OK button to save the form file. Visual Basic prompts you for the name of the project.

■ Enter a filename for the project in the File Name box, then click the OK button.

To run a Visual Basic application:

■ Click the Run icon in the toolbar ▣ (or Click Run, then click Start; you can also press [F5]).

To stop running a Visual Basic application:

■ If necessary, click the form's Restore button so that the Visual Basic menu bar and toolbar are visible.

■ Click the Stop icon in the toolbar ▣ (or Click Run, then click End).

To open a new project:

■ Click File, then click New Project.

To open an existing project:

■ Launch Visual Basic, click the Open Project icon ▣ (or click File, then click Open Project...), then select the appropriate drive and directory location of the project file.

■ Scroll through the File Name list box until the project name appears in the list, then click the project name, and then click the OK button to open the project. (If you were working on a project before choosing the Open Project option and you did not save that form and/or project, Visual Basic will display one or more dialog boxes asking if you want to save the current form and/or project before opening another project.)

■ Click the View Form button in the Project window.

To exit Visual Basic:

■ Double-click the Microsoft Visual Basic Control menu box (or click the Microsoft Visual Basic Control menu box, then click Close; you can also click File, then click Exit).

■ Double-click the Program Manager icon to maximize it, if necessary.

■ Double-click the Visual Basic Control menu box to close the Visual Basic group window.

Q U E S T I O N S

1. You design your user interface in a _____ .
   a. design bar
   b. form
   c. menu bar
   d. Properties window
   e. toolbar

2. The tools you use when designing your application are found in the _____ .
   a. design bar
   b. Toolbox
   c. toolbar
   d. user interface
   e. user screen

3. In which window do you set the characteristics that control an object's appearance and behavior?
    a. Main
    b. Form
    c. Project
    (d.) Properties
    e. Toolbox

4. When you save a form, which of the following extensions does Visual Basic add to the filename you enter?
    a. .ff
    b. .ffl
    c. .for
    d. .form
    (e.) .frm

5. When you save a project, which of the following extensions does Visual Basic add to the filename you enter?
    a. .frm
    (b.) .mak
    c. .prg
    d. .prj
    e. .pro

6. Refer to Figure 1-19. Identify the location of the following Visual Basic components by writing the appropriate letter on the line to the left of the component.

    H Form window   F Properties list
    A Main window   G Properties window
    C Menu bar   E Settings box
    D Object box   B Toolbar
    I Project window   J Toolbox window

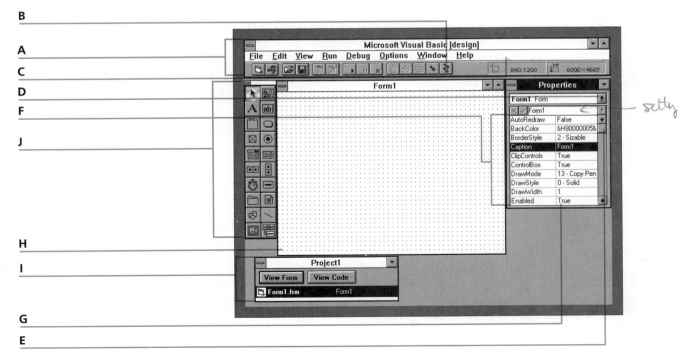

Figure 1-19: Visual Basic screen

7. Explain the procedure for removing a file from a project.

8. Explain the difference between a form's Caption property and a form's Name property.

9. Explain how to open a new project.

10. Explain how to open an existing project.

11. Explain how to display the Project window and the Properties window.

E X E R C I S E S

1. If necessary, launch Visual Basic and open a new project.
   a. Remove the .VBX files from the project.
   b. Size and arrange the windows so they do not overlap each other.
   c. Set the following properties for the form:
      Caption: Charities Unlimited
      BackColor: Blue
      Name: FrmCharity
      WindowState: 2-Maximized
   d. Save the form and the project as T1LAE1 (Tutorial 1, Lesson A, Exercise 1) in either the tut1\ver2 or tut1\ver3 directory.
   e. Run the application. Then stop the application.

2. If necessary, launch Visual Basic and open a new project.
   a. Remove the .VBX files from the project.
   b. Size and arrange the windows so they do not overlap each other.
   c. Set the following properties for the form:
      Caption: Photos Inc.
      Name: FrmPhotos
      BackColor: Green
      WindowState: 2-Maximized
   d. Save the form and the project as T1LAE2 (Tutorial 1, Lesson A, Exercise 2) in either the tut1\ver2 or tut1\ver3 directory.
   e. Run the application.

As you learned in Lesson A, some properties have predefined settings and some do not. You can tell if a property has predefined settings by looking in the Settings box of the Properties window. Use the following key to complete Exercise 3.

   A This property has no predefined settings.
   B This property does have predefined settings. The Settings box will display a drop-down list of the valid choices.
   C This property does have predefined settings. The Settings box will display a color palette or a dialog box.

3. Below are the names of 10 properties for a form. Launch Visual Basic and open a new project, if necessary. Select each of the 10 properties, one at a time, in the Properties list. On the line to the left of the property, write A, B, or C, according to the key mentioned above.

   B Caption   C ForeColor
   B Enabled   C Icon
   C FillColor   ___ Left
   C FontItalic   ___ Name
   B FontSize   ___ Picture

LESSON B
objectives

In this lesson you will learn how to:

■ Access the Visual Basic Help screens
■ Add a Label control to a form
■ Move and size a control
■ Delete a control from a form
■ Select multiple controls
■ Save files under a different name

Working with Controls

Getting Help in Visual Basic

Let's begin this lesson by spending some time looking at the Visual Basic Help screens. If you encounter any problems during the tutorials or if you have any questions, you will then be able to get help on your own.

To start this lesson:

1   Launch Visual Basic, if necessary.

2   Click the **Open Project icon** 🖻 to open the T1A.MAK project that you created in Lesson A. Depending on your version of Visual Basic, the T1A.MAK file is located in either the tut1\ver2 or the tut1\ver3 directory on your Student Disk.

3   Click the **View Form button** to view the FrmCopyright form.

Visual Basic has an on-line Help system that you can access using either the Help menu Contents option or the Help menu Search For Help On... option (called Search... in Version 2.0), or by pressing [F1]. You can practice with each of these methods right now, beginning with the Help menu Contents option.

To access Help through the Help menu Contents option:

1   Click **Help,** then click **Contents.** Visual Basic displays a Help screen showing various topics for which you can get help. Notice the Glossary topic, which allows you to look up the definitions of words.

You can display additional Help screens by clicking any of the underlined words. For example, let's view the information on Properties.

2   Position the mouse pointer anywhere on the Properties topic. The pointer turns into ↳, as shown in Figure 1-20.

3   Click **Properties**. Another Help screen appears. This Help screen displays a list of Visual Basic properties. Notice that each property is underlined, which means you can click on it to display another, more specific, Help screen.

4   Double-click the **Control menu box** in the upper-left corner of the second Help screen. The second Help screen closes.

5   Double-click the **Control menu box** in the upper-left corner of the first Help screen. The first Help screen closes.

click here to look up the
definitions of words

Version 3.0 only

*Introducing and Learning
Visual Basic* in Version 2.0

mouse pointer becomes
a pointing hand

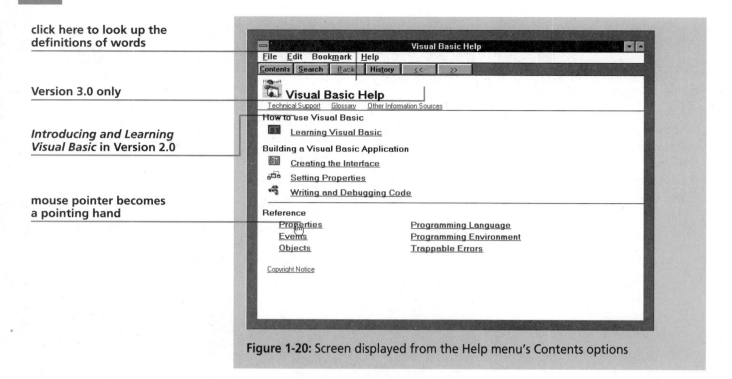

Figure 1-20: Screen displayed from the Help menu's Contents options

Another way to get help is to use the Search For Help On... option (called Search... in Version 2.0) on the Help menu. This option lets you search for help on a specific topic.

Let's say you would like to get some information on the Toolbox window. You can practice with the Help menu Search For Help On... (or Search... in Version 2.0) option by searching for a Help screen on that topic.

To access Help through the Help menu Search For Help On... (or Search... in Version 2.0) option:

1   Click **Help** to open the Help menu.

2   *If you are using Version 2.0,* click **Search...** in the Help menu. Visual Basic displays the Search dialog box shown in Figure 1-21.

If you are using Version 3.0, click **Search For Help On...** in the Help menu. Visual Basic displays the Search dialog box shown in Figure 1-21.

Search dialog box instructions

**options are slightly
different in Version 2.0**

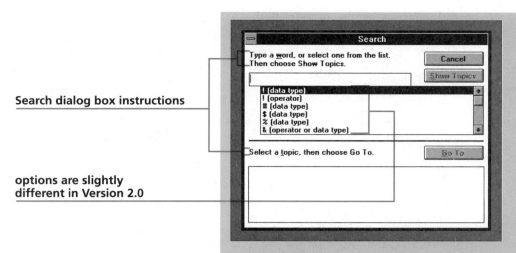

Figure 1-21: Search dialog box

You can either type a topic into the text box at the top of the Search dialog box or select one of the topics from the list. The topics in the list are in alphabetical order.

3　Type **toolbox** in the text box. The selection bar moves to the Toolbox topic.

4　Click the **Show Topics button** to have Visual Basic display a list of topics associated with the word you entered. Two topics appear in the list box. The Toolbox topic is currently selected.

5　Click the **Go To button** to view the Help screen for the selected topic. The Help screen for the Toolbox topic appears. See Figure 1-22. Remember that you can view additional Help screens for an underlined word or phrase by simply clicking the word or phrase. (You can also maximize a Help screen to read more of its contents.)

**Visual Basic Help
Control menu box**

Maximize button

**click underlined words
for additional help**

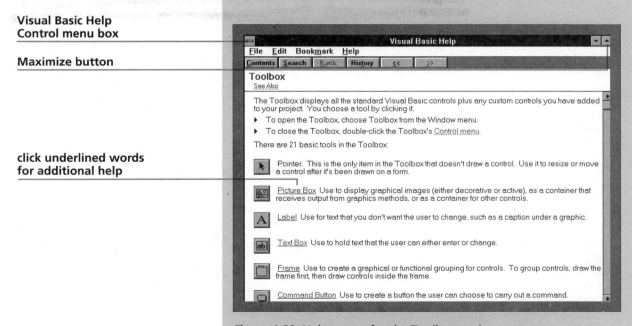

Figure 1-22: Help screen for the Toolbox topic

6   If you are connected to a printer, click **File**, then click **Print Topic** to print the Help screen.

7   Double-click the **Visual Basic Help Control menu box** to close the Help screen.

In addition to using the Contents option and the Search For Help On... (or Search...) option in the Help menu, you can also access the Help screens by pressing [F1]. [F1] provides you with context-sensitive help. That means Visual Basic displays a Help screen for whatever is currently selected. In many instances [F1] is a faster way of getting help. You can use [F1], for example, to display the Help screen for the Toolbox window, but you must first select that window.

To use [F1] to display the Help screen for the Toolbox window:

1   Click the **Toolbox window title bar**. The Toolbox window's title bar is now highlighted, which means that the Toolbox is the currently selected window.

2   Press [**F1**] to display a Help screen for the Toolbox window. The same Help screen shown earlier in Figure 1-22 appears on the screen.

3   Double-click the **Visual Basic Help Control menu box** to close the Help screen.

Be sure to refer to the Help screens if you have any questions or problems while you are working in Visual Basic. Now let's add some objects to the current form.

Adding a Control to a Form

The tools in the Toolbox allow you to add graphical objects, called **controls**, to a form. The terms "object" and "control" are often used interchangeably in Visual Basic. Technically, however, a control refers to an object placed on a form. Although the form itself is an object, it is not a control. (The tutorials in this book use "object" to refer both to a form and a control; "control" refers only to the objects placed on the form—not the form itself.)

The first tool you will use is the Label tool—the large letter A located in the left column, second row of the Toolbox. The **Label tool** creates a Label control (graphical object) that you can use to display text you don't want the user to modify. In other words, when your application is run, Visual Basic will not allow the user to make any changes to the contents of a Label control. In this application, you do not want the user to modify the information on the copyright screen, so a Label control is the correct control to use.

tips

· ·

▶ If a Label control does not appear in the center of the form, double-click the Label tool again.

To have Visual Basic create a default-size Label control in the center of the form:

1   Double-click the **Label tool** Ⓐ in the Toolbox. A default-size Label control appears in the center of the form, with the default caption Label1. See Figure 1-23.

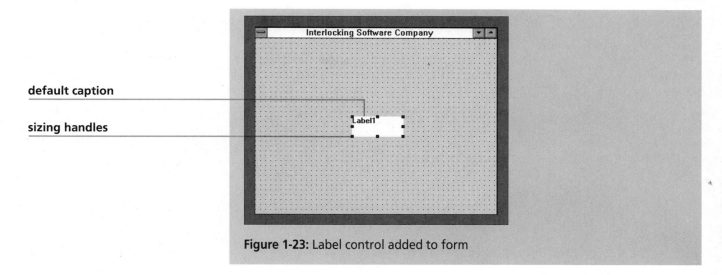

default caption

sizing handles

Figure 1-23: Label control added to form

Notice that a Label control's caption—in this case, Label1—appears inside the control. Visual Basic also assigns Label1 as the default setting of this control's Name property. You can verify that, if you want, by scrolling the Properties list in the Properties window until you see the Name property.

In order to use Visual Basic efficiently, you must know how to size, move, and delete the controls you've placed on the form. You will learn these three skills next.

Sizing, Moving, and Deleting a Control

You size, move, and delete a Visual Basic control in the same manner as you do in any Windows application. First, you must select the control that you want to size, move, or delete. You select a control by clicking it; when a control is selected, sizing handles appear around it. For example, notice the sizing handles around the Label1 control in Figure 1-23, indicating that the control is selected. Let's practice sizing, moving, and deleting the Label1 control.

To size, move, and then delete the Label1 control, which is currently selected:

1   Place the mouse pointer on the Label control's lower-right sizing handle until the mouse pointer becomes a double-headed arrow. Then drag the sizing handle until the object is a little larger than the default size. Then release the mouse button. (You don't need to worry about the exact size.)

2   Now to move the Label1 control, position the mouse pointer anywhere on the Label1 control, except on a sizing handle. Drag the Label1 control to the upper-left corner of the screen, then release the mouse button. (Don't worry about the exact location.)

3   The Label1 control should still be selected, so press the **Delete key** to delete the control.

Now that you know how to add, size, move, and delete controls, you can continue building the copyright screen.

Adding Label Controls to the Copyright Screen

The copyright screen application requires two Label controls: one for the name of the application's author and the other for the copyright year.

> To add two Label controls to the copyright screen:
> 1 Double-click the **Label tool** A in the Toolbox. The Label1 control appears in the center of the form.
> 2 Drag the Label1 control to the upper-left corner of the screen. (Don't worry about the exact location.)
> 3 Double-click the **Label tool** A in the Toolbox again. The Label2 control appears in the center of the form.
> 4 Drag the Label2 control to a location immediately below the Label1 control.

Now that the controls are on the form, the next step is setting their properties.

Setting the Properties of a Label Control

The first property you will set is the Name property. Recall that you use the Name property to assign meaningful names to objects. Following the naming convention discussed earlier, you will assign the name LblAuthor to the first Label control and the name LblYear to the second Label control. The "Lbl" identifies the objects as Label controls, and "Author" and "Year" indicate each control's purpose in the form.

tips

If you accidentally double-clicked the Label1 control, you will see a smaller window in the center of the screen. Double-click the smaller window's Control menu box to close the window.

> To set the Name property of the Label controls:
> 1 Click the **Label1 control** in the form to select it. Sizing handles appear around the control. The Properties window also shows that the Label1 control is the currently selected object.
> 2 Click the **Name** property in the Properties list to select it, then type **LblAuthor** and press [Enter] to enter a new name for this control. LblAuthor appears as the value of the Name property in the Properties list.
> 3 Click the **Label2 control** in the form to select it. Sizing handles appear around the control.
> The Name property is already selected in the Properties list.
> 4 Type **LblYear** and press [Enter] to enter a new name for this control. LblYear appears as the value of the Name property in the Properties list.

Like forms, Label controls also have a Caption property, which controls the text that appears inside the Label control. In this application you want the words "Written By" and your name to appear in the LblAuthor control, and the word "Copyright" and the year 1997 to appear in the LblYear control, so you will need to set both controls' Caption properties accordingly.

▶ If you opened the Object box, click the down arrow again to close it.

▶ If you minimized the Properties window, double-click its icon to display it.

To set the Caption property for the two Label controls:

1 The LblYear Label control is currently selected, so just click the **Caption property** in the Properties list to select that property.

2 Type **Copyright 1997** and press **[Enter]**. The new caption appears in the LblYear control.

Because the caption is longer than the width of the control, some of the information wraps around to the next line. You can use the sizing handles to size the Label control until the entire caption appears on one line, or you can change the Label control's AutoSize property. The AutoSize property does just what its name implies: It automatically sizes the control to fit its current contents. Let's set the AutoSize property.

3 Click the **AutoSize** property in the Properties list. Notice that the down arrow button in the Settings box darkens, which means this property has predefined settings.

4 Click the **down arrow button** in the Settings box, located immediately above the Properties list in the Properties window, to see the valid settings for the AutoSize property. A drop-down list appears.

As the drop-down list indicates, Visual Basic allows you to set the AutoSize property to either True or False. (Many of the other properties shown in the Properties list also have only these two settings.) The True setting turns the property on; the False setting turns the property off. To tell Visual Basic to size the selected control automatically, you will set the control's AutoSize property to True.

5 Click **True** in the drop-down list. The Label control automatically stretches to fit the caption.

Now set the AutoSize and Caption properties for the LblAuthor control.

6 Click the **LblAuthor Label control**. Sizing handles appear around the control. See Figure 1-24.

LblAuthor control

LblYear control

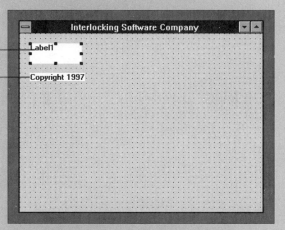

Figure 1-24: LblAuthor control selected in form

The AutoSize property is still selected in the Properties list.

7 Click the **down arrow button in the Settings box**, located immediately above the Properties list in the Properties window, then click **True** in the drop-down list.

8 Click the **Caption** property in the Properties list to select that property.

9 Type **Written By**, then press the **spacebar**, then type your name and press **[Enter]**. (Actually type your name, not the words "your name.")

Now let's concentrate on the placement of these two Label controls on the form.

Setting the Left and Top Properties

Recall that you can drag a control to any position on the form. So that your screen agrees with the figures in the book, however, you will sometimes be given the value of each control's Left property and Top property. These two properties control the position of the upper-left corner of the object. Let's use the Left and Top properties to move the LblYear control to its proper position on the form. This time, instead of selecting the control by clicking it on the form, you will use the Object box to select the control.

To select a control using the Object box, and then set the control's Left property and its Top property:

1 Click the **down arrow button in the Object box,** located immediately below the Properties window's title bar, to display its drop-down list. The list shows the name and type of all objects included in the form.

2 Click **LblYear Label** in the drop-down list to select that Label control. The LblYear control is now selected, as the sizing handles indicate.

3 Click the **Left** property in the Properties list to select it.

The location of an object in a form is measured in twips from the edges of the form. A **twip** is 1/1440 of an inch. If you set the Left property to 1440, Visual Basic positions the control 1" from the left edge of the form. (Actual physical distances on the screen vary according to the size of the monitor.) Let's position the LblYear control 2" from the left edge of the form.

4 Type **2880** as the Left property and press **[Enter]** to position the selected control 2" from the left edge of the form. Visual Basic moves the object accordingly.

5 Click the **Top** property in the Properties list, type **4320**, and press **[Enter]** to position the control 3" from the top of the form. Visual Basic positions the control accordingly. (Don't worry if the control disappears from view. You will see the control when you maximize the form in the next section.)

You can now set the Left and Top properties of the other Label control.

6 Click the **down arrow button** in the Object box, located immediately below the Properties window's title bar, to display the drop-down list of objects, and then click **LblAuthor Label** to select that Label control.

Since the Top property is already selected in the Properties list, you'll set that property first.

7 Type **3360**, and press **[Enter]** to set the Top property. The Label control moves to its proper position on the top.

8 Click the **Left** property in the Properties list, type **2880** and press **[Enter]** to set the Left property. The control moves to its proper position on the form.

twips

The final modification you will make to these Label controls is to set their FontSize property. As you will see in the next section, you can set the FontSize property for both controls at the same time.

Selecting More Than One Control

Many of the Visual Basic controls have font properties that determine the appearance of the text displayed in the control. For example, the FontName property controls the type of font Visual Basic uses to display text in the form. (A **font** is the general shape of the characters in the text.) Another font property is FontSize, which controls the size of the font. You can make the text in the two Label controls more noticeable by increasing the size of the font Visual Basic uses. You can set the value of the FontSize property for both controls at the same time by clicking one control and then pressing and holding down the Control key as you click the other control in the form. (You must hold down the Control key as you click the control in the form; you can't hold down the Control key and click the control's name in the Object box.) You can use the Control-click method to select as many controls as you want. You cancel the selection by clicking on the form or on any unselected control in the form.

If the **LblAuthor** is not selected, click the **LblAuthor** control to select it.

To select both Label controls and then set their FontSize property:

1   The LblAuthor control should still be selected. Verify that by looking in the Object box in the Properties window or by looking for sizing handles around the control.

2   Click the **form's Maximize button** so that you can see the LblYear control.

3   Press and hold down the **Ctrl key** as you click the **LblYear control**, and then press **[F4]** to display the Properties window. Both Label controls are now selected, as shown in Figure 1-25.

no values shown when more than one control is selected

both Label controls are selected

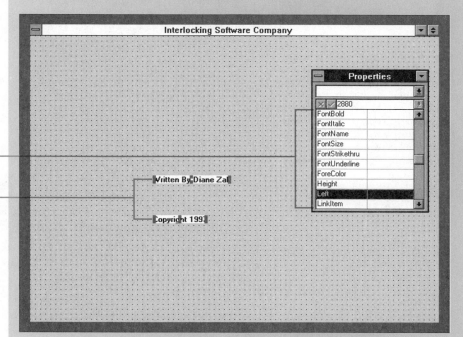

Figure 1-25: Both Label controls selected

Notice that no values appear in the right column of the Properties list when you have more than one control selected.

4 Click the **FontSize** property in the Properties list. The darkened down arrow button in the Settings box indicates that this property has predefined settings.

5 Click the **down arrow button in the Settings box** to display the drop-down list of predefined settings.

The size of a font is measured in points. One **point** equals 1/72 of an inch.

6 Click **18** (or a number close to 18) to increase the font size to 18 points. The text in the two Label controls is displayed in the new font size.

7 Click the **form** to cancel the selection of the Label controls, then click the **form's Restore button** to restore the form to its standard size.

Saving Files under a Different Name

Before ending Lesson B, you will save what you have completed so far and then run the application to see how it looks. Usually you save the form and the project using its original name. In this case, however, you will give the form and the project a different name. By saving the form and the project under a different name, you can repeat this lesson as often as you want because the original files from Lesson A will still be on your Student Disk. One very important note: You must save the form under a different name before saving the project under a different name.

To save the form and the project under a different name:

1 Click **File**, then click **Save File As...** to save the form. The Save File As dialog box appears with the current name of the form, t1a.frm, offered in the File Name box. (The File Name box also shows the current drive and the current directory.)

2 Type **t1b** in the File Name box, then click the **OK button** to save the form under the new name. A copy of the FrmCopyright form is now saved as t1b.frm on your Student Disk.

Notice that Visual Basic updates the Project window to reflect the new name of the form file, T1B.FRM. That's why you must give the form a new name before giving the project a new name. (Notice that the name of the form within the .frm file, however, is still FrmCopyright.) You can now save the project.

3 Click **File**, then click **Save Project As...** to save the project. The Save Project As dialog box appears with the current name of the project, t1a.mak, offered in the File Name box. (The File Name box also shows the current drive and the current directory.)

4 Type **t1b** in the File Name box, then click the **OK button** to save the project under the new name. A copy of the project is now saved as t1b.mak on your Student Disk.

Now that the files are saved, you can run the project.

5 Click the **Run icon** ▣ in the toolbar. (Or press [F5].) The copyright screen appears. See Figure 1-26.

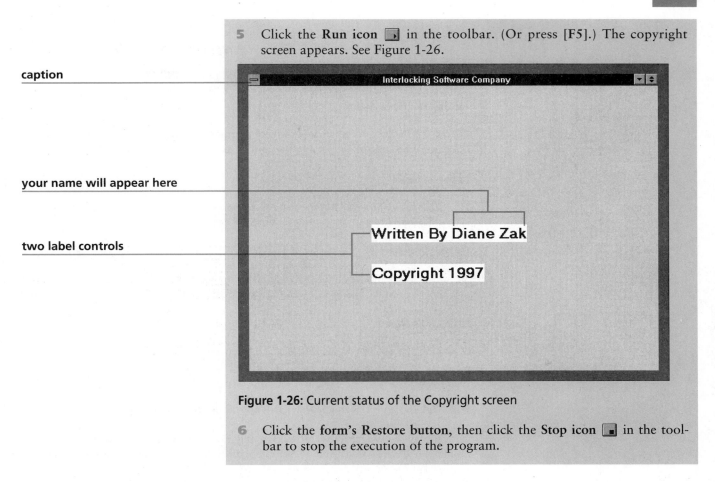

caption

your name will appear here

two label controls

Written By Diane Zak

Copyright 1997

Figure 1-26: Current status of the Copyright screen

6 Click the **form's Restore button**, then click the **Stop icon** ▣ in the toolbar to stop the execution of the program.

Now you can either take a break or complete the end-of-lesson questions and exercises. In Lesson C you will complete the copyright screen.

S U M M A R Y

To access the Visual Basic Help screens:

Using the Help Menu Contents option:
■ Click Help in the menu bar, then click Contents. You can then click any of the underlined words or phrases to display additional Help screens.

Using the Help Menu Search For... (or Search...) option:
■ Click Help in the menu bar.
■ If you are using Version 2.0, click Search.... If you are using Version 3.0, click Search For Help On.... A dialog box appears.
■ In the dialog box, enter the word or phrase for which you want help, or select a topic from the list in the dialog box.
■ Click the Show Topics button. A list of associated topics displays.
■ Click the topic you want, then click the Go To button. Visual Basic displays the appropriate Help screen. You can then click any of the underlined words or phrases to display additional Help screens.

Using the F1 key:
- Select the object, window, property, and so on for which you want help.
- Press F1. A context-sensitive Help screen appears. You can then click any of the underlined words or phrases to display additional Help screens.

To add a control to a form:

- In the Toolbox, double-click the tool representing the control you want to add.
- Move the control and/or size the control as necessary.

To size an object:

- Click the object you want to size. Then position the mouse pointer on one of the sizing handles and drag until the object is the desired size.

To move an object:

- Position the mouse pointer on the object you want to move, being careful not to position the pointer on any of the sizing handles. Then drag the object to its new location.

To delete an object:

- Select the object you want to delete, then press the Delete key.

To select an object:

- Click the object. Sizing handles will appear around the object.
  or
- Display the Properties window, click the down arrow button in the Object box, then click the name of the object in the drop-down list. Sizing handles will appear around the object.

To select multiple controls:

- Click the first control you want to select in the form.
- Press and hold down the Control key as you click the other controls you want to select. You must do this procedure on the controls in the form, not their names in the Object box.

To cancel the selection of multiple controls:

To cancel the selection of one of the selected controls:
- Press and hold down the Control key as you click the control.

To cancel the selection of all of the selected controls:
- Click on the form or on any unselected control in the form.

To save the open form and project using a different name:

- Click File, then click Save File As... to save the form. Enter the new name for the form in the File Name box, select the appropriate drive and directory, then click the OK button. If the filename already exists on the disk, Visual Basic will display a dialog box stating that the file already exists and asking if you want to replace the existing file. If you want to replace the form file on the disk with the current form, click Yes; otherwise, click No.

■ Click File, then click Save Project As... to save the project. Enter the new name for the project in the File Name box, select the appropriate drive and directory, then click the OK button. If the filename already exists on the disk, Visual Basic will display a dialog box stating that the file already exists and asking if you want to replace the existing file. If you want to replace the project file on the disk with the current project, click Yes; otherwise, click No.

Q U E S T I O N S

1. You can open context-sensitive Help screens by selecting an object and pressing _____.
   a. [F1]
   b. [F2]
   c. [F3]
   d. [F4]
   e. [F5]

2. The _____ tool creates a control in which you display text that you don't want the user to change.
   a. Caption
   b. Command
   c. Control
   d. Label
   e. Text

3. The location of an object in a form is measured in _____ from the edges of the form.
   a. characters
   b. inches
   c. points
   d. twips
   e. twups

4. The size of a font is measured in _____.
   a. characters
   b. inches
   c. points
   d. twips
   e. twups

5. Which of the following properties tells a Label control to adjust automatically to the size of its caption?
   a. AutoAdjust
   b. AutoCaption
   c. AutoControl
   d. AutoLblSize
   e. AutoSize

6. Explain how to select more than one control.

7. Explain how to save an existing form file and an existing project file under a different name.

8. Explain the three ways of accessing the Visual Basic Help screens.

EXERCISES

1. Launch Visual Basic (if necessary) and open the T1LAE1 project.
   a. Click the View Form button to view the FrmCharity form.
   b. Add a Label control to the form.
   c. Set the following properties for the Label control:
      Caption: Charities Unlimited
      Name: LblTitle
      Left: 800 twips
      FontSize: 24 points
      AutoSize: True
      Top: 1000 twips
   d. Use the File menu's Save File As and Save Project As options to save the form and the project as T1LBE1.
   e. Run the application. Then stop the application.

2. Launch Visual Basic (if necessary) and open the T1LAE2 project.
   a. Click the View Form button to view the FrmPhotos form.
   b. Add two Label controls to the form.
   c. Set the following properties for the first Label control:
      Caption: Welcome To   FontSize: 24 points
      Name: LblLine1   AutoSize: True
      Left: 800 twips   Top: 1000 twips
   d. Set the following properties for the second Label control:
      Caption: Photos Inc.   FontSize: 24 points
      Name: LblLine2   AutoSize: True
      Left: 800 twips   Top: 2400 twips
   e. Use the File menu's Save File As and Save Project As options to save the form and the project as T1LBE2.
   f. Run the application. Then stop the application.

3. Use the Search For Help On... (or Search...) option on the Visual Basic Help menu to find and then print the Help screen for each of the following topics:
   a. applications: creating EXE
   b. assigning icons (to a form)
   c. BackStyle (property)
   d. Caption (property)
   e. changing properties
   f. Command button (control)
   g. Code window (Guidelines for Entering and Editing Code)
   h. drawing controls
   i. twip (definition)

LESSON C

objectives

In this lesson you will learn how to:

- Add an Image control to the form
- Add a Command button to the form
- Open and close an object's Code window
- Enter code in a Code window
- Print the form, the form text, and the code
- Make an executable file

Writing Code

Adding an Image Control to the Form

According to the sketch of the copyright screen (Figure 1-1), you need to include the Interlocking Software Company logo in your application. You can use either the Image tool or the Picture box tool to add a picture (or icon) to a form. One advantage of the Image tool over the Picture box is that the Image tool requires less memory. You will use the Image tool to create an Image control for the copyright screen.

To add an Image control to the form:

1 Launch Visual Basic, if necessary. Click the **Open Project icon** 🗁 to open the T1B.MAK project that you created in Lesson B. Depending on your version of Visual Basic, the T1B.MAK file is in either the tut1\ver2 or the tut1\ver3 directory on your Student Disk.

2 Click the **View Form button** to view the FrmCopyright form.

3 Double-click the **Image tool** 🖾 in the Toolbox. An empty rectangular box with sizing handles appears in the center of the form. This is the Image control into which you will place the company's logo. You place (or load) a picture into an Image control by setting the control's Picture property.

4 If necessary, click the **Picture property** in the Properties list to select it. An ellipsis (...) button appears in the Settings box located above the Properties list in the Properties window.

5 Click the **... button** (ellipsis button) in the Properties window's Settings box. The Load Picture dialog box appears.

6 Click the **down arrow button in the Drives box**, then click the letter of the drive containing your Student Disk, then double-click **a:** (or **b:**) in the Directories list box, then double-click **tut1** in the Directories list box.

7 *If you are using Visual Basic Version 2.0*, double-click **ver2** in the Directories list box. A list of filenames appears in the File Name list box.

If you are using Visual Basic Version 3.0, double-click **ver3** in the Directories list box. A list of filenames appears in the File Name list box.

8 Click **inter.bmp** in the File Name box, then click the **OK button**. The Interlocking Software logo appears in the Image control in the center of the form.

You will now set the Name property of the Image control, and then position the upper-left corner of the Image control by setting its Left and Top properties.

To set the Name, Left, and Top properties of the Image control:

1   Click the **form's Maximize button** to maximize the form, then press **[F4]** to display the Properties window.

2   Set the following properties for the Image control:

Left: **6700**

Name: **ImgLogo** ("Img" identifies the object as an Image control.)

Top: **240**

3   Click the **form** to remove the Properties window. See Figure 1-27.

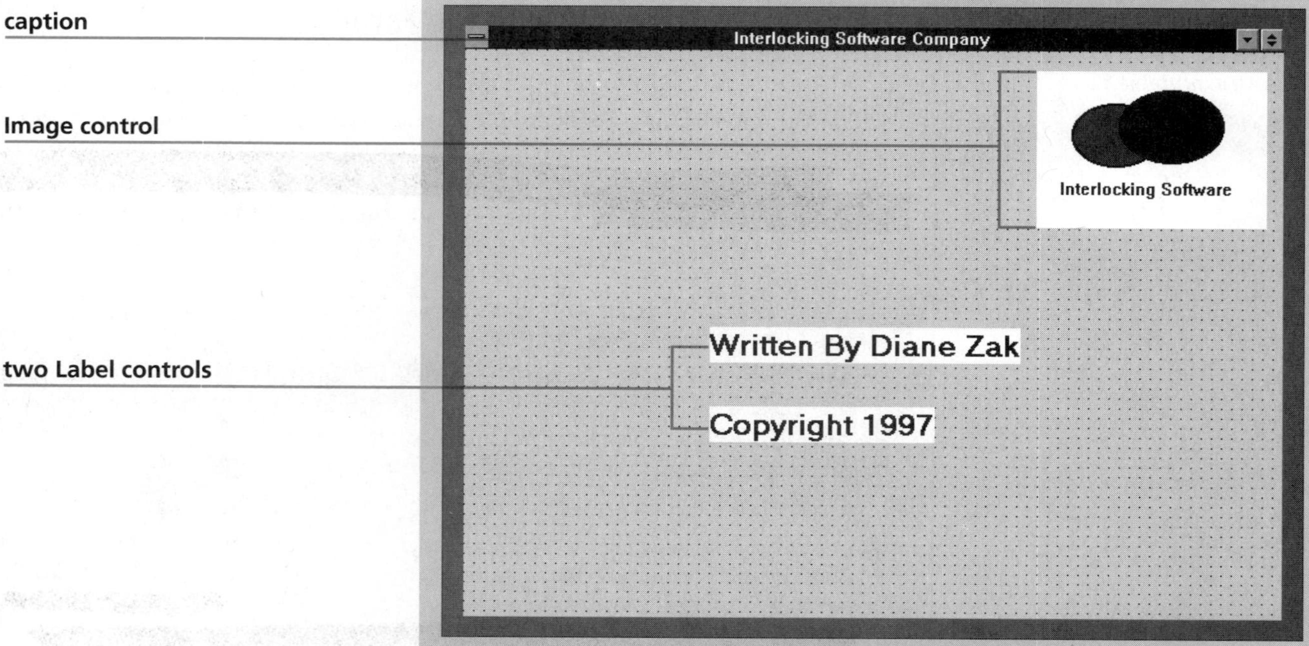

caption

Image control

two Label controls

Figure 1-27: Copyright screen with Image control added

4   Click the **form's Restore button** to restore the form to its standard size.

According to the sketch (Figure 1-1), the copyright screen is almost complete. All that remains is to add the Exit button.

Adding a Command Button to the Form

Every Windows application should give the user a way to quit the program. Most Windows applications provide either an Exit option on a File menu or an Exit button. As you saw earlier, the copyright screen uses an Exit button. You create the Exit button by using the Command button tool, which is the third tool in the right column of the Toolbox.

In Windows applications, Command buttons perform an immediate action when clicked. The OK and Cancel buttons are examples of Command buttons found in many applications. In the copyright screen, the Exit Command button will end the application when the button is clicked by the user.

To add a Command button control to the form:

1 Double-click the **Command button tool** in the Toolbox. A default-size button appears in the center of the form. The default name and caption of this control is Command1.

You will now set the Name, Caption, and FontSize properties for this control. You will also move the Command button to the bottom right corner of the screen. Remember that you can position a control on the form either by dragging it or by setting its Left and Top properties. (Recall that the values of the Left and Top properties are given to you just so that your screen agrees with the figures in the book. Otherwise you could simply drag the control to the proper position.)

2 Click the **form's Maximize button**, then press **[F4]** to display the Properties window.

3 Set the Command button's properties as follows:

Name: **CmdExit**   Caption: **Exit**   FontSize: **24**

Left: **7500**   Top: **5760**

The "Cmd" in the Name property identifies the control as a Command button. "Exit" identifies the purpose of this control.

4 Click the **form** to remove the Properties window. See Figure 1-28.

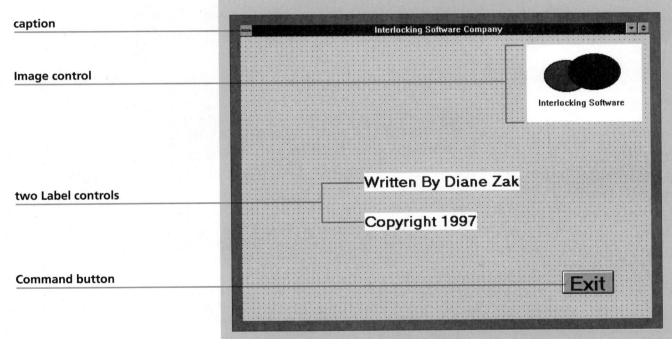

caption

Image control

two Label controls

Command button

Figure 1-28: Copyright screen with Command button added

5 Click the **form's Restore button** to restore the form to its standard size.

Although the Exit button appears on the screen and its properties are set, you're not done with this control yet, as you'll see in the next section.

Writing Visual Basic Code

Think about the Windows environment for a moment. Did you ever wonder why the OK and Cancel buttons respond the way they do when you click them, or how the Exit option on the File menu knows to quit the application? The answer to these questions is very simple: A programmer gave the buttons and menu options explicit instructions on how to respond to the actions of the user. Those actions—such as clicking, double-clicking, and scrolling—are called **events**. The Visual Basic instructions, or **code**, that tells an object how to respond to an event is called an **event procedure**.

At this point, the Exit button in the copyright screen does not know what it is supposed to do; you must tell it what to do by writing an event procedure for it. You write the event procedure in the object's Code window, which is a window you have not yet seen. Each object has its own Code window. You open a Code window by double-clicking the object.

Let's open the Code window for the Exit button. Inside the Code window, you will enter instructions that tell the button to end the application when the button is clicked by the user.

To open the Command button's Code window:

1   Click the **form's Maximize button** to maximize the form.

2   Double-click the **Exit Command button** on the form. The button's Code window opens. See Figure 1-29.

Control menu box

Object box

input area

current event procedure

Proc (Procedure) box

Proc box down arrow button

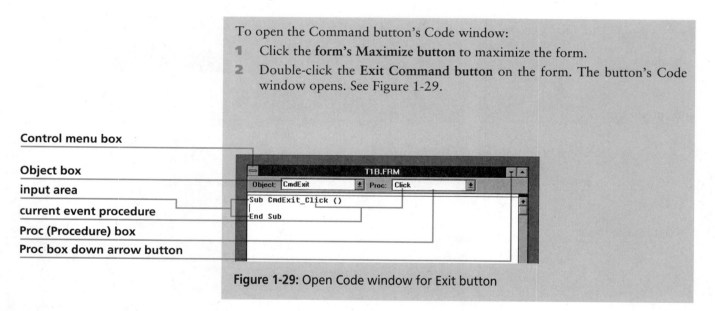

Figure 1-29: Open Code window for Exit button

The Visual Basic Code window contains an Object box, a Proc (Procedure) box, and an input area. The Object box performs the same function as the Object box in the Properties window; both allow you to choose other objects on the form. You can also use the Object box to verify the name of a control while you are writing instructions in the Code window.

The Proc (Procedure) box in the Code window lists the event procedures to which the selected object is capable of responding. The Proc box shows that the current event procedure—the event procedure shown in the input area of the Code window—is Click. You can see what other event procedures an object can recognize by clicking the down arrow button in the Proc box. Let's see what other event procedures a Command button can recognize.

To display the event procedures in the Proc box:

1   Click the **down arrow button in the Proc box** located in the Code window. A drop-down list of event procedures appears. See Figure 1-30.

**event procedures for
selected objects (Version 2
list will be different)**

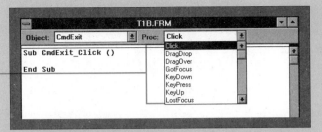

Figure 1-30: Drop-down list of event procedures

If you are using Version 2.0, you will not see scroll bars on the drop-down list. If you are using Version 3.0, the scroll bars on the list box indicate that not all of the event procedures are currently displayed. You would need to scroll down the list box to see the remaining event procedures. To change to another event procedure, simply click the one you want in the list. Let's try this.

2   Click **GotFocus** in the Proc box. Notice that both the Sub statement and the Proc box now show that the GotFocus event procedure is the current one. See Figure 1-31.

current event procedure

Proc box down arrow button

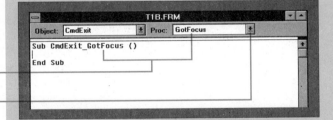

Figure 1-31: GotFocus event procedure

Because you need to enter the instruction to end the application in the Click event, you will need to switch back to that procedure.

3   Click the **down arrow button in the Proc box** to open the drop-down list of event procedures.

4   *If you are using Visual Basic Version 2.0*, click the **Click** event procedure. The Click event procedure is now the current procedure. See Figure 1-32.

   If you are using Visual Basic Version 3.0, scroll the Proc box until the Click event is visible, then click the **Click** event procedure. The Click event procedure is now the current procedure. See Figure 1-32.

Control menu box

name of the control

input area

event (action) that causes the
control to respond

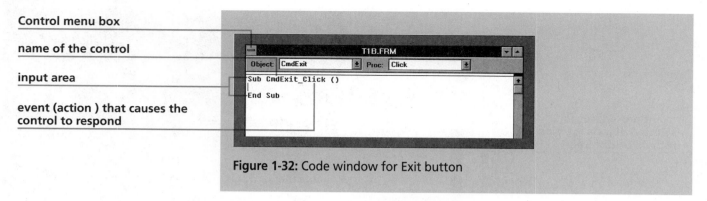

Figure 1-32: Code window for Exit button

You will notice that the input area of the Code window already contains some Visual Basic code (instructions). To help you follow the rules of its language, called **syntax**, Visual Basic provides you with a code template for every event procedure. The code template begins with the word Sub. (In programming terminology, blocks of code that perform a specific task are called **subprocedures** or **subroutines**. The Sub in Visual Basic's code is an abbreviation of these terms.) Following the word "Sub" is the name of the control (CmdExit), an underscore (_), the name of the current event (Click), and parentheses. The code template ends with the two words "End Sub." You must enter your Visual Basic instructions between the Sub and End Sub lines. The instructions in the Code window tell the control (CmdExit) how to respond to the current event (Click).

If you are using a color monitor, notice that the words "Sub," "End Sub," and the parentheses appear in a different color than both the control's name and the word "Click." Visual Basic displays keywords and key symbols in a different color to help you quickly identify these elements in the Code window. In this case, the color coding helps you easily locate the beginning and ending of the event procedure. Now let's enter the instruction that will tell the Exit button to end the application when clicked by the user.

The blinking insertion point located in the input area of the Code window means that Visual Basic is waiting for you to type something in the window. In this case you want to tell the Exit button to end the application whenever the button is clicked. For this you need to use the "End" instruction, which has a very specific meaning in Visual Basic; it tells Visual Basic to terminate the current application. You'll indent the code in the Code window to make the instructions easier to read.

To enter the code into the open Code window:

1 Press [Tab], then type **end** in the Code window, and then press [Enter]. See Figure 1-33.

Control menu box

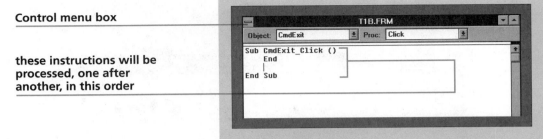

these instructions will be processed, one after another, in this order

Figure 1-33: End instruction entered in Code window

· · · · · · · · · · · · · · · · · ·

▶ If you accidentally closed the form instead of the Code window, double-click the Code window's Control menu box to close the Code window, then click the View Form button in the Project window to display the form.

When the user clicks the Exit button, Visual Basic reads and processes the instructions entered in the Code window. It is probably no surprise to you that Visual Basic processes the instructions, one after another, in the order in which the instructions are entered in the Code window. In programming, this is referred to as **sequential processing** or as the **sequence structure**. (You will learn about two other programming structures, selection and repetition, in future tutorials.) You're finished with the Code window, so you can close it.

2   Double-click the **Code window's Control menu box** to close the window, then click the **form's Restore button** to restore the form to its standard size.

Your next step is to save the application, then run it to make sure it is working properly. Here again, you will save the form and the project under a different name so that both the T1B.FRM form file and the T1B.MAK project file remain intact. This approach will allow you to practice Lesson C as often as you like.

To save and then run the application:

1   Click **File**, click **Save File As...**, type **t1c** in the File Name box, and then click the **OK button** to save the form under the new name. A copy of the FrmCopyright form is now saved as t1c.frm on your Student Disk. (Recall that you must save the form before you save the project.)

2   Click **File**, click **Save Project As...**, type **t1c** in the File Name box, then click the **OK button** to save the project under the new name. A copy of the project is now saved as t1c.mak on your Student Disk.

Now that the files are saved, you can run the project to see if it is working correctly.

3 Click the **Run icon** ☐ in the toolbar. (Or press [F5].) The copyright screen appears. See Figure 1-34.

Control menu box

Minimize button

Restore / Maximize button

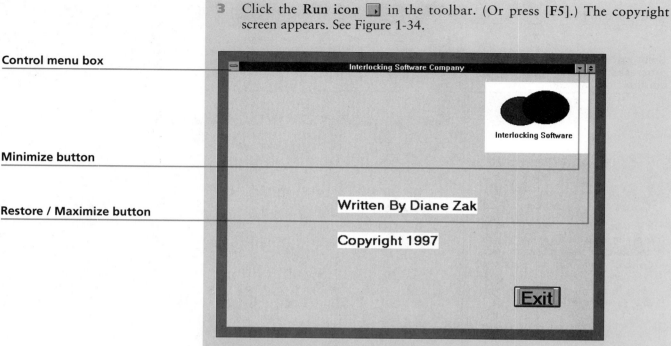

Figure 1-34: Copyright screen with border elements

Let's see if the Exit button ends the application when it is clicked.

4 Click the **Exit button** in the user interface. (Or, because the Exit button is currently selected, as indicated by the dotted rectangle around the button's caption, you could also press [**Enter**]. Recall that Windows applications allow you to choose a Command button either by clicking it or by pressing the Enter key when the button is selected. Visual Basic will perform the "End" instruction when either of these two methods is used to choose the Exit button, even though the instruction is entered in the Click event procedure.)

Now that you know your application is working correctly, you can remove its Control menu box and the Minimize and Maximize buttons. Removing those elements will prevent the user from sizing your copyright screen and from exiting without clicking the Exit button. You can remove the Control menu box and the Minimize and Maximize buttons by setting the form's BorderStyle property.

Setting the BorderStyle Property

The BorderStyle property determines the border style of an object. The default BorderStyle for a form is 2-Sizable. If you want to prevent the user from sizing the user interface or from exiting using the Control menu box, you can reset the BorderStyle property to 0-None.

tips
. . . .
▶ If a dialog box appears on the screen with the message "Syntax error," click the OK button, type the End command correctly in the Exit button's Code window, double-click the Code window's Control menu box, and then click the Run icon again.

To change the form's BorderStyle property, then save and run the project:

1   If necessary, click the **form** to select it. The form's title bar is now high-lighted.

2   Click the **BorderStyle** property in the Properties list, then press **[F1]** to view the Help screen for this property. The Help screen appears.

Notice the four BorderStyle property settings for a form. You want the 0-None setting, which removes the border and its related elements.

3   Double-click the **Help screen's Control menu box** to close the Help screen.

4   Click the **down arrow in the Settings box**, then click the **0-None** setting. Visual Basic will remove the form's border when the application is run.

5   Click the **Save Project icon** 🖫 in the toolbar, then click the **Run icon** 🔘 in the toolbar. Notice that the border is no longer displayed when you run the application. See Figure 1-35.

Border elements removed

Figure 1-35: Copyright screen without border elements

6   Click the **Exit button** to end the application. Visual Basic returns to the design screen.

Be sure you do not change the BorderStyle property to 0-None until after you have tested your application and you are sure it is working correctly; otherwise, the only way to end the application is to reboot the computer with [Ctrl][Alt][Del].

Your first application is finally complete. All that remains is to print the application, then make it into an executable (.EXE) file that can be run directly from Windows, like the applications in the Overview and in Lesson A of this tutorial.

Printing a Visual Basic Application

You should always print a copy of the form, the properties of the objects included in the form (called the form text), and the code you wrote. This information, called **documentation**, will help you understand and maintain the application in the future.

tips

· · · · · · · · · · · · · · · · · ·

▶ If the Print Manager displays a dialog box telling you it can't print your application, check that the printer is on, that it is on-line, and that it has paper. If none of these seems to be the problem, ask your technical support person for assistance.

▶ If the output from the printer doesn't look anything like the form, you may have the wrong printer selected in the Print Manager. Ask your technical support person for assistance.

To print the application:

1   Click **File** to open the File menu. The File menu opens.

The File menu contains an option called Print.... If you choose that option to print the form, however, only the portion of the form currently showing on the screen will print. Notice that you can also print by using the Control P combination. ([Ctrl][P] means to press and hold down the Control key as you type the letter P.) You can use the Control P combination to print the entire form, but first you need to maximize the form.

2   Click **File** to close the File menu. The File menu closes.

3   Click the **Maximize button** in the Interlocking Software Company title bar. The form fills the entire screen.

4   Press [Ctrl][P]. (Press and hold down the Control key as you type the letter P.) The Print dialog box appears.

You will print the form first.

5   Click **Form**, then click the **OK button** to print the form.

6   Click the **form's Restore button** to restore the form.

You will print the Form Text and the Code next. The Form Text option prints the property settings of the objects in the application. The Code option prints the Visual Basic instructions entered in the Code windows.

7   Click **File**, then click **Print...** to open the Print dialog box.

8   Click **Form Text**, click **Code**, and then click the **OK button**. Visual Basic prints the property settings of the objects in the application. Visual Basic also prints the contents of the Exit button's Code window.

The final topic in this lesson is to make the copyright screen into an executable (.EXE) file that can be run directly from Windows. (Recall that the Monthly Payment application in the Overview and the copyright screen you previewed in Lesson A of Tutorial 1 were run directly from the Windows Program Manager.)

Making an Executable (.EXE) File

In the Overview you learned that high-level languages require either an interpreter or a compiler to convert the English-like instructions into machine code—the 0s and 1s the computer can understand. Recall that both interpreters and compilers are separate programs. An interpreter translates the high-level instructions into machine code, line by line, as the program is executing. For example, when you click the Run icon to run the copyright screen application, Visual Basic's interpreter translates your application, line by line, into the machine code the computer can understand. Visual Basic's interpreter makes that translation each time you click the Run icon.

Recall that a compiler translates the entire program into machine code before executing the program. Visual Basic's compiler saves the machine code in a separate file on your disk. The file has an .EXE extension on its name; the .EXE extension stands for "executable." Whenever you want to run your application, you simply tell the computer to execute the .EXE file. Because the .EXE file already contains the machine code version of your application, the computer does not need to re-translate the application, which means that your application will run faster.

Another reason for using Visual Basic's compiler to create an executable (.EXE) file is that the .EXE file can run on any computer system that is running Windows, even if the system does not have Visual Basic installed on it. You simply need to give the user a copy of the .EXE file and a copy of the VBRUN300.DLL (VBRUN200.DLL in Version 2.0) file. The VBRUN300.DLL (or VBRUN200.DLL) file comes with Visual Basic, and Microsoft allows you to distribute this file with your applications without violating any licensing agreement. Let's make the copyright screen into an executable file and then try running it directly from Windows.

To make an executable (.EXE) file and then run it from the Program Manager:

1   Click **File**, then click **Make EXE File...**. The Make EXE File dialog box appears.

2   Type **t1c** in the File Name box, then verify the entries in the Drives box and in the Directories box. You want to save the t1c file in the tut1\ver3 (or tut1\ver2) directory on your Student Disk.

3   After entering the filename and verifying both the drive and the directory, click the **OK button**. Visual Basic's compiler translates your application into machine code, which it saves in the t1c.exe file on your Student Disk. See Figure 1-36.

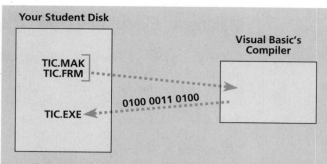

Figure 1-36: Visual Basic's compiler translates the project and form files into machine code

You can now exit Visual Basic and then run the T1C.EXE file from the Program Manager.

4   Click **File**, then click **Exit** to exit Visual Basic. If you are asked if you want to save the form, click **Yes**. If you are asked if you want to save the project, click **Yes**.

5   If the Program Manager appears as an icon, double-click the **Program Manager icon** to maximize it, then click **File** in the Program Manager's menu bar, then click **Run....**

6   Click the **Browse... button**, then locate the t1c.exe file, which is saved in either the tut1\ver2 or the tut1\ver3 directory on your Student Disk.

7   Click **t1c.exe**, then click the **OK button** to close the Browse dialog box.

8   Click the **OK button** to close the Run dialog box and run the application. The copyright screen appears.

9   Click the **Exit button** to end the application.

Now you can either take a break or complete the end-of-lesson questions and exercises.

S U M M A R Y

To open an object's Code window:

■   Double-click the object whose Code window you want to open.

To close an object's Code window:

■   Double-click the Control menu box in the Code window's title bar.

To print a Visual Basic Form:

■   Maximize the form, then press [Ctrl][P].
■   Click the Form check box to print the form, then click the OK button to start printing.

To print the Visual Basic Form text and code:

- ◼ Click File, then click Print....
- ◼ Click the Form Text check box to print the properties of the objects, click the Code check box to print the contents of the Code windows.
- ◼ Click the OK button to start printing.

To make an executable (.EXE) file:

- ◼ Click File, then click Make EXE File.... The Make EXE File dialog box appears.
- ◼ If necessary, enter a filename and select the appropriate drive and directory.
- ◼ Click the OK button.

Q U E S T I O N S

1. If you want to print an entire form during design time, maximize the form on the screen and press _____ .
   a. [Alt][P]
   b. [Ctrl][P]
   c. [Ctrl][F]
   d. [Shift][P]
   e. [Shift][F]

2. You load a picture into an Image control by setting the control's _____ property.
   a. ControlImage
   b. Icon
   c. Image
   d. Load
   e. Picture

3. The _____ instruction tells Visual Basic to stop an application.
   a. Done
   b. End
   c. Finish
   d. Stop
   e. Timer

4. Printing the _____ will print the properties of the objects included in the form.
   a. Code
   b. Form
   c. Form Text
   d. Properties
   e. Text

5. You tell an object what you want it to do by entering instructions in the object's _____ window.
   a. Code
   b. Form
   c. Instruction
   d. Main
   e. Text

6. Explain how to open an object's Code window.

7. Write a one-sentence definition of an "event procedure."

8. Explain the purpose of the Code window's Object box and its Proc (Procedure) box.

9. Write a one-sentence definition of "syntax."

E X E R C I S E S

1. Launch Visual Basic (if necessary) and open the T1LBE1 project.
   a. Click the View Form button to view the FrmCharity form.
   b. Add an Image control to the form and a Command button to the form.
   c. Set the following properties for the Image control:
      Left: 1500 twips   Top: 2000 twips
      Name: ImgLogo
      Picture: Load the LOGO1.BMP file from your Student Disk
   d. Set the following properties for the Command button:
      Left: 150 twips   Top: 150 twips   FontSize: 24 points
      Caption: Exit   Name: CmdExit
   e. Open the Command button's Code window and enter the End instruction.
   f. Use the File menu's Save File As and Save Project As options to save the form and the project as T1LCE1.
   g. Run the application. Then exit the application using the Exit button.
   h. Print the form, the form text, and the code.
   i. Make the application an executable (.EXE) file. Then run the application from Windows.

2. Launch Visual Basic (if necessary) and open the T1LBE2 project.
   a. Click the View Form button to view the FrmPhotos form.
   b. Add an Image control and a Command button to the form.
   c. Set the following properties for the Image control:
      Left: 6000 twips   Top: 3000 twips
      Name: ImgPicture
      Picture: Load the LOGO1.BMP file from your Student Disk
   d. Set the following properties for the Command button:
      Left: 150 twips   Top: 150 twips   FontSize: 18 points
      Caption: Exit   Name: CmdExit
   e. Open the Command button's Code window and enter the End instruction.
   f. Use the File menu's Save File As and Save Project As options to save the form and the project as T1LCE2.
   g. Run the application. Then exit the application using the Exit button.
   h. Print the form, the form text, and the code.
   i. Make the application an executable (.EXE) file. Then run the application from Windows.

Exercises 3 and 4 are Discovery Exercises, which allow you to "discover" the solutions to problems on your own. Discovery Exercises include topics that are not covered in the tutorial.

discovery ▶ 3. a. Design your own display screen. Be sure to include an Exit button that will end the application. Also use Label controls and Image controls as desired. Use the Image control's Picture property to load a Visual Basic icon. The Visual Basic icons are located in the vb\icons directory on the local hard drive or on the network drive. (Verify the location of the icon files with your instructor.)

b. Find the property that will allow you to size an icon stored in an Image control, then make the icon larger than its default size.

c. Use the Save Project icon in the toolbar to save the form and the project as T1LCE3.

d. Run the application. Then exit the application using the Exit button.

e. Print the form, the form text, and the code.

f. Make the application an executable (.EXE) file. Then run the application from Windows.

discovery ▶ 4. a. Add an Image control and three Command buttons to a form. The Captions for the three Command buttons should be On, Off, and Exit.

b. Use the Image control's Picture property to load a Visual Basic icon. The Visual Basic icons are located in the vb\icons directory on the local hard drive or on the network drive. (Verify the location of the icon files with your instructor.)

c. In the Exit button, enter the command to end the application.

d. Find the property that will allow you to hide and display the Image control. In the On button's Click event procedure, include an instruction to hide the Image control. In the Off button's Click event procedure, include an instruction to display the Image control.

e. Run and test the application. Print the form and the code.

D E B U G G I N G

Technique

The simplest technique a programmer uses for debugging an application is to print the application's Form Text and Code. In the Form Text printout, the programmer looks for a property that is set incorrectly. In the Code printout, the programmer looks for an instruction that is either in the wrong object's Code window or in the wrong event procedure.

At the end of each tutorial you will find a Debugging Section. In programming, the term "debugging" refers to the process of finding the errors in a program. Each Debugging Section will include debugging techniques, from the simple to the more complex, as well as exercises designed to let you practice debugging applications.

Tutorial 1's Debugging Section contains three debugging exercises. In each exercise you will open and then run an application that is not working correctly. Your task is to find and correct the errors in the application—in other words, to debug the application—using this tutorial's debugging technique.

Exercises 1. Open the T1D1.MAK (Tutorial 1, Debugging exercise 1) project, which is in either the tut1\ver2 or the tut1\ver3 directory on your Student Disk.

a. Click the View Form button to view the form.

b. Run the application. Notice two problems: The form does not fill the entire screen, and the title bar does not say Glamour-Us (the name of the beauty salon).

c. Stop the application, then print the Form Text. Find the problems and mark the corrections on the Form Text printout. Then correct the two problems; run the application to make sure it works correctly.

d. Use the File menu's Save File As... option to save the form as T1D1DBGD. (The "DBGD" stands for "debugged.")

e. Use the File menu's Save Project As... option to save the project as T1D1DBGD. (The "DBGD" stands for "debugged.")

2. Open the T1D2 (Tutorial 1, Debugging exercise 2) project, which is in either the tut1\ver2 or the tut1\ver3 directory on your Student Disk.
   a. Click the View Form button to view the form.
   b. Run the application. Notice two problems: The caption in the Label control does not fit on one line, and the form does not fill the entire screen.
   c. Stop the application, then print the Form Text. Find the problems and mark the corrections on the Form Text printout. Then correct the two problems; run the application to make sure it works correctly.
   d. Use the File menu's Save File As... and Save Project As... options to save the form and the project as T1D2DBGD.

3. Open the T1D3.MAK (Tutorial 1, Debugging exercise 3) project, which is in either the tut1\ver2 or the tut1\ver3 directory on your Student Disk.
   a. Click the View Form button to view the form.
   b. Run the application. Notice two problems: The Command button should say Exit, and the Command button does not work (it should end the application when clicked by the user).
   c. Stop the application, then print the form text and the code. Find the problems and mark the corrections on the Form Text printout. Then correct the two problems, and run the application to make sure it works correctly.
   d. Use the File menu's Save File As and Save Project As options to save the form and the project as T1D3DBGD.

TUTORIAL

2

Designing Applications

Creating an Order Screen

case ▶ During your second week at Interlocking Software, you and Chris Statton, the senior programmer, meet with the sales manager of Skate-Away Sales. The sales manager tells you that his company sells skateboards by phone. The skateboards are priced at $100 each and are available in two colors—red and blue. He further explains that Skate-Away Sales employs 20 salespeople to answer the phones. The salespeople record each order on a form that contains the customer's name, address, and the number of red and blue skateboards ordered. They then calculate the total number of skateboards ordered and the total price of the skateboards, including a 5% sales tax.

Skate-Away's sales manager feels that having the salespeople manually perform the necessary calculations is much too time-consuming and prone to errors. Also, the company now wants to send confirmation notices to the customers, and the handwritten form the salespeople currently complete is too informal to send. The sales manager at Skate-Away Sales wants Interlocking to create a computerized application that will solve the problems of the current order-taking system.

Solving the Problem Using a Procedure-Oriented Approach

As you learned in the Overview, procedure-oriented languages preceded object-oriented/event-driven languages. Recall that in procedure-oriented languages, the emphasis of a program is on *how* to accomplish a task. The programmer must instruct the computer every step of the way, from the start of the task to the completion of the task.

The procedure-oriented approach to problem solving requires a programmer to think in a step-by-step, top-to-bottom fashion. Planning tools such as flowcharts and pseudocode make this approach easier. A flowchart uses standardized symbols to show the steps needed to solve a problem. Pseudocode uses English-like phrases to represent the required steps. Some programmers prefer to use flowcharts, while others prefer pseudocode; it's really a matter of personal preference. (You will learn more about pseudocode in this tutorial, and about flowcharts in Tutorial 3, as these planning tools are also useful in object-oriented/event-driven programming.) Let's look at a procedure-oriented approach to solving Skate-Away's problem. Figure 2-1 shows the solution written in pseudocode; Figure 2-2 shows the solution using a flowchart.

1. Get customer name, address, number of red skateboards, number of blue skateboards
2. Calculate total skateboards = number of red skateboards + number of blue skateboards
3. Calculate total price = total skateboards * $100 * 105%
4. Print customer name, address, number of red skateboards, number of blue skateboards, total skateboards, total price
5. End

Figure 2-1: Pseudocode for the procedure-oriented solution

You will notice that both planning tools (Figure 2-1 and Figure 2-2) indicate the sequence of steps the computer must take to process an order. Using the flowchart, pseudocode, or both as a guide, the programmer then translates the solution into a procedure-oriented language that the computer can understand. Figure 2-3 shows the pseudocode, flowchart, or both translated into Microsoft's QuickBASIC language. QuickBASIC, a procedure-oriented language, is a predecessor of Visual Basic.

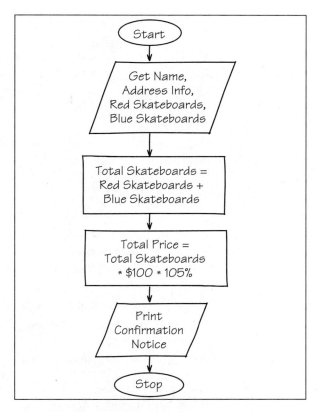

Figure 2-2: Flowchart of the procedure-oriented solution

```
Input "Enter Customer Name: ",Names$
Input "Enter Address: ",Address$
Input "Enter City: ",City$
Input "Enter State: ",State$
Input "Enter Zip: ",Zip$
Input "Enter Number of Red skateboards: ",Red
Input "Enter Number of Blue skateboards: ",Blue
Totboards = Red + Blue
Totprice = Totboards * 100 * 1.05
Print "Customer Name: ",Names$
Print "Address: ",Address$
Print "City: ",City$
Print "State: ",State$
Print "Zip: ",Zip$
Print "Red skateboards: ",Red
Print "Blue skateboards: ",Blue
Print "Total Skateboards: ",Totboards
Print "Total Price: $",Totprice
Input "Type E to End",Ans$
End
```

Figure 2-3: Procedure-oriented solution written in QuickBASIC

Let's see this procedure-oriented program in action.

To run the procedure-oriented program:

1   Launch Windows and make sure the Program Manager window is open and your Student Disk is in the appropriate drive. If necessary, click the Minimize on Use option on the Options menu to minimize the Program Manager on use.

2   Using the **Run...** command on the Program Manager's **File** menu, run the **ordrproc.exe** program, which is located in either the tut2\ver2 or the tut2\ver3 directory on your Student Disk. A prompt requesting a customer's name appears on the screen.

Assume that Sport Warehouse wants to place an order for 10 red skateboards and 20 blue skateboards. Let's enter the order information using the procedure-oriented program on the screen.

To enter the information using the procedure-oriented program:

1   Type **Sport Warehouse** and press [**Enter**]. Don't be concerned if the computer beeps when you press [**Enter**]. The screen requests the address next.

2   Type **123 Main** and press [**Enter**], then type **Glendale** for the city and press [**Enter**], then type **IL** for the state and press [**Enter**], and then type **60134** for the zip code and press [**Enter**]. The screen is now requesting the number of red skateboards ordered.

3   Type **10** as the number of red skateboards ordered, then press [**Enter**]. The screen is now requesting the number of blue skateboards ordered.

4   Type **20** as the number of blue skateboards ordered, then press [**Enter**]. The program computes the total skateboards ordered (30) and the total price of the order (3150). (Recall that skateboards are $100 each and there is a 5% sales tax.) See Figure 2-4.

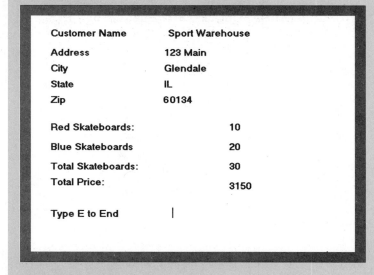

Customer Name	Sport Warehouse
Address	123 Main
City	Glendale
State	IL
Zip	60134
Red Skateboards:	10
Blue Skateboards	20
Total Skateboards:	30
Total Price:	3150
Type E to End	

Figure 2-4: Results of procedure-oriented program

5   Type e to end the program. The program ends.

Although Skate-Away Sales could use this procedure-oriented program to record its phone orders, the program has one very important limitation that is inherent in all procedure-oriented programs: The user has little, if any, control over the processing of the program. Recall, for example, that you could not control the sequence in which the customer information was entered. What if the customer wants to order the blue skateboards before the red skateboards? Also recall that you couldn't change the information once you entered it. What if the customer changes his or her mind about how many red skateboards to order? And, last, recall that you had no control over when the program calculated the total order and the total price. What if the customer wants to know the total price of the red skateboards before placing the blue skateboard order?

Now let's look at the object-oriented/event-driven approach to programming.

Solving the Problem Using an Object-Oriented/Event-Driven (OOED) Approach

As you learned in the Overview, in object-oriented/event-driven languages, the emphasis of a program is on the *objects* included in the user interface (such as scroll bars or buttons) and the *events* that occur on those objects (such as scrolling or clicking). Unlike the procedure-oriented approach to problem solving, in the OOED approach the programmer does not view the solution as a step-by-step, top-to-bottom process; instead, the OOED programmer's goal is to give the user as much control over the program as possible.

When using the OOED approach to problem solving, the programmer begins by identifying the tasks the application needs to perform. Then the programmer decides on the appropriate objects to which those tasks will be assigned, and on the event(s) necessary to trigger those objects to perform their assigned task(s). For example, in Tutorial 1, the copyright screen had to provide the user with a way to end the application. Recall that you assigned that task to the Exit Command button. The event that triggered the Exit button to perform its assigned task was the Click event. In this book, you will use a TOE (Task, Object, Event) chart to assist you in planning your object-oriented/event-driven programs.

Before we discuss planning OOED applications further, let's run an OOED application designed to solve Skate-Away's problem. (The OOED application is written using Visual Basic.) This application contains a new control, a Text box. You use a Text box to provide areas in the form where the user can enter information.

To run the OOED application:

1   Using the **Run...** command on the Program Manager's **File** menu, run the **ordrooed.exe** program, which is located in either the tut2\ver2 or the tut2\ver3 directory on your Student Disk. The order screen appears. See Figure 2-5.

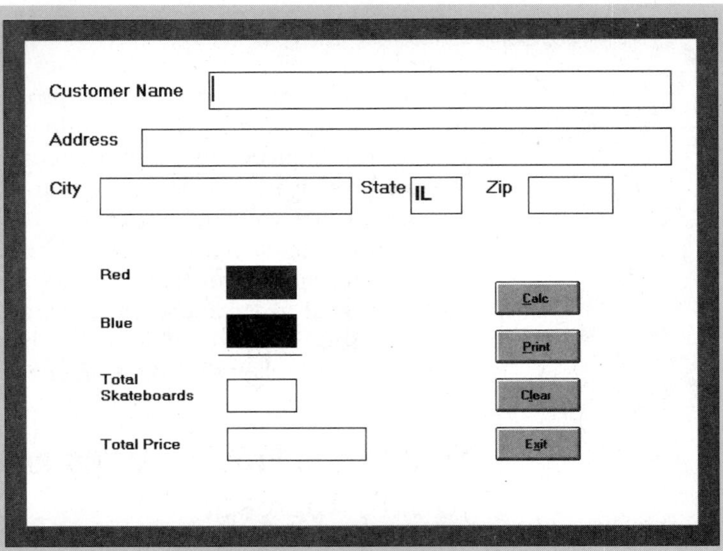

Figure 2-5: Order screen created by the OOED program

Now let's enter Sport Warehouse's information using the OOED program on the screen. You will notice that Visual Basic displays a blinking insertion point in the first Text box. The Label control to the left of the Text box identifies the information the user should enter—in this case, the customer's name.

To enter the information using the OOED application:

1   Type **Sport Warehouse**, then press [**Tab**] two times. The blinking insertion point appears in the City Text box.

2   Type **Glendale** as the city, then press [**Shift**][**Tab**] (press and hold down the Shift key as you press the Tab key) to move the insertion point to the Address Text box. (You can also click inside the Address Text box to move the insertion point into that box.)

3   Type **123 Main** as the address, then press [**Tab**] two times, then type **60134** as the zip code, then press [**Tab**]. The blinking insertion point appears in the Red skateboards Text box. (Notice that the screen already contains "IL" in the State Text box. Because most of Skate-Away's customers come from Illinois, the OOED application already enters the state for the user. You can change the state, if necessary, by clicking inside the State text box.)

Notice that you can enter the customer information in any order.

4   Type **10** as the number of red skateboards ordered, then click the **Calc button**. Notice that the OOED application allows you to tell the customer how much the red skateboards will cost ($1,050.00).

5 Click inside the **Blue Text box**, type **20**, then click the **Calc button**. The application recalculates the total skateboards (30) and the total price ($3,150.00).

Now assume that Sport Warehouse wants to change her order to 20 red skateboards.

6 Click to the **immediate left of the 10 in the Red Text box**, press [Delete] to remove the 1, then type **2**. The number of red skateboards ordered should now say 20.

7 Click the **Calc button**. The application recalculates the total skateboards ordered (40) and the total price ($4,200.00). See Figure 2-6.

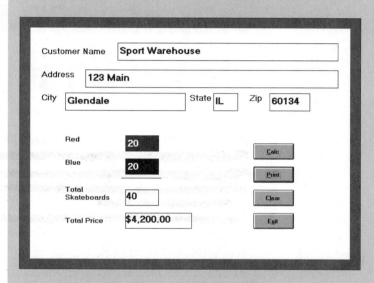

Figure 2-6: Completed order using the OOED program

8 If you are connected to a printer, click the **Print button**. The confirmation notice prints on the printer.

When the salesperson is finished with an order, he or she can use the Clear button to clear the screen for the next order.

9 Click the **Clear button** to clear the screen for the next order. The previous customer's information disappears, and the blinking insertion point is placed in the Customer Name Text box.

10 Click the **Exit button** to end the application. If the Program Manager appears as an icon, double-click the Program Manager icon to restore the Program Manager.

Unlike the procedure-oriented program, the OOED application gives users a lot of control over the program. Users can enter information in any order, change what they entered at any time, and calculate a subtotal whenever they like.

In Lesson A, you will learn how a Visual Basic programmer plans an OOED application. Then, in Lesson B and Lesson C, you will create the OOED application that you just saw.

In this lesson you will learn how to:

■ Plan an OOED application in Visual Basic

■ Complete a TOE (Task, Object, Event) chart

Planning an OOED Application in Visual Basic

Planning an OOED application in Visual Basic requires the following steps:

1. Identify the tasks the application needs to perform.
2. Identify the objects to which you will assign those tasks.
3. Identify the events required to trigger an object into performing its assigned tasks.
4. Draw a sketch of the user interface.

You can use a TOE (**T**ask, **O**bject, **E**vent) chart to plan your Visual Basic applications. A blank TOE chart is shown in Figure 2-7.

Task	Object	Event

Figure 2-7: TOE chart

Let's complete a TOE chart for the Skate-Away Sales application. We'll start by identifying the tasks.

Identify the Application's Tasks

When identifying the tasks an application needs to perform, it is helpful to ask the following questions:

■ What information, if any, will the user need to enter?

- What information, if any, will the application need to calculate?
- What information, if any, will the application need to display or print?
- How will the user end the application?
- Will previous information need to be cleared from the screen before new information is entered?

The answers to these questions will help you identify the application's major tasks. Let's answer each question for the Skate-Away Sales application.

What information, if any, will the user need to enter into the user interface? In the Skate-Away Sales application, the salesperson (the user) must enter the order information (customer name and address, and the number of red and blue skateboards ordered). You can enter this task in the TOE chart as "Get order information from the user."

What information, if any, will the application need to calculate? The Skate-Away Sales application needs to calculate the total number of skateboards ordered and the total price of the order. You can enter this task in the TOE chart as "Calculate total skateboards and total price."

What information, if any, will the application need to display or print? (Display refers to the screen; print refers to the printer.) In addition to calculating the total number of skateboards ordered and the total price of the order, the application must display the result of those calculations. You can list this in the TOE chart as "Display total skateboards and total price." Also recall that the sales manager wants the application to "Print a confirmation notice."

How will the user end the application? In Tutorial 1, you learned that all applications should give the user a way to exit the program. The Skate-Away Sales application needs to provide a way to "End the application."

Will previous information need to be cleared from the screen before new information is entered? After Skate-Away's salesperson enters and prints an order, he or she will need to clear the previous order's information from the screen before the next order is entered. You can list this task as "Clear the screen for the next order."

Figure 2-8 shows the Skate-Away Sales application's tasks listed in the TOE chart. Unlike procedure-oriented planning, OOED planning does not require the TOE chart tasks to be in any particular order. In this case, they are listed in the order in which they were identified in this lesson.

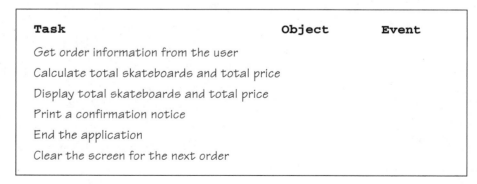

Task	Object	Event
Get order information from the user		
Calculate total skateboards and total price		
Display total skateboards and total price		
Print a confirmation notice		
End the application		
Clear the screen for the next order		

Figure 2-8: Tasks entered in TOE chart

Identify the Objects

After completing the Task column of the TOE chart, you then assign each task to an object in the user interface. For this application, the only objects you will use, besides the form itself, are the Command button, the Label control, and the Text box. As you learned in Tutorial 1, you use a Label control to display information that you don't want the user to change while your application is running, and you use a Command button to perform an action immediately after it is clicked by the user. As you saw in the OOED application you ran earlier, you use a Text box to give the user an area in which to enter data. Let's assign each of the tasks in the TOE chart to an object.

The first task listed in Figure 2-8 is "Get order information from the user." For each order, the salesperson will need to enter the customer's name, address, city, state, zip code, and the number of red and blue skateboards ordered. Because you need to provide the salesperson with areas in which to enter that information, you will assign the first task to seven Text boxes—one for each item of information.

The second task listed in the TOE chart is "Calculate total skateboards and total price." So that the salesperson can calculate these amounts at any time, you will assign the task to a Command button that we'll call Calc.

The third task listed in the TOE chart is "Display total skateboards and total price." Recall that the total skateboards and the total price are not entered by the user; they are calculated by the Calc Command button and should not be changed by the user. You will therefore assign the display task to two Label controls. Recall that Label controls do not allow the user to change their contents when the application is running.

The last three tasks listed in the TOE chart are "Print a confirmation notice," "End the application," and "Clear the screen for the next order." So that the user has control over when these tasks are performed, you will assign the tasks to Command buttons. Let's call the Command buttons Print, Exit, and Clear. Figure 2-9 shows the TOE chart with the Task and Object columns completed.

Task	Object	Event
Get order information from the user	7 Text boxes	
Calculate total skateboards and total price	Command button (Calc)	
Display total skateboards and total price	2 Label controls	
Print a confirmation notice	Command button (Print)	
End the application	Command button (Exit)	
Clear the screen for the next order	Command button (Clear)	

Figure 2-9: Tasks and objects entered in TOE chart

After defining the application's tasks and assigning those tasks to objects in the user interface, you must then determine which objects will need an event (such as clicking or double-clicking) to occur for the object to do its assigned task. (Not all objects in the user interface will need an event to occur.) Let's look at the tasks and the objects listed in Figure 2-9's TOE chart.

Identify Events

The seven Text boxes listed in the TOE chart in Figure 2-9 are assigned the task of getting the order information. Text boxes automatically accept information from the user, so no special event is necessary for them to do their assigned task.

The two Label controls listed in the TOE chart are assigned the task of displaying the total number of skateboards and the total price of the order. Label controls automatically display their contents so, here again, no special event needs to occur.

The remaining objects listed in the TOE chart are the four Command buttons, which are assigned the tasks of calculating, printing, exiting, and clearing. In this application you will have the Command buttons perform their assigned tasks when they are clicked by the user. Figure 2-10 shows the completed TOE chart.

Task	Object	Event
Get order information from the user	7 Text boxes	None
Calculate total skateboards and total price	Command button (Calc)	Click
Display total skateboards and total price	2 Label controls	None
Print a confirmation notice	Command button (Print)	Click
End the application	Command button (Exit)	Click
Clear the screen for the next order	Command button (Clear)	Click

Figure 2-10: Completed TOE chart

After completing the TOE chart, the next step is to draw a sketch of the user interface.

Draw a Sketch of the User Interface

Figure 2-11 shows a sketch of the user interface for the Skate-Away Sales application. Notice that additional Label controls are used to identify the information to be entered into the Text boxes.

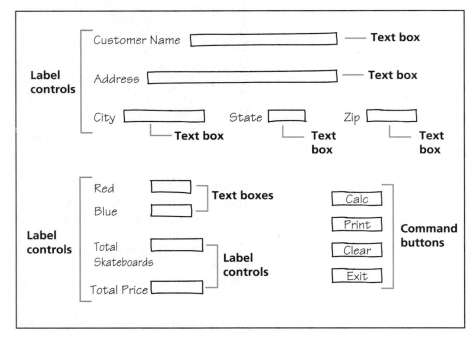

Figure 2-11: Sketch of the user interface

You have now completed the four planning steps:
1. Identify the tasks the application needs to perform.
2. Identify the objects to which you will assign those tasks.
3. Identify the events required to trigger an object into performing its assigned tasks.
4. Draw a sketch of the user interface.

In Lesson B you will create the Skate-Away Sales application. Now you can either take a break or complete the exercises and questions at the end of Lesson A.

S U M M A R Y

To plan an OOED application in Visual Basic:

■ Identify the tasks the application needs to perform.
■ Identify the objects to which you will assign those tasks.
■ Identify the events required to trigger an object into performing its assigned tasks.
■ Draw a sketch of the user interface.

To assist you in identifying the tasks an application needs to perform, ask the following questions:

■ What information, if any, will the user need to enter?
■ What information, if any, will the application need to calculate?
■ What information, if any, will the application need to display or print?
■ How will the user end the application?
■ Will prior information need to be cleared from the screen before new information is entered?

Q U E S T I O N S

1. You use a _____*label*_____ control to display information you don't want the user to change.
   a. Command button
   b. Form
   c. Label
   d. Text box
   e. User

2. You use a _____*text box*_____ control to accept or display information you will allow the user to change.
   a. Changeable
   b. Command button
   c. Form
   d. Label
   e. Text box

3. You use a _____*Command button*_____ control to perform an immediate action when it is clicked by the user.
   a. Changeable
   b. Command button
   c. Form
   d. Label
   e. Text box

4. You can use a _____*TOE*_____ chart to plan your OOED applications.
   a. EOT
   b. ETO
   c. OET
   d. OTE
   e. TOE

5. Listed below are the four steps you should follow when planning an OOED application. Put them in the proper order by placing a number (1 to 4) on the line to the left of the step.
   _4_ Draw a sketch of the user interface.
   _2_ Identify the objects to which you will assign those tasks.
   _1_ Identify the tasks the application needs to perform.
   _3_ Identify the events required to trigger an object into performing its assigned tasks.

E X E R C I S E S

1. Sarah Brimley is the accountant at Paper Products. The salespeople at Paper Products are paid a commission, which is a percentage of the sales they make. The current commission rate is 10%. (In other words, if you sell $2,000, your commission is $200.) Sarah wants you to create an application that will compute the commission after she enters the salesperson's name and sales. She also wants to print this information on the printer.
   a. Prepare a TOE chart.
   b. Draw a sketch of the user interface.

2. Recall that 1440 twips is equal to one inch. Create an application that allows you to enter the number of twips, then convert the twips to inches and print the user interface.

   a. Prepare a TOE chart.

   b. Draw a sketch of the user interface.

3. John Lee wants an application in which he can enter the following three pieces of information: his cash balance at the beginning of the month, the amount of money he earned during the month, and the amount of money he spent during the month. He wants the application to compute his ending balance, then print the information on the printer.

   a. Prepare a TOE chart.

   b. Draw a sketch of the user interface.

4. Lana Jones wants an application that will compute and print the average of any three numbers she enters.

   a. Prepare a TOE chart.

   b. Draw a sketch of the user interface.

5. Martha Arito, manager of Bookworms Inc., needs an inventory application. Martha will enter the title of a book, the number of paperback versions of the book currently in inventory, the number of hardcover versions of the book currently in inventory, the cost of the paperback version, and the cost of the hardcover version. Martha wants the application to compute the value of the paperback versions of the book, the value of the hardcover versions of the book, the total number of paperback and hardcover versions, and the total value of the paperback and hardcover versions. Martha will need to print this information.

   a. Prepare a TOE chart.

   b. Draw a sketch of the user interface.

6. Jackets Unlimited is having a 25% off sale on all its merchandise. The store manager asks you to create an application that requires the clerk simply to enter the original price of a jacket. The application should then compute and print both the discount and the new price.

   a. Prepare a TOE chart.

   b. Draw a sketch of the user interface.

7. Typing Salon charges $.10 per typed envelope and $.25 per typed page. The company accountant wants an application to help her prepare bills. She will enter the customer's name, the number of typed envelopes, and the number of typed pages. The application should compute and print the total bill.

   a. Prepare a TOE chart.

   b. Draw a sketch of the user interface.

8. Suman Gadhari, the payroll clerk at Sun Projects, wants an application that will compute net pay. She will enter the employee's name, hours worked, and rate of pay. For this application, you do not have to worry about overtime, as this company does not allow anyone to work more than 40 hours. Suman wants the application to compute the gross pay, the federal withholding tax (FWT), the social security tax (FICA), the state income tax, and the net pay. Suman also wants to print the payroll information on the printer. Use the following information when computing the three taxes:

   FWT   20% of gross pay

   FICA   8% of gross pay

   state income tax   2% of gross pay

   a. Prepare a TOE chart.

   b. Draw a sketch of the user interface.

9. Management USA, a small training center, plans to run two full-day seminars on December 1. The seminars are called "How to Be an Effective Manager" and "How to Run a Small Business." Each seminar costs $200. Registration for the seminars will be done by phone. When a company calls to register its employees, the phone representative will ask the following information: the company's name, address (including city, state, and zip), the number of employees registering for the "How to Be an Effective Manager" seminar, and the number of employees registering for the "How to Run a Small Business" seminar. Claire Jenkowski, the owner of Management USA, wants the application to calculate the total number of employees the company is registering and the total cost. Ms. Jenkowski also wants to print the company information.
   a. Prepare a TOE chart.
   b. Draw a sketch of the user interface.

10. R&M Sales divides its sales territory into two regions: South and West. Robert Gonzales, the sales manager, wants an application in which he can enter the current year's sales for each region and the projected increase (expressed as a percentage) in sales for each region. He then wants the application to compute next year's projected sales for each region. (For example, if Robert enters 10000 as the current sales for the South region, and then enters a 10% projected increase, the application should display 11000 as next year's projected sales.) He also wants to print the information on the printer.
    a. Prepare a TOE chart.
    b. Draw a sketch of the user interface.

LESSON B

objectives

In this lesson you will learn how to:

- Use a TOE chart to create a Visual Basic application
- Add a Text box control to a form
- Control the focus with the TabStop and TabIndex properties and the SetFocus method
- Write an assignment statement
- Print a form with the PrintForm method
- Use pseudocode to plan an object's code
- Hide and display a control
- Internally document the program code

Creating an OOED Application

Creating a Visual Basic Application

Once you have planned your Visual Basic application, you can begin creating it. Creating a Visual Basic application involves five steps:

1. Create the user interface, using the sketch you drew when you planned the application. The user interface includes the form and the controls you place on the form, such as scroll bars and buttons.
2. Set the properties of the objects. Recall that a property controls the appearance and behavior of the objects included in the interface, such as the object's font, size, and so on.
3. Plan and then write the Visual Basic program instructions, called **program code**, to tell the objects how to respond when scrolled, clicked, and so on. Your TOE chart will tell you which objects are responsible for which tasks. You can use either a flowchart or pseudocode to help you plan the steps each object will need to take to accomplish its assigned task.
4. Test the application with sample data. If necessary, find and correct any errors in the application. (This is known as debugging the application.)
5. Document the application.

Some programmers create the entire interface before setting the properties of each object; other programmers change the properties of each object as it is added to the form. Either way will work, so it's really just a matter of preference. Step 3, planning and writing the program code, is usually done after the interface is created. It is a good programming practice to write the code for one object at a time and then test and debug (Step 4) that object's code before coding the next object. The last step, documenting the application, refers to placing your planning tool (flowchart or pseudocode) and a printout of the application (form, form text, and code) in a safe place, so you can refer to them if you need to change the application in the future. (You can also document a program internally, as you will learn in this tutorial.)

To save you time, your Student Disk contains a partially completed application for Skate-Away Sales. When you open the application, you will notice that most of steps 1 and 2 (creating the user interface and setting the properties) have already been done for you. This will allow you to concentrate on planning and writing the code, as well as testing and debugging the application.

To open the partially completed project and then save the files under a new name:

1 Launch Visual Basic and open the **t2a.mak** project, which is in either the tut2\ver2 or tut2\ver3 directory on your Student Disk.

2 Click the **View form button** in the Project window to view the FrmOrder form.

3 Use the **Save File As...** option on the **File** menu to save the form as **T2B**.

4 Use the **Save Project As...** option on the **File** menu to save the project as **T2B**.

5 Click the **form's Maximize button** to maximize the form. Figure 2-12 identifies the controls already included in the application.

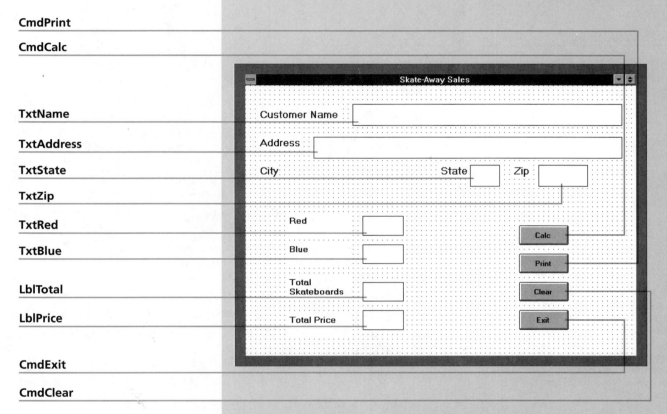

Figure 2-12: Partially completed Skate-Away Sales application

You will notice that Figure 2-12 shows only the names of those controls whose names were changed from their default values. Only objects that will contain code or objects that will be referred to in code need to have their names changed to more meaningful ones.

One control is missing from the form: the Text box control in which the user enters the city. You'll add the missing control in the next section. First, let's enter the *End* instruction in the Exit button's Click event procedure so that you will have a convenient way of quitting the application.

To code the Exit button:

1 Double-click the **Exit button** to open the button's Code window. The current event procedure is Click.

2 Press [**Tab**], type **end** and then press [**Enter**]. See Figure 2-13.

Object box

Control menu box

these instructions will be processed in the order in which they appear

Proc (procedure) box

```
                          T2B.FRM
Object:  CmdExit          Proc:  Click
Sub CmdExit_Click ()
    End

End Sub
```

Figure 2-13: Exit button's Code window

As you learned in Tutorial 1, when the user clicks the Exit button, Visual Basic processes the instructions entered in the Code window, one instruction after another, in the order in which the instructions appear. Recall from Tutorial 1 that programmers refer to this as sequential processing. The series of instructions executed sequentially is known as the sequence structure. The sequence structure is one of three programming structures. You will learn the other two structures—selection and repetition—in future tutorials.

3 Double-click the **Code window's Control menu box** to close the Code window.

Let's make sure the Exit button is working properly before coding another object. Whenever possible, you should always test the object you just coded before coding another object. If the application is not working correctly, you then will know which object is causing the problem.

4 Click the **form's Restore button** to restore the form to its standard size.

5 Click the **Save Project icon** ▣ in the toolbar, then click the **Run icon** ▣ in the toolbar (or press [**F5**]) to run the project. (From now on you will be instructed to simply **save and run** the project.)

6 Click the **Exit button** to see if it is working correctly. The application ends and Visual Basic returns to the design screen.

If a dialog box appears on the screen with the message "Syntax error," click the OK button, type the End command correctly in the Exit button's Code window, double-click the Code window's Control menu box, and then click the Save Project icon and the Run icon again.

Now let's add the missing Text box to the form.

Adding a Text Box Control to the Form

Recall that a Text box control provides an area in the form where the user can enter data. Let's add the missing Text box control to the form and then set its properties.

To add the Text box control to the form, then set its properties:

1 Double-click the **Text box tool** in the Toolbox. A Text box control appears in the middle of the form.

The Text1 text you see inside the Text box is the current setting of this control's Text property. The Text property for a Text box is similar to the Caption property for a Label control. Both properties manage the text shown inside their respective controls. Because you don't want the Text1 to appear when the application is run, you will delete the contents of this control's Text property.

2 Double-click the **Text** property in the Properties list, located in the Properties window. Visual Basic highlights the Text1 text in the Settings box of the Properties window, as shown in Figure 2-14.

Text property highlighted in Settings box

Text property

Figure 2-14: Text property highlighted in Settings box

3 Press [**Delete**] and then press [**Enter**] to remove the highlighted text. The Text box is now empty.

4 Now set the following six properties for this Text box control:

FontSize: **13.5**   Name: **TxtCity** ("Txt" means Text box)

Height: **555**   Top: **2040**

Left: **1000**   Width: **3600**

Let's save and run the project to see if it is working correctly.

5 **Save and run** the project. A blinking insertion point appears in the customer name Text box (the TxtName control).

The blinking insertion point indicates that this Text box is the active control. In Windows terminology, the Text box has the focus. When a control has the **focus**, the control is ready to receive input from you. Let's try this now.

6 Type **Sport Warehouse** as the customer name. Notice that the Text box displays the information it receives from you. The information is recorded in the TxtName control's Text property.

You can move the focus from one control to another by pressing the Tab key.

tips

If the Text1 text is not highlighted in the Settings box, double-click the Text property again until the Text1 text is highlighted.

7 Press [**Tab**] to move the focus to the address Text box (the TxtAddress control), then type **123 Main**. The city entry is next.

8 Press [**Tab**] to move the focus to the city Text box (the TxtCity control). Notice that the focus skips the city Text box and moves to the state Text box.

Let's stop the application and discuss why this happened.

9 Click the **Exit button** to end the application. The application ends, and Visual Basic returns to the design screen.

Controlling the Focus with the TabStop and TabIndex Properties

The TabStop and TabIndex properties control if and when an object receives the focus. By default, Visual Basic sets the TabStop property to True for all controls capable of receiving the focus. When a control's TabStop property is set to True, it means you can use the Tab key to move the focus to that control. (The Tab key allows the user to move the focus easily from one control to another.) Setting a control's TabStop property to False tells Visual Basic to bypass that control when the user is tabbing.

The TabIndex property, on the other hand, determines the order in which a control receives the focus when the user is tabbing. Whenever you add a control to a form, Visual Basic sets the control's TabIndex property to a number representing the order in which that control was added to the form. Keep in mind that when assigning these numbers Visual Basic starts counting at 0 (zero). In other words, the TabIndex property for the first control added to a form is 0 (zero), the TabIndex property for the second control is 1, and so on. Visual Basic uses the TabIndex property to determine the Tab order for the controls.

To get a better idea of how this works, let's check the TabIndex and TabStop properties for the address Text box (TxtAddress), the state Text box (TxtState), and the city Text box (TxtCity).

To view the TabIndex and TabStop properties:

1 Click the **form's Maximize button**, then click the **TxtAddress control** (the address Text box). Sizing handles appear around the Text box. You now need to display the Properties window.

The easiest way to display the Properties window when the form is maximized is to press [F4].

2 Press [**F4**] to display the Properties window, scroll the Properties list (if necessary) until you can see the TabIndex and TabStop properties, and then click the **TabStop** property. Notice that Visual Basic set the TabStop property for the TxtAddress control to True and the TabIndex property to 6. (A TabIndex property of 6 means that this was the seventh control added to the form.)

Now let's look at both the TabStop and the TabIndex property for the TxtState control (the state Text box).

tips

If the TabIndex property is not 6, you might have selected the address Label control instead of the address Text box. Click the TxtAddress Text box.

3   Click the **down arrow button in the Object box** (located below the Properties window title bar) to display the list of objects in the form. A drop-down list of object names appears.

4   Click **TxtState TextBox** in the drop-down list to select that control. Sizing handles appear around the control. Notice that the control's TabStop property is set to True and its TabIndex property is set to 7. A control with a TabIndex of 7 will receive the focus immediately after the control with a TabIndex of 6 (in this case, the TxtAddress Text box).

Now let's look at both the TabStop and the TabIndex properties for the city Text box, which was the last control added to the form.

5   Click the **down arrow button in the Object box** (located below the Properties window title bar) to display the list of objects in the form, then click **TxtCity TextBox** in the drop-down list to select that control. Notice that the control's TabStop property is set to True and its TabIndex property is set to 21.

To tell Visual Basic that you want the city Text box to receive the focus immediately after the address Text box, you need to change the TabIndex property of the TxtCity control to 7, which is one number greater than the TabIndex of the address Text box (6). Figure 2-15 shows the current TabIndex values for the TxtAddress, TxtCity, and TxtState controls and what their TabIndex values should be.

Control	Original TabIndex	New TabIndex
TxtAddress	6	6
TxtCity	21	7
TxtState	7	8

Figure 2-15: TabIndex values

The first TabIndex you will need to change is the one for the TxtCity control.

To change the TabIndex property and then save and run the project:

1   The TxtCity control should already be selected, so just click **TabIndex** in the Properties list, then type **7** and press **[Enter]** to change the TabIndex property for the TxtCity control.

Changing the TabIndex for this control causes Visual Basic to renumber the controls on the form, beginning with the control that originally had a TabIndex of 7. For example, the TabIndex of the TxtState control, which was originally 7, will now have a TabIndex of 8. The control that had a TabIndex of 8 will now have a TabIndex of 9, and so on. (You can verify the renumbering by selecting the TxtState control and looking at its TabIndex value.)

2   Click the **form's Restore button** to restore the form, then **save and run** the project.

3   Type **Sport Warehouse** as the customer name, then press [**Tab**] to move the focus to the address Text box.

4   Type **123 Main** as the address, then press [**Tab**]. Notice that the focus now moves to the city Text box.

Let's check the focus order of the remaining controls. You can do that by simply pressing the Tab key.

5   The focus is currently in the city Text box. Press [**Tab**]. The state Text box now has the focus, which is correct.

6   Press [**Tab**], slowly, eight times. The focus correctly moves to the following controls: the zip code Text box, the red skateboard Text box, the blue skateboard Text box, the Calc Command button (notice the highlighted border around the Command button and the dotted rectangle around the button's caption), the Print command button, the Clear Command button, the Exit Command button, and finally back to the customer name Text box.

The Tab key moves the focus forward, and the Shift-Tab key combination moves the focus backward.

7   Press [**Shift**][**Tab**]. (Press and hold down the Shift key as you press the Tab key.) The focus moves to the Exit button, as indicated by its highlighted border and the dotted rectangle around its caption.

8   Click the **Exit button** (or, since the Exit button has the focus, press [**Enter**]) to end the application. The application ends and Visual Basic returns to the design screen.

Now let's see how the TabStop property operates. Assume that most of Skate-Away's customers are in Illinois. Instead of having the salesperson enter IL in the state Text box for each customer, it would be more efficient to have IL automatically appear in the Text box when the application is run. You can display IL in the state Text box by setting the TxtState control's Text property to IL. You can then set the TxtState control's TabStop property to False, which tells Visual Basic to bypass that control when the user is tabbing.

To set the Text property and the TabStop property of the TxtState control:

1   Click the **down arrow button in the Object box** (located below the Properties window title bar), scroll the Object box, and then click **TxtState TextBox** in the drop-down list. Sizing handles appear around the TxtState control.

2   If necessary, click the **Text** property in the Properties list.

3   Type **IL** and press [**Enter**]. IL is the current value of this control's Text property.

Now let's change the TabStop property to False.

4   Click the **TabStop** property in the Properties list, click the **down arrow button in the Settings box** (located above the Properties list in the Properties window), then click **False** in the drop-down list. Visual Basic will now bypass the TxtState control when the user is tabbing.

5 **Save and run** the project. When the form appears on the screen, notice IL in the state Text box.

6 Press [**Tab**] three times. Notice that Visual Basic bypasses the state Text box.

Although the state Text box is bypassed when the user is tabbing, the user can still make an entry in that Text box.

7 Click to the immediate left of IL in the state Text box, press [**Delete**] two times to remove the IL, then type **CA**. CA appears in the state Text box.

8 Click the **Exit button**. The application ends and Visual Basic returns to the design screen.

After creating the user interface and setting the properties of the objects, you then plan and write the Visual Basic instructions (code) to tell the objects how to respond to events. You'll do that next.

Planning and Writing Visual Basic Code

The third step in creating a Visual Basic application is planning and writing the program instructions (code). You will need to write code for each object that has an event listed in the third column of the TOE chart you created in Lesson A. That TOE chart is shown in Figure 2-16.

Task	Object	Event
Get order information from user	7 Text boxes	None
Calculate total skateboards and total price	Command button (Calc)	Click
Display total skateboards and total price	2 Label controls	None
Print a confirmation notice	Command button (Print)	Click
End the application	Command button (Exit)	Click
Clear the screen for the next order	Command button (Clear)	Click

Figure 2-16: Completed TOE chart

According to the TOE chart, you will need to write code for the four Command buttons, as they are the only objects with an event listed in the third column of the chart. You've already written the code for the Exit button, so you'll do the Print button next.

Coding the Print Command button

According to the TOE chart, the Print button is assigned the task of printing the form. You can use Visual Basic's PrintForm method to accomplish that task. A **method** is a predefined Visual Basic procedure. The syntax of the

PrintForm method [handwritten margin note]

PrintForm method is *Form.PrintForm* where *Form* is the name of the form you want to print and *PrintForm* is the name of the method. Notice that you use a period to separate the name of the form from the name of the method. If you want to print only the current form, you can omit the form's name and just use the syntax *PrintForm*. According to your TOE chart, the instruction to print the form must be placed in the Click event procedure.

To code the Print Command button and then save and run the project:

1   Click the **form's Maximize button**, then double-click the **Print button** to open the button's Code window. The Code window opens and shows that the current event procedure is Click.

2   Press [**Tab**], type **printform** and press [**Enter**], and then double-click the **Code window's Control menu box** to close the Code window.

3   Click the **form's Restore button**, then **save** **and run** the project.

4   If you are not connected to a printer, continue to the next step. If you are connected to a printer, click the **Print button**. Visual Basic prints the form. See Figure 2-17.

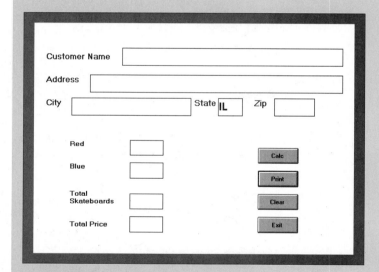

Figure 2-17: Printed confirmation notice

5   Click the **Exit button** to end the application. Visual Basic returns to the design screen.

Notice that the Command buttons appear in the printout shown in Figure 2-17. Having the Command buttons print on a customer's confirmation notice is not very professional-looking. It would be better if you could temporarily hide those buttons immediately before printing the form, then display them again after the form is printed. Figure 2-18 lists what you want the Print Command button to do.

Print button

1. Hide the 4 Command buttons
2. Print the form
3. Display the 4 Command buttons

Figure 2-18: Pseudocode for the Print Command button

Notice that the list shown in Figure 2-18 is composed of short, English-like statements. The statements represent the steps the Print button needs to follow in order to print the form without the Command buttons showing. In programming terms, the list of steps shown in Figure 2-18 is called pseudocode.

Pseudocode is a tool programmers use to help them plan the steps that an object will need to take to perform its assigned task. Even though the word *pseudocode* might be unfamiliar to you, you've already written pseudocode without even realizing it. Think about the last time you gave directions to someone. You wrote each direction down on paper, in your own words; that is pseudocode. Let's translate the Print button's pseudocode into the appropriate Visual Basic instructions. The first step is to hide the four Command buttons before printing the form. You can use the Help screens to see if there is a way to hide Command buttons temporarily.

To display a context-sensitive Help screen on Command buttons:

1 Click (don't double-click) the **Command button tool** 🔲 in the Toolbox, then press [F1]. A Help screen on Command button controls appears.

Notice that you can use the Help screen to display the <u>Properties</u>, <u>Events</u>, and <u>Methods</u> for Command buttons. Let's begin by looking at the properties of a Command button; remember, we are searching for a property that will allow us to hide a control temporarily.

2 Click **<u>Properties</u>** at the top of the Help screen. A list of properties appears. See Figure 2-19.

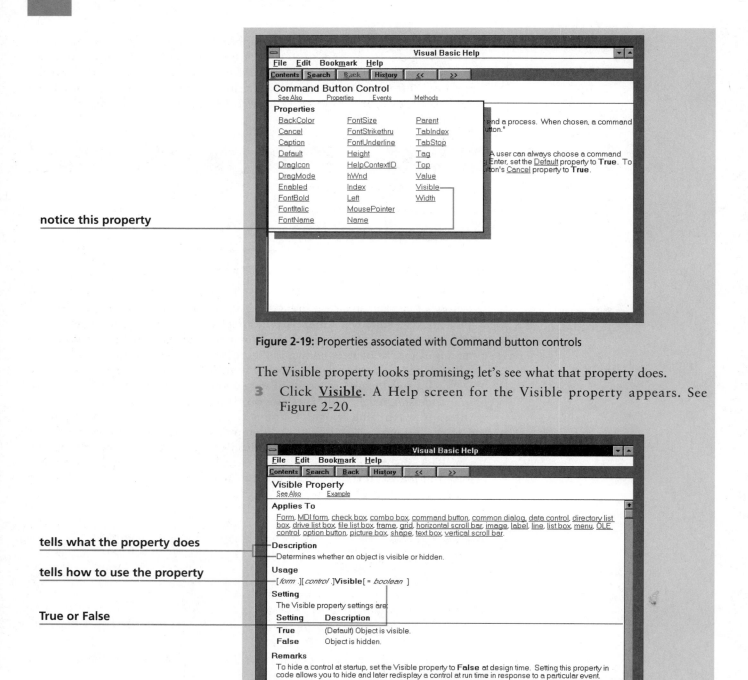

Figure 2-19: Properties associated with Command button controls

The Visible property looks promising; let's see what that property does.

3   Click **Visible**. A Help screen for the Visible property appears. See Figure 2-20.

Figure 2-20: Visible Property Help screen

Notice that the Visible property determines whether an object is visible or hidden. The property has two predefined settings: True and False. (These settings are called **Boolean** values, named after the English mathematician George Boole.) If the property is set to True, the Command button appears on the form; if the property is set to False, the Command button is hidden from view. You can use this property to first hide and then display the Command buttons.

4 Double-click the **Help screen's Control menu box** to close the Help screen, then click the **form's title bar** to select the form. The form's title bar is now highlighted.

You can use an assignment statement, which is simply a Visual Basic instruction, to assign a value to the property of an object while the application is running. (You can also use an assignment statement to assign a value to a variable. You'll learn about variables in Tutorial 3.) In this case you want to tell Visual Basic to assign the False value to the Visible property of each of the four Command buttons when the Print button is clicked. Assigning the False value to the Visible property will hide the Command buttons. Then, after the form is printed, you want to tell Visual Basic to assign the True value to the Visible property of each of the Command buttons. Assigning the True value to the Visible property will display the buttons on the form.

Writing an Assignment Statement

An assignment statement that assigns a value to the property of an object must follow this syntax: *Form.Object.Property = value*. *Form* is the name of the form in which the object is located, *Object* is the name of the object, and *Property* is the name of the property to which you want the value assigned. Notice that you use a period to separate the form's name from the object's name, and the object's name from the property name. You follow the *Form.Object.Property* information with an equal sign (=) and the value you want to assign to the object's property. If the object is in the current form, you can omit the form name and simply use the syntax: *Object.Property = value*. For example, the assignment statement to change the Calc button's Visible property to False, which will hide the Calc button from view, could be written as *FrmOrder.CmdCalc.Visible = False* or simply as *CmdCalc.Visible = False*. When Visual Basic sees an assignment statement in a Code window, Visual Basic assigns the value on the right side of the equal sign to the object and property appearing on the left side of the equal sign. For example, the *CmdCalc.Visible = False* assignment statement tells Visual Basic to assign the Boolean value of False to the Visible property of the CmdCalc control.

Using the pseudocode shown earlier in Figure 2-18, let's enter the code to tell the Print button to hide the four Command buttons before printing the form and then to display the Command buttons after printing the form.

To code the Print button:

1   Maximize the form, then open the Print button's Code window.

The blinking insertion point is at the beginning of the second line in the Code window (the line that says PrintForm).

2   Press [Enter] to add a new line above the PrintForm instruction, then press the **up arrow key** to move the insertion point into the new line.

3   Type **CmdCalc.visible = false** and press [Enter].

4   Type **CmdPrint.visible = false** and press [Enter].

5   Type **CmdClear.visible = false** and press [Enter].

6   Type **CmdExit.visible = false**. See Figure 2-21.

these instructions will hide the four command buttons

this instruction will print the form

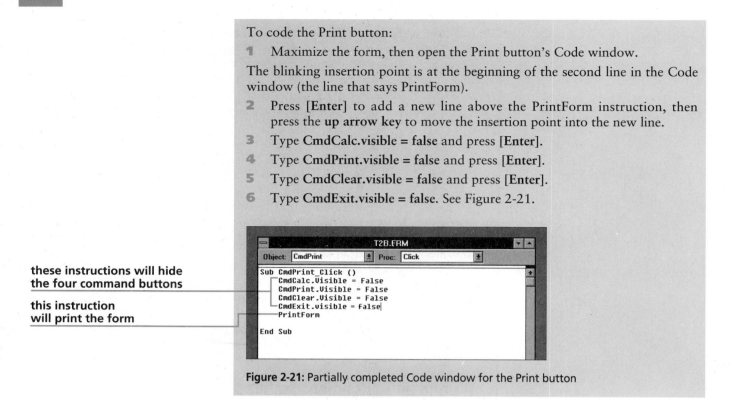

Figure 2-21: Partially completed Code window for the Print button

The code entered into the Print button's Code window will hide the four Command buttons before printing the form. After the form is printed, you need to display the four buttons for the user. To do that you must enter four additional assignment statements into the Code window. These assignment statements will set the Visible property of the four Command buttons to True. Instead of typing the four additional statements, let's copy the assignment statements you already entered to the Windows Clipboard and paste them into the Code window, below the PrintForm instruction. Then, in each of the copied statements, you can simply change the False to True.

To complete the Print button:

1   Position the I-bar I at the beginning of the first assignment statement in the Code window. Press and hold down the left mouse button and drag until all four assignment statements are highlighted, then release the mouse button. See Figure 2-22.

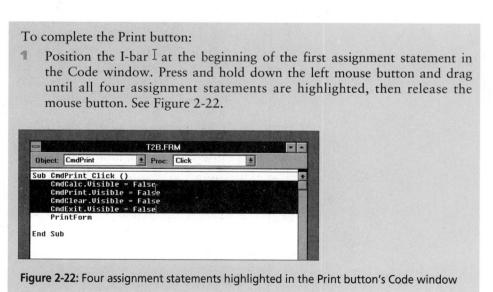

Figure 2-22: Four assignment statements highlighted in the Print button's Code window

2   Press [Ctrl][c] to copy the assignment statements to the Clipboard.

3   Position the I-bar I in the empty line below the PrintForm statement (immediately below the P), then click at that location. The blinking insertion point appears at that location.

4   Press [Ctrl][v] to paste the four assignment statements into the Code window.

5   In the four assignment statements you just copied, change the False to True, as shown in Figure 2-23.

changed to True

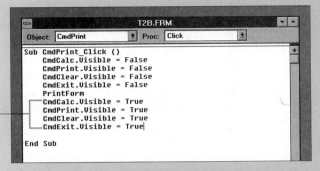

Figure 2-23: Four additional assignment statements copied into the Code window

Internally Documenting the Program Code

It's always a good idea to leave yourself some messages as reminders in the Code window. Programmers refer to this as **internal documentation**. Visual Basic provides an easy way to document a program internally. You simply place an apostrophe (') before the statement you want Visual Basic to treat as a comment. Visual Basic ignores everything after the apostrophe on that line. Let's add some comments to the Print button's Code window.

To document the Print button's code internally:

1   Position the I-bar at the end of the first line in the Code window (the line with the Sub instruction), then click at that location. The blinking insertion point appears at that location.

2   Press [Enter] to insert a new line, then type **'Hide Command buttons before printing the form**. Don't type the period, but be sure to type the apostrophe (').

3   Position the I-bar after the PrintForm instruction, then click at that location. Notice that the internal documentation changes to a different color when you move the insertion point to another line. Recall from Tutorial 1 that Visual Basic displays keywords and key symbols in a different color to help you quickly identify these elements in the Code window. In this case, the color coding helps you easily locate the internal documentation.

4   Press [Enter], then press [Backspace] to cancel the indentation.

5   Type **'Display Command buttons after the form is printed.** Don't type the period, but be sure to type the apostrophe ('). See Figure 2-24.

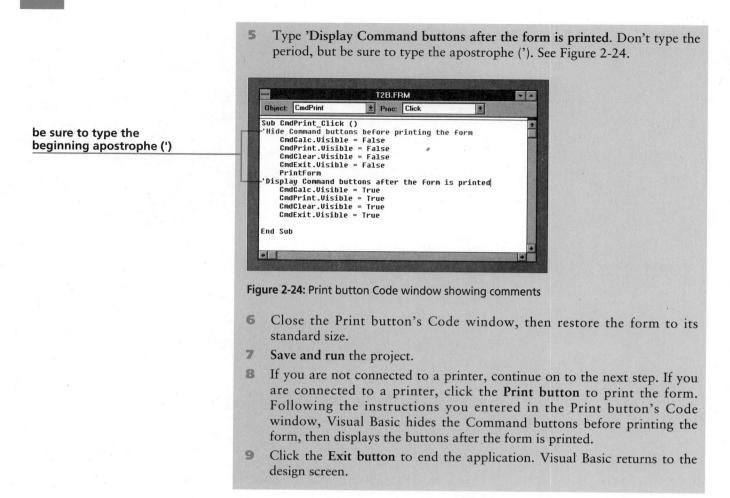

be sure to type the beginning apostrophe (')

```
                              T2B.FRM
Object: CmdPrint          ±   Proc: Click             ±
Sub CmdPrint_Click ()
'Hide Command buttons before printing the form
      CmdCalc.Visible = False
      CmdPrint.Visible = False
      CmdClear.Visible = False
      CmdExit.Visible = False
      PrintForm
'Display Command buttons after the form is printed
      CmdCalc.Visible = True
      CmdPrint.Visible = True
      CmdClear.Visible = True
      CmdExit.Visible = True

End Sub
```

Figure 2-24: Print button Code window showing comments

6   Close the Print button's Code window, then restore the form to its standard size.

7   **Save and run** the project.

8   If you are not connected to a printer, continue on to the next step. If you are connected to a printer, click the **Print button** to print the form. Following the instructions you entered in the Print button's Code window, Visual Basic hides the Command buttons before printing the form, then displays the buttons after the form is printed.

9   Click the **Exit button** to end the application. Visual Basic returns to the design screen.

Let's code the Clear button next.

Coding the Clear Command Button

According to the TOE chart, the Clear button is assigned the task of clearing the screen for the next order. Here again, you can use an assignment statement to accomplish this task. Recall that the text displayed in a Label control is recorded in the Caption property, whereas the text displayed in a Text box control is recorded in the Text property. To clear the prior customer information from the screen, you will need to remove the contents of the Text property for the seven Text boxes, as well as the entries recorded in the Caption property of the two Label controls. Figure 2-25 lists the steps—the pseudocode—you want the Clear button to follow.

Clear button

1. Clear the Text property of the 7 Text boxes (customer name, address, city, state, zip code, red skateboards, blue skateboards)

2. Clear the Caption property of the 2 Label controls (total skateboards and total price)

Figure 2-25: Pseudocode for the Clear button

You can use assignment statements to clear both the Text property of the seven Text boxes and the Caption property of the two Label controls. The assignment statements will assign a zero-length string to eight of those nine controls, and the string "IL" to the TxtState control. A **string** is a group of characters enclosed in quotation marks. For example, the word "Jones" is considered a string because it is a group of characters enclosed in quotation marks. Likewise, "45" is a string, but 45 is not (45 is a number). "Jones" is a string with a length of five because there are five characters between the quotation marks; "45" is a string with a length of two because there are two characters between the quotation marks. Following this logic, a zero-length string is a set of quotation marks with nothing between them, like this: "". You will assign a zero-length string, also called a **null string**, to the Text property of six of the seven Text boxes and to the Caption property of the two Label controls. Assigning the zero-length string to the Text property and to the Caption property will clear the prior customer's information from the controls.

To code the Clear button:

1   Maximize the form, then open the Clear button's Code window. The Code window opens.

First, let's include some documentation in the Code window.

2   Type **'Clear prior information from the screen** and press **[Enter]**. Don't type the period, but be sure to type the apostrophe (').

Recall that the names of the Text boxes are TxtName, TxtAddress, TxtCity, TxtState, TxtZip, TxtRed, and TxtBlue.

3   Press **[Tab]**, then type **TxtName.Text = ""** and press **[Enter]**. (Don't type any spaces between the quotation marks.) You don't need the form name in the assignment statement because the TxtName control is in the current form.

4   Copy the TxtName.Text = "" assignment statement to the Clipboard, then paste the assignment statement into the Code window six times, between the original assignment statement and the End Sub instruction.

5 Change the names of the controls in the assignment statements to match Figure 2-26. Be sure to change the "" to "IL" in the TxtState control's assignment statement. Also be sure to position the insertion point in the blank line immediately below the last assignment statement, as shown in Figure 2-26.

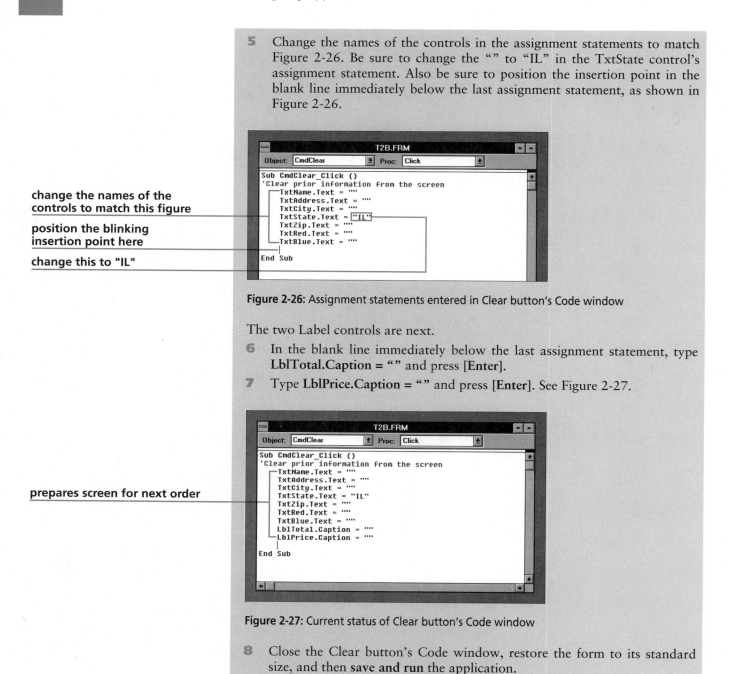

change the names of the controls to match this figure

position the blinking insertion point here

change this to "IL"

Figure 2-26: Assignment statements entered in Clear button's Code window

The two Label controls are next.

6 In the blank line immediately below the last assignment statement, type **LblTotal.Caption = ""** and press **[Enter]**.

7 Type **LblPrice.Caption = ""** and press **[Enter]**. See Figure 2-27.

prepares screen for next order

Figure 2-27: Current status of Clear button's Code window

8 Close the Clear button's Code window, restore the form to its standard size, and then **save** and **run** the application.

9   To test the application, enter **your name and address information**. Then enter **10** for the number of red skateboards and **10** for the number of blue skateboards. Then click the **Clear button**. The information disappears from the screen.

Notice that the Clear button retains the focus after clearing the information from the screen. (You can tell that the Clear button has the focus because it has a highlighted border and a dotted rectangle around its caption.) It would be more convenient for the user if the focus were in the customer name Text box. Then the user would not have to click in that area to enter a new order. Let's exit the application and find a way to fix this problem.

10 Click the **Exit button** to end the application. Visual Basic returns to the design screen.

As usual, we'll use the Help screens to look for a property, event, or method that will allow us to control *where* the focus is placed. This time, because we want the focus sent to a Text box (the TxtName control), we will need to look at a Help screen on Text boxes to see what properties, events, and methods that control can understand.

To view a Help screen on the Text box control:

1   Click (don't double-click) the **Text box tool** [abl] in the Toolbox, then press **[F1]**. The Text Box Control Help screen appears.

Let's look at the methods for a Text box control.

2   Click **Methods**. The list of Text box methods appears.

The SetFocus method looks promising. Let's see what this method does.

3   Click **SetFocus** in the list. The Help screen indicates that you can use this method to set the focus to a form or control, which is exactly what you want to do.

Notice that the syntax of the SetFocus method is *object.SetFocus* where *object* is the name of the object in which you want the focus, and *SetFocus* is the name of the method.

4   Close the Help screen, maximize the form, then open the Clear button's Code window,

5   Position the I-bar at the beginning of the blank line immediately above the End Sub instruction and click at that location, then type **'Set the focus to the customer name** and press **[Enter]**. Be sure to type the apostrophe (') at the beginning of the documentation.

6 Press [Tab], then type **TxtName.SetFocus** and press [Enter]. See Figure 2-28.

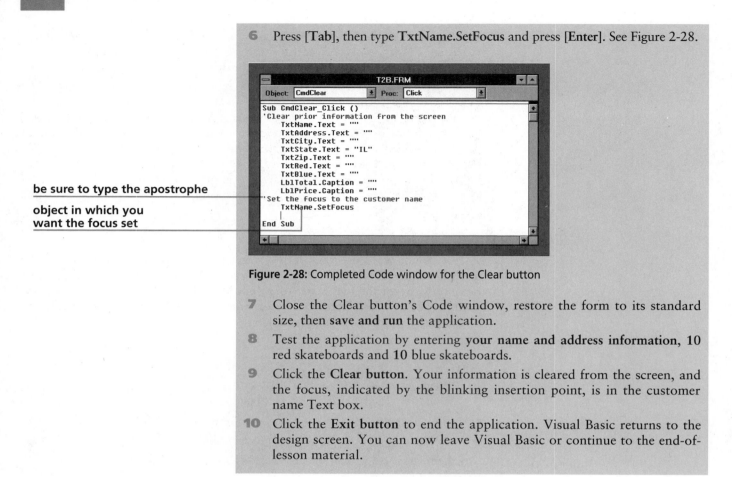

be sure to type the apostrophe

object in which you
want the focus set

Figure 2-28: Completed Code window for the Clear button

7 Close the Clear button's Code window, restore the form to its standard size, then **save and run** the application.

8 Test the application by entering **your name and address information, 10** red skateboards and **10** blue skateboards.

9 Click the **Clear button**. Your information is cleared from the screen, and the focus, indicated by the blinking insertion point, is in the customer name Text box.

10 Click the **Exit button** to end the application. Visual Basic returns to the design screen. You can now leave Visual Basic or continue to the end-of-lesson material.

The Calc Command button is the only object that still needs to be coded. You'll do that in Lesson C. You will also learn ways to make your application more professional-looking. For now, you can either take a break or complete the end-of-lesson questions and exercises.

S U M M A R Y

To create a Visual Basic application:

■ Create the user interface, using the sketch you drew when you planned the application..

■ Set the properties of the objects.

■ Plan and then write the Visual Basic program instructions (program code) to tell the objects how to respond when scrolled, clicked, and so on.

■ Test the application with sample data. If necessary, find and correct (debug) any errors in the application.

■ Document the application.

To use the Tab key to move the focus to a control:

■ Set the control's TabStop property to True.

To bypass a control when using the Tab key:

■ Set the control's TabStop property to False.

To set the tab order:

■ Set each control's TabIndex property to a number that represents the order in which you want that control to receive the focus. Remember to begin with 0 (zero).

To move the focus to an object while the program is running:

■ Use the SetFocus method (*Object.Setfocus*) in the Code window.

To print a form:

■ Use the PrintForm method (*Form.PrintForm* or *PrintForm*) in the Code window.

To assign a value to the property of an object:

■ Use an assignment statement (*Form.Object.Property = value* or *Object.Property = value*) in the Code window.

To document Visual Basic code with comments:

■ Begin the comment with an apostrophe (') in the Code window.

To clear an object's property:

■ Use an assignment statement to assign a zero-length string (""), also called a null string, to the object's property.

Q U E S T I O N S

1. The ___TabIndex___ property determines the order in which a control receives the focus when the user is tabbing.
   a. OrderTab
   b. SetOrder
   c. TabIndex
   d. TabOrder
   e. TabStop

2. The ___TabStop___ property controls whether the control is bypassed when the user is tabbing.
   a. OrderTab
   b. SetOrder
   c. TabIndex
   d. TabOrder
   e. TabStop

3. The ___Print Form___ method prints a form.
   a. Form
   b. FormPrint
   c. Print
   d. Printer
   e. PrintForm

4. Which of the following is a valid assignment statement?
   a. TxtName.Caption = "Jones"
   b. TxtName.Caption = "Jones"
   c. TxtName.Text = 'Jones'
   d. TxtName.Text = "Jones" ✓
   e. None of the above is valid

5. Which of the following is a valid assignment statement?
   a. LblName.Caption = Jones
   b. TxtName.Caption = "Jones" ✓
   c. TxtName.Caption = 'Jones'
   d. CmdExit.Visible = "False"
   e. None of the above is valid

6. Listed below are the five steps you should follow when creating an OOED application. Put them in the proper order by placing a number (1 to 5) on the line to the left of the step.
   __3__ Plan and then write the Visual Basic program instructions (program code) to tell the objects how to respond when scrolled, clicked, and so on.
   __1__ Create the user interface, using the sketch you drew when you planned the application.
   __4__ Test the application with sample data. If necessary, find and correct (debug) any errors in the application.
   __2__ Set the properties of the objects.
   __5__ Document the application.

E X E R C I S E S

tips
• • • • • • • • • • • • • • • • •

▶ Place your Text box controls on the form first, in the order in which you need them. Then you won't need to spend a lot of time setting the TabIndex property.

▶ Either write the objects' names on the sketch you created in Lesson A or create and then print the user interface (form) and write the objects' names on it. This process will help you remember the names as you are coding.

1. a. Use the TOE chart and sketch you created in Lesson A to create the user interface for the Paper Products application. (See tips box following.)
   b. Write the pseudocode for the appropriate objects. Then write the code for all but the Calc Command button.
   c. Save the form and the project as T2LBE1.
   d. Test the application with the following data:
      Salesperson's Name: John Smith
      Sales: 2000
   e. Print the application with the test data showing.
   f. Print the code.

2. a. Use the TOE chart and sketch you created in Lesson A to create the user interface for the twips to inches application.
   b. Write the pseudocode for the appropriate objects. Then write the code for all but the Calc Command button.
   c. Save the form and the project as T2LBE2.
   d. Test the application with the following data:
      Twips: 2880
   e. Print the application with the test data showing.
   f. Print the code.

3.   a. Use the TOE chart and sketch you created in Lesson A to create the user interface for John Lee's application.
     b. Write the pseudocode for the appropriate objects. Then write the code for all but the Calc Command button.
     c. Save the form and the project as T2LBE3.
     d. Test the application with the following data:
       Beginning cash balance: 5000
       Earnings: 2500
       Expenses: 3000
     e. Print the application with the test data showing.
     f. Print the code.

4.   a. Use the TOE chart and sketch you created in Lesson A to create the user interface for Lana Jones' application.
     b. Write the pseudocode for the appropriate objects. Then write the code for all but the Calc Command button.
     c. Save the form and the project as T2LBE4.
     d. Test the application with the following data:
       First Number: 27
       Second Number: 9
       Third Number: 18
     e. Print the application with the test data showing.
     f. Print the code.

5.   a. Use the TOE chart and sketch you created in Lesson A to create the user interface for the Bookworms Inc. application.
     b. Write the pseudocode for the appropriate objects. Then write the code for all but the Calc Command button.
     c. Save the form and the project as T2LBE5.
     d. Test the application with the following data:
       Book Title: An Intro to Visual Basic
       Paperback versions: 100
       Paperback cost: 40
       Hardcover versions: 50
       Hardcover cost: 75
     e. Print the application with the test data showing.
     f. Print the code.

6.   a. Use the TOE chart and sketch you created in Lesson A to create the user interface for the Jackets Unlimited application.
     b. Write the pseudocode for the appropriate objects. Then write the code for all but the Calc Command button.
     c. Save the form and the project as T2LBE6.
     d. Test the application with the following data:
       Jacket's original price: 50
     e. Print the application with the test data showing.
     f. Print the code.

7.   a. Use the TOE chart and sketch you created in Lesson A to create the user interface for the Typing Salon application.
     b. Write the pseudocode for the appropriate objects. Then write the code for all but the Calc Command button.
     c. Save the form and the project as T2LBE7.
     d. Test the application with the following data:
       Customer's name: Alice Wong
       Number of typed envelopes: 250
       Number of typed pages: 200

    e. Print the application with the test data showing.

    f. Print the code.

8. a. Use the TOE chart and sketch you created in Lesson A to create the user interface for the Sun Projects application.

    b. Write the pseudocode for the appropriate objects. Then write the code for all but the Calc Command button.

    c. Save the form and the project as T2LBE8.

    d. Test the application with the following data:

    Employee's name: Susan Reha

    Hours worked: 40

    Rate of pay: 12

    e. Print the application with the test data showing.

    f. Print the code.

9. a. Use the TOE chart and sketch you created in Lesson A to create the user interface for the Management USA application.

    b. Write the pseudocode for the appropriate objects. Then write the code for all but the Calc Command button.

    c. Save the form and the project as T2LBE9.

    d. Test the application with the following data:

    Company Name: ABC Company

    Address: 345 Main St.

    City, State, Zip: Glen, TX 70122

    "How to Be an Effective Manager" registrants: 10

    "How to Run a Small Business" registrants: 5

    e. Print the application with the test data showing.

    f. Print the code.

10. a. Use the TOE chart and sketch you created in Lesson A to create the user interface for the R&M Sales application.

    b. Write the pseudocode for the appropriate objects. Then write the code for all but the Calc Command button.

    c. Save the form and the project as T2LBE10.

    d. Test the application with the following data:

    South region's current year's sales: 20000

    South region's projected increase: .03 (3%)

    West region's current year's sales: 11500

    West region's projected increase: .05 (5%)

    e. Print the application with the test data showing.

    f. Print the code.

LESSON C

In this lesson you will learn how to:

■ Write Visual Basic equations
■ Use the Val function
■ Add a Line control
■ Use the Format function

Writing Equations

Writing Visual Basic Equations

Most applications require the computer to perform some calculations. You instruct the computer to perform a calculation by writing an arithmetic equation in an object's Code window. The mathematical operators you can use in your arithmetic equations, along with their precedence numbers, are listed in Figure 2-29. The precedence numbers represent the order in which Visual Basic performs the mathematical operations in an equation. You can, however, use parentheses to override the order of precedence. Operations within parentheses are always performed before operations outside of parentheses.

Operator	Operation	Precedence Number
^	Exponentiation (raises a number to a power)	1
−	Negation	2
*, /	Multiplication and Division	3
\	Integer Division	4
Mod	Modulo Arithmetic	5
+, −	Addition and Subtraction	6

Figure 2-29: Mathematical operators and their order of precedence

When you create an arithmetic equation, keep in mind that Visual Basic follows the same order of precedence as you do when solving equations; that is, an operation with a lower precedence number is done before one with a higher precedence number. If the equation contains more than one operator having the same priority, those operators are evaluated from left to right. For example, in the equation 3+9/3*5, the division (/) would be done first, then the multiplication (*), and then the addition (+). In other words, Visual Basic would first divide 9 by 3, then multiply by 5, and then add 3. The equation evaluates to 18. You can use parentheses to change the order in which the operators will be evaluated. For example, the equation (3+9)/3*5 (notice the parentheses around the 3+9) evaluates to 20, not 18. That's because the parentheses tell Visual Basic to add 3 + 9 first, then divide by 3, and then multiply by 5.

Two of the mathematical operators listed in Figure 2-29 might be less familiar to you; these are the integer division operator (\) and the modulo arithmetic operator (Mod). The integer division operator (\), like the standard division operator (/), is used to divide two numbers. Unlike the standard division operator, however, the integer division operator returns an integer (whole number) result. For example, the expression 211\4 results in 52, whereas the expression 211/4 results in 52.75.

The modulo arithmetic operator is also used to divide two numbers, but it results in the remainder of the division. For example, 211 Mod 4 equals 3 (the remainder of 211 divided by 4).

In addition to the mathematical operators, Visual Basic also allows you to use relational operators and logical operators in your equations. You will learn about those two types of operators in Tutorial 4. For now, you will need to know only the mathematical operators in order to complete the Skate-Away Sales application.

Let's open the T2B project and code the Calc Command button.

Coding the Calc Command Button

Before you can code the Calc button, you will need to open the T2B project that you created in Lesson B. Let's do this now.

To open the T2B project and then save the form file and the project file under a new name:

1. Launch Visual Basic and open the **t2b.mak** project, which is in either the tut2\ver2 or tut2\ver3 directory on your Student Disk.

2. Click the **View Form button** to view the FrmOrder form. The FrmOrder form from Lesson B appears.

3. Use the **Save File As...** option on the **File** menu to save the form as **T2C**.

4. Use the **Save Project As...** option on the **File** menu to save the project as **T2C**.

5. Click the **form's Maximize button** to maximize the form.

According to your TOE chart for this application, the Calc button is responsible for calculating the total number of skateboards ordered and the total price of the order. The instructions to accomplish the Calc button's task must be placed in the Click event. Let's write the pseudocode defining the steps the Calc button will need to take. See Figure 2-30.

Calc button

1. Calculate total skateboards = red skateboards + blue skateboards
2. Calculate total price = total skateboards * $100 * 105%

Figure 2-30: Pseudocode for the Calc button

The first step listed in the pseudocode shown in Figure 2-30 is to calculate the total number of skateboards. To do this, the Calc button will need to add the number of red skateboards to the number of blue skateboards. Recall that the number of red skateboards is recorded in the Text property of the TxtRed control as the user enters that information. Likewise, the number of blue skateboards is recorded in the Text property of the TxtBlue control. Recall from your TOE chart that the LblTotal control is responsible for displaying the total number of skateboards. You can use an assignment statement to add the two Text properties and then assign the sum to the Caption property of the LblTotal control. This is illustrated in Figure 2-31.

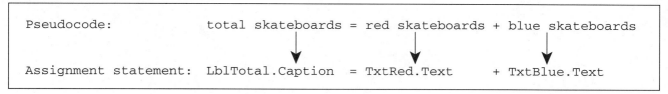

Figure 2-31: Illustration of the total skateboards calculation

The next step shown in the pseudocode is to compute the total price of the order. To do this, the application needs to multiply the total number of skateboards (recorded in the LblTotal control) by $100, and then multiply that amount by 105% (recall that you need to include a 5% sales tax in the price). The total price equation is illustrated in Figure 2-32.

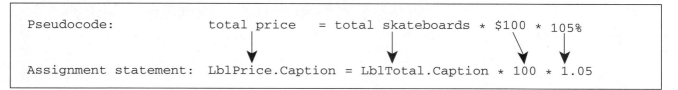

Figure 2-32: Illustration of the total price calculation

Notice that the total price equation, written in Visual Basic code, does not include the dollar sign ($) or the percent sign (%). When entering a percentage in Visual Basic, you must convert the percentage to its decimal equivalent. In this case, for example, 105% was converted to 1.05. Let's open the Calc button's Code window and write the necessary code.

To code the Calc button:

1 Open the **Calc button's Code window**. The current event procedure is Click, which is the event you want.

2 Type **'Calculate total number of skateboards** and press [**Enter**].

3 Press [**Tab**], then type **LblTotal.Caption = TxtRed.Text + TxtBlue.Text** and press [**Enter**].

4 Press [**Backspace**], then type **'Calculate total price** and press [**Enter**].

5 Press [Tab], then type **LblPrice.Caption = LblTotal.Caption * 100 * 1.05** and press [Enter]. See Figure 2-33.

be sure to type the apostrophe in the documentation lines

```
Object:  CmdCalc          Proc:  Click

Sub CmdCalc_Click ()
'Calculate total number of skateboards
    LblTotal.Caption = TxtRed.Text + TxtBlue.Text
'Calculate total price
    LblPrice.Caption = LblTotal.Caption * 100 * 1.05

End Sub
```

assignment statements

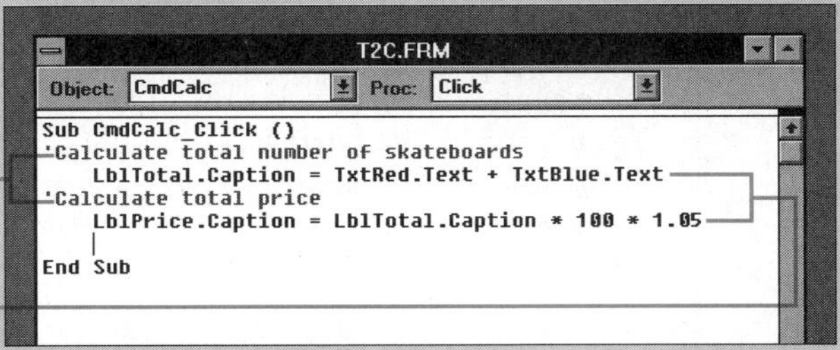

Figure 2-33: Calc button's Code window

6 Close the **Calc button's Code window**, restore the form to its standard size, then **save and run** the application.

7 Press [Tab] four times until the focus is in the red skateboard Text box, type **5**, then press [Tab].

8 Type **10** in the blue skateboard Text box, then press [Tab]. The Calc button receives the focus next, as indicated by its highlighted border and the dotted rectangle around its caption.

9 Press [Enter] to select the Calc button. The Calc button calculates the total skateboards and the total price according to the instructions in its Code window. See Figure 2-34.

Skate-Away Sales

Customer Name

Address

City   State **IL**   Zip

Red   **5**   Calc

Blue   **10**   Print

Total Skateboards   **510**   Clear

Total Price   **53550**   Exit

these figures are incorrect

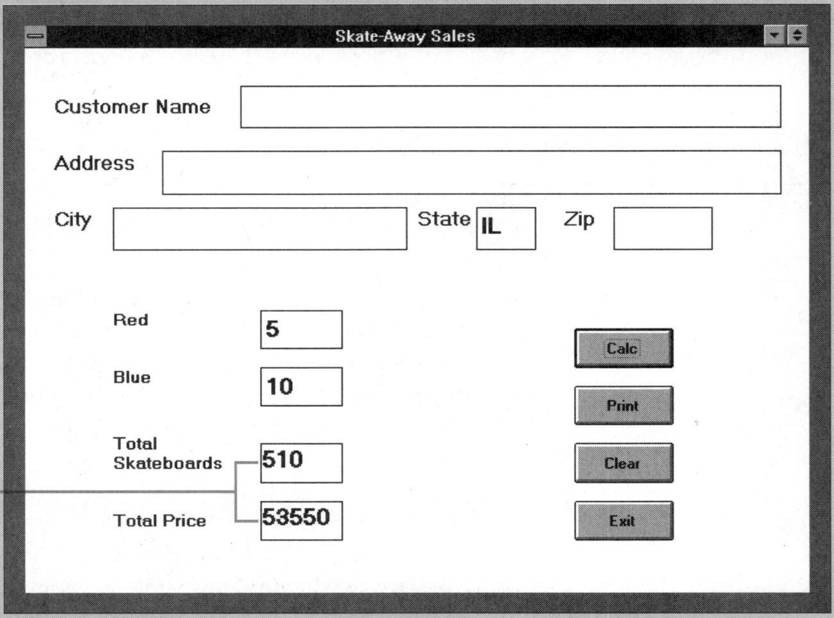

Figure 2-34: Screen showing incorrect figures calculated by Calc button

Notice that the application shows 510 as the total number of skateboards.
Instead of mathematically adding the two order quantities together, which
should have resulted in a total of 15, Visual Basic appended the second order
quantity to the end of the first order quantity, giving 510. When the total
skateboards figure is incorrect, it follows that the total price figure will also be
incorrect, as the total skateboards figure is used in the total price equation.
Let's exit the application and discuss what went wrong.

10 Click the **Exit button** to end the application. Visual Basic returns to the
    design screen.

The Val Function

The *LblTotal.Caption = TxtRed.Text + TxtBlue.Text* equation you entered in the
Calc button's Code window is supposed to calculate the total skateboards, but
the equation is not working correctly. Instead of the plus sign (+) adding the red
skateboard quantity to the blue skateboard quantity, the plus sign appends the
latter quantity to the end of the first one. This occurs because the plus sign (+) in
Visual Basic performs two roles: It adds numbers together and it **concatenates**
(links together) strings. You will learn about string concatenation in Tutorial 3.
(Recall that strings are groups of characters enclosed in quotation marks.)

In Visual Basic, values in the Caption property and the Text property of
controls are treated as strings, not numbers, even though you don't see the quotation marks. Adding strings together will not give you the same result as adding
numbers together. As you saw in the Skate-Away Sales application, adding the
string "5" to the string "10" results in the string "510," whereas adding
the number 5 to the number 10 results in the number 15. To fix this problem,
you need to tell Visual Basic to treat the entries in the Text property of the red
and blue skateboard Text boxes as numbers, not as strings. For this, you need to
use the Val function.

A **function** is a predefined procedure that performs a specific task. Unlike a
method, a function results in a value. For example, the **Val function**, which tells
Visual Basic to treat a character string as a numeric value, results in a number.
The Val function has the following syntax: Val(*StringExpression*). The
StringExpression is the character string you want treated as a number. Because
Visual Basic must be able to interpret the *StringExpression* as a numeric value,
the expression cannot include a dollar sign, commas, or the percent sign (%). To
fix the assignment statement entered in the Calc button's Code window, you will
use the Val function to tell Visual Basic to treat the Text property of the red and
blue Text boxes as numbers (not strings).

To include the Val function in the Calc button's Code window and then print
the confirmation notice:

1 Maximize the form, open the Calc button's Code window, and then maximize the Code window. The Code window fills the screen.

2 Change the *LblTotal.Caption = TxtRed.Text + TxtBlue.Text* assignment
   statement to ***LblTotal.Caption = Val(TxtRed.Text) + Val(TxtBlue.Text)***.
   Be sure to watch the placement of the parentheses. See Figure 2-35.

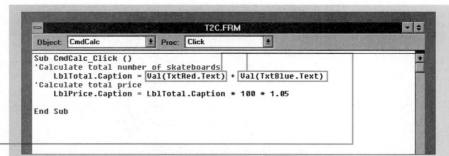

enter Val function in two places

Figure 2-35: Calc button's Code window showing Val function

You do not need to enter the Val function in the equation that computes the total price because that equation does not use the plus sign (+) to add the properties of controls. In the total price equation (which involves multiplication, not addition), Visual Basic will automatically treat the contents of the LblTotal control as a number when it performs the calculation.

3   Close the Code window, restore the form to its standard size, then **save and run** the project.

4   Press [**Tab**] four times to move the focus to the red skateboards Text box, type **5** as the number of red skateboards ordered, then press [**Tab**], then type **10** as the number of blue skateboards ordered, and then press [**Tab**]. The Calc button has the focus.

5   Press [**Enter**] to select the Calc button. The application correctly calculates the total skateboards (15) and the total price (1575).

Notice that the focus remains in the Calc button, which means that the salesperson will either have to click the Print button or press the Tab key and then press [Enter] to print the confirmation notice. Because the salesperson will usually print the confirmation notice after calculating the order, it would be more efficient to have the Calc button move the focus to the Print button immediately after the calculations are made. You can use the SetFocus method you learned earlier to place the focus in the Print button. Before you do that, you'll print the current confirmation notice.

6   Click the **Print button** to print the confirmation notice. The confirmation notice prints on the printer, and the customer name Text box receives the focus.

After printing a confirmation notice, the salesperson will usually clear the screen for the next order. Here again, you can use the SetFocus method to place the focus in the Clear button after the confirmation is printed.

7   Click the **Exit button**. Visual Basic returns to the design screen.

Now let's enter the SetFocus method in the Calc button's Code window and in the Print button's Code window.

To enter the SetFocus method in the two Code windows:

1   Maximize the form, then open the Calc button's Code window.

2   Position the I-bar at the beginning of the blank line above the End Sub instruction. Click at that location, then type **'Set the focus to the Print button** and press [Enter].

3   Press [Tab], then type **CmdPrint.SetFocus** and press [Enter].

4   Click the **down arrow button in the Code window's Object box**, then click **CmdPrint** in the drop-down list. The CmdPrint Code window, showing the Click event procedure, appears.

5   Position the I-bar at the beginning of the blank line above the End Sub instruction. Click at that location, then type **'Set the focus to the Clear button** and press [Enter].

6   Press [Tab], then type **CmdClear.SetFocus** and press [Enter].

7   Close the Code window, restore the form to its standard size, then **save and run** the project.

8   Enter the following order:

   Tom Lee Sports, 345 Main, Woodstock, 60884, 20 red skateboards, 30 blue skateboards

9   Click the **Calc button** (or press [Enter]). The application calculates the total skateboards (50) and the total price (5250). The Print button now has the focus.

10 Click the **Print button** (or press [Enter]). The confirmation notice prints and the focus moves to the Clear button. Click the **Clear button** (or press [Enter]). The information is cleared from the screen, and the focus moves to the customer name Text box. Click the **Exit button**. Visual Basic returns to the design screen.

Now that you have completed and tested the Skate-Away Sales application, you can concentrate on improving its appearance.

Improving the Appearance of an Application

You can improve the appearance of the Skate-Away Sales application in five ways:
1. Remove the form's title bar so the user cannot size the user interface.
2. Add a horizontal line between the blue skateboard Text box and the total skateboard Label control.
3. Add color to the user interface.
4. Display a dollar sign ($) and a comma in the total price Label control.
5. Assign access keys to objects in the user interface. (Access keys allow the user to select objects by pressing the Alt key along with a letter. This is helpful in cases where the user's mouse is not working.)

Removing the Form's Title Bar

In Tutorial 1 you learned that you remove the form's title bar by setting the BorderStyle property to 0-None. Let's do this now.

To remove the form's title bar:

1   If necessary, click the **form's title bar** to select the form, then click **BorderStyle** in the Properties list.

2   Click the **down arrow button in the Settings box** (located in the Properties window), then click **0-None** in the drop-down list. Visual Basic will now remove the form's title bar when you run the application.

Next let's draw a line between the blue skateboard Text box and the total skateboard Label control.

Drawing a Line Control on the Form

You use the Line Tool to draw a Line control. You can place a Line control on the form in the usual manner—by double-clicking the Line tool in the Toolbox. You can also draw a Line control on the form by first clicking the Line tool in the Toolbox, moving the mouse pointer onto the form, and then dragging the mouse pointer until the control is the size you want. Let's try the latter method now.

To add a Line control to the user interface:

1   Click the **Line tool** ◩ in the Toolbox and move the mouse pointer onto the form. The mouse pointer becomes a cross hair +.

2   Click the **form's Maximize button** to maximize the form.

3   Position the + as shown in Figure 2-36.

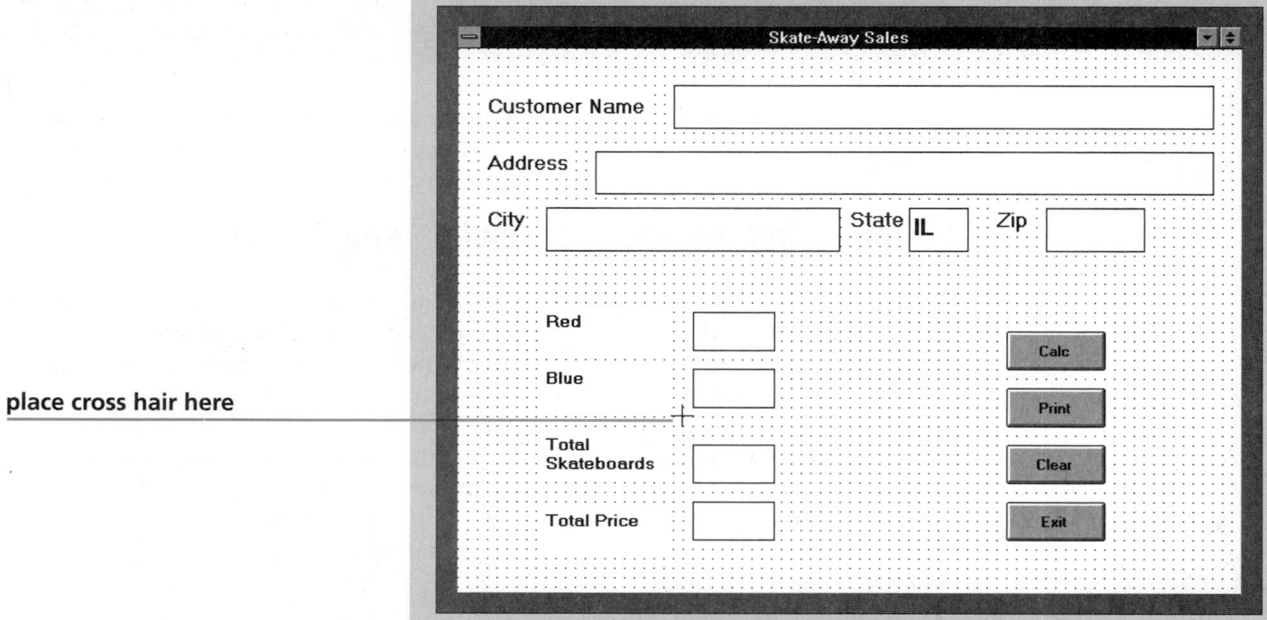

place cross hair here

Figure 2-36: Screen showing placement of cross hair

4 Press and hold down the left mouse button as you drag the + to the right until the Line control is about one inch long, then release the mouse button. The Line control appears on the form. See Figure 2-37.

sizing handle

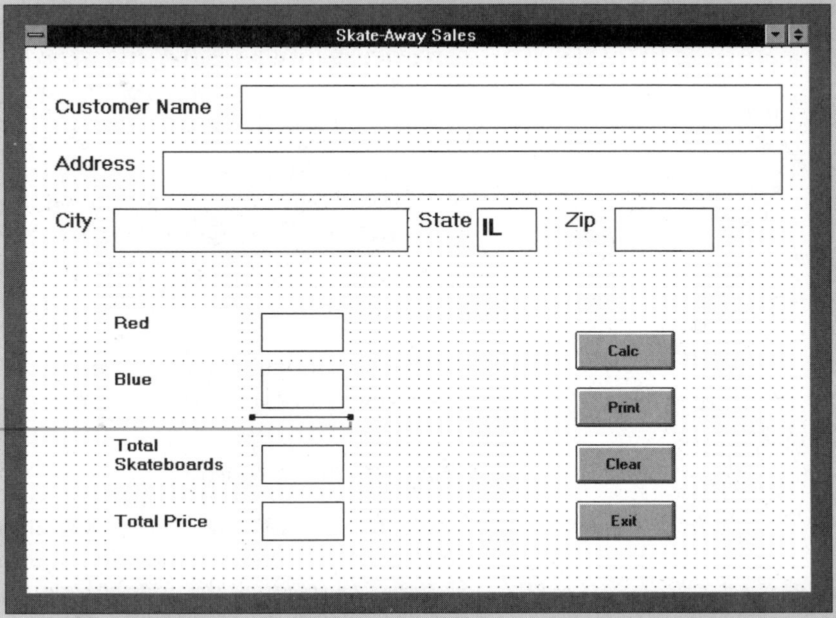

Figure 2-37: Screen showing Line control

You can use the "click and draw" method to add any of the Toolbox controls to the form. Next, let's include some color in the user interface.

Adding Color to the User Interface

Color adds interest to the interface and helps the user identify specific areas in the form. You will change the BackColor property of the red Text box to red, and the BackColor property of the blue Text box to blue. The red and blue colors will indicate where the red and blue skateboard orders should be entered. You will then change the ForeColor of the two Text boxes to white. The ForeColor controls the color of the text inside the control.

To add color to the user interface:

1 If you do not have a color monitor, skip to the next section—"Using the Format Function."

2 Click the **TxtRed control** (the red skateboard Text box) to select that control, then press [**F4**] to display the Properties window.

3 Click **BackColor** in the Properties list, click the **...** **button** in the Settings box, then click a red square in the color palette. The Text box is now red.

4 Click **ForeColor** in the Properties list, click the **...** **button** in the Settings box, then click a white square in the color palette.

5 Click the **TxtBlue control** (the blue skateboard Text box) to select that control, then press [F4] to display the Properties window.

The ForeColor property is already selected.

6 Click the **...** **button** in the Settings box, then click a white square in the color palette once again.

7 Click **BackColor** in the Properties list, click the **...** **button** in the Settings box, then click a blue square in the color palette. The Text box is now blue.

8 Click the form to remove the Properties window.

Next, you will have the application display a dollar sign ($) and a comma in the total price Label control.

Using the Format Function

You can use the Format function to improve the appearance of the numbers in your application. The syntax of the Format function is : Format(*expression,fmt*). *Expression* specifies the number, date, time, or string whose appearance you want to format. *Fmt* is either the name of a predefined Visual Basic format or, if you want more control over the appearance of the *expression*, a string containing special symbols that tell Visual Basic how you want the *expression* displayed. (You can display the Help screen for the Format function to learn more about these special symbols.) In this case, you will use one of Visual Basic's predefined formats, some of which are explained in Figure 2-38.

Format Name	Description
Currency	Displays a number with a dollar sign and two decimal places; if appropriate, displays a number with a thousand separator; negative numbers are enclosed in parentheses
Fixed	Displays a number with at least one digit to the left and two digits to the right of the decimal point
Standard	Displays a number with two decimal places; if appropriate, displays a number with a thousand separator; negative numbers are enclosed in parentheses
Percent	Multiplies a number by 100 and displays the number with a percent sign (%); displays two digits to the right of the decimal point

Figure 2-38: Some of Visual Basic's predefined formats

Because you want a dollar sign and a comma to display in the total price Label control, you will use the "Currency" format in the Format function. You can include the Format function on the assignment statement that computes the total price. Recall that that assignment statement is in the Calc button's Code window.

To include the Format function in the Calc button's Code window:

1   Open the **Calc button's Code window**, then click the **Code window's Maximize button**. The Code window fills the screen.

2   Change the *LblPrice.Caption = LblTotal.Caption * 100 * 1.05* assignment statement to ***LblPrice.Caption = format(LblTotal.Caption * 100 * 1.05, "currency")***, as shown in Figure 2-39. Be sure to watch the placement of the comma, the parentheses, and the quotation marks.

be sure to type the parentheses

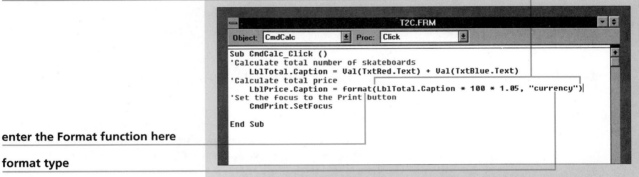

enter the Format function here

format type

Figure 2-39: Format function entered in Calc button's Code window

3   Close the Code window.

You will need to make the LblPrice control wider to accommodate the additional characters (dollar sign and comma).

4   Click the **LblPrice control** (the total price control), press [**F4**], click Width in the Properties list, type **2000** and press [**Enter**].

5   Restore the form to its standard size, then **save and run** the project.

6   Enter the following order:

   Sport Warehouse, 123 Main, Glendale, 60134, 100, 150

7   Click the **Calc button**. The application calculates the total skateboards and total price, as shown in Figure 2-40.

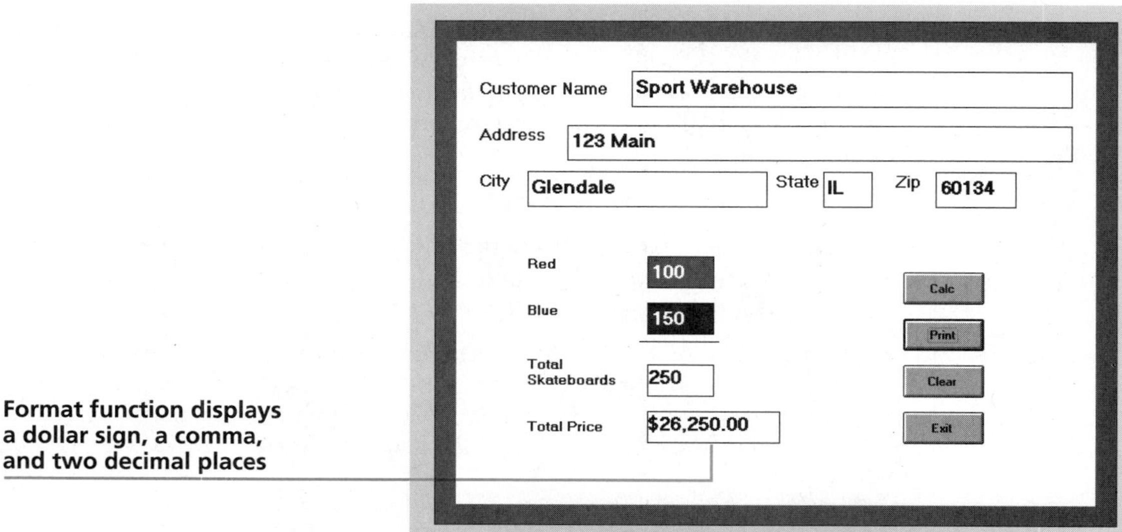

Format function displays
a dollar sign, a comma,
and two decimal places

Figure 2-40: Total price displayed using the Format function

8   Click the **Exit button.** Visual Basic returns to the design screen.

The final change you will make to the Skate-Away Sales application is to assign access keys to the Command buttons.

Assigning Access Keys

An access key allows the user to select an object using the Alt key in combination with a letter. (For example, you can use [Alt][F] to open Visual Basic's File menu. The letter "F" is the File menu's access key.) You can assign an access key to any control that has a Caption property. You create an access key for a control by including an ampersand (&) in the control's caption. You enter the ampersand to the immediate left of the character you want to designate as the access key. In the Skate-Away Sales application, you will assign an access key to each of the four Command buttons. Then, instead of clicking the Command button, the user can simply press the Alt key along with the access key.

To assign an access key to each of the four Command buttons:

1   Click the **down arrow button in the Object box** (located below the Properties window's title bar), click **CmdCalc CommandButton** in the drop-down list, then click **Caption** in the Properties list to select that property.

2   In the Properties window's Settings box, click to the left of the first "C" in Calc, type **&** (ampersand), then press **[Enter]**. The Properties window should look like Figure 2-41.

enter an ampersand to the left of the C

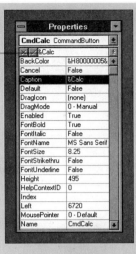

Figure 2-41: Properties window showing access key character

Next, assign an access key to the Clear button.

3   Click the **down arrow button in the Object box**, then click **CmdClear CommandButton** in the drop-down list.

The Caption property is still selected. You can't use the letter "C" for the access key because that is the access key for the Calc Command button; each object must have a unique access key. The letter "L" will be the access key for this control.

4   In the Properties window's Settings box, click to the left of the "l" in Clear, type **&** (ampersand), and then press **[Enter]**. The Caption property should say C&lear.

Now assign an access key to the Exit button.

5   Click the **down arrow button in the Object box**, then click **CmdExit CommandButton** in the drop-down list.

In Windows applications, the letter "X" is customarily the access key for an Exit button.

6   In the Properties window's Settings box, click to the left of the "x" in Exit, type **&** (ampersand), and then press **[Enter]**. The Caption property should say E&xit.

Finally, assign an access key to the Print button.

7   Click the **down arrow button in the Object box**, then click **CmdPrint CommandButton** in the drop-down list.

8   In the Properties window's Settings box, click to the left of the "P" in Print, type **&** (ampersand), and then press **[Enter]**. The Caption property should say &Print.

9   Maximize the form. Notice the underlined access keys in each of the Command buttons. See Figure 2-42.

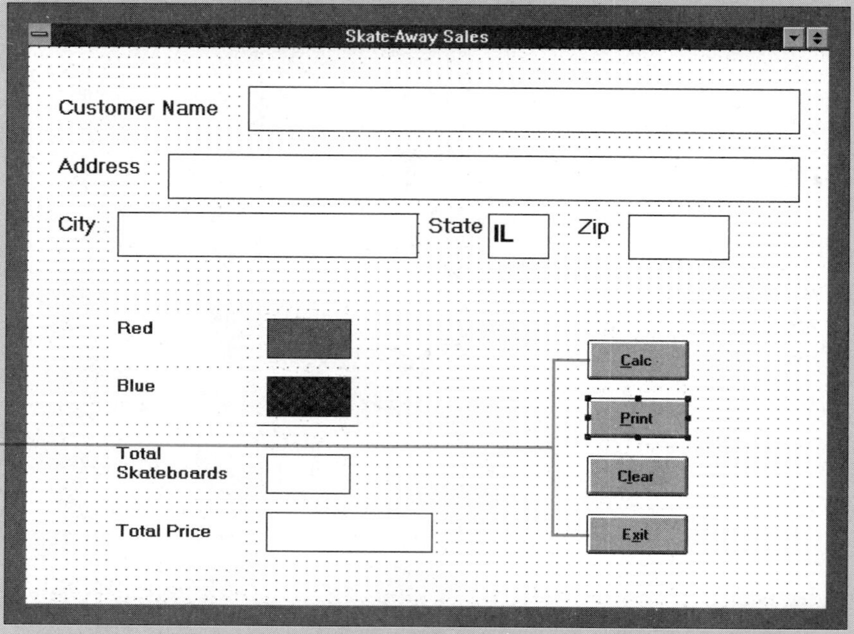

the underlined letter is the button's access key

Figure 2-42: Screen showing access keys for Command buttons

Let's run the application and test the access keys.

To test the access keys:

1   Restore the form to its standard size, then **save and run** the application.

2   Enter **your own name and address**, then enter **10** in the red skateboard Text box, press [**Tab**], then enter **40** in the blue skateboard Text box.

3   Press [**Alt**][**c**] to access the Calc button. The application calculates the total skateboards (50) and the total price ($5,250.00).

4   Press [**Alt**][**p**] to access the Print button. The application prints the confirmation notice.

5   Press [**Alt**][**l**] (the letter "l") to access the Clear button. The screen is cleared for the next order.

6   Press [**Alt**][**x**] to access the Exit button. The application ends, and Visual Basic returns to the design screen.

Making an Executable (.EXE) File

Now that the Skate-Away Sales application is complete, you can have Visual Basic's compiler translate the application into machine code. Recall that the compiler saves the machine code in a file with an .EXE extension. You can run the .EXE file directly from Windows.

To make the Skate-Away application into an executable file:

1 Click **File**, then click **Make EXE File....** The Make EXE File dialog box appears.
2 Type **t2c.exe** in the File Name box, then click the **OK button**. Visual Basic's compiler translates your application into machine code, which it saves in the t2c.exe file on your Student Disk.
3 Exit Visual Basic. If you are asked if you want to save the changes to the T2C.MAK project, click the **Yes button**.
4 To test the T2C.EXE file, run the file directly from the Program Manager.

The Skate-Away Sales application is finally complete. You can either take a break or complete the end-of-lesson questions and exercises.

S U M M A R Y

To tell Visual Basic to treat a character string as a numeric value:

▪ Use the Val function in the Code window. Its syntax is Val(*StringExpression*).

To add a line to the form:

▪ Double-click the Line tool in the Toolbox.
  or
▪ Click the Line tool in the Toolbox.
▪ Move the mouse pointer onto the form. The mouse pointer becomes a +.
▪ Position the + on the screen wherever you want the upper-left corner of the control to appear.
▪ Drag the + until the control is the size you want, then release the mouse button.

To add color to the user interface:

▪ Set the BackColor and ForeColor properties of an object.

To remove the title bar from the form:

▪ Set the form's BorderStyle property to 0-None.

To improve the appearance of numbers in the user interface:

▪ Use the Format function in the Code window. Its syntax is Format (*expression, fmt*).

To assign an access key to an object:

■ In the object's Caption property, type an ampersand (&) to the immediate left of the letter you want to designate as the access key.

To access an object that has an access key:

■ Press and hold down the Alt key as you press the access key.

QUESTIONS

1. Which of the following assignment statements will not calculate correctly?
   a. TxtTotal.Text = Val(TxtRed.Text) + Val(TxtBlue.Text)
   b. TxtTotal.Text = Val(LblRed.Caption) + Val(LblBlue.Caption)
   c. TxtTotal.Text = TxtRed.Text * 2
   d. TxtTotal.Text = LblBlue.Caption * 1.1
   e. All of the above are correct

2. You use the _____ character to assign an access key to a control.
   a. &
   b. *
   c. @
   d. $
   e. ^

3. Only objects having a(n) _____ property can have an access key.
   a. Access
   b. Caption
   c. Key
   d. KeyAccess
   e. Text

4. You use the _____ function to display dollar signs and commas in numbers.
   a. Focus
   b. Format
   c. PrintForm
   d. SetFocus
   e. Val

5. The _____ function tells Visual Basic to treat a string as a numeric value.
   a. Focus
   b. Format
   c. PrintForm
   d. SetFocus
   e. Val

E X E R C I S E S

1. a. Open the T2LBE1 project. Complete the Paper Products application by coding the Calc button.
   b. Improve the appearance of the application using what you learned in Lesson C.
   c. Save the form and the project as T2LCE1.
   d. Test the application with the following data:
      Salesperson's Name: John Smith
      Sales: 2000
   e. Calculate and print the application with the test data showing.
   f. Print the code.
   g. Make an executable (.EXE) file.

2. a. Open the T2LBE2 project. Complete the twips to inches application by coding the Calc button.
   b. Improve the appearance of the application using what you learned in Lesson C.
   c. Save the form and the project as T2LCE2.
   d. Test the application with the following data:
      Twips: 2880
   e. Calculate and print the application with the test data showing.
   f. Print the code.
   g. Make an executable (.EXE) file.

3. a. Open the T2LBE3 project. Complete John Lee's application by coding the Calc button.
   b. Improve the appearance of the application using what you learned in Lesson C.
   c. Save the form and the project as T2LCE3.
   d. Test the application with the following data:
      Beginning cash balance: 5000
      Earnings: 2500
      Expenses: 3000
   e. Calculate and print the application with the test data showing.
   f. Print the code.
   g. Make an executable (.EXE) file.

4. a. Open the T2LBE4 project. Complete Lana Jones' application by coding the Calc button.
   b. Improve the appearance of the application using what you learned in Lesson C.
   c. Save the form and the project as T2LCE4.
   d. Test the application with the following data:
      First Number: 27
      Second Number: 9
      Third Number: 18
   e. Calculate and print the application with the test data showing.
   f. Print the code.
   g. Make an executable (.EXE) file.

5. a. Open the T2LBE5 project. Complete the Bookworms Inc. application by coding the Calc button.
   b. Improve the appearance of the application using what you learned in Lesson C.
   c. Save the form and the project as T2LCE5.
   d. Test the application with the following data:
      Book Title: An Intro to Visual Basic
      Paperback versions: 100
      Paperback cost: 40

       Hardcover versions: 50
       Hardcover cost: 75
- e. Calculate and print the application with the test data showing.
- f. Print the code.
- g. Make an executable (.EXE) file.

6.
- a. Open the T2LBE6 project. Complete the Jackets Unlimited application by coding the Calc button.
- b. Improve the appearance of the application using what you learned in Lesson C.
- c. Save the form and the project as T2LCE6.
- d. Test the application with the following data:
  Jacket's original price: 50
- e. Calculate and print the application with the test data showing.
- f. Print the code.
- g. Make an executable (.EXE) file.

7.
- a. Open the T2LBE7 project. Complete the Typing Salon application by coding the Calc button.
- b. Improve the appearance of the application using what you learned in Lesson C.
- c. Save the form and the project as T2LCE7.
- d. Test the application with the following data:
  Customer's name: Alice Wong
  Number of typed envelopes: 250
  Number of typed pages: 200
- e. Calculate and print the application with the test data showing.
- f. Print the code.
- g. Make an executable (.EXE) file.

8.
- a. Open the T2LBE8 project. Complete the Sun Projects application by coding the Calc button.
- b. Improve the appearance of the application using what you learned in Lesson C.
- c. Save the form and the project as T2LCE8.
- d. Test the application with the following data:
  Employee's name: Susan Reha
  Hours worked: 40
  Rate of pay: 12
- e. Calculate and print the application with the test data showing.
- f. Print the code.
- g. Make an executable (.EXE) file.

9.
- a. Open the T2LBE9 project. Complete the Management USA application by coding the Calc button.
- b. Improve the appearance of the application using what you learned in Lesson C.
- c. Save the form and the project as T2LCE9.
- d. Test the application with the following data:
  Company Name: ABC Company
  Address: 345 Main St.
  City, State, Zip: Glen, TX 70122
  "How to Be an Effective Manager" registrants: 10
  "How to Run a Small Business" registrants: 5
- e. Calculate and print the application with the test data showing.
- f. Print the code.
- g. Make an executable (.EXE) file.

10. a. Open the T2LBE10 project. Complete the R&M Sales application by coding the Calc button.

    b. Improve the appearance of the application using what you learned in Lesson C.

    c. Save the form and the project as T2LCE10.

    d. Test the application with the following data:

       South region's current year's sales: 20000

       South region's projected increase: .03 (3%)

       West region's current year's sales: 11500

       West region's projected increase: .05 (5%)

    e. Calculate and print the application with the test data showing.

    f. Print the code.

    g. Make an executable (.EXE) file.

Exercises 11 through 17 are Discovery Exercises, which allow you to "discover" the solutions to problems on your own. Discovery Exercises may include topics that are not covered in the tutorial.

discovery ▶ **11.** Plan and create an application that allows the user to enter the quantity of an item in inventory and how many of the item can be packed in a box for shipping. When the user clicks the Calculate button, the application will compute and display the number of full boxes that can be packed and how many of the item are left over. Test the application using the following data:

    a. A company has 45 skateboards in inventory. If six skateboards can fit into a box for shipping, how many full boxes could the company ship, and how many skateboards will remain in inventory? Write the answers on a piece of paper, then print the application's code.

discovery ▶ **12.** Plan and create an application that will allow the user to enter the length of four sides of a polygon. When the user clicks the Calculate button, the application will compute and display the perimeter of the polygon. Test the application using the following data:

    a. Each day you ride your bike around a park that has side lengths of 1/2 mile, 1 mile, 1/2 mile, and 1 mile. How far do you ride your bike each day? Write the answer on a piece of paper, then print the application's code.

discovery ▶ **13.** Plan and create an application that will allow the user to enter both the diameter of a circle and the price of railing material per foot. When the user clicks the Calculate button, the application will compute and display the circumference of the circle and the total price of the railing material. (Use 3.14 as the value of π.) Test the application using the following data:

    a. You are building a railing around a circular deck having a diameter of 36 feet. The railing material costs $2 per foot. What is the circumference of the deck and the total price of the railing material? Write the answers on a piece of paper, then print the application's code.

discovery ▶ **14.** Plan and create an application that will allow the user to enter the number of hours worked. When the user clicks the Calculate button, the application will compute and display the number of weeks (assume a 40-hour week), days (assume an 8-hour day), and hours worked. For example, if the user enters the number 70, the application will display 1 week, 3 days, and 6 hours. Test the application three times using the following data:

    a. Hours worked: 88

    b. Hours worked: 111

    c. Hours worked: 12

Write the answers on a piece of paper, then print the application's code.

discovery ▶ 15.   Plan and create an application that will allow the user to enter the length and width, in feet, of a rectangle, and the price of a square foot of tile. When the user clicks the Calculate button, the application will compute and display the area of the rectangle and the total price of the tile. Test the application using the following data:

 a. You are tiling a floor in your home. The floor is 12 feet long and 14 feet wide. The price of a square foot of tile is $1.59. What is the area of the floor and how much will the tile cost? Write the answers on a piece of paper, then print the application's code.

discovery ▶ 16.   Plan and create an application that will allow the user to enter the length, width, and height of a rectangle. When the user clicks the Calculate button, the application will compute and display the volume of the rectangle. Test the application using the following data:

 a. The swimming pool at a health club is 100 feet long, 30 feet wide, and 4 feet deep. How many cubic feet of water will the pool contain? Write the answer on a piece of paper, then print the application's code.

discovery ▶ 17.   Plan and create an application that will allow the user to enter the amount of a loan, the interest rate, and the term of the loan (in years). When the user clicks the Calculate button, the application will compute and display the total amount of interest and the total amount to be repaid. Test the application using the following data:

 a. You borrowed $9000 to buy a new car. The loan is for three years at an annual interest rate of 12%. How much will you pay in interest over the three years, and what is the total amount to be repaid? Write the answers on a piece of paper, then print the application's code.

D E B U G G I N G

Technique   Visual Basic's Options menu contains an option, called Environment..., that displays a dialog box showing the current status of the Visual Basic environment. The dialog box contains an option called Syntax Checking. Before entering code in the Code windows, you should verify that the Syntax Checking option is set to Yes. When it is set to Yes, Visual Basic checks to make sure the instructions you enter into an object's Code window follow the rules, called syntax, of the Visual Basic language. If you violate one of the rules, Visual Basic informs you of the error. (Even with the Syntax Checking option set to Yes, some errors will not be caught until you run the project. The point when Visual Basic catches the error as you are entering the instruction into the Code window or when the project is run depends on the type of error you have made.)

First, let's make sure that the Syntax Checking option is set to Yes.

To view the Syntax Checking option:

1 Launch Visual Basic, if necessary. Click **Options**, then click **Environment...** The Environment Options dialog box appears.

2 If the Syntax Checking option is set to Yes, go to step 3. If the Syntax Checking option is set to No, double-click Syntax Checking to set it to Yes.

3 Click the **OK button** to leave the Environment Options dialog box.

Following are four debugging exercises that will allow you to see the effects of the Syntax Checking option.

To complete the debugging exercises:

■ Add one Label control to a blank form. Move the Label control to the upper-left corner of the form.

■ Add two Command button controls to the form. Move the Command1 button to the lower-right corner of the form. Leave the Command2 button in the center.

Exercises

1. a. Open the Command1 Code window, press [Tab], and type **end?** in the Code window. Be sure to type the question mark (?) after the word End. (You are making an intentional typing error here in order to see what the Syntax Checking option does when the option is set to Yes.) Visual Basic won't catch the error until you press the Enter key.

    b. Press [Enter]. Visual Basic displays a message dialog box informing you of an error in the instruction you entered. The message says *Expected: Function or If or Select or Sub or Type or end-of-statement*. Click the OK button to remove the dialog box. Notice that Visual Basic highlights the question mark (?) after the End instruction to indicate that the question mark is what is causing the error.

    c. Delete the entire End? instruction from the Code window, then close the Code window.

2. a. Open the Command1 Code window, press [Tab], type **Ens**, and press [Enter]. Notice that Visual Basic did not catch this error. Some errors will not be caught until you run the project.

    b. Close the Code window, then run the project. Visual Basic displays a message box containing the message *Syntax error*. A "Syntax error" means that you violated one of the rules of the Visual Basic language. Click the OK button to remove the message dialog box.

    c. Type **End** correctly in the Code window, close the Code window, run the project, then click the Command1 button to test the button. The application ends and Visual Basic returns to the design screen.

3. a. Open the Command2 Code window, press [Tab], type **Label1.Text = "Hello"** and press [Enter]. Recall that Label controls have a Caption property, not a Text property. Let's see what Visual Basic does when you run the project.

    b. Close the Code window, then run the project. Visual Basic displays a message box with the message *Property 'Text' not found*.

    c. Click the OK button to remove the message box. Visual Basic highlights the word Text in the Code window. Replace the word Text with **Caption**, close the Code window, and run the project.

    d. Click the Command2 button to place the word "Hello" in the Label control, then click the Command1 button to end the project.

4. a. Open the Command2 Code window. If you completed debugging exercise 3, remove the *Label1.Caption = "Hello"* instruction from the Code window.

    b. Press [Tab], then type **Label 1.Caption = "Joe"**. Don't type the ending period, but be sure to type the space between the letter l and the number one in the instruction. Press [Enter]. Visual Basic displays a message box with the message *Expected: end-of-statement*.

    c. Click the OK button to remove the message box, then remove the space between the letter l and the number 1. Close the Code window, run the project, click the Command2 button to place the word "Joe" in the Label control, then click the Command1 button to end the application.

You can now exit Visual Basic. You do not need to save the form or the project.

TUTORIAL 3

Storing Data in Variables

The Dots & Stripes Application

case ▶ Chris Statton tells you that Ahmad Hadkari, another Interlocking Software programmer, is currently working on an application for the Dots & Stripes wallpaper store. Unfortunately, Ahmad is going out of town for a while and he won't be able to finish the project. Chris wants you to complete the project for Ahmad.

Ahmad gives you the TOE chart and the flowcharts for the Dots & Stripes application. He tells you that he already created the user interface; the necessary objects are in place, and their properties have been set. All that remains is to write the Visual Basic code that tells the objects how to respond to the user.

Previewing the Completed Application

The Dots & Stripes application calculates the amount of wallpaper, in rolls, that a customer will need to purchase. Let's preview the completed Dots & Stripes application.

To preview the completed application:

1 Launch Windows and make sure the Program Manager window is open and your Student Disk is in the appropriate drive. If necessary, click the **Minimize on** Use option on the Options menu to minimize the Program Manager on use. Click **File** in the Program Manager's menu bar, then click **Run....** The Run dialog box appears.

2 *If you are using Visual Basic Version 2.0*, run the DOTS.EXE file, which is in the tut3\ver2 directory on your Student Disk. The Dots & Stripes application appears on the screen. See Figure 3-1.

   If you are using Visual Basic Version 3.0, run the DOTS.EXE file, which is in the tut3\ver3 directory on your Student Disk. The Dots & Stripes application appears on the screen. See Figure 3-1.

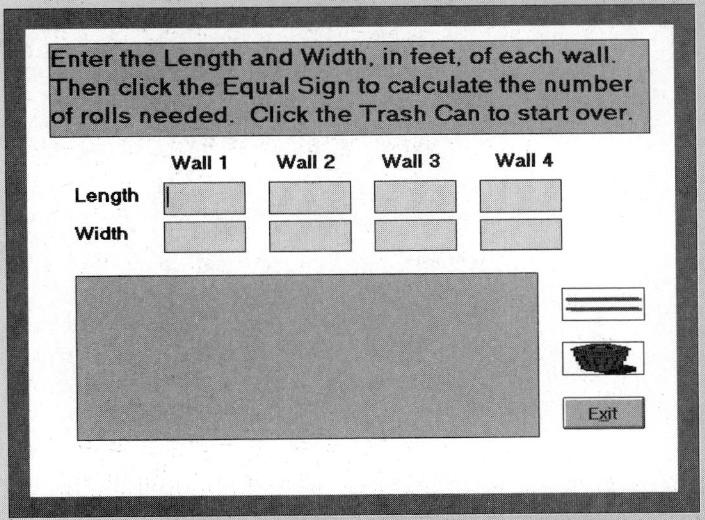

Figure 3-1: The Dots & Stripes application

The user must enter the length and width, in feet, of each wall to be wall-papered. Let's assume the customer wants to wallpaper two walls.

3 Type **10** as the length of the first wall and press [**Tab**]. Then type **12** as the width of the first wall and press [**Tab**].

4 Type **10** as the length of the second wall and press [**Tab**]. Then type **10** as the width of the second wall.

   After entering the length and width of the walls, the user must click the equal sign.

5 Click the **equal sign**. A dialog box appears and requests the style code of the wallpaper. The dialog box was created with the InputBox function, which you will learn about in Lesson B.

6   Type **AB45 - Flowers** and press [**Enter**] (or click the **OK button**). Another dialog box appears and requests the roll coverage (the number of square feet covered by a roll).

7   Type **35** as the roll coverage and press [**Enter**] (or click the **OK button**). The application calculates the number of rolls of wallpaper the customer will need to purchase. It then uses string concatenation, which you will learn about in Lesson A, to display that information in a message to the user. See Figure 3-2.

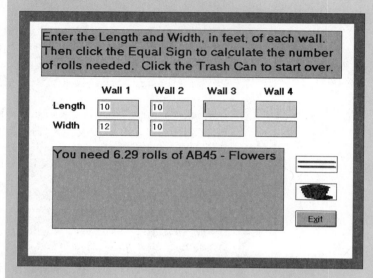

Figure 3-2: Information entered in the Dots & Stripes application

Because you can't purchase a partial roll of wallpaper, the customer will need to purchase seven rolls.

8   Click the **trash can** to clear the screen, then click the **Exit button** to leave the application. The Dots & Stripes application ends.

In Lesson A you will learn how to store information, temporarily, in memory locations inside the computer. You will also learn how to concatenate (link together) strings. The InputBox function, which allows you to prompt the user for information, is covered in Lesson B. Also in Lesson B, you will use Ahmad's TOE chart and flowcharts to begin writing the Visual Basic code for the Dots & Stripes application. You will complete the Dots & Stripes application in Lesson C.

LESSON A
objectives

In this lesson you will learn how to:

- Create a variable
- Assign a data type to a variable
- Control the scope of a variable
- Concatenate strings
- Remove a control containing code

Creating Variables

Using Variables to Store Information

In Tutorial 2's application for Skate-Away Sales, all the skateboard information was stored, temporarily, in the properties of various controls on the form. For example, recall that the number of red skateboards ordered was stored in the Text property of the TxtRed control, and the number of blue skateboards ordered was stored in the Text property of the TxtBlue control. Also recall that the assignment statement—*LblTotal.Caption = Val(TxtRed.Text) + Val(TxtBlue.Text)*—added the value stored in the Text property of the TxtRed control to the value stored in the Text property of the TxtBlue control, and then assigned that sum to the Caption property of the LblTotal control.

Besides storing data in the properties of controls, a programmer can also store data, temporarily, in memory locations inside the computer. These memory locations are called **variables** because the contents of the locations can change as the program is running. (It may be helpful to picture a variable as a tiny box inside the computer. You can enter and store data in the box, but you can't actually *see* the box.) One use for a variable is to hold information that is not stored in a control on the user interface. For example, if the Skate-Away Sales application (from Tutorial 2) did not require you to display the total number of skateboards ordered, you could eliminate the LblTotal control from the form and store that information in a variable instead. You would then use the variable, instead of the LblTotal control, to compute the total price of the skateboard order.

Each variable (each tiny box in memory) must be given a name by the programmer.

Naming Variables

The name that a programmer assigns to a variable must follow several specific rules. These rules are listed in Figure 3-3, along with examples of valid and invalid variable names.

You should use a descriptive name for each variable; the name should help you remember the purpose of the variable. For example, although S is a valid name for a variable, it is not as descriptive as the name Sales. In the latter case, the name reminds you that the purpose of the variable is to store a sales amount.

In addition to assigning a name, the programmer also assigns a data type to each variable. The data type determines the type of data the variable (memory location) can store.

Data Types

Visual Basic has seven basic data types, which are described in Figure 3-4.

Rules for variable names

1. The name must begin with a letter.

2. The name must contain only letters, numbers, and the underscore. No punctuation characters or spaces are allowed in the name.

3. The name cannot be more than 40 characters in length.

4. The name cannot be a reserved word, (such as Print), because reserved words have special meaning in Visual Basic.

Valid Variable Names	Invalid Variable Names	
Hourswkd	Hour	(reserved word)
Sales94	94Sales	(name must begin with a letter)
Region_West	Region West	(name cannot contain a space)
Names	Name	(reserved word)
Eastsales	East.Sales	(name cannot contain punctuation)

Figure 3-3: Rules for naming variables

Type	Stores
Integer	Integers in the range of -32,768 to 32,767
Long	Integers in the range of -2,147,483,648 to 2,147,483,647
Single	Floating-point numbers in the range of: -3.402823E38 to -1.401298E-45 for negative values 1.401298E-45 to 3.402823E38 for positive values
Double	Floating-point numbers in the range of: -1.79769313486232D308 to -4.94065645841247D-324 for negative values 4.94065645841247D-324 to 1.79769313486232D308 for positive values
Currency	Fixed-point numbers in the range of: -922337203685477.5808 to 922337203685477.5807
String	String of characters in the range of 0 to approximately 65,500 characters
Variant	Integer, floating-point number, fixed-point number, string, date, and time

Figure 3-4: Seven basic data types

Figure 3-4 shows that both the Integer type variable and the Long type variable can store an integer. An **integer** is a whole number, which means a number without any decimal places. The differences between the Integer type and the Long type are in the range of numbers each type can store and the amount of memory each type needs to store the numbers. For example, although a Long type variable can also store numbers in the Integer type range of −32768 to 32767, the Long data type takes twice as much memory to do so. Therefore, use an Integer variable to store a person's age; use a Long variable to store the population of a large city.

Figure 3-4 also shows that both the Single type variable and the Double type variable can store a floating-point number. A **floating-point number** is a number that is expressed as a multiple of some power of 10. In Visual Basic, floating-point numbers are written in E (exponential) notation, which is similar to scientific notation. For example, the number 3,200,000 written in E (exponential) notation is 3.2E6; written in scientific notation it is 3.2×10^6. Notice that exponential notation simply replaces "$\times 10^6$" with the letter E followed by the power number—in this case, 6. The 3.2E6 (or 3.2D6 for the Double type) means 3.2 times 10 to the sixth power (10 * 10 * 10 * 10 * 10 * 10).

Another way of viewing the 3.2E6 (or 3.2D6) is that the positive number after the E (or D) indicates how many places to the right to move the decimal point. In this case, E6 says to move the decimal point six places to the right; so 3.2E6 becomes 3,200,000. Moving the decimal point six places to the right is the same as multiplying the number by 10 to the sixth power.

Floating-point numbers can also have a negative number after the E (or D). For example, 3.2E–6 means 3.2 divided by 10 to the sixth power, or .0000032. The negative number after the E (or D) tells you how many places to the left to move the decimal point. In this case, E–6 means to move the decimal point six places to the left.

Floating-point numbers, which can be stored in either a Single type variable or a Double type variable, are used to represent both extremely small and extremely large numbers. The differences between the Single type and the Double type are in the range of numbers each type can store and the amount of memory each type needs to store the numbers. Although the Double type can store numbers in the Single type's range, the Double type takes twice as much memory to do so.

The Currency data type listed in Figure 3-4 stores numbers with a fixed decimal point. Unlike floating-point numbers, fixed-point numbers are not expressed as a multiple of some power of 10. For example, the number 32000 expressed in the Single data type is 3.2E4, but that same number expressed in the Currency data type is simply 32000. Calculations involving fixed-point numbers are not subject to the small rounding errors that may occur when floating-point numbers are used. In most cases, these small rounding errors create no problems in the application. One exception, however, is when the application deals with money, where you need accuracy to the penny. In those cases, the Currency data type is the best type to use.

Also listed in Figure 3-4 is the String data type, which can store from zero to approximately 65,500 characters. Recall that a string is a group of characters enclosed in quotation marks. "Desk" and "AB345" are two examples of strings.

The last data type listed in Figure 3-4 is Variant. If you don't assign a specific data type to a variable, Visual Basic assigns the Variant data type to it. Unlike other variables, a Variant variable can store many different types of data, and it also can freely change the type of stored data while the program is running. You can store the number 40 in a Variant variable at the beginning of the program and then, later on in the program, store the string "John Smith" in that same variable. Although the Variant data type is the most flexible, in many cases it is less efficient than the other data types. At times it uses more memory than necessary to store a value and, because the variable has to determine which type of data is currently stored at that location, your application will run more slowly.

Assigning an appropriate data type to the variables in a program will make the application run more efficiently. Here are some guidelines to follow when assigning the data type:

■ Assign the Integer or Long data type when you are sure that a variable will always contain whole numbers. Which type you choose, Integer or Long, will depend on the size of the numbers you expect to store in the variable.

■ Assign either the Single, Double, or Currency data type when you need to store numbers with a decimal fraction. Here again, which type you choose will depend on the size of the numbers you expect to store in the variable and whether the variable will hold money values.

■ Assign the String data type if the variable will always contain a string.

■ Assign the Variant data type if your variable needs to be flexible about the type of data it will store and if you are not concerned with speed and the amount of memory used.

In the next section you will learn how to create a variable in Visual Basic.

Creating a Variable

You use the Dim statement to create, or declare, a variable. (Dim comes from the word "dimension.") "Declaring" a variable tells Visual Basic to create the variable in memory. The format of the Dim statement, *Dim variablename [as datatype]*, allows you to assign both a name and a data type to the variable you are creating. Although the *as datatype* part of the instruction is optional, as indicated by the brackets, you should always assign a specific data type to each variable. If you don't assign a data type, Visual Basic assigns the Variant type, which may not be the most efficient data type. Figure 3-5 shows examples of Dim statements used to create (declare) variables.

Dim Statement	Explanation
Dim Hours as Integer	Creates an Integer variable named Hours
Dim Discount as Single	Creates a Single variable named Discount
Dim Price as Currency	Creates a Currency variable named Price
Dim Fname as String	Creates a String variable named Fname
Dim Temp as Variant	Creates a Variant variable named Temp

Figure 3-5: Examples of Dim statements

It's easy to forget to declare a variable, so Visual Basic provides a way to help you remember. You simply enter Visual Basic's *Option Explicit* statement in the general Declarations section of the form. (You have not yet seen the general Declarations section of a form.) Then if your code contains the name of an undeclared variable, Visual Basic informs you of the error. You will learn more about the *Option Explicit* statement in this lesson and in the Debugging section.

When you create an Integer, Long, Single, Double, or Currency variable, Visual Basic automatically stores the value of 0 (zero) in the variable. This is referred to as **initializing** the variable—in other words, giving the variable a beginning value. Visual Basic initializes String and Variant variables by assigning a zero-length string to them. (Recall from Tutorial 2 that a zero-length string is called a null string.) You can use an assignment statement to store other data in the variable, as you will see in the next section.

Storing Data in a Variable

An assignment statement is one way of storing data in a variable. In Tutorial 2 you learned that the format of an assignment statement that assigns a value to an object's property is *Form.Object.Property = value.* Similarly, the format of an assignment statement that stores a value in a variable is *Variablename = value.* The assignment statement *Sales = 500,* for example, stores the number 500 in a variable named Sales. The number 500 is called a **constant,** which is a value that does not change while the program is running. The string "Mary Smith" is another example of a constant. You store constants in variables (memory locations). (Visual Basic also allows you to create **symbolic constants** with Visual Basic's Const statement; they are memory locations whose contents cannot be changed while the program is running. You will learn about symbolic constants in Tutorial 7.)

It's important to remember that, like an object's property, a variable can store only one item of data at any one time. When you use an assignment statement to assign another item to the variable, the new data replaces the existing data. For example, assume that the Click event procedure for a Command button contains the following three lines of code: *Dim Sales as Currency, Sales = 500, Sales = Sales * 2.* When you run the application and click the Command button, the three lines of code are processed as follows:

- The Dim statement creates the Sales variable in memory. (Here again, picture the Sales variable as a tiny box inside the computer.) Because the Sales variable is a Currency type variable, Visual Basic initializes it to 0. (In other words, Visual Basic places the number 0 inside the box.)
- The *Sales = 500* assignment statement removes the zero from the Sales variable and stores the number 500 there instead. (The box now contains the number 500 only.)
- The *Sales = Sales * 2* assignment statement first multiplies the contents of the Sales variable (500) by the number 2, giving 1000. The assignment statement then removes the number 500 from the Sales variable and stores the number 1000 there instead. Notice that Visual Basic performs the calculation appearing on the right side of the equal sign before assigning the result to the variable whose name appears on the left side.

As you can see, after data is stored in a variable, you can use the data in calculations, just as you can with the data stored in the properties of controls. When you refer to a variable's name, the computer uses the value stored inside the variable.

You now know how to create a variable and how to store data inside it. There's just one more thing about variables that you need to learn. In addition to a name and a data type, every variable also has a scope. A variable's **scope** indicates which procedures in the application can use the variable.

The Scope of a Variable

A variable's scope is determined by *where* you declare the variable—in other words, where you enter the Dim statement. You can declare a variable in three places:

- the event procedure of an object
- the general Declarations section of a form
- the general Declarations section of a code module

(You have not yet seen the general Declarations section of either a form or a code module.) In this tutorial you will learn how to declare a variable in an event procedure and also in the general Declarations section of a form. You'll learn how to declare variables in the general Declarations section of a code module in Tutorial 9.

When you declare a variable in an event procedure, only that event procedure can use the variable. For example, if you enter the *Dim Sales as Currency* statement in the Click event procedure of a Command button, only the Click event procedure for that Command button can use the Sales variable. A variable declared in an event procedure is called a **local variable** because its use is limited to only the procedure in which it is declared. No other procedures in the application are allowed to use the variable. (No other procedures in the application will even know that the variable exists.) When the event procedure ends, Visual Basic removes the local variable from the computer's memory.

If you declare a variable in the general Declarations section of a form, on the other hand, all procedures in that form, including the procedures of the objects contained on the form, can use the variable. For example, if you enter the *Dim Sales as Currency* statement in the form's general Declarations section, every procedure in the form can use the Sales variable. A variable declared in a form's general Declarations section is called a **form-level variable**. Form-level variables remain in memory until the application ends. (Variables declared in the general Declarations section of a code module are called **global variables**. Global variables, which you will learn about in Tutorial 9, are used in applications containing multiple forms. Global variables are available to every procedure in every form in the application.)

The difference between local variables and form-level variables is best illustrated with a few examples.

To illustrate the difference between local variables and form-level variables:

1 Launch Visual Basic, if necessary. Be sure your Student Disk is in the appropriate disk drive. Open the **t3a_var.mak** project which is in either the tut3\ver2 or the tut3\ver3 directory on your Student Disk. Click the **View Form button**. The T3A_VAR form appears on the screen. Figure 3-6 shows the names of the controls included in the user interface.

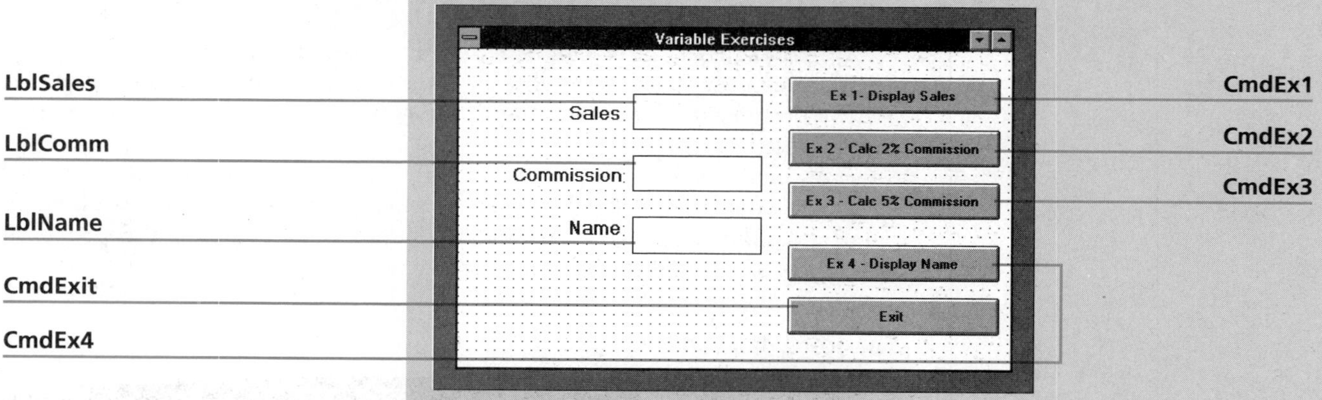

Figure 3-6: The T3A_VAR form

2   Save the form as **t3a_var2** and save the project as **t3a_var2**.

The Exit button already contains the End instruction. Before coding the other Command buttons, you will enter the *Option Explicit* statement in the general Declarations section of the form. The *Option Explicit* statement tells Visual Basic to warn you if you use the name of an undeclared variable in your code. An **undeclared variable** is a variable whose name does not appear in a Dim statement.

3   Double-click the **form** to open its Code window. The form's Load event procedure appears in the Code window. Click the **down arrow in the Code window's Object box**, then scroll the drop-down list until you see (general), which is at the top of the drop-down list. Click **(general)** in the drop-down list. The general Declarations section of the form appears.

Instructions entered in the general Declarations section of the form are automatically processed when the application is run.

4   Type **option explicit** and press [**Enter**]. See Figure 3-7.

general Declarations section of the T3A_VAR2 form

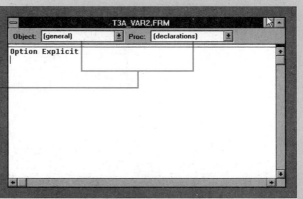

Figure 3-7: Option Explicit statement entered in the form's general Declarations section

Now let's code the Ex 1 - Display Sales button (the CmdEx1 control).

5   Click the **down arrow in the Code window's object box**, then click **CmdEx1** in the drop-down list. CmdEx1's Click event procedure appears in the Code window.

First declare a local variable named Sales.

6   Press [**Tab**], type **dim Sales as currency** and press [**Enter**]. When the application is run, this statement will create and initialize (to zero) a local variable named Sales.

Now use an assignment statement to store data in the local Sales variable.

7   Type **Sales = 500** and press [**Enter**]. When the application is run, this instruction will assign the number 500 to the local Sales variable. (In other words, it will store the number 500 in the memory location named Sales.)

Now display the contents of the Sales variable in the LblSales control. You can do that by assigning the contents of the Sales variable to the Caption property of the LblSales control. (Recall that a Label control's caption appears inside the control.)

8   Type **LblSales.Caption = Sales** and press [Enter]. See Figure 3-8.

declares (creates) the variable

assigns a value to the variable

assigns the contents of the
variable to the Label control

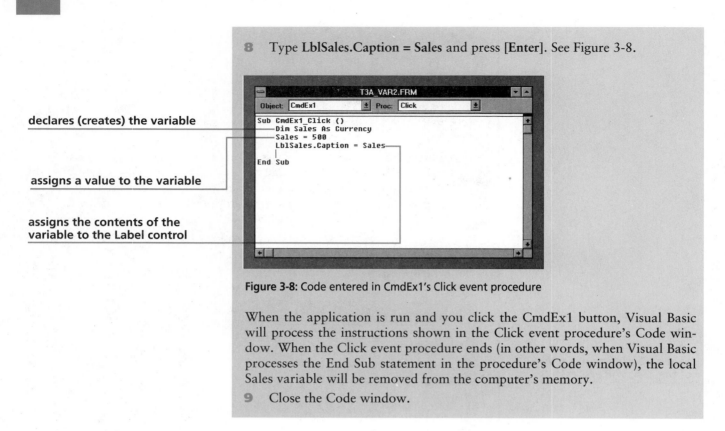

Figure 3-8: Code entered in CmdEx1's Click event procedure

When the application is run and you click the CmdEx1 button, Visual Basic will process the instructions shown in the Click event procedure's Code window. When the Click event procedure ends (in other words, when Visual Basic processes the End Sub statement in the procedure's Code window), the local Sales variable will be removed from the computer's memory.

9   Close the Code window.

Let's run the application to see if the Ex 1 - Display Sales button (the CmdEx1 control) works correctly.

If an error message box appears on the screen, read the message and then click the OK button. Visual Basic will highlight the error in the Code window. Check your code with the code shown in Figure 3-8, then correct the code and repeat steps 1 and 2.

To test the Ex 1 - Display Sales button (the CmdEx1 control):

1   **Save and run** the application. Visual Basic processes the *Option Explicit* statement found in the general Declarations section of the form. (Recall that instructions in the general Declarations section of the form are processed automatically when the application is run.)

2   Click the **Ex 1 - Display Sales button** (the CmdEx1 control). Following the instructions entered in the control's Click event procedure, Visual Basic creates a local variable named Sales, assigns the number 500 to it, and then displays the contents of the Sales variable (500) in the LblSales control.

3   Click the **Exit button** to end the application. Visual Basic returns to the design screen.

As this example shows, a local variable can be used by the event procedure in which it is declared. Now let's see if another event procedure can use the variable. You will do that by coding the Ex 2 - Calc 2% Commission button (the CmdEx2 control). The CmdEx2 control should calculate a 2% commission on the sales entered in the Sales variable and then display the result in the LblComm control.

To code the CmdEx2 Command button:

1 Double-click the **Ex 2 - Calc 2% Commission button** (the CmdEx2 control) to open its Code window. The Code window for CmdEx2's Click event procedure appears.

2 Press [**Tab**], type **LblComm.Caption = Sales * .02** and press [**Enter**]. This instruction tells Visual Basic to multiply the contents of the Sales variable by .02 and then assign the result to the Caption property of the LblComm control.

3 Close the Code window, then **save and run** the application. Visual Basic displays the warning message shown in Figure 3-9.

Figure 3-9: Warning message caused by an undeclared variable

4 Click the **OK button** to remove the "Variable not defined" message from the screen. Visual Basic highlights the name of the undefined variable, Sales. (An undefined variable is the same as an undeclared variable.) Notice that the undefined variable is in CmdEx2's Click event procedure. See Figure 3-10.

event procedure containing the undefined variable

undefined (undeclared) variable

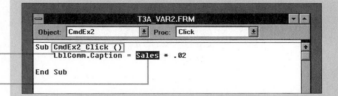

Figure 3-10: Undefined (undeclared) variable in Code window

Recall that the *Option Explicit* statement, which you entered in the general Declarations section of the form, tells Visual Basic to display a warning message if you use the name of an undeclared variable. In this case the undeclared (undefined) variable is the Sales variable appearing in CmdEx2's Click event procedure. At this point you may be thinking "But I did declare the Sales variable." Recall, however, that you declared the Sales variable in CmdEx1's Click event procedure; only CmdEx1's Click event procedure can use that variable. CmdEx2's Click event procedure doesn't know about the Sales variable, so it treats it as undefined variable. In other words, a local variable can be used only by the event procedure in which it is declared.

Next, let's see what happens if you declare the same variable in two event procedures. Specifically, you will declare the Sales variable in CmdEx1's Click event procedure and also in CmdEx2's Click event procedure. The *Dim Sales as Currency* statement is already in CmdEx1's Click event procedure, so you just need to enter the same statement in CmdEx2's Click event procedure.

To enter the *Dim Sales as Currency* statement in CmdEx2's Click event procedure:

1. The Code window showing CmdEx2's Click event procedure should still be open. Position the mouse pointer[1] after the) in the *Sub CmdEx2_Click ( )* instruction and click at that location, then press [**Enter**] to insert a blank line below the Sub instruction.

2. In the blank line below the Sub instruction, press [**Tab**], type **dim Sales as currency** and then close the Code window.

3. **Save and run** the application. This time, Visual Basic does not display a "Variable not defined" message.

4. Click the **Ex 1 - Display Sales button** (the CmdEx1 control). The contents of CmdEx1's local Sales variable (500) appears in the LblSales control. When the Click event procedure ends, CmdEx1's Sales variable is removed from memory.

Let's see what happens when you click the CmdEx2 control, which contains the *Dim Sales as Currency* instruction and the *LblComm.Caption = Sales * .02* instruction.

5. Click the **Ex 2 - Calc 2% Commission button** (the CmdEx2 control). A zero appears in the LblComm control. The correct commission, however, should be 10 (2% of the $500 sales).

The zero appears because the *Dim Sales as Currency* instruction in CmdEx2's Click event procedure creates and initializes (to zero) its own local Sales variable. The *LblComm.Caption = Sales * .02* instruction multiplies the contents of CmdEx2's local Sales variable (0) by .02, giving zero, and then assigns the zero to the Caption property of the LblComm control. When CmdEx2's Click event procedure ends, its local Sales variable is removed from the computer's memory.

6. Click the **Exit button** to end the application. Visual Basic returns to the design screen.

As this example shows, when you use the same name to declare a variable in more than one event procedure, each procedure creates its own local variable. Although the variables have the same name, each refers to a different location (box) in memory.

But what if you want both Command buttons to use the same Sales variable? In that case you will need to declare the variable in the general Declarations section of the form. Recall that variables declared in the form's general Declarations section are called form-level variables. Form-level variables can be used by every procedure in the form, and they remain in memory until the application ends. Let's declare the Sales variable as a form-level variable.

To declare the Sales variable as a form-level variable:

1. Double-click the **form** to open its Code window. The form's Load event procedure appears. Click the **down arrow in the Code window's Object box**, then click (**general**) in the drop-down list. The general Declarations section of the form appears. All form-level variables must be declared in this section of the form.

2 Press the **down arrow key** to position the blinking insertion point in the blank line immediately below the Option Explicit statement, then type **dim Sales as currency** and press [**Enter**].

You will need to remove the Dim Sales as Currency statement in both the CmdEx1 and the CmdEx2 Click event procedures, as those Dim statements tell Visual Basic to create two local Sales variables.

3 Click the **down arrow in the Code window's Object box**, then click **CmdEx1** in the drop-down list. The Code window for CmdEx1's Click event procedure appears.

4 Highlight only the *Dim Sales as Currency* statement in the Code window, then press [**Delete**] to remove the highlighted statement from the Code window. If the blinking insertion point appears at the far left in the blank line, press [**Delete**] again to remove the blank line, then press [**Tab**]. If the blinking insertion point appears at the first tab position, press [**Delete**] to remove the blank line.

5 Click the **down arrow in the Code window's Object box**, then click **CmdEx2** in the drop-down list. The Code window for CmdEx2's Click event procedure appears.

6 Highlight only the *Dim Sales as Currency* statement in the Code window, then press [**Delete**] to remove the highlighted statement from the Code window. If the blinking insertion point appears at the far left in the blank line, press [**Delete**] again to remove the blank line, then press [**Tab**]. If the blinking insertion point appears at the first tab position, press [**Delete**] to remove the blank line.

7 Close the Code window, then **save and run** the application. The *Dim Sales as Currency* statement in the general Declarations section of the form creates and initializes a form-level variable named Sales.

Let's see what happens when you click the CmdEx1 control.

8 Click the **Ex 1 - Display Sales button** (the CmdEx1 control). Visual Basic processes the instructions in the control's Click event procedure. The *Sales = 500* instruction stores the number 500 in the form-level Sales variable. The *LblSales.Caption = Sales* displays the contents of the form-level Sales variable (500) in the LblSales control.

Let's see what happens when you click the CmdEx2 control.

9 Click the **Ex 2 - Calc 2% Commission button** (the CmdEx2 control). Visual Basic processes the instructions in the control's Click event procedure. The *LblComm.Caption = Sales * .02* instruction multiplies the contents of the form-level Sales variable (500) by .02, giving 10. The instruction then displays the result (10) in the LblComm control.

10 Click the **Exit button** to end the application. Visual Basic removes the form-level Sales variable from the computer's memory and then returns to the design screen.

As this example shows, when you declare a form-level variable in the general Declarations section of the form, every procedure in the form can use the variable. Finally, let's see what happens if you declare a variable both as a form-level variable and as a local variable.

To see what happens when you declare a variable both as a form-level variable and as a local variable:

1 Double-click the **Ex 3 - Calc 5% Commission button** (the CmdEx3 control) to open its Code window. The Click event procedure appears.

2 Press [**Tab**], then type **dim Sales as currency** and press [**Enter**].

The CmdEx3 control should calculate a 5% commission on the sales.

3 Type **LblComm.Caption = Sales * .05** and press [**Enter**].

4 Close the **Code window**, then **save and run** the application.

Recall that when the application is run, the *Dim Sales as Currency* instruction in the form's general Declarations section instructs Visual Basic to create and initialize a form-level variable named Sales. The form-level Sales variable will remain in memory until the application ends.

5 Click the **Ex 1 - Display Sales button** (the CmdEx1 control). The *Sales = 500* instruction stores the number 500 in the form-level Sales variable. The *LblSales.Caption = Sales* instruction displays the contents of the form-level Sales variable (500) in the LblSales control.

6 Click the **Ex 2 - Calc 2% Commission button** (the CmdEx2 control). The *LblComm.Caption = Sales * .02* instruction multiplies the contents of the form-level Sales variable (500) by .02, giving 10. The instruction then displays the result (10) in the LblComm control.

7 Click the **Ex 3 - Calc 5% Commission button** (the CmdEx3 control). A zero appears in the LblComm control. The zero appears because the *Dim Sales as Currency* instruction in CmdEx3's Click event procedure creates and initializes (to zero) a local variable named Sales. The local Sales variable is different from the form-level Sales variable. The next instruction in the Click event procedure, *LblComm.Caption = Sales * .05*, multiplies the contents of the local Sales variable (0) by .05, giving 0 (zero). The instruction then displays the result (0) in the LblComm control. When the Click event procedure ends, Visual Basic removes the local Sales variable from the computer's memory. The form-level Sales variable, however, remains in memory.

8 Click the **Exit button** to end the application. Visual Basic removes the form-level Sales variable from the computer's memory and then returns to the design screen.

As this example shows, if you use the same name to declare both a form-level variable and a local variable, the event procedure in which the local variable is declared will use its local variable, not the form-level variable.

Let's recap what you have learned about local and form-level variables:

- Local variables are declared in an event procedure, and they can be used only by the event procedure in which they are declared.
- If a variable with the same name is declared in more than one event procedure, each event procedure creates and uses its own variable with that name.
- Form-level variables are declared in the form's general Declarations section, and they can be used by every event procedure in the form.
- If a variable with the same name is declared as a local variable and as a form-level variable, the event procedure declaring the local variable uses the local variable. All other procedures use the form-level variable.

The previous examples used a numeric variable, which is a variable that contains a number. The next example uses a string variable, which is a variable that contains a string. (Recall that a string is a group of characters enclosed in quotation marks.)

String Variables

To save you time, CmdEx4's Click event procedure already contains some code. Let's look at that code right now.

To open CmdEx4's Code window:

1 Double-click the **Ex 4 - Display Name button** (the CmdEx4 control) to open its Code window. The Click event procedure appears, as shown in Figure 3-11.

declares two String variables

assigns values to the String variables

```
                    T3A_VAR2.FRM

Object: CmdEx4            Proc: Click

Sub CmdEx4_Click ()
    Dim Fname As String
    Dim Lname As String
    Fname = "Sue"
    Lname = "Chen"

End Sub
```

Figure 3-11: Code in CmdEx4's Click event procedure

The Dim statements declare two String variables: Fname and Lname. (Fname stands for first name; Lname stands for last name.) The assignment statements assign a string to each variable. Notice that the strings are enclosed in quotation marks, but the names of the string variables are not. The quotation marks differentiate a string from a variable name. In other words, "Sue" is a string, but Sue (without quotation marks) is the name of a variable.

Let's display the contents of the Fname variable in the LblName control. Recall that you can do that by assigning the contents of the Fname variable to the Label control's Caption property.

2 Press the **down arrow key** four times. The blinking insertion point should be positioned in the blank line above the End Sub statement. Press [**Tab**], then type **LblName.Caption = Fname** and press [**Enter**].

3 Close the Code window, **save and run** the application, then click the **Ex 4 - Display Name** button (the CmdEx4 control). The string "Sue" (without the quotes) appears in the LblName control. (You will learn how to display the contents of the Lname variable in the next section.)

4 Click the **Exit button** to end the application. Visual Basic returns to the design screen.

You can also connect (or link) strings together, which means placing one string immediately after another. Let's see how that works.

Concatenating Strings

Connecting (or linking) strings together is called **concatenating**. In Visual Basic, you concatenate strings with the **concatenation operator**—the ampersand (&). You can also use the plus sign (+) to concatenate strings. To avoid confusion, however, you should use the plus sign for addition and the ampersand for concatenation. Figure 3-12 shows some examples of string concatenation. (Notice that you can also concatenate a number with a string. In those cases, Visual Basic treats the number as if it were a string.)

Assume you have the following variables:

Variable	Data Type	Contents
Fname	String	"Sue"
Lname	String	"Chen"
Age	Integer	21

Concatenated String	Result
Fname & Lname	SueChen
Fname & " " & Lname	Sue Chen
Lname & ", " & Fname	Chen, Sue
"She is " & Age & "!"	She is 21!

Figure 3-12: Examples of string concatenation

When concatenating strings, you must be sure to include a space before and after the concatenation operator—the ampersand (&). If you do not enter a space before and after the ampersand, Visual Basic will not recognize the ampersand as the concatenation operator. Let's use the concatenation operator to link the Lname variable to the Fname variable, and display the result in the LblName control.

tips

• • • • • • • • • • • • • • • • •

▶ If an error message box appears on the screen, read the message and then click the OK button. Visual Basic will highlight the error in the Code window. Correct the code and repeat Step 3.

To concatenate the Lname variable to the Fname variable:

1   Double-click the **Ex 4 - Display Name button** (the CmdEx4 control) to open its Code window. The Click event procedure appears.

2   Change the *LblName.Caption = Fname* instruction to

LblName.Caption = Fname & Lname.

Don't type the period at the end. Also, be sure to enter a space before and after the ampersand (&).

3   Close the Code window, **save and run** the application, then click the **Ex 4 - Display Name button** (the CmdEx4 control). The string "SueChen" (without the quotes) appears in the LblName control.

Notice that the contents of the Lname variable (Chen) appears immediately after the contents of the Fname variable (Sue). The string would look better if a space separated the first name from the last name. Let's stop the application and fix this problem.

4 Click the **Exit button** to end the application. Visual Basic returns to the design screen.

5 Double-click the **Ex 4 - Display Name button** (the CmdEx4 control) to open its Code window. The Click event procedure appears.

To separate the first and last name with a space, you simply concatenate a space between the Fname variable and the Lname variable in the *LblName.Caption = Fname & Lname* instruction. A space, which is a string, is written like this: " " (one blank space between two quotation marks).

6 Change the *LblName.Caption = Fname & Lname* instruction to **LblName.Caption = Fname & " " & Lname**. Be sure to enter a space between the quotation marks. Also be sure to enter a space before and after each ampersand (&). See Figure 3-13.

one blank space

be sure to include a space before and after each concatenation operator

concatenation operator

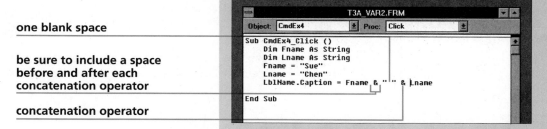

```
                    T3A_VAR2.FRM
Object: CmdEx4        Proc: Click

Sub CmdEx4_Click ()
    Dim Fname As String
    Dim Lname As String
    Fname = "Sue"
    Lname = "Chen"
    LblName.Caption = Fname & " " & Lname

End Sub
```

Figure 3-13: Code window showing string concatenation

7 Close the Code window, **save and run** the application, then click the **Ex 4 - Display Name button** (the CmdEx4 control). This time, the string "Sue Chen" (without the quotes) appears in the LblName control.

8 Click the **Exit button** to end the application. Visual Basic returns to the design screen.

The last topic you'll learn about in Lesson A is how to remove a coded control from the form.

Removing a Coded Control from the Form

If a control does not contain any code, you can remove the control from the form by selecting the control and pressing the Delete key. If a control contains code, however, you should delete the code that you entered in its Code window(s) before deleting the control from the form; otherwise, Visual Basic retains the unnecessary code in your application, even though the control is gone. Just for practice, let's remove the CmdEx3 control from the form.

tips

● ● ● ● ● ● ● ● ● ● ● ● ● ● ● ● ●

▶ If you want to verify that the code from a deleted control was removed from the application, open the form's general Declarations section and click the down arrow in the Code window's Proc (procedure) box. If the name of the deleted control appears in the list, then your application still contains the control's code. To remove the code, click the control's name in the drop-down list, then highlight the instructions in its Code window (including the Sub and End Sub instructions), and then press Delete.

To remove the CmdEx3 control from the form:

1 Double-click the **Ex 3 - Calc 5% Commission button** (the CmdEx3 control) to open its Code window. The Click event procedure appears.

The only procedure coded for the CmdEx3 button is the Click event procedure, so that is the only code you will need to delete before removing the control from the form.

2 Highlight **all of the instructions in the Code window**, including the Sub and the End Sub instructions, then press [**Delete**] to delete the instructions in the Code window. Visual Basic removes CmdEx3's Code window from the screen. CmdEx4's Click event procedure now appears in the Code window.

3 Close the Code window. The Ex 3 - Calc 5% Commission button (the CmdEx3 control) should still be selected, so just press [**Delete**] to remove the control from the form. The CmdEx3 control is now removed from the form.

4 **Save** the application.

In Lesson B you will begin coding the Dots & Stripes application. For now, you can either take a break or complete the end-of-lesson questions and exercises.

S U M M A R Y

To tell Visual Basic to check for undeclared variables:

■ Enter the *Option Explicit* statement in the general Declarations section of the form.

To create a local variable:

■ Enter the *Dim variablename [as datatype]* statement in an event procedure's Code window.
■ See naming rules in Figure 3-3 and data types listed in Figure 3-4.

To create a form-level variable:

■ Enter the *Dim variablename [as datatype]* statement in the form's general Declarations section.
■ See naming rules in Figure 3-3 and data types listed in Figure 3-4.

To use an assignment statement to assign data to a variable:

■ Use the format *Variablename = value*.

To concatenate strings:

■ Use the concatenation operator—the ampersand (&). Be sure to enter a space before and after the ampersand; otherwise, Visual Basic will not recognize the ampersand as the concatenation operator.

To remove a coded control from the form:

- Select the control you want to remove from the form.
- Delete the code that you entered in the control's Code window(s).
- Press [Delete] to remove the control from the form.

To verify that a deleted control's code was removed from the application:

- Open the general Declarations section of the form and click the down arrow in the Code window's Proc (procedure) box.
- If the name of the deleted control appears in the list, click the control's name in the drop-down list, then highlight the instructions in its Code window (including the Sub and End Sub instructions), and then press [Delete].

Q U E S T I O N S

1. _____ are memory locations in which you store information, temporarily.
   a. Boxes
   b. Forms
   c. Labels
   d. Variables
   e. Variances

2. Which of the following are valid variable names? (You can choose more than one.)
   a. 94income
   b. Inc 94
   c. Income
   d. Inc_94
   e. IncomeTax

3. Which of the following is the correct data type to use for a variable that will always contain whole numbers in the range 0 to 20000?
   a. Currency
   b. Integer
   c. Long
   d. Single
   e. Variant

4. Which of the following is the only data type that can store numbers and strings?
   a. Currency
   b. Integer
   c. Long
   d. Single
   e. Variant

5. A variable known only to the procedure in which it is declared is called a(n) _____ variable.
   a. Event
   b. Form-level
   c. Local
   d. Procedure
   e. Protected

6. Which of the following is the concatenation operator?
   a. @
   b. #
   c. $
   d. &
   e. *

7. Assume the Reg1 variable contains the string "North" and the Reg2 variable contains the string "West". Which of the following will display the string "NorthWest" in the LblRegion control?
   a. LblRegion.Caption = Reg1 & Reg2
   b. LblRegion.Caption = Reg1&Reg2
   c. LblRegion.Caption = Reg1 $ Reg2
   d. LblRegion.Caption = Reg1 # Reg2
   e. LblRegion.Caption = Reg1 @ Reg2

8. Assume the City variable contains the string "Boston" and the State variable contains the string "MA". Which of the following will display the string "Boston, MA" (the city, a comma, a space, and the state) in the LblAddress control?
   a. LblAddress.Caption = City & , & State
   b. LblAddress.Caption = "City" & ", " & "State"
   c. LblAddress.Caption = "City&", "&State
   d. LblAddress.Caption = City & ", " & State
   e. LblAddress.Caption = "City, " & "State"

EXERCISES

1. Assume your application needs to store an item's name and its price. On a piece of paper, write the appropriate Dim statements to create the necessary variables.

2. Assume your application needs to store the name of an item in inventory and its height and weight. On a piece of paper, write the appropriate Dim statements to create the necessary variables.

3. Assume your application needs to store the name of an inventory item, the number of units in stock at the beginning of the current month, the number of units purchased during the current month, the number of units sold during the current month, and the number of units in stock at the end of the current month. On a piece of paper, write the appropriate Dim statements to create the necessary variables.

4. Assume your application needs to store the name and the population of a city. On a piece of paper, write the appropriate Dim statements to create the necessary variables.

5. Assume your application needs to store the part number of an item and its cost. (An example of a part number for this application is A103.) On a piece of paper, write the appropriate Dim statements to create the necessary variables.

6. On a piece of paper, write an assignment statement that assigns Miami to an existing variable named City.

7. On a piece of paper, write an assignment statement that assigns the part number AB103 to an existing variable named Partno.

8. On a piece of paper, write the assignment statements that will assign the word Desk to an existing variable named Itemname, the number 40 to an existing variable named In_stock, and the number 20 to an existing variable named On_order.

9. On a piece of paper, write an assignment statement that will add the contents of the Reg1sales variable to the contents of the Reg2sales variable, then assign that sum to an existing variable named Totalsales.

10. On a piece of paper, write an assignment statement that will multiply the contents of the Salary variable by the number 1.5, then assign that result to the Salary variable.

11. Assume your application contains two Command buttons: CmdSalary and CmdBonus. Both buttons' Click event procedures need to use the Empname variable. On a piece of paper, write the appropriate Dim statement to declare the Empname variable. Also write down where you will need to enter the Dim statement and whether the variable is a form-level variable or a local variable.

12. Assume your application contains two Command buttons: CmdWest and CmdSouth. The Click event procedure for the CmdWest button needs to use a variable named Westsales. The Click event procedure for the CmdSouth button needs to use a variable named Southsales. Both buttons' Click event procedures need to use the Company variable. On a piece of paper, write the appropriate Dim statements to declare the Westsales variable, the Southsales variable, and the Empname variable. Also write down where you will need to enter each Dim statement and whether each variable is a form-level variable or a local variable.

Use the following information to answer questions 13–15.

Variable Name	Contents
City	"Madison"
State	"WI"
Zip	53711

13. On a piece of paper, write an assignment statement that will display the string "Madison, WI" in the LblAddress control. Be sure to use the information shown above.

14. On a piece of paper, write an assignment statement that will display the string "I live in Madison, WI." in the LblAddress control. Be sure to use the information shown above.

15. On a piece of paper, write an assignment statement that will display the string "My zip code is 53711." in the LblAddress control. Be sure to use the information shown above.

In this lesson you will learn how to:

■ Read the symbols in a flowchart
■ Use a flowchart to help you code
■ Use the InputBox function

Coding a Flowchart

The Dots & Stripes Application

Recall that Dots & Stripes, a local wallpaper store, has hired Interlocking Software to create an application that will compute the number of rolls of wallpaper a customer needs to purchase. (To review the Dots & Stripes application, run the DOTS.EXE file from the Program Manager before continuing with this lesson.) You have been asked to complete the application for Ahmad Hadkari. Let's begin by opening the partially completed Dots & Stripes application.

To open the partially completed Dots & Stripes application:

1 Launch Visual Basic (if necessary) and open the **t3a.mak** project, which is in either the tut3\ver2 or tut3\ver3 directory on your Student Disk.

2 Click the **View form button** in the Project window to view the FrmDots form. The FrmDots form appears on the screen.

3 Click the **form's Maximize button** to maximize the form. Figure 3-14 identifies the controls already included in the application.

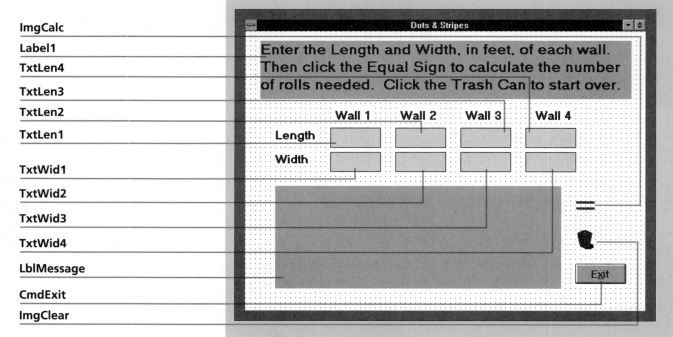

ImgCalc
Label1
TxtLen4
TxtLen3
TxtLen2
TxtLen1
TxtWid1
TxtWid2
TxtWid3
TxtWid4
LblMessage
CmdExit
ImgClear

Figure 3-14: Dots & Stripes user interface

The ImgCalc's Picture property contains the calc.ico icon file (an equal sign). The ImgClear's Picture property contains the trsh.ico icon file (a trash can). The TabStop property of the CmdExit control was set to False to prevent the user from tabbing into the control and accidentally exiting the application.

4 Restore the form to its standard size, then save the form file as **t3b** and the project file as **t3b**.

Because the Dots & Stripes application will use variables, you will enter the *Option Explicit* statement in the general Declarations section of the form.

To enter the *Option Explicit* statement in the form's general Declarations section:

1 Double-click the **form** to open its Code window, click the **down arrow in the Code window's Object box**, and click (**general**) in the drop-down list. The form's general Declarations section appears.

2 Type **option explicit** and press [**Enter**], then close the Code window. Now, when the application is run, Visual Basic will warn you if you use the name of an undeclared variable in your code.

The TOE chart Ahmad created for the Dots & Stripes application is shown in Figure 3-15.

Task	Object	Event
Get wall length and width, in feet	8 Text boxes	None
Get the style code and the roll coverage, in sq. ft.		
Calculate the area of each wall		
Calculate the required number of rolls	Image control (ImgCalc)	Click
Display the required number of rolls and the style code		
Clear the screen	Image control (ImgClear)	Click
End the application	Command button (Exit)	Click

Figure 3-15: Dots & Stripes TOE chart

According to the TOE chart, only the Click event procedures of the two Image controls (ImgCalc and ImgClear) and the Click event procedure of the Exit Command button will need to be coded. The ImgCalc control (the equal sign) will get the style code and the roll coverage (the number of square feet a roll of wallpaper covers) from the user. The control will also calculate the area of each wall and the number of rolls of wallpaper the customer will need. It will then display the required number of rolls and the style code. The ImgClear control will clear the screen, and the Exit Command button will end the application.

To complete the Dots & Stripes application, you will need to enter code in the Click event procedures for the ImgClear control and the ImgCalc control only. The Exit button already contains the End instruction, so you won't need to code that control.

You will now use Ahmad's flowcharts to assist you in coding the two Image controls. Let's begin with the flowchart for the ImgClear control.

The Flowchart for the ImgClear Control

Recall that a flowchart uses standardized symbols to represent the steps needed to solve a problem. The flowchart for the ImgClear control is shown in Figure 3-16.

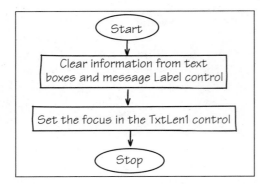

Figure 3-16: Flowchart for the ImgClear control

Let's take a closer look at the symbols used in the flowchart. The first symbol, called the **start/stop oval**, identifies the beginning of the flowchart. You will notice that the start/stop oval is also the last symbol in the flowchart. In that position it marks the end of the flowchart.

Between the start and the stop ovals are two rectangles called **process symbols**. You use the process symbol to represent tasks such as declaring variables, clearing information from the screen, assigning values to variables and to the properties of controls, setting the focus, and for calculations. The first process symbol, for example, represents an assignment task. The second process symbol is used to set the focus to a control.

The lines connecting the flowchart symbols are called **flowlines**. To translate the flowchart into Visual Basic code, you will start at the top of the flowchart and write the code for each symbol as you follow the flowlines down to the bottom of the flowchart. Some symbols in a flowchart may require more than one line of code. The only symbol that is not coded is the start oval. Let's use the flowchart to code the ImgClear control.

Coding the ImgClear Control

Because the start oval is not coded, the first symbol you will translate into Visual Basic code is actually the second symbol in the flowchart, a process symbol. That process symbol tells you to clear the information from the Text boxes and the message Label control. Recall that you can do that by assigning the null string ("") to the Text property of the Text boxes and to the Caption property of the Label control.

tips

▶ Enter the first two assignment statements in the Code window. Then highlight both assignment statements and copy them to the Windows Clipboard. Then paste the copied assignment statements into the Code window three times and change the copied statements to match Figure 3-17. Don't forget to type the last assignment statement, which is different from the first eight.

assigning the null string will clear any text from these controls

two quotation marks

To clear the information from the Text boxes and the Label control:

1 Maximize the form, then double-click the **ImgClear control** (the trash can) to open its Code window. The ImgClear control's Click event procedure appears.

As you learned in Tutorial 2, it's a good idea to document the Code window.

2 Type **'Clear Text boxes and Label control** and press [**Enter**] to document the Code window. (Be sure to type the apostrophe at the beginning of the documentation.)

3 Press [**Tab**], then enter the nine assignment statements shown in Figure 3-17.

The next symbol in the ImgClear flowchart (Figure 3-16) is the process symbol that tells you to set the focus in the TxtLen1 control.

4 In the blank line immediately below the last assignment statement, type **TxtLen1.SetFocus** and press [**Tab**], then type **'Move focus to TxtLen1 control** and press [**Enter**]. (Be sure to type the apostrophe.) Notice that you can enter the documentation on the same line as the code; but the documentation must come after the code, not before it.

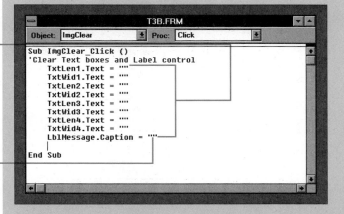

Figure 3-17: ImgClear's Code window showing nine assignment statements

The last symbol in the ImgClear flowchart is the oval that says Stop. Visual Basic's *End Sub* statement, which is already entered in the Code window, corresponds to the stop oval. That means you have completed coding the ImgClear Click event procedure. You will test the ImgClear control by first entering some text in the length and width Text boxes and then clicking the trash can icon to see if the code removes the text from the Text boxes. (Because you can't enter text in a Label control while the application is running, you will not be able to verify that the code clears the text from the LblMessage control until later on.)

5 Close the Code window, restore the form to its standard size, then **save and run** the application.

6 Type **1** in the TxtLen1 box and press [**Tab**], type **2** in the TxtWid1 box and press [**Tab**]. On your own, type any numbers you want in the remaining six Text boxes.

7 When each of the Text boxes contains some text, click the **ImgClear control** (the trash can). The Text boxes should now be empty.

8 Click the **Exit button** to end the application. Visual Basic returns to the design screen.

tips

▶ If the "Element not defined" error message box appears, click the OK button. Visual Basic will highlight the error in the Code window. The "Element not defined" message means that Visual Basic does not recognize the name of a control. Compare your code with the code shown in Figure 3-17. You can also verify the name of a variable by opening the Code window's Object box. Correct the mistyped control's name, close the Code window, then save and run the application again.

Next, let's look at the flowchart for the ImgCalc control.

The Flowchart for the ImgCalc Control

The flowchart for the ImgCalc control is shown in Figure 3-18. This flowchart contains a new symbol, a parallelogram. The parallelogram, which is called the **input/output symbol,** is used to represent input tasks (such as getting information from the user) and output tasks (such as displaying information). Figure 3 18's flowchart shows three input/output symbols: two are for input and one is for output. We'll use this flowchart to code the ImgCalc control.

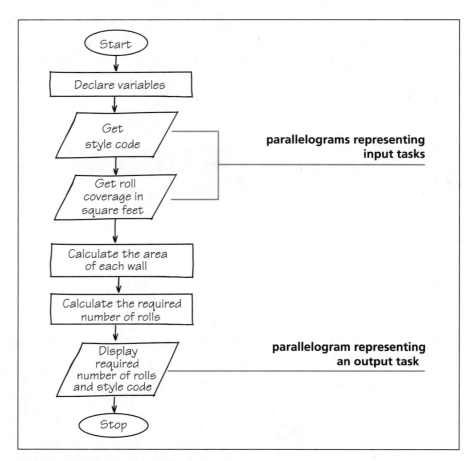

Figure 3-18: Flowchart for the ImgCalc control

Coding the ImgCalc Control

Recall that the start oval is not coded. So the first symbol you will translate into Visual Basic code is the process symbol (the rectangle), which tells you to declare the variables you will use in the application. To determine the necessary variables, scan the flowchart for places where you will need to store information temporarily. When searching for such places in a flowchart, look at all parallelograms and all rectangles. A parallelogram that represents an input task, such as requesting information from the user, may need a memory variable in which to store the information. Any rectangle that represents an assignment statement may also need a memory variable. Figure 3-18's flowchart shows two parallelograms that represent input tasks and two rectangles. (The third parallelogram in the flowchart represents an output task, so it will not need a variable.) Let's look at the input parallelograms and the rectangles to see if any of them will require a variable. Start with the two parallelograms.

The first parallelogram in Figure 3-18 says to "Get style code" from the user. The Dots & Stripes user interface does not provide a control in which the style code can be stored, so you will need to store the style code in a variable, which you can name Style. Because style codes can contain letters and numbers, you will assign the String data type to the Style variable. In addition to assigning a name and a data type to a variable, recall that you also must determine a variable's scope—in other words, which procedures need to use the variable. According to the TOE chart (Figure 3-15), only ImgCalc's Click event procedure needs to use the style code. So the Style variable can be declared as a local variable in the ImgCalc Click event procedure.

The second parallelogram shown in Figure 3-18's flowchart says to "Get roll coverage in square feet" from the user. (Roll coverage is the number of square feet a roll of wallpaper covers.) Here again, the user interface does not provide a control in which that information can be stored, so you will need to store the roll coverage in a variable, which you can name Rollcov. Because the Rollcov variable might need to store a number containing a decimal fraction (for example, 37.5), you will assign the Single data type to it. According to the TOE chart, no other procedure will need the Rollcov variable, so you can declare it as a local variable in the ImgCalc Click event procedure. Now let's look at the two rectangles (process symbols) in the flowchart.

The first process symbol says to "Calculate the area of each wall." Because the user interface does not provide a control in which to store the area of each wall, you will need to store that information in four variables: one for each wall's area. You can name the variables Area1, Area2, Area3, and Area4. Because these variables might need to store numbers containing a decimal fraction, you will assign the Single data type to them. According to the TOE chart, no other procedure will need these variables, so you can declare them as local variables in the ImgCalc Click event procedure.

The second process symbol says to "Calculate the required number of rolls." Here again, because the user interface does not provide a control in which to store the required number of rolls, you will store that information in a variable named Totalrolls. You will assign the Single data type to the Totalrolls variable and declare it as a local variable in the ImgCalc Click event procedure. Figure 3-19 recaps the variables that the ImgCalc control will need to perform its assigned tasks.

Name	Type	Used by	Declare in / Declare as
Style	String	ImgCalc Click event	ImgCalc Click event / local
Rollcov	Single	ImgCalc Click event	ImgCalc Click event / local
Area1	Single	ImgCalc Click event	ImgCalc Click event / local
Area2	Single	ImgCalc Click event	ImgCalc Click event / local
Area3	Single	ImgCalc Click event	ImgCalc Click event / local
Area4	Single	ImgCalc Click event	ImgCalc Click event / local
Totalrolls	Single	ImgCalc Click event	ImgCalc Click event / local

Figure 3-19: Variables needed by the ImgCalc control

Now let's declare these local variables in the ImgCalc Click event procedure.

You can declare more than one variable in a Dim statement, but you must be sure to include the appropriate data type on each variable. For example, you could have declared five of the variables in one Dim statement as follows: **Dim Area1 As Single, Area2 As Single, Area3 As Single, Area4 As Single, Totalrolls As Single**. The entire Dim statement would have to be typed on one line in the Code window. If you omit the data type, Visual Basic assigns the Variant data type.

To declare the local variables in the ImgCalc Click event procedure:

1 Maximize the form, then double-click the **ImgCalc control** (the equal sign) to open its Code window. The Click event procedure appears.

2 Enter the code shown in Figure 3-20.

Figure 3-20: Dim statements entered in ImgCalc Click event procedure

Now that the "Declare variables" rectangle is coded, you can code the next flowchart symbol, which is the "Get style code" parallelogram. You will use Visual Basic's InputBox function to get the style code from the user.

The InputBox Function

You can use the InputBox function to display a message in a dialog box, along with an OK button, a Cancel button, and an input area in which the user can enter information. The message in the dialog box should prompt the user to enter the appropriate information in the input area of the dialog box. The user will then need to click either the OK button or the Cancel button in order to continue the application.

The format of the InputBox function is *InputBox(prompt)*, where *prompt* is the message you want displayed inside the dialog box. The *prompt* must be enclosed in quotation marks. (You can also include other information in the InputBox function. If you want to see more about the InputBox function, use the Help menu to search for its Help screen.) Recall that a function is a predefined procedure that returns a value; in the case of the InputBox function, the value returned to the application is the value entered by the user in response to the prompt. You will use the InputBox function to prompt the user to enter the style code, which you will store in the Style variable.

To continue coding the ImgCalc control:

1   The Code window for the ImgCalc Click event procedure should still be open. The blinking insertion point should be positioned in the blank line below the last Dim statement. Press [**Backspace**] to remove the indentation, then type '**Get style code** and press [**Enter**]. (Be sure to type the apostrophe.)

2   Press [**Tab**], then type **Style = inputbox("Enter style code")** and press [**Enter**]. When the application is run, the InputBox function will display a dialog box containing the "Enter style code" prompt, as well as an area in which the user can enter his or her response, and an OK and a Cancel button. After the user enters the appropriate information in the input area of the dialog box and clicks the OK button, the user's response is stored in the Style variable.

The next flowchart symbol you will code is the "Get roll coverage in square feet" parallelogram. Here again, you can use the InputBox function to prompt the user to enter the roll coverage, then store the response in the Rollcov variable.

3   Press [**Backspace**] to remove the indentation, then type '**Get roll coverage** and press [**Enter**].

4   Press [**Tab**], then type **Rollcov = inputbox("Enter roll coverage in square feet")** and press [**Enter**].

Before writing any more code, let's save and run the application to make sure that the code you've entered so far is working correctly.

5   Close the Code window, restore the form to its standard size, then **save and run** the application.

6   Click the **equal sign** (the ImgCalc control). A dialog box requesting the style code appears on the screen. See Figure 3-21.

prompt

input area

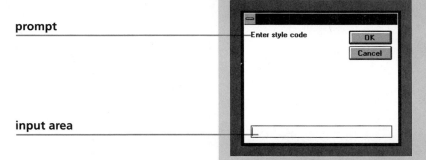

Figure 3-21: Dialog box created by the InputBox function

7   Type **AB45 - Flowers** and press [**Enter**] (or click the **OK button**). Visual Basic stores your response in the local Style variable. A dialog box requesting the roll coverage appears on the screen.

8   Type **35** and press [**Enter**] (or click the **OK button**). Visual Basic stores your response in the local Rollcov variable.

The code does not result in any error messages, so it appears to be working correctly. You will test it again later on.

9   Click the **Exit button** to end the application. Visual Basic returns to the design screen.

Let's continue translating the ImgCalc flowchart into Visual Basic code. The next flowchart symbol you will code is the process symbol (the rectangle) that says "Calculate the area of each wall." You calculate the area of a wall by multiplying its length times its width. Because you must calculate the area of each of the four walls, this flowchart symbol will require four lines of code. Let's write the first line now.

To continue coding the ImgCalc Click event procedure:

1   Maximize the form, then double-click the **ImgCalc control** (the equal sign) to open its Code window. The Click event procedure appears.

2   Maximize the Code window so that you can view more of the code, then position the mouse pointer[1] in the blank line immediately above the End Sub statement, and click at that location. (The blinking insertion point should be at the far left in the blank line.)

3   Type '**Calculate the area of each wall** and press [**Enter**]. (Be sure to type the apostrophe.)

You calculate the area of a wall by multiplying its length times its width. The length of wall 1 is stored in the Text property of the TxtLen1 control, and the width of wall 1 is stored in the Text property of the TxtWid1 control. You can store the area of wall 1 in the Area1 variable.

4   Press [**Tab**], then type **Area1 = TxtLen1.Text * TxtWid1.Text** and press [**Enter**].

The assignment statements that calculate the areas of the other walls will be similar to the assignment statement you just entered. You can simply copy the assignment statement to the Windows Clipboard, paste the statement into the Code window three times, and then make the necessary changes.

5 Copy the *Area1 = TxtLen1.Text * TxtWid1.Text* assignment statement to the Windows Clipboard, then paste the assignment statement into the Code window three times. Then make the changes shown in Figure 3-22.

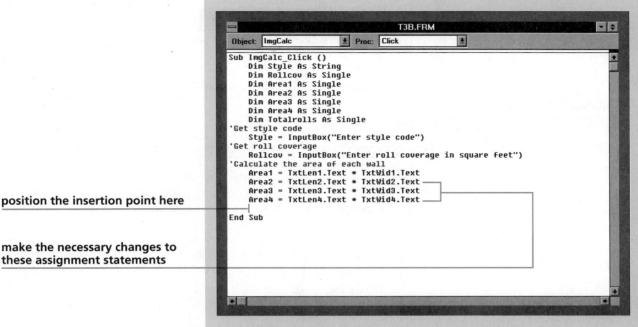

position the insertion point here

make the necessary changes to these assignment statements

```
                    T3B.FRM
Object: ImgCalc        ± Proc: Click          ±

Sub ImgCalc_Click ()
    Dim Style As String
    Dim Rollcov As Single
    Dim Area1 As Single
    Dim Area2 As Single
    Dim Area3 As Single
    Dim Area4 As Single
    Dim Totalrolls As Single
'Get style code
    Style = InputBox("Enter style code")
'Get roll coverage
    Rollcov = InputBox("Enter roll coverage in square feet")
'Calculate the area of each wall
    Area1 = TxtLen1.Text * TxtWid1.Text
    Area2 = TxtLen2.Text * TxtWid2.Text
    Area3 = TxtLen3.Text * TxtWid3.Text
    Area4 = TxtLen4.Text * TxtWid4.Text

End Sub
```

Figure 3-22: Assignment statements entered in Code window

6 Position the blinking insertion point in the blank line immediately below the last assignment statement, as shown in Figure 3-22.

The next flowchart symbol you will code is the process symbol (the rectangle) that says "Calculate the required number of rolls." That amount is calculated by adding the areas of each wall and then dividing that sum by the roll coverage (the number of square feet covered by a roll). You will assign the result of the calculation to the Totalrolls variable.

7 Press [Backspace] to remove the indentation, then type **'Calculate required number of rolls** and press [Enter].

8 Press [Tab], type **Totalrolls = (Area1 + Area2 + Area3 + Area4) / Rollcov** and press [Enter]. Be sure to type the parentheses.

Before writing any more code, let's test the code you've entered so far. Assume the customer wants to wallpaper only one wall.

9 Close the Code window, restore the form to its standard size, then **save and run** the application.

10 Type **10** as the length of the first wall, press [Tab], type **12** as the width of the first wall, then click the **equal sign** (the ImgCalc control). Type **CA33 - Stripes** as the style code and press [Enter], then type **35** as the roll coverage and press [Enter]. Visual Basic displays a "Type mismatch" error message on the screen and highlights the *Area2 = TxtLen2.Text * TxtWid2.Text* instruction in the Code window. See Figure 3-23.

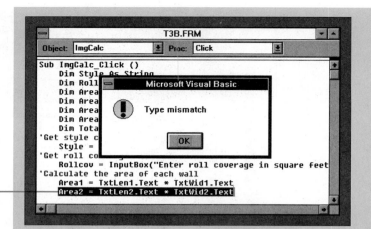

Visual Basic highlights the instruction causing the error

Figure 3-23: Type mismatch error in Code window

A "Type mismatch" error means that Visual Basic has encountered something that it wasn't expecting in an instruction—for example, a string where a number is required or a number where a string is needed. In this case, Visual Basic expected to find numbers stored in the Text property of the two Text boxes (TxtLen2 and TxtWid2). Because the Text boxes were empty, Visual Basic found the null string ("") stored there instead. (In Visual Basic, the Text property of an empty Text box contains the null string.) You can't use the null string in an equation involving multiplication, so Visual Basic displays the "Type mismatch" error message. What you need here is a way to tell Visual Basic to treat the null string as a number—specifically, the number 0. You can use the Val function, which you learned in Tutorial 2, to do that. Let's return to the design screen to fix this problem.

11   Click the **OK button** to remove the error message box. Close the Code window, restore the form to its standard size, then click the **Stop icon** ■.

Recall that the Val function results in the numeric equivalent of a string. In Visual Basic, the numeric equivalent of the null string is the number 0. Therefore, you can use the Val function to tell Visual Basic to treat the Text property of an empty Text box as a number (the number 0) instead of a string (the null string). Because it is possible that all eight of the length and width Text boxes might be empty (the user might accidentally click the equal sign without entering any data), you will include the Val function in each of the area equations. Let's do that now.

To include the Val function in the four area equations:
1   Maximize the form, then double-click the **equal sign** (the ImgCalc control). The Click event procedure appears.

2   Maximize the Code window and make the changes shown in Figure 3-24.

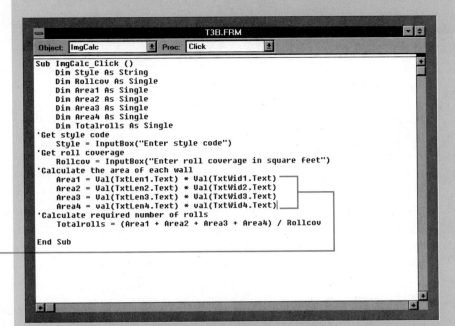

include the Val function on the eight length and width Text boxes

Figure 3-24: Val function entered in Code window

Before testing the application, let's finish coding the ImgCalc flowchart. The "Display required number of rolls and style code" parallelogram is next. You will display that information in the LblMessage control.

3   Click the blank line immediately above the End Sub instruction. Be sure the insertion point is above the E in End.

4   Type 'Display required number of rolls and style code and press [Enter].

Let's include a message along with the required number of rolls and the style code. For example, if the customer needs three rolls of style code AB45 - Flowers, let's display the following message: "You need 3 rolls of AB45 - Flowers". You will use string concatenation to display the message in the LblMessage control. The message consists of the following: the string "You need ", the variable Totalrolls, the string " rolls of ", and the variable Style.

5   Press [Tab], then type **LblMessage.Caption = "You need " & Totalrolls & " rolls of " & Style** and press [Enter]. Compare your code to the instructions shown in Figure 3-25.

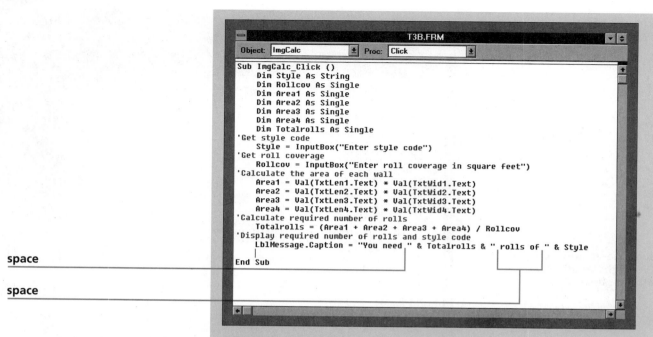

```
                              T3B.FRM
Object: ImgCalc         ±  Proc: Click              ±

Sub ImgCalc_Click ()
    Dim Style As String
    Dim Rollcov As Single
    Dim Area1 As Single
    Dim Area2 As Single
    Dim Area3 As Single
    Dim Area4 As Single
    Dim Totalrolls As Single
'Get style code
    Style = InputBox("Enter style code")
'Get roll coverage
    Rollcov = InputBox("Enter roll coverage in square feet")
'Calculate the area of each wall
    Area1 = Val(TxtLen1.Text) * Val(TxtWid1.Text)
    Area2 = Val(TxtLen2.Text) * Val(TxtWid2.Text)
    Area3 = Val(TxtLen3.Text) * Val(TxtWid3.Text)
    Area4 = Val(TxtLen4.Text) * Val(TxtWid4.Text)
'Calculate required number of rolls
    Totalrolls = (Area1 + Area2 + Area3 + Area4) / Rollcov
'Display required number of rolls and style code
    LblMessage.Caption = "You need " & Totalrolls & " rolls of " & Style

End Sub
```

space

space

Figure 3-25: Code window showing string concatenation

The last symbol in the ImgCalc flowchart is the stop oval. Recall that the *End Sub* instruction, which is already entered in the Code window, corresponds to that symbol. That means you have completed coding the ImgCalc flowchart, so you can close the Code window.

6   Close the Code window and restore the form to its standard size.

Now let's test the entire application.

To test the application:

1   **Save and run** the application. Type **10** as the length of wall 1, press [**Tab**], type **10** as the width of wall 1, press [**Tab**], type **10** as the length of wall 2, press [**Tab**], type **10** as the width of wall 2, then click the **equal sign** (the ImgCalc control). The dialog box requesting the style code appears.

2   Type **AB45 - Flowers** as the style code and press [**Enter**]. The dialog box requesting the roll coverage appears. Type **25** as the roll coverage and press [**Enter**]. Visual Basic displays the required rolls of wallpaper (8) and the style code in the LblMessage control.

3   Click the **trash can** (the ImgClear control). Visual Basic removes the information from the length and width Text boxes and from the message Label control. The focus is in the TxtLen1 control.

Now let's test the application again. This time you will notice a small problem that you will fix in Lesson C.

4   Type **8** as the length of wall 1, press [**Tab**], type **10** as its width, press [**Tab**]. Type **8** as the length of wall 2, press [**Tab**], type **10** as its width, press [**Tab**]. Type **8** as the length of wall 3, press [**Tab**], type **8** as its width, press [**Tab**]. Type **8** as the length of wall 4, press [**Tab**], type **8** as its width.

5 Click the **equal sign** (the ImgCalc control), type **BD78 - Kitchen pots and pans** and press **[Enter]**, then type **35** and press **[Enter]**. Visual Basic displays the required number of rolls (8.228572) and the style code in the TxtMessage control.

Notice that the required rolls is displayed with a lot of decimal places, which the user might find confusing. You will correct this problem in Lesson C.

6 Click the **Exit button** to end the application.

You have now completed Lesson B. In Lesson C you will learn ways to make the application more professional-looking. For now, you can either take a break or complete the end-of-lesson questions and exercises.

SUMMARY

To create a flowchart:

■ Use the start/stop oval to mark the beginning and the end of the flowchart.
■ Use the input/output parallelogram to represent steps that get data from the user and steps that display or print information.
■ Use the process rectangle to represent steps that declare variables, assign values to variables or properties, and for calculations.

To display a dialog box containing a prompt, an input area, an OK button, and a Cancel button:

■ Use the *InputBox(prompt)*. The prompt must be enclosed in quotes ("").

QUESTIONS

1. The _____ symbol is used in a flowchart to represent a calculation task.
   a. input
   b. output
   c. process
   d. start
   e. stop

2. The _____ symbol is used in a flowchart to represent a step that gets information from the user.
   a. input
   b. output
   c. process
   d. start
   e. stop

3. The process symbol is the _____ .
   a. circle
   b. oval
   c. parallelogram
   d. rectangle
   e. square

4. The input/output symbol is the ______________ .
   a. circle
   b. oval
   c. parallelogram
   d. rectangle
   e. square
5. The InputBox displays a dialog box containing which of the following? (You can choose more than one answer.)
   a. Cancel button
   b. Exit button
   c. input area
   d. OK button
   e. prompt

E X E R C I S E S

1. a. Create the user interface shown in Figure 3-26. (Load the calc.ico file into the ImgCalc control. Load the trsh.ico file into the ImgClear control.)

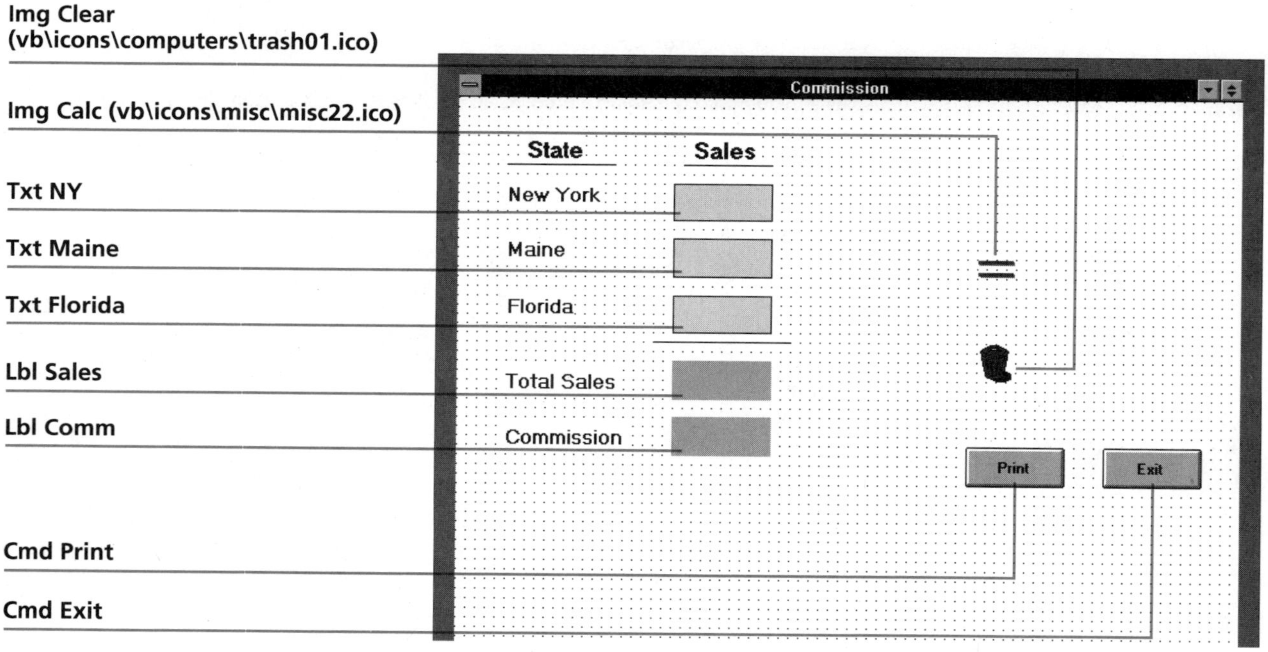

Img Clear (vb\icons\computers\trash01.ico)
Img Calc (vb\icons\misc\misc22.ico)
Txt NY
Txt Maine
Txt Florida
Lbl Sales
Lbl Comm
Cmd Print
Cmd Exit
Commission
State
Sales
New York
Maine
Florida
Total Sales
Commission
Print
Exit

Figure 3-26

b. Code the Exit button so that it ends the application when it is clicked.

c. Code the ImgClear control's Click event procedure so that it clears the screen. (Note: Clear the sales Text boxes, the total sales Label control, and the Commission Label control.)

d. Code the CmdPrint control's Click event procedure so that it prints the form.

e. Use the flowchart shown in Figure 3-27 to code the ImgCalc control's Click event procedure. Use the InputBox function to get the commission rate from the user.

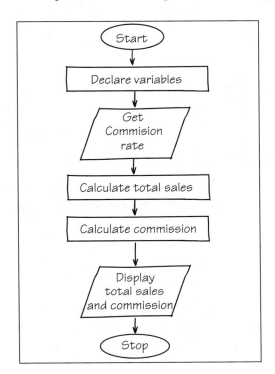

Figure 3-27

f. Save the form and the project as T3LBE1.

g. Run, test, and print the application using the following data:

New York sales: 26000
Maine sales: 34000
Florida sales: 17000
Commission rate: .1 (10%)

(Check figures: The total sales will be 77000. The commission will be 7700.)

h. Exit the application. Print the code.

2. a. Create the user interface shown in Figure 3-28. (Load the calc.ico file into the ImgCalc control. Load the trsh.ico file into the ImgClear control.)

LblJc2

LblJc1

TxtJc1

TxtJc2

TxtJc3

LblJc3

ImgCalc (vb\icons\misc\misc22.ico)

ImgClear
(vb\icons\computers\trash01.ico)

CmdPrint

CmdExit

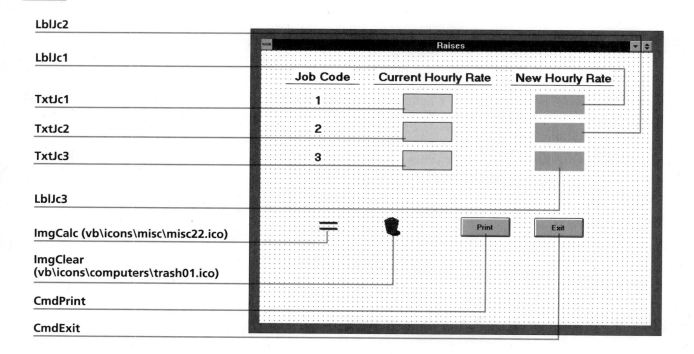

Figure 3-28

b. Code the Exit button so that it ends the application when it is clicked.

c. Code the ImgClear control's Click event procedure so that it clears the screen. (Note: Clear the current hourly rate Text boxes and the new hourly rate Label controls.)

d. Code the CmdPrint control's Click event procedure so that it prints the form.

e. Use the flowchart shown in Figure 3-29 to code the ImgCalc control. Use the InputBox function to get the raise percentage.

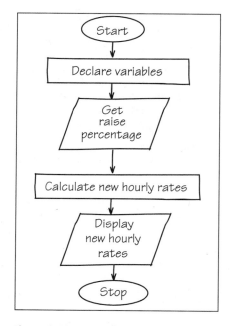

Figure 3-29

f. Save the form and the project as T3LBE2.

g. Run, test, and print the application using the following data:

Current hourly rate for job code 1:   5.00

Current hourly rate for job code 2:   6.25

Current hourly rate for job code 3:   7.75

Raise rate: .06

(Check figure: New hourly rate for job code 1 is 5.30.)

h. Exit the application. Print the code.

3. a. Create the user interface shown in Figure 3-30.

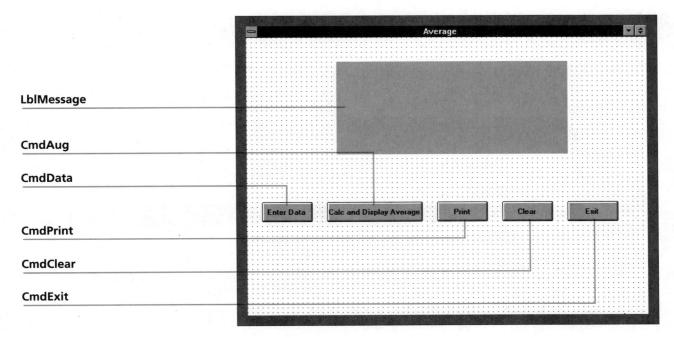

Figure 3-30

b. Code the Exit button so that it ends the application when it is clicked.

c. Code the CmdClear control's Click event procedure so that it clears the screen. (Note: Clear the LblMessage control.)

d. Code the CmdPrint control's Click event procedure so that it prints the form.

e. Use the flowcharts shown in Figure 3-31 to code the Click event procedures for the CmdData and the CmdAvg controls. Use the InputBox function to get the student's name and the three test scores. (Note: Use four InputBox functions— one for each piece of data. You will also need to use form-level variables in this application.)

f. Save the form and the project as T3LBE3.

g. Run, test, and print the application using the following data:

Name: Mary Kaye

Test 1 score: 75

Test 2 score: 87

Test 3 score: 99

(Check figure: The average will be 87.)

h. Exit the application. Print the code.

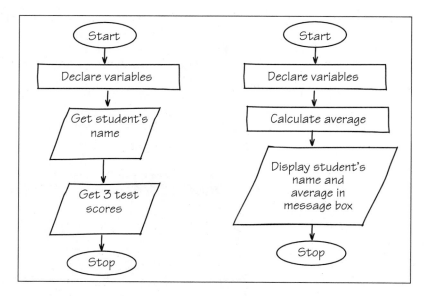

Figure 3-31

4.   a. Create the user interface shown in Figure 3-32.

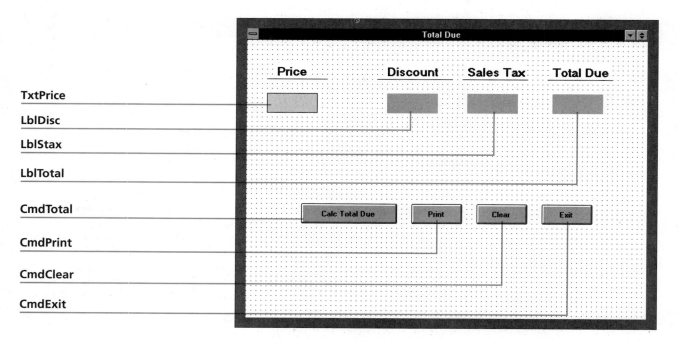

Figure 3-32

    b. Code the Exit button so that it ends the application when it is clicked.
    c. Code the CmdClear control's Click event procedure so that it clears the screen.
       (Note: Clear the TxtPrice, LblDisc, LblStax, and LblTotal controls.)

d. Code the CmdPrint control's Click event procedure so that it prints the form.

e. Use the flowchart shown in Figure 3-33 to code the Click event procedure of the CmdTotal control. Use the InputBox function to get the discount rate; use another InputBox function to get the sales tax rate.

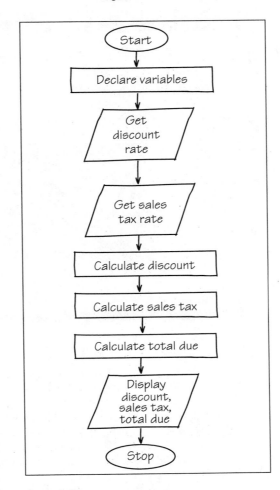

Figure 3-33

f. Save the form and the project as T3LBE4.

g. Run, test, and print the application using the following data:

Price: 125
Discount rate: .1 (10%)
Sales tax rate: .05 (5%)

(Check figure: The total due should be 118.125.)

h. Exit the application. Print the code.

5. a. Create the user interface shown in Figure 3-34.

LblBlue

LblRed

TxtRed

TxtBlue

CmdCalc

CmdPrint

LblMessage

CmdClear

CmdExit

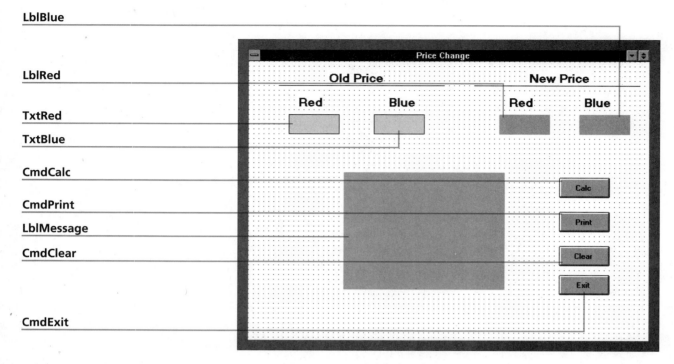

Figure 3-34

b. Code the Exit button so that it ends the application when it is clicked.
c. Code the CmdClear control's Click event procedure so that it clears the screen. (Note: Clear the TxtRed, TxtBlue, LblRed, LblBlue, and LblMessage controls.)
d. Code the CmdPrint control's Click event procedure so that it prints the form.
e. Use the flowchart shown in Figure 3-35 to code the Click event procedure of the CmdCalc button. Use the InputBox function to get the price increase percentage. Display the following message (without the quotes) in the LblMessage control: "New prices reflect a <price increase>% increase". In other words, if the price increase is .2, then the message should say (without the quotes): "New prices reflect a 20% price increase".
f. Save the form and the project as T3LBE5.
g. Run, test, and print the application using the following data:
   Price of red skateboards: 75
   Price of blue skateboards: 65
   Price increase: .2
   (Check figure: The new price of the red skateboards should be 90.)
h. Exit the application. Print the code.

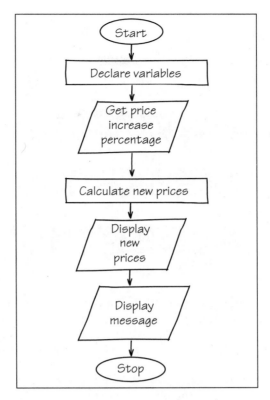

Figure 3-35

In this lesson you will learn how to:

- Use the BorderStyle property to put a border around a control
- Use the Stretch property of an Image control

Improving the Application's Appearance

When you tested the Dots & Stripes application in Lesson B, the required rolls of wallpaper was displayed with too many decimal places. You will fix this problem before we discuss other ways of improving the appearance of the application. First, open the t3b.mak project, which you created in Lesson B.

To open the t3b.mak project:

1 Launch Visual Basic (if necessary) and open the **t3b.mak** project, which you created in Lesson B. The t3b.mak file is in either the tut3\ver2 or tut3\ver3 directory on your Student Disk.

2 Click the **View form button** in the Project window to view the FrmDots form, then save the form as **t3c** and save the project as **t3c**.

You can use the Format function, which you learned in Tutorial 2, to limit the number of decimal places displayed in the number of required rolls.

Using the Format Function

As you learned in Tutorial 2, you can use the Format function to improve the appearance of the numbers in your application. Recall that the syntax of the Format function is: Format(*expression,fmt*). *Expression* specifies the number, date, time, or string whose appearance you want to format. *Fmt* is either the name of a predefined Visual Basic format or, if you want more control over the appearance of the *expression*, a string containing special symbols that tell Visual Basic how you want the *expression* displayed. In this case, you will use one of Visual Basic's predefined formats—the Fixed format—to display no more than two digits to the right of the decimal point. (You could also use the Standard format to display the required rolls with no more than two decimal places.)

To include the Format function in the ImgCalc control's Code window:

1   Maximize the form, double-click the **ImgCalc control** (the equal sign) to open its Code window, then maximize the Code window so you can see more of the code.

2   In the *LblMessage.Caption* = *"You need"* & *Totalrolls* & *"rolls of"* & *Style* statement, change Totalrolls to **Format(Totalrolls, "fixed")**. Be sure to watch the placement of the comma, the parentheses, and the quotation marks. The instruction should now be *LblMessage.Caption* = *"You need"* & *Format(Totalrolls, "fixed")* & *"rolls of"* & *style*.

Let's test this now.

3   Close the Code window, restore the form to its standard size, then **save and run** the application.

4   Type **10** as the length of wall 1, type **12** as the width of wall 1, type **10** as the length of wall 2, type **8** as the width of wall 2, then click the **equal sign** (the ImgCalc control).

5   Type **AB45 - Flowers** as the style code and press **[Enter]**, then type **37.5** as the roll coverage and press **[Enter]**. The required rolls of wallpaper (5.33) is displayed with two decimal places only.

6   Click the **Exit button** to end the application. Visual Basic returns to the design screen.

Now let's work on improving the appearance of the Dots & Stripes user interface.

Improving the Appearance of the User Interface

You can improve the appearance of the Dots & Stripes application in four ways:

1.   Remove the border from the form.
2.   Put a border around the Label control at the top of the screen (Label1) and around the LblMessage control. The border will make both messages more noticeable.
3.   Put a border around the two Image controls so they look more like buttons.
4.   Size the two Image controls to make the icons larger.

You can accomplish the first three items in the list by changing each object's BorderStyle property.

Changing the BorderStyle Property

In Tutorial 1 you learned that the BorderStyle property determines the border style of an object. The default setting of a form's BorderStyle property, for example, is 2-Sizable, which means that the form contains a Control menu box, a title bar, and Minimize and Maximize buttons. If you want to remove those items from the form, which will prevent the user from sizing the user interface or from exiting using the Control menu box, you simply reset the form's BorderStyle property to 0-None. Let's do that now.

To change the BorderStyle property of the form:

1   The form should be selected. (Verify that by looking in the Object box in the Properties window.) Click **BorderStyle** in the Properties list, click the **down arrow in the Settings box**, then click **0 - None** in the drop-down list.

Label controls and Image controls also have a BorderStyle property. The default setting of their BorderStyle property, however, is 0-None. Setting their BorderStyle property to 1-Fixed Single will display a border (a rectangle) around the control. Let's change the BorderStyle property of the two Label controls and the two Image controls to 1-Fixed Single.

To change the BorderStyle property of the two Label controls and the two Image controls:

1   Click the **Label1 control at the top of the form** (the Label control that contains the instructions). Sizing handles appear around the Label1 control.

2   [Ctrl]-click the **LblMessage** control. Sizing handles appear around both Label controls.

3   Double-click **BorderStyle** in the Properties list until the BorderStyle property says 1-Fixed Single. A border (rectangle) appears around both Label controls.

4   Maximize the form, click the **ImgCalc control** (the equal sign), and then [Ctrl]-click the **ImgClear control** (the trash can). Sizing handles appear around both Image controls.

5   Press [F4] to display the Properties window, double-click **BorderStyle** in the Properties list until the BorderStyle property says 1-Fixed Single, then click the **form** to remove the Properties window. A border appears around the two Image controls. Notice that the border makes the Image controls look like buttons.

Next, let's size the Image controls to make them larger.

Using the Stretch Property

The equal sign and the trash can would look much better if they were larger. As you learned in Tutorial 1, you size a control by dragging one of its sizing handles until the control is the desired size. Let's try that now.

To size the Image controls:

1   Click the **ImgCalc control** (the equal sign). Sizing handles appear around the Image control.

2   Place the mouse pointer on the center-right sizing handle until it becomes a double-ended arrow, then drag to the right until the control is approximately the width of the Exit button, and then release the mouse button.

Notice that the control gets larger, but the icon does not. If you want the icon to be sized with the control, you will need to set the control's Stretch property to True.

3   Press [F4] to display the Properties window, then double-click **Stretch** in the Properties list until the Stretch property says True, and then click the **form** to remove the Properties window. The icon stretches to fit the control.

Now let's change the Stretch property of the ImgClear control and then size that control.

4   Click the **ImgClear control** (the trash can), press **[F4]** to display the Properties window, double-click **Stretch** in the Properties list until the Stretch property says True, and then click the **form** to remove the Properties window.

5   Click the **ImgClear control** (the trash can), place the mouse pointer on the center-right sizing handle until it becomes a double-ended arrow, then drag to the right until the control is approximately the width of the other Image control, and then release the mouse button. This time the icon sizes along with the control.

Finally, let's save, run, and test the entire application again.

To save, run, and test the application:

1   Restore the form to its standard size, then **save and run** the application. The form appears without a border. (Your application should now match the completed application shown in Figure 3-1.)

2   On your own, enter a **length and a width for each of the four walls**, then click the **ImgCalc control** (the equal sign). Type **AB45 - Flowers** as the style code and press **[Enter]**, then type **35** as the roll coverage and press **[Enter]**. Visual Basic displays the required rolls of wallpaper and the style code in the LblMessage control.

3   Click the **Exit button** to end the application.

Before ending Lesson C, you will make the Dots & Stripes application into an executable file.

Making an Executable (.EXE) File

Now that the Dots & Stripes application is complete, you can have Visual Basic's compiler translate the application into machine code. Recall that the compiler saves the machine code in a file with an .EXE extension, which you can run directly from Windows.

To make the Dots & Stripes application into an executable file:

1   Click **File**, then click **Make EXE File....** The Make EXE File dialog box appears.

2   Type **t3c** in the File Name box, then click the **OK button**. Visual Basic's compiler translates your application into machine code, which it saves in the t3c.exe file on your Student Disk.

3   Exit Visual Basic. If a prompt appears asking if you want to save the project file, click the **Yes button**.

4   On your own, run the t3c.exe file directly from the Program Manager to verify that it works correctly.

The Dots & Stripes application is finally complete. You can either take a break or complete the end-of-lesson questions and exercises.

S U M M A R Y

To put a border around a control:

■ Set the control's BorderStyle property to 1-Fixed Single.

To size the picture in an Image control:

■ Set the Image control's Stretch property to True.

To improve the appearance of numbers in the user interface:

■ Use the Format function. Its syntax is Format(*expression,fmt*). *Fmt* is either the name of a predefined Visual Basic format or a string containing special symbols that tell Visual Basic how you want the *expression* displayed.

Q U E S T I O N S

1. The _____ property specifies the style of border placed around a control.
   a. Border
   b. BorderStyle
   c. ControlBorder
   d. Style
   e. StyleBorder

2. To size a picture in an Image control, set the Image control's _____ property to True.
   a. Image
   b. ImageSize
   c. Size
   d. SizeImage
   e. Stretch

3. To place a border around a Label control, set its BorderStyle property to _____ .
   a. 0 - None
   b. 1 - Fixed Single
   c. False
   d. True
   e. Yes

4. To remove the border from a form, set its BorderStyle property to _____ .
   a. 0 - None
   b. 1 - Fixed Single
   c. False
   d. True
   e. Yes

5. You can use the _____ function to improve the appearance of the numbers in the application.
   a. Appearance
   b. Fixed
   c. Format
   d. Number
   e. Picture

E X E R C I S E S

1. a. Open the T3LBE1 project that you created in Lesson B. Save the form and the project as T3LCE1.
   b. Use the Format function to format the Commission to Currency.
   c. Put a border around the following controls: LblSales, LblComm, ImgCalc, ImgClear.
   d. Size the Image controls and their icons to make them larger.
   e. Save, run, test, and print the application using the following data:

New York sales:	26000
Maine sales:	34000
Florida sales:	17000
Commission rate:	.1 (10%)

2. a. Open the T3LBE2 project that you created in Lesson B. Save the form and the project as T3LCE2.
   b. Use the Format function to format the new hourly rates to Currency.
   c. Put a border around the following controls: LblJc1, LblJc2, LblJc3, ImgCalc, ImgClear.
   d. Size the Image controls and their icons to make them larger.
   e. Save, run, test, and print the application using the following data:

Current hourly rate for job code 1:	5.00
Current hourly rate for job code 2:	6.25
Current hourly rate for job code 3:	7.75
Raise rate:	.06

3. a. Open the T3LBE3 project that you created in Lesson B. Save the form and the project as T3LCE3.
   b. Use the Format function to format the average to Fixed.
   c. Put a border around the LblMessage control.
   d. Save, run, test, and print the application using the following data:

Name:	Mary Kaye
Test 1 score:	75
Test 2 score:	87
Test 3 score:	99

4. a. Open the T3LBE4 project that you created in Lesson B. Save the form and the project as T3LCE4.
   b. Use the Format function to format the discount, sales tax, and total due to Standard.
   c. Put a border around the following controls: LblDisc, LblStax, LblTotal.
   d. Save, run, test, and print the application using the following data:

Price:	125
Discount rate:	.1 (10%)
Sales tax rate:	.05 (5%)

5. a. Open the T3LBE5 project that you created in Lesson B. Save the form and the project as T3LCE5.
 b. Put a border around the following controls: LblRed, LblBlue, LblMessage.
 c. Save, run, test, and print the application using the following data:

Price of red skateboards:	75
Price of blue skateboards:	65
Price increase:	.2

Exercises 6 through 8 are Discovery Exercises, which allow you to "discover" the solutions to problems on your own. Discovery Exercises might include topics that are not covered in the tutorial.

discovery ▶ 6. a. Open the iconwrks.mak project, which is in the samples\iconwrks directory of the Visual Basic main directory (located on your network or your local hard drive).
 b. Run the iconwrks.mak project. Maximize the IconWorks Editor window. Then use the Help screens to learn how to create your own icon.
 c. Create an icon of your own design.
 d. Save the icon as T3LCE6.ICO on your Student Disk. Then close the IconWorks Viewer and exit the IconWorks editor.
 e. Open a new Visual Basic project. (If you are asked if you want to save the changes to the ICONWRKS.MAK project, click No.)
 f. Add an Image control to the form. Load your icon into the Image control. Make the control and your icon larger.
 g. Print the form to show your icon. You do not need to save the form.

discovery ▶ 7. a. Open the iconwrks.mak project, which is in the samples\iconwrks directory of the Visual Basic main directory (located on your network or your local hard drive).
 b. Run the iconwrks.mak project. The IconWorks Editor window appears. Maximize the IconWorks Editor window.
 c. Click File, then click Open.... The IconWorks Viewer appears.
 d. Double-click the icons folder in the directories box. The directories containing the Visual Basic icon files appear.
 e. To view the icons in the computer directory, double-click the computer folder in the directories box, then click Options, and then click Show all Icons.
 f. Click any .ico file, or click any icon. The icon you select appears at the top of the IconWorks Viewer.
 g. Click Edit, then click Copy to copy the icon to the Windows Clipboard. Close the IconWorks Viewer. Visual Basic returns to the IconWorks Editor.
 h. Click Edit, then click Paste to paste the icon into the IconWorks Editor. You can now make any changes you want to the icon.
 i. Save the changed icon to T3LCE7.ICO on your Student Disk. Then close the IconWorks Viewer and exit the IconWorks Editor.
 j. Open a new Visual Basic project. (If you are asked if you want to save the changes to the ICONWORKS.MAK project, click No.)
 k. Add an Image control to the form. Load your icon into the Image control. Make the control and your icon larger.
 l. Print the form to show your icon. You do not need to save the form.

discovery ▶ 8. a. Open the t3c.mak project. Save the form and the project as T3LCE7.
 b. Change the form's BorderStyle property to 2-Sizable.
 c. Save and run the project. Enter 8 as wall 1's length, enter 8 as wall 1's width, then click the equal sign.
 d. Type AB45 - Flowers as the style code, then press [Enter].
 e. Don't enter anything in response to the wall coverage prompt. Instead, just press [Enter]. Visual Basic displays an error message box on the screen.

f. Click the OK button to remove the error message. Visual Basic highlights the problem instruction in the Code window.

g. Close the Code window. Restore the form to its standard size, then stop the application.

h. Use the Help screens to find information about the InputBox function. Specifically, look at what the function returns when the user clicks either the OK button or the Cancel button without entering information into the input area.

i. Fix the application so that it doesn't result in an error message if the user neglects to enter the roll coverage. Here are two hints:

    1) You can't use the Val function in this case because division by zero is not allowed.

    2) Read the Help screen on the If...Then...Else statement.

j. Save, run, and test the code using your own data.

k. Print the code.

D E B U G G I N G

Technique

One of the most common errors made in writing code is mistyping the name of a variable. When you don't keep a variable's name consistent throughout the code, you create a bug in the program. You can have Visual Basic help you find this type of bug by entering the Option Explicit statement in the general Declarations section of the form. Then if you use the name of a variable that has not been previously declared, Visual Basic will inform you of the error when you run the application.

You can have Visual Basic automatically enter the Option Explicit statement in the general Declarations section of all new forms by opening Visual Basic's Options menu, then clicking Environment..., and then setting the Require Variable Declaration option to Yes. Keep in mind that the Require Variable Declaration option affects only new forms, not forms that already contain controls or code.

To see how an application that does not contain the Option Explicit statement handles a bug created by mistyping a variable's name in the code:

1   Launch Visual Basic and open a new project (if necessary). Be sure you have a blank form on the screen.

2   Double-click the **form** to open its Code window, click the **down arrow in the Code window's Object box,** and then click **(general)** in the drop-down list. The general Declarations section of the form appears.

3   If the general Declarations section contains the *Option Explicit* statement, delete the statement from the Code window

4   Close the **Code window.**

5   Add a Command button and a Label control to the form. Position the Label control above the Command button. Double-click the **Command1 button** to open its Code window. The Click event procedure for the Command1 button appears.

6   Press [Tab], then type **dim Hourswkd as integer** and press [Enter]. This instruction declares a variable named Hourswkd.

Now you will purposely mistype a variable's name in the code.

7   Type **Hourwkd = 40** and press [Enter]. Notice that this is Hourwkd, not Hourswkd.

8   Type **Label1.Caption = Hourswkd** and press [Enter].

9   Close the **Code window, run** the application, then click the **Command1 button**. A zero, instead of 40, appears in the Label control. That's because the Hourwkd variable, not the Hourswkd variable, contains the number 40. Notice that Visual Basic did not catch the bug created by the mistyped variable name.

10   Click the **Stop icon** ▣ (or click **Run**, then click **End**) to end the application. Visual Basic returns to the design screen.

Now let's see what happens when you enter the *Option Explicit* statement in the general Declarations section of the form.

1   Double-click the **form** to open its Code window, then click the **down arrow in the Code window's Object box**, then click **(general)** in the drop-down list. The general Declarations section of the form appears.

2   Type **option explicit** and press [**Enter**], then close the Code window.

3   **Run** the application. Visual Basic displays the "Variable not defined" error message.

4   Click the **OK button** (or press [**Enter**]) to remove the error message. Notice that Visual Basic highlights the mistyped variable name, Hourwkd.

5   Change Hourwkd to **Hourswkd** in the Code window, then close the Code window.

6   **Run** the application, then click the **Command1 button**. This time the number 40 appears in the Label control.

7   Click the **Stop icon** ▣ to end the application. Visual Basic returns to the design screen. You do not need to save the corrected application.

Entering the *Option Explicit* statement in the form's general Declarations section will help you locate bugs caused by mistyping a variable's name.

Here's an application for you to debug on your own:

Exercises

a.   Launch Visual Basic (if necessary) and open the T3D1.MAK project, which is in either the tut3\ver2 or tut3\ver3 directory on your Student disk. Click the View Form button, then run the project. ,

b.   Click the Compute Average button, type **300** as the first number and press [**Enter**], then type **100** as the second number and press [**Enter**]. Notice that the application is not working correctly.

c.   Click the Exit button to end the application.

d.   Print the code.

e.   To help you find some of the errors in the code, enter the Option Explicit statement in the general Declarations section of the form.

f.   Run the application and correct the errors. (Note: The Option Explicit statement will not find all the errors. You will need to run the application more than once.)

g.   After all of the errors are corrected, test the application with the following data:

First number: 300
Second number: 100

The average should be 200.

h.   When the application is working correctly, print the code. You do not need to save the corrected application.

TUTORIAL 4

The Selection Structure

The Sweet-Tooth Application

case ▶ On Monday you meet with Susan Chen, the manager of the Sweet-Tooth Ice Cream Parlor. Susan asks you to create an application that her clerks can use to calculate the price of a sundae. Figure 4-1 shows the Sweet-Tooth menu, which you will use to plan the application.

```
┌─────────────────────────────────────────────┐
│            Sweet-Tooth Menu                   │
│                                               │
│   Scoop Price        Topping Price            │
│                                               │
│   Ice Cream   .95    One topping      Free    │
│                                               │
│   Yogurt      .85    Two toppings     .20     │
│                                               │
│                      Three Toppings   .25     │
│                                               │
│                 Additional Charges            │
│                                               │
│                 Nuts            .15           │
│                                               │
│                 Whipped Cream   .10           │
│                                               │
└─────────────────────────────────────────────┘
```

Figure 4-1: Sweet-Tooth menu

The Sweet-Tooth menu indicates that the price of a scoop of ice cream is $.95; the price of a scoop of yogurt is $.85. There is an additional charge for more than one topping, as well as for nuts and whipped cream.

Previewing the Completed Application

Let's begin by previewing the completed Sweet-Tooth application.

To preview the completed application:

1 Launch Windows and make sure the Program Manager window is open and your Student Disk is in the appropriate drive. If necessary, click the **Minimize on Use option** on the Options menu to minimize the Program Manager on use. Click **File** in the Program Manager's menu bar, then click **Run....** The Run dialog box appears.

The file you will run is called SWEET.EXE. You can use the Browse... button to find that file on your Student Disk, or you can simply type the filename in the Run dialog box, as shown in the next step.

2 *If you are using Visual Basic Version 2.0*, run the SWEET.EXE file in the **tut4\ver2** directory on your Student Disk. The Sweet-Tooth user interface appears on the screen. See Figure 4-2.

If you are using Visual Basic Version 3.0, run the SWEET.EXE file in the **tut4\ver3** directory on your Student Disk. The Sweet-Tooth user interface appears on the screen. See Figure 4-2.

The Sweet-Tooth application contains several new controls—Option buttons, Check boxes, and Frames. You will learn about these controls in Lesson B.

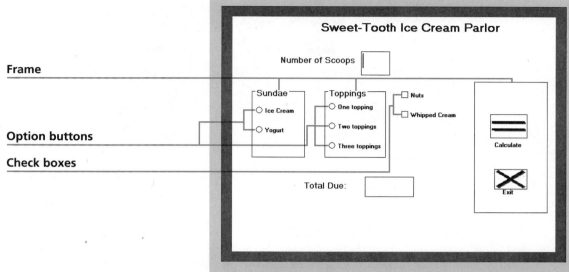

Frame

Option buttons

Check boxes

Figure 4-2: Sweet-Tooth user interface

3 Type **3** as the number of scoops, then click the **Ice Cream Option button**. A black dot appears in the center of the button to indicate that the Option button is on.

4 Click the **One topping Option button** to turn it on, then click the **=** (the equal sign). The application displays the total due ($2.85) for three scoops of ice cream with one topping.

5 Click the **Yogurt Option button** to turn it on. Notice that the Yogurt button turns on as the Ice Cream button turns off. When Option buttons are used in an application, only one Option button in each group can be on at any one time.

6 Click the **Two toppings Option button** to turn it on. The One topping Option button turns off as the Two toppings button turns on.

7 Click the **=** (the equal sign). The application displays the total due ($2.75) for three scoops of yogurt with two toppings.

Notice that the total due depends on which type of sundae you order (ice cream or yogurt) and the number of toppings. Now let's try the Check boxes.

To continue previewing the application:

1 Click the **Whipped Cream Check box** to turn it on. An X appears inside the Check box. The X indicates that the Check box is on.

2 Click the **Nuts Check box** to turn it on. An X appears inside the Nuts Check box. Clicking the Nuts Check box, however, does not turn off the Whipped Cream Check box. Unlike Option buttons, any number of Check boxes can be on at any one time.

tips

If the total due does not appear on the form, click the equal sign again. Be sure to click directly on the equal sign.

3 Click the **Whipped Cream Check box** to turn it off. The X disappears from the Check box. Now click the **=** (the equal sign). The application displays the total due ($2.90) for three scoops of yogurt with two toppings and nuts.

Notice that the total due also depends on whether the sundae includes nuts or whipped cream, or both.

4 Click the **Img Exit control** (the large X). The Sweet-Tooth application ends.

Before you can begin coding the Sweet-Tooth application, you will need to learn about the selection structure.

The Selection Structure

The applications you created in the previous three tutorials used the sequence programming structure only, where each of the program instructions was processed, one after another, in the order in which it appeared in the Code window. In many applications, however, the next instruction to be processed will depend on the result of a decision or a comparison that the program must make. For example, a payroll program might need to decide if an employee worked overtime. Assuming a 40-hour work week, the program can make that determination by comparing the number of hours the employee worked with the number 40. Based on the result of that comparison, the program will then select either an instruction that computes regular pay or an instruction that computes overtime pay.

You use the **selection structure**, also called the **decision structure**, when you want a program to make a decision or comparison and then, based on the result of that decision or comparison, to select one of two paths. (You can think of the selection structure as being a fork in the road.) The selection structure, you might recall, is one of three programming structures. The other two are sequence and repetition. (The sequence structure was covered in the previous tutorials. The repetition structure will be covered in Tutorials 5 and 6.) You will need to use the selection structure in Lesson C to complete the Sweet-Tooth application.

In Lesson A you will learn more about the selection structure. In Lesson B you will complete the Sweet-Tooth interface as you learn how to use three new controls. In Lesson C you will write the Visual Basic code for the Sweet-Tooth application.

LESSON A
objectives

In this lesson you will learn how to:

- Write pseudocode for the selection structure
- Draw a flowchart of the selection structure
- Use Visual Basic's If...Then...Else statement
- Use relational operators and logical operators
- Write a nested selection structure

The If...Then...Else Statement

Making Decisions

Each day you probably make hundreds of decisions, some so minor that you might not even realize you've made them. For example, every morning you have to decide if you are hungry and, if you are, what you are going to eat. Figure 4-3 shows other decisions you might have to make today.

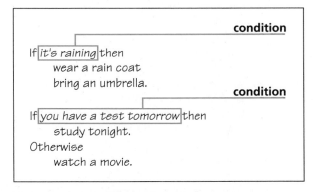

Figure 4-3: Decisions you might need to make today

In the examples shown in Figure 4-3, the portion in *italics*, called the **condition**, specifies the decision you are making and is phrased so that it results in either a true (yes) or a false (no) answer only. For example, either it's raining (true/yes) or it's not raining (false/no); either you have a test tomorrow (true/yes) or you don't have a test tomorrow (false/no).

If the condition is true, you perform a specific set of tasks. If the condition is false, however, you might or might not need to perform a different set of tasks. For instance, look at the first example shown in Figure 4-3. If it's raining (a true condition), then you will wear a raincoat and bring an umbrella. Notice, however, that you don't have anything in particular to do if it's not raining (a false condition). Compare this to the second example shown in Figure 4-3. If you have a test tomorrow (a true condition), then you will study tonight. If you don't have a test tomorrow (a false condition), however, then you will watch a movie.

Writing Pseudocode for the Selection Structure

Like you, the computer can also evaluate a condition and then select the appropriate tasks to perform based on that evaluation. The programmer must be sure to phrase the condition so that it results in either a true or a false answer only. The programmer must also specify the tasks to be performed when the condition is true and, if necessary, the tasks to be performed when the condition is false. Programmers refer to this as the selection structure (or the decision structure). Figure 4-4 shows two examples of the selection structure written in pseudocode.

<u>Selection with a true path only</u>	<u>Selection with both true and false paths</u>
If *Partnumber = "AB203"* Then	If *Sales > 1500* Then
Item = "Desk"	Commission = .02 * Sales
Price = 56.60	Else
End If	Commission = .01 * Sales
	End If

Figure 4-4: Two examples of the selection structure written in pseudocode

Although pseudocode is not standardized—every programmer has his or her own version—you will find some similarities among the various versions. For example, many programmers begin the selection structure with the word If and end the structure with the two words End If. The reason for the similarity in pseudocode is quite simple: The pseudocode written by many programmers greatly resembles the programming language they are using to code the program. Because many programming languages require the keywords "If" and "End If" in the selection structure code, those words generally appear in the programmer's pseudocode.

In the examples shown in Figure 4-4, the *italicized* portion of the instruction indicates the condition to be evaluated. Notice that each condition results in either a true or a false answer only. Either the Partnumber variable contains the string "AB203" or it doesn't contain the string "AB203." Either the sales variable contains a number that is greater than the number 1500, or it doesn't contain a number that is greater than 1500.

When the condition is true, the set of instructions following the word "Then" is selected for processing. The instructions following "Then" are referred to as the true path—the path you follow when the condition is true. The true path ends when you come to the "Else" or, if there is no "Else," when you come to the end of the selection structure (the "End If"). After the true path instructions are processed, the instruction following the "End If" is processed.

The instructions selected for processing when the condition is false—the false path—depend on whether the If instruction contains an "Else." When there is no "Else" in the If instruction, as in the first example shown in Figure 4-4, the instruction following the "End If" is processed when the condition is false. When there is an "Else" in the If instruction, as in the second example shown in Figure 4-4, the set of instructions between the "Else" and the "End If" are processed first and then the instruction after the "End If" is processed. Now let's look at a flowchart of the selection structure.

The Selection Structure in a Flowchart

Unlike pseudocode, a flowchart uses standardized symbols to represent the steps needed to solve a problem. The flowchart symbol for the selection structure is a diamond. Figure 4-5 shows the flowcharts for the selection structures in Figure 4-4.

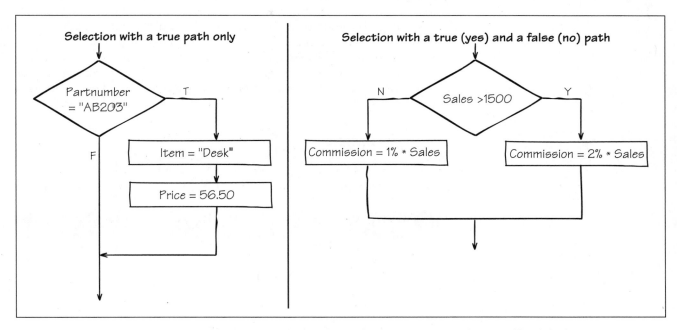

Figure 4-5: Two examples of the selection structure drawn in flowchart form

Inside each diamond is a question that has a true (yes) or false (no) answer only. Each diamond also has one flowline entering the symbol and two flowlines leaving the symbol. The two flowlines leading out of the diamond should be marked so that anyone reading the flowchart can distinguish the true path from the false path. You can mark the flowlines either with a "T" and an "F" (for true and false) or a "Y" and an "N" (for yes and no).

Now let's look at how you code the selection structure in Visual Basic.

Coding the Selection Structure in Visual Basic

You use the If...Then...Else statement to code the selection structure in Visual Basic. The format of the If...Then...Else instruction is shown in Figure 4-6.

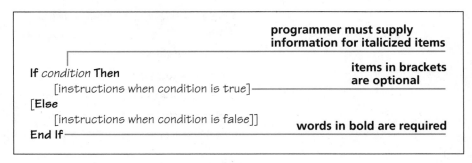

Figure 4-6: Format of Visual Basic's If...Then...Else statement

In the format, the items in square brackets ([ ]) are optional. For example, the Else portion of the format, referred to as the Else clause, is optional; you don't need to include an Else clause in an If...Then...Else instruction. Words in **bold**, however, are essential components of the If...Then...Else statement. The words If, Then, and End If, for instance, must be included in the instruction. (The word Else must be included only if the instruction uses the Else clause.) Items in *italics* indicate where the programmer must supply information pertaining to the current application. For instance, the programmer must supply the condition to be evaluated. The condition can contain variables, constants, properties, functions, mathematical operators, relational operators, and logical operators. You already know about variables, constants, properties, functions, and the mathematical operators. You will learn about the relational operators and the logical operators in the next two sections. We'll begin with the relational operators.

Relational Operators

Figure 4-7 lists the relational operators you can use in the If...Then...Else statement's condition.

Relational Operator	Meaning
=	Equal to
>	Greater than
>=	Greater than or equal to
<	Less than
<=	Less than or equal to
<>	Not equal to

Figure 4-7: Relational operators

Unlike the mathematical operators, the relational operators do not have an order of precedence. If an expression contains more than one relational operator, Visual Basic evaluates the relational operators from left to right in the expression. Keep in mind, however, that relational operators are evaluated after any mathematical operators in the expression. In other words, in the expression $5 - 2 > 1 + 2$, the two mathematical operators ($-$, $+$) will be evaluated before the relational operator ($>$). The result of the expression is false, as shown in Figure 4-8.

Original expression:	$5 - 2 > 1 + 2$
Evaluation Steps	**Result**
5 – 2 is evaluated first	3 > 1 + 2
1 + 2 is evaluated second	3 > 3
3 > 3 is evaluated last	False

Figure 4-8: Evaluation steps for an expression containing mathematical and relational operators

All expressions containing a relational operator will result in either a true or a false answer only. Let's try a few examples of the If...Then...Else statement using relational operators in the condition. On your Student Disk is a partially completed project, named T4A_IF.MAK, which you will use to practice various If...Then...Else instructions.

To open the T4A_IF.MAK project:

1　Launch Visual Basic, if necessary, and open the **t4a_if.mak** project, which is in either the tut4\ver2 directory or the tut4\ver3 directory on your Student Disk.

2　Click the **View Form button** in the Project window, then **save** the form and the project as **t4a_if2**.

3　Maximize the form. The T4A_IF project appears on the screen, as shown in Figure 4-9.

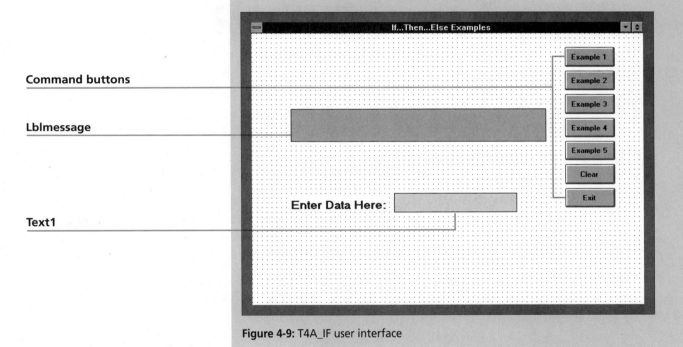

Command buttons

Lblmessage

Text1

Figure 4-9: T4A_IF user interface

Some of the Command buttons have been coded for you. For example, the Exit button contains the End instruction. The Clear button contains the following three instructions: *LblMessage.Caption = " "*, *Text1.Text = " "*, and *Text1.SetFocus*. These instructions clear the contents of the Label control and the Text box, then place the focus in the Text box. You will now code the Click event procedure for the Example 1 Command button.

Example 1

Assume you are creating a checkbook application. You will enter the amount of a transaction (a number) in the Text box on the screen. If the number entered in the Text box is less than 0 (zero), you want to display the string "Withdrawal" in the Label control. Figure 4-10 shows both the flowchart and the Visual Basic instructions to accomplish this.

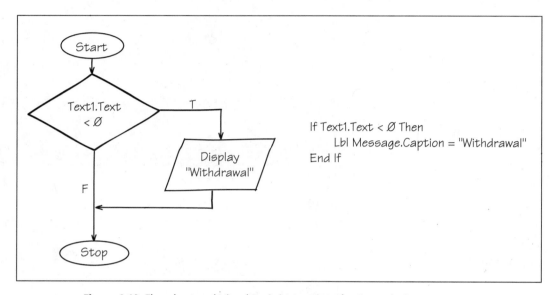

Figure 4-10: Flowchart and Visual Basic instructions for Example 1

The *Text1.Text < 0* condition tells Visual Basic to compare the contents of the Text1 control's Text property with the number 0. If the condition is true, which means the number entered is less than 0, then the string "Withdrawal" (without the quotes) will appear in the Label control. If the condition is false, which means the number entered is not less than 0 (in other words, it's greater than or equal to 0), nothing will appear in the Label control. Let's code the Click event procedure for the Example 1 button.

To code the Example 1 button:

1 Double-click the **Example 1 button** to open its Code window. The Click event procedure appears.

2 Press [**Tab**], then type **if Text1.Text < 0 then** and press [**Enter**]. (Be sure to type the number 0, and not the letter O.)

Now enter the true path instructions. Programmers usually indent these instructions for easier readability.

3 Press [**Tab**], then type **LblMessage.Caption = "Withdrawal"** and press [**Enter**].

Example 2   VB 191

4   Press [**Backspace**] to cancel the indentation, then type **end if** and press [**Enter**]. Compare your instructions with Figure 4-11.

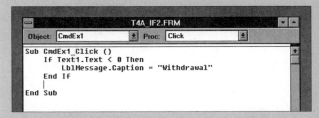

Figure 4-11: Code window for Example 1

5   Close the **Code window**. Restore the form to its standard size, then **save and run** the application.

6   Type **-25** (be sure to type the leading hyphen) in the Text box, then click the **Example 1 button** to process the instructions in the Click event procedure. The string "Withdrawal" (without the quotes) appears in the Label control, then the Click event procedure ends. In this case, because the number entered in the Text box is less than zero, Visual Basic processes the true path instruction before processing the instruction following the End If (the End Sub instruction).

7   Click the **Clear button** to clear the contents of the Text box and the Label control.

8   Type **500** in the Text box, then click the **Example 1 button**. This time nothing appears in the Label control. Notice that when the number in the Text box is not less than zero—a false condition—the instruction in the true path is not processed. Instead, Visual Basic processes the instruction following the End If (the End Sub instruction).

9   Click the **Exit button**. Visual Basic returns to the design screen.

Let's try another example.

Example 2

This time you will display the string "Withdrawal" when the number entered in the Text box is less than 0 (zero) and the string "Deposit" when the number is greater than or equal to 0. Figure 4-12 shows both the flowchart and the pseudocode to accomplish this.

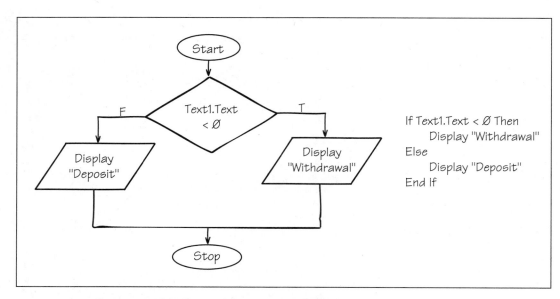

Figure 4-12: Flowchart and pseudocode for Example 2

To save you time, the Visual Basic instructions have already been entered in Example 2's Click event procedure. Let's open Example 2's Code window to view the instructions.

To view the instructions in Example 2's Click event procedure:

1   Maximize the form, then double-click the **Example 2 button** to open its Code window. The Click event procedure appears as shown in Figure 4-13.

enter on a separate line ─────────────

```
                          T4A_IF2.FRM
Object:  CmdEx2          Proc:  Click

Sub CmdEx2_Click ()
    If Text1.Text < 0 Then
        LblMessage.Caption = "Withdrawal"
    Else
        LblMessage.Caption = "Deposit"
    End If

End Sub
```

Figure 4-13: Code window for Example 2

Notice that the Else must be entered on its own line.

2   Close the **Code window**. Restore the form to its standard size, then **save and run** the application.

Example 2   VB 193

If "Deposit" (without the quotes) does not appear in the Label control, you might have clicked the wrong button. Click the Example 2 button again.

3   Type -15 (be sure to type the leading hyphen) in the Text box, then click the **Example 2 button**. "Withdrawal" appears in the Label control, then the Click event procedure ends.

4   Click the **Clear button**, type 5 in the Text box, then click the **Example 2 button**. This time, "Deposit" appears in the Label control, then the Click event procedure ends.

5   Click the **Exit button**. Visual Basic returns to the design screen.

Recall that you can also use logical operators to form the If...Then...Else condition. Visual Basic has six logical operators—the most commonly used ones are Not, And, and Or. (If you want to see information about the other logical operators, use the Help menu to search for a Help screen on logical operators.) Let's discuss the Not, And, and Or logical operators next.

Logical Operators

You can use the logical operators to combine several conditions into one compound condition. Figure 4-14 shows the three most commonly used logical operators, their meaning, and their order of precedence.

Logical Operator	Meaning	Precedence
Not	Reverses the value of the condition; True becomes False, False becomes True	1
And	All conditions connected by the And operator must be true for the compound condition to be true	2
Or	Only one of the conditions connected by the Or operator needs to be true for the compound condition to be true	3

Figure 4-14: Logical operators

The **truth tables** in Figure 4-15 summarize how Visual Basic evaluates the logical operators in an expression.

As Figure 4-15 indicates, the Not operator reverses the truth value of the condition (referred to as A). If A (the condition) is true, then Not A is evaluated as false. Likewise, if A is false, then Not A is true. As you can see, the Not operator can be confusing; it's best to avoid using it if possible. (In Tutorial 6, which covers sequential files, you will see a useful purpose for the Not operator. For now you don't need to worry about the Not operator; just be aware that it exists.)

Truth Table for NOT	
Value of A	Value of NOT A
T	F
F	T

Truth Table for AND		
Value of A	Value of B	Value of A AND B
T	T	T
T	F	F
F	T	F
F	F	F

Truth Table for OR		
Value of A	Value of B	Value of A OR B
T	T	T
T	F	T
F	T	T
F	F	F

Figure 4-15: Truth tables for the logical operators

Now look at the truth tables for the And and Or operators. Notice that when you use the And operator to combine two conditions (A And B), the resulting compound condition is true only when both conditions are true. If either condition is false or if both conditions are false, then the compound condition is false. Compare that to the Or operator. When you combine conditions using the Or operator (A Or B), notice that the compound condition is false only when both conditions are false. If either condition is true or if both conditions are true, then the compound condition is true. Two examples might help to clarify the difference between the And and the Or operators.

Examples of the And and the Or Operators Let's say that you want to pay a bonus to the salespeople in Virginia whose sales total more than $10,000. To receive a bonus, the salesperson must live in the state of Virginia and he or she must sell more than $10,000. Assuming the application uses the two variables, State and Sales, you can phrase condition A as *State = "Virginia"* and condition B as *Sales > 10000*. Now the question is "Should you use the And operator or the Or operator to combine both conditions into one compound condition?" To answer this question, you will need to look at the truth tables for the And and the Or operators.

Example 2   VB 195

To receive a bonus, remember that both condition A (*State = "Virginia"*) and condition B (*Sales > 10000*) must be true at the same time. If either condition is false, or if both conditions are false, then the compound condition should be false, and the salesperson should not receive a bonus. According to the truth tables, both the And and the Or operators will evaluate the compound condition as true when both conditions are true. Only the And operator, however, will evaluate the compound condition as false when either one or both of the conditions is false. (Notice that the only time the Or operator evaluates the compound condition as false is when both conditions are false.) Therefore, the correct compound condition to use here is *State = "Virginia" And Sales > 10000*.

Now let's say that you want to send a letter to all customers living in Virginia and all customers living in Texas. Assuming the application uses the variable State, you can phrase condition A as *State = "Virginia"* and condition B as *State = "Texas"*. Now which operator do you use—And or Or? (Here's a hint: Recall from Tutorial 3 that a variable can store only one item of data at a time.)

At first it might appear that the And operator is the correct one to use. That's probably because the example says to send the letter to "all customers living in Virginia **and** all customers living in Texas." In our everyday conversations, you'll find that we sometimes use the word "and" when what we really mean is "or." Although both words do not mean the same thing, using "and" instead of "or" generally doesn't cause a problem because we are able to infer what another person means. Computers, however, cannot infer anything; they simply process the directions you give them, word for word. In this case, you actually want to send a letter to all customers living either in Virginia or in Texas, so you will need to use the Or operator. The Or operator is the only operator that will evaluate the compound condition as true if either one of the conditions is true. The correct compound condition to use here is *State = "Virginia" Or State = "Texas"*.

Like expressions containing relational operators, expressions containing logical operators always result in either a true or a false answer. The logical operators have an order of precedence as follows: The Not operator is evaluated first, then the And operator, and then the Or operator. Logical operators are evaluated after any mathematical operators or relational operators in the expression. In other words, in the expression, 12 > 0 And 12 < 10 * 2, the mathematical operator (*) will be evaluated first, followed by the two relational operators (>, <), followed by the logical operator (And). The expression evaluates to true, as shown in Figure 4-16.

Original expression: **12 > 0 And 12 < 10 * 2**

Evaluation Steps	Result
10 * 2 is evaluated first	12 > 0 And 12 < 20
12 > 0 is evaluated second	True And 12 < 20
12 < 20 is evaluated third	True And True
True And True is evaluated last	True

Figure 4-16: Evaluation steps for an expression containing mathematical, relational, and logical operators

Let's practice using the logical operators in an If...Then...Else statement.

Example 3

Assume you want the Example 3 button to display the string "In-range" when the number entered in the Text box is greater than or equal to 1500, but less than 3000. If the number does not fall in that range, then you want to display the string "Out-of-range". Figure 4-17 shows both the pseudocode and the flowchart to accomplish this.

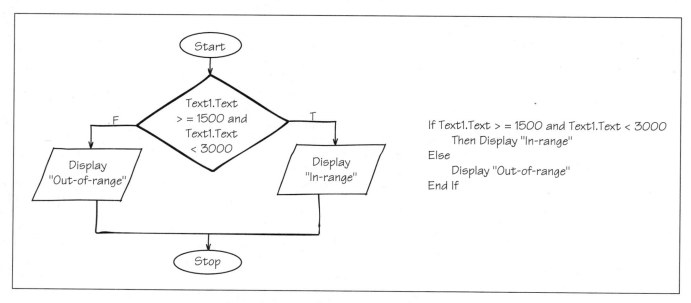

Figure 4-17: Flowchart and pseudocode for Example 3

The necessary Visual Basic instructions have already been entered into the Example 3 button's Code window. Let's look at those instructions and then run the application to test the Example 3 button.

To view Example 3's code, then run the application:

1   Maximize the form, then double-click the **Example 3 button** to open its Code window. The Click event procedure appears as shown in Figure 4-18.

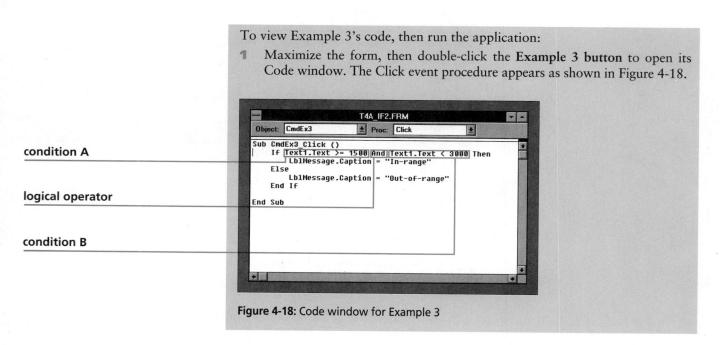

Figure 4-18: Code window for Example 3

Example 3   VB 197

2   Close the **Code window**. Restore the form to its standard size, then **save and run** the application.

3   Type **2500** in the Text box, then click the **Example 3 button**. The string "In-range" (without the quotes) appears in the Label control because the number 2500 satisfies both of the conditions listed in the compound condition—it is greater than or equal to 1500 and it is less than 3000.

4   Click the **Clear button**, type **6500** in the Text box, then click the **Example 3 button**. The string "Out-of-range" (without the quotes) appears in the Label control because the number 6500 does not satisfy both of the conditions listed in the compound condition. Although 6500 is greater than or equal to 1500, it is not less than 3000.

5   Click the **Exit button**. Visual Basic returns to the design screen.

Now let's modify Example 3's code to see what happens when you use the Or operator, instead of the And operator, in the If...Then...Else statement.

To modify the instruction in Example 3's Code window, then run the application:

1   Maximize the form, then double-click the **Example 3 button** to open its Code window. In the Click event procedure, change the And in the If instruction to an Or. The If instruction should now say *If Text1.Text >= 1500 Or Text1.Text < 3000 Then*.

2   Close the **Code window**. Restore the form to its standard size, then **save and run** the application.

3   Type **2500** in the Text box, then click the **Example 3 button**. The string "In-range" appears in the Label control because the number 2500 satisfies both conditions listed in the compound condition.

4   Click the **Clear button**, type **6500** in the Text box, then click the **Example 3 button**. The string "In-range" appears in the Label control because the number 6500 satisfies one of the conditions listed in the compound condition—specifically, the number 6500 is greater than or equal to the number 1500. Remember, when you use the Or operator, only one of the conditions needs to be true for the compound condition to be true.

5   Click the **Clear button**, type **3** in the Text box, then click the **Example 3 button**. The string "In-range" appears in the Label control because the number 3 satisfies one of the conditions listed in the compound condition—specifically, the number 3 is less than the number 3000.

6   Click the **Exit button**. Visual Basic returns to the design screen.

By changing the And to an Or, the condition *Text1.Text >= 1500 Or Text1.Text < 3000*, will always evaluate as true; it will never evaluate as false.

7   Maximize the form, then double-click the **Example 3 button** to open its Code window, then change the Or back to an And in the If statement.

8   Close the Code window.

Now let's see how to include a string comparison in an If...Then...Else statement.

Example 4

Assume you want the Example 4 button to display the word "Pass" if the Text box contains the letter P and the word "Fail" if the Text box contains anything else. The Visual Basic instructions that would accomplish this have already been entered in the Code window of Example 4's Click event procedure, as shown in Figure 4-19. (You can open the Code window and verify that, if you want.)

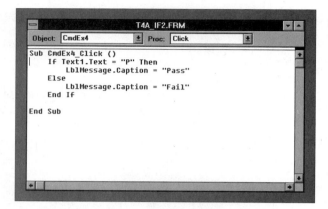

```
                        T4A_IF2.FRM
Object: CmdEx4          ±   Proc: Click              ±
Sub CmdEx4_Click ()
    If Text1.Text = "P" Then
        LblMessage.Caption = "Pass"
    Else
        LblMessage.Caption = "Fail"
    End If

End Sub
```

Figure 4-19: Code window for Example 4

Let's run the application and then test Example 4's Click event procedure.

tips

If, after pressing [F5], you are asked if you want to save the changes, click the No button.

To run the application and test the Example 4 button:

1   Press [F5] to run the application, type **P** (be sure to use an uppercase letter P) in the Text box, then click the **Example 4 button**. The string "Pass" appears in the Label control.

Now let's enter a letter other than the letter P.

2   Click the **Clear button**, type **K** (in uppercase) in the Text box, then click the **Example 4 button**. The string "Fail" appears in the Label control.

Now let's enter a lowercase letter p.

3   Click the **Clear button**, type **p** (be sure to type a lowercase letter p) in the Text box, then click the **Example 4 button**.

Although you were probably expecting the word "Pass" to appear, the word "Fail" appears instead. Let's stop the application and discuss why this happened.

4   Click the **Exit button**. Visual Basic returns to the design screen.

The UCase Function

As is true in many programming languages, string comparisons in Visual Basic are case sensitive. That means that the uppercase version of a letter is not the same as its lowercase counterpart. So, although a human recognizes "P" and "p" as being the same letter, a computer does not; to a computer, a "P" is different from a "p". As you saw in Example 4, a problem occurs when you need to include a string, entered by the user, in a comparison. The problem occurs because you can't control the case in which the user enters the string.

One way of handling the string comparison problem is to include the UCase (uppercase) function in your string comparisons. The format of the UCase function is UCase(*string expression*). The function temporarily converts the *string expression* to uppercase letters. (The UCase function does not actually change the *string expression* to uppercase; the function just treats the *string expression* as though it contained uppercase letters.) Figure 4-20 shows some examples of the UCase function.

If UCase(Text1.Text) = "YES" Then	Compares the uppercase version of the string entered in the Text box to the string "YES"
If UCase(Text1.Text) > UCase(Item)	Compares the uppercase version of the string entered in the Text box with the uppercase version of the string contained in the Item variable
If "RENO" = UCase(LblCity.Caption)	Compares the string "RENO" to the uppercase version of the string contained in the Label control
TxtName.Text = UCase(Empname)	Assigns the uppercase version of the string contained in the Empname variable to the Text property of the Text box

Figure 4-20: Examples of UCase function

In Example 4, you will need to change the condition in the If statement from *Text1.Text = "P"* to *UCase(Text1.Text) = "P"*. Then when Visual Basic processes the If statement, the UCase function will temporarily convert, to uppercase, the string entered in the Text box. Visual Basic will then compare the uppercase version of the string to the uppercase letter "P." If both are equal, Visual Basic will process the true path instructions; otherwise, it will process the false path instructions.

When using the UCase function, be sure that everything you are comparing is in uppercase. In other words, *UCase(Text1.Text) = "p"* is incorrect because it tells Visual Basic to compare the uppercase version of a string with the lowercase letter p; this condition would always evaluate as false. (Visual Basic also has an LCase function that temporarily converts a string expression to lowercase. The correct condition using the LCase function would be *LCase(Text1.Text) = "p"*.)

Let's modify Example 4 to include the UCase function.

To modify the If instruction in Example 4's Click event procedure:

1 Maximize the form, then double-click the **Example 4 button** to open its Code window. Enter the UCase function as shown in Figure 4-21.

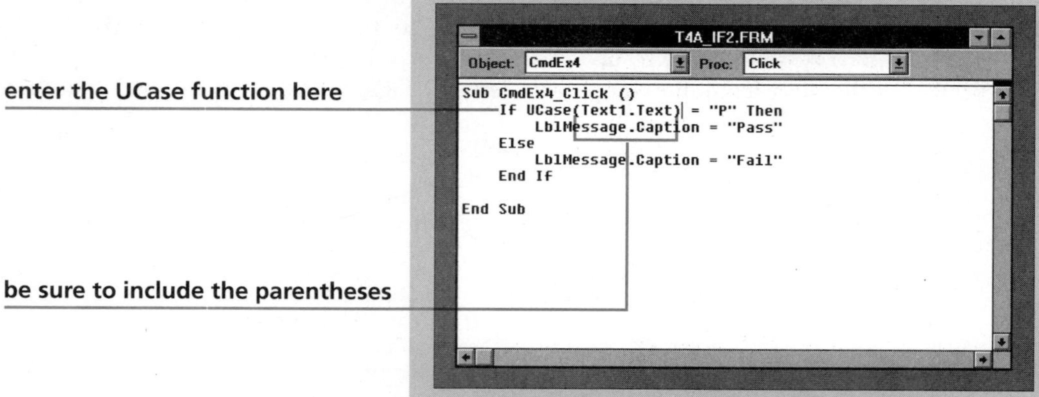

enter the UCase function here ──────

be sure to include the parentheses ──────

```
─                          T4A_IF2.FRM                      ▼ ▲
Object: CmdEx4              ±   Proc:  Click              ±
Sub CmdEx4_Click ()                                           ▲
    If UCase(Text1.Text)| = "P" Then
        LblMessage.Caption = "Pass"
    Else
        LblMessage.Caption = "Fail"
    End If

End Sub

                                                              ▼
  ◀                                                        ▶
```

Figure 4-21: UCase function in Example 4's Code window

2 Close the **Code window**. Restore the form to its standard size, then **save and run** the application.

3 Type **p** in the Text box, then click the **Example 4 button**. This time "Pass" appears in the Label control.

4 Click the **Exit button**. Visual Basic returns to the design screen.

You can also nest If...Then...Else statements, which means you can place one If...Then...Else statement inside another If...Then...Else statement. You will learn how to do that in the next section.

Nested If...Then...Else Statements

A nested If...Then...Else statement is one in which either the Then clause or the Else clause includes yet another If...Then...Else statement. Figures 4-22 and Figure 4-23 show examples of writing a nested selection structure both in pseudocode and in a flowchart. Figure 4-22 shows the nested If on the Then clause; Figure 4-23 shows the nested If on the Else clause. (The lines connecting the If, Else, and End If in the pseudocode are not necessary. They are included in the figures to help you see which clauses match up with each other.)

Figure 4-24 shows two ways of writing the format of the nested selection structure in Visual Basic—with the nested If on the Then clause and with the nested If on the Else clause.

Notice that each If...Then...Else statement is matched with an "End If." The "End If" marks the end of that If...Then...Else statement. Let's look at a nested If...Then...Else statement in a Code window.

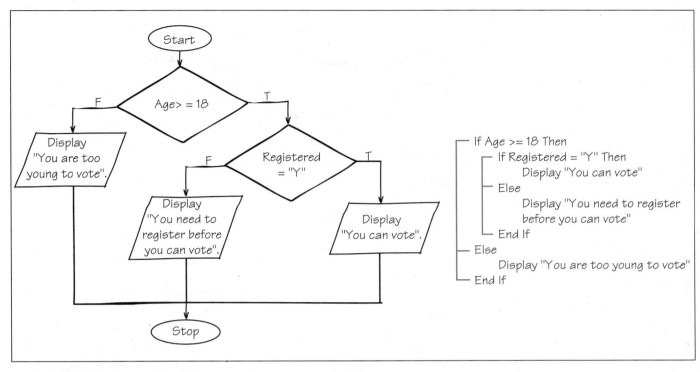

Figure 4-22: Pseudocode and flowchart showing the nested If on the Then clause

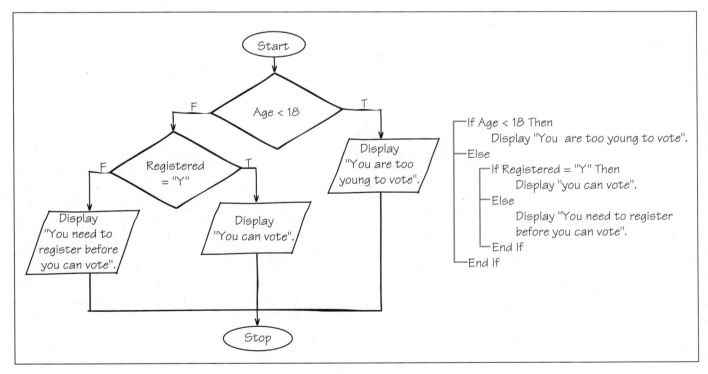

Figure 4-23: Pseudocode and flowchart showing the nested If on the Else clause

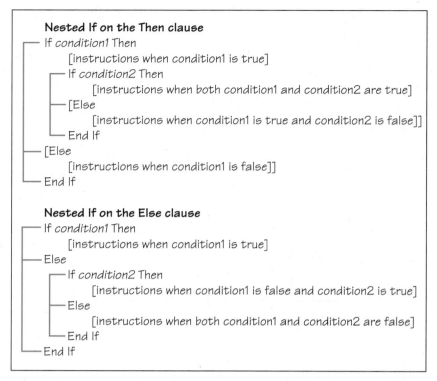

Nested If on the Then clause
```
If condition1 Then
      [instructions when condition1 is true]
      If condition2 Then
            [instructions when both condition1 and condition2 are true]
      [Else
            [instructions when condition1 is true and condition2 is false]]
      End If
[Else
      [instructions when condition1 is false]]
End If
```

Nested If on the Else clause
```
If condition1 Then
      [instructions when condition1 is true]
Else
      If condition2 Then
            [instructions when condition1 is false and condition2 is true]
      Else
            [instructions when both condition1 and condition2 are false]
      End If
End If
```

Figure 4-24: Formats of Visual Basic's nested selection structure

Example 5

The Example 5 button's Click event procedure contains a nested selection structure with the nested If on the Else clause.

To open Example 5's Code window:

1   Maximize the form, double-click the **Example 5 button** to open its Code window, then maximize the Code window. The Click event procedure appears, as shown in Figure 4-25.

The nested selection structure first compares the contents of the Text box to the number 18. If the number entered in the Text box is less than 18, then Visual Basic processes the instruction in the true path (the *LblMessage.Caption = "You are too young to vote."* instruction); otherwise, it processes the instructions in the false path. Notice that the false path contains an assignment statement that uses the InputBox function to ask the user if he or she is registered to vote, and then stores the response in the Registered variable. The false path also contains another If...Then...Else statement. This If...Then...Else statement compares the uppercase version of the user's response, stored in the Registered variable, to the letter "Y." If the Registered

Example 5   **VB 203**

variable contains either "Y" or "y," then Visual Basic processes the instruction in the nested If statement's true path (the *LblMessage.Caption = "You can vote."* instruction); otherwise, it processes the instruction in the false path (the *LblMessage.Caption = "You need to register before you can vote."* instruction). Now let's test the Example 5 button.

```
                              T4A_IF.FRM
Object: CmdEx5              ↕   Proc: Click              ↕

Sub CmdEx5_Click ()
    'Declare variables
    Dim Registered As String

    'Verify age and registration
    If Text1.Text < 18 Then
        LblMessage.Caption = "You are too young to vote."
    Else
        Registered = InputBox("Are you registered to vote?")
        If UCase(Registered) = "Y" Then
            LblMessage.Caption = "You can vote."
        Else
            LblMessage.Caption = "You need to register before you can vote."
        End If
    End If

End Sub
```

Figure 4-25: Code window for Example 5 showing nested If on the Else clause

tips

If you are asked if you want to save the changes, click the No button.

2   Close the Code window and press [F5] to run the application.

First enter the number 17 in the Text box. A person who is 17 years old is too young to vote.

3   Type **17** in the Text box, then click the **Example 5 button**. The "You are too young to vote." message appears in the Label control.

Now let's try the number 21. A person who is 21 years old can vote, but only if he or she is registered.

4   Click the **Clear button**, type **21** in the Text box, then click the **Example 5 button**. The InputBox function displays a dialog box containing the "Are you registered to vote?" prompt.

5   Type **y** and press [**Enter**] (or click the **OK button**). The "You can vote." message appears in the Label control.

Now let's try the number 21 again, but this time you'll answer "n" to the "Are you registered to vote?" prompt.

6   Click the **Clear button**, type **21** in the Text box, then click the **Example 5 button**. Type **n** in answer to the "Are you registered to vote?" prompt and press [**Enter**]. The "You need to register before you can vote." message appears in the Label control.

7   Click the **Exit button** to end the application. Visual Basic returns to the design screen.

8   Restore the form to its standard size. You can then exit Visual Basic. Or, you can open a new or an existing project. You do not need to save the current project.

In Tutorial 5 you will learn another form of the selection structure, called Case. When a selection structure has several paths from which to choose, it is most times simpler and clearer to use the Case format of the selection structure instead of the nested If format.

You have now completed Lesson A. You can either take a break or complete the exercises and questions at the end of the lesson.

S U M M A R Y

To evaluate an expression containing mathematical, relational, and logical operators:

■   Evaluate the mathematical operators first, then evaluate the relational operators, and then evaluate the logical operators.

To code a selection structure:

■   Use the If...Then...Else statement. The format is:

> If *condition* Then
>   [instructions when condition is true]
> [Else
>   [instructions when condition is false]]
> End If

To code a nested selection structure:

■   Use the nested If...Then...Else statement. Both formats are shown in Figure 4-24.

To temporarily convert a string expression to uppercase:

■   Use the UCase function. The format is UCase(*string expression*).

To temporarily convert a string expression to lowercase:

■   Use the LCase function. The format is LCase(*string expression*).

Q U E S T I O N S

1. Which of the following is a valid condition for an If...Then...Else statement? (Choose three.)
   a. TxtAge.Text > 65
   b. LblPrice.Caption <= 10
   c. Sales > 500 And < 800
   d. Cost > 100 And Cost <= 1000
   e. UCase(State) = "Alaska" and UCase(State) = "Hawaii"

2. You can use the _____ function to temporarily convert a string to uppercase.
   a. Caseupper
   b. CaseU
   c. LCase
   d. UCase
   e. Upper

3. Assume you want to compare the string contained in the Text property of the TxtName control with the name Bob. Which of the following conditions should you use in the If...Then...Else statement? (Be sure the condition will handle Bob, BOB, bob, and so on.)
   a. TxtName.Text = "BOB"
   b. TxtName.Text = UCase("BOB")
   c. TxtName.Text = UCase("Bob")
   d. UCase(TxtName.Text) = "Bob"
   e. UCase(TxtName.Text) = "BOB"

4. Which of the following will change the contents of the TxtName Text box to uppercase?
   a. TxtName.Text = UCase(TxtName.Text)
   b. TxtName.Text = TXTNAME.TEXT
   c. TxtName.Text = "TXTNAME.TEXT"
   d. UCase(TxtName.Text) = TxtName.Text
   e. Upper(TxtName.Text) = "TxtName.Text"

5. The three logical operators are listed below. Indicate their order of precedence by placing a number (1, 2, or 3) on the line to the left of the operator.

   _____ And   _____ Not   _____ Or

6. An expression can contain mathematical, relational, and logical operators. Indicate the order of precedence for the three types of operators by placing a number (1, 2, or 3) on the line to the left.

   _____ Mathematical   _____ Logical   _____ Relational

7. Evaluate the following expression: 3 > 6 And 7 > 4
   a. True   b. False

8. Evaluate the following expression: 4 > 6 Or 10 < 2 * 6
   a. True   b. False

9. Evaluate the following expression: 7 >= 3 + 4 Or 6 < 4 And 2 < 5
   a. True   b. False

Use the following information to answer questions 10–16:

    X=5, Y=3, Z = 2, A=True, B=False.

10. Evaluate the following expression: X – Y = Z
    a. True   b. False

11. Evaluate the following expression: $X * Z > X * Y$ And A
    a. True   b. False

12. Evaluate the following expression: $X * Z < X * Y$ Or A
    a. True   b. False

13. Evaluate the following expression: A And B
    a. True   b. False

14. Evaluate the following expression: A Or B
    a. True   b. False

15. Evaluate the following expression: $X * Y > Y \wedge Z$
    a. True   b. False

16. Evaluate the following expression: $X * Y > Y \wedge Z$ And A Or B
    a. True   b. False

Use the following selection structure to answer questions 17–19.

```
If Number1 <= 100 Then
    Number1 = Number1 * 2
Else
    If Number1 > 500 Then
        Number1 = Number1 * 3
    End If
End If
```

17. Assume the Number1 variable contains the number 90. What value will be in the Number1 variable after the above selection structure is processed?
    a. 0
    b. 90
    c. 180
    d. 270
    e. null

18. Assume the Number1 variable contains the number 1000. What value will be in the Number1 variable after the above selection structure is processed?
    a. 0
    b. 1000
    c. 2000
    d. 3000
    e. null

19. Assume the Number1 variable contains the number 200. What value will be in the Number1 variable after the above selection structure is processed?
    a. 0
    b. 200
    c. 400
    d. 600
    e. null

E X E R C I S E S

1. Draw the flowchart that corresponds to the following Visual Basic code.

    ```
    If Hours > 40 Then
        LblMsg.Caption = "Overtime"
    Else
        LblMsg.Caption = "Regular"
    End If
    ```

2. Display the string "Pontiac" in a Label control named LblType if the Text property of the TxtCar control contains the string "Grand Am" (in any case).
    a. Draw the flowchart, write the pseudocode, and then write the Visual Basic code.

3. Display the string "Entry error" in the LblMsg control if the Units variable contains a number that is less than 0; otherwise, display the string "Valid Number". (Do not include the period.)
    a. Draw the flowchart, write the pseudocode, and then write the Visual Basic code.

4. Display the string "Reorder" in the LblMsg control if the Price variable contains a number that is less than 10; otherwise, display the string "OK". (Do not include the period.)
    a. Draw the flowchart, write the pseudocode, then write the Visual Basic code.

5. Assign the number 10 to the Bonus variable if the Sales variable contains a number that is less than or equal to $250; otherwise, assign the number 15.
    a. Draw the flowchart, then write the Visual Basic code.

6. Display the number 25 in the LblShipping control if the State variable contains the string "Hawaii" (in any case); otherwise, display the number 50.
    a. Draw the flowchart, then write the Visual Basic code.

7. Assume you want to calculate a 3% sales tax if the State variable contains the string "Colorado" (in any case); otherwise, you want to calculate a 4% sales tax. You can calculate the sales tax by multiplying the tax rate by the contents of the Sales variable. Display the sales tax in the LblStax control.
    a. Draw the flowchart, then write the Visual Basic code.

8. Assume you want to calculate an employee's gross pay. Employees working more than 40 hours should receive overtime pay (time and one-half) for the hours over 40. Use the variables Hours, Rate, Gross. Display the contents of the Gross variable in the LblGross control.
    a. Draw the flowchart, write the pseudocode, then write the Visual Basic code.

9. Display the string "Dog" in the LblType control if the Animal variable contains the letter "D" (in any case); otherwise, display the string "Cat". (Do not include the period.)
    a. Draw the flowchart, write the pseudocode, then write the Visual Basic code.

10. Assume you want to calculate a 10% discount on desks sold to customers in Colorado. Use the variables Item, State, and Sales. Format the discount to Currency and display it in the LblDisc control. (You don't know the case of either the Item or the State variables. In other words, the contents of those two variables can be in uppercase, lowercase, or a combination of uppercase and lowercase letters.)
    a. Draw the flowchart, then write the Visual Basic code.

11. Assume you want to calculate a 10% discount on sales made to customers in California and in Texas. You can use the variables State and Sales. Format the discount to Currency and display it in the LblDisc control. (You don't know the case of the State variable. In other words, the contents of the variable can be in uppercase, lowercase, or a combination of uppercase and lowercase letters.)
    a. Draw the flowchart, then write the Visual Basic code.

12. Display the string "Valid Entry" in the LblEntry control if the user enters either the number 1 or the number 2 in the TxtEntry Text box; otherwise, display the string "Entry Error". (Do not include the period.)

    a. Draw the flowchart, then write the Visual Basic code.

13. Assume you want to calculate a 2% price increase on all red shirts, but a 1% price increase on all other items. In addition to calculating the price increase, also calculate the new price. You can use the variables Color, Item, Origprice, Increase, and Newprice. Format the original price to Currency and display it in the LblOrig control. Format the price increase to Standard and display it in the LblIncrease control. Format the new price to currency and display it in the LblNew control. (You don't know the case of either the Color variable or the Item variable. In other words, the contents of those variables can be in uppercase, lowercase, or a combination of uppercase and lowercase letters.)

    a. Draw the flowchart, write the pseudocode, then write the Visual Basic code.

14. Display the string "Dog" in the LblAnimal control if the Animal variable contains the number 1. Display the string "Cat" if the Animal variable contains the number 2. Display the string "Bird" if the Animal variable contains anything other than the number 1 or the number 2.

    a. Draw the flowchart, write the pseudocode, then write the Visual Basic code.

15. Assume you offer programming seminars to companies. Your price per person depends on the number of people the company registers. (For example, if the company registers 7 people, then the total amount owed by the company is $560.)

Number of registrants	Charge
1 – 4	$ 100 per person
5 – 10	$ 80 per person
11 and over	$ 60 per person

    The number of people registered is stored in the Text property of the TxtReg control. Calculate the total amount owed by the company. Store the amount in the Totaldue variable.

    a. Draw the flowchart, write the pseudocode, then write the Visual Basic code.

16. Recall that string comparisons in Visual Basic are case sensitive, which means that a "P" is different from a "p." In Lesson A you learned how to use the UCase function (and the LCase function) to handle the string comparison problem. Recall that the Example 4 button's Click event procedure contains the following code:

    ```
    If UCase(Text1.Text) = "P" Then
        LblMessage.Caption = "Pass"
    Else
        LblMessage.Caption = "Fail"
    End If
    ```

    a. Not all languages have a UCase function or an LCase function. Just for practice, let's assume that Visual Basic does not have either function. Without using either the UCase function or the LCase function, rewrite the If statement's condition so that it displays the "Pass" message when the user enters the letter "P" in either lowercase or uppercase.

More Visual Basic Controls

The Sweet-Tooth Ice Cream Parlor Application

Recall that Susan Chen, the owner of the Sweet-Tooth Ice Cream Parlor, has hired you to create an application that will calculate the price of a sundae. The sketch of the user interface is shown in Figure 4-26.

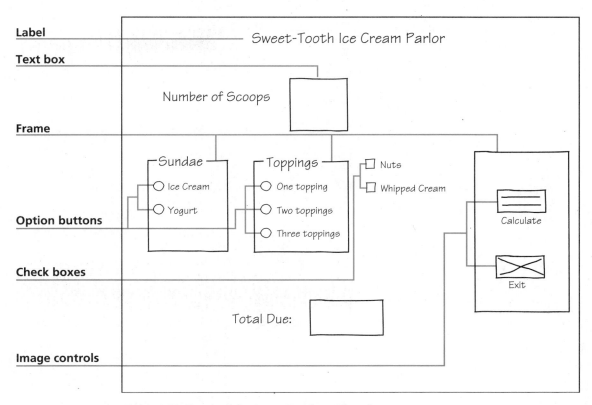

Figure 4-26: Sketch of the Sweet-Tooth user interface

According to the sketch, the Sweet-Tooth application will contain one Text box, five Option buttons, two Check boxes, two Image controls, three Frame controls, and various Label controls. To save you time, your Student Disk contains a partially completed application for Sweet-Tooth Ice Cream. When you open the application, you will notice that most of the user interface has already been created and the properties of the existing objects have been set. You will finish creating the user interface in this lesson.

To open the partially completed application:

1 Launch Visual Basic (if necessary) and open the **t4a.mak** project, which is in either the tut4\ver2 or tut4\ver3 directory on your Student Disk. Click the **View form button** in the Project window to view the FrmSweet form, then **save** the form and the project as **t4b**.

2 Click the **form's Maximize button** to maximize the form. Figure 4-27 identifies the controls already included in the application.

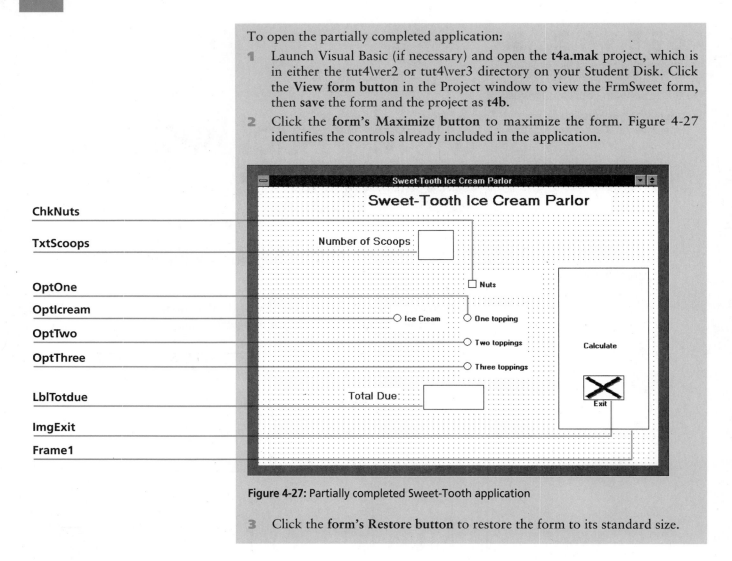

Figure 4-27: Partially completed Sweet-Tooth application

3 Click the **form's Restore button** to restore the form to its standard size.

Now you can begin adding the missing controls. You'll start with the Yogurt Option button.

Adding an Option Button to the Form

The Option button tool draws an Option button control. When Option buttons are grouped together, only one of the buttons in the group can be on at any time. The Option button is the control to use in situations where you want to limit the user to only one of two or more choices. In the Sweet-Tooth application, for example, you want to limit the type of sundae to either ice cream or yogurt. Let's add the missing Option button right now.

To add an Option button to the form:

1 Double-click the **Option button tool** in the Toolbox. An Option button appears on the form.

2 Set the Option button's properties as follows:

Name: **OptYogurt**   Caption: **Yogurt**

3 Either drag the Yogurt Option button to a location immediately below the Ice Cream Option button or set the Yogurt button's properties as follows:

Left: **3240**   Top: **3600**

4 **Save and run** the application. Click the **Ice Cream Option button**. A black dot appears inside the button. The black dot indicates that the button is on.

5 Click the **Yogurt Option button**. Visual Basic turns the Ice Cream button off as it turns the Yogurt button on.

6 Click the **One topping Option button**. Visual Basic turns the Yogurt button off and the One topping button on.

You should see a problem with the way the Option buttons are working. Choosing one of the topping buttons turns the buttons for type of sundae (ice cream or yogurt) off. That means the user will not be able to choose the type of sundae and the number of toppings at the same time. You actually want Visual Basic to treat the buttons for type of sundae (ice cream or yogurt) as a separate group, independent of the three topping buttons. You create a separate group of Option buttons by placing the buttons in a Frame, which is another Visual Basic control.

7 Click the **ImgExit control** (the large X) to end the application. Visual Basic returns to the design screen.

Adding a Frame to the Form

You use the Frame tool to draw a Frame control, which is necessary if you want more than one group of Option buttons in a form. You can also use a Frame to visually separate other types of controls from one another. You can think of a Frame control as being a container for other controls. You will group the Ice Cream and the Yogurt Option buttons in one Frame control.

To add a Frame control to the form:

1 Double-click the **Frame tool** 🔲 in the Toolbox. The Frame2 control appears on the form. (The form already contains the Frame1 control.)

2 Set the properties of the **Frame2 control** as follows:

Caption: **Sundae**   FontSize: **12**

3 Maximize the **form**.

You will now position the Frame control and also make it larger. Recall that you can move a control by dragging it to its new position or by setting its Left and Top properties. You can size a control by dragging the control's borders or by setting its Height and Width properties. It is much easier to use the dragging method to move and size a control, so you'll use that method in the next step.

4 Size and drag the **Frame control** as shown in Figure 4-28.

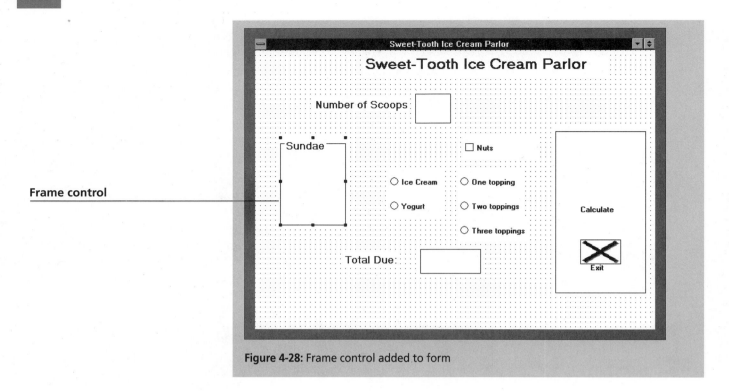

Frame control

Figure 4-28: Frame control added to form

The objects you add to a form belong to the form itself. Therefore, if you want to put the existing Option buttons in a Frame, you will need to detach the Option buttons from the form first. In Windows terminology, you will cut the buttons from the form. That process will place the Option buttons on the Windows Clipboard. You can then paste the Option buttons from the Windows Clipboard into the Frame control. (You can't just drag the Option buttons into the Frame. You must cut and paste them.)

To cut both the Ice Cream and the Yogurt Option buttons from the form and then paste them into the Frame:

1   Click the **Ice Cream Option button** to select it. Sizing handles appear around the control.

Recall from Tutorial 1 that you can select more than one object at a time by clicking the first object (as you just did) and then [Ctrl]-clicking the other objects. ([Ctrl]-clicking means to hold down the Control key as you click.)

2   [Ctrl]-click the **Yogurt Option button**. Sizing handles appear around the Yogurt Option button also.

You can now cut the selected controls from the form and then paste them into the Frame.

3   Press [**Ctrl**]x to cut the selected Option buttons from the form. Visual Basic removes the two buttons from the form and places them on the Windows Clipboard.

4   Click the **Sundae Frame control**. Sizing handles appear around the Frame. Now press [**Ctrl**]v to paste the Option buttons into the Sundae Frame, then place the mouse pointer ⟍ on the selected Option buttons, as shown in Figure 4-29. (Notice that the mouse pointer is on one of the selected controls.)

place the mouse pointer on one of the selected controls

both buttons are selected

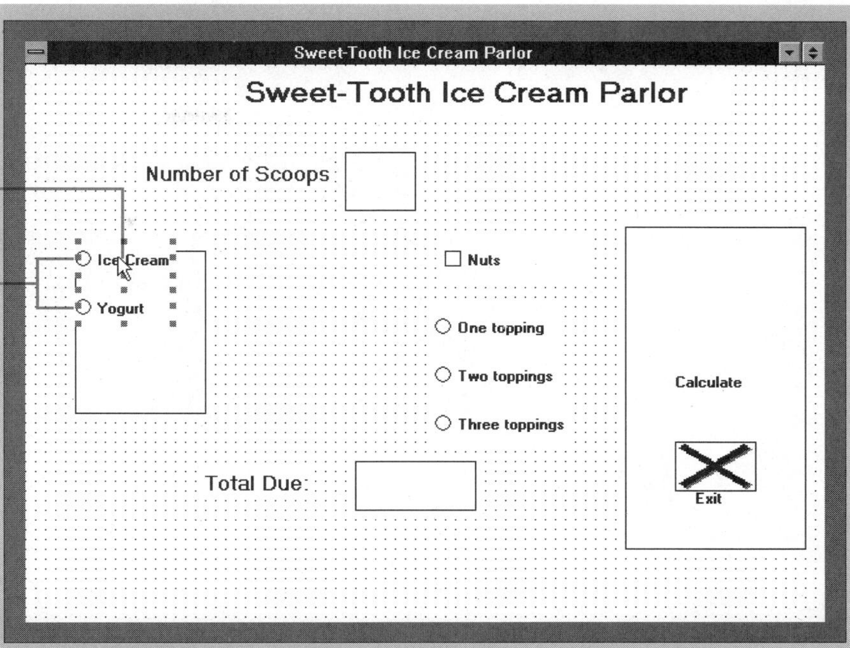

Figure 4-29: Option buttons in Frame control

tips

If you accidentally deselect the Option buttons, simply click the Ice Cream button, then [Ctrl]-click the Yogurt button, then place the mouse pointer on one of the selected Option buttons, and then drag the Option buttons further into the Frame control.

5 With the mouse pointer on the selected Option buttons, drag the **Option buttons** further into the Frame control, as shown in Figure 4-30.

drag the selected button further into the frame

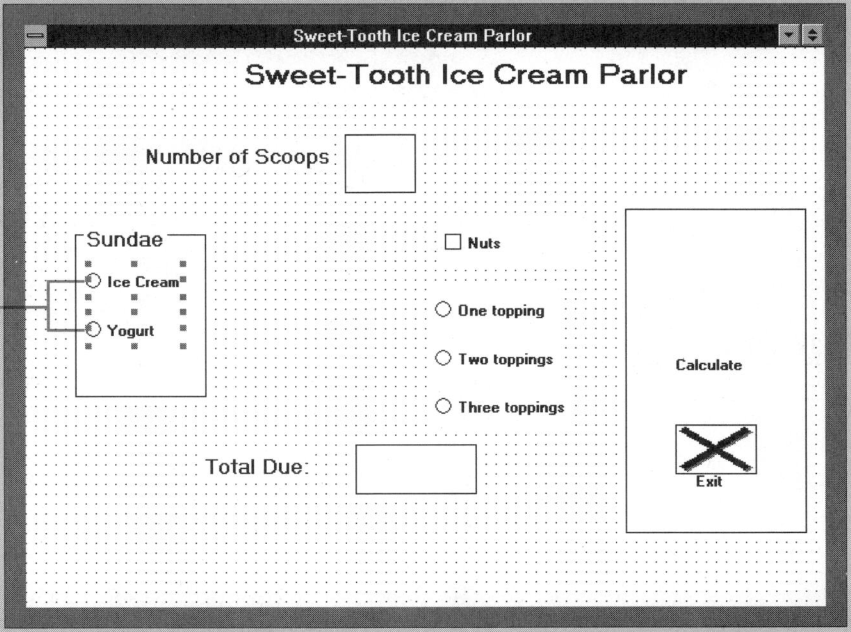

Figure 4-30: Option buttons positioned in Frame control

6 Click the **form** to deselect the Option buttons, click the **form's Restore button**, then **save and run** the application.

7   Click the **Yogurt Option button**, then click the **Two toppings Option button**. Notice that the topping Option button does not turn off the Yogurt Option button.

8   On your own, try clicking the other Option buttons. You should notice that when the Ice Cream button is turned on, the Yogurt button turns off; when the Yogurt button is turned on, the Ice Cream button turns off. The Ice Cream and Yogurt buttons, however, have no effect on the topping buttons. Also notice that turning a topping Option button on turns the previously selected topping button off, but it has no effect on the Ice Cream or the Yogurt buttons.

9   Click the **ImgExit control** (the large X). Visual Basic returns to the design screen.

Although you don't need to put the topping Option buttons in their own Frame for the buttons to work, you will do so anyway. The Frame will improve the appearance of the user interface by visually separating the topping Option buttons from the other controls on the form.

To group the topping Option buttons in a Frame control:

1   Double-click the **Frame tool** 🔲 in the Toolbox. The Frame3 control appears on the form.

2   Maximize the **form**, press [F4] to display the Properties window, then set the Frame3 control's following properties:

Caption: **Toppings**   FontSize: **12**

3   Size and drag the **Frame control** as shown in Figure 4-31.

Frame 3 control

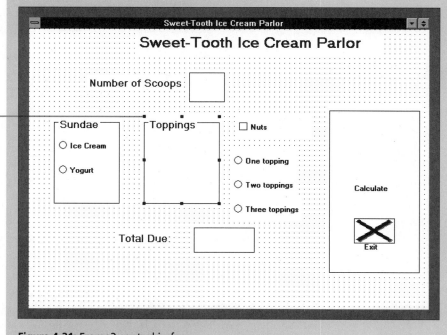

Figure 4-31: Frame3 control in form

4 Click the **One topping button**, [Ctrl]-click the **Two toppings button**, then [Ctrl]-click the **Three toppings button**. All three of the topping Option buttons are now selected.

5 Press **[Ctrl]x** to cut the selected buttons from the form, click the **Toppings Frame control** to select it, then press **[Ctrl]v** to paste the Option buttons into the Frame.

6 With the mouse pointer on one of the selected Option buttons, drag the **Option buttons** further inside the Frame, then click the **form** to deselect the buttons.

7 Click the **form's Restore button**, then **save and run** the application.

8 On your own, try clicking each of the Option buttons to make sure they are still working correctly. Then click the **ImgExit control** (the large X). Visual Basic returns to the design screen.

tips

▶ If you accidentally deselect the Option buttons, simply select each Option button again, then place the mouse pointer on one of the selected Option buttons, and then drag the Option buttons further into the Frame control.

An easier way to place a control in a Frame is simply to draw the control right inside the Frame.

Drawing Controls in a Frame

Recall from Tutorial 2 that you can draw a control by first clicking the appropriate tool in the Toolbox, then moving the mouse pointer onto the user interface, and then dragging the mouse pointer until the control is the size you want. Let's use this method to draw the missing Calculate Image control.

To draw a control inside a Frame:

1 Click (don't double-click) the **Image control** 🖾, then click the **form's Maximize button**. When you move the mouse pointer onto the form, it becomes a crosshair +.

2 Place the crosshair + inside the Frame, as shown in Figure 4-32. (Don't worry about the exact location.)

3 Press and hold down the left mouse button as you drag the mouse down and to the right. When the Image control is about the same size as the ImgExit control (the large X), release the mouse button. Your screen should look similar to Figure 4-33.

place the crosshair here

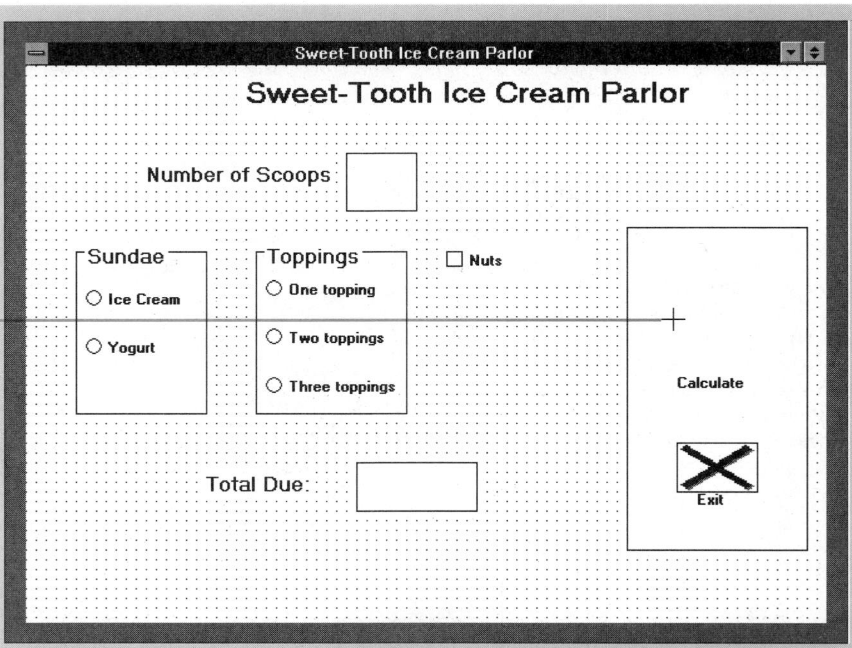

Figure 4-32: Placement of crosshair in Frame control

Image control

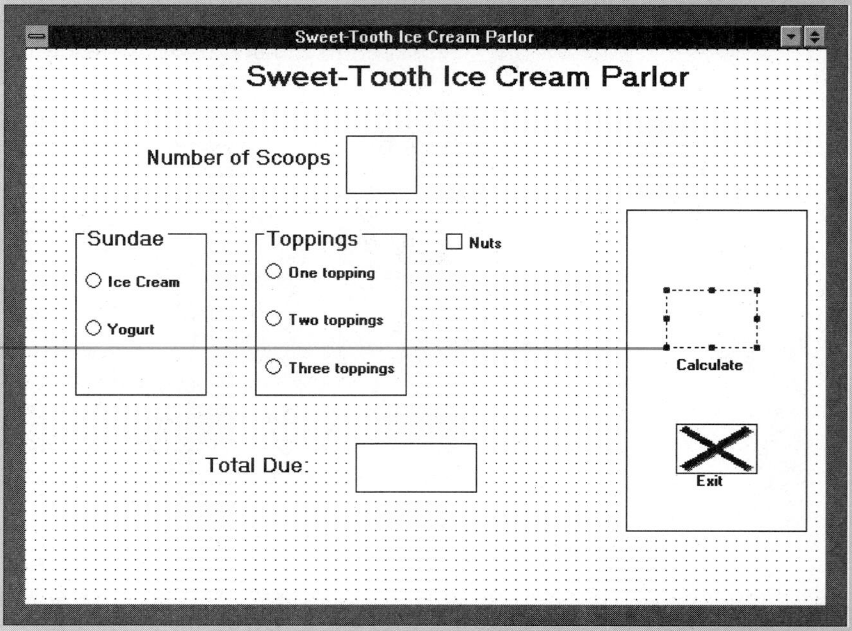

Figure 4-33: Image control drawn in Frame

Because you drew the Image control directly inside the Frame, the Image control belongs to the Frame, not to the form.

4   Press [F4] to display the Properties window, click **Name** in the Properties list, then type **ImgCalc** and press [Enter].

If you don't see the Stretch property, you chose the Picture box control instead of the Image control. Delete the Picture box and draw the Image control inside the Frame.

5   Double-click **Stretch** in the Properties list until the property says True. As you learned in Tutorial 3, when the Stretch property is set to True, it will resize the picture to fit the Image control.

6   Click **Picture** in the Properties list, then click the **... button** (ellipsis button) in the Properties window's Settings box. The Load Picture dialog box appears.

7   Double-click **icons** in the Directories list box to open the icons directory, where the Visual Basic icons are stored. (The icons directory should be on the local hard drive or on the network drive.)

The various Visual Basic icons are grouped by category. The icon you will use is in the misc (miscellaneous) folder. (Pictures of the various icons can be found in the *Microsoft Visual Basic Programmer's Guide* manual.)

8   Scroll the Directories list box until the misc directory is visible. Double-click **misc** to display the names of the icon files contained in the misc category. The names of the icon files appear in the File Name list box. Notice that icon files have an .ico filename extension.

9   Scroll the File Name list box until you locate the misc22.ico file, then double-click **misc22.ico.**, then click the **form** to remove the Properties window. An equal sign (=) appears in the Image control.

Recall from Tutorial 3 that you use the BorderStyle property to place a border around an Image control. The border makes an Image control look more like a button.

10   Click the **ImgCalc control** (the large =) to select it. Press **[F4]** to display the Properties window, then double-click **BorderStyle** in the Properties list until the property says 1-Fixed Single. A border appears around the equal sign. Click the **form** to remove the Properties window, then click the **form's Restore button**. The form returns to its standard size.

Before coding the application, let's add the last control to the form—a Check box control.

Adding a Check Box to the Form

Like Option buttons, Check boxes can be turned on and off only. Unlike Option buttons, however, any number of Check boxes on a form can be selected at the same time.

To add a Check box to the Form:

1   Double-click the **Check box tool** ☒ in the Toolbox. A Check box control appears on the form.

2   Set the following properties for the Check box:
    Name: **ChkWcream**   Caption: **Whipped Cream**
    (Don't worry that the entire caption does not fit inside the control.)

3   Click the **form's Maximize button** to maximize the form, then size and drag the Check box to match Figure 4-34.

Check box

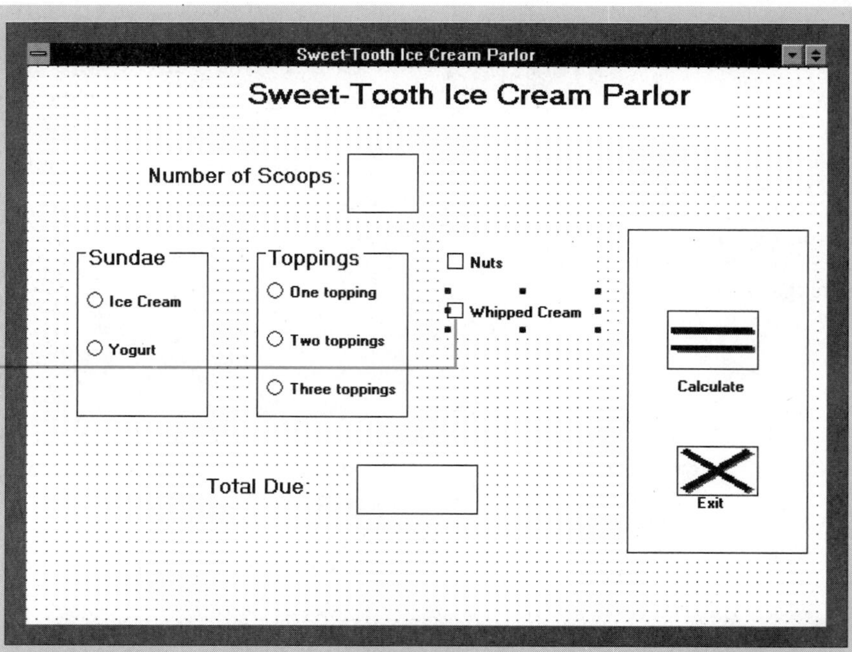

Figure 4-34: Whipped Cream Check box added to form

4 Click the **form's Restore button**, then **save and run** the application.

5 Click the **Nuts Check box** to turn it on. An X appears inside the Nuts Check box. Now click the **Whipped Cream Check box** to turn it on. An X appears inside the Whipped Cream Check box. Notice that one Check box does not turn off the other Check box.

6 Click the **Nuts Check box** to turn it off. The X disappears from the Check box.

7 Click the **ImgExit control** (the large X). Visual Basic returns to the design screen.

You have now created the user interface and set the properties of its objects. Planning and then writing the Visual Basic program instructions (code) is next, followed by testing, debugging, and documenting. You will do all of that in Lesson C.

S U M M A R Y

To limit the user to only one of several choices:

■ Use the Option button tool 🔘.

To allow the user to select one or more choices:

■ Use the Check box tool 🗵.

To create separate groups of Option buttons or to visually separate areas of the form:

■ Use the Frame tool ▢.

To place an existing control into a Frame:

■ Cut the existing control from the form, then select the Frame, and then paste the control into the Frame.

To draw a control in a Frame:

■ Click (do not double-click) the appropriate tool in the Toolbox.
■ Position the crosshair inside the Frame, then drag until the control is the desired size.

Q U E S T I O N S

1. Which of the following controls allows the user to select only one choice?
   a. Check box
   b. Command button
   c. Label
   d. Option button
   e. Shape

2. Which of the following controls allows the user to select one or more choices?
   a. Check box
   b. Command button
   c. Label
   d. Option button
   e. Shape

3. If you want to create separate groups of Option buttons, you will need to place each group in its own _____ control.
   a. Check box
   b. Circle
   c. Container
   d. Frame
   e. Shape

4. Assume the form contains a Command button named CmdExit. How could you place this control in a Frame?

5. How do you draw a control in a Frame?

6. Assume the form contains three Option buttons. (The buttons are not in a Frame control.) How many Option buttons can be on at any one time?
   a. One
   b. Two
   c. Three
   d. Four
   e. Five

7. Assume the form contains two Frame controls. Each Frame control contains three Option buttons. How many Option buttons can be on at any time?
   a. One
   b. Two
   c. Three
   d. Four
   e. Five

8. Assume the form contains three Check boxes. (The Check boxes are not in a Frame control.) How many Check boxes can be on at any one time?
    a. One
    b. Two
    c. Three
    d. Four
    e. Five

9. Assume the form contains two Frame controls. Each Frame control contains two Check boxes. How many Check boxes can be on at any time?
    a. One
    b. Two
    c. Three
    d. Four
    e. Five

10. Assume the form contains two Frame controls. One Frame control contains two Option buttons; the other Frame control contains three Check boxes. What is the total number of Option buttons and Check boxes that can be on at any one time?
    a. One
    b. Two
    c. Three
    d. Four
    e. Five

E X E R C I S E S

1. a. Create the user interface shown in Figure 4-35.

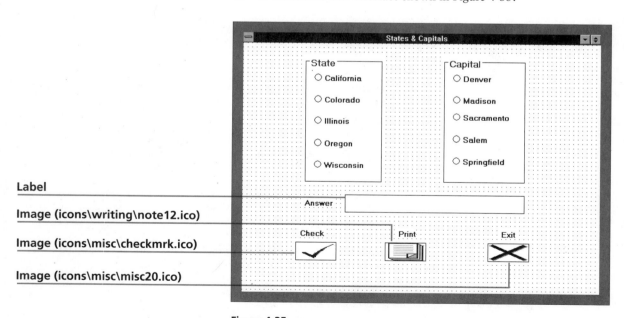

Figure 4-35

    b. Save the form and the project as T4LBE1.
    c. Code the Exit control so that it ends the application.
    d. Code the Print control so that it prints the form.

e. Save and run the application.

f. Use the Print control to print the form. Use the Exit control to end the application.

2. a. Create the user interface shown in Figure 4-36.

Image (icons\misc\misc20.ico)

Image (icons\misc\misc21.ico)

Label

Command buttons

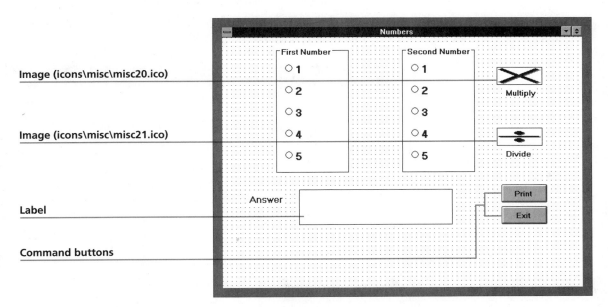

Figure 4-36

b. Save the form and the project as T4LBE2.

c. Code the Exit control so that it ends the application.

d. Code the Print control so that it prints the form.

e. Save and run the application.

f. Use the Print control to print the form. Use the Exit control to end the application.

3. a. Create the user interface shown in Figure 4-37.

Labels

Frame

Image (icons\misc\misc22.ico)

Image (icons\writing\note12.ico)

Image (icons\misc\misc20.ico)

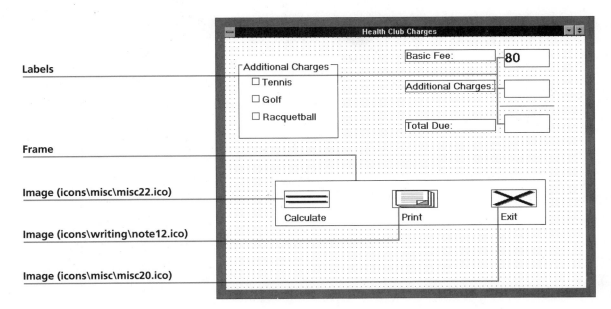

Figure 4-37

b. Save the form and the project as T4LBE3.
c. Code the Exit control so that it ends the application.
d. Code the Print control so that it prints the form.
e. Save and run the application.
f. Use the Print control to print the form. Use the Exit control to end the application.

4. a. Create the user interface shown in Figure 4-38.

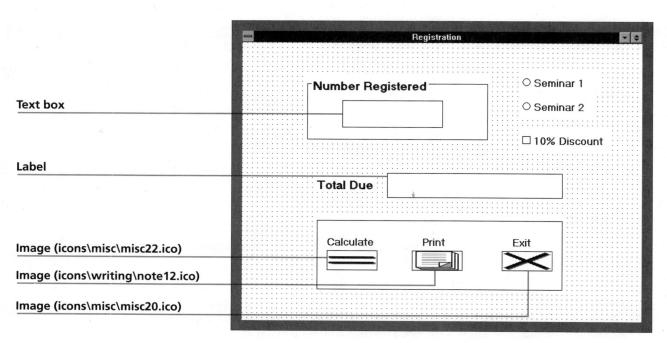

Figure 4-38

b. Save the form and the project as T4LBE4.
c. Code the Exit control so it ends the application.
d. Code the Print control so it prints the form.
e. Save and run the application.
f. Use the Print control to print the form. Use the Exit control to end the application.

L E S S O N   C
o b j e c t i v e s

In this lesson you will learn how to:

■ Use the Value property
■ Use the Print method
■ Include the If...Then...Else statement in an application

Coding the Sweet-Tooth Application

The Sweet-Tooth Ice Cream Parlor Application

Recall that Susan Chen, the owner of the Sweet-Tooth Ice Cream Parlor, has hired you to create an application that will calculate the price of a sundae. The TOE chart for the application is shown in Figure 4-39.

Task	Object	Event
Get number of scoops from user	1 Text box (TxtScoops)	None
Assign price of a single scoop	2 Option buttons (OptIcream, OptYogurt)	Click
Assign toppings charge	3 Option buttons (ChkOne, ChkTwo, ChkThree)	Click
Assign nuts charge	1 Check box (ChkNuts)	Click
Assign whipped cream charge	1 Check box (ChkWcream)	Click
Calculate total due	1 Image control (ImgCalc)	Click
End the application	1 Image control (ImgExit)	Click

Figure 4-39: TOE chart for the Sweet-Tooth application

According to the TOE chart, you will need to write code for the five Option buttons, the two Check boxes, and the two Image controls. You need to enter the code in each control's Click event procedure. Let's begin by opening the T4B.MAK project that you created in Lesson B.

To open the T4B.MAK project:

1   Launch Visual Basic (if necessary) and open the **t4b.mak** project, which is in either the tut4\ver2 or tut4\ver3 directory on your Student Disk. Click the **View form button** in the Project window to view the FrmSweet form, then save the form and the project as **t4c**.

2   Click the **form's Maximize button** to maximize the form. Figure 4-40 identifies the controls already included in the application.

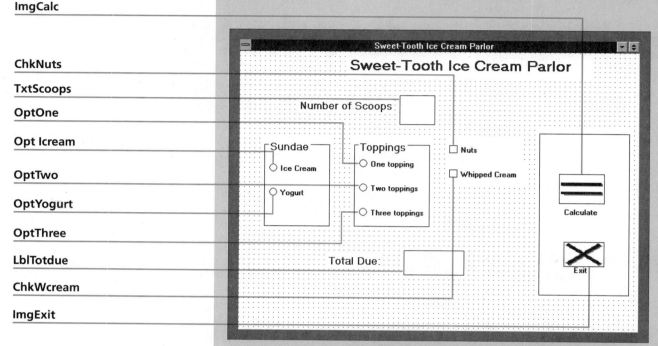

ImgCalc

ChkNuts

TxtScoops

OptOne

Opt Icream

OptTwo

OptYogurt

OptThree

LblTotdue

ChkWcream

ImgExit

Figure 4-40: Completed Sweet-Tooth user interface

Before coding the application, you will enter the Option Explicit statement in the general Declarations section of the form. Recall from Tutorial 3 that you should always include the Option Explicit statement in an application. Then if you use the name of an undeclared variable in the program code, Visual Basic will inform you of the error when you run the application.

3   Double-click the **form** to open its Code window, then click the **down arrow in the Code window's Object box**. A drop-down list of objects appears. Scroll until you see (general) at the top of the drop-down list, then click **(general)** in the drop-down list. The general Declarations section of the form appears.

4   Type **option explicit** and press [Enter], then close the Code window and restore the form to its standard size.

You will now concentrate on planning and writing the Visual Basic code, as well as testing and debugging the application. You can begin with the Ice Cream and the Yogurt Option buttons.

Planning the Code for the Ice Cream Option Button and the Yogurt Option Button

According to the TOE chart, both the Ice Cream Option button and the Yogurt Option button are responsible for assigning the price of a single scoop. Figure 4-41 shows the flowchart and the pseudocode for these Option buttons.

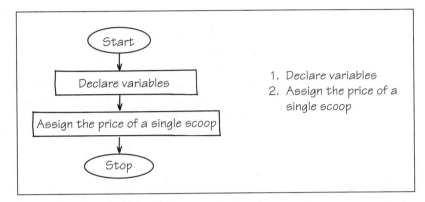

Figure 4-41: Flowchart and pseudocode for the Ice Cream and the Yogurt Option buttons

Coding the Ice Cream and Yogurt Option Buttons

The first step listed in Figure 4-41 is to declare the necessary variables. To determine the necessary variables, recall that you look in the flowchart, or the pseudocode, for places where you will need to store information temporarily. According to Figure 4-41, the Option buttons will need a variable in which to store the price of a single scoop. You can call the variable Price and declare it as a Currency data type. The Price variable will be used by the Ice Cream Option button, the Yogurt Option button, and the ImgCalc control. (The ImgCalc control will need the price of a single scoop to calculate the total due.) Because the variable must be available to three procedures—the OptIcream Click event, the OptYogurt Click event, and the ImgCalc Click event—you will declare the variable as a form-level variable in the general Declarations section of the form.

To declare Price as a form-level variable:

1   Double-click the **form** to open its Code window, then click the **down arrow in the Code window's Object box.** Scroll the drop-down list until you see (general), then click **(general)** in the drop-down list. The general Declarations section of the form appears.

2   Click in the **line below the Option Explicit** statement, type **dim Price as currency** and press [Enter], then close the **Code window.**

The next step shown in Figure 4-41 is to assign the price of a single scoop to the Price variable. The assignment statement to accomplish that should be entered in the Click event procedure of both the Ice Cream Option button and the Yogurt Option button. The assignment statement you will enter into the Ice Cream button's Click event procedure will assign .95 (95 cents) to the Price variable when the user clicks that button. The assignment statement you will enter into the Yogurt button's Click event procedure will assign .85 (85 cents) to the Price variable when the user clicks that button.

To code the Ice Cream Option button and the Yogurt Option button:

1   Double-click the **Ice Cream Option button** to open its Code window. The Click event procedure appears. Press [**Tab**], then type **Price = .95** and press [**Enter**]. When the user clicks the Ice Cream Option button, the application will assign .95 to the Price variable.

Now use the Code window's Object box to open the Yogurt button's Code window.

2   Click the **down arrow in the Code window's Object box**, then click **OptYogurt** in the drop-down list. The Click event procedure for the Yogurt Option button appears. Press [**Tab**], then type **Price = .85** and press [**Enter**]. When the user clicks the Yogurt Option button, the application will assign .85 to the Price variable.

Before coding another control, you should verify that, when clicked, the Option buttons do, in fact, assign the appropriate values to the Price variable. You can verify that by using Visual Basic's Print method to print the contents of the Price variable on the form.

The Print Method

The format of the Print method that prints information on a form is *Print [expressionlist]*. Notice that the *expressionlist* part of the instruction is optional, as indicated by the brackets; if you omit the *expressionlist*, the Print method prints a blank line. (You can also include other information in the Print method. To learn more about the Print method, use the Help menu to search for its Help screen.)

You will enter, temporarily, a *Print Price* instruction in the ImgCalc control's Code window. The *Print Price* instruction will print the contents of the Price variable on the form. You will remove the Print instruction after you have finished verifying the status of the variables used in the application.

To enter the Print instruction in the ImgCalc's Click event procedure, then test the Option buttons:

1   The Code window should still be open. Click the **down arrow in the Code window's Object box**, then click **ImgCalc** in the drop-down list. The Click event procedure for the ImgCalc control appears.

2   Type **print Price** and press [**Enter**], then close the Code window.

3   **Save and run** the application.

4   Click the **Ice Cream Option button**, then click the **ImgCalc control** (the =). The contents of the Price variable, .95, appear in the upper-left corner of the form.

5   Now click the **Yogurt Option button**, then click the **ImgCalc control** (the =). The contents of the Price variable, .85, appear below the .95.

The Option buttons are working correctly, so you can exit the application.

6   Click the **ImgExit** control (the large X). Visual Basic returns to the design screen.

You will leave the Print statement in the ImgCalc's Code window. You will use the statement to test the other variables in the application. Let's code the topping Option buttons next.

Planning the Code for the Topping Option Buttons

According to the TOE chart, the three topping Option buttons are responsible for assigning the appropriate charge, if any, for extra toppings. Figure 4-42 shows the flowchart and the pseudocode for these three Option buttons.

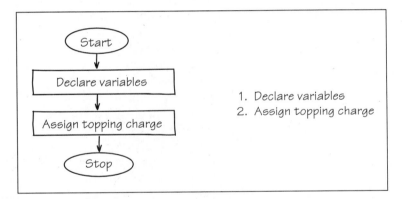

Figure 4-42: Flowchart and pseudocode for the topping Option buttons

Coding the Toppings Option Buttons

The first step is to declare the necessary variables. According to Figure 4-42, the topping Option buttons will need a variable in which to store the topping charge. You can call the variable Toppings and declare it as a Currency data type. The Toppings variable will be used by the three topping Option buttons and also by the ImgCalc control. (The ImgCalc will need the topping charge in order to calculate the total due.) Therefore, you will need to declare the Toppings variable as a form-level variable in the general Declarations section of the form.

To declare Toppings as a form-level variable:

1 Double-click the **form** to open its Code window, then click the **down arrow in the Code window's Object box**. Scroll the drop-down list until you see (general), then click (**general**) in the drop-down list. The general Declarations section of the form appears.

2 Click in the line immediately below the existing Dim statement, type **dim Toppings as currency** and press [**Enter**], and then close the **Code window**.

The next step shown in Figure 4-42 is to assign the price of the topping to the Toppings variable. The appropriate assignment statement should be entered in the Click event procedures of the three topping Option buttons. According to the Sweet-Tooth menu (Figure 4-1), there is no charge for one topping. The charge for two toppings, however, is .2 (20 cents), and the charge for three toppings is .25 (25 cents).

To code the topping Option buttons, then test the buttons:

1 Double-click the **One topping Option button** to open its Code window. The Click event procedure appears. Press [**Tab**], then type **Toppings = 0** (zero) and press [**Enter**]. When the user clicks the One topping Option button, the application will assign 0 (zero) to the Toppings variable.

2 Click the **down arrow in the Code window's Object box**, then click **OptTwo**. The Click event procedure for the Two toppings Option button appears. Press [**Tab**], then type **Toppings = .2** and press [**Enter**]. When the user clicks the Two toppings Option button, the application will assign .2 to the Toppings variable.

3 Click the **down arrow in the Code window's Object box**, then click **OptThree**. The Click event procedure for the Three toppings Option button appears. Press [**Tab**], then type **Toppings = .25** and press [**Enter**]. When the user clicks the Three toppings Option button, the application will assign .25 to the Toppings variable.

Let's verify that these three Option buttons are assigning the appropriate values to the Toppings variable. You can do that by changing the *Print Price* instruction in the ImgCalc control's Code window to *Print Toppings*.

4 Click the **down arrow in the Code window's Object box**, then click **ImgCalc** in the drop-down list. In the ImgCalc's Click event procedure, change *Print Price* to **Print Toppings**.

5 Close the Code window, then **save and run** the application.

6 Click the **One topping Option button**, then click the **ImgCalc control** (the =). The charge for one topping, 0, appears on the form. Now click the **Two toppings Option button**, then click the **ImgCalc control**. The charge for two toppings, .2, appears on the form. Now click the **Three toppings Option button**, then click the **ImgCalc control**. The charge for three toppings, .25, appears on the form.

The Option buttons are working correctly, so you can exit the application.

7 Click the **ImgExit control** (the large X). Visual Basic returns to the design screen.

Let's code the two Check boxes next.

Planning the Code for the Nuts Check Box

According to the TOE chart, the Nuts Check box is responsible for assigning the appropriate charge, if any, for nuts. Figure 4-43 shows the flowchart and the pseudocode for the Nuts Check box.

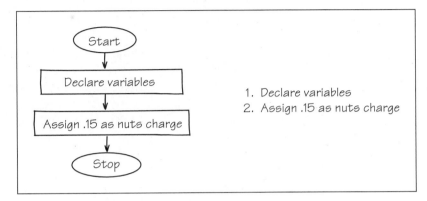

Figure 4-43: Flowchart and pseudocode for Nuts Check box

Coding the Nuts Check Box

According to Figure 4-43, the Nuts Check box will need a variable in which to store the charge for nuts. You can call the variable Nuts and declare it as a Currency data type. The Nuts variable will be used by the ChkNuts Check box and the ImgCalc control. (The ImgCalc control will use the charge for nuts, if any, in the total due calculation.) Therefore, you will need to declare the Nuts variable as a form-level variable in the general Declarations section of the form.

To declare Nuts as a form-level variable:

1   Open the general Declarations section of the form. Click in the blank line immediately below the last Dim statement, then type **dim Nuts as currency** and press **[Enter]**, and then close the Code window.

The next task shown in Figure 4-43 is to enter the appropriate assignment statement in the Click event procedure of the Nuts Check box. The extra charge for nuts is .15 (15 cents).

To code the Nuts Check box:

1   Double-click the **Nuts Check box** to open its Code window. The Click event procedure appears. Press **[Tab]**, then type **Nuts = .15** and press **[Enter]**. When the user clicks the Nuts Check box, the Check box will assign 15 cents to the Nuts variable.

You can verify that the Check box is working correctly by changing the Print instruction in the ImgCalc control's Code window to *Print Nuts*.

2 Click the **down arrow in the Code window's Object box**, then click **ImgCalc** in the drop-down list. The Click event for the ImgCalc control appears. Change the Print instruction to **Print Nuts**, then close the Code window.

3 **Save and run** the application.

4 Click the **Nuts Check box** to turn it on, then click the **ImgCalc control** (the =). The charge for nuts, .15, appears on the form.

5 Click the **Nuts Check box** again. The Nuts Check box turns off. Now click the **ImgCalc control** (the =). The .15 prints on the form again, which is not correct. Let's stop the application and discuss why this happened.

6 Click the **ImgExit control** (the large X). Visual Basic returns to the design screen.

Recall that the ChkNuts Click event procedure contains the *Nuts = .15* assignment statement. That statement tells Visual Basic to assign the .15 value to the Nuts variable whenever the Nuts Check box is clicked, whether it is clicked on or off. What you really want is to assign the .15 value to the Nuts variable when the Nuts Check box is clicked on, but assign 0 (zero) to the Nuts variable when the Nuts Check box is clicked off. You can use the selection structure, which you learned in Lesson A, to do that. First, however, let's correct both the flowchart and pseudocode. Figure 4-44 shows the corrected flowchart and pseudocode for the Nuts Check box.

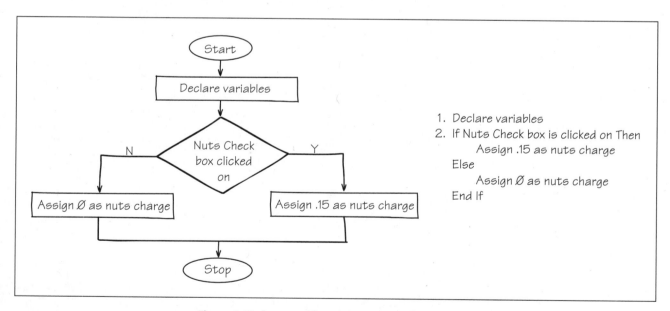

Figure 4-44: Corrected flowchart and pseudocode for Nuts Check box

Now let's correct the code.

Modifying the Click Event Procedure for the Nuts Check Box

You can determine if a Check box is on or off by looking at its Value property. If the Check box is on, then its Value property contains the number 1. If the Check box is off, then its Value property contains the number 0. (Option buttons also have a Value property. If an Option button is on, however, its Value property contains the Boolean value True. If the Option button is off, its Value property contains the Boolean value False.) The following If statement will assign a .15 value to the Nuts variable when the ChkNuts Check box is on, and a 0 value when the ChkNuts Check box is off:

```
If ChkNuts.Value = 1 Then
        Nuts = .15
Else
        Nuts = 0
End If
```

To modify the Click event procedure for the Nuts Check box:

1   Double-click the **Nuts Check box**. Modify the Code window to match Figure 4-45. (Be sure to press [Tab] and type the apostrophe before the documentation.)

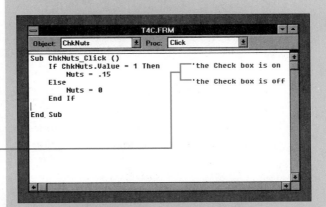

be sure to type the apostrophe

Figure 4-45: ChkNuts Click event procedure showing corrected code

2   Close the Code window, then **save and run** the application to test it again.

3   Click the **Nuts Check box** to turn it on, then click the **ImgCalc control** (the =). The .15 prints on the form. Click the **Nuts Check box** to turn it off, then click the **ImgCalc control**. This time a 0 (zero) prints on the form, which is correct.

4   Click the **ImgExit control** (the large X). Visual Basic returns to the design screen.

The Whipped Cream Check box is next.

Planning the Code for the Whipped Cream Check Box

According to the TOE chart, the Whipped Cream Check box is responsible for assigning the appropriate charge, if any, for whipped cream. Figure 4-46 shows the flowchart and the pseudocode for the Whipped Cream Check box.

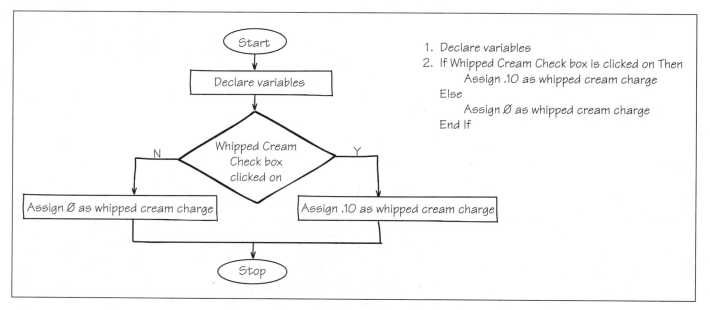

Figure 4-46: Flowchart and pseudocode for Whipped Cream Check box

Coding the Whipped Cream Check Box

According to Figure 4-46, the Whipped Cream Check box will need a variable in which to store the whipped cream charge, if any. You can call the variable Wcream and declare it as a Currency data type. The Wcream variable will be used by the ChkWcream Check box and the ImgCalc control. (The ImgCalc will use the whipped cream charge, if any, in the total due calculation.) Therefore, you will need to declare the Wcream variable as a form-level variable in the general Declarations section of the form.

To declare Wcream as a form-level variable, and then code the ChkWcream Check box:

1   Open the general Declarations section of the form, click in the blank line immediately below the Dim statements, then type **dim Wcream as currency** and press [Enter]. Close the Code window.

You can now enter the appropriate instructions in the Click event procedure of the Whipped Cream Check box. The extra charge for whipped cream is .10 (10 cents).

2   Double-click the **Whipped Cream Check box** to open its Code window. The Click event procedure appears. Enter the code shown in Figure 4-47. (Be sure to enter the apostrophe before the documentation.)

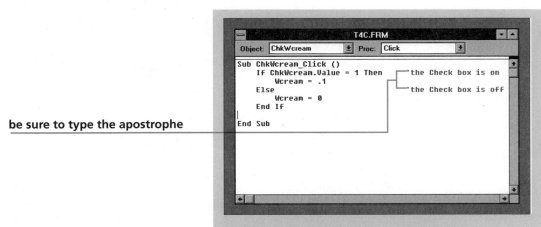

be sure to type the apostrophe

Figure 4-47: ChkWcream Click event procedure

3 On your own, change the Print instruction in the ImgCalc control's Click event procedure to **Print Wcream**.

4 Close the Code window, then **save and run** the application.

5 On your own, test the Whipped Cream Check box to verify that it is working correctly. (The ImgCalc control should print .1 on the form when the Whipped Cream Check box is on and 0 (zero) when it is off.)

6 Click the **ImgExit control** (the large X). Visual Basic returns to the design screen.

The ImgCalc control is the last control you need to code.

Planning the Code for the ImgCalc Control

According to the TOE chart, the ImgCalc control is responsible for calculating the total price of the sundae. Figure 4-48 shows the flowchart and the pseudocode for the ImgCalc control.

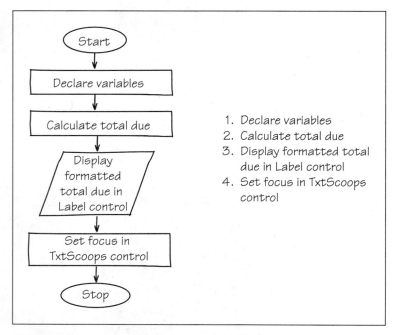

Figure 4-48: Flowchart and pseudocode for ImgCalc control

Coding the ImgCalc Control

According to Figure 4-48, the ImgCalc control will need a variable in which to store the total due after it has been calculated. You can call the variable Total and declare it as a Currency data type. The Total variable will be used by the ImgCalc control only, so it can be declared as a local variable in the ImgCalc control's Click event procedure.

To declare Total as a local variable and then code the ImgCalc control:

1 Maximize the **form**, then double-click the **ImgCalc control** (the =). The Click event procedure for the ImgCalc control appears.

2 Maximize the Code window, remove the entire *Print Wcream* instruction from the Code window, then enter the code shown in Figure 4-49.

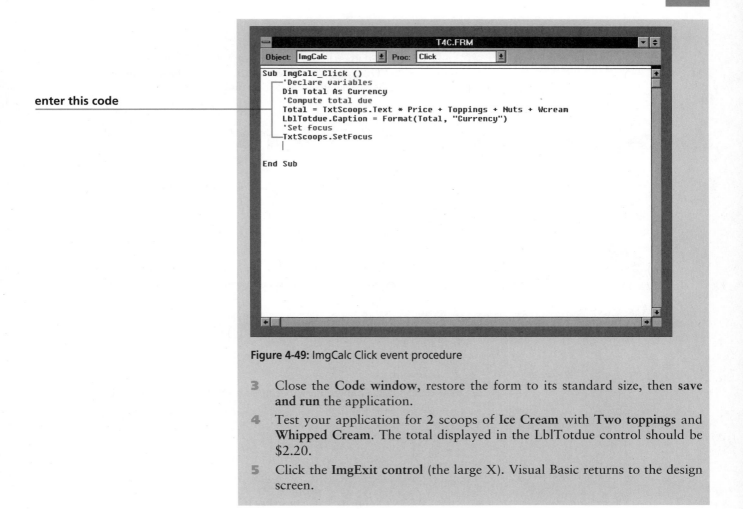

enter this code

Figure 4-49: ImgCalc Click event procedure

3 Close the **Code window**, restore the form to its standard size, then **save and run** the application.

4 Test your application for **2** scoops of **Ice Cream** with **Two toppings** and **Whipped Cream**. The total displayed in the LblTotdue control should be $2.20.

5 Click the **ImgExit control** (the large X). Visual Basic returns to the design screen.

You have now completed Lesson C. You can either take a break or complete the exercises and questions at the end of the lesson.

S U M M A R Y

To have Visual Basic inform you if your code contains the name of an undeclared variable:

◼ Enter the Option Explicit statement in the general Declarations section of the form.

To print the contents of a variable on a form:

◼ Use the Print method; its format is *Print [expressionlist]*.

To determine if a Check box is on or off:

◼ Look at the Check box's Value property. If the Value property contains the number 1, then the Check box is on. If the Value property contains the number 0, then the Check box is off.

To determine if an Option button is on or off:

■ Look at the Option button's Value property. If the Value property contains the Boolean value True, then the Option button is on. If the Value property contains the Boolean value False, then the Option button is off.

Q U E S T I O N S

1. The _____ statement tells Visual Basic to inform you if a Code window contains an undeclared variable.
   a. Explicit
   b. Explicit Option
   c. Options Explicit
   d. Option Explicit

2. If a variable will be used by more than one procedure, you should declare it as a _____ variable.
   a. form
   b. form-level
   c. global
   d. local
   e. local-form

3. A variable known only to the procedure in which it is defined is called a _____ variable.
   a. form
   b. form-level
   c. global
   d. local
   e. local-form

4. If a Check box is on, its Value property is set to _____ .
   a. 0 (zero)
   b. 1 (One)
   c. False
   d. True
   e. Yes

5. If an Option button is off, its Value property is set to _____ .
   a. 0 (zero)
   b. 1 (One)
   c. False
   d. True
   e. Yes

6. You can use the _____ method to print information on the form.
   a. Display
   b. FormPrint
   c. Print
   d. PrintForm
   e. Show

E X E R C I S E S

1. a. Open the T4LBE1 project that you created in Lesson B, then save the form and the project as T4LCE1.

    After selecting a state and its corresponding capital, the user will click the Check Image control (the checkmark) to verify that the capital he or she chose is correct. If the capital is correct, "Correct" should appear in the Label control; otherwise, "Incorrect" should appear in the Label control.

    b. Use the flowcharts shown in Figure 4-50 to finish coding the application.
    c. Save and run the application.
    d. Test the application by choosing Denver from one group and Colorado from the other group. Click the Check control. Then click the Print control.
    e. Test the application again by choosing Salem from one group and Wisconsin from the other group. Click the Check control. Then click the Print control.
    f. Exit the application, then print the code.

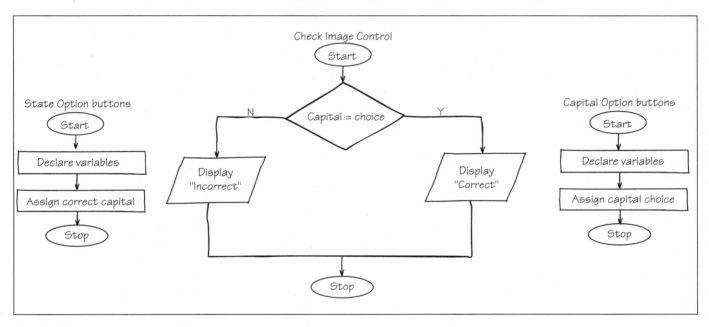

Figure 4-50

2. a. Open the T4LBE2 project that you created in Lesson B, then save the form and the project as T4LCE2.

    After selecting a first number and a second number, the user will click either the Multiply Image control (the large X) or the Divide Image control (the division sign). If he or she clicks the Multiply Image control, the application will multiply the first number by the second number, then display the result in the Label control. If he or she clicks the Divide Image control, the application will divide the first number by the second number, then display the result in the Label control.

    b. Draw the flowcharts or write the pseudocode for the First Number Option buttons, the Second Number Option buttons, the Multiply Image control, and the Divide Image control.
    c. Use your flowcharts or pseudocode to finish coding the application.
    d. Save and run the application.

    e. Test the application by choosing the number 3 from the First Number group and the number 5 from the Second Number group. Click the Multiply Image control. Then click the Print Command button.

    f. Test the application again by choosing the number 4 from the First Number group and the number 2 from the Second Number group. Click the Divide Image control. Then click the Print Command button.

    g. Exit the application, then print the code.

3.   a. Open the T4LBE3 project that you created in Lesson B, then save the form and the project as T4LCE3.

After selecting the additional charges, the user will click the Calculate Image control (the equal sign) to calculate and display the total additional charge and the total due. (The total due is calculated by adding the basic fee to the additional charges.) The additional charges are as follows:

Tennis	$ 30 per month
Golf	$ 25 per month
Racquetball	$ 20 per month

    b. Draw the flowcharts or write the pseudocode for each of the Check boxes and for the Calculate Image control.

    c. Use your flowcharts or pseudocode to finish coding the application.

    d. Save and run the application.

    e. Test the application by choosing Golf. Click the Calculate Image control, then click the Print Image control.

    f. Test the application again by choosing Tennis and Racquetball. Click the Calculate Image control, then click the Print Image control.

    g. Exit the application, then print the code.

4.   a. Open the T4LBE4 project that you created in Lesson B, then save the form and the project as T4LCE4.

The user will first enter the number registered in the Text box. He or she will then select either the Seminar 1 Option button or the Seminar 2 Option button. (A person can register for only one of the seminars.) The user can also select the 10% discount Check box. After the selections are made, the user will click the Calculate Image control to calculate the total registration fee for a seminar. Seminar 1 is $100 per person and Seminar 2 is $120 per person. The total registration fee should be displayed in the Total Due Label control.

    b. Draw the flowcharts or write the pseudocode for the Option buttons, the Check box, and the Calculate Image control.

    c. Use your flowcharts or pseudocode to finish coding the application.

    d. Save and run the application.

    e. Test the application by entering 10 in the Text box and then choosing Seminar 2. Click the Calculate Image control. Then click the Print Image control.

    f. Test the application again by entering 5 in the Text box and then choosing Seminar 1 and the 10% discount. Click the Calculate Image control, then click the Print Image control.

    g. Exit the application, then print the code.

5.   a. Create the user interface shown in Figure 4-51.

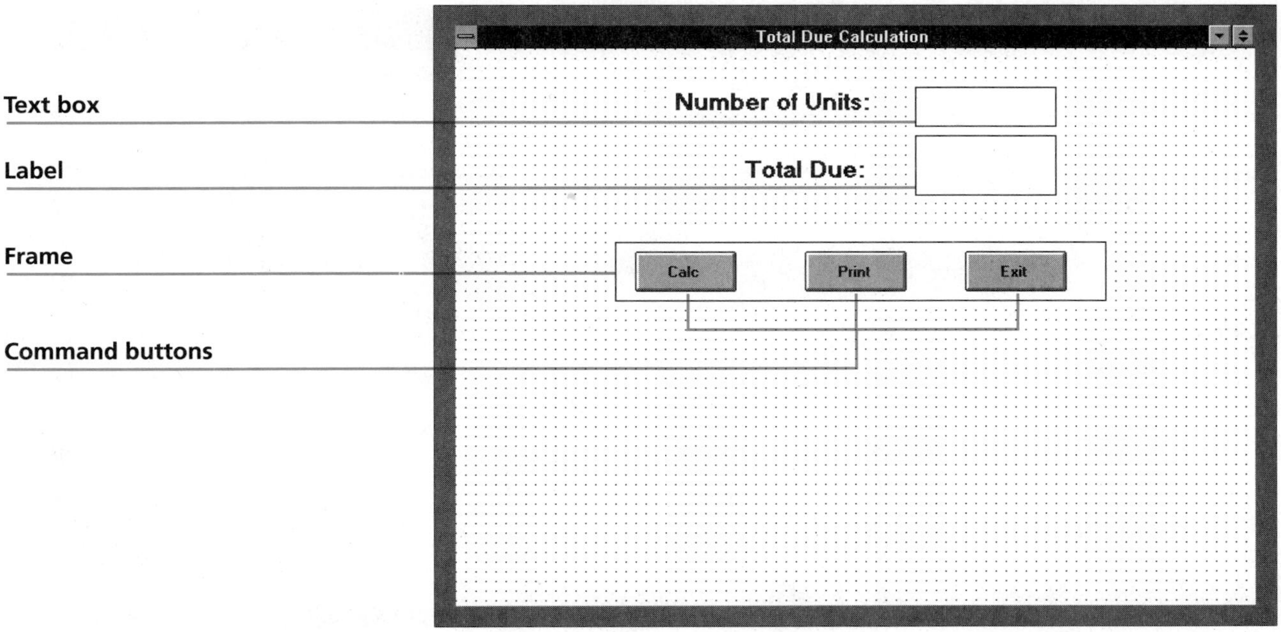

Text box

Label

Frame

Command buttons

Figure 4-51

b. Save the form and the project as T4LCE5.

c. Code the Exit Command button so that it ends the application. Code the Print Command button so that it prints the form.

The user will enter the units ordered in the Text box. He or she will click the Calc Command button to calculate the total due (number of units times price per unit). The price per unit depends on how many units are ordered. Use the following information to determine the price per unit:

Number of units ordered	Price
1 – 4	$10 per unit
5 – 10	9 per unit
11 and over	7 per unit

Display the total due in the Total Due Label control.

d. Draw the flowchart or write the pseudocode for the Calc Command button.

e. Use your flowchart or pseudocode to finish coding the application.

f. Save and run the application.

g. Test the application by entering 10 in the Text box. Click the Calc Command button. (The total due should be 90.) Then click the Print Command button.

h. Test the application again by entering 15 in the Text box. Click the Calc Command button, then click the Print Command button.

i. Test the application again by entering 2 in the Text box. Click the Calc Command button, then click the Print Command button.

j. Exit the application, then print the code.

6. a. Create the user interface shown in Figure 4-52.

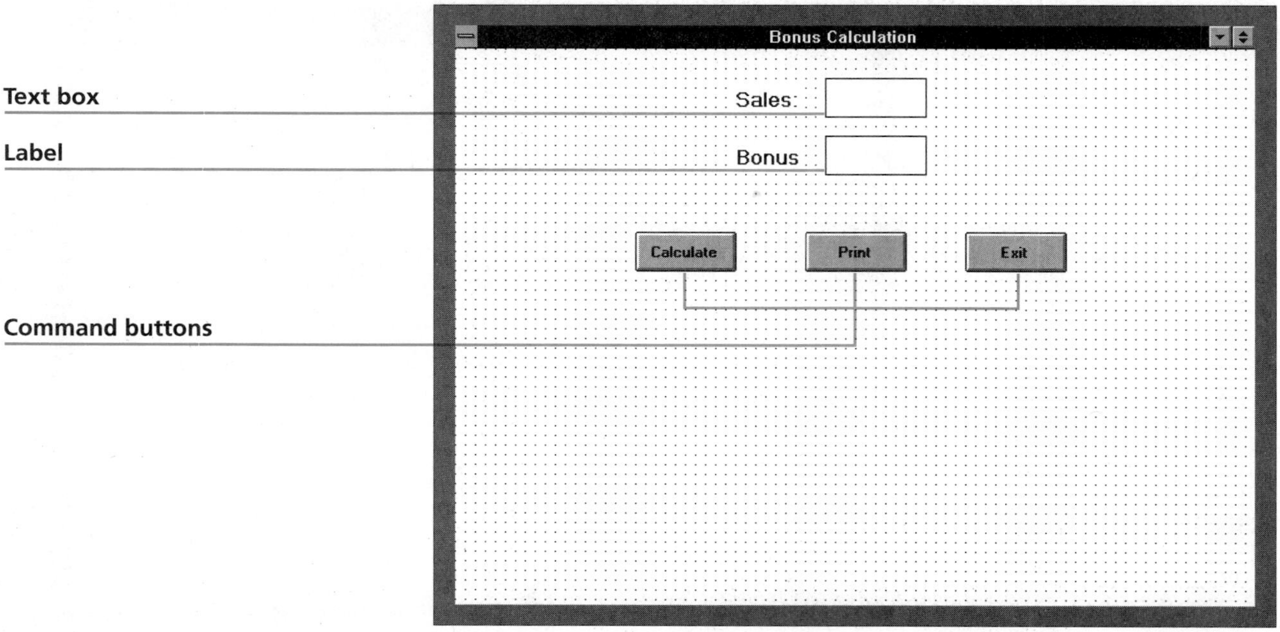

Text box

Label

Command buttons

Figure 4-52:

b. Save the form and the project as T4LCE6.

c. Code the Exit button so that it ends the application. Code the Print button so that it prints the form.

The user will enter the sales in the Text box. He or she will then click the Calculate Command button to calculate and display the bonus. The bonus depends on the amount of sales, as follows:

Amount of Sales	Bonus
0 – 1000.99	$ 0
1001 – 5000.99	50
5001 – 9999.99	100
10000 and over	250

d. Draw the flowchart or write the pseudocode for the Calculate Command button.

e. Use your flowchart or pseudocode to finish coding the application.

f. Save and run the application.

g. Test the application by entering 900 in the Text box. Click the Calculate Command button. Then click the Print Command button.

h. Test the application again by entering 4999.50 in the Text box. Click the Calculate Command button, then click the Print Command button.

i. Test the application again by entering 9000 in the Text box. Click the Calculate Command button, then click the Print Command button.

j. Test the application again by entering 20000 in the Text box. Click the Calculate Command button, then click the Print Command button.

k. Exit the application, then print the code.

Exercises 7 and 8 are Discovery Exercises, which allow you to "discover" the solutions to problems on your own. Discovery Exercises can include topics that are not covered in the tutorial.

discovery ▶ **7.** a. Create a user interface that contains one Image control and two Command buttons.

b. Set the Caption of one Command button to Exit. Set the Caption of the other Command button to On/Off. Load an icon of your choice into the Image control.

c. Code the Click event procedure of the On/Off Command button so that the Command button can be used to either hide or display the Image control. (In other words, each time the On/Off Command button is clicked, the Image control will either be hidden or displayed.)

d. Save the form and the project as T4LCE7.

e. Exit the application, then print the form and the code.

discovery ▶ 8.   a. Create the user interface shown in Figure 4-53.

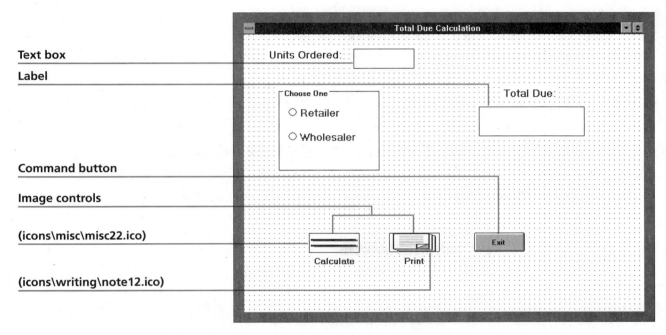

Text box

Label

Command button

Image controls

(icons\misc\misc22.ico)

(icons\writing\note12.ico)

Figure 4-53

b. Save the form and the project as T4LCE8.

c. Code the Exit button and the Print Image control. The Exit button should end the application. The Print Image control should print the form.

The user will enter the units ordered in the Text box. He or she will then select either the Retailer Option button or the Wholesaler Option button. After the data is entered and the selection is made, the user will click the Calculate Image control to calculate the total due (units ordered times price per unit). The price per unit depends on both the customer type and the number of units ordered. Use the following information to determine the price per unit:

Wholesaler:

Number of units ordered	Price
1 – 4	$ 10 per unit
5 and over	9 per unit

Retailer:

Number of units ordered	Price
1 – 3	$ 15 per unit
4 – 8	14 per unit
9 and over	12 per unit

d. In this application, put all of the necessary code in the Calculate Image control's Click event procedure. Do not put any code in the Option buttons' procedures. (The purpose of this application is to show you another way of coding an application that contains Option buttons.) Draw the flowchart or write the pseudocode for the Calculate Image control. (Hint: Have the Calculate Image control determine which Option button is on and then assign the correct price per unit.)

e. Use your flowchart or pseudocode to finish coding the application.

f. Save and run the application.

g. Test the application by entering 10 in the Text box. Choose Retailer, then click the Calculate Image control. (The total due should be 120.) Click the Print Image control.

h. Test the application again by choosing Wholesaler. (Leave the number 10 in the Text box.) Click the Calculate Image control, then click the Print Image control.

i. Test the application again by entering 5 in the Text box. Choose Retailer, then click the Calculate Image control, then click the Print Image control.

j. Exit the application, then print the code.

D E B U G G I N G

Technique　　Use the Print method to verify the contents of the variables in the application.

Exercises　　Tutorial 4's Debugging section contains two debugging exercises.

1. a. Open the T4D1.MAK project, which is in either the tut4\ver2 or the tut4\ver3 directory on your Student Disk. Click the View Form button to view the form.

b. Print the code, then run the application. This application computes the total cost of the tapes, records, and CDs ordered by a customer.

c. Type 5 as the number of tapes, type 5 as the number of records, type 5 as the number of CDs, then click the Calc button. (Be sure to enter all three numbers.) The application calculates and displays the total price of the order ($149.35). Notice that the application does not display the individual totals for the tapes, records, and CDs.

d. Click the Exit button to end the application. You will now use the Print method to print the contents of the Tottape, Totrecord, and Totcd variables on the form. The sum of these three variables should equal the total price of the order.

e. Open the Calc button's Code window. In the blank line immediately above the *End Sub* instruction, type **Print Tottape, Totrecord, Totcd** and press [Enter]. Notice that you can include more than one item on a Print instruction. You can separate each item with either a comma (,) or a semicolon (;). Using the comma to separate the items allows you to take advantage of Visual Basic's preset tabs. The comma tells Visual Basic to tab to the next print zone before printing; each print zone is 14 columns wide. If you use a semicolon to separate one item from another, the second item prints immediately after the first item. (When printing positive numbers, Visual Basic prints the number with both a leading and a trailing space. When printing negative numbers, Visual Basic prints the number with a negative sign on the left and a trailing space on the right.)

f. Close the Code window, then run the application. You do not need to save the application.

g. Type **5** as the number of tapes, type **5** as the number of records, type **5** as the number of CDs, then click the Calc button. The total price ($149.35) appears in the Label control. The contents of the Tottape variable (49.95), the Totrecord variable (39.95), and the Totcd variable (59.45) appear in the upper-left corner of the form. Click the Exit button to end the application, then print the code.

2. a. If necessary, open the T4D1.MAK project, which is in either the tut4\ver2 or the tut4\ver3 directory on your Student Disk. Click the View Form button to view the form.

b. If you did not do Debugging Exercise 1, then print the code for this application.

c. Run the application. This application computes the total cost of the tapes, records, and CDs ordered by a customer.

d. Type **5** as the number of tapes, then click the Calc button. Visual Basic displays a "Type mismatch" error message on the screen. As you learned in Tutorial 3, a "Type mismatch" error means that Visual Basic has encountered something that it wasn't expecting in an instruction—for example, a string where a number is required, or a number where a string is needed.

e. Click the OK button to remove the error message. Visual Basic highlights the *Totrecord = Recordprice * TxtRecord.Text* instruction. In this case, Visual Basic expected to find numbers stored in the Text property of the Text boxes (TxtTape, TxtRecord, and TxtCd). Because the TxtRecord Text box was empty, Visual Basic found the null string ("") stored there instead. Recall that you can't use the null string in an equation involving multiplication. You will use the Val function, as you did in Tutorial 3, to fix this problem.

f. Click the Stop icon ■ to stop the application. Open the Calc button's Code window. Change the *Tottape = Tapeprice * TxtTape.Text* instruction to **Tottape = Tapeprice * Val(TxtTape.Text)**.

g. Change the *Totrecord = Recordprice * TxtRecord.Text* to **Totrecord = Recordprice * Val(TxtRecord.Text)**.

h. Change the *Totcd = Cdprice * TxtCd.Text* to **Totcd = Cdprice * Val(TxtCd.Text)**.

i. Close the Code window, then run the application. You do not need to save the application.

j. Type **10** as the number of Tapes, then click the Calc button. The total price ($99.90) appears in the Label control. If you completed Debugging Exercise 1, the numbers 99.9, 0, and 0 appear in the upper-left corner of the form.

k. Click the Exit button to end the application, then print the code. You can now exit Visual Basic. You do not need to save the application.

Repetition and More on Selection

The Grade Calculation Application

case ▶ Next Monday is Career Day at your alma mater. Professor Carver, one of your computer programming instructors, has asked you to be a guest speaker in his Introduction to Programming class. You gladly accept this speaking engagement and begin planning your presentation. You decide to show the students how to create an application that will calculate their grade in Professor Carver's class.

Previewing the Completed Application

Let's begin by previewing the completed grade application.

To preview the completed application:

1. Launch Windows and make sure the Program Manager window is open and your Student Disk is in the appropriate drive. If necessary, click the Minimize on Use option on the Options menu to minimize the Program Manager on use. **Run** the GRADE.EXE file, which is in either the tut5\ver2 or the tut5\ver3 directory on your Student Disk. The grade application's user interface appears on the screen. See Figure 5-1.

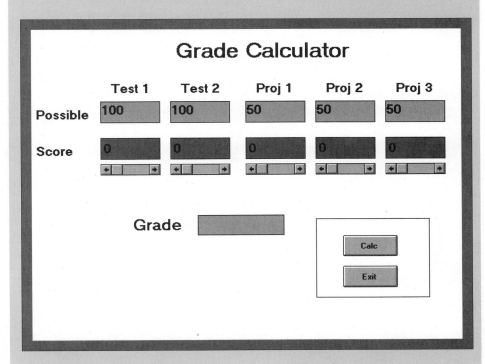

Figure 5-1: The grade application

This application contains a new control, the Horizontal scroll bar, which you will learn about in Lesson B.

2. **In the first scroll bar** on the left, click the **right scroll arrow button**. Notice that the scroll box moves to the right and a number greater than 0 appears in the text box above the scroll bar. Continue clicking until **90** appears in the Text box. (If you see a number greater than 90, click the left scroll arrow button until 90 appears.)

3. Click the **right scroll arrow button in each of the remaining four scroll bars** until the following numbers appear in the Text boxes:

Test 2	85	Proj 2	45
Proj 1	40	Proj 3	50

4. Click the **Calc button**. The grade in Professor Carver's class, a "B" (without the quotes), appears in the Label control on the screen.

5   Now click the **right or left scroll arrow buttons in each of the five scroll bars** until the following numbers appear in the Text boxes:

Test 1	75	Proj 1	35
Test 2	75	Proj 2	35
		Proj 3	35

6   Click the **Calc button**. A "C" (without the quotes) appears in the Label control.

7   Click the **Exit button**. The application ends.

In this tutorial you will learn about two Visual Basic statements, Select Case and For...Next, which you will use to complete the grade application. The Select Case statement is another form of the selection structure, which you learned about in Tutorial 4. The For...Next statement is one of three forms of the Repetition structure. (You will learn the other two forms of the Repetition structure in Tutorial 6.) You will learn the Select Case statement and the For...Next statement in Lesson A. In Lesson B you will learn about scroll bars and control arrays. You will begin coding the grade application in Lesson B and then complete the application in Lesson C.

Writing the Select Case and the For...Next Statements

More on the Selection Structure

In Tutorial 4 you learned how to use Visual Basic's If...Then...Else statement to code the selection structure. Recall that the If...Then...Else statement first evaluates the condition specified in the If clause. Based on that evaluation, the statement then selects and processes the instructions in one of two paths—either the true path (the Then) or the false path (the Else). In many cases you can have more than two paths for a selection structure to choose from. For example, suppose your application needs to display a message based on a letter grade that the user enters in a Text box. The letter grades and their corresponding messages are as follows:

Letter Grade	Message
A	Excellent
B	Above Average
C	Average
D, F	Below Average
I	Incomplete
W	Withdrawal
Other	Incorrect Grade

You could use a nested If...Then...Else statement to code this selection structure. However, when a selection structure has several paths to choose from, it is usually clearer to use the Case format of the selection structure instead of the nested If...Then...Else format. The Case format is sometimes referred to as an **extended selection structure**. Figure 5-2 shows the flowchart and the pseudocode for the Case selection structure that would display a message based on the grade contained in a Text box named TxtData.

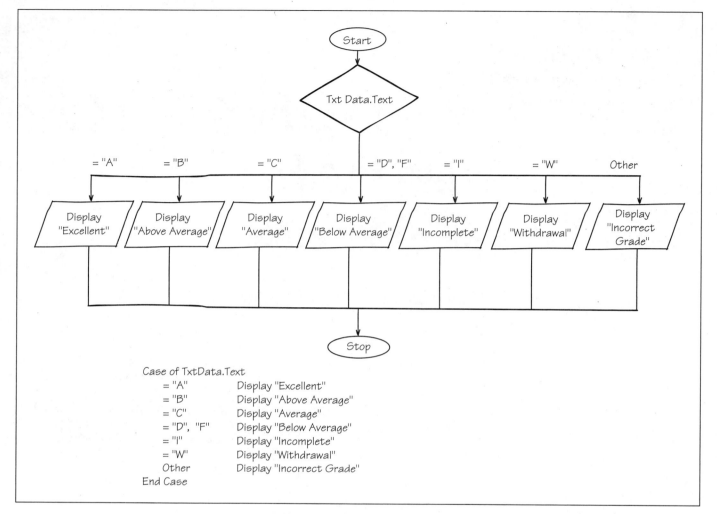

Figure 5-2: Flowchart and pseudocode of Case structure

Let's take a closer look at the flowchart shown in Figure 5-2. In Tutorial 4, you learned that the flowchart symbol for the selection structure is a diamond. Unlike the If...Then...Else diamond you saw in Tutorial 4, however, the Case diamond does not contain a condition requiring a true/false (yes/no) answer. Instead, the Case diamond contains an expression—in this case, TxtData.Text—whose value will control which path is chosen. (An **expression** is any combination of variables, constants, functions, operators, and properties.)

Like the If...Then...Else diamond, the Case diamond has one flowline leading into the symbol. Unlike the If...Then...Else diamond, however, the Case diamond has many flowlines leading out of the symbol. Each flowline represents a possible path for the selection structure. The flowlines must be marked appropriately, indicating which value(s) are necessary for each path to be chosen.

Now let's look at how you code the Case selection structure in Visual Basic.

The Select Case Statement

You use Visual Basic's Select Case statement to code the Case selection structure. Figure 5-3 shows the format of the Select Case statement. It also shows the Select Case statement that will display a message based on the grade entered in the TxtData Text box.

Format	Example
Select Case *testexpression*	Select Case TxtData.Text
Case *expressionlist1*	Case "A"
[*instructions for the first Case*]]	LblMsg.Caption = "Excellent"
[**Case** *expressionlist2*	Case "B"
[*instructions for the second Case*]]	LblMsg.Caption = "Above Average"
Case *expressionlistn*	Case "C"
[*instructions for the nth Case*]]	LblMsg.Caption = "Average"
Case Else	Case "D", "F"
[*instructions for when the*	LblMsg.Caption = "Below Average"
testexpression does not match	Case "I"
any of the expressionlists]]	LblMsg.Caption = "Incomplete"
End Select	Case "W"
	LblMsg.Caption = "Withdrawal"
	Case Else
	LblMsg.Caption = "Incorrect Grade"
	End Select

Figure 5-3: The format and an example of the Case structure

In the format, the items in square brackets ([]) are optional. Words in bold, however, are essential components of the Select Case statement. Items in *italics* indicate where the programmer must supply information pertaining to the current application.

The Select Case statement begins with the Select Case clause and ends with the two words End Select. Between the Select Case clause and the End Select are the individual Case clauses. Each Case clause represents a different path that the selection structure can follow. You can have as many Case clauses as necessary in a Select Case statement.

Notice that the Select Case clause must include a *testexpression*. The *testexpression* can be any numeric or string expression, which means it can contain a combination of variables, constants, functions, operators, and properties. In the example shown in Figure 5-3, the *testexpression* is TxtData.Text.

Each of the individual Case clauses, except the Case Else, must contain an *expressionlist*, which can include one or more numeric or string expressions. (To include more than one expression in an *expressionlist*, simply separate each expression with a comma, as in *Case "D", "F"*.) The data type of the expressions must be compatible with the data type of the *testexpression*. In other words, if the *testexpression* is numeric, the expressions must be numeric. Likewise, if the *testexpression* is a string, the expressions must be strings. In the example shown in Figure 5-3, the *testexpression* (TxtData.Text) is a string, and so are the expressions—"A", "B", "C", "D", "F", "I", "W"—as the surrounding quotation marks indicate. (Recall from Tutorial 2 that the value in the Text property of a control is treated as a string, not as a number.)

When processing the Select Case statement, Visual Basic first compares the value of the *testexpression* with the expressions (values) listed in *expressionlist1*. If a match is found, Visual Basic processes the instructions for the first Case and then skips to the instruction following the End Select. If a match is not found in *expressionlist1*, Visual Basic skips to the second Case clause, where it compares the *testexpression* with the values listed in *expressionlist2*. If a match is found, Visual Basic processes the instructions for the second Case clause and then skips to the instruction following the End Select. If a match is not found, Visual Basic skips to the third Case clause and so on. If the *testexpression* value does not match any of the values listed in any of the expressionlists, Visual Basic then processes the instructions listed in the Case Else clause or if there is no Case Else clause, it processes the instruction following the End Select. (If the *testexpression* value matches a value in more than one Case clause, only the instructions in the first match are processed.)

The T5A_CASE.MAK project on your Student Disk contains three examples of the Select Case statement. Let's open that project now.

To open the T5A_CASE.MAK project:

1 Launch Visual Basic, if necessary. Open the **t5a_case.mak** file, which is in either the tut5\ver2 or the tut5\ver3 directory on your Student Disk. Click the **View Form button**, then maximize the form. The user interface appears on the screen, as shown in Figure 5-4.

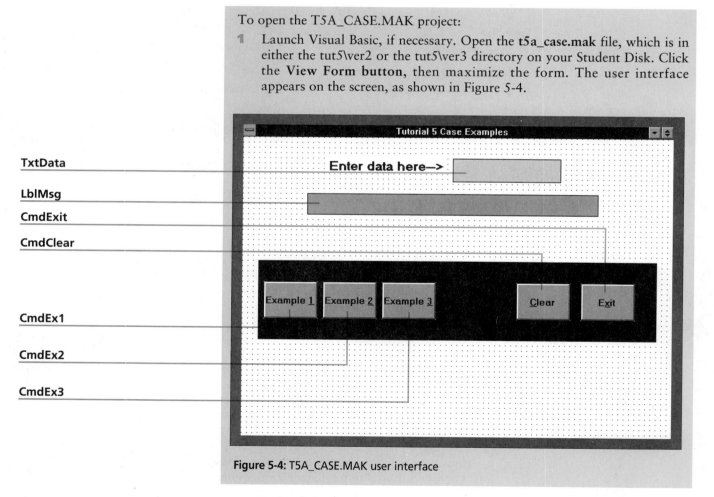

Figure 5-4: T5A_CASE.MAK user interface

Each of the Command buttons has been coded for you. (You can verify that if you want.) First let's look at the code for Example 1.

Example 1

Example 1 uses the Select Case statement to display a message based on the grade entered in the TxtData Text box. (The flowchart and pseudocode for this example are shown in Figure 5-2.)

To view the code for Example 1, and then test the Example 1 button:

1   Double-click the **Example 1 button** to open its Code window, then maximize the Code window. The CmdEx1's Click event procedure appears on the screen, as shown in Figure 5-5.

temporarily converts Text property to uppercase →

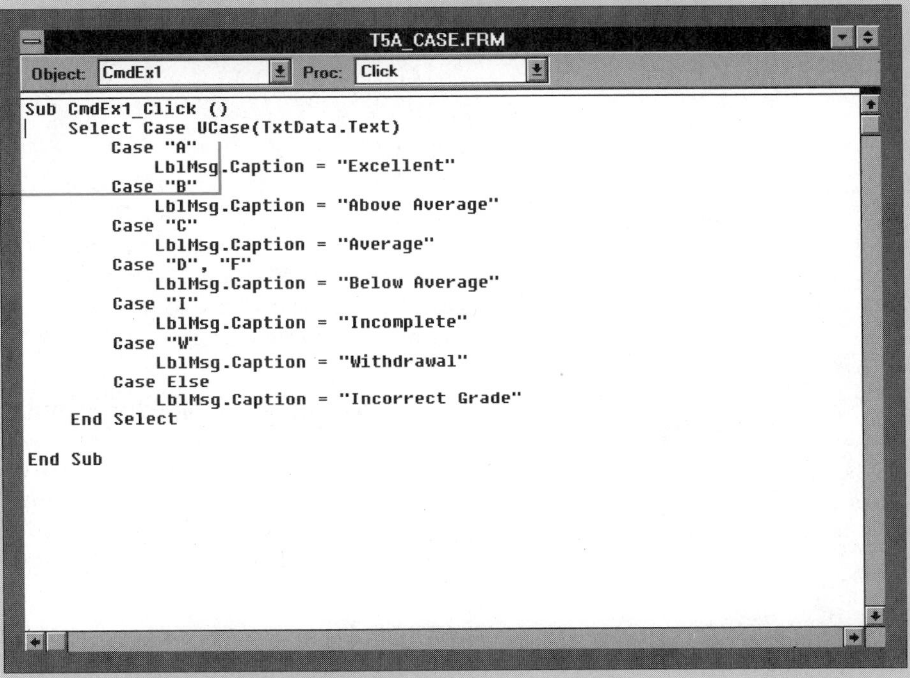

```
                              T5A_CASE.FRM
Object:  CmdEx1          ±   Proc:  Click          ±

Sub CmdEx1_Click ()
    Select Case UCase(TxtData.Text)
        Case "A"
            LblMsg.Caption = "Excellent"
        Case "B"
            LblMsg.Caption = "Above Average"
        Case "C"
            LblMsg.Caption = "Average"
        Case "D", "F"
            LblMsg.Caption = "Below Average"
        Case "I"
            LblMsg.Caption = "Incomplete"
        Case "W"
            LblMsg.Caption = "Withdrawal"
        Case Else
            LblMsg.Caption = "Incorrect Grade"
    End Select

End Sub
```

Figure 5-5: Example 1's Click event procedure

Notice that the code uses the UCase function, which you learned about in Tutorial 4, to temporarily convert the contents of the Text box to uppercase before comparing it to the uppercase letter grades. This way the user can enter the grade in upper- or lowercase.

2   Close the Code window, then press [F5] to run the application. (If you are asked if you want to save the form, click No.) Type **c** in the Text box, then click the **Example 1 button**. Visual Basic processes the instructions in CmdEx1's Click event procedure. "Average" (without quotes) appears in the Label control.

So how does the Example1 button work? (Refer back to Figure 5-5 as you read the following explanation.) First, Visual Basic temporarily converts the contents of the TxtData's Text property ("c") to uppercase, giving "C". It then compares the "C" with the value listed in the first Case's expressionlist ("A"). Because "C" does not match "A", Visual Basic skips to the second Case clause where it compares "C" with that Case's expressionlist ("B").

Because "C" does not match "B", Visual Basic skips to the third Case clause where it compares "C" with that Case's expressionlist ("C"). Here there is a match, so Visual Basic processes the *LblMsg.Caption* = *"Average"* instruction, which displays the string "Average" (without the quotes) in the Label control. Visual Basic then skips the remaining instructions in the Select Case statement and processes the instruction after the End Select (the End Sub instruction). (Notice that the string "Average" is centered in the Label control. You will learn how to center the Caption property in Lesson C.)

Now let's see what happens if you enter an incorrect grade in the Text box.

3   Click the **Clear button** to clear the Label control and the Text box, type **t** in the Text box, then click the **Example 1 button**. Because the value in the Text box does not match any of the values listed in any of the Case clauses, the Case Else instruction is processed and the string "Incorrect Grade" appears in the Label control. Visual Basic then processes the instruction following the End Select (the End Sub instruction).

4   Click the **Exit button** to end the application. Visual Basic returns to the design screen.

In the next two examples, you will learn how to specify a range of values in an expressionlist—such as the values 1 through 4, and values greater than 10. You will also learn how to use numbers, instead of strings, in the *testexpression* and in the expressionlists.

Using "To" and "Is" in an Expressionlist

You can use either the keyword "To" or the keyword "Is" to specify a range of values in an expressionlist. (A **keyword** is a word that has a specific meaning in a programming language.) The specified values can be either numeric or strings. You will use the keyword "To" in Example 2 and the keyword "Is" in Example 3.

Example 2

XYZ Corporation offers programming seminars to a variety of companies. The price per person depends on the number of people the company registers, as shown in the following chart.

Number of registrants	Charge
1 – 4	$ 100 per person
5 – 10	$ 80 per person
More than 10	$ 60 per person

Figure 5-6 shows the flowchart and the pseudocode for this example.

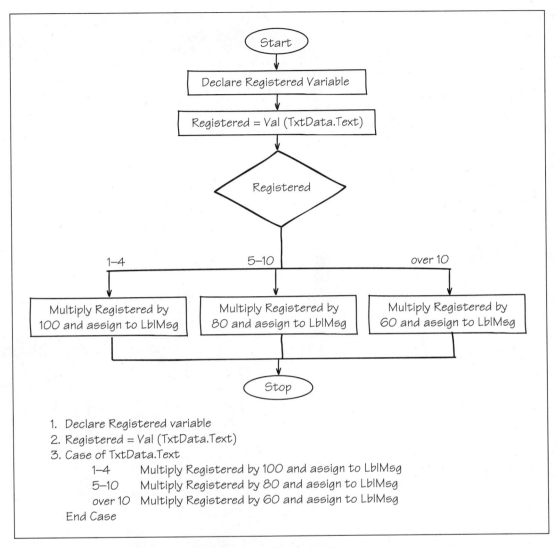

1. Declare Registered variable
2. Registered = Val (TxtData.Text)
3. Case of TxtData.Text
   - 1–4   Multiply Registered by 100 and assign to LblMsg
   - 5–10   Multiply Registered by 80 and assign to LblMsg
   - over 10 Multiply Registered by 60 and assign to LblMsg
   - End Case

Figure 5-6: Example 2's flowchart and pseudocode

Now let's look at the corresponding Visual Basic code in the Example 2 button's Click event procedure.

To view the code for Example 2 and then test the Example 2 button:

1. Double-click the **Example 2 button** to open its Code window, then maximize the Code window. The CmdEx2's Click event procedure appears on the screen, as shown in Figure 5-7.

declares an Integer
variable

stores numeric
equivalent of Text
property in Integer variable

specifies a range of values

handles numbers over 10

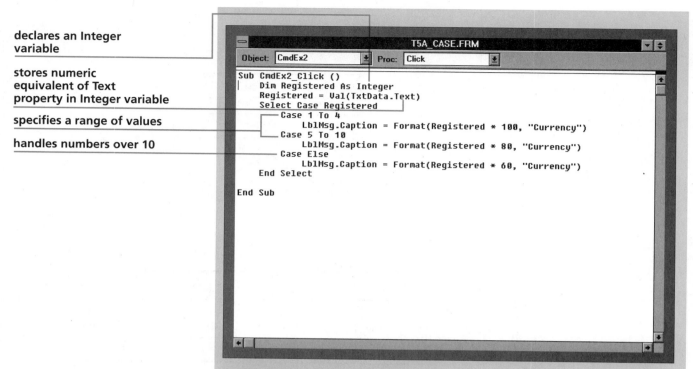

```
                                      T5A_CASE.FRM
Object:  CmdEx2          ±   Proc:  Click              ±
Sub CmdEx2_Click ()
    Dim Registered As Integer
    Registered = Val(TxtData.Text)
    Select Case Registered
       Case 1 To 4
           LblMsg.Caption = Format(Registered * 100, "Currency")
       Case 5 To 10
           LblMsg.Caption = Format(Registered * 80, "Currency")
       Case Else
           LblMsg.Caption = Format(Registered * 60, "Currency")
    End Select

End Sub
```

Figure 5-7: Example 2's Click event procedure

The code first declares an Integer variable named Registered. It then uses the Val function to assign the numeric equivalent of the TxtData control's Text property to the Registered variable. The Registered variable, instead of the TxtData's Text property, is then used as the *testexpression* in the Select Case clause. Because the Registered variable contains a number, the values listed in each expressionlist must be numeric.

According to the XYZ Corporation's chart, the charge for one to four registrants is $100 each. You could, therefore, write the first Case clause as *Case 1, 2, 3, 4*. A more convenient way of writing that range of numbers, however, is to use the keyword "To," but you must follow this format: *smallest value in the range* **To** *largest value in the range*. The expression *1 To 4* in the first Case clause, for example, specifies the range of numbers from 1 to 4, inclusive. The expression *5 To 10* in the second Case clause specifies the range of numbers from 5 to 10, inclusive. When you use the keyword "To," the value preceding the "To" must always be smaller than the value after the "To." In other words, *10 To 5* is not a correct expression. (Visual Basic will not display an error message if the value preceding the "To" is greater than the value after the "To"; instead, the selection structure simply will not give the correct results. This is another reason why it is always important to test your code.) In Example 2, the Case Else clause will be processed when the number of registrants is greater than 10.

2   Close the Code window, then press [F5] to run the application. (If you are asked if you want to save the form, click No.)

Assume a company registers seven people.

3 Type **7** in the Text box, then click the **Example 2 button.** $560.00, which is 7 times $80 (the charge for 5 to 10 registrants), appears in the Label control. That's because the number 7 matches a number in the range specified in the *Case 5 To 10* clause.

4 Click the **Clear button.** On your own, verify that 3 registrants will cost $300.00—3 times the $100 charge for 1 to 4 registrants. Also verify that 15 registrants will cost $900.00—15 times the $60 charge for more than 10 registrants. (The charge for the 15 registrants will be calculated by the Case Else clause.)

Always keep in mind that users will, at times, make mistakes when entering data. Let's see what the Example 2 button does if the user accidentally enters a negative number.

5 Click the **Clear button,** type **–3** (be sure to type the minus sign) in the Text box, then click the **Example 2 button.** The negative number, ($180.00), appears in the Label control. (Note that the parentheses indicate a negative currency value.)

Because the –3 did not fall into either the *1 To 4* range or the *5 To 10* range, Visual Basic processed the *LblMsg.Caption = Format(Registered * 60, "Currency")* instruction in the Case Else clause, which multiplied the –3 times the $60 charge. It would be better if the application displayed a message alerting the user that an input error was made. You will learn how to display such a message in Example 3.

6 Click the **Exit button** to end the application. Visual Basic returns to the design screen.

Example 3

Example 3 is the same as Example 2, except that it requires the application to print an error message if the user enters an incorrect number of registrants. An incorrect number would include 0 (zero), a negative number, or a letter.

Number of registrants	Charge
1 – 4	$ 100 per person
5 – 10	$ 80 per person
More than 10	$ 60 per person
0, negative number, letter	"Incorrect Data"

Most of the code for Example 3 will be similar to the code for Example 2. Example 3, however, will include one additional Case clause, and its Case Else clause will be different. Let's look at Example 3's code now.

To view the code for Example 3 and then test the Example 3 button:

1 Double-click the **Example 3 button** to open its Code window, then maximize the Code window. The CmdEx3's Click event procedure appears on the screen, as shown in Figure 5-8.

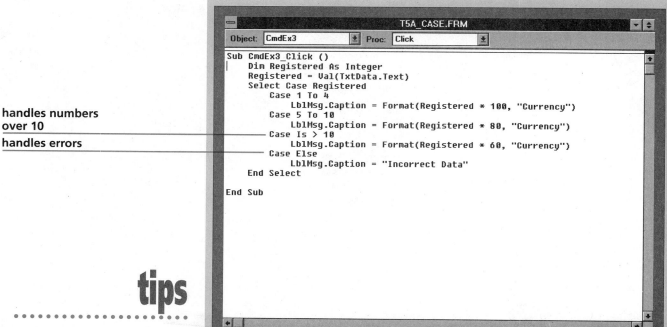

handles numbers
over 10

handles errors

Figure 5-8: Example 3's Click event procedure

You also could have written Example 3's Select Case statement with *Case Is <= 0* as the first Case, *Case 1 To 4* as the second Case, *Case 5 to 10* as the third Case, and then let the Case Else clause handle the numbers greater than 10. The difference between both Select Case statements is the position of the error checking clause—the clause that catches the input errors. Unless you expect the user to enter mostly incorrect values, you can save computer time by putting the error checking at the end of the Case structure, as shown in Example 3, instead of at the beginning of the structure.

If you want to learn more about the Select Case statement, use Visual Basic's Help menu to search for the *Select Case* topic, then print the topic and close the Help screen.

Notice the third Case clause, *Case Is > 10*, which was not included in Example 2's code. (You also could have written the clause as *Case Is >= 11*.) In addition to the keyword "To," you can also use the keyword "Is" to specify a range of values. You use the "Is" keyword in combination with the relational operators, like this: Is relational operator *value*. (Recall that the relational operators are =, <, <=, >, >=, and <>.) The expression *Is > 10*, for example, specifies all numbers greater than the number 10. (If you forget to type the "Is" in the expression, Visual Basic types it in for you. In other words, if you enter *Case > 10*, Visual Basic changes the clause to *Case Is > 10*.)

Notice that, in this example, the Case Else clause is used to display an "Incorrect Data" message when the user enters something that is not included in any of the Case clauses—namely, a 0 (zero), a negative number, or a letter. (In Visual Basic, the numeric equivalent of a letter is zero.)

2   Close the Code window, then press [F5] to run the application. (If you are asked if you want to save the form, click No.)

Now let's see what the application will do if the user enters a negative number.

3   Type –3 in the Text box, then click the **Example 3 button**. "Incorrect Data" (without the quotes) appears in the Label control.

4   Click the **Clear button**. On your own, verify that the application will display the "Incorrect Data" message when the user enters a letter.

5   Click the **Exit button** to end the application, then restore the form to its standard size.

In addition to the Case selection structure, you will also use the repetition structure in the grade application for Professor Carver's class.

The Repetition Structure (Looping)

Programmers use the repetition structure, also called **looping**, to tell the computer to repeat one or more instructions contained in a program. The three forms of the repetition structure are: For...Next, Do...While, and Do...Until. You will learn about the For...Next loop in this tutorial and about the other two loops in Tutorial 6.

The For...Next (Automatic Counter) Loop

The For...Next loop, also called an **automatic counter loop**, repeats a block of statements a specified number of times. You use Visual Basic's For...Next statement to code the automatic counter loop. Figure 5-9 shows both the format and an example of the For...Next statement. The example repeats a Print instruction three times.

Format of For...Next	Example of For...Next
For *counter = startvalue* **To** *endvalue* [**Step** *stepvalue*] [instructions]	For X = 1 to 3 Step 1 Print X
Next *counter*	Next X

Figure 5-9: Format and an example of the For...Next statement

Notice that the For...Next loop begins with the For statement and ends with the Next statement. Between those two statements, you enter the instructions you want the loop to repeat. In the format, *counter* is the name of a numeric variable, which is a variable that can store a number. Visual Basic uses the numeric variable to keep track of the number of times the loop instructions are processed. The name of the numeric variable in Figure 5-9's example is X.

The *startvalue*, *endvalue*, and *stepvalue* items control how many times to process the loop instructions. The *startvalue* tells the loop where to begin, the *endvalue* tells the loop when to stop, and the *stepvalue* tells the loop how much to add to (or subtract from) the *startvalue* each time the loop is processed. In Figure 5-9's example, the *startvalue* is 1, the *endvalue* is 3, and the *stepvalue* is 1. Those values tell the loop to start counting at 1 and, counting by 1's, stop at 3—in other words, count 1, 2, and then 3.

Startvalue, *endvalue*, and *stepvalue* must be numeric and they can be either positive or negative, integer or non-integer. If *stepvalue* is positive, then *startvalue* must be less than or equal to *endvalue* for the loop instructions to be processed. In other words, *For X = 1 To 3 Step 1* is correct, but *For X = 3 To 1 Step 1* is not correct because you can't count from 3 (the *startvalue*) to 1 (the *endvalue*) by adding increments of 1 (the *stepvalue*). If, on the other hand, *stepvalue* is negative, then *startvalue* must be greater than or equal to *endvalue* for the loop instructions to be processed. For example, *For X = 3 To 1 Step –1* is correct, but *For X = 1 To 3 Step –1* is not correct because you can't count from 1 to 3 by subtracting increments of 1. (If you omit the *stepvalue*, Visual Basic uses a *stepvalue* of a positive 1.)

The For...Next loop performs the following three tasks:

1. The loop initializes the *counter* (the numeric variable) to the *startvalue*. This is done only once, at the beginning of the loop.

2. If the *stepvalue* is positive, the loop checks if the value in the *counter* is greater than the *endvalue*. (Or, if the *stepvalue* is negative, the loop checks if the value in the *counter* is less than the *endvalue*.) If it is, the loop stops; if it's not, the instructions within the loop are processed and task 3 (below) is performed.

3. The loop adds the *stepvalue* to the *counter*. It then repeats steps 2 and 3 until the *counter* is greater than (or less than, if the stepvalue is negative) the *endvalue*.

On your Student Disk is a project named T5A_FOR.MAK, which contains two examples of the For...Next loop. Before opening the project, however, let's look at the flowchart and the pseudocode for the For...Next loop structure that will print the numbers 1 through 3 on the form. Both are shown in Figure 5-10.

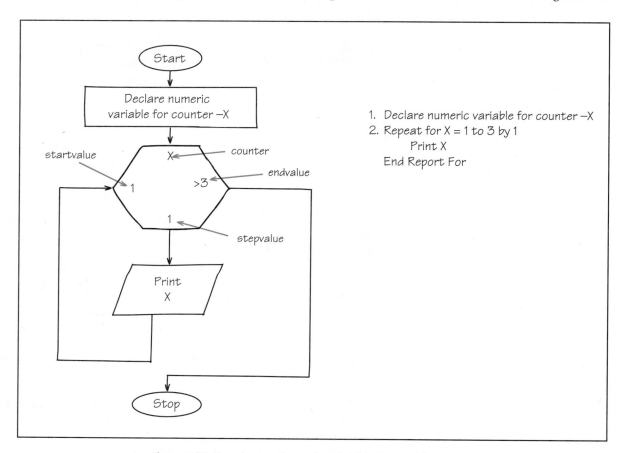

Figure 5-10: Flowchart and pseudocode of For...Next (automatic counter)

The For...Next loop is represented in a flowchart by a hexagon—a six-sided symbol. Four values are recorded inside the hexagon: the name of the *counter*, the *startvalue*, the *stepvalue*, and the *endvalue*. Notice that the *endvalue* is preceded by a > (greater-than sign). That's to remind you that the loop will stop when the value in the *counter* is greater than the *endvalue*. (If the *stepvalue* is negative, however, a < (less-than sign) should precede the *endvalue*, as that loop will stop when the value in the *counter* is less than the *endvalue*.) Now let's open the T5A_FOR.MAK project.

To open the T5A_FOR.MAK project:

1   Open the **t5a_for.mak** project on your Student Disk. (If you are asked if you want to save the form, click No.) Click the **View Form button**, then maximize the form. The user interface appears on the screen, as shown in Figure 5-11.

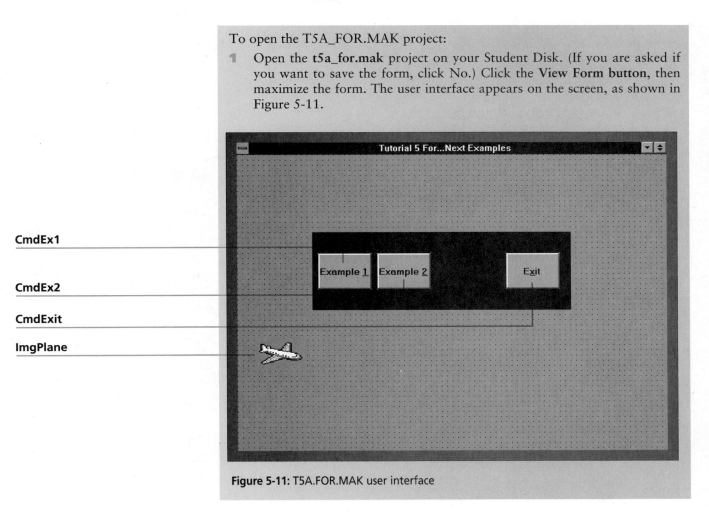

Figure 5-11: T5A.FOR.MAK user interface

Each of the Command buttons has been coded for you. (You can verify that if you want.) Let's look at the code for Example 1.

Example 1

The Example 1 button contains the code that will display the numbers 1 through 3 on the form.

To view the code for Example 1 and then test the Example 1 button:

1   Double-click the **Example 1 button** to open its Code window. The CmdEx1's Click event procedure appears on the screen, as shown in Figure 5-12.

declares the counter

prints the counter's
value on the form
three times

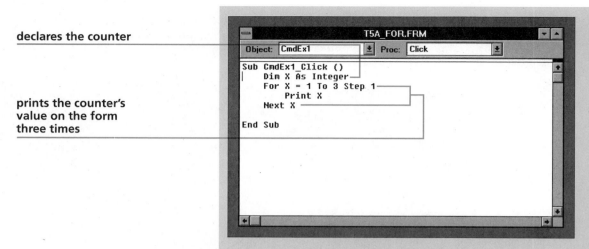

```
                        T5A_FOR.FRM
Object:  CmdEx1          ±    Proc:  Click          ±

Sub CmdEx1_Click ()
    Dim X As Integer
    For X = 1 To 3 Step 1
        Print X
    Next X

End Sub
```

Figure 5-12: Example 1's Click event procedure

The code first declares a numeric variable, X, which will be used as the *counter* in the For...Next loop. Because the *counter* will contain only whole numbers, the X variable is declared as an Integer type. The For...Next loop then instructs Visual Basic to print the contents of X on the form three times.

2   Close the Code window, then press [F5] to run the application. (If you are asked if you want to save the form, click No.)

3   Click the **Example 1 button**. Visual Basic processes the For...Next loop, as shown in Figure 5-13, and the numbers 1, 2, and 3 appear in the upper-left corner of the form.

4   Click the **Exit button** to end the application. Visual Basic returns to the design screen.

Steps in Processing Example 1's For...Next Loop

1. Loop initializes the counter, X, to 1 (*startvalue*).
2. Loop checks if value in X is greater than 3 (*endvalue*). It's not.
3. Visual Basic prints 1 (contents of X) on the form.
4. Loop adds 1 (*stepvalue*) to X, giving 2.
5. Loop checks if value in X is greater than 3 (*endvalue*). It's not.
6. Visual Basic prints 2 (contents of X) on the form.
7. Loop adds 1 (*stepvalue*) to X, giving 3.
8. Loop checks if value in X is greater than 3 (*endvalue*). It's not.
9. Visual Basic prints 3 (contents of X) on the form.
10. Loop adds 1 (*stepvalue*) to X, giving 4.
11. Loop checks if value in X is greater than 3 (*endvalue*). It is.
12. Loop stops.

Figure 5-13: Processing steps for Example 1's For...Next Loop

In Example 2, you will use the For...Next loop to move an object across the screen.

Example 2

You can move an object across the screen by setting its Left property within a For...Next loop. Let's open Example 2's Code window to see how this is done.

To view the code for Example 2 and then test the Example 2 button:

1 Double-click the **Example 2 button** to open its Code window. The CmdEx2's Click event procedure appears on the screen, as shown in Figure 5-14.

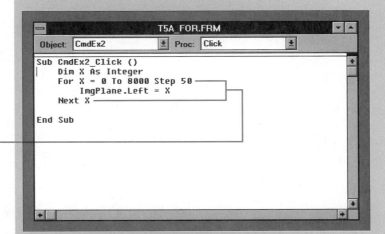

moves Image control from left to right

```
┌─ T5A_FOR.FRM ──────────────────────── ▼ ▲ ┐
│ Object: CmdEx2        ▼  Proc: Click          ▼  │
├──────────────────────────────────────────── ↑ │
│ Sub CmdEx2_Click ()                             │
│     Dim X As Integer                            │
│     For X = 0 To 8000 Step 50 ──┐               │
│         ImgPlane.Left = X        │              │
│     Next X ──────────────────────┘              │
│                                                 │
│ End Sub                                         │
│                                              ↓  │
│ ←───────────────────────────────────────── →   │
└─────────────────────────────────────────────────┘
```

Figure 5-14: Example 2's Click event procedure

In this example, the For...Next loop controls the value of the Image control's Left property. When you run the application and click the Example 2 button, the loop will initialize the Left property to 0 twips, which will place the Image control at the left edge of the form. (Recall that the Left property is measured in twips from the left edge of the form.) It will then add 50 twips to the Left property each time the loop is processed—in other words, the Left property will be increased from 0 to 50, then to 100, and so on. As the value in the Left property increases, the Image control moves farther away from the left edge of the form. When the Left property contains a number that is greater than 8,000 (the endvalue), the loop will stop and the Image control will be on the right side of the form. (In this example, the loop will stop when the Left property reaches a value of 8,050, which is 50—the stepvalue—more than the endvalue of 8,000.) Let's see how this code works.

2 Close the Code window, then press [F5] to run the application. (If you are asked if you want to save the form, click No.)

3 Click the **Example 2 button**. The airplane icon moves from the left edge of the screen to the right edge of the screen.

4 Click the **Example 2 button** again. The airplane icon again moves from left to right across the screen.

5 Click the **Exit button** to end the application. Visual Basic returns to the design screen.

6   If necessary, restore the form to its standard size. Click **File**, then click **New Project** to open a new project. If you are asked if you want to save the form, click No.

You have now completed Lesson A. You can either take a break or complete the exercises and questions at the end of the lesson.

S U M M A R Y

To code a Case (an extended selection) structure:

■   Use the Select Case statement. The format is:
> **Select Case** *testexpression*
> > [**Case** *expressionlist1*
> > > [*instructions for the first Case*]]
> > [**Case** *expressionlist2*
> > > [*instructions for the second Case*]]
> > [**Case** *expressionlistn*
> > > [*instructions for the nth Case*]]
> > [**Case Else**
> > > [*instructions when testexpression does not match any of the expressionlists*]]
> **End Select**

To specify a range of values in a Case clause's expressionlist:

■   Use the keyword "To" in the following format: *smallest value in the range* **To** *largest value in the range*. Examples: 1 To 4, "A" To "C".
■   Use the keyword "Is" in the following format: **Is** *relational operator value*. Examples: Is > 10, Is <= "Jones".

To code the For...Next (automatic counter) loop:

■   Use the For...Next statement. The format is:
> **For** *counter* = *startvalue* **To** *endvalue* [**Step** *stepvalue*]
> > [*instructions*]
> **Next** *counter*
■   The loop performs the following three tasks:
1.   The loop initializes the counter (the numeric variable) to the *startvalue*. This is done only once, at the beginning of the loop.
2.   If the *stepvalue* is positive (negative), the loop checks if the value in the counter is greater (less) than the *endvalue*. If it is, the loop stops; if it's not, the instructions within the loop are processed.
3.   The loop adds the *stepvalue* to the *counter*. It then repeats steps 2 and 3 until the *counter* is greater than the *endvalue* (or, if the *stepvalue* is negative, until the *counter* is less than the *endvalue*) .

To move a control across the screen (from left to right or from right to left):

■   Use a For...Next loop to set the control's Left property.

QUESTIONS

1. Which of the following flowchart symbols represents the Case selection structure?
    a. diamond
    b. hexagon
    c. oval
    d. parallelogram
    e. rectangle

2. Which of the following flowchart symbols represents the For...Next loop?
    a. diamond
    b. hexagon
    c. oval
    d. parallelogram
    e. rectangle

3. If the *testexpression* used in the Select Case clause is the numeric variable Sales, which of the following Case clauses are valid? (Choose two.)
    a. Case 2, 4, 6, 8
    b. Case "1" To "3"
    c. Case Is < "6"
    d. Case Is >= 8
    e. Case 4.5 Through 8.5

4. Assume the application uses a string variable named State. If the *testexpression* used in the Select Case clause is UCase(State), which of the following Case clauses are valid? (Choose three.)
    a. Case "TEXAS"
    b. Case "ALABAMA" And "ARKANSAS"
    c. Case Is > "Illinois"
    d. Case "COLORADO", "CALIFORNIA"
    e. Case "ALABAMA" To "ARKANSAS"

5. Assuming X is a numeric variable, how many times will the Print X instruction be processed?

    > For X = 1 to 6 Step 1
    >> Print X
    > Next X

    a. 0
    b. 1
    c. 5
    d. 6
    e. 7

6. What is the value of X when the loop in question 5 stops?
    a. 1
    b. 5
    c. 6
    d. 7
    e. 8

7. Assuming X is a numeric variable, how many times will the Print X instruction be processed?

        For X = 4 to 10 Step 2

            Print X

        Next X

    a. 0
    b. 3
    c. 4
    d. 5
    e. 12

8. What is the value of X when the loop in question 7 stops?
    a. 4
    b. 6
    c. 10
    d. 11
    e. 12

9. When the *stepvalue* in a For...Next loop is positive, the instructions within the loop are processed only when the *counter* is _____ the *endvalue*.
    a. equal to   d. less than
    b. greater than   e. less than or equal to
    c. greater than or equal to

10. When the *stepvalue* in a For...Next loop is negative, the instructions within the loop are processed only when the *counter* is _____ the *endvalue*.
    a. equal to   d. less than
    b. greater than   e. less than or equal to
    c. greater than or equal to

11. Which of the following are valid For instructions? (Choose two.)
    a. For X = 1.5 To 5 Step .5
    b. For X = 5 To 1 Step .25
    c. For X = 1 To 3 Step −1
    d. For X = 3 To 1
    e. For X = 1 To 10

12. The For...Next loop performs three tasks, as shown below. Put these tasks in their proper order by placing the numbers 1 through 3 on the line to the left of the task.

    _____ Adds the *stepvalue* to the *counter*.

    _____ Initializes the *counter* to the *startvalue*.

    _____ Checks if the value in the *counter* is greater (less) than the *endvalue*.

13. If you omit the *stepvalue* in a For...Next statement, Visual Basic uses a *stepvalue* of

    _____ .
    a. 0
    b. 1
    c. −1
    d. It results in an error message

14. Use the Help menu to search for a Help screen on the Select Case statement. Print the Help screen. How would you write an expressionlist that would match strings falling between the word "nuts" and the word "soup"? (Assume you don't know the case of the strings.)

15. Use the Help menu to search for a Help screen on the For...Next statement. Print the Help screen. Can you nest For...Next loops? _____

E X E R C I S E S

1. Draw the flowchart that corresponds to the following Visual Basic code:

   ```
   Select Case Sales
   Case Is >= 10000
           Commission = .1 * Sales
   Case Is >= 5000
           Commission = .05 * Sales
   Case Else
           Commission = 0
   End Select
   ```

2. Draw the flowchart that corresponds to the following Visual Basic code:

   ```
   Select Case Hours
   Case Is > 40
           LblMsg.Caption = "Overtime"
   Case Else
           LblMsg.Caption = "Regular"
   End Select
   ```

3. Write the Visual Basic code that corresponds to the flowchart shown in Figure 5-15.

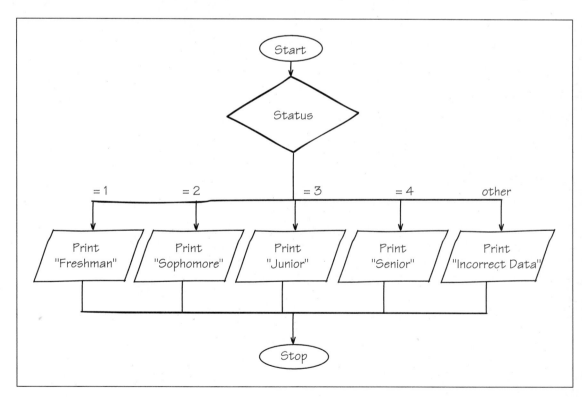

Figure 5-15

4. Write the Visual Basic code that corresponds to the flowchart shown in Figure 5-16.

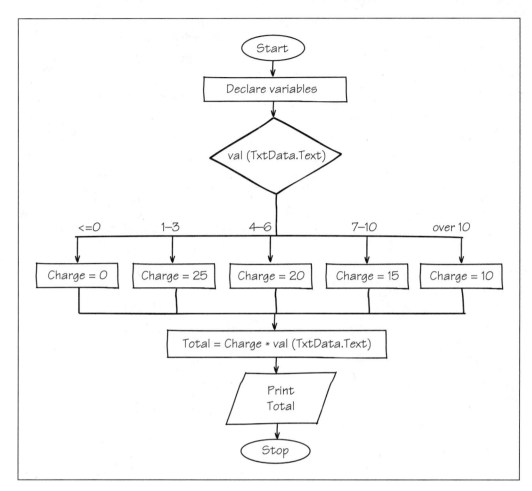

Figure 5-16

5. Display the string "Dog" in the LblAnimal control if the Animal variable contains the number 1. Display the string "Cat" if the Animal variable contains the number 2. Display the string "Bird" if the Animal variable contains anything other than the number 1 or the number 2.
   a. Draw the flowchart or write the pseudocode.
   b. Write the Visual Basic code.

6. An application needs to display a shipping charge based on the state entered in the TxtState control. Use the Case selection structure to display the shipping charge in the LblShip control. Use the chart below. (The state could be typed by the user in either uppercase or lowercase.)

State entered in TxtState control	Shipping charge
Hawaii	$25.00
Oregon	$30.00
California	$32.50

(Any other state should result in an "Incorrect State" message.)

   a. Draw the flowchart or write the pseudocode.
   b. Write the Visual Basic code.

7. The price of a concert ticket depends on the seat location entered in a Text box named TxtSeat. Use the Case selection structure to display the price in the LblPrice control. Use the chart below. (The seat location could be entered by the user in either uppercase or lowercase.)

Seat location	Concert ticket price
Box	$75.00
Pavilion	$30.00
Lawn	$21.00

(Any other seat location should result in an "Incorrect Seat Location" message.)

a. Draw the flowchart or write the pseudocode.
b. Write the Visual Basic code.

8. In most companies the amount of vacation you receive depends on the number of years you've been with the company. The number of years is entered in a Text box named TxtYears. Store the numeric equivalent of the years in an Integer variable named Years. Use the Case selection structure to display the weeks of vacation in the LblWeeks control. Use the following chart:

Years with the company	Weeks of vacation
Less than 1	0
1 to 5	1
6 to 10	2
11 and over	3

a. Draw the flowchart or write the pseudocode.
b. Write the Visual Basic code.

9. XYZ Corporation pays its salespeople a commission based on the amount of their sales. The sales amount is entered in a Text box named TxtSales. Store the numeric equivalent of the sales amount in a Currency variable named Sales. Use the Case selection structure to calculate and display the commission. (*Hint:* Commission is calculated by multiplying the sales by the commission rate.) Use the following chart:

Sales	Commission rate
$10,000.01 and over	10.0%
$5,000.01 – $10,000	7.5%
$1.00 – $5,000	5.0%
0 and under	Data Error

a. Draw the flowchart or write the pseudocode.
b. Write the Visual Basic code.

10. Assume you want to calculate a 10% discount on sales made to customers in California and in Texas, a 7% discount on sales made to customers in Oregon and New Mexico, and a 6% discount on sales made to customers in all other states. The state is entered in the TxtState control, and the sales amount is entered in the TxtSales control. Format the discount to Currency and display it in the LblDisc control. (You don't know the case of the State variable. In other words, the contents of the variable might be in uppercase, lowercase, or a combination of uppercase and lowercase letters.)

a. Draw the flowchart or write the pseudocode.
b. Write the Visual Basic code.

11. Draw the flowchart that corresponds to the following Visual Basic code.

```
For Number = 1 To 10 Step 1
    Print "Hello"
Next Number
```

12. a. Open a new project. Add one Command button to the form.

   b. Open the Command button's Code window. In the Click event procedure, enter a For...Next loop that will print the numbers 0 through 117, in increments of 9, on the form. Use X as the numeric variable in the For...Next loop. What value will X have when the loop stops? (*Hint:* Enter a Print X statement after the For...Next loop.)

   c. Run the project. (You don't need to save it.) Click the Command1 button to test your code. Mark down the value X has when the loop stops, then exit the application.

   d. Print the code. On the printout, mark the value X has when the loop stops.

13. An application needs to calculate and display the square of the even numbers from 2 to 12. Use the For...Next loop and the Print method to display the squares on the form.

   a. Draw the flowchart or write the pseudocode, then write the Visual Basic code.

   b. Open a new project. Add one Command button to the form.

   c. Open the Command button's Code window. Enter the Visual Basic code.

   d. Run the project. (You don't need to save it.) Click the Command1 button to test your code. Mark down the squares of the even numbers from 2 through 12, then exit the application.

   e. Print the code. On the printout, mark the squares of the even numbers from 2 through 12.

14. a. Open the T5A_FOR.MAK project, then save the form and the project as T5A_FOR2.

   b. Open Example 2's Code window. Add another For...Next statement that will move the Image control from right to left. (Enter the additional For...Next statement above the End Sub statement. Use 8000 as the *startvalue*, use −50 as the *stepvalue*, and use 0 as the *endvalue*.)

   c. Save, run, and test the Example 2 button. Then print the code.

Exercises 15 through 17 are Discovery Exercises.

discovery ▶ 15. a. Open the T5A_FOR.MAK project or, if you completed Exercise 14, then open the T5A_FOR2.MAK project. Save the form and the project as T5A_FOR2.

   b. Add two Command buttons to the form. Name one of the Command buttons CmdEx3 and change its Caption to Example 3. Name the other Command button CmdEx4 and change its Caption to Example 4.

   c. Open Example 3's Code window. In the Click event procedure, enter a For...Next statement that will move the Image control from the top of the screen to the bottom of the screen.

   d. Open Example 4's Code window. In the Click event procedure, enter a For...Next statement that will move the Image control diagonally from the top left corner of the screen to the bottom right corner of the screen.

   e. Save, run, and test the Example 3 and Example 4 Command buttons. Print the form and the code.

discovery ▶ 16. a. Create a user interface that contains three Command buttons. Name one of the Command buttons CmdTest and change its Caption to Test. Name another Command button CmdExit and change its Caption to Exit. Name the remaining Command button CmdPrint and change its Caption to Print.

   b. Save the form and the project as T5LAE16.

   c. Open the CmdTest control's Code window. In the Click event procedure, enter a For...Next statement that will print the first 10 Fibonacci numbers (1, 1, 2, 3, 5, 8, 13, 21, 34, 55) on the form. (Hint: Notice that, beginning with the third number in the series, each Fibonacci number is the sum of the prior two numbers. In other words, two is the sum of one plus one, three is the sum of one plus two, five is the sum of two plus three, and so on.)

   d. Code the CmdPrint control's Click event procedure so that it will print the form on the printer.

    e. Code the CmdExit control's Click event procedure so that it will end the application.

    f. Save and run the application. Click the Test button, then click the Print button, and then click the Exit button.

    g. Print the code.

discovery ▶ 17. a. Open the T5FORMUL.MAK project which is in either the tut5\ver2 or the tut5\ver3 directory on your Student Disk. Save the form and the project as T5LAE17. This application can be used to calculate the area of a square, rectangle, parallelogram, circle, or triangle.

    b. When the user clicks an option button, set the focus to the appropriate Text box.

    c. Use the Select Case statement in the Calculate button's Click event procedure to calculate the appropriate area. (For example, when the user selects the Square button, the area of a square should be calculated and then displayed in the LblAns1 control.)

    d. Save and run the application. Test the application with the following data: Square side measurement of 4, Rectangle length of 5 and width of 3, Parallelogram base of 3 and height of 4, Circle radius of 2, Triangle base of 4 and height of 3.

    e. Print the application with all of the test data and areas showing, then exit the application. Also print the form and the code.

LESSON B
objectives

In this lesson you will learn how to:

■ Add a scroll bar to a form
■ Code a Change event and a Scroll event
■ Create and code a control array

Using Scroll Bars and Control Arrays

Using Scroll Bars in an Application

Before working on the grade application for Professor Carver's class, let's take some time to learn about scroll bars. Scroll bars offer another way of getting numeric information from the user. For example, instead of having the user type a number in a Text box—a time-consuming process that can result in typing errors—you can use a scroll bar to display a predefined set of numbers. The user can then select the number he or she wants. Your Student Disk contains a project named T5B_HSB.MAK in which you will practice creating a scroll bar. Let's open that project now.

> **To open the T5B_HSB.MAK project:**
>
> **1** Launch Visual Basic (if necessary) and open the **t5b_hsb.mak** project, which is in either the tut5\ver2 or the tut5\ver3 directory on your Student Disk. Click the **View Form button** to view the form. Only one control, a Text box named TxtNums, appears on the form.

The Visual Basic Toolbox contains a Horizontal scroll bar tool and a Vertical scroll bar tool. The Horizontal scroll bar has arrows facing left and right while the Vertical scroll bar has arrows facing up and down. All scroll bar controls have three parts: the scroll arrow buttons, the scroll box, and the scroll bar. These parts are shown in Figure 5-17.

scroll arrow button
scroll bar
scroll box
scroll arrow button

Figure 5-17: Scroll bar control

As you probably know from using other Windows-based applications, you can scroll by clicking either the scroll arrow buttons or the scroll bar, or by dragging the scroll box along the scroll bar. Now let's see why a scroll bar works the way it does.

Five key properties control the three parts of a scroll bar control. These five properties are Value, Min, Max, SmallChange, and LargeChange. The Value property contains a number that represents the current location, or value, of the scroll box in the scroll bar. When you run the application, Visual Basic changes the contents of the Value property as you move the scroll box along the scroll bar.

During design time, you set the Min property to a number that represents the minimum value for the scroll bar. This is the number Visual Basic assigns to the Value property when the scroll box is at the leftmost location in a Horizontal scroll bar or at the top in a Vertical scroll bar. (Setting the Min property during design time automatically sets the Value property to the same amount. When you run the application, the scroll box will be located at the scroll bar's minimum location.) You set the Max property to a number that represents the maximum value for the scroll bar. Visual Basic assigns this number to the Value property when the scroll box is at the rightmost location of a Horizontal scroll bar or at the bottom in a Vertical scroll bar. You can set the Min and Max properties to any integer (whole number) between –32768 and 32767, inclusive.

The SmallChange property determines how far the scroll box will move when the user clicks the scroll arrow buttons in the scroll bar. The LargeChange property, on the other hand, determines how far the scroll box will move when the user clicks the scroll bar between the scroll box and the scroll arrow buttons. You can set the SmallChange and LargeChange properties to any integer between 1 and 32767, inclusive. These two properties allow you to scroll more quickly through the numbers in the scroll bar. Figure 5-18 recaps the five properties of a scroll bar control.

Property	Description
Value	A number representing the current location of the scroll box
Min	A number representing the minimum value in the scroll bar
Max	A number representing the maximum value in the scroll bar
SmallChange	A number that determines how far the scroll box moves when the user clicks a scroll arrow button
LargeChange	A number that determines how far the scroll box moves when the user clicks the scroll bar between the scroll box and the scroll arrow buttons

Figure 5-18: Primary properties of a scroll bar control

In the next set of steps, you will add a Horizontal scroll bar to the form. You will leave the scroll bar's Min property at its 0 setting, but you will set its Max property to 100. By doing so, the Horizontal scroll bar will display numbers ranging from 0 to 100. To allow the user to scroll more quickly through this range of numbers, you will set the scroll bar's SmallChange property to 5 and its LargeChange property to 10. Then when the user clicks a scroll arrow button, he or she can view the numbers in increments of 5—for example: 5, 10,

15, and so on. And when the user clicks the scroll bar between the scroll box and the scroll arrow buttons, he or she can view the numbers in increments of 10—for example: 10, 20, 30, and so on.

To add a Horizontal scroll bar to the form:

1 Double-click the **Horizontal scroll bar tool** 🔲 in the Toolbox. A Horizontal scroll bar appears in the middle of the form.

2 Set the following properties for the Horizontal scroll bar:

LargeChange: **10**

Max: **100**

Name: **HsbNums** ("Hsb" stands for Horizontal scroll bar.)

SmallChange: **5**

Responding to a Change Event

Now that you have set the scroll bar's properties, you need to write the Visual Basic code that tells the scroll bar control to display, in the TxtNums Text box, the current location of the scroll box in the scroll bar. Remember, the location of the scroll box in the scroll bar represents the number that the user wants to select.

To code the Horizontal scroll bar:

1 Double-click the **HsbNums control** (the Horizontal scroll bar) to open its Code window.

Recall that the event procedure that appears when you open an object's Code window is typically the most commonly used procedure for that object; usually that's the Click event procedure. Notice, however, that the most common event procedure for a scroll bar control is Change. A Change event occurs when the position of the scroll box changes. Because you are usually interested in tracking changes in the position of the scroll box, the Change event procedure is the most commonly used procedure for scroll bar controls.

In this application you want to display, in the TxtNums Text box, the value corresponding to the current position of the scroll box. You do this by writing an assignment statement to assign the scroll bar's Value property, which keeps track of the scroll box's location, to the Text box's Text property. Recall that the Text property manages the text appearing inside a Text box control.

2 Press [**Tab**], then type **TxtNums.Text = HsbNums.Value** and press [**Enter**]. This assignment statement tells Visual Basic to assign the contents of the Horizontal scroll bar's Value property to the Text box's Text property. When the application is run and the user drags the scroll box or clicks either the scroll bar or the scroll arrow buttons, the value corresponding to the location of the scroll box will appear in the Text box.

3 Close the Code window, then **run** the application. (You don't need to save the application.) Click the **scroll bar's right scroll arrow button** three times. The number 5 appears in the Text box, then 10, and then 15. Clicking the right scroll arrow button displays the scores in increments of 5—the value in the SmallChange property.

4   Click the **scroll bar's left scroll arrow button** three times. Now 10 appears in the Text box, followed by 5, and then 0. Clicking the left scroll arrow button decreases the score by the value in the SmallChange property—5.

5   Click the **scroll bar between the scroll box and the right scroll arrow button** several times. The score increases by 10—the value in the LargeChange property—each time you click. Click the **scroll bar between the scroll box and the left scroll arrow button** several times. The score decreases by 10—the value in the LargeChange property—each time you click.

In addition to clicking the scroll arrow buttons and the scroll bar, you can also drag the scroll box along the scroll bar.

6   Slowly drag the scroll box all the way to the right, then release the mouse button. The number 100 appears in the Text box. Notice, however, that the Text box does not reflect the change in the position of the scroll box until you release the mouse button.

Because the Text box isn't updated until after you release the mouse button, you don't know when to stop dragging to reach a specific number. It would be much better to have the Text box display the location of the scroll box as it moves along the scroll bar. You can do so by coding the scroll bar's Scroll event procedure. Let's return to the design screen to make this change.

7   Click the **Stop icon** ▣. Visual Basic returns to the design screen.

Responding to a Scroll Event

A Scroll event occurs while the user drags the scroll box along the scroll bar. To have the Text box display the current location of the scroll box as the scroll box is dragged, you will need to enter the same assignment statement in the Scroll event procedure as you did in the Change event procedure. Instead of retyping the instruction, you can copy the instruction from the Change event procedure's Code window to the Scroll event procedure's Code window.

To enter the assignment statement in the Scroll event and then run and test the application:

1   Double-click the **HsbNums control** (the Horizontal scroll bar) to open the Code window. The Change event procedure appears.

2   On your own, copy the TxtNums.Text = HsbNums.Value assignment statement to the Windows Clipboard. Click the **down arrow in the Code window's Proc box** to open the drop-down list of event procedures, then click **Scroll** in the drop-down list. (You might need to scroll the drop-down list in the Proc box.) Finally, paste the assignment statement into the Scroll event procedure.

3   Close the Code window, then **run** the application. (You don't need to save the application.) Slowly drag the scroll box to the right, then release the mouse button. Notice that the value displayed in the Text box changes as you drag the scroll box.

You are finished with this application, so you can close it. You don't need to save it.

4   Click the **Stop icon** ▣ to stop the application. Click **File**, then click **New Project**, and then click the **No button** to open a new project. A blank form appears.

Now that you know how to use a scroll bar, you can start working on the grade application for Professor Carver's class.

The Grade Application

Recall that your task in this tutorial is to create an application that will allow Professor Carver's programming class to calculate their grades. (To refamiliarize yourself with the grade application, you might want to run the GRADE.EXE file from the Program Manager before continuing with this lesson.) The sketch of the user interface is shown in Figure 5-19.

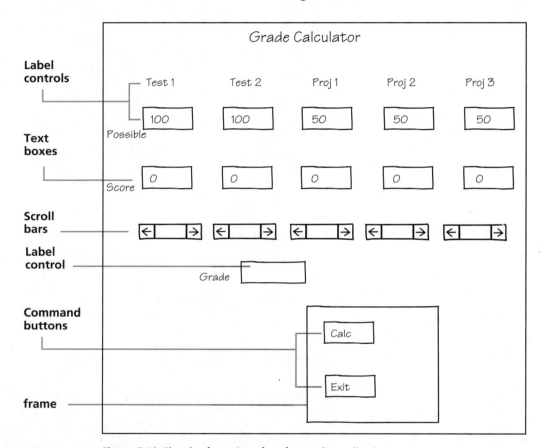

Figure 5-19: Sketch of user interface for grade application

According to the sketch, the grade application will contain various Label controls, Text boxes, Horizontal scroll bars, Command buttons, and a Frame control. The Label controls at the top of the user interface are for documentation; they show the maximum possible score that the student can attain on each of the tests and projects. The five scroll bars will allow the student to enter his or her scores in each of the Text boxes. (Because the scores are recorded in Text boxes, instead of Label controls, the user also has the option of entering the scores from the keyboard.) When the student clicks the Calc button, the application will calculate his or her grade in Professor Carver's class.

To save you time, your Student Disk contains a partially completed grade application. When you open the application you will notice that most of the user interface has already been created and most of the properties of the existing objects have been set. You will finish creating the user interface in this lesson. You will also begin coding the application.

To open the partially completed application:

1   Open the **t5a.mak** project, which is in either the tut5\ver2 or tut5\ver3 directory on your Student Disk, then click the **View form button** in the Project window to view the FrmGrade form.

2   Save the form and the project as **t5b**.

3   Click the **form's Maximize button** to maximize the form. The maximized form appears, as shown in Figure 5-20.

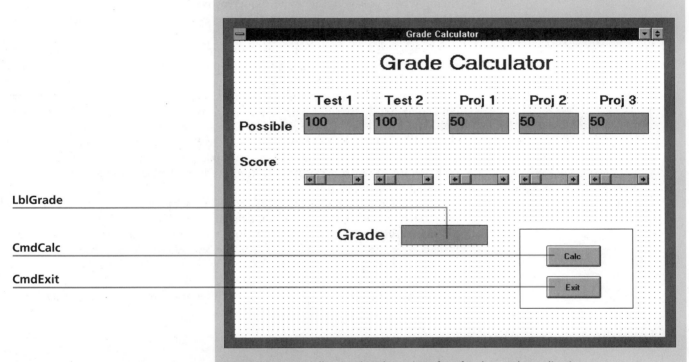

LblGrade

CmdCalc

CmdExit

Figure 5-20: Partially completed user interface for the grade application

Notice that the user interface is not complete; you still need to add the five Text boxes to it. Also, although the five scroll bars are already in the user interface, their Name properties have not been changed from their original values. You will do that in the next section. Each scroll bar's Min, SmallChange, LargeChange, and Max property, however, have been set. The Min property for each is set to 0, the SmallChange property is set to 5, and the LargeChange property is set to 10. The Max property for the two test scroll bars is set to 100, and the Max property for the three project scroll bars is set to 50.

4   Click the **form's Restore button** to restore the form to its standard size.

The grade application will use variables, so you should enter the Option Explicit statement in the general Declarations section of the form.

Open the general Declarations section of the form. If necessary, type **option explicit** and press **[Enter]**, then close the Code window.

First let's give a more meaningful name to each of the five scroll bars.

Control Arrays

Many times an application will contain a group of controls, of the same type, that perform essentially the same task. In the grade application, for example, each of the five Horizontal scroll bars will be used to enter a numeric score. Instead of giving each of the related controls a different name, which can be difficult to remember, Visual Basic allows you to assign the same name to each of them. When you give the same name to more than one control, you create a **control array**—a group of controls of the same type that have the same name and share the same set of event procedures. All of the controls in an array must be of the same type. In other words, they must all be Text boxes, or Label controls, or Option buttons, and so on. (You can also have an array of variables, which you will learn about in Tutorial 8.)

Visual Basic assigns a unique number, called an **index**, to each of the controls in an array. It might help to picture a control array as a group of mailboxes on a street. The name of the array is the name of the street, and the index is the address on each mailbox. The index reflects the control's position in the array, just as the address reflects a mailbox's position on a street. The first control (mailbox) in an array has an index (address) of 0, the second control has an index of 1, and so on.

You refer to each control in an array by the array's name (street name) and the control's index (address). The index is specified in a set of parentheses immediately following the name. For example, the first control in an array named HsbScore is referred to as HsbScore(0), the second control is HsbScore(1), and so on. The name of the array is stored in each control's Name property; the index is stored in each control's Index property.

Let's make the five Horizontal scroll bars into a control array named HsbScore.

To create a control array:

1   Click the **first scroll bar on the left** (under the Test 1 Text box) to select that control. Scroll the Properties list, if necessary, until both the Name property and the Index property are visible. The default name of the first scroll bar is HScroll1. Notice that the Index property is empty. When the Index property is empty, it means that the control is not a member of an array.

2   Click **Name** in the Properties list (if necessary), then type **HsbScore** and press **[Enter]**. HsbScore appears both in the Name property and in the Object box, and the Index property is still empty. (Be sure to verify, in the Properties window, that you have typed HsbScore correctly.)

3 Click the **second scroll bar** to select that control, type **HsbScore** in the Name property, and press [**Enter**]. The message dialog box shown in Figure 5-21 appears.

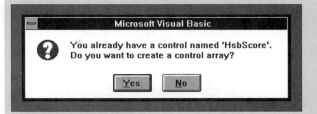

Figure 5-21: Message dialog box

The message in the dialog box tells you that you already have a control named HsbScore, and it asks if you want to create a control array.

4 Click the **Yes button** to create the control array. HsbScore appears in the Name property, 1 (one) appears in the Index property, and HsbScore(1) HScrollBar appears in the Object box.

Let's see what changes Visual Basic made to the properties of the first scroll bar.

5 Click the **first scroll bar**. The Name property says HsbScore, as it did before, but the Index property now says 0 (zero) and the Object box now says HsbScore(0) HScrollBar. Both the zero in the Index property and the (0) after the name in the Object box indicate that the control is the first control in an array.

Now let's name the remaining three scroll bars.

6 Click the **third scroll bar**, type **HsbScore** in the Name property, and press [**Enter**]. Look in the Properties window to verify that HsbScore appears in the Name property, 2 appears in the Index property, and HsbScore(2) appears in the Object box. HsbScore(2) indicates that this is the third control in the array.

7 Maximize the form, click the **fourth scroll bar**, press [**F4**] to display the Properties window, then type **HsbScore** in the Name property and press [**Enter**]. Look in the Properties window to verify that HsbScore appears in the Name property, 3 appears in the Index property, and HsbScore(3) HScrollBar appears in the Object box. The HsbScore(3) control is the fourth control in the array.

8 Click the **form** to remove the Properties window, then click the **fifth scroll bar**. Press [**F4**] to display the Properties window, then type **HsbScore** in the Name property and press [**Enter**]. Look in the Properties window to verify that HsbScore appears in the Name property, 4 appears in the Index property, and HsbScore(4) HScrollBar appears in the Object box. This control is the fifth control in the HsbScore array.

9 Restore the form to its standard size.

You have now finished creating the Horizontal scroll bar array. Next you will add the missing Text boxes to the form. These five Text boxes all perform essentially the same task—they display a score—so you will make them into a control array also. Earlier you saw how to create a control array when the controls were already on the form. In the next section you will learn how to use the "copy and paste" method to create a control array as you add the controls to the form.

Creating a Control Array While Adding Controls to the Form

Before you can use the "copy and paste" method to create a control array, you need to add the first array control—in this case, a Text box—to the form and then set its properties.

To add the first Text box to the form and then use the "copy and paste" method to create a control array:

1 Double-click the **Text box tool** ▦ in the Toolbox, then drag the Text box until it is positioned immediately above the first scroll bar. (You can look ahead to Figure 5-22 to see the new location of the text box.)

You will now set the BackColor property of the Text box to a dark pink, its FontSize property to 13.5, its Text property to 0 (zero), and its Width property to 1335.

2 Click **BackColor** in the Properties list, click the **... button in the Settings box,** then click a **dark pink** in the color palette. (Skip this step if you are using a black-and-white monitor.)

3 Click **FontSize** in the Properties list, click the **down arrow button in the Settings box,** and then click **13.5** in the drop-down list. Click **Text** in the Properties list, type **0** (a zero), and press **[Enter]**. Click **Width** in the Properties list, type **1335,** and press **[Enter]**.

You will now set the Name property to TxtScore. This will become the name of the control array when the array is created.

3 Scroll the Properties window, if necessary, until both the Index property and the Name property are visible. Click **Name** in the Properties list, then type **TxtScore** and press **[Enter]**.

Now that the Text box is on the form and its properties are set, you can use the "copy and paste" method to create the control array. First, you need to copy the Text box to the Windows Clipboard.

4 Click the **TxtScore control** to return to the form, press **[Ctrl][c]** to copy the Text box to the Windows Clipboard, then press **[Ctrl][v]** to paste a copy of the Text box on the form. When you are asked if you want to create a control array, click the **Yes button.** Another Text box appears in the upper-left corner of the form. See Figure 5-22.

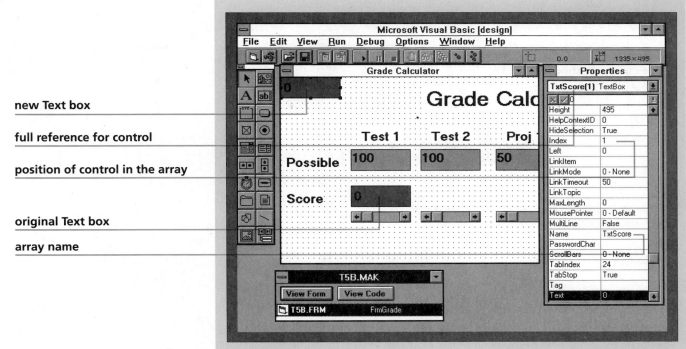

new Text box

full reference for control

position of control in the array

original Text box

array name

Figure 5-22: Form showing new Text box copied to upper-left corner

The Properties window shows TxtScore (the name of the control array) in this control's Name property and the number 1 (one) in its Index property. TxtScore(1)—the full reference to this control—appears in the Object box. Visual Basic also copies the BackColor, FontSize, Text, and Width property values from the original Text box to the new Text box. (You can scroll the Properties window to verify that, if you want.)

5   Drag the TxtScore(1) control to a position above the second scroll bar.

The Text box is still on the Windows Clipboard, so you just need to paste it into the form three more times.

6   Maximize the form, press [Ctrl][v] to paste another Text box on the form, then drag the Text box to a position above the third scroll bar. Press [Ctrl][v] again, then drag the Text box to a position above the fourth scroll bar. Press [Ctrl][v] one last time, then drag the Text box to a position above the fifth scroll bar.

Now let's verify that the controls were named correctly.

7   Restore the form to its standard size, then click the **down arrow button in the Object box** (located in the Properties window) to open the Object box. The names of the five Text boxes in the TxtScore array should appear as shown in Figure 5-23.

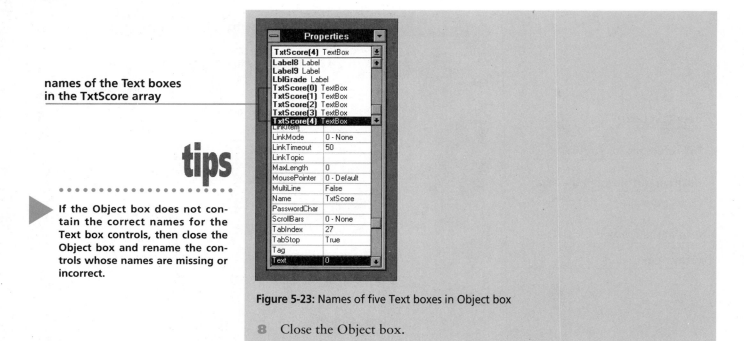

names of the Text boxes
in the TxtScore array

tips

▶ **If the Object box does not contain the correct names for the Text box controls, then close the Object box and rename the controls whose names are missing or incorrect.**

Figure 5-23: Names of five Text boxes in Object box

8   Close the Object box.

The controls in an array not only share the same name, they also share the same event procedures. That means that the code you enter in an array's Code window applies to all of the controls in the array. In other words, when you code one of the controls in an array, you're actually coding all of the controls in the array. The Code window associated with a control array differs slightly from the Code windows you've seen so far—specifically, the Code window includes an additional item of information. Before you begin coding the grade application, let's open the Code window for the HsbScore scroll bar array to see what a control array's Code window looks like. Because the controls in an array share the same event procedures, you can open their Code window by double-clicking any one of the controls in the array.

To open the Horizontal scroll bar array's Code window:

1   Double-click **one of the Horizontal scroll bars.** The Code window opens as shown in Figure 5-24.

argument (parameter)

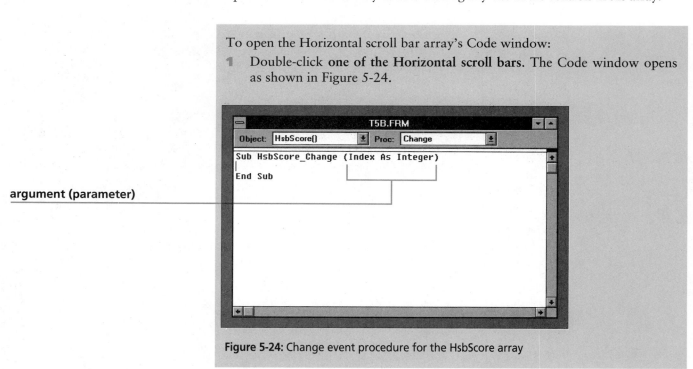

Figure 5-24: Change event procedure for the HsbScore array

In the Code windows you've seen so far, an empty set of parentheses followed the name of the event procedure. If a Code window belongs to a control array, however, *Index as Integer* will appear inside the parentheses. Items inside the parentheses are called **arguments** or **parameters**; they are used by Visual Basic to pass information to the event procedures. The information passed to the event procedures of control arrays is the Index of the control that is receiving the event. In this case, for example, if the user scrolls the first scroll bar, Visual Basic records the first scroll bar's index—0 (zero)—in the Index argument that is sent to the Change event procedure. If the user scrolls the second scroll bar, Visual Basic records the second scroll bar's index—1 (one)—in the Index argument, and so on. You can prove this by entering a *Print Index* instruction, temporarily, in the Change event's Code window. The Print instruction will print the value of the Index argument on the form. Let's do that now.

To enter the Print instruction in the Change event procedure and then save, run, and test the application:

1   The HsbScore's Code window, showing the Change event procedure, should still be open. Type **print Index** in the open Code window and press [**Enter**].

Recall that the code in the Code window applies to each of the controls in the array. In other words, Visual Basic will process the *Print Index* instruction when any one of the scroll bars is scrolled.

2   Close the Code window, then **save and run** the application.

Let's see what Visual Basic assigns to the Index argument when you scroll the first scroll bar.

3   Drag the first scroll bar's scroll box all the way to the right. When you release the mouse button, Visual Basic prints a 0 (zero), the first scroll bar's index, in the upper-left corner of the form.

4   On your own, drag the scroll box in each of the other scroll bars all the way to the right. Visual Basic will print the numbers 1, 2, 3, and 4 when you scroll the second, third, fourth, and fifth scrolls bars, respectively.

Now that you know what values Visual Basic records in the Index argument when the Change event occurs, you can stop the application, open the HsbScore's Code window, and delete the *Print Index* instruction.

5   Click the **Exit button** to stop the application. Double-click **any one of the Horizontal scroll bars** to open the array's Code window, delete the *Print Index* instruction from the Code window, then close the Code window.

You can now begin coding the grade application. The TOE chart for this application is shown in Figure 5-25.

Task	Object	Event
Get scores from user	5 Horizontal scroll bars	Change, Scroll
	5 Text boxes	None
Calculate grade	1 Command button (CmdCalc)	Click
Display the grade	1 Label control	None
End the application	1 Command button (CmdExit)	Click

Figure 5-25: TOE chart for the grade application

You need to code only the Horizontal scroll bars and the Calc Command button. (The Exit Command button already contains the End instruction.) You will code the scroll bars in this lesson and the Calc button in Lesson C. The flowchart and pseudocode for the Horizontal scroll bars are shown in Figure 5-26.

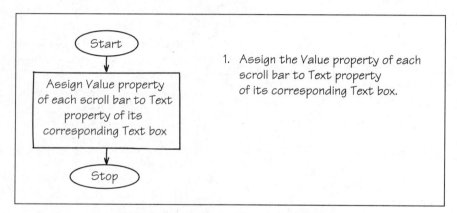

Figure 5-26: Flowchart and pseudocode for the Horizontal scroll bars

Let's code the Horizontal scroll bar array.

Coding the Horizontal Scroll Bar Array

According to Figure 5-26, you need to assign the Value property of each scroll bar in the HsbScore array to the Text property of a Text box in the TxtScore array. Recall that the Value property keeps track of the current location of the scroll box in the scroll bar. In this case, the Value property of each scroll bar will represent the student's score. The first scroll bar's Value property should be assigned to the first Text box's Text property, the second scroll bar's Value property should be assigned to the second Text box's Text property, and so on. Figure 5-27 illustrates this point.

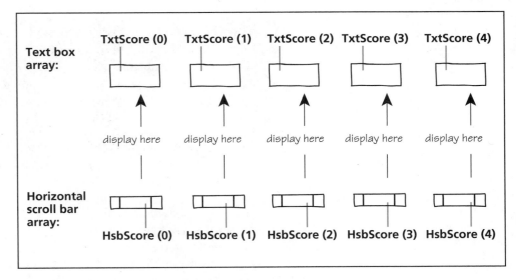

Figure 5-27: Relationship of controls in both arrays

Notice that each scroll bar has the same index as the Text box in which its Value property (student score) is to be displayed. For example, the first scroll bar in the HsbScore array and the first Text box in the TxtScore array both have an index of 0. Likewise, the second scroll bar and its associated Text box both have an index of 1. The same relationship is true for the remaining scroll bars and Text boxes contained in the two arrays. Arrays whose controls are related by their position in the arrays—in other words, by their index—are called **parallel arrays**. Let's open the HsbScore array's Code window and begin entering the code.

To code the HsbScore array, then save, run, and test the application:

1 Double-click **one of the scroll bar controls** to open the array's Code window. The HsbScore array's Change event procedure appears.

Recall that Visual Basic records, in the Index argument, the index of the control receiving the event—in this case, the index of the scroll bar that is currently being scrolled. You can use the Index argument to assign the Value property of the scroll bar being scrolled to the Text property of its corresponding Text box. You will use the following assignment statement to do so: *TxtScore(Index).Text = HsbScore(Index).Value*. This assignment statement tells Visual Basic to assign the Value property of the scroll bar, whose index is recorded in the index argument, to the Text box having the same index. If the student scrolls the first scroll bar, for example, the index argument will contain a 0 and Visual Basic will assign the Value property of the first scroll bar in the HsbScore array to the Text property of the first Text box in the TxtScore array. (Recall that the first control in an array has an index of 0.) You will enter the assignment statement in both the Change event procedure and the Scroll event procedure for the HsbScore array. You'll begin with the Change event procedure, which is currently open.

2 Press [Tab], then type **TxtScore(Index).Text = HsbScore(Index).Value** and press [Enter]. (Be sure to type the proper number of parentheses.)

You will now copy this assignment statement to the Scroll event procedure.

3   Highlight the assignment statement in the Code window, then press [Ctrl][c] to copy the instruction to the Windows Clipboard.

4   Click the **down arrow in the Code window's Proc (procedure) box**, then click **Scroll** in the drop-down list (you might need to scroll the drop-down list to locate the Scroll event). The Scroll event procedure appears in the Code window. Press [Ctrl][v] to paste the assignment statement into the Code window, then press [Enter].

5   Close the Code window, then **save and run** the application. Click the **right scroll arrow button in each of the scroll bars**, slowly, three times. The score in the corresponding Text box increases by 5—the value in the SmallChange property.

6   Click **each scroll bar between its scroll box and its right scroll arrow button** several times. The score in the corresponding Text box increases by 10—the value in the LargeChange property.

7   Drag **any one of the scroll boxes** to the right, then release the mouse button. Because you coded the scroll bar array's Scroll event procedure, the score changes as you drag.

8   Click the **Exit button**. Visual Basic returns to the design screen.

You have now completed Lesson B. You can either take a break or complete the questions and exercises at the end of the lesson. You will complete the grade application in Lesson C.

SUMMARY

To create a control array when the controls are already on the form:

■   Enter the same name in the Name property for each of the controls to be included in the array. When you are asked if you want to create a control array, click the Yes button.

To create a control array as you are entering the controls on the form:

■   Add the first control to the form and set its properties. Then press [Ctrl][c] (or click Edit, then click Copy) to copy the control to the Windows Clipboard.

■   Press [Ctrl][v] (or click Edit, then click Paste) to paste a copy of the control on the form. When you are asked if you want to create a control array, click the Yes button. Continue pasting copies of the control until the entire array is created.

To allow the user to scroll through a predefined set of numbers:

■   Use either the Horizontal scroll bar tool 🔲 or the Vertical scroll bar tool 🔲 .

■   Set the Name property. Set the Min and Max properties to integers between −32768 and 32767, inclusive. Set the LargeChange and SmallChange properties to integers between 1 and 32767, inclusive. Visual Basic stores the current location of the scroll box in the control's Value property.

■   Enter code in the scroll bar's Change event procedure and its Scroll event procedure.

Q U E S T I O N S

1. This property contains a number that represents the current location of the scroll box in the scroll bar.
    a. BoxLoc
    b. BoxVal
    c. ScrollLoc
    d. ScrollVal
    e. Value

2. When you move the scroll box in the scroll bar, Visual Basic changes the value in this property.
    a. LargeChange
    b. Max
    c. Min
    d. SmallChange
    e. Value

3. The value of the leftmost location of the scroll box in a Horizontal scroll bar is set with this property.
    a. LargeChange
    b. Max
    c. Min
    d. SmallChange
    e. Value

4. This property determines how far the scroll box will move when the user clicks the scroll arrow buttons in the scroll bar.
    a. LargeChange
    b. Max
    c. Min
    d. SmallChange
    e. Value

5. This event procedure appears when you open the Code window for a scroll bar control.
    a. Change
    b. Click
    c. DblClick
    d. Load
    e. Scroll

6. Assume you have a scroll bar named HsbNumber and a Text box named TxtNumber. This assignment statement will display the scroll box's position in the Text box.
    a. HsbNumber.Text = TxtNumber.Value
    b. HsbNumber.Value = TxtNumber.Text
    c. TxtNumber.Text = HsbNumber.BoxPos
    d. TxtNumber.Text = HsbNumber.Value
    e. TxtNumber.Value = TxtNumber.Text

7. This event procedure occurs while the user drags the scroll box along the scroll bar.
    a. Drag
    b. DragBox
    c. Move
    d. Push
    e. Scroll

8. When you give the same name to more than one control, you create a
   _____ .
   a. control array
   b. control group
   c. group
   d. name array
   e. name group

9. Visual Basic assigns a unique number, called a(n) _____ , to each of the
   controls in an array.
   a. address
   b. control number
   c. control value
   d. index
   e. value

10. Which of the following is the name of a control in an array?
    a. TxtName.1
    b. TxtName-1
    c. TxtName[1]
    d. TxtName_1
    e. TxtName(1)

11. The index of the fourth control is an array is _____ .
    a. 3
    b. 4
    c. 5

12. Items appearing within the parentheses after an event procedure's name are called
    _____ or _____ . (Choose two answers.)
    a. arguments
    b. controls
    c. parameters
    d. properties
    e. values

13. Arrays that have corresponding elements are called _____ arrays.
    a. associated
    b. coordinated
    c. matching
    d. parallel
    e. same

14. Assume the user interface contains four Option buttons. Explain how to make these
    Option buttons into a control array named OptChoice. What values will be con-
    tained in each of the button's Index properties?

15. Assume you want to create a control array named ChkChoice that contains three
    Check boxes. The Check boxes are not, as yet, on the form. Explain how to create
    the array at the same time as you add the controls to the form. What values will be
    contained in each of the Check boxes' Index properties?

EXERCISES

Note: In the following exercises you will begin coding controls in a number of applications. You will complete the applications in the exercises for Lesson C.

1. a. Create the user interface shown in Figure 5-28.

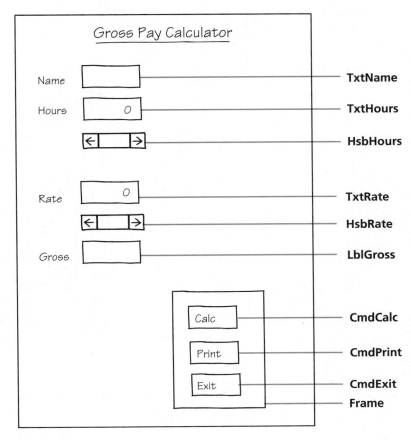

Figure 5-28

     b. Set the following properties for the HsbHours control:
       Name: HsbHours   Min: 1   Max: 40
       SmallChange: 1   LargeChange: 5
     c. Set the following properties for the HsbRate control:
       Name: HsbRate   Min: 5   Max: 10
       SmallChange: 1   LargeChange: 2
     d. Save the form and the project as T5LBE1.
     e. Code the scroll bars so they display the hours and rate in the appropriate Text boxes.
     f. Code the Exit control so it ends the application.
     g. Code the Print control so it prints the form.
     h. Save and run the application. Test the application with the following data: Your name, 25 hours, and a rate of 7.
     i. Use the Print control to print the form with the test data showing. Use the Exit control to end the application.
     j. Print the code.

2.   a. Create the user interface shown in Figure 5-29.

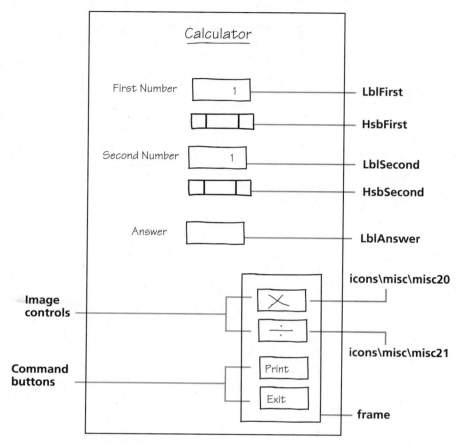

Figure 5-29

    b. Set the following properties for the HsbFirst control:
        Name: HsbFirst   Min: 1   Max: 10
        SmallChange: 1   LargeChange: 2
    c. Set the following properties for the HsbSecond control:
        Name: HsbSecond   Min: 1   Max: 10
        SmallChange: 1   LargeChange: 2
    d. Save the form and the project as T5LBE2.
    e. Code the scroll bars so they display the numbers in the appropriate Label controls.
    f. Code the Exit control so it ends the application.
    g. Code the Print control so it prints the form.
    h. Save and run the application. Test the application with the following data: a first number of 5 and a second number of 5.
    i. Use the Print control to print the form with the test data showing. Use the Exit control to end the application.
    j. Print the code.

3. a. Create the user interface shown in Figure 5-30. Make the scroll bars into a control array named HsbSales. Make the Text boxes into a control array named TxtSales.

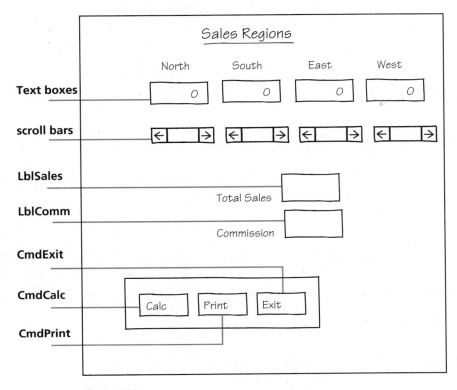

Figure 5-30

b. Set the following properties for the scroll bars:
   Name: HsbSales   Min: 0   Max: 30000
   SmallChange: 1000   LargeChange: 10000
c. Save the form and the project as T5LBE3.
d. Code the scroll bar array so it displays the sales in the appropriate Text boxes.
e. Code the Exit control so it ends the application.
f. Code the Print control so it prints the form.
g. Save and run the application. Test the application with the following data: North region sales of 20000, South region sales of 25000, East region sales of 1000, and West region sales of 5000.
h. Use the Print control to print the form with the test data showing. Use the Exit control to end the application.
i. Print the code.

4. a. Create the user interface shown in Figure 5-31. Make the Home team's scroll bars into a control array named HsbHome. Make the Home team's Text boxes into a control array named TxtName. Make the Visitor team's scroll bars into a control array named HsbVisitor. Make the Visitor team's Text boxes into a control array named TxtVisitor.

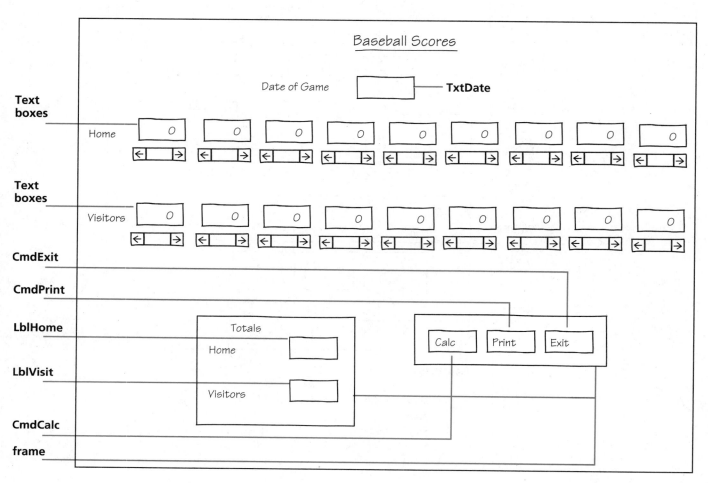

Figure 5-31

b. Set the following properties for the Home team's scroll bars:
   Name: HsbHome   Min: 0   Max: 20
   SmallChange: 1   LargeChange: 2
c. Set the following properties for the Visitor team's scroll bars:
   Name: HsbVisitor   Min: 0   Max: 20
   SmallChange: 1   LargeChange: 2
d. Save the form and the project as T5LBE4.
e. Code the scroll bar arrays so they display the scores in the appropriate Text boxes.
f. Code the Exit control so it ends the application.
g. Code the Print control so it prints the form.
h. Save and run the application. Test the application with the following data: A game date of 8/20/97. Display the number 2 in each of the Home team's Text boxes. Display the number 3 in each of the Visitor team's Text boxes.
i. Use the Print control to print the form with the test data showing. Use the Exit control to end the application.
j. Print the code.

5. a. Create the user interface shown in Figure 5-32. Make the State option buttons into a control array named OptState. Make the Capital option buttons into a control array named OptCapital.

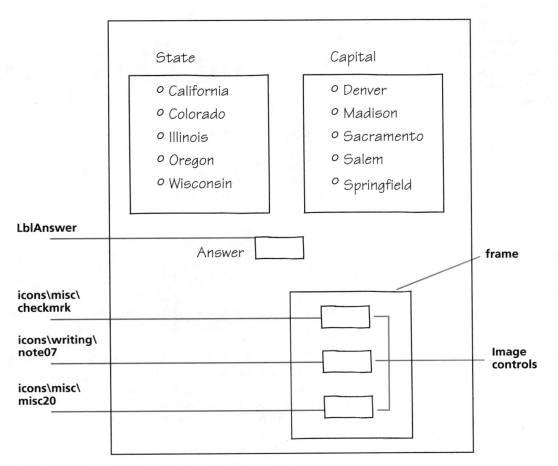

Figure 5-32

b. Save the form and the project as T5LBE5.
c. Code the Exit control so it ends the application.
d. Code the Print control so it prints the form.
e. Save and run the application.
f. Use the Print control to print the form. Use the Exit control to end the application.

In this lesson you will learn how to:

- Include the For...Next loop in the grade application
- Include the Select...Case statement in the grade application
- Center the Caption in a Label control

Coding the Calc Button

Coding the Calc Button

The grade application is almost complete; you just need to code the Calc button, which you will do in this lesson. First you will need to open the T5B.MAK project that you created in Lesson B.

To open the t5b.mak project:

1   Launch Visual Basic (if necessary) and open the **t5b.mak** project, which is in either the tut5\ver2 or tut5\ver3 directory on your Student Disk. Click the **View form button** in the Project window to view the FrmGrade form.

2   Save the form and the project as **t5c**.

The flowchart and pseudocode for the Calc button are shown in Figure 5-33. Let's take a closer look at the steps the Calc button needs to take to calculate the grade. Notice that the Calc button uses the For...Next (automatic counter) loop and the Case selection structure. The first step shown in Figure 5-33 is to declare the necessary variables. The For...Next loop will need a numeric variable to use as the *counter*. You will call the variable X and define it as an Integer type. The For...Next loop will also need a variable in which it can accumulate (add together) the five student scores. You will call the variable Totalscore and define it as an Integer type. Let's open the Calc button's Code window and declare the variables.

To declare the variables in the Calc button's Code window:

1   Maximize the form, double-click the **Calc button** to open its Code window, then maximize the Code window. The Click event procedure appears.

2   Type **'Declare variables** and press **[Enter]** to document the first line of code.

3   Press **[Tab]**, type **dim X as integer, Totalscore as integer** and press **[Enter]**. Recall that you can declare more than one variable in a Dim statement, but you must be sure to include the data type in each one.

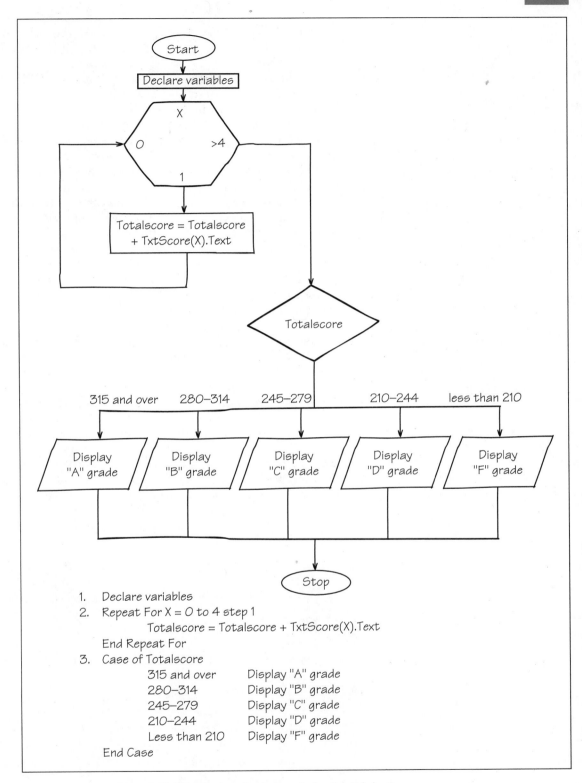

1. Declare variables
2. Repeat For X = 0 to 4 step 1
         Totalscore = Totalscore + TxtScore(X).Text
   End Repeat For
3. Case of Totalscore
         315 and over   Display "A" grade
         280–314   Display "B" grade
         245–279   Display "C" grade
         210–244   Display "D" grade
         Less than 210   Display "F" grade
   End Case

Figure 5-33: Flowchart and pseudocode for the Calc button

After the necessary variables are declared, the Calc button needs to sum the scores contained in the five Text boxes. Recall that the names of those Text boxes are TxtScore(0), TxtScore(1), TxtScore(2), TxtScore(3), and TxtScore(4). You could use the following assignment statement to add the scores together—*Totalscore = TxtScore(0) + TxtScore(1) + TxtScore(2) + TxtScore(3) + TxtScore(4)*—but that instruction is fairly lengthy. (Imagine what the assignment statement would look like if you needed to sum the scores in 20 Text boxes.) The For...Next (automatic counter) loop provides a more convenient way of summing the scores in the Text box array.

The For...Next loop shown in Figure 5-33 uses its *counter* (X) to refer to each of the Text boxes in the TxtScore array. First the loop will initialize X (the *counter*) to 0. The value in X (0) is not greater than the *endvalue* (4), so the assignment statement inside the loop will be processed. That assignment statement will add the contents of the first Text box, TxtScore(0), to a variable named Totalscore. X (the *counter*) will then be incremented by 1 (the *stepvalue*), giving 1. (Note that "incremented" is a shorter way of saying "increased by an increment of.") The value in X (1) will not be greater than 4 (the *endvalue*), so the instruction inside the loop will be processed once again. This time the assignment statement will add the contents of the second Text box, TxtScore(1), to the Totalscore variable. Each time through the loop, X will be incremented by one and the assignment statement will add the contents of the next Text box to the Totalscore variable. The loop stops when the value in X is greater than 4 (the *endvalue*).

At this point the Totalscore variable will contain the sum of the scores. The Totalscore variable is called an **accumulator**, which is a variable or a control that is used to accumulate, or sum, a group of numbers. You will learn much more about accumulators in Tutorial 6. You will also learn about **counters**, which are variables or controls used for counting. Many applications require data to be accumulated and/or counted. Accumulators are used to answer the question "How much?"—for example, "How much did the salespeople sell this quarter?" Counters, on the other hand, are used to answer the question "How many?"—for example, "How many salespeople live in Virginia?" Let's enter the For...Next loop into the open Code window.

To enter the For...Next statement in the Calc button's Code window:

1   The Calc button's Code window should still be open, so you just need to press [**Backspace**] to remove the indentation, then type '**Accumulate scores** and press [**Enter**].

According to Figure 5-33, the loop's *startvalue* should be 0 (zero), its *endvalue* should be 4, and its *stepvalue* should be 1. Translated into Visual Basic code, that becomes *For X = 0 to 4 Step 1*. (This For instruction will repeat the loop five times.)

2   Press [**Tab**], then type **for X = 0 to 4 step 1** and press [**Enter**]. (Be sure to type the number 0, not the letter O.)

You will now enter the *Totalscore = Totalscore + TxtScore(X).Text* assignment statement, which tells Visual Basic to add the contents of the TxtScore(X) Text box to the Totalscore variable and place the result back in the Totalscore variable. (Recall that Visual Basic first evaluates the right side of the equal sign in an assignment statement and then places the result in the variable whose name appears on the left side of the equal sign.)

3 Press [Tab], type **Totalscore = Totalscore + TxtScore(X).Text**, and press [Enter].

You can now end the loop.

4 Press [Backspace] to delete one tabstop, then type **next X** and press [Enter].

After the scores are summed, the Calc button uses the Case selection structure to display the appropriate grade in the Label control. The grade is based on the value contained in the Totalscore variable, as follows.

Value in Totalscore variable	Grade
315 and over	A
280 – 314	B
245 – 279	C
210 – 244	D
less than 210	F

You can use Visual Basic's Select Case statement to code this Case structure.

To enter the Select Case statement in the Calc button's Code window:

1 Press [Backspace] to cancel the indentation, type **'Assign grade** and press [Enter].

2 Press [Tab], then enter the Select Case statement shown in Figure 5-34.

enter these instructions

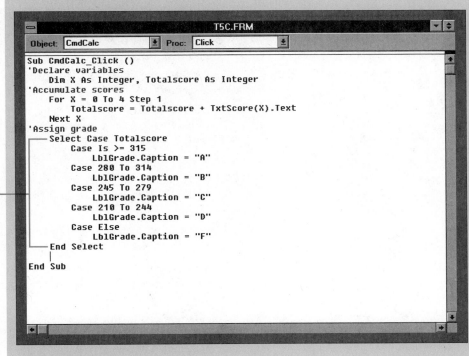

```
                              T5C.FRM
Object: CmdCalc        Proc: Click

Sub CmdCalc_Click ()
'Declare variables
    Dim X As Integer, Totalscore As Integer
'Accumulate scores
    For X = 0 To 4 Step 1
        Totalscore = Totalscore + TxtScore(X).Text
    Next X
'Assign grade
    Select Case Totalscore
        Case Is >= 315
            LblGrade.Caption = "A"
        Case 280 To 314
            LblGrade.Caption = "B"
        Case 245 To 279
            LblGrade.Caption = "C"
        Case 210 To 244
            LblGrade.Caption = "D"
        Case Else
            LblGrade.Caption = "F"
    End Select

End Sub
```

Figure 5-34: CmdCalc Code window

According to the flowchart and the pseudocode, you are finished coding the Calc button.

3   Compare your code to the code shown in Figure 5-34. Close the Code window, restore the form to its standard size, then **save and run** the application.

4   Test the application using the following scores: **95** for Test 1, **90** for Test 2, **45** for project 1, **45** for project 2, and **50** for project 3. Click the **Calc button**; the grade should be an A.

5   Test the application again using the following scores: **65** for test 1, **80** for test 2, **40** for project 1, **40** for project 2, and **40** for project 3. Click the **Calc button**; the grade should be a C.

6   Click the **Exit button** to end the application. Visual Basic returns to the design screen.

Now that the application is working correctly, you can improve its appearance by centering the grade in the Label control and also removing the form's border. You'll do that in the next section.

Improving the Appearance of the Application

First you will center the grade in the LblGrade control, and then you will remove the form's border.

To improve the appearance of the grade application:

1   Click the **down arrow button in the Object box** (located in the Properties window), then click **LblGrade Label** in the drop-down list (you will need to scroll the drop-down list). Notice that you can select a control even when it's not in view.

You center the contents of a Label control by setting its Alignment property to 2-Center.

2   Click **Alignment** in the Properties list, click the **down arrow in the Settings box** (located in the Properties window), and then click **2-Center** in the drop-down list.

Now let's remove the form's border.

3   Click the **form** to select it, then click **Borderstyle** in the Properties list. Click the **down arrow in the Settings box**, and then click **0-None** in the drop-down list.

You can now save, run, and test the application.

4   **Save and run** the application. The form appears without a border.

5   Test the application using the following scores: **100** for test 1, **100** for test 2, **50** for project 1, **50** for project 2, and **50** for project 3. Click the **Calc button**, the grade should be an A. The A is centered in the Label control.

6   Click the **Exit button** to end the application. Visual Basic returns to the design screen.

You have now completed Lesson C. You can either take a break or complete the questions and exercises at the end of the lesson.

S U M M A R Y

To align the Caption property in a Label control:

■ Set the Label control's Alignment property to 0-Left Justify, 1-Right Justify, or 2-Center.

Q U E S T I O N S

1. You can align the Caption property of a Label control by setting the control's _____ property.
   a. Align
   b. Alignment
   c. Caption
   d. Justify
   e. Location

2. Which one of the following is an incorrect For instruction?
   a. For X = 1 To 3 Step 1
   b. For X = 3 To 1 Step 1
   c. For X = 3 To 1 Step −1
   d. For X = 100 To 200 Step 10
   e. For X = 75 to 100

3. Assume the application contains a control array named TxtSales. The TxtSales array contains three Text boxes. Which of the following loops will accumulate the contents of each Text box in the array? (X is an Integer variable; Total is a single variable.)

   a. For X = 2 To 0 Step −1   c. For X = 1 To 3 Step 1
       Total = Total + TxtSales(X).Text   Total = Total + TxtSales(X).Text
   Next X   Next X

   b. For X = 3 To 1 Step −1   d. For X = 0 To 2 Step 1
       Total = Total + TxtSales(X).Text   Total(X) = Total(X) + TxtSales.Text
   Next X   Next X

4. In question 3, what will be the value of X when the loop stops?
   a. −1
   b. 0
   c. 1
   d. 2
   e. 3

5. Which of the Select Case statements will print the shipping charges, shown below, based on the sales contained in the Sales variable? (Choose two answers.)

Sales	Shipping charge
$0 to 100	15
$100.01 to $500	10
$500.01 and up	5

a. Select Case Sales
    Case Is >= 0
      Print 15
    Case Is >= 100.01
      Print 10
    Case Else
      Print 5
End Select

b. Select Case Sales
    Case Is >= 500.01
      Print 5
    Case Is >= 100.01
      Print 10
    Case Else
      Print 15
End Select

c. Select Case Sales
    Case Is < 100
      Print 15
    Case Is < 500
      Print 10
    Case Else
      Print 5
End Select

d. Select Case Sales
    Case Is <= 100
      Print 15
    Case Is <= 500
      Print 10
    Case Else
      Print 5
End Select

E X E R C I S E S

1.   a. Open the T5LBE1 project that you created in Lesson B, then save the form and the project as T5LCE1.
     After entering the employee's name, hours, and rate, the user will click the Calc Command button to calculate and display the gross pay.
    b. Use the flowchart shown in Figure 5-35 to finish coding the application.
    c. Save and run the application.
    d. Test the application with the following data: Your name, 25 hours, and a rate of 7. Click the Calc button, then click the Print button.
    e. Exit the application, then print the code.

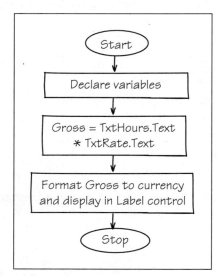

Figure 5-35

2. a. Open the T5LBE2 project that you created in Lesson B, then save the form and the project as T5LCE2.

   After entering both numbers, the user will click either the Multiply control or the Divide control to calculate and display either the product or the quotient.

   b. Use the flowchart shown in Figure 5-36 to finish coding the application.

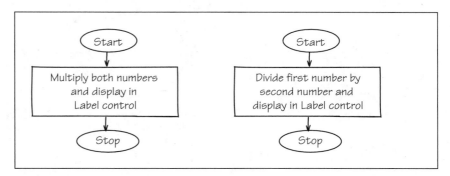

Figure 5-36

   c. Save and run the application.

   d. Test the application with the following data: a first number of 5 and a second number of 5. Click the Multiply control, then click the Print button.

   e. Now test the application with the following data: a first number of 10 and a second number of 2. Click the Divide control, then click the Print button.

   f. Exit the application, then print the code.

3. a. Open the T5LBE3 project that you created in Lesson B, then save the form and the project as T5LCE3.

   After entering the sales for each region, the user will click the Calc button to calculate and display the total sales and the commission. The commission rate is .01 (1%) for sales from 0 to $20,000; .03 (3%) for sales from $20,001 to $40,000; and .05 (5%) for sales over $40,000.

   b. Use the flowchart shown in Figure 5-37 to finish coding the application.

   c. Save and run the application.

   d. Test the application with the following data: North region sales of 20000, South region sales of 25000, East region sales of 1000, and West region sales of 5000. Click the Calc button, then click the Print button.

   e. Exit the application, then print the code.

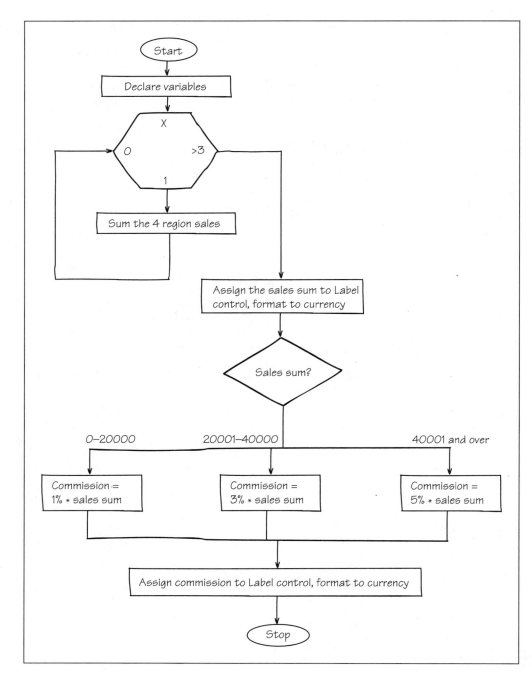

Figure 5-37

4. a. Open the T5LBE4 project that you created in Lesson B, then save the form and
        the project as T5LCE4.
        After entering the date and the scores, the user will click the Calc button to
        calculate and display the total score for each team.
    b. Use the flowchart shown in Figure 5-38 to finish coding the application.
    c. Save and run the application.
    d. Test the application with the following data: A game date of 8/20/97. Display the
        number 2 in each of the Home team's Text boxes. Display the number 3 in each
        of the Visitor team's Text boxes. Click the Calc button, then click the Print button.
    e. Exit the application, then print the code.

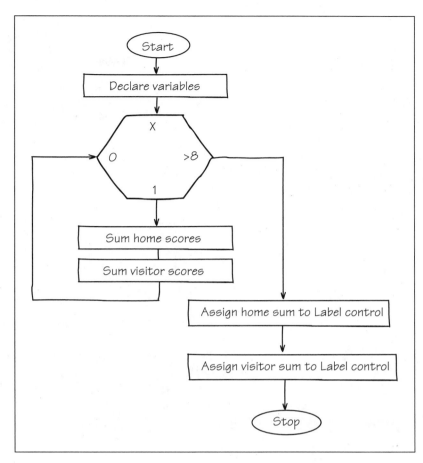

Figure 5-38

Exercises 5 and 6 are Discovery Exercises.

discovery ▶ **5.** a. Open the T5LBE5 project that you created in Lesson B, then save the form and the project as T5LCE5.

After selecting a state and its corresponding capital, the user will click the Check Image control (the checkmark) to verify that the capital he or she chose is correct. If the capital is correct, "Correct" should appear in the Label control; otherwise, "Incorrect" should appear in the Label control.

b. Use the flowchart shown in Figure 5-39 to finish coding the application.

c. Center the Caption in the Label control.

d. Save and run the application.

e. Test the application by choosing Denver from one group and Colorado from the other group. Click the Check control, then click the Print control.

f. Test the application again by choosing Salem from one group and Wisconsin from the other group. Click the Check control, then click the Print control.

g. Exit the application, then print the code.

discovery ▶ **6.** a. Launch Write. Open the T5LCE6.WRI document which is in either the tut5\ver2 or the tut5\ver3 directory on your Student Disk. Print the T5LCE6.WRI document, which contains the directions for how to complete Exercise 6.

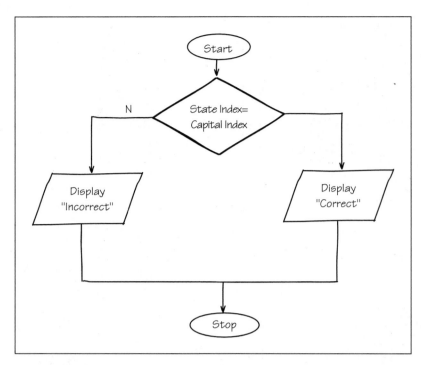

Figure 5-39

D E B U G G I N G

Technique

Many new programmers make the mistake of testing their applications with valid data only. It's wise to keep in mind, however, that users do make mistakes when entering data. For example, users sometimes enter letters where numbers are required. It's also common for a user to forget to supply all of the required information. Generally these types of entry errors will either cause the application to end abruptly (usually with an error message) or to give incorrect results. Your application should be able to deal with these entry errors.

Follow these steps when testing your applications:

1. Ensure that the application works with valid data.
2. On a piece of paper, jot down possible mistakes the user could make when entering the data.
3. Test your application again, making the same mistakes you think the user might make.
4. If the application ends incorrectly, or if it gives incorrect results, enter additional code to deal with the errors.

Below are two possible errors the user could make in the grade application created in the tutorial:

1. Recall that the student's scores are entered in Text boxes either by scrolling the scroll bars or by typing the scores from the keyboard. When the keyboard is used to enter a score, it is possible that the user might accidentally enter a letter instead of a number.
2. After calculating the grade, the student might need to change one of the scores. If, after changing a score, the student forgets to click the Calc button again, the grade displayed in the LblGrade control will be incorrect.

To run the grade application and make these entry errors:

1 Launch Visual Basic (if necessary) and open the **T5C.MAK** project, which is in either the tut5\ver2 or the tut5\ver3 directory on your Student Disk. Click the **View Form button** to view the form, then save the form and the project as **t5cdbgd**. (The "dbgd" stands for "debugged.")

Before running the application, you will change the BorderStyle property from 0-None to 2-Sizable. When debugging an application, be sure that the BorderStyle property is *not* set to 0-None. When it is set to 0-None and the program ends abruptly because of an error, the only way to exit the application is to press [Ctrl][Alt][Del].

2 Click **BorderStyle** in the Properties list, click the **down arrow button in the Settings box**, and then click **2-Sizable** in the drop-down list.

3 **Save and run** the application. Delete the 0 from the first Text box, type the letter **k** inside the Text box, and then click the **Calc button**. A dialog box containing the error message "Type mismatch" appears on the screen.

Recall that a "Type mismatch" error means that the application has encountered something that it wasn't expecting—for example, a string instead of a number, or a number instead of a string. Let's see which of the instructions is causing the "Type mismatch" error.

4 Click the **OK button**. Visual Basic highlights the instruction that is causing the error—*Totalscore = Totalscore + TxtScore(X).Text*. In this case the assignment statement expected to find a number in each of the TxtScore array Text boxes, but it found a letter there instead. Your application should be able to deal with this error.

5 Close the **Code window**, restore the **form**, then click the **Stop icon** ▪ to end the application.

Now let's see what the application will do if the user makes a change to a score and forgets to click the Calc button.

6 **Run** the application. Use the scroll bars to enter the following grades: 50 for test 1, 50 for test 2, 50 for project 1, 50 for project 2, and 50 for project 3. Click the **Calc button**. A grade of C appears in the Label control.

7 Change the first test score to 100. Notice that the grade is still a C, when it should be a B. Click the **Calc button** to recalculate the grade. The grade is now B. Removing the grade from the Label control if the user makes any changes to the scores would be a better idea.

8 Click the **Exit button** to end the application.

Entry Error #1 — Entering a Letter Instead of a Number

You will use the selection structure along with the Isnumeric function (which you have not yet learned) to verify that each Text box contains a number. If a Text box does not contain a number, the application will display the word "Error" in the Label control and will not calculate the grade.

Visual Basic's Isnumeric function has the following format: Isnumeric(*expression*). If the *expression* is numeric, or if it can be converted to a number, then the Isnumeric function returns the Boolean value True. If the *expression* is not numeric, then the function returns the Boolean value False. Let's enter the selection structure and the Isnumeric function in the Calc button's Code window.

To fix entry error #1:

1   Maximize the form, then double-click the **Calc button** to open its Code window. The Click event procedure appears. Change the For...Next loop in the Code window to match Figure 5-40.

change the For...Next statement as shown

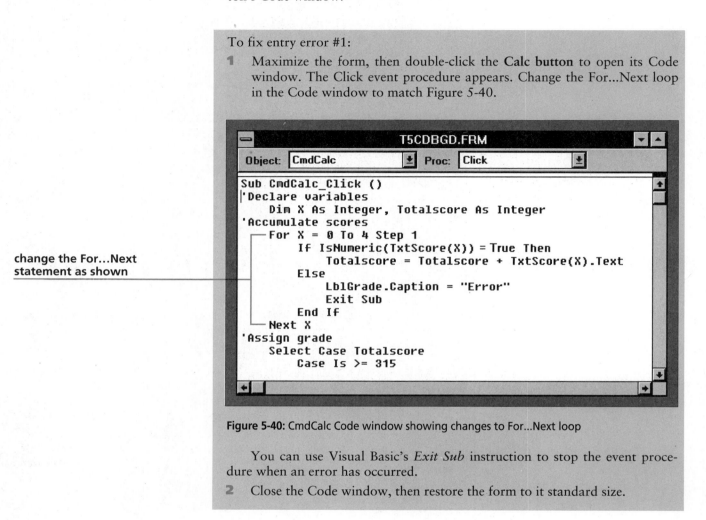

```
T5CDBGD.FRM

Object: CmdCalc          Proc: Click

Sub CmdCalc_Click ()
'Declare variables
    Dim X As Integer, Totalscore As Integer
'Accumulate scores
    For X = 0 To 4 Step 1
        If IsNumeric(TxtScore(X)) = True Then
            Totalscore = Totalscore + TxtScore(X).Text
        Else
            LblGrade.Caption = "Error"
            Exit Sub
        End If
    Next X
'Assign grade
    Select Case Totalscore
        Case Is >= 315
```

Figure 5-40: CmdCalc Code window showing changes to For...Next loop

You can use Visual Basic's *Exit Sub* instruction to stop the event procedure when an error has occurred.

2   Close the Code window, then restore the form to it standard size.

You will enter the code to fix entry error #2 before saving and testing the application.

Entry Error #2 — Forgetting to Recalculate the Grade After Making a Change

You can fix this entry error by clearing the contents of the LblGrade control whenever a change is made to the contents of any of the Text boxes. Recall that you clear a Label control by setting its Caption property to the null string, like this: *LblGrade.Caption* = "". You will enter this assignment statement in the Change event procedure for the TxtScore Text box array.

To fix entry error #2, then save, run, and test the application:

1 Double-click the **first Text box**. The Change event procedure for the TxtScore array appears. Press [**Tab**], then type **LblGrade.Caption = ""** and press [**Enter**]. Close the Code window.

2 **Save and run** the application. Delete the 0 from the first Text box, type the letter k inside the Text box, and then click the **Calc button**. "Error" (without the quotes) appears in the LblGrade control.

3 Use the scroll bars to enter the following grades: **50** for test 1, **50** for test 2, **50** for project 1, **50** for project 2, and **50** for project 3. Click the **Calc button**. A grade of C appears in the Label control.

4 Now change the grade for test 2 to **100**. Notice that Visual Basic clears the grade from the Label control.

5 Click the **Exit button** to end the application. Visual Basic returns to the design screen.

TUTORIAL

6

Sequential Access Files and More on Repetition

The UFO Application

case ▶ Each year the Chicago UFO Club passes out a questionnaire to the people attending the air and water show held at Navy Pier. After collecting the completed questionnaires (usually about 100–150 are completed), the club's secretary tabulates the responses and issues a report to the club. The questionnaire and the report are shown in Figure 6-1.

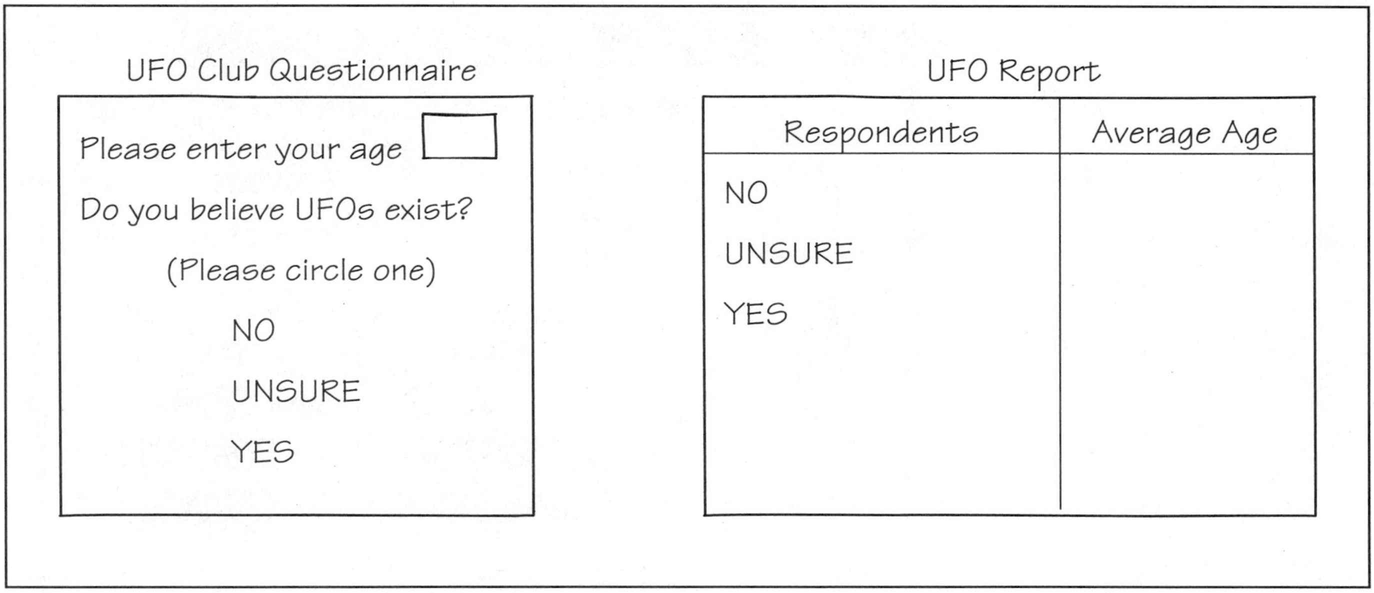

Figure 6-1: UFO Club questionnaire and report

Tabulating the data and creating the report is a time-consuming and tedious job. The club's president wants you to create an application that will simplify this process.

Previewing the Completed Application

As you've done in previous tutorials, you will preview the application before creating it.

To preview the completed application:

1 Launch Windows and make sure the Program Manager window is open and your Student Disk is in the appropriate drive. If necessary, click the Minimize on Use option on the Options menu to minimize the Program Manager on use.

2 *If you are using Version 2 and your Student Disk is in drive A*, then run the **A2_UFO.EXE** file, which is in the tut6\ver2 directory on your Student Disk. The UFO application's user interface appears on the screen. See Figure 6-2.

If you are using Version 2 and your Student Disk is in drive B, then run the **B2_UFO.EXE** file, which is in the tut6\ver2 directory on your Student Disk. The UFO application's user interface appears on the screen. See Figure 6-2.

If you are using Version 3 and your Student Disk is in drive A, then run the **A3_UFO.EXE** file, which is in the tut6\ver3 directory on your Student Disk. The UFO application's user interface appears on the screen. See Figure 6-2.

If you are using Version 3 and your Student Disk is in drive B, then run the **B3_UFO.EXE** file, which is in the tut6\ver3 directory on your Student Disk. The UFO application's user interface appears on the screen. See Figure 6-2.

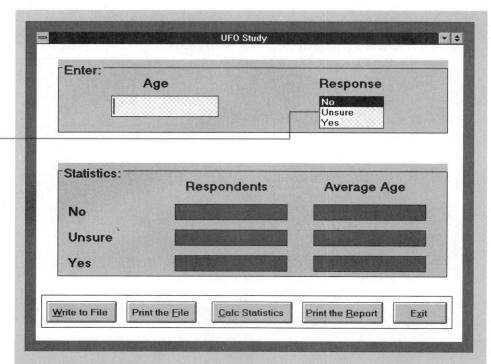

Figure 6-2: UFO application

This application contains a new control, a List box, which you will learn about in Lesson B. The application saves the information you enter in a sequential access data file. You will learn about sequential access data files in Lesson B. Let's enter some information right now.

3   Type **22** in the Age Text box, then click **Yes** in the List box. Click the **Write to File button.** The age and response to the question "Do you believe UFOs exist?" are saved in a sequential access data file on your Student Disk.

You can verify that the record was added to the data file by printing the file.

4   If your computer is connected to a printer, then click the **Print the File button.** The data in the data file prints on the printer, as shown in Figure 6-3. (The data file already contained the information from three questionnaires. If this is the second or subsequent time you have run this application, your data file will contain more records than are shown in Figure 6-3.)

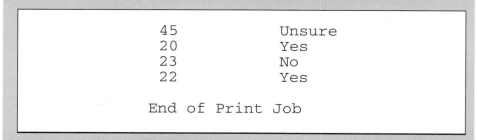

Figure 6-3: Printout of data file

Finally, let's calculate the number of No, Unsure, and Yes responses, and the average age of the people choosing each of those responses.

5   Click the **Calc Statistics button**. The number and average age of the respondents in each category appear under the Respondents and Average Age headings.

6   Click the **Exit button**. The UFO application ends.

In Lesson A you will learn how to use the remaining two forms of the repetition structure: the Do...While loop and the Do...Until loop. (Recall that you learned the other form of the repetition structure—the For...Next loop—in Tutorial 5.) You will also learn how to use counters and accumulators. The List box control and sequential access data files are covered in Lesson B. You will complete the UFO application in Lesson C.

Loops, Counters, and Accumulators

More on the Repetition Structure (Looping)

Recall that programmers use the repetition structure, also called looping, to tell the computer to repeat one or more program instructions. The three forms of the repetition structure (or loops) are: For...Next, Do...While, and Do...Until. You can use either loop to repeat a set of instructions a specified number of times, although the For...Next loop, which you learned in Tutorial 5, is usually used in those situations. When you don't know precisely how many times the loop instructions should be repeated, which is the case in many applications, then you must use either the Do...While loop or the Do...Until loop.

The Do...While and the Do...Until Loops

The Do...While loop repeats a block of instructions *while* a condition is true, whereas the Do...Until loop repeats a block of instructions *until* a condition becomes true. You can use Visual Basic's *Do While...Loop* statement to code the Do...While loop, and Visual Basic's *Do...Loop Until* statement to code the Do...Until loop. Figure 6-4 shows the format for each loop. It also gives an example of how you could use either loop to display the numbers 1 through 3 on the form.

loop instructions ─

condition ─

condition ─
loop instructions ─

tips

Recall that, in a statement syntax, words in **bold** are required, and items in *italics* represent areas where the programmer must supply information specific to the application.

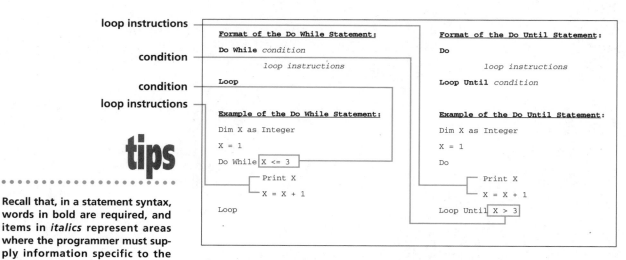

```
Format of the Do While Statement:
Do While condition
        loop instructions
Loop


Example of the Do While Statement:
Dim X as Integer
X = 1
Do While X <= 3
        ┌ Print X
        └ X = X + 1
Loop
```

```
Format of the Do Until Statement:
Do
        loop instructions
Loop Until condition


Example of the Do Until Statement:
Dim X as Integer
X = 1
Do
        ┌ Print X
        └ X = X + 1
Loop Until X > 3
```

Figure 6-4: Formats and examples of the Do...While and the Do...Until loops

The Do...While loop begins with the Do While statement and ends with the Loop statement. The Do...Until loop, on the other hand, begins with the Do statement and ends with the Loop Until statement. Between each loop's beginning and ending statements, you enter the instructions you want the loop to repeat.

Both loops require a *condition*, which is located at the top of the Do...While loop and at the bottom of the Do...Until loop. The *condition* can contain variables, constants, properties, functions, mathematical operators, relational operators, and logical operators. Like the *condition* used in the If...Then...Else statement (which you learned in Tutorial 4), the loop *condition* must also evaluate to either true or false. The *condition* determines if the loop instructions will be processed. In the Do...While loop, the loop instructions are processed only if the *condition* evaluates to true; if the *condition* evaluates to false, the loop instructions are not processed. In the Do...Until loop, the loop instructions are processed only if the *condition* evaluates to false; if the *condition* evaluates to true, the loop instructions are not processed.

Programmers call the Do...While loop a **pretest loop** because the loop evaluates (tests) the *condition* before processing any of the instructions within the loop. (The For...Next loop is also a pretest loop.) Depending on the condition, the instructions in a Do...While loop not be processed at all. For example, if the condition evaluates initially to false, Visual Basic skips the instructions within the loop; processing then continues with the instruction immediately following the end of the loop.

Programmers call the Do...Until loop a **posttest loop** because the loop evaluates (tests) the *condition* after processing the instructions within the loop. The Do...Until loop always processes the loop instructions at least once.

Let's look closer at the two examples shown in Figure 6-4. We'll begin with the example of the Do...While loop, which will display the numbers 1 through 3 on the form. The example first declares and initializes (to 1) an Integer variable named X. The Do While statement then evaluates the condition, $X <= 3$, to determine if the instructions within the loop should be processed. If X contains a number that is less than or equal to 3, the loop instructions, which display the value of X on the form and also add 1 to X, are processed. Then the Loop statement, which marks the end of the loop, sends the program back to the beginning of the loop (the Do While statement), where the *condition* is tested again. If the value in X is still less than or equal to 3, the loop instructions are processed again, and so on.

If X does not contain a number that is less than or equal to 3 (in other words, if X is greater than 3), the loop stops—that is, the instructions within the loop are not processed. Processing then continues with the instruction following the Loop statement.

To summarize, the Do...While loop repeats the loop instructions as long as the *condition* evaluates to true. When the *condition* evaluates to false, the Do...While loop stops. Now let's look at the Do...Until example, which also displays the numbers 1 through 3 on the form.

The Do...Until example first declares and initializes (to 1) an Integer variable named X. The Do statement, which simply marks the beginning of the loop, is processed next. Visual Basic then processes the loop instructions, which display the value of X on the form and also add 1 to X. The Loop Until statement then evaluates the condition, *X > 3*, to determine if the loop instructions should be processed again. (Notice that the *condition* is not evaluated until after the loop instructions are processed the first time.) If X contains a number that is greater than 3, the loop stops; processing then continues with the instruction following the Loop Until statement. If X contains a number that is not greater than 3 (in other words, if it's less than or equal to 3), the loop instructions are processed again.

To summarize, the Do...Until loop repeats the loop instructions as long as the *condition* evaluates to false. When the *condition* evaluates to true, the Do...Until loop stops. Now let's look at the flowchart for both loops.

Flowchart for the Do...While and the Do...Until Loops

The flowcharts for the Do...While and the Do...Until loops that display the numbers 1 through 3 on the form are shown in Figure 6-5.

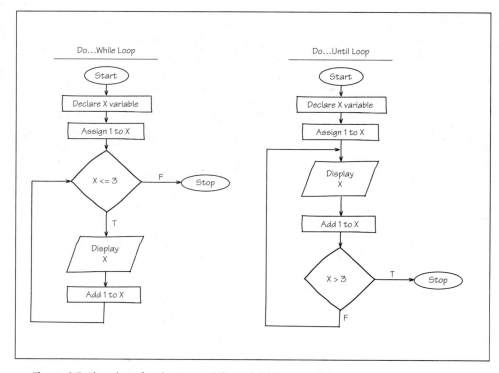

Figure 6-5: Flowchart for the Do...While and the Do...Until loops

Both loops are represented in a flowchart by a diamond. Like the selection diamond you learned in Tutorial 4, the repetition diamond contains a question that has a true (yes) or false (no) answer only. Also like the selection diamond, the repetition diamond has one flowline leading into the diamond and two flowlines leading out of the diamond.

On your Student Disk is a project named t6_loop1.mak that contains the code for the flowcharts shown in Figure 6-5. Let's look at that code now.

To view the code for the loop examples:

1   Launch Visual Basic and open the **t6_loop1.mak** file, which is in either the tut6\ver2 or the tut6\ver3 directory on your Student Disk. Click the **View Form button,** then maximize the form. The user interface appears on the screen, as shown in Figure 6-6.

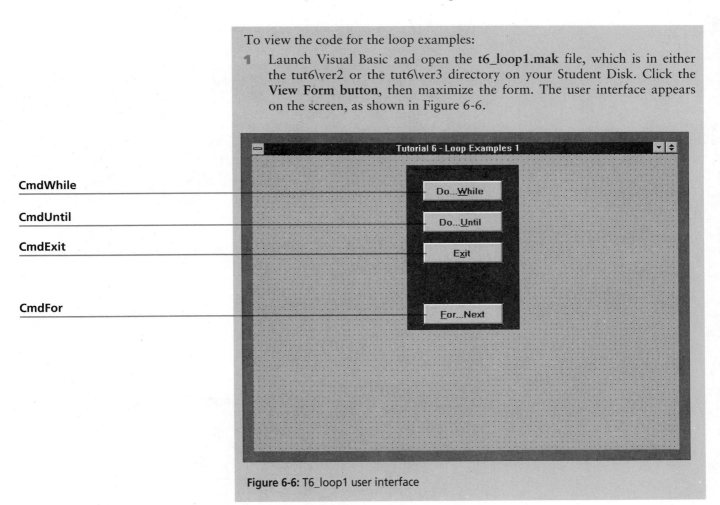

CmdWhile

CmdUntil

CmdExit

CmdFor

Figure 6-6: T6_loop1 user interface

The Do...While button and the Do...Until button have already been coded for you. Each will display the numbers 1 through 3 on the form. (The For...Next button, which is included for your reference only, also contains the code that will display the numbers 1 through 3 on the form. If you want to compare the For...Next loop with the loops you are learning in this tutorial, or if you want to review the For...Next loop, you can simply open the button's Code window and look at the code.) Let's begin with the Do...While button.

Do...While Example

The Do...While Command button uses the **Do While...Loop** statement to display the numbers 1 through 3 on the form.

To look at the code, then test the Do...While button:

1 Double-click the **Do...While button** to open its Code window. The CmdWhile's Click event procedure appears on the screen, as shown in Figure 6-7.

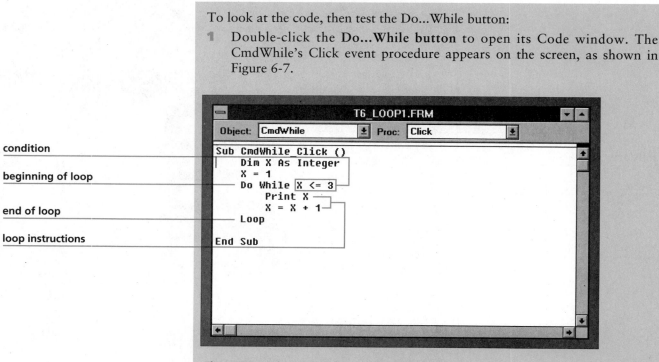

Figure 6-7: Code window for the Do...While button

2 Close the Code window, then press [F5] to run the application. (If you are asked if you want to save the form, click the No button.) Click the **Do...While button**. Visual Basic processes the instructions as shown in Figure 6-8, and the numbers 1, 2, and 3 appear in the upper-left corner of the form.

Do...While Example

1. X variable is declared as an Integer.

2. X variable is assigned the number 1.

3. Do While statement checks if the value in X is less than or equal to 3. It is.

4. Visual Basic prints 1 (the contents of X) on the form.

5. Visual Basic adds 1 to X, giving 2.

6. Loop statement sends the program to the beginning of the loop (to the Do While statement).

7. Do While statement checks if the value in X is less than or equal to 3. It is.

8. Visual Basic prints 2 (the contents of X) on the form.

9. Visual Basic adds 1 to X, giving 3.

10. Loop statement sends the program to the beginning of the loop (to the Do While statement).

11. Do While statement checks if the value in X is less than or equal to 3. It is.

12. Visual Basic prints 3 (the contents of X) on the form.

13. Visual Basic adds 1 to X, giving 4.

14. Loop statement sends the program to the beginning of the loop (to the Do While statement).

15. Do While statement checks if the value in X is less than or equal to 3. It's not.

16. Loop stops.

17. End Sub statement ends the Click event procedure.

Figure 6-8: Processing steps for Do...While example

3 Click the **Exit button** to end the application. Visual Basic returns to the design screen.

Now let's look at the Do...Until button.

Do...Until Example

The Do...Until Command button uses the Do...Loop Until statement to display the numbers 1 through 3 on the form.

To look at the code, then test the Do...Until button:

1   Double-click the **Do...Until button** to open its Code window. The CmdUntil's Click event procedure appears on the screen, as shown in Figure 6-9.

loop instructions

beginning of loop

end of loop

condition

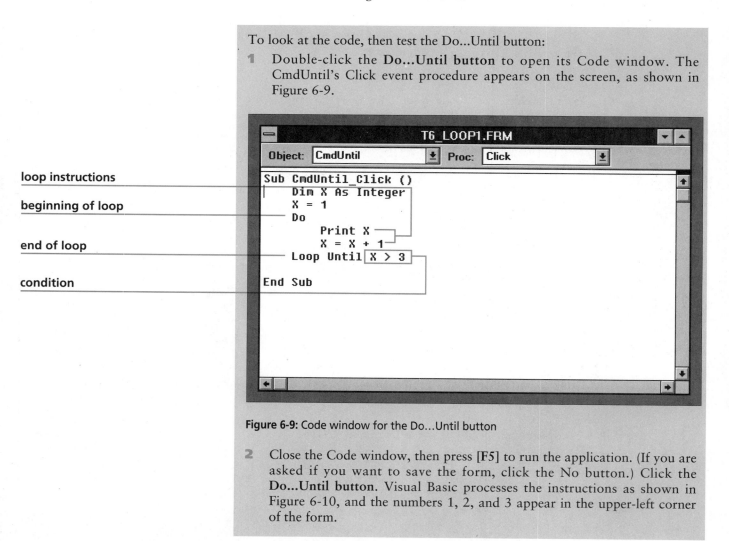

Figure 6-9: Code window for the Do...Until button

2   Close the Code window, then press [F5] to run the application. (If you are asked if you want to save the form, click the No button.) Click the **Do...Until button.** Visual Basic processes the instructions as shown in Figure 6-10, and the numbers 1, 2, and 3 appear in the upper-left corner of the form.

Do...Until Example

1. X variable is declared as an Integer.

2. X variable is assigned the number 1.

3. Do statement marks the beginning of the loop.

4. Visual Basic prints 1 (the contents of X) on the form.

5. Visual Basic adds 1 to X, giving 2.

6. Loop Until statement checks if the value in X is greater than 3. It's not.

7. Loop Until statement sends the program to the beginning of the loop (to the Do statement).

8. Visual Basic prints 2 (the contents of X) on the form.

9. Visual Basic adds 1 to X, giving 3.

10. Loop Until statement checks if the value in X is greater than 3. It's not.

11. Loop Until statement sends the program to the beginning of the loop (to the Do statement).

12. Visual Basic prints 3 (the contents of X) on the form.

13. Visual Basic adds 1 to X, giving 4.

14. Loop Until statement checks if the value in X is greater than 3. It is.

15. Loop stops.

16. End Sub statement ends the Click event procedure.

Figure 6-10: Processing steps for the modified Do...Until example

> **3** Click the **Exit button** to end the application. Visual Basic returns to the design screen.

Although it appears that the Do...While loop and Do...Until loop work identically—in this case, both loops displayed the numbers 1 through 3 on the form—that will not always be the case. In other words, the two loops are not always interchangeable. The difference between the Do...While (pretest) loop and the Do...Until (posttest) loop will be more apparent in the next set of steps.

To see the difference between the Do...While and the Do...Until loops:

1 Double-click the **Do...While button** to open its Code window. The CmdWhile's Click event procedure appears.

Let's change the initial value of X from 1 to 10.

2 Change the *X = 1* instruction to **X = 10**.

By setting the initial value of X to 10, the loop's *condition* (X <= 3) will evaluate to false, so Visual Basic will skip the loop instructions. Let's see if that is, in fact, what happens.

3 Close the Code window, then press [F5] to run the application. (If you are asked if you want to save the application, click the No button.) Click the **Do...While button**. As expected, the numbers 1 through 3 do not appear in the upper-left corner of the form. Because the Do...While loop's *condition* (X <= 3) evaluated to false, the instructions within the loop were not processed. Figure 6-11 shows how Visual Basic processed the Do...While Command button's code.

```
Modified Do...While Example

1.    X variable is declared as an Integer.

2.    X variable is assigned the number 10.

3.    Do While statement checks if the value in X is less than or equal to 3.

      It's not.

4.    Loop stops.

5.    End Sub statement ends the Click event procedure.
```

Figure 6-11: Processing steps for the modified Do...While example

---

4 Click the **Exit button**. Visual Basic returns to the design screen.

Now let's make the same change to the Do...Until button.

5 Double-click the **Do...Until button** to open its Code window. Change the *X = 1* instruction to **X = 10**.

Let's see how the Do...Until loop handles this change.

6 Close the Code window, then press [F5] to run the application. (If you are asked if you want to save the application, click the No button.) Click the **Do...Until button**. This time the number 10 appears in the upper-left corner of the form. Because the Do...Until loop instructions are processed before the *condition* (X > 3) is tested, the value in X, 10, appears on the form. Figure 6-12 shows how Visual Basic processed the Do...Until Command button's code.

<u>Modified Do...Until Example</u>

1.   X variable is declared as an Integer.

2.   X variable is assigned the number 10.

3.   Do statement marks the beginning of the loop.

4.   Visual Basic prints 10 (the contents of X) on the form.

5.   Visual Basic adds 1 to X, giving 11.

6.   Loop Until statement checks if the value in X is greater than 3. It is.

7.   Loop stops.

8.   End Sub statement ends the Click event procedure.

Figure 6-12: Processing steps for the modified Do...Until example

As this example shows, it is possible for the Do...While and the Do...Until loops to give different results. When deciding which loop to use, keep in mind that the Do...Until loop will always process the loop instructions at least once, whereas the Do...While loop might not process the instructions at all.

7 Click the **Exit button**. Visual Basic returns to the design screen.

You're finished with the current project, so you can remove it from the screen.

8 Restore the form to its standard size. Click **File** in the menu bar, then click **New Project**. When you are asked if you want to save the form, click the **No button**.

Now that you know how to use the Do...While and the Do...Until repetition structures, you can learn about counters and accumulators. You will often find either a counter or an accumulator, or both, within a repetition structure.

Counters and Accumulators

Counters and accumulators are used within a repetition structure to calculate subtotals, totals, and averages. A **counter** is a numeric variable used for counting something—such as the number of employees paid in a week. An **accumulator** is a numeric variable used for accumulating (adding together) something—such as the total dollar amount of a week's payroll.

Two tasks are associated with counters and accumulators: initializing and updating. **Initializing** means to assign a beginning value to the counter or accumulator. Although that beginning value is usually zero, counters and accumulators can be initialized to any number.

Updating, also called **incrementing,** means adding a number to the value stored in the counter or the accumulator. A counter is always incremented by a constant value, whereas an accumulator is incremented by a value that varies. The assignment statement that updates a counter or an accumulator is placed within the repetition structure.

On your Student Disk is a project that contains examples of a counter and an accumulator. Both examples will show you how to use a counter and an accumulator to calculate the average of the sales amounts that are entered by the user. One example uses the Do...While loop; the other uses the Do...Until loop. Before opening the project, let's look at the flowcharts, shown in Figure 6-13, for each of the examples.

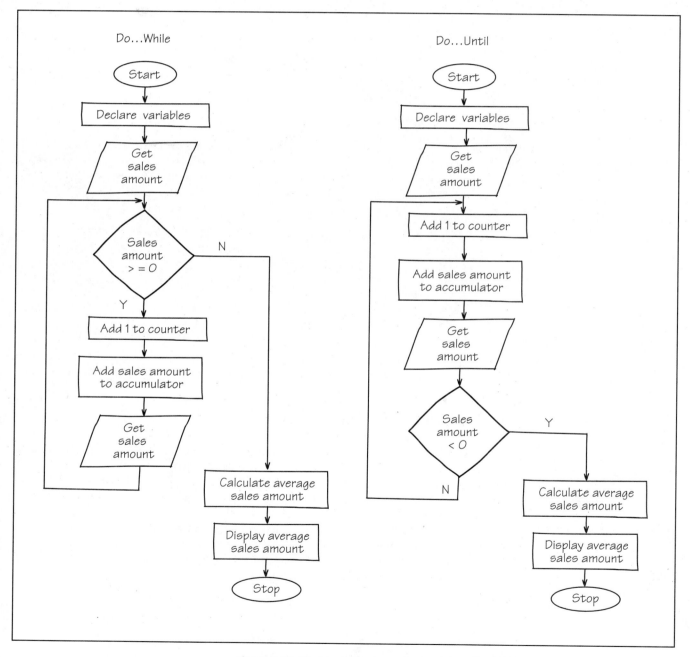

Figure 6-13: Flowcharts for examples in t6_loop2 project

The Do...While loop first declares the necessary variables and then gets a sales amount from the user. The loop then tests if the sales amount that the user entered is greater than or equal to zero. If it is, the counter is incremented by one, the accumulator is incremented by the sales amount, and another sales amount is requested from the user. The program then returns to the beginning of the loop where the *condition* is tested again. If the user enters a sales amount that is not greater than or equal to zero, the loop stops and the average sales amount is calculated and displayed.

The Do...Until loop also first declares the necessary variables and gets a sales amount from the user. The loop then increments both the counter by one and the accumulator by the sales amount before requesting another sales amount from the user. The loop then tests if the sales amount that the user entered is less than zero. If it's not, the program returns to the beginning of the loop and processes the loop instructions again; if it is, the loop stops and the average sales amount is then calculated and displayed.

Now let's open the t6_loop2.mak project on your Student Disk.

To look at the examples in the t6_loop2 project:

1 Open the **t6_loop2.mak** project, which is in either the tut6\ver2 or the tut6\ver3 directory on your Student Disk. Click the **View Form button** to view the t6_loop2 form.

2 Maximize the form. The user interface appears, as shown in Figure 6-14.

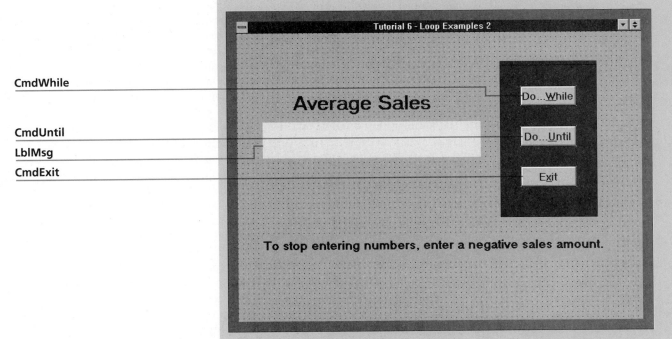

Figure 6-14: T6_Loop2 user interface

The Do...While and the Do...Until Command buttons have already been coded for you. Let's look at the code for the Do...While button first.

3 Double-click the **Do...While button**, then maximize the Code window. The maximized Code window appears, as shown in Figure 6-15.

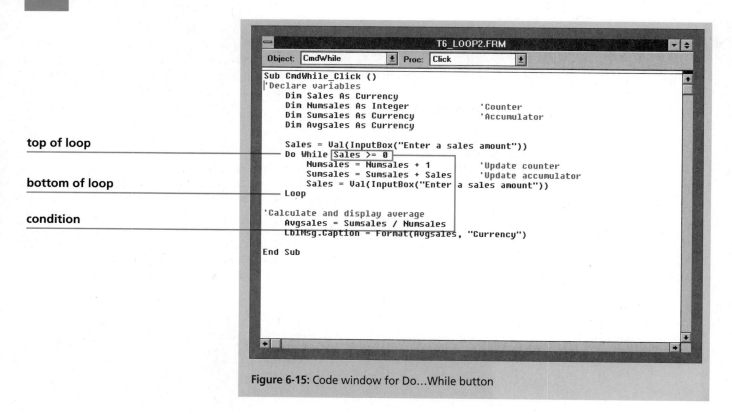

top of loop

bottom of loop

condition

```
                        T6_LOOP2.FRM
Object: CmdWhile            Proc: Click

Sub CmdWhile_Click ()
'Declare variables
    Dim Sales As Currency
    Dim Numsales As Integer              'Counter
    Dim Sumsales As Currency             'Accumulator
    Dim Avgsales As Currency

    Sales = Val(InputBox("Enter a sales amount"))
    Do While Sales >= 0
        Numsales = Numsales + 1          'Update counter
        Sumsales = Sumsales + Sales      'Update accumulator
        Sales = Val(InputBox("Enter a sales amount"))
    Loop

'Calculate and display average
    Avgsales = Sumsales / Numsales
    LblMsg.Caption = Format(Avgsales, "Currency")

End Sub
```

Figure 6-15: Code window for Do…While button

The code begins by declaring four variables: Sales, Numsales, Sumsales, and Avgsales. Three of the variables—Sales, Sumsales, and Avgsales—will store dollar amounts and are declared as Currency type variables. The Sales variable will store the sales amounts entered by the user, Sumsales (the accumulator variable) will store the total of the sales amounts, and Avgsales will store the average sales amount. The remaining variable, Numsales, is the counter variable that will count the number of sales amounts entered. Numsales is declared as an Integer type variable because it will store whole numbers only.

Recall that counters and accumulators must be initialized (given a beginning value). Because the Dim statement automatically assigns a zero to Integer variables and Currency variables when the variables are created, you do not need to enter any additional code to initialize the Numsales counter or the Sumsales accumulator—in other words, the Dim statement initializes the variables for you. If you want to initialize a counter or an accumulator to a value other than zero, however, you would need to include the appropriate assignment statement in your code. For example, to initialize the Numsales counter to 1, you would need to include the *Numsales = 1* assignment statement in your code. (The statements to initialize counters and accumulators to a value other than zero are usually entered after any Dim statements in the Code window.) In this application, you want both the counter and the accumulator initialized to zero, so no assignment statements are necessary.

After the variables are declared, the Inputbox function (which you learned about in Tutorial 3) asks the user to enter a sales amount. The numeric equivalent of the user's response is stored in the Sales variable. The Do While statement then evaluates the condition, *Sales >= 0*, to determine if the loop instructions should be processed. If the sales amount entered by the user is greater than or equal to zero, the loop instructions are processed; if the sales amount is not greater than or equal to zero (in other words, if it's less than zero), the loop instructions are not processed. Let's take a closer look at the instructions within the loop.

The *Numsales = Numsales + 1* instruction updates the counter by a constant value of 1. Notice that the counter variable, Numsales, appears on both sides of the assignment statement. The statement tells Visual Basic to add 1 to the contents of the Numsales variable, then place the result back in the Numsales variable. Numsales will be incremented by 1 each time the loop is processed.

The *Sumsales = Sumsales + Sales* instruction updates the accumulator. Notice that the accumulator variable, Sumsales, also appears on both sides of the assignment statement. The statement tells Visual Basic to add the contents of the Sales variable to the contents of the Sumsales variable, then place the result back in the Sumsales variable. Sumsales will be incremented by a sales amount, which will vary, each time the loop is processed.

After the counter and the accumulator are updated, the Inputbox function is used again to ask the user for another sales amount. Notice that the *Sales = Val(Inputbox("Enter a sales amount"))* instruction appears twice in the code—before the Do...While loop and within the Do...While loop. You may be wondering why you need to repeat the same instruction. Recall that the Loop statement sends the program to the top of the loop—to the Do While statement. Because the first Inputbox instruction is located before the Do While statement, the program will never return to that instruction once the loop begins. (It may help to refer to the flowchart shown in Figure 6-13.) In other words, the *Sales = Val(Inputbox("Enter a sales amount"))* instruction located above the loop gets only the first sales amount from the user. The *Sales = Val(Inputbox("Enter a sales amount"))* located within the loop gets each of the remaining sales amounts, if any, from the user.

After the user enters another sales amount, the Loop statement sends the program to the Do While statement where the *condition* is tested again. If the *condition* is true, the loop instructions are processed again. If the *condition* is false—in this case, if the user enters a sales amount that is less than 0—the loop stops and the instruction after the Loop statement is processed. That statement calculates the average sales amount by dividing the contents of the accumulator variable (Sumsales) by the contents of the counter variable (Numsales). The next instruction displays the average sales amount, formatted as currency, in the LblMsg control. Let's run the program and test the Do...While Command button.

To run the application and test the Do...While button:

1 Close the Code window, then press [F5] to run the application. (If you are asked if you want to save the form, click the No button.)

Recall that the Do...While button will calculate the average of the sales amounts that are entered by the user. Let's enter two sales amounts: 3000 and 4000.

2 Click the **Do...While button**, type **3000** in the dialog box, and press [Enter]. Because the sales amount is not less than zero, the loop instructions are processed. Those instructions add 1 to the Numsales variable, giving 1, and also add 3000 to the Sumsales variable, giving 3000. The user is then prompted for another sales amount.

3   Type **4000** in the dialog box and press [**Enter**]. Because the sales amount is not less than zero, the loop instructions are processed again. Those instructions add 1 to the Numsales variable, giving 2, and also add 4000 to the Sumsales variable, giving 7000.

Now let's stop the loop. Recall that you stop the loop by entering a negative sales amount.

4   Type **–1** in the dialog box and press [**Enter**]. Because the sales amount is less than zero, the loop stops. The average sales amount, $3,500.00, is calculated and displayed in the LblMsg control, and the Click event procedure ends.

In Tutorial 5's Debugging section you learned that you should always test your application with both correct and incorrect data. (Recall that incorrect data is data that the application is not expecting.) Let's see what happens if the user clicks the Do...While button and enters a negative value as the first sales amount.

5   Click the **Do...While button**, type **–1** in the dialog box, and press [**Enter**]. The Do...While button's Code window and a dialog box containing an "Overflow" error message appear on the screen, as shown in Figure 6-16.

Visual Basic highlights the instruction causing the error

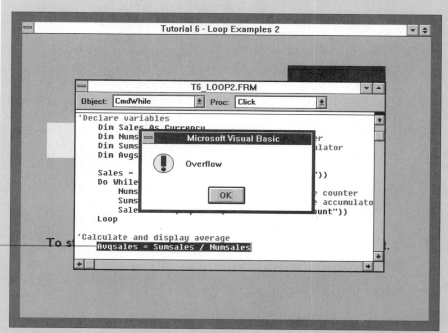

Figure 6-16: Dialog box showing Overflow error message

6   Click the **OK button** to remove the error message dialog box. Visual Basic highlights the *Avgsales = Sumsales / Numsales* instruction in the Code window.

When you enter a negative number as the first sales amount, the loop instructions are never processed. That means that the Numsales variable is not updated from its initial value of zero. Because division by zero is not allowed,

Visual Basic displays the "Overflow" error message when it attempts to process the *Avgsales* = *Sumsales* / *Numsales* assignment statement. Let's return to the design screen to fix this problem.

7   Close the Code window, click the **Restore button**, then click the **Stop icon** ◼. Visual Basic returns to the design screen.

You can use a selection structure to correct the division-by-zero problem. Before calculating the average sales amount, you will first determine if the value in Numsales is greater than zero. If it is, you will calculate and display the average sales amount; otherwise you will display a "No sales were entered." message in the LblMsg control.

8   If necessary, maximize the form, then double-click the **Do…While button** to open its Code window. Maximize the Code window and enter the selection structure shown in Figure 6-17.

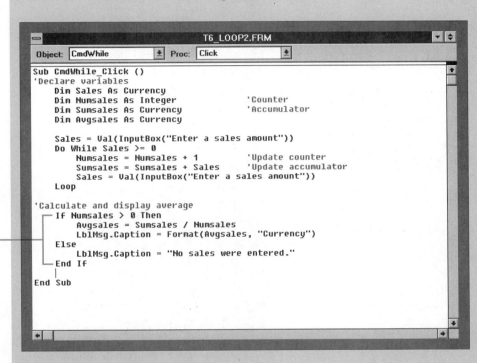

enter this selection structure

```
                                    T6_LOOP2.FRM
Object:  CmdWhile         ▼   Proc:  Click            ▼

Sub CmdWhile_Click ()
'Declare variables
    Dim Sales As Currency
    Dim Numsales As Integer           'Counter
    Dim Sumsales As Currency          'Accumulator
    Dim Avgsales As Currency

    Sales = Val(InputBox("Enter a sales amount"))
    Do While Sales >= 0
        Numsales = Numsales + 1           'Update counter
        Sumsales = Sumsales + Sales       'Update accumulator
        Sales = Val(InputBox("Enter a sales amount"))
    Loop

'Calculate and display average
    If Numsales > 0 Then
        Avgsales = Sumsales / Numsales
        LblMsg.Caption = Format(Avgsales, "Currency")
    Else
        LblMsg.Caption = "No sales were entered."
    End If

End Sub
```

Figure 6-17: Selection structure entered in Code window for the Do…While button

9   Close the Code window, then press [F5] to run the application. (If you are asked if you want to save the form, click the No button.) Click the **Do…While button**, then type **-1** and press [Enter]. The "Overflow" error does not occur and the "No sales were entered." message appears in the LblMsg control.

10 Click the **Exit button** to end the application. Visual Basic returns to the design screen.

Now let's look at the same example written with the Do…Until loop.

To view the code in the Do...Until button:

1   If necessary, maximize the form and double-click the **Do...Until button**, then maximize the Code window. The Code window appears, as shown in Figure 6-18.

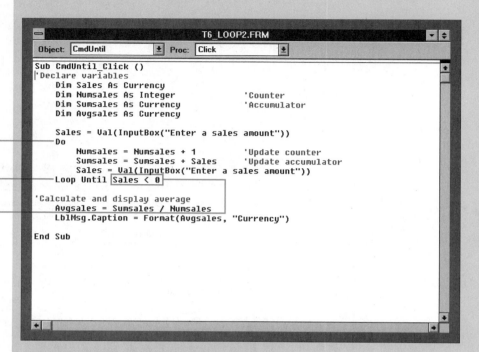

top of loop

bottom of loop

condition

Figure 6-18: Code window for the Do...Until button

Notice that the *condition*, *Sales < 0*, appears at the bottom of the Do...Until loop.

2   Close the Code window, then press [**F5**] to run the application. (If you are asked if you want to save the form, click the No button.) Now let's enter the two sales amounts, 3000 and 4000.

3   Click the **Do...Until button**, then type **3000** in the dialog box and press [**Enter**]. The loop instructions add 1 to Numsales, giving 1, and add 3000 to Sumsales, giving 3000. The user is then prompted to enter another sales amount.

4   Type **4000** in the dialog box and press [**Enter**]. Because the sales amount is not less than zero, the loop instructions are processed again. Those instructions add 1 to Numsales, giving 2, and add 4000 to Sumsales, giving 7000. The user is then prompted to enter another sales amount.

Now let's stop the Do...Until loop by entering a negative number.

5   Type **–1** in the dialog box and press [**Enter**]. Because the sales amount is less than zero, the loop stops and the average sales amount, $3,500.00, is calculated and displayed in the LblMsg control.

As we did with the Do...While loop, let's see what happens if the user clicks the Do...Until button and then enters a negative number as the first sales amount.

6   Click the **Do...Until button**, then type **–1** in the dialog box and press [**Enter**]. The loop instructions add 1 to Numsales and add a –1 to Sumsales. Another dialog box requesting another sales amount appears.

Because the Do...Until loop's *condition* (*Sales* < 0) is not tested until after the second sales amount is entered, you will need to enter another negative number to stop the loop.

7 Type **–1** and press **[Enter]**. The loop stops and ($1.00), which is probably not what you were expecting, appears in the LblMsg control. The ($1.00) is the result of dividing the contents of Sumsales (–1) by the contents of Numsales (1).

Because you can never be sure what a user might do, it is usually safer to use the Do...While loop instead of the Do...Until loop. Use the Do...Until loop only in situations where you know that the loop definitely can and will be processed at least once.

8 Click the **Exit button** to end the application. Visual Basic returns to the design screen.

You're finished viewing the t6_loop2 application, so you can remove it from the screen.

9 If necessary, restore the form to its standard size. Click **File** in the menu bar, then click **New Project**. When you are asked if you want to save the form, click the No button.

You have now completed Lesson A. You can either take a break or complete the end-of-lesson questions and exercises.

S U M M A R Y

To code the Do...While loop:

■ Use the Do While...Loop statement. Its syntax is:
> **Do While** *condition*
> > *loop instructions*
> **Loop**

To code the Do...Until loop:

■ Use the Do...Loop Until statement. Its syntax is:
> **Do**
> > *loop instructions*
> **Loop Until** *condition*

To use a counter:

■ Initialize the counter, if necessary.
■ Use an assignment statement, within a repetition structure, to update the counter. You update a counter by incrementing its value by a constant amount.

To use an accumulator:

■ Initialize the accumulator, if necessary.
■ Use an assignment statement, within a repetition structure, to update the accumulator. You update an accumulator by incrementing its value by an amount that varies.

QUESTIONS

1. The three forms of the repetition structure are: (Select three)
   a. Do...For
   b. Do...Until
   c. Do...While
   d. For...Now
   e. For...Next

2. You can use the _____ loop(s) when you don't know how many times the loop instructions should be processed.
   a. Do...Until
   b. Do...While
   c. For...Next
   d. a or b
   e. a, b, or c

3. You can use the _____ loop(s) when you know precisely how many times the loop instructions should be processed.
   a. Do...Until
   b. Do...While
   c. For...Next
   d. a or b
   e. a, b, or c

4. Programmers call the _____ loop a pretest loop because the condition is tested at the beginning of the loop.
   a. Do...Until
   b. Do...While
   c. For...Next
   d. a and c
   e. b and c

5. Programmers call the _____ loop a posttest loop because the condition is tested at the end of the loop.
   a. Do...Until
   b. Do...While
   c. For...Next
   d. a and c
   e. b and c

6. The _____ loop repeats the loop instructions as long as the condition is true. Once the condition becomes false, this loop stops.
   a. Do...Until
   b. Do...While

7. The _____ loop repeats the loop instructions as long as the condition is false. Once the condition becomes true, this loop stops.
   a. Do...Until
   b. Do...While

8. The _____ loop processes the loop instructions at least once, whereas the _____ loop instructions might not be processed at all.
   a. Do...Until, Do...While
   b. Do...While, Do...Until

9. A(n) _____ is a numeric variable used for counting something.
   a. accumulator
   b. adder
   c. constant
   d. counter
   e. integer

10. A(n) _____ is a numeric variable used for accumulating something.
    a. accumulator
    b. adder
    c. constant
    d. counter
    e. integer

11. The tasks associated with counters and accumulators are: (Select two)
    a. adding
    b. counting
    c. initializing
    d. printing
    e. updating

12. A(n) _____ is always incremented by a constant amount, whereas a(n) _____ is incremented by an amount that varies.
    a. accumulator, counter
    b. counter, accumulator

13. Which of the following will correctly update the counter variable named Number?
    a. Number = 0
    b. Number = 1
    c. Number = Number + Number
    d. Number = Number + Sales
    e. Number = Number + 1

14. Which of the following will correctly update the accumulator variable named Total?
    a. Total = 0
    b. Total = 1
    c. Total = Total + Total
    d. Total = Total + Sales
    e. Total = Total + 1

15. Counters and accumulators are automatically initialized to zero by _____ .
    a. an assignment statement
    b. the Dim statement
    c. the Initialize statement
    d. the Update statement

E X E R C I S E S

1. Complete the following code by using the Do...While loop to print the word "Hello" on the form 10 times.

    ```
    Dim X as Integer
    X = 1
    Do _____
            Print "Hello"
            X = X + 1
    Loop
    ```

2. Complete the following code by using the Do...Until loop to print the word "Hello" on the form 10 times.

    ```
    Dim X as Integer
    X = 1
    Do
            Print "Hello"
            X = X + 1
    Loop _____
    ```

3. Write a Do While statement that tells Visual Basic to stop the loop when the value in the Sales variable is equal to zero.

4. Write a Loop Until statement that tells Visual Basic to stop the loop when the value in the Sales variable is equal to zero.

5. Write a Do While statement that tells Visual Basic to stop the loop when the user enters the word "Done" (in either uppercase or lowercase letters) in the Fname variable.

6. Write a Loop Until statement that tells Visual Basic to stop the loop when the user enters the word "Done" (in either uppercase or lowercase letters) in the Fname variable.

7. What will print on the form when the following code is processed?

    ```
    Dim X as Integer
    Do While X < 5
            Print X
            X = X + 1
    Loop
    ```

8. What will print on the form when the following code is processed?

    ```
    Dim X as Integer
    Do
            Print X
            X = X + 1
    Loop Until X > 5
    ```

9. An instruction is missing from the following code. What is the missing instruction and where does it belong in the code?

    ```
    Dim Num as Integer
    Num = 1
    Do While Num < 5
            Print Num
    Loop
    ```

10. An instruction is missing from the following code. What is the missing instruction and where does it belong in the code?

    ```
    Dim Num as Integer
    Num = 10
    Do
            Print Num
    Loop Until Num = 0
    ```

11. The following code should print the commission (Sales*.1) for each sales amount that is entered. The code is not working properly because an instruction is missing. What is the missing instruction and where does it belong in the code?

    ```
    Dim Sales as Currency
    Sales = Val(Inputbox("Enter a sales amount"))
    Do While Sales > 0
            Print Sales *.1
    Loop
    ```

12. The following code should print the commission (Sales*.1) for each sales amount that is entered. The code is not working properly. What is wrong with the code and how will you fix it?

    ```
    Dim Sales as Currency
    Sales = Val(Inputbox("Enter a sales amount"))
    Do
            Sales = Val(Inputbox("Enter a sales amount"))
            Print Sales *.1
    Loop Until Sales <= 0
    ```

13. Write an assignment statement that updates a counter variable, named X, by 1.

14. Write an assignment statement that updates a counter variable, named Total, by 5.

15. Write an assignment statement that updates an accumulator variable, named Totsales, by the value in the Sales variable.

16. Write an assignment statement that updates an accumulator variable, named Totalgross, by the value in the Gross variable.

17. Write an assignment statement that initializes a counter variable, named Employees, to 1.

18. Look at the following two assignment statements. Which will correctly update a counter, and which will correctly update an accumulator? How do you know which one updates a counter and which one updates an accumulator?

    ```
    Total = Total + 1
    Total = Total + Sales
    ```

19. What will print when the following code is processed?

    ```
    Dim Totemp as Integer
    Do While Totemp <= 5
            Print Totemp
            Totemp = Totemp + 2
    Loop
    ```

20. What will print when the following code is processed?

    ```
    Dim Totemp as Integer
    Totemp = 1
    Do
            Print Totemp
            Totemp = Totemp + 2
    Loop Until Totemp >= 3
    ```

LESSON B

objectives

In this lesson you will learn how to:

■ Use a List box

■ Open and close a sequential access data file

■ Write data to a sequential access data file

Sequential Access Data Files

The UFO Application

Recall that the president of the Chicago UFO Club wants you to create an application that will tabulate the responses to the UFO questionnaire and produce the UFO report. (The questionnaire and the report are shown in Figure 6-1). Figure 6-19 shows the sketch of the user interface for the UFO application.

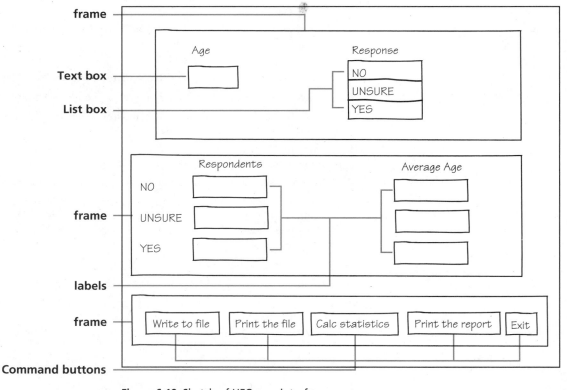

frame

Text box

List box

Age

Response

NO
UNSURE
YES

frame

Respondents

Average Age

NO

UNSURE

YES

labels

frame

Command buttons

Write to file   Print the file   Calc statistics   Print the report   Exit

Figure 6-19: Sketch of UFO user interface

On your Student Disk is a partially completed application for the Chicago UFO Club. Let's open that application right now.

To open the partially completed application:

1 Launch Visual Basic (if necessary) and open the **t6a.mak** file, which is in either the tut6\ver2 or the tut6\ver3 directory on your Student Disk. (The Option Explicit statement has already been entered into the general Declarations section of the form.)

2 **Save** the form and the project as **t6b**. Click the **View Form button**, then maximize the form. The form appears, as shown in Figure 6-20.

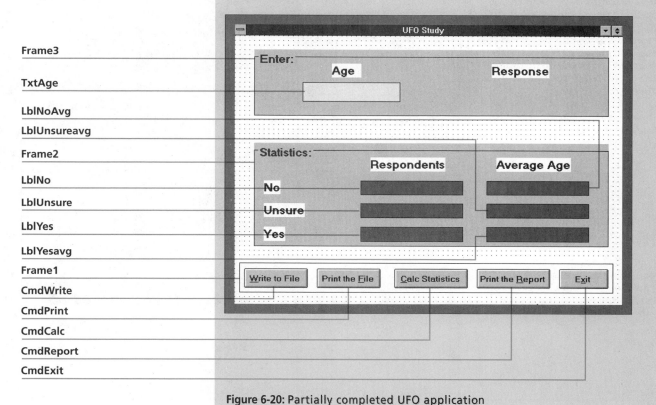

Frame3
TxtAge
LblNoAvg
LblUnsureavg
Frame2
LblNo
LblUnsure
LblYes
LblYesavg
Frame1
CmdWrite
CmdPrint
CmdCalc
CmdReport
CmdExit

Figure 6-20: Partially completed UFO application

One control is missing from the form—a List box. You will learn how to create that now.

Creating a List Box

For each completed questionnaire, the club's secretary will enter, into the user interface, both an age and a response—either No, Unsure, or Yes. You will use a Text box to get the age and a List box to get the response. Like Option buttons (which you learned about in Tutorial 4), a List box also can be used to display a set of choices from which the user can select only one. Unlike Option buttons, however, a List box does not require you to display all of the choices on the screen at the same time. You can make a List box any size you want, and if you have more items than will fit into the List box, Visual Basic will automatically supply scroll bars on the box, which you can use to view the undisplayed items. So if you have many possible choices, you can save space on the form by using a List box instead of Option buttons. (Although this application needs to offer only three responses to the user, you will use a List box instead of Option buttons to display those responses.) Let's add the missing List box right now.

tips

▶ If your control says Combo1, you accidentally double-clicked the Combo box tool. Press [Delete] to remove the Combo box control, then double-click the List box tool, which is the fifth tool in the right-hand column of the Toolbox.

▶ Don't set a property for BackColor if you have a monochrome monitor.

tips

▶ If [Ctrl][X] does not cut the List box from the form, repeat Step 3. This time, be sure to click the LstResponse List box before pressing [Ctrl][X].

To create a List box:

1　Restore the form to its standard size, then double-click the **List box tool** in the Toolbox. The List1 List box appears in the middle of the form.

2　Set the following properties for the List box control:

Width: **1455**　　　　　BackColor: **Choose a pale yellow**

TabIndex: **1**　　　　　FontSize: **9.75**

Name: **LstResponse** (The Lst stands for List box.)

Don't worry that the LstResponse name appears inside the List box; the name won't appear when you run the application. To place the List box inside the Frame control, recall that you first need to cut the control from the form, which places the control on the Windows Clipboard. You can then paste the control from the Clipboard into the Frame.

3　Click the **LstResponse List box** to return to the form and select that control. Press [**Ctrl**][**X**] to cut the List box from the form, click the **Frame3 control** (the one located at the top of the form shown in Figure 6-20) to select that control, then press [**Ctrl**][**V**] to paste the List box into the Frame3 control.

4　Maximize the form, then drag the List box further into the Frame3 control, as shown in Figure 6-21.

List box control ───────────

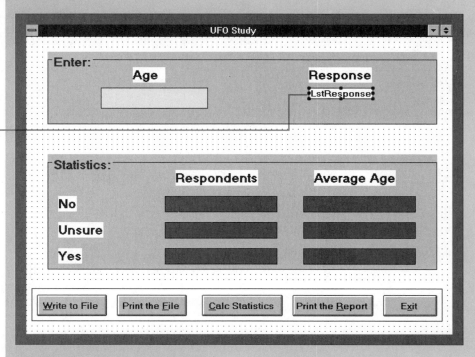

Figure 6-21: List box in Frame3 control

Now that the missing List box control is on the form, you need to tell Visual Basic what items you want displayed in the List box. You do that by writing Visual Basic code.

Responding to a Load Event

Because you want the List box to display its values when the form first appears on the screen, you will need to define the List box items in the form's Load event procedure. A Load event occurs when the application is run and the form is loaded into the computer's memory. Visual Basic automatically executes the instructions contained in the Load event procedure's Code window when the Load event occurs. These instructions give a beginning value to initialize the form and its controls. In this case, you will be initializing the form's List box.

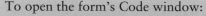

To open the form's Code window:

1 Double-click the **form** to open the form's Code window. The form's Code window appears. (Be sure to double-click the form, not a control in the form.) Notice that Load is the default event procedure for a form.

If you don't see the form's Load event procedure, click the down arrow in the Code window's Object box, then click Form in the drop-down list.

The AddItem Method

You use Visual Basic's AddItem method to specify the items you want displayed in a List box control. The syntax of the AddItem method is *Control.AddItem item*. *Control* is the name of the control to which you want the item added, *AddItem* is the name of the method, and *item* is the string expression you want displayed in the control. (If you want a number displayed, be sure to surround the number with quotation marks.) To complete the LstResponse List box, you need to enter three AddItem instructions—one for each of the three responses you want displayed in the List box. Let's add the instructions right now.

To enter the AddItem instructions for the LstResponse List box:

1 The form's Code window should still be open. Enter the instructions shown in Figure 6-22 into the form's Load event procedure.

One way to organize the items in a List box is to place the most frequently chosen items at the top of the list. By doing so, the user will not need to scroll the list as often. For example, if the majority of people answering the UFO questionnaire are expected to answer "Yes," then "Yes" should be the first item in the list. Another way to organize the items in a List box is to place them in alphabetical order. You will learn how to do that in the next section.

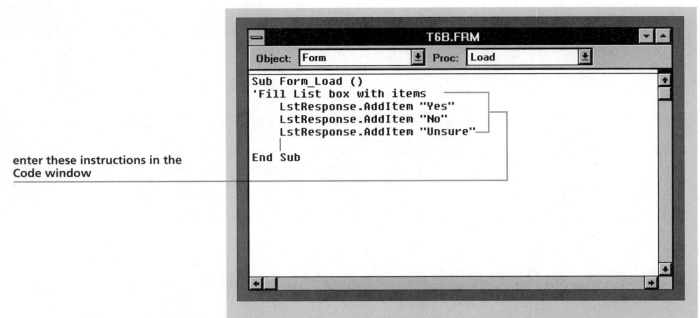

Figure 6-22: AddItem instructions in form's Load event procedure

enter these instructions in the Code window

When you run this application and the form is loaded into the computer's memory, Visual Basic will fill the LstResponse List box with the values you entered in the Load event procedure's Code window. Let's try that now.

2   Close the Code window, restore the form to its standard size, then **save and run** the application. Visual Basic displays the form on the screen, as shown in Figure 6-23.

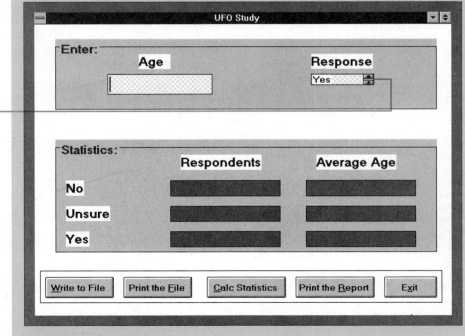

scroll bars

Figure 6-23: List box with scroll bars

Because the List box is too small to display the three items at the same time, Visual Basic supplies scroll bars on the box. You can use those scroll bars to scroll through the various choices.

3 Scroll the List box until the No response appears, then click **No** to highlight it. When you select an item from a List box, that item is assigned to the List box's Text property. In this case, the string "No" (without the quotes) is assigned to the Text property of the LstResponse List box.

You will improve the LstResponse List box by making some modifications. First you will make the List box larger so that all three choices are displayed; then the user will not need to waste time scrolling. Second, you will put the List box items in alphabetical order so they are easier for the user to locate. Third, you will tell Visual Basic to select the first item in the list automatically when the application is run. Let's return to the design screen and make these three modifications.

4 Click the **Exit button**, which already contains the End statement. Visual Basic returns to the design screen.

First let's make the List box larger so the three responses will be displayed at the same time.

5 Maximize the form, then click the **LstResponse List box** to select that control. Press [F4] to display the Properties window, then change the Height property to **750**. Now all three responses will appear in the List box when the application is run. (If part of the List box is out of the Frame, simply drag the List box further into the Frame.)

Next let's put the List box items in alphabetical order. Arranging information in either alphabetical or numerical order is called **sorting**.

The Sorted Property

If you want the List box items to appear in alphabetical order, you can either add them to the List box in the correct order—in other words, add the "No" item to the List box first, then add the "Unsure" item, and then add the "Yes" item—or you can simply set the List box's Sorted property to True. Setting the List box's Sorted property to True automatically sorts the items as they are loaded into the List box. Let's set the Sorted property of the LstResponse List box to True so that the responses appear in alphabetical order.

To sort the List box items:

1 The LstResponse List box should still be selected and the Properties window should still be displayed. Double-click **Sorted** in the Properties list until the property says True. Now Visual Basic will sort the items as they are being added to the List box.

You will now tell Visual Basic to select the first item in the List box automatically.

The ListIndex Property

Just as the TabIndex property (which you learned about in Tutorial 2) keeps track of the various objects in a form, the ListIndex property keeps track of the various items in a List box. The first item in a List box has a ListIndex of 0 (zero), the second item has a ListIndex of 1, and so on. In order to have the first item selected when the form appears on the screen, you need to add an instruction to the form's Load event procedure. The instruction will set the ListIndex to a number that represents the location of the first item in the list—zero.

tips

· ·

▶ If you don't see the form's Load event procedure, click the down arrow in the Code window's Object box, then click Form in the drop-down list.

To select the first item in the LstResponse List box automatically:

1 Double-click the **form** to open the Load event procedure's Code window. The Load event procedure, showing the AddItem instructions, appears.

2 Place the I-bar I in the blank line immediately below the last AddItem instruction and then click at that location. Type **LstResponse.listindex = 0** and then press [**Enter**]. (Be sure to type the number 0 and not the letter O.) This assignment statement tells Visual Basic to select the first item in the LstResponse List box automatically.

3 Close the Code window, restore the form to its standard size, then **save and run** the application. Visual Basic displays the form on the screen.

Because the List box is now large enough to display all three of the choices, Visual Basic does not supply scroll bars on the box. Also notice that the items appear in alphabetical order and the first item in the list is automatically selected.

4 Click the **Exit button** to end the application. Visual Basic returns to the design screen.

The user interface is finally complete. Before you can begin coding the application, however, you will need to learn about data files.

Data Files

In previous tutorials you saved the form and the project in separate files on your Student Disk. Those files, called **program files**, contain the instructions that create the user interface and tell the objects how to respond to events. Although the form and the project were saved, recall that the data entered into the user interface—for example, the student's scores in Tutorial 5's grade application—was not saved. That means you will need to enter the data (the student's scores) each time the grade application is run. So that the UFO Club's secretary will not have to enter the UFO data—the ages and the responses—every time he or she wants to prepare a report, you will save that information in a file, called a data file, on your Student Disk.

The information in a data file is organized into fields and records. A **field**, also called a **data element**, is a single item of information about a person, place, or thing—for example, a social security number, a city, or a price. A **record** is a group of related fields that contain all of the necessary data about a specific person, place, or thing. For example, the college you are attending keeps a student record on you. Your student record contains the following fields: your social security number, name, address, phone number, credits earned, grades earned, grade point average, and so on. The place where you are employed also keeps a record on you. Your employee record contains your social security number, name, address, phone number, starting date, salary or hourly wage, and so on. A collection of related records is called a **data file**. The collection of records for each of the students in your class forms the class data file; the collection of employee records forms the employee data file.

In the UFO application, only two elements of data are important—the respondent's age and his or her response. Together, those two fields form each respondent's record. The collection of respondents' records forms the UFO data file. Figure 6-24 illustrates the concept of a field, a record, and a data file.

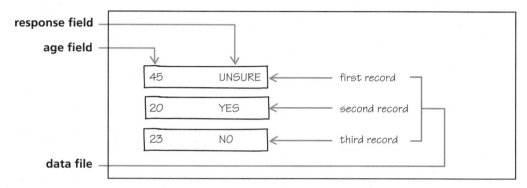

Figure 6-24: Illustration of fields and records in a data file

Visual Basic has three types of data files: sequential, random, and binary. The data file type refers to how the data is accessed. For example, the data in a sequential access file is always accessed sequentially—in other words, in consecutive order. The data in a random access file, on the other hand, can be accessed either in consecutive order or in random order. The data in a binary access file can be accessed by its byte location in the file. You will learn about sequential access files in this tutorial and random access files in Tutorial 7. Binary access files are beyond the scope of this book.

Sequential Access Files

Sequential access files are similar to cassette tapes in that each record in the file, like each song on a cassette tape, is both stored and retrieved in consecutive order (sequentially). Sequential access files have the advantage of being very easy to create. The drawback of this file type is the same drawback encountered with cassette tapes: The records in a sequential access data file, like the songs on a cassette tape, can be processed only in the order in which they are stored. In other words, if you want to listen to the third song on a cassette tape, you must play (or fast-forward through) the first two songs. Likewise, if you want to read the third record in a sequential access file, you must first read the two records that precede it. Sequential access files work best when you want to process either a small file, like the one needed by the UFO Club, or a file consisting only of text, such as a file created with a typical text editor.

In this lesson you will learn how to create, open, write records to, and close a sequential access file. You will learn how to both read and print the records in a sequential access file in Lesson C.

Let's begin coding the UFO application. The TOE chart is shown in Figure 6-25.

Task	Object	Event
Get age from the user	Text box	None
Get response from the user	List box	Click
Write the respondent's data to a data file	Command button (CmdWrite)	Click
Print the respondent's data from the data file	Command button (CmdPrint)	Click
Calculate the number of respondents and the average age in each response	Command button (CmdCalc)	Click
Print the UFO report	Command button (CmdReport)	Click
End the application	Command button (CmdExit)	Click

Figure 6-25: TOE chart for the UFO application

According to the TOE chart, five Command buttons need to be coded. (You don't need to code the List box's Click event. When you click an item in a list box, Visual Basic assigns the item to the List box's. Text property automatically.) You, however, will need to code only four of the five buttons because the Exit button already contains the End command. We'll begin with the CmdWrite Command button (the Write to File button), which is responsible for saving each respondent's age and response in a data file on your Student Disk.

Coding the Write to File Button

For each returned questionnaire, recall that the club's secretary will enter the age into the TxtAge Text box and the response into the LstResponse List box. After entering a respondent's data into the user interface, the secretary will then click the Write to File button to write the record to the data file. The flowchart for the Write to File button is shown in Figure 6-26.

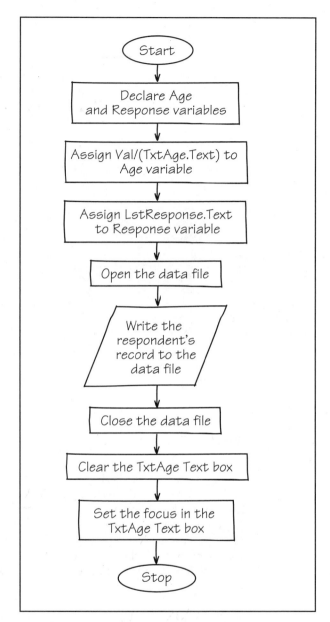

Figure 6-26: Flowchart for the Write to File button

The first step is to declare two variables, Age and Response. You will declare Age as an Integer variable because it will store whole numbers only; you will declare Response as a String variable because it will store characters only. After declaring the variables, you will then assign the numeric equivalent of the TxtAge control's Text property to the Age variable. You will also assign the Text property of the LstResponse List box to the Response variable. Although it's not necessary to assign the Text property of those controls to variables, doing so allows you to use shorter and more meaningful names when referring to the data later in your code. Response, for example, is much shorter and clearer than LstResponse.Text. More importantly, however, assigning the Text property of controls to variables allows you to control how the data is stored in the file. For example, recall that the value stored in the Text property of a control is treated as a string. Assigning the numeric equivalent of a string to an Integer variable tells Visual Basic to store the number as an integer. Let's declare the variables and assign the appropriate values to them before continuing with the flowchart.

To begin coding the Write to File button:

1   Maximize the form, then double-click the **Write to File button**. The CmdWrite control's Click event procedure appears.

2   Enter the code shown in Figure 6-27. (Recall that you can enter more than one variable on a Dim statement, but you must be sure to declare a data type for each.)

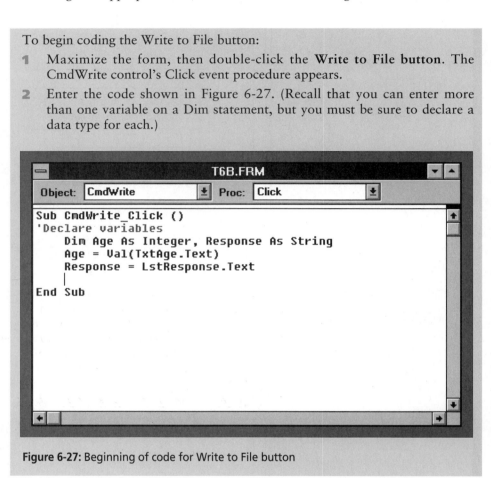

```
Sub CmdWrite_Click ()
'Declare variables
    Dim Age As Integer, Response As String
    Age = Val(TxtAge.Text)
    Response = LstResponse.Text
|
End Sub
```

Figure 6-27: Beginning of code for Write to File button

Now that the variables have been declared and their values assigned, you can proceed to the next step shown in Figure 6-26's flowchart. That step tells you to open the data file. You must always open a data file before you can use it.

Opening a Data File

You open a data file with Visual Basic's Open statement. Its syntax is **Open** *filename* **For** *mode* **As #** *filenumber*. *Filename* is the name of the file you want to open; it should include the drive letter and path, and it must be enclosed in quotation marks. For sequential access files, *mode* can be Input, Output, or Append. (Two other modes, Random and Binary, are used with random access and binary access files, respectively. Random access files are covered in Tutorial 7. Binary access files are beyond the scope of this book.) You open a sequential access file for **Input** when you want to read its contents. You open the file for **Output** when you want to create a new sequential access file and then write data to it. (If the file already exists, Visual Basic erases its contents before writing the new information.) You open a file for Append when you want to add data to the end of an existing sequential access file. (If the file does not already exist, Visual Basic creates it before adding the data to it.) Figure 6-28 recaps the three modes.

Open statement modes:	Use for:
Append	Adding data to an existing sequential access data file. The file is created if it doesn't already exist.
Input	Reading data from an existing sequential access data file. The file must already exist in order to be read.
Output	Creating a new sequential access data file and writing data to it. If the file already exists, its contents are erased before the new data is written.

Figure 6-28: Recap of Open statement modes

Filenumber is a number that you assign to the file; it must be an integer between 1 and 255, inclusive. When the Open statement is processed, Visual Basic associates the *filenumber* with the file. You use the *filenumber* to refer to the file in other statements. The *filenumber* will be associated with the file as long as the file is open. Figure 6-29 shows examples of the Open statement.

Examples of the Open statement for sequential access data files:

Open "a:\tut6\ver3\test.dat" for append as #1	Opens a sequential access data file for append.
Open "a:\tut6\ver2\myfile.dat" for output as #2	Opens a sequential access data file for output.
Open "a:\tut6\ver3\employee.dat" for input as #1	Opens a sequential access data file for input.

Figure 6-29: Examples of the Open statement

Because the club's secretary will be adding new records to the file as the questionnaires are returned, you will need to open the UFO file for Append; new records will then be added automatically to the end of the data file. You will name the data file t6b.dat and assign the number 1 to it. (A .dat extension is commonly used on a file's name to indicate that the file is a data file).

To enter the Open statement:

1   Type one of the following Open statements into the Code window. Which statement you type will depend on your version of Visual Basic and the location of your Student Disk. For example, if you are using Version 3 and your Student Disk is in drive A, then you would type *Open "a:\tut6\ver3\t6b.dat" for append as #1*. Be sure to type the backslash (\), not the slash (/).

> **open "a:\tut6\ver2\t6b.dat" for append as #1**
>
> **open "b:\tut6\ver2\t6b.dat" for append as #1**
>
> **open "a:\tut6\ver3\t6b.dat" for append as #1**
>
> **open "b:\tut6\ver3\t6b.dat" for append as #1**

2   Press [**Enter**].

When the application is run and the user clicks the Write to File button, the Open statement will open the sequential access data file named t6b.dat. If the t6b.dat file does not exist, the Open statement will create the data file before opening it.

The next step in the flowchart (shown in Figure 6-26) is to write the respondent's record to the data file—in other words, to enter the record in the file.

Writing to a File

Recall that a respondent's record consists of his or her age and response to the UFO question. You use Visual Basic's Write # statement to write a record to a sequential access file. The syntax of the Write # statement is *Write # filenumber [, expressionlist]*. *Filenumber* is the number used in the Open statement to open the sequential access file and *expressionlist* is one or more numeric or string expressions, separated by commas. Figure 6-30 shows examples of the Write # statement.

Examples of the Write statement for sequential access data files:

```
Write #1, TxtCity.Text    Writes the Text property of the TxtCity control to the
                          sequential access data file opened as file #1.

Write #2, Sales           Writes the contents of the Sales variable to the sequential
                          access data file opened as file #2.

Write #1, City, Sales     Writes the contents of the City variable and the Sales
                          variable to the sequential access data file opened as file #1.
```

Figure 6-30: Examples of the Write statement

In this case you want to write the respondent's age, which is stored in the Age variable, and the response, which is stored in the Response variable, to the data file.

To add the Write # statement to the open Code window:

1 Type **write #1, Age, Response** and press [**Enter**]. This statement will write the contents of the Age and Response variables to the t6b.dat file on your Student Disk.

When you are finished with a data file, you should close it.

Closing a File

You use Visual Basic's Close statement to close a file. Its syntax is **Close [#** *filenumber*], where *filenumber* is the number used in the Open statement to open the file. A Close statement with no arguments closes all open files. When a file is closed, its *filenumber* is disassociated from the file. The *filenumber* can then be used by another file. In this case you want to close the file opened as #1.

To complete the Write to File button's code:

1 Type **close #1** and press [**Enter**].

According to the flowchart shown in Figure 6-26, you still need to enter the code to clear the TxtAge Text box and also set the focus to that control.

2 Maximize the Code window. Type **TxtAge.Text = " "** and press [**Enter**], then type **TxtAge.setfocus** and press [**Enter**].

3 Enter the documentation shown in Figure 6-31.

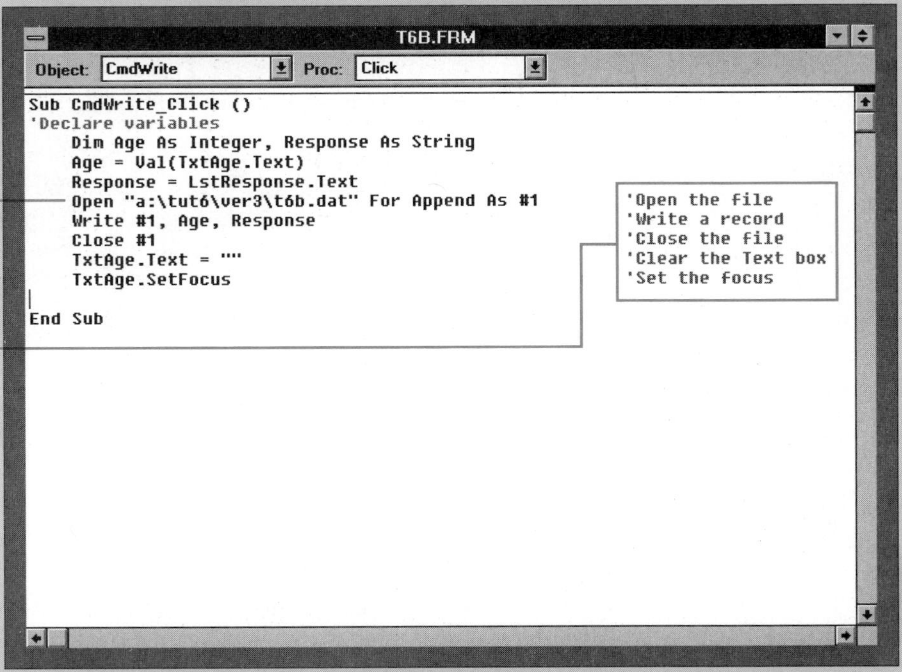

your drive letter and version number might be different

enter this documentation

```
T6B.FRM
Object: CmdWrite    Proc: Click

Sub CmdWrite_Click ()
'Declare variables
    Dim Age As Integer, Response As String
    Age = Val(TxtAge.Text)
    Response = LstResponse.Text
    Open "a:\tut6\ver3\t6b.dat" For Append As #1    'Open the File
    Write #1, Age, Response                         'Write a record
    Close #1                                        'Close the file
    TxtAge.Text = ""                                'Clear the Text box
    TxtAge.SetFocus                                 'Set the focus

End Sub
```

Figure 6-31: Completed Code window showing documentation

4   Compare your code with the code shown in Figure 6-31. Make any necessary corrections before continuing to the next step.

5   Close the Code window and restore the form to its standard size.

Let's test the Write to File button by entering the data from three completed questionnaires. The first questionnaire is from a 45-year-old person who is unsure about his or her belief in UFOs. (If you have already completed this lesson and are now practicing it again, then switch to File Manager and delete the t6b.dat from your Student Disk before running the application; otherwise, the records will be added to the existing t6b.dat file.)

To test the Write the File button:

1   **Save and run** the application. Type **45** in the Age Text box, click **Unsure** in the List box, then click the **Write to File button**. Visual Basic creates the Age and Response variables and assigns the appropriate values to them. Visual Basic then creates the t6b.dat file on your Student Disk (recall that the file doesn't, as yet, exist), writes the record to the file, closes the t6b.dat file, clears the Text box, and sets the focus. The Click event procedure then ends.

The second questionnaire is from a 20-year-old person who believes in UFOs.

2   Type **20** in the Age Text box, click **Yes** in the List box, then click the **Write to File button**. Visual Basic creates the Age and Response variables and assigns the appropriate values to them. This time Visual Basic opens the existing t6b.dat file on your Student Disk, writes the second record to the file, closes the file, clears the Text box, and sets the focus. The Click event procedure then ends.

The third questionnaire is from a 23-year-old person who does not believe in UFOs.

3   Type **23** in the Age Text box, click **No** in the List box, then click the **Write to File button**. Visual Basic creates the Age and Response variables and assigns the appropriate values to them. Visual Basic then opens the existing t6b.dat file, writes the third record to the file, closes the file, clears the Text box, and sets the focus. The Click event procedure then ends.

4   Click the **Exit button**. Visual Basic returns to the design screen.

You can use Notepad, one of the applications that comes with Microsoft Windows, to verify that the records were written to the data file. Let's learn how to do that next.

Using Notepad to View the Contents of a File

You can use Notepad to view the contents of a data file quickly and easily. You can also make changes to the data file while you are in Notepad, but you must be careful not to add any unnecessary characters—for example, don't leave any blank lines in the file by unnecessarily pressing the Enter key—or Visual Basic will have trouble reading the file. You also must be careful not to remove any needed punctuation. Let's switch to Notepad and open the t6b.dat file.

To switch to Notepad and view the contents of the t6b.dat file:

1   Hold down the **Ctrl** key and continue holding it down while you press [**Esc**]. When the Task List appears, click **Program Manager**, then click the **Switch To button**. The Program Manager appears.

2   Double-click the **Accessories icon** to open the Accessories group window, then double-click the **Notepad icon** to launch Notepad.

3   Click **File** in the Notepad's menu bar, then click **Open....** The Open dialog box appears.

4   Click the **down arrow in the Drives box**, then click the **drive containing your Student Disk**. Double-click the **a:** (or **b:**) in the Directories list box, then double-click **tut6** in the Directories list box.

5   *If you are using Version 2*, double-click **ver2** in the Directories list box.
    If you are using Version 3, double-click **ver3** in the Directories list box.

6   Click the **down arrow in the List Files of Type box**, then click **All Files** (*.*) in the drop-down list. A list of files appears in the File Name list box.

7   Click **t6b.dat** in the File Name list box, then click the **OK button**. The t6b.dat file appears, as shown in Figure 6-32.

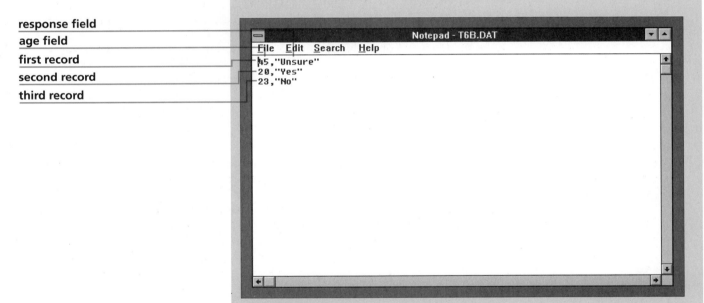

response field
age field
first record
second record
third record

Notepad - T6B.DAT
File Edit Search Help

45,"Unsure"
20,"Yes"
23,"No"

Figure 6-32: t6b.dat data file in Notepad

Each line represents a record and each record is composed of two fields, age and response. The two fields are separated by a comma. The age field is numeric and the response field is a string, as indicated by the surrounding quotation marks. When you write a record to a data file, Visual Basic automatically supplies the quotation marks around the string data and separates the data in each field by commas. Let's use Notepad to print the data in the file.

tips

....

▶ If Visual Basic does not appear on the screen, hold down the Ctrl key and press [Esc]. When the Task List appears, click Microsoft Visual Basic and then click the Switch To button.

8 If your computer is connected to a printer, click **File** in Notepad's menu bar, then click **Print** to print the file. After printing the file, click **File** in Notepad's menu bar, then click **Exit** to exit Notepad. (You do not need to save the file in Notepad.) Visual Basic appears on the screen.

You have now completed Lesson B. You can either take a break or complete the end-of-lesson questions and exercises.

(If you want to practice this lesson again, be sure to switch to File Manager and delete the t6b.dat from your Student Disk; otherwise, the records will be added to the existing t6b.dat file.)

S U M M A R Y

To create a List box:

- Use the List box tool .
- Use the AddItem method to specify the items you want to display in the List box. The syntax of the AddItem method is *Control.AddItem item*. Enter the AddItem instructions in the appropriate event procedure, which is usually the form's Load event procedure.
- Use the ListIndex property to refer to the location of an item in a List box.

To execute instructions automatically when a form is loaded into memory:

- Enter the instructions in the form's Load event procedure.

To open a sequential access file:

- Use the Open statement. Its syntax is **Open** *filename* **For** *mode* **As #** *filenumber*.
- *Filename* is the name of the file, including the drive letter and path, and must be enclosed in quotation marks.
- *Mode* can be Input, Output, or Append. Use Input mode to open the file for reading. Use Output mode to create a new file and write records to it. Use Append mode to add records to an existing file.
- *Filenumber* is an integer expression with a value between 1 and 255, inclusive.

To write a record to an open sequential access file:

- Use the Write # statement. Its syntax is **Write #** *filenumber* [, *expressionlist*]. *Filenumber* is the number used in the Open statement to open the sequential access file. *Expressionlist* is one or more numeric or string variables separated by a comma.

To close a file:

- Use the Close statement. Its syntax is **Close** [# *filenumber*][, # *filenumber*].... *Filenumber* is the number used in the Open statement to open the file. A Close statement with no arguments closes all open files.

Q U E S T I O N S

1. You use this method to define the items in a List box.
   a. AddItem
   b. AddList
   c. ItemAdd
   d. ItemDefine
   e. ListAdd

2. This event occurs when an application is run.
   a. Copy_Form
   b. Form_Run
   c. Load
   d. Run
   e. Run_Form

3. This is the default procedure for a form.
   a. Change
   b. Click
   c. Form_Run
   d. Load
   e. Run_Form

4. Which of the following will add the word DESK to a List box named LstOffice?
   a. AddItem.LstOffice DESK
   b. AddItem.LstOffice "DESK"
   c. ItemAdd.LstOffice "DESK"
   d. LstOffice.AddItem "DESK"
   e. LstOffice.ItemAdd DESK

5. Which of the following will display 1997 in a List box named LstYear?
   a. AddItem.LstYear 1997
   b. AddItem.LstYear "1997"
   c. ItemAdd.LstYear "1997"
   d. LstYear.AddItem "1997"
   e. LstYear.ItemAdd 1997

6. This property keeps track of the items in a List box.
   a. ItemList
   b. ListIndex
   c. ListItem
   d. ListNum
   e. NumItem

7. The second item in a List box has a ListIndex of _____.
   a. 1
   b. 2
   c. 3

8. This assignment statement will select the first item in a List box named LstTerm.
   a. LstTerm.ItemList = 0
   b. LstTerm.ListIndex = 0
   c. LstTerm.ListIndex = 1
   d. LstTerm.ListItem = 1
   e. LstTerm.ListNum = 0

9. A _____ , also called a data element, is a single item of information about a person, place, or thing.
   a. data file
   b. field
   c. program file
   d. record

10. A group of related data elements that contain all of the data about a specific person, place, or thing is called a _____ .
   a. data file
   b. field
   c. program file
   d. record

11. A collection of related records is called a _____ .
   a. data file
   b. field
   c. program file
   d. record collection

12. You open a file for _____ when you want to read its contents.
   a. Append
   b. Input
   c. Output
   d. Read
   e. Sequential

13. You open a file for _____ when you want to create a new file and write information to it.
   a. Append
   b. Input
   c. Output
   d. Read
   e. Sequential

14. You open a file for _____ when you want to add information to an existing file.
   a. Append
   b. Input
   c. Output
   d. Read
   e. Sequential

15. Which of the following is a valid Open statement?
   a. Open a:\data.dat for sequential as #1
   b. Open a:\data.dat for "append" as #1
   c. Open "a:\data.dat" for append as #1
   d. Open "a:\data.dat" for append
   e. Open "a:\data.dat" for sequential as #1

16. Which of the following is a valid Write statement?
   a. Write #1, Lname, Fname
   b. Write, Lname, Fname to #1
   c. Write to #1, Lname, Fname
   d. Write, #1, Lname, Fname
   e. Write Lname, Fname, to #1

17. Which of the following will close a file opened as file number #3?
   a. Close filenumber 3
   b. Close #3 file
   c. Close file #3
   d. Close #3
   e. Close file 3

E X E R C I S E S

1.   a. Create the user interface shown in Figure 6-33.

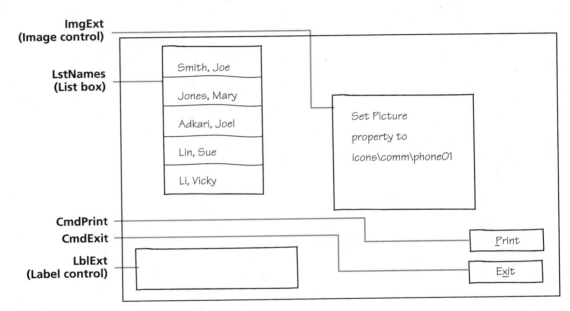

Figure 6-33

Using this application, the user can click an employee's name in the List box and then click the telephone icon to display the employee's extension. The user can also print the form.
   b. Save the form and the project as t6lbe1.
   c. Set the List box's FontSize property to 12. Set its Sorted property to True.
   d. Code the form's Load event so that it fills the List box with data, then selects the first item in the list.
   e. Set the Label control's FontSize property to 18. Set its Alignment property to 2-Center.
   f. Code the Exit button so that it ends the application when clicked. Code the Print button so that it prints the form when clicked.
   g. Code the ImgExt control according to the flowchart shown in Figure 6-34. (Use the Case selection structure.)
   h. Save and run the application. Test the application by selecting Sue Lin's entry in the List box, then clicking the telephone. Print the form with the test data showing.
   i. Exit the application. Print the code.

2.   a. Create the user interface shown in Figure 6-35.
      Using this application, the user can click a city name in the List box and then click the mailbox icon to display the city's Zip code. The user can also print the form.

b. Save the form and the project as t6lbe2.
c. Set the List box's FontSize property to 12. Set its sorted property to True. After the form's Load event fills the List box with data, have the application automatically select the Downers Grove item in the list

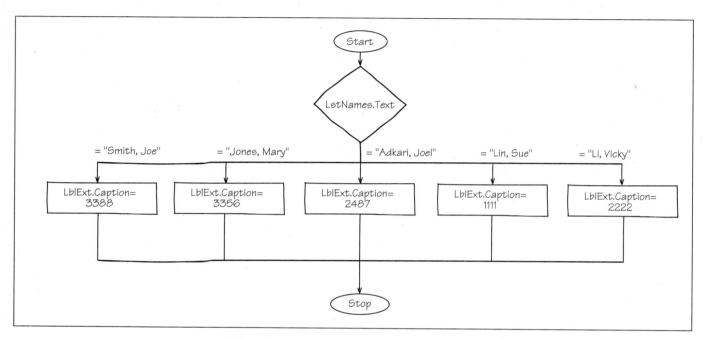

Figure 6-34

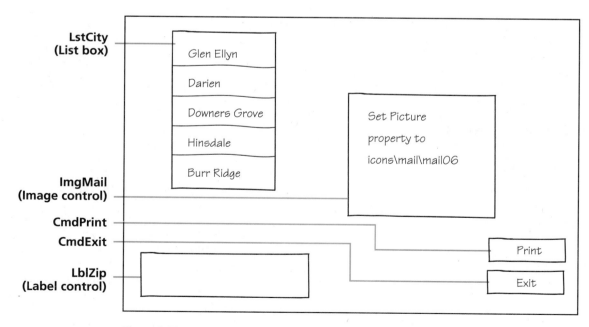

Figure 6-35

d. Set the Label control's FontSize property to 18. Set its Alignment property to 2-Center.

e. Code the Exit button so that it ends the application when clicked. Code the Print button so that it prints the form when clicked.

f. Code the ImgMail control according to the flowchart shown in Figure 6-36. (Use nested If...Then...Else statements.)

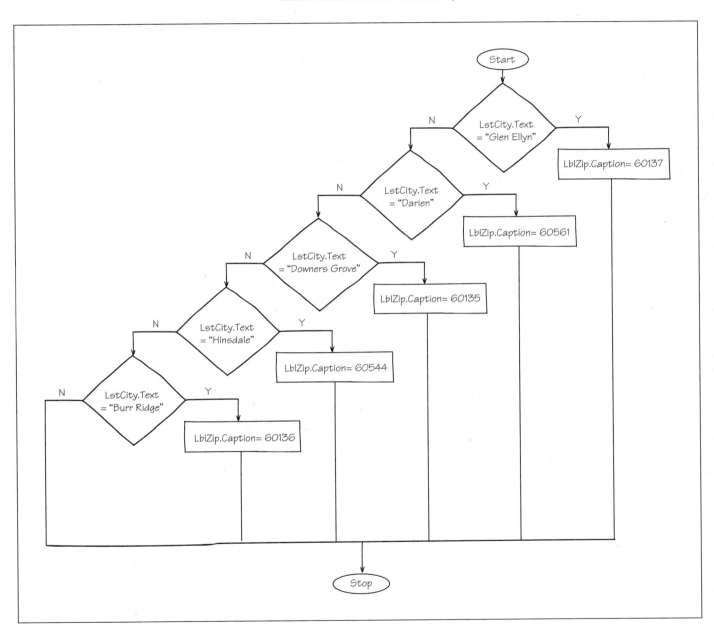

Figure 6-36

g. Save and run the application. Test the application by selecting Hinsdale in the List box, then clicking the ImgMail control. Print the form with the test data showing.

h. Exit the application. Print the code.

3. a. Create the user interface shown in Figure 6-37.

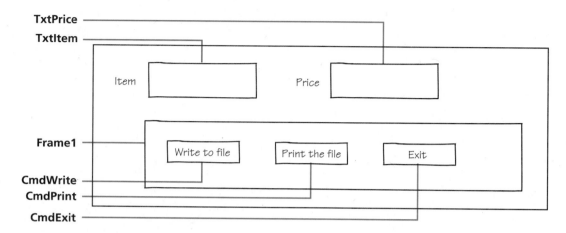

Figure 6-37

Using this application, the user can enter an item's name and price into a sequential access file. The user can also print the contents of the file.

b. Save the form and the project as t6lbe3.

c. Code the Exit button so that it ends the application when clicked. You will code the Print the File button in Lesson C.

d. Code the Write to File button according to the flowchart shown in Figure 6-38. Call the sequential access data file t6item.dat.

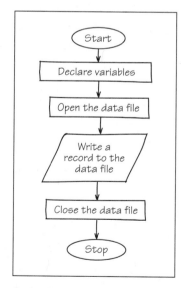

Figure 6-38

e. Save and run the application. Test the application by entering each of the following records. After entering each record, be sure to click the Write to File button to write the record to the file.

Item	Price
Desk	25.59
Chair	15.99
Lamp	9.85

f. Exit the application. Print the code.

g. Switch to Notepad. Open the t6item.dat file and print the file.

h. Exit Notepad. Do not save the file in Notepad. Switch back to Visual Basic.

4. a. Create the user interface shown in Figure 6-39.

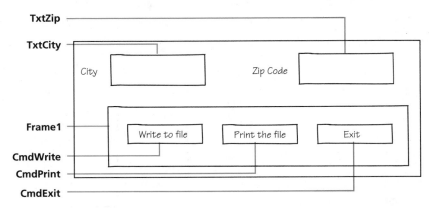

Figure 6-39

Using this application, the user can enter a city's name and Zip code into a sequential access file. The user can also print the contents of the file.

b. Save the form and the project as t6lbe4.

c. Code the Exit button so that it ends the application when clicked. You will code the Print the File button in Lesson C.

d. Code the Write to File button according to the flowchart shown in Figure 6-40. Call the sequential access data file t6zip.dat.

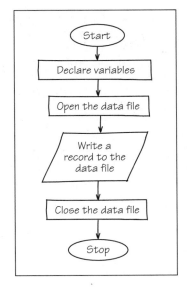

Figure 6-40

e. Save and run the application. Test the application by entering each of the following records. After entering each record, be sure to click the Write to File button to write the record to the file.

City	Zip
Darien	60561
Hinsdale	60544
Glen Ellyn	60137
Downers Grove	60135
Burr Ridge	60136

f. Exit the application. Print the code.

g. Switch to Notepad. Open the t6zip.dat file and print the file.

h. Exit Notepad. Do not save the file in Notepad. Switch back to Visual Basic.

discovery ▶ 5. a. Create the user interface shown in Figure 6-41.

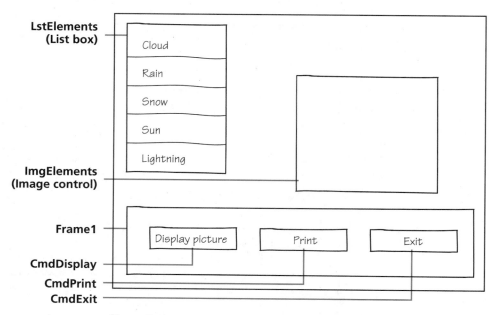

Figure 6-41

Using this application, the user can click an element in the List box and then click the Display Picture button to display a corresponding icon. The user can also print the form.

b. Save the form and the project as t6lbe5.

c. Set the List box's FontSize property to 12. Set its Sorted property to True. After the form's Load event fills the List box with data, have the application automatically select the first item in the list.

d. Set the Image control's BorderStyle property to 1-Fixed Single. Set its Stretch property to True.

e. Code the Exit button so that it ends the application when clicked. Code the Print button so that it prints the form when clicked.

f. Code the Display Picture button according to the flowchart shown in Figure 6-42.

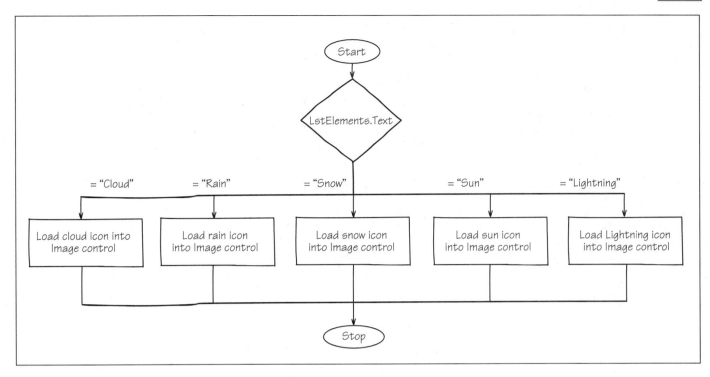

Figure 6-42

This application uses a new function, LoadPicture(), to load an icon into an Image control during run time. The syntax of the LoadPicture function is **LoadPicture(***filename***).** The icon files you will load are shown below. **Be sure to verify the location of these files with your instructor.**

"c:\vb\icons\elements\cloud.ico"

"c:\vb\icons\elements\rain.ico"

"c:\vb\icons\elements\snow.ico"

"c:\vb\icons\elements\sun.ico"

"c:\vb\icons\elements\litening.ico"

g. Save and run the application. Test the application by selecting Snow in the List box, then click the Display Picture button. Print the form with the test data showing.

h. Exit the application. Print the code.

discovery ▶ **6.**   a. Open the t6b.mak project that you created in Lesson B.

b. Save the form and the project as t6lbe6.

c. Open the CmdWrite control's Click event procedure. Change the file name in the Open statement to t6lbe6.dat.

d. Change the code in the CmdWrite control's Click event procedure so that it writes the record (age and response) to the data file only if the age is greater than zero.

e. Print the Help screen for the MsgBox statement.

f. Use the MsgBox statement in the CmdWrite control's Click event procedure to display the message "Record added to file" if the record was written to the data file. Display the message "Please enter the respondent's age" if the record was not written to the data file.

g. Save and run the application. To test the application, click the Write to File button without entering an age. The "Please enter the respondent's age" message should appear in a dialog box. Remove the dialog box from the screen. Now enter an age of 35 and a "Yes" response, then click the Write to File button. The "Record added to file" message should appear in a dialog box. Remove the dialog box from the screen.

h. Exit the application. Print the code.

In this lesson you will learn how to:

■ Read a record from a sequential access file

■ Print a sequential access file

■ Include a counter and an accumulator in an application

■ Change the BackStyle property of a Label control

Completing the UFO Application

Coding the Print the File Button

To complete the UFO application, you still need to code the Print the File button, the Calc Statistics button, and the Print the Report button. Let's begin with the Print the File button, which is responsible for printing the contents of the data file on the printer. The flowchart is shown in Figure 6-43.

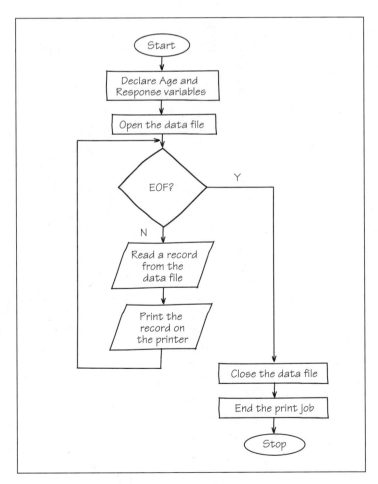

Figure 6-43: Flowchart for the Print the File button

Before coding the Print the File button, let's look briefly at the logic shown in Figure 6-43. The first two tasks are to declare the necessary variables, Age and Response, and open the data file. You will then use the Do...While loop to have Visual Basic read and print each record in the file, one at a time. The loop will stop when there are no more records to read, a point referred to by programmers as "EOF" ("end of file"). When all the records have been read and printed, you will close the file and end the print task by printing a blank line and an "End of File" message. Let's begin coding the Print the File button.

To begin coding the Print the File (CmdPrint) button:

1 Launch Visual Basic (if necessary) and open the **t6b.mak** file, which is in either the tut6\ver2 or the tut6\ver3 directory on your Student Disk. Save the form and the project as **t6c**. Click the **View Form button**, then maximize the form. The form appears, as shown in Figure 6-44.

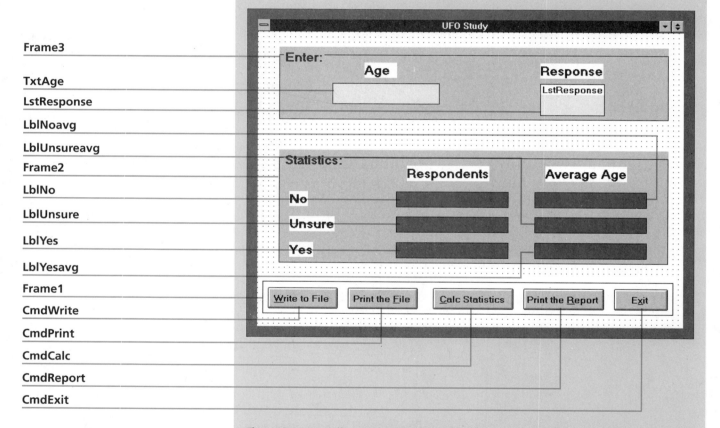

Figure 6-44: Partially completed UFO application

2 Double-click the **Print the File button**. The CmdPrint Click event procedure appears.

First let's declare the variables.

3 Type '**Declare variables** and press [Enter]. Press [Tab], then type **dim Age as integer, Response as string** and press [Enter].

In order to read the records in a data file, you must open the file for Input.

4   Type one of the following Open statements according to your version of Visual Basic and the location of your Student Disk.

open "a:\tut6\ver2\t6b.dat" for input as #1

open "b:\tut6\ver2\t6b.dat" for input as #1

open "a:\tut6\ver3\t6b.dat" for input as #1

open "b:\tut6\ver3\t6b.dat" for input as #1

5   Press **[Enter]**.

According to the flowchart shown in Figure 6-43, you will now use a Do...While loop to tell Visual Basic to repeat the loop instructions while there are records to read—in other words, while it is not the end of the file. (You know that it's the Do...While loop because the test is at the beginning of the loop, not at the end of the loop as in the Do...Until loop.) You might be wondering how Visual Basic will know when the end of the file is reached. Visual Basic uses a record pointer to keep track of which record it is looking at in the file. When you first open a data file for input, Visual Basic sets the record pointer to the first record in the file. Each time you read a record, the record pointer moves to the next record in the file. (Recall that sequential access files are read sequentially—one record after another in the order in which they were written to the file.)

You can use the EOF function, which stands for "end of file," along with the Not logical operator to test for the end of the file. The syntax of the EOF function is **EOF**(*filenumber*), where *filenumber* is the number of the file used in the Open statement. When the record pointer is at the end of the file, the EOF function returns the Boolean value True; otherwise, the function returns the Boolean value False. *Do While Not EOF(1)* tells Visual Basic to repeat the loop instructions while it is not the end of the file. When the end of the file is reached, the loop will stop.

6   Type **do while not eof(1)** and press **[Enter]**. When the application is run, this instruction will tell Visual Basic to look in the t6b.dat file to see if the record pointer is at the end of the file.

tips

If a file opened for Input does not exist, Visual Basic will display an error message. It will not create the file as it does with either Append mode or Output mode.

Now that the file is opened, you can use Visual Basic's Input # statement to read a record from it.

Reading a Record from a Sequential Access File

You can use Visual Basic's Input # statement to read a record from a sequential access file. The syntax of the Input # statement is **Input #** *filenumber*, *variablelist*, where *filenumber* is the number used in the Open statement to open the sequential access file and *variablelist* is one or more numeric or string variables, separated by commas. Each variable in the list is associated with a field in the record. When Visual Basic reads a record from the file, the value in each field is stored in a variable listed in the *variablelist*. In this case, for example, because each record in the t6b.dat file contains two fields—an age followed by a response—the *variablelist* will contain two variables, Age and Response. Visual Basic will use the variables to store the age and response information from the record. Let's include the Input # statement in the Code window.

To continue coding the Print the File button:

1. The CmdPrint's Code window, showing the Click event procedure, should still be open. Press [Tab] to indent the loop instructions, then type **input #1, Age, Response** and press [Enter].

According to the flowchart, shown in Figure 6-43, you now need to print the record on the printer.

Printing a Record on the Printer

Recall that you can use the Print instruction to print the contents of a variable on the form. For example, *Print Age, Response* will print the contents of both variables on the form. To print information on the printer, simply include both the keyword "Printer" (without the quotes) and a period before the Print instruction, like this: *Printer.Print Age, Response*. The keyword "Printer" tells Visual Basic to print the information on the printer instead of on the form.

To continue coding the Print the File button:

1. Type **Printer.print Age, Response** and press [Enter].

   You can now end the Do...While loop and close the file.

2. Press [Backspace], then type **loop** and press [Enter] to mark the end of the Do...While loop. Type **close #1** and press [Enter] to close the t6b.dat file.

   You will tell Visual Basic to print a blank line and the message "End of Print Job" on the printer. Programmers often include an "End of Print Job" message so they can quickly verify that the entire file was printed.

3. Type **Printer.print** and press [Enter]. If you don't include a *variablelist* in the Print statement, Visual Basic prints a blank line. Now type **Printer.print "End of Print Job"** and press [Enter].

   You use the EndDoc method to tell the printer that the end of the document has been reached, so the printer should print the page and then eject the paper to the next page. The syntax of the EndDoc method is simply Printer.EndDoc.

4. Type **Printer.enddoc** and press [Enter].

5. Maximize the Code window, then enter the documentation shown in Figure 6-45. Also be sure to compare your code and make any necessary corrections before continuing to the next step.

6. Close the Code window. Restore the form to its standard size, then **save and run** the application. If your computer is connected to a printer, then click the **Print the File button** to print the sequential access data file. Visual Basic prints the contents of the sequential access data file—the three records that you entered in Lesson B—on the printer.

7. Click the **Exit button** to end the application. Visual Basic returns to the design screen.

Let's code the Calc Statistics button next.

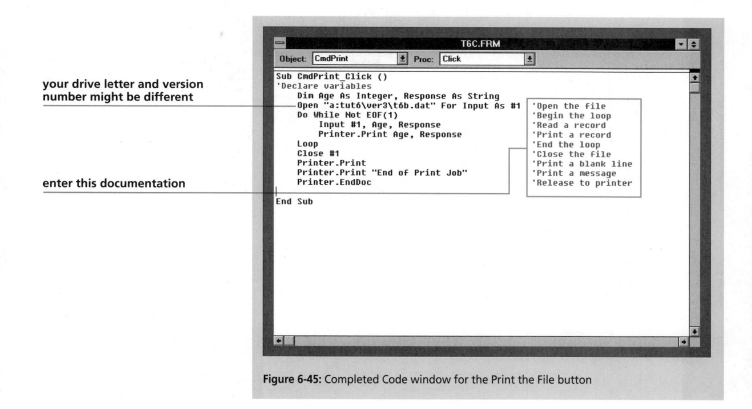

your drive letter and version number might be different

enter this documentation

```
T6C.FRM

Object: CmdPrint          Proc: Click

Sub CmdPrint_Click ()
'Declare variables
    Dim Age As Integer, Response As String
    Open "a:tut6\ver3\t6b.dat" For Input As #1    'Open the file
    Do While Not EOF(1)                           'Begin the loop
        Input #1, Age, Response                   'Read a record
        Printer.Print Age, Response               'Print a record
    Loop                                          'End the loop
    Close #1                                      'Close the file
    Printer.Print                                 'Print a blank line
    Printer.Print "End of Print Job"              'Print a message
    Printer.EndDoc                                'Release to printer

End Sub
```

Figure 6-45: Completed Code window for the Print the File button

Coding the Calc Statistics Button

The flowchart for the Calc Statistics button is shown in Figure 6-46.

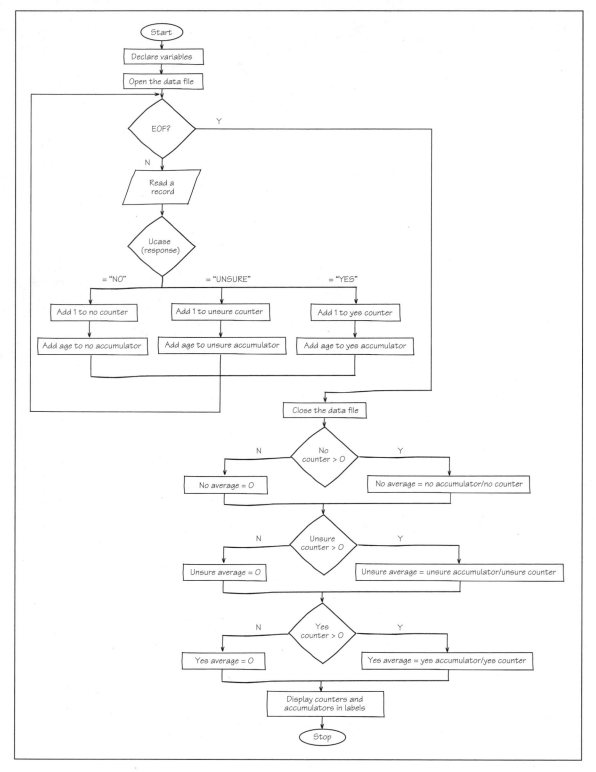

Figure 6-46: Flowchart for Calc Statistics button

The first task is to declare the necessary variables. This button will need the 11 variables shown in Figure 6-47

Variable Name	Data Type	Purpose
Age	Integer	Store the respondent's age
Response	String	Store the respondent's response
Nocount	Integer	Count the number of No responses
Yescount	Integer	Count the number of Yes responses
Uscount	Integer	Count the number of Unsure responses
Nosum	Integer	Accumulate the No response ages
Yessum	Integer	Accumulate the Yes response ages
Ussum	Integer	Accumulate the Unsure response ages
Noavg	Integer	Store the No response average
Yesavg	Integer	Store the Yes response average
Usavg	Integer	Store the Unsure response average

Figure 6-47: Eleven variables used in Calc Statistics button

The Age variable and the Response variable will store the information read from each record. Because this application calculates the average ages of the people selecting each of the three responses, you will need three counters, three accumulators, and three variables in which to calculate and store the three averages. Let's declare the 11 variables right now.

To begin coding the CmdCalc button:

1   Maximize the form, double-click the **Calc Statistics button**, then maximize the Code window. Enter the instructions shown in Figure 6-48 into the CmdCalc control's Click event procedure.

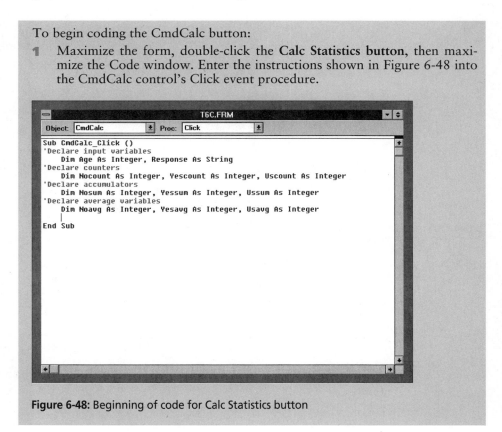

Figure 6-48: Beginning of code for Calc Statistics button

The next task is to open the data file. Because you will need to read from the file, you will open it for Input.

2   Type one of the following Open statements according to your version of Visual Basic and the location of your Student Disk.

open "a:\tut6\ver2\t6b.dat" for input as #1

open "b:\tut6\ver2\t6b.dat" for input as #1

open "a:\tut6\ver3\t6b.dat" for input as #1

open "b:\tut6\ver3\t6b.dat" for input as #1

3   Press [**Enter**].

Next is the Do...While loop, which will test for the end of the file, and the Input statement, which will read a record.

4   Type **do while not eof(1)** and press [**Enter**].

5   Press [**Tab**], then type **input #1, Age, Response** and press [**Enter**].

Which counter and which accumulator you update depends on the value stored in the Response variable. You can use either the If...Then...Else structure or the Select Case structure to look at the contents of the Response variable and select the correct counter and accumulator to update. Let's use the Case structure.

To enter the Case structure:

1   Enter the code shown in Figure 6-49. Be sure to type the "NO," "UNSURE," and "YES" responses in uppercase.

enter this case structure

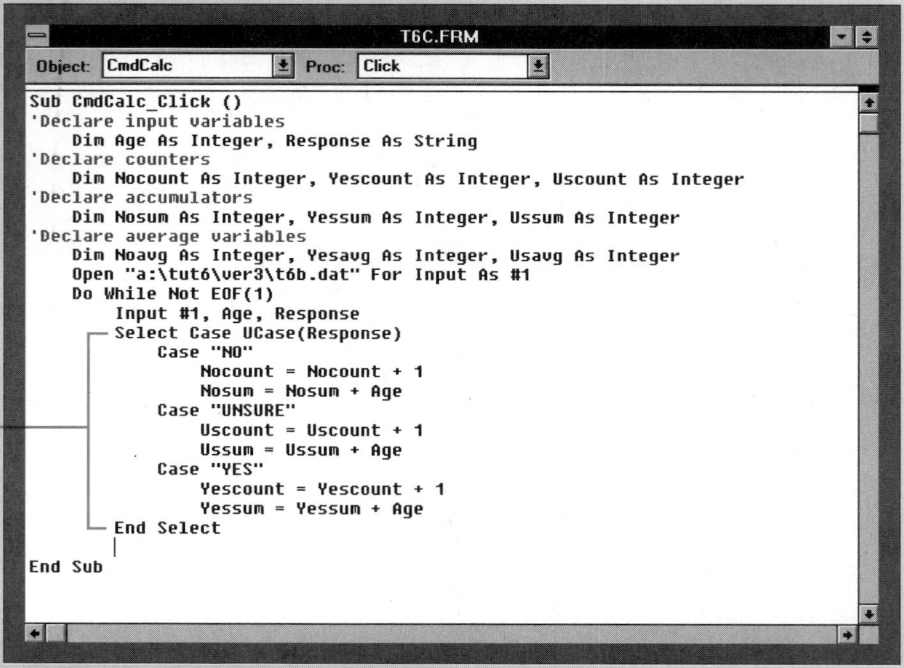

```
                              T6C.FRM
Object: CmdCalc            Proc: Click

Sub CmdCalc_Click ()
'Declare input variables
    Dim Age As Integer, Response As String
'Declare counters
    Dim Nocount As Integer, Yescount As Integer, Uscount As Integer
'Declare accumulators
    Dim Nosum As Integer, Yessum As Integer, Ussum As Integer
'Declare average variables
    Dim Noavg As Integer, Yesavg As Integer, Usavg As Integer
    Open "a:\tut6\ver3\t6b.dat" For Input As #1
    Do While Not EOF(1)
        Input #1, Age, Response
        Select Case UCase(Response)
            Case "NO"
                Nocount = Nocount + 1
                Nosum = Nosum + Age
            Case "UNSURE"
                Uscount = Uscount + 1
                Ussum = Ussum + Age
            Case "YES"
                Yescount = Yescount + 1
                Yessum = Yessum + Age
        End Select

End Sub
```

Figure 6-49: Case structure entered in Code window for Calc Statistics button

At this point you might be wondering why the Select Case statement uses the UCase function to compare the value in the Response variable to the different responses. It might seem unnecessary because, you might recall, the application enters the responses (NO, UNSURE, YES) in uppercase into the data file. Keep in mind, however, that it is possible for a user to enter a record manually into the data file. For example, the user could open the data file in Notepad and then add a record to the file. The response he or she enters might be typed in uppercase, lowercase, or a combination of both. If you do not use the UCase function in the Select Case statement, only the responses typed in uppercase will be included in the statistics; the other responses will be ignored. By using the UCase function in the Select Case statement, you are assured that every "yes," "no," and "unsure" response will be counted.

According to the flowchart, the Case structure is the last instruction within the loop, so you can end the loop and close the file.

2 Press [**Backspace**], then type **loop** and press [**Enter**], and then type **close #1** and press [**Enter**] two times. (Separating groups of instructions with one or more blank lines makes your code easier to read.)

You can now calculate the average age in each response category. Keep in mind that there is no guarantee that each of the responses will be chosen by at least one respondent. If no one chooses a particular response, that response's counter variable will not be updated from its initial value of zero. In Lesson A you used a selection structure to verify that the counter contained a value that was greater than zero. Let's verify that the three counters used in this application contain values greater than zero.

3 Enter the one line of documentation and the three If...Then...Else statements shown in Figure 6-50.

enter these statements

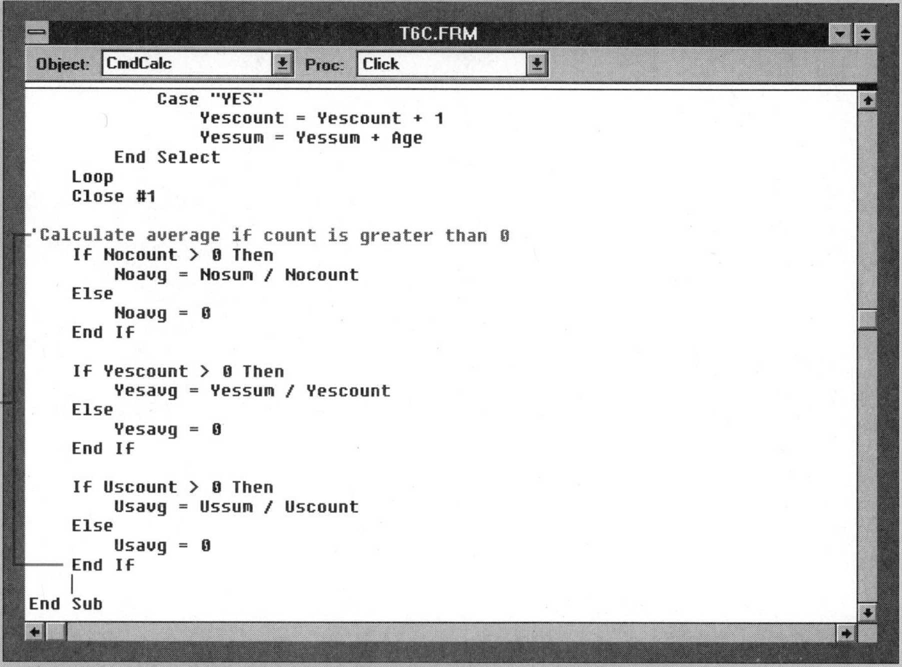

```
                    Case "YES"
                        Yescount = Yescount + 1
                        Yessum = Yessum + Age
                End Select
          Loop
          Close #1

'Calculate average if count is greater than 0
          If Nocount > 0 Then
                Noavg = Nosum / Nocount
          Else
                Noavg = 0
          End If

          If Yescount > 0 Then
                Yesavg = Yessum / Yescount
          Else
                Yesavg = 0
          End If

          If Uscount > 0 Then
                Usavg = Ussum / Uscount
          Else
                Usavg = 0
          End If

End Sub
```

Figure 6-50: If...Then...Else statements in Code window for Calc Statistics button

All that remains is to display the number of respondents and their average age in the appropriate Label controls on the form. Let's do that now.

4   Enter the one line of documentation and the remaining assignment statements shown in Figure 6-51.

enter this code

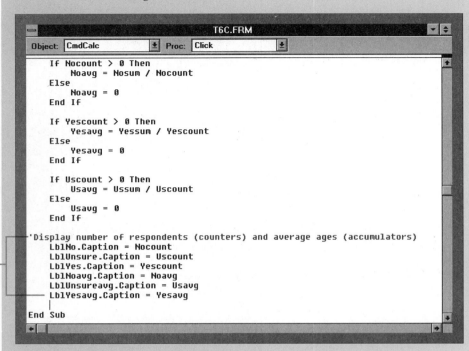

```
                                    T6C.FRM
Object:  CmdCalc            Proc:  Click

    If Nocount > 0 Then
        Noavg = Nosum / Nocount
    Else
        Noavg = 0
    End If

    If Yescount > 0 Then
        Yesavg = Yessum / Yescount
    Else
        Yesavg = 0
    End If

    If Uscount > 0 Then
        Usavg = Ussum / Uscount
    Else
        Usavg = 0
    End If

    'Display number of respondents (counters) and average ages (accumulators)
    LblNo.Caption = Nocount
    LblUnsure.Caption = Uscount
    LblYes.Caption = Yescount
    LblNoavg.Caption = Noavg
    LblUnsureavg.Caption = Usavg
    LblYesavg.Caption = Yesavg

End Sub
```

Figure 6-51: Assignment statements entered in Code window for Calc Statistics button

5   Close the Code window, restore the form to its standard size, then **save and run** the application. Click the **Calc Statistics button**. The number of respondents in each response category (1, 1, and 1) and their average ages (23, 45, and 20) appear on the screen. (Recall that you entered these three records into the sequential access data file in Lesson B.)

6   Click the **Exit button** to end the application. Visual Basic returns to the design screen.

The last button you need to code is the Print the Report button.

Coding the Print the Report Button

The flowchart for the Print the Report button is shown in Figure 6-52.

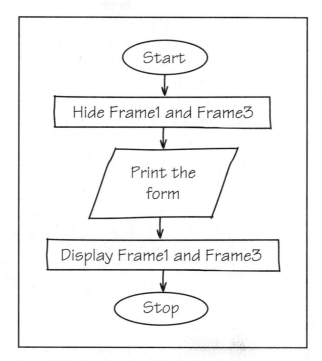

Figure 6-52: Flowchart for Print the Report button

To code the Print the Report button:

1   Maximize the form, then double-click the **Print the Report button**. The CmdReport button's Click event procedure appears.

First you want to hide the Frame control at the top of the form (Frame3) and the Frame control at the bottom of the form (Frame1). You also want to hide the controls contained within those two controls. One advantage of using a Frame control as a container for other controls is that when you hide the Frame control, Visual Basic automatically hides the controls contained in the Frame. In this case, therefore, only two instructions are necessary to hide the two Frame controls as well as the controls contained within those Frames.

2   Enter the code shown in Figure 6-53.

Now let's test the Print the Report button.

3   Close the Code window, restore the form to its standard size, then **save and run** the application. Click the **Calc Statistics button** to calculate the statistics. If your computer is connected to a printer, then click the **Print the Report button** to print the report. Visual Basic prints the report on the printer.

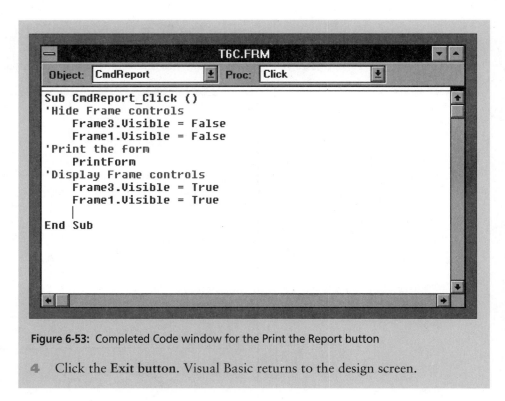

Figure 6-53: Completed Code window for the Print the Report button

4   Click the **Exit button**. Visual Basic returns to the design screen.

The final modification you will make to this application is to change the BackStyle property of some of the Label controls.

The BackStyle Property

A Label control's BackStyle property determines whether the label is transparent or opaque. The default setting is 1-Opaque, which means that the control's BackColor property setting, which is white in many of the Label controls used in this application, fills the control and obscures any color behind it. When the BackStyle property is set to 0-Transparent, any background color shows through the Label control. Let's change the BackStyle property for the Label controls to 0-Transparent.

To change the BackStyle property:

1   Maximize the form. Click **Age**, then [Ctrl][click] **Response** to select both the Age and Response headings in the top Frame control.

2   Press [**F4**] to display the Properties window, then double-click **BackStyle** in the Properties list until the property says 0-Transparent. Notice that the Frame's background color now shows through both Label controls.

3   Click **No**, [Ctrl][click] **Unsure**, [Ctrl][click] **Yes**, [Ctrl][click] **Respondents**, and [Ctrl][click] **Average Age**. Five Label controls are now selected in the center Frame.

4   Press **[F4]** to display the Properties window, then double-click **BackStyle** in the Properties list until the property says 0-Transparent. The Frame's background color now shows through the Label controls.

5   Click the **form** to cancel the selection of the Label controls, restore the form to its standard size, then **save and run** the application.

6   Test the application by entering your age and response to the "Do you believe in UFOs?" question, then click the **Write to File button**. After the record is written to the file, click the **Print the File button** to verify that your record is in the file. Click the **Calc Statistics button** to calculate the statistics, then click the **Print the Report button** to print the report. Finally, click the **Exit button** to end the application and return to the design screen.

You have now completed Lesson C and the UFO application. You can either take a break or complete the exercises and questions at the end of the lesson.

S U M M A R Y

To read a record from an open sequential access file:

■   Use the Input # statement. Its syntax is **Input #** *filenumber, variablelist*. *Filenumber* is the number used in the Open statement to open the sequential access file. *Variablelist* is one or more numeric or string variables, separated by commas. Each variable in the list is associated with a field in the record.

To test for the end of the file:

■   Use the EOF function. Its syntax is **EOF**(*filenumber*). *Filenumber* is the number of the file used in the Open statement.

To print information on the printer:

■   Use the Print method. Its syntax is **Printer.Print**.

To tell the printer to print the page and then eject to the next page:

■   Use the EndDoc method. Its syntax is **Printer.EndDoc**.

To make a Label control transparent:

■   Change the Label control's BackStyle property from 1-Opaque to 0-Transparent.

QUESTIONS

1. You open a file for _____ when you want to read its contents.
   a. Append
   b. Input
   c. Output
   d. Read
   e. Sequential

2. Which of the following is a valid Open statement?
   a. Open a:\data.dat for sequential as #1
   b. Open a:\data.dat for "input" as #1
   c. Open "a:\data.dat" for input as #1
   d. Open "a:\data.dat" for input
   e. Open "a:\data.dat" for sequential as #1

3. Which of the following will correctly update a counter named Total?
   a. Total = Total + Sales
   b. Total = Total + 1
   c. Total + Sales = Total
   d. Total + 1 = Total
   e. Total = 1

4. Which of the following will close a file opened as file number #1?
   a. Close filenumber 1
   b. Close #1 file
   c. Close file #1
   d. Close #1

5. Which of the following will stop the loop when the record pointer is at the end of the file opened as #1? (Select two.)
   a. Do While EOF(1)
   b. Do Until EOF(1)
   c. Do While Not EOF(1)
   d. Do Until Not EOF(1)

6. Which of the following will print the contents of the Sales variable on the printer?
   a. Print Sales
   b. Print.Sales Printer
   c. Printer.Sales Print
   d. Printer.Sales
   e. Printer.Print Sales

7. The "EOF" in the EOF function stands for _____ .
   a. each open file
   b. end of file
   c. end of function
   d. every open file

8. If you want to see the background color behind a Label control, set the Label control's _____ to 0-Transparent.
   a. BackColor
   b. Background
   c. BackgroundColor
   d. BackStyle
   e. Color

EXERCISES

1. a. Open the t6lbe3 project that you created in Lesson B's Exercise 3.
   b. Save the form and the project as t6lce1.
   c. Code the Print the File button so that, when clicked, it prints the contents of the t6item.dat sequential data file on the printer. (You created the t6item.dat file in Lesson B's Exercise 3.)
   d. Save and run the application. To test the application:
      1) Click the Print the File button.
      2) Enter an item and a price of your choice, then click the Write to File button.
      3) Click the Print the File button.
   e. Exit the application. Print the code.

2. a. Open the t6lbe4 project that you created in Lesson B's Exercise 4.
   b. Save the form and the project as t6lce2.
   c. Code the Print the File button so that, when clicked, it prints the contents of the t6zip.dat sequential file on the printer. (You created the t6zip.dat file in Lesson B's Exercise 4.)
   d. Save and run the application. To test the application:
      1) Click the Print the File button.
      2) Enter a city and a Zip code of your choice, then click the Write to File button.
      3) Click the Print the File button.
   e. Exit the application. Print the code.

3. a. Create the user interface shown in Figure 6-54.

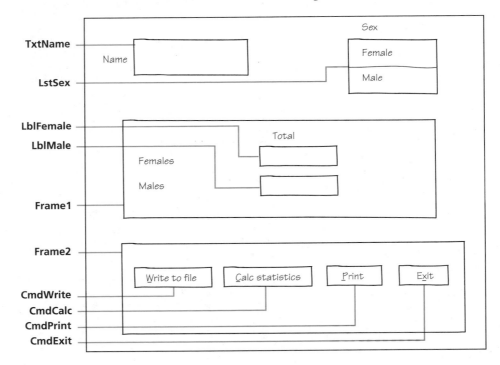

Figure 6-54

Using the application, the user can both enter and save the name and sex of the people registered for a seminar. The user can also calculate how many males and females are registered. The application will also print the form.

   b. Save the form and the project as t6lce3.

c. Set the List box's FontSize property to 12. Set its Sorted property to True. After filling the List box with data, have the application automatically select the first item in the list.

d. Set the FontSize property of both the LblMale and the LblFemale control to 18. Set their Alignment property to 2-Center.

e. Code the Exit button so that it ends the application when clicked. Code the Print button so that it prints the form when clicked.

f. Code the Write to File button so that, when clicked, it writes the records to a sequential access data file named t6names.dat.

g. Code the Calc Statistics button so that, when clicked, it calculates and displays the number of males and the number of females in the data file.

h. Save and run the application. Test the application by entering each of the following records. After entering each record, be sure to click the Write to File button to write the record to the file.

Name	Sex
Mary	Female
Terri	Female
Jim	Male
George	Male
Paula	Female
Fred	Male

i. After entering the records, click the Calc Statistics button, then click the Print button.

j. Exit the application. Print the code.

4. a. Create the user interface shown in Figure 6-55.

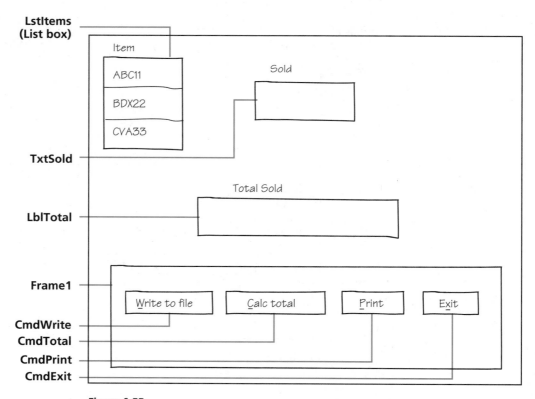

Figure 6-55

Using the application, the user can both enter and save an item's ID and its amount sold. The user can calculate the total amount sold and can also print the form.

b. Save the form and the project as t6lce4.

c. Set the List box's FontSize property to 12. Set its Sorted property to True. After filling the List box with data, have the application automatically select the first item in the list.

d. Set the FontSize property of both the LblTotal and the TxtSold controls to 18. Set their Alignment property to 2-Center.

e. Code the Exit button so that it ends the application when clicked. Code the Print button so that it prints the form when clicked.

f. Code the Write to File button so that, when clicked, it writes the records to a sequential access data file named t6sold.dat.

g. Code the Calc Total button so that, when clicked, it calculates and displays the total number sold for all of the items in the file.

h. Save and run the application. Test the application by entering each of the following records. After entering each record, be sure to click the Write to File button to write the record to the file.

Item	Sold
BDX22	100
ABC11	150
BDX22	250
CVA33	100
ABC11	200

i. After entering the records, click the Calc Total button, then click the Print button.

j. Exit the application. Print the code.

5. a. Open the t6lce4 project that you created in Exercise 4. Save the form and the project as t6lce5.

b. Add another Command button to the form. Change the Command button's Name property to CmdItem, change its Caption property to Calc by Item. Cut the CmdItem button from the form and paste it into the Frame1 control. Drag the CmdItem button to a position immediately below the CmdTotal button.

c. Code the Calc by Item button so that, when clicked, it calculates and displays the total sold for only the item the user chooses in the List box. (In other words, if the user clicks the ABC11 item in the List box, the Calc by Item button will calculate and display only the total sold for the ABC11 item.)

d. Save and run the application. Test the application by clicking the BDX22 item in the List box, then click the Calc by Item button, and then click the Print button.

e. Exit the application. Print the code.

6. a. Create the user interface shown in Figure 6-56.
Using the application, the user can both enter and save a city's name and population. The user can calculate the average population and can also print the form.

b. Save the form and the project as t6lce6.

c. Code the Exit button so that it ends the application when clicked. Code the Print button so that it prints the form when clicked.

d. Code the Write to File button so that it writes the city and its population to a sequential access data file named t6pop.dat.

e. Code the Calc Avg Population button so that it calculates the average population of the cities in the t6pop.dat data file. Display the average population in the LblPop control.

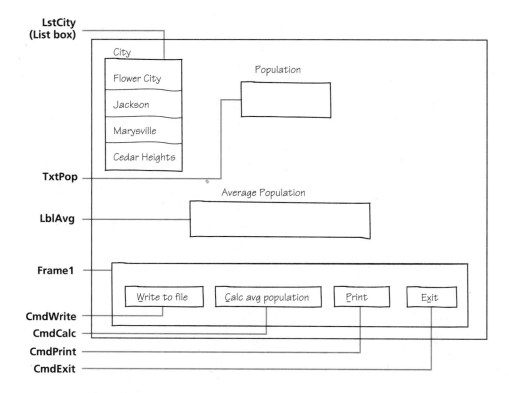

Figure 6-56

f. Save and run the application. Test the application by entering each of the follow-ing records. After entering each record, be sure to click the Write to File button to write the record to the file.

City	Population
Flower City	2000
Jackson	15000
Marysville	25000
Cedar Heights	1500

g. After entering the records, click the Calc Avg Population button, then click the Print button.

h. Exit the application. Print the code.

Exercises 7 through 10 are Discovery Exercises.

discovery ▶ 7. In this exercise you will use a Do...While loop and a sequential access file to fill a List box with items.

a. Open the t6lbe2 project that you created in Lesson B's Exercise 2. Save the form and the project as t6lce7.

b. Remove the AddItem instructions and the ListIndex instruction from the form's Load event procedure. In the form's Load event procedure, open the data file that you created in Lesson B's Exercise 4. The name of the data file is t6zip.dat. Use a Do...While loop to read the records from the t6zip.dat data file and add each city to the List box.

c. If you completed Lesson C's Exercise 2, then change the ImgMail control's Click event procedure to include the city that you added.

d. Save and run the application. Test the application by selecting Hinsdale in the List box and clicking the Image control. The correct Zip code should appear in the LblZip control. Print the application with the test data showing.

e. Exit the application. Print the code.

discovery ▶ 8. In this exercise you will find and then display the lowest price contained in a sequential access file.

    a. Create a user interface that contains one Label control and three Command buttons. Name the Label control LblPrice. Change one Command button's Caption to Display Lowest Price and its Name to CmdLow. Change another Command button's Caption to Print and its name to CmdPrint. Change the remaining Command button's Caption to Exit and its name to CmdExit.

    b. Save the form and the project as t6lce8.

    c. Code the Exit Command button so that it ends the application when clicked.

    d. Code the Print Command button so that it prints the form when clicked.

    e. In Lesson B's Exercise 3, you created a data file named t6item.dat. The data file contained the following three records:

Item	Price
Desk	25.59
Chair	15.99
Lamp	9.85

    Code the Display Lowest Price button so that it opens the t6item.dat file, finds the lowest price contained in the file, displays that price in the LblPrice control, and then closes the file.

    f. Save and run the application. Click the Display Lowest Price button, click the Print button, and then click the Exit button.

    g. Switch to Notepad. Open the t6item.dat data file and add the following three records to the file:

Item	Price
Pens	5.59
Markers	4.35
Pencils	8.56

    h. Save the t6item.dat file. Print the t6item.dat file.

    i. Close Notepad and switch to Visual Basic.

    j. Run the t6lce8 application. Click the Display Lowest Price button, click the Print button, and then click the Exit button.

    k. Print the code.

discovery ▶ 9. In this exercise you will find and then display the lowest price and the highest price contained in a sequential access file. You will also display the names of the items corresponding to the lowest and the highest price.

    a. Open the t6lce8.mak project that you created in Exercise 8. Add another Label control to the form. Also add another Command button to the form. Name the Label control LblItem. Change the Command button's Caption to Display Highest Price and its name to CmdHigh.

    b. Save the form and the project as t6lce9.

    c. Change the code in the Display Lowest Price button so that, in addition to displaying the lowest price in the LblPrice control, it also displays that item's name in the LblItem control.

    d. Code the Display Highest Price button so that it opens the t6item.dat file, finds the highest price contained in the file, displays that price in the LblPrice control and its name in the LblItem control, and then closes the file.

    e. Save and run the application. Click the Display Lowest Price button, then click the Print button. Click the Display Highest Price button, then click the Print button. Last, click the Exit button.

    f. Print the code.

discovery ▶ 10. In this exercise you will use Notepad to create a new sequential access file that contains the names of five cities. You will then create an application that uses a List box to sort the names of the cities. The application will then write the sorted names to a new sequential access file.

a. Use Notepad to create the following sequential access file. Save the file as t6city.dat.
   "Darien"
   "Hinsdale"
   "Glen Ellyn"
   "Downers Grove"
   "Burr Ridge"

b. Print the t6city.dat file. Close Notepad and switch to Visual Basic.

c. Create a user interface that contains one List box and two Command buttons. Name the List box LstCity. Change one of the Command button's Caption property to Sort and its name to CmdSort. Change the other Command button's Caption property to Exit and its name to CmdExit.

d. Set the List box's Sorted property to True.

e. Save the form and the project as t6lce10.

f. Code the Exit button so that it ends the application when clicked.

g. Code the Form's Load event procedure so that it opens the t6city.dat data file, enters the cities into the LstCity List box, and then closes the t6city.dat file.

h. Code the Sort button so that it writes the sorted cities, which are contained in the List box, to a new sequential access file named t6city.srt.

i. Save and run the application. Test the application by clicking the Sort button, then clicking the Exit button.

j. Switch to Notepad. Open the t6city.srt file and print its contents. Close Notepad.

D E B U G G I N G

Technique   You can use Visual Basic's Debug window to help in debugging your code. The Debug window consists of the Immediate pane and the Watch pane. You will learn about the Immediate pane in this Debugging Section and the Watch pane in Tutorial 7's Debugging Section.

In the Immediate pane, which is located below the Debug window's title bar (or below the Watch pane if the Watch pane is displayed), you can enter code that you want executed immediately. You can use the Debug window for such tasks as printing the value stored in a variable or in the property of a control, changing a variable's value or a control's property, and testing the effect a new line of code will have on the application.

On your Student Disk is a project named t6_debug.mak that is not working correctly. You will use the Debug window to help you debug the project.

To debug the project:

1 Launch Visual Basic (if necessary) and open the **t6_debug.mak** project, which is in either the tut6\ver2 or the tut6\ver3 directory on your Student Disk. Click the **View Form button** to view the form, then save the form and the project as **t6dbgd.** (The "dbgd" stands for "debugged.")

2 Maximize the form.

The three Command buttons have already been coded for you. The Print the File button will print the contents of a sequential access data file named t6debug.dat. The Calc button will calculate the average sales made in California and the average sales made in Oregon. The Exit button will exit the application.

Before you can run this application, you will need to modify the Open statement entered in two of the Code windows: the Print the File button's Click event procedure and the Calc button's Click event procedure.

3 Double-click the **Print the File button** to open its Code window. The Click event procedure appears.

4 Remove the <insert filename> from the Open statement and type one of the filenames listed below in its place. Which filename you type will depend on your version of Visual Basic and the location of your Student Disk. For example, if you are using version 3 and your Student Disk is in drive A, then your Open statement should read *Open "a:\tut6\ver3\t6debug.dat" for Input as #1.*

> "a:\tut6\ver2\t6debug.dat"

> "b:\tut6\ver2\t6debug.dat"

> "a:\tut6\ver3\t6debug.dat"

> "b:\tut6\ver3\t6debug.dat"

5 Click the **down arrow in the Code window's Object box**. Scroll the drop-down list until CmdCalc is visible, then click **CmdCalc** in the drop-down list. The Calc button's Click event procedure appears.

6 Repeat Step 4 to change the Open statement in the CmdCalc's Code window.

7 Close the Code window, restore the form to its standard size, then **save and run** the application.

First let's print the sequential access file.

8 If your computer is connected to a printer, then click the **Print the File button**. Five records should appear on the printout. The first field in each record is the state, and the second field is the sales.

Now let's calculate the average sales made in both states.

9 Click the **Calc button** to calculate the average sales in each state. Visual Basic displays a dialog box with the "Division by zero" error message. Click the **OK button** to remove the dialog box. The *Oreavg = Oreaccum / Orecount* instruction is highlighted in the Code window.

Let's use the Debug window to verify that the Orecount variable contains a zero.

To use the Debug window:

1   Press [Ctrl][b] to display the Debug window. The Debug window appears, as shown in Figure 6-57.

Immediate pane

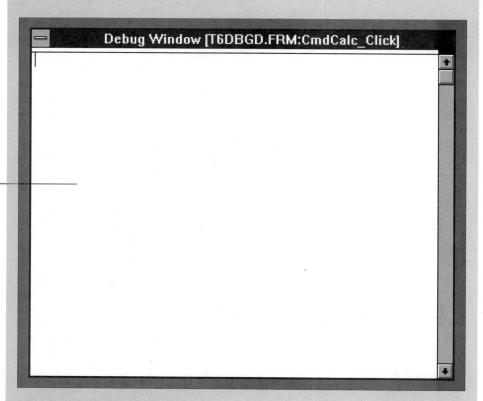

Figure 6-57: Debug window

2   Type **print orecount** in the Debug window and press [Enter]. A 0 (zero) appears below the print instruction.

Let's see why the Orecount variable contains a zero.

3   Close the Debug window, then maximize the Code window. Scroll the Code window so that all of the code is visible. If you look closely at the code in the Case structure shown in Figure 6-58, you will notice that the assignment statement to update the Orecount counter variable is missing.

Let's fix the code right now.

4   Click in the blank line below the *Oreaccum = Oreaccum + Sales* instruction, then type **Orecount = Orecount + 1**.

Now let's use the Debug window to change the value stored in the Orecount variable so that processing can continue.

tips

If you accidentally closed the Code window, then press [F5] again and click the OK button to remove the Error Message dialog box. Maximize the Code window, then scroll until all of the code is showing.

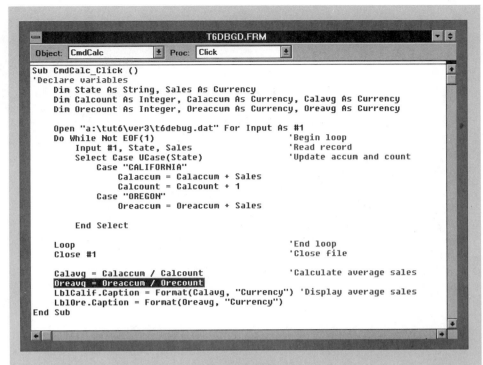

```
                              T6DBGD.FRM
Object: CmdCalc            Proc: Click

Sub CmdCalc_Click ()
'Declare variables
    Dim State As String, Sales As Currency
    Dim Calcount As Integer, Calaccum As Currency, Calavg As Currency
    Dim Orecount As Integer, Oreaccum As Currency, Oreavg As Currency

    Open "a:\tut6\ver3\t6debug.dat" For Input As #1
    Do While Not EOF(1)                        'Begin loop
        Input #1, State, Sales                 'Read record
        Select Case UCase(State)               'Update accum and count
            Case "CALIFORNIA"
                    Calaccum = Calaccum + Sales
                    Calcount = Calcount + 1
            Case "OREGON"
                    Oreaccum = Oreaccum + Sales

        End Select

    Loop                                       'End loop
    Close #1                                    'Close file

    Calavg = Calaccum / Calcount               'Calculate average sales
    Oreavg = Oreaccum / Orecount
    LblCalif.Caption = Format(Calavg, "Currency") 'Display average sales
    LblOre.Caption = Format(Oreavg, "Currency")
End Sub
```

Figure 6-58: CmdCalc control's Click event procedure

5 Press [**Ctrl**][**b**] to display the Debug window.

To continue processing the application, you will need to change the value in Orecount to any number other than zero. (Remember, the zero in the Orecount variable is the cause of the "Division by zero" error message.) In this case the data file contains two Oregon records, so you will change the value to 2. (If you didn't know how many Oregon records were in the file, you could simply change the Orecount value to 1 and processing would continue.)

6 Type **orecount = 2** in the Debug window and press [**Enter**]. This statement changes the value stored in the Orecount variable to 2.

Let's verify the contents of the Orecount variable.

7 Type **print orecount** in the Debug window and press [**Enter**]. A 2 appears in the Debug window. Close the Debug window, then close the Code window.

To continue processing the application, you simply need to press [F5]. Processing will resume with the statement that caused the error—in this case, the *Oreavg = Oreaccum / Orecount* statement. Now, however, the Orecount variable will contain the number 2, not a zero.

8 Press [**F5**] to resume processing of the application. The average sales made in both states ($30,000.00 and $60,000.00) appear on the screen. Click the **Exit button** to end the application.

Recall that you added the *Orecount = Orecount + 1* instruction to the Code window. You will need to save the application for that change to be saved.

9. **Save** the application. Now **run** the application and click the **Calc button**. This time the application runs without any errors and the average sales made in both states appear on the screen. Click the **Exit button** to end the application. Visual Basic returns to the design screen. You can now exit Visual Basic.

TUTORIAL

7

Random Access Files and Multiple Forms

The Cole's Playhouse Application

case ▶ Every Sunday afternoon, Cole's Playhouse, a small community theater, performs plays featuring local talent. The theater holds only 48 seats, which must be reserved in advance of the performance. No tickets are sold at the door. The manager of the playhouse, Max Phillips, asks you to create an application that will keep track of each patron's name and phone number.

Before submitting a completed application, you decide to create a **prototype** (a sample or demo version) to be sure the manager is satisfied that you are on the right track. Let's take a look at the prototype now.

Previewing the Prototype

As you've done in previous tutorials, you will preview the application before creating it.

To preview the demo:

1   Launch Windows and make sure the Program Manager window is open and your Student Disk is in the appropriate drive. If necessary, click the Minimize on Use option on the Options menu to minimize the Program Manager on use.

2   Run the **COLE.EXE** file, which is in either the tut7\ver2 or the tut7\ver3 directory on your Student Disk. The first user interface in the Cole's Playhouse application appears on the screen. See Figure 7-1

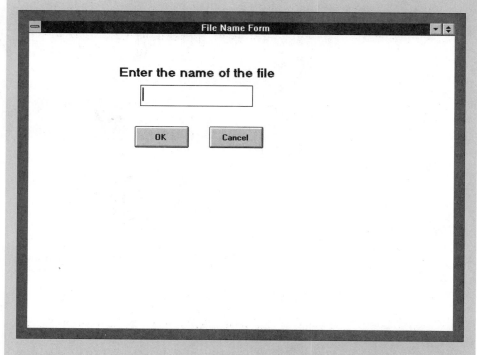

Figure 7-1: First user interface for the Cole's Playhouse application

This form is used to enter the name of the data file you want to open.

3   Depending on your version of Visual Basic and the location of your Student disk, type one of the following in the TxtFile Text box:

a:\tut7\ver2\t7cole.dat   a:\tut7\ver3\t7cole.dat

b:\tut7\ver2\t7cole.dat   b:\tut7\ver3\t7cole.dat

4   Click the **OK button.** The second user interface in the Cole's Playhouse application appears on the screen, as shown in Figure 7-2.

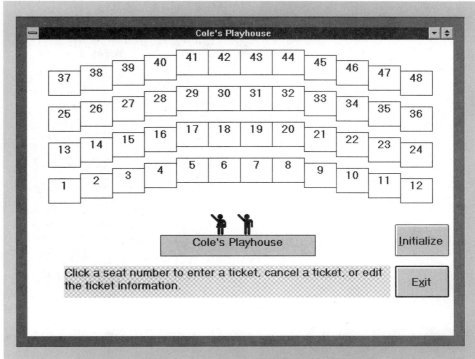

Figure 7-2 : Second user interface for the Cole's Playhouse application

This form displays the 48 seats in the Cole's Playhouse theater. To reserve a seat, you simply click it.

5   Click **seat number 8**. The third user interface in the Cole's Playhouse application appears on the screen, as shown in Figure 7-3.

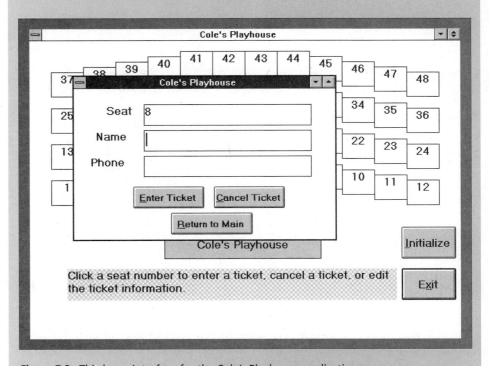

Figure 7-3 : Third user interface for the Cole's Playhouse application

This form is used to enter or cancel patron information as well as to return to the screen that displays the theater seats.

6   Type **Sue Jones** as the name, press [**Tab**], then type **111–1111** as the phone number. Click the **Enter Ticket button**. Visual Basic saves the name and phone number in a random access file on your Student Disk. Notice that seat number 8 is colored red, which indicates that the seat is reserved.

Let's see what happens if Sue Jones cancels her reservation.

7   Click **seat number 8**. Sue Jones's information appears on the screen. Click the **Cancel Ticket button**. Notice that seat number 8 is now colored white, which indicates that the seat is available.

8   Experiment a bit by entering data of your choosing. Then press the **Initialize** button. This will cause all data to be removed from the file. The manager can think of several situations where this would be useful, and you indicate that there will be a warning message present whenever this button is pressed. (You will add the warning message in the Exercises for Lesson C of this tutorial.)

9   Click the **Exit button**. The first user interface, which requests the filename, appears. Click the **Cancel button**. The Cole's Playhouse application ends.

Mr. Phillips is both surprised and pleased that you were able to create a prototype in such a short time. You explain that Visual Basic has many powerful features that make programming easy and fun. You are instructed to proceed with the project.

As you can see from viewing the prototype, an application can have more than one form. The Cole's Playhouse application will have three when it's completed—one for selecting a file, a second for selecting a seat, and a third for entering and editing patron data. Data for each patron will be stored in a random access file.

In Lesson A you will learn how to use random access files in an application. You will learn how to create applications containing more than one form as you complete the Cole's Playhouse application in Lessons B and C. Some important modifications and useful enhancements will be left as exercises.

LESSON A
objectives

In this lesson you will learn how to:

- Create a user-defined data type
- Open and close a random access file
- Write data to a random access file
- Read data from a random access file
- Initialize a random access file

Random Access Files

Random Access Files

As you learned in Tutorial 6, you can save the data that the user enters, such as the student scores from Tutorial 5 or the UFO responses from Tutorial 6, in a data file. A **data file**, you may remember, is organized into fields and records. A **field**, also called a data element, is a single item of information about a person, place, or thing—for example, a social security number, a city, or a price. A **record** is a group of related fields that contain all of the necessary data about a specific person, place, or thing.

Recall that Visual Basic has three types of data files—sequential access, random access, and binary access. (Binary access files are beyond the scope of this book.) A sequential access file is similar to a cassette tape in that each record in the file, like each song on a cassette tape, is both stored and retrieved in consecutive order from the beginning of the file to the end of the file. A random access file, on the other hand, is similar to a compact disc (CD) in that each record in the file, like each song on a CD, can be stored and retrieved in any order. That means, for example, that you can read or write the third record in a random access file without first reading or writing the two records that precede it.

As you may know, each song on a CD is associated with a unique number. The number indicates the position of the song on the CD; it allows you to access the song directly. Each record in a random access file also has a unique number, called a **record number**, that indicates its position in the file. The first record in the file is record number 1, the second record is number 2, and so on. You can access a record in a random access file, directly, by its record number. For this reason, random access files are also referred to as **direct access files**.

The ability to access a record directly allows quick retrieval of information, which accounts for the extensive use of random access files for on-line activities, such as making airline reservations, looking up the prices of items at a store, and approving credit card purchases. In a random access file, you can access record number 500 just as quickly as record number 1. Accessing record number 500 in a sequential access file would take much longer because the program would have to read the previous 499 records first.

You may be wondering why programmers use sequential files at all if random access files are so much faster for retrieving data. Sequential access files are generally used when all the data needs to be in the computer's memory at once. A grade book application is a good example. A teacher needs to be able to access information pertaining to a class as a whole—not just individual students. Sequential access files are also preferable when you are dealing with records that do not all have the same number of fields.

Before we look at a sample application involving a random access file, let's compare the way records are stored in a sequential access file with the way records are stored in a random access file. This will give you a better insight into how the computer accesses the records in each of the two file types, and why the records in a random access file can be processed so much faster than the records in a sequential access file.

Sequential Access Files vs. Random Access Files

Recall that you can use Notepad to view the records in a data file. Figure 7-4 shows a sequential access file, displayed in Notepad, that contains three records.

name field

record

price field

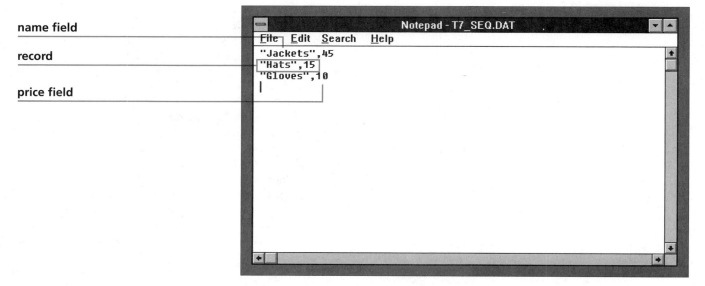

Figure 7-4: Sequential access file displayed in Notepad

Notice that each record appears on a separate line; that's because Visual Basic appends a carriage return character to the end of each record as it writes the record to the file. (You can't see the carriage return character.) Each record in the file contains two fields: a name field and a price field. The name field stores strings, as indicated by the quotation marks around the data. The price field stores numbers. The comma, which separates the fields in a sequential access file, indicates where the name field ends and the price field begins.

In a sequential access file, the number of characters contained in a field usually varies from record to record. In Figure 7-4, for example, notice that each of the names stored in the name field is a different length. Because the field lengths are not the same in each record, the length of each record in a sequential access file will vary. That's why records in a sequential access file are referred to as **variable-length records**. Now let's look at these same three records in a random access file.

Figure 7-5 shows a random access file, displayed in Notepad, containing the same three records shown in Figure 7-4.

binary representation of price field

name

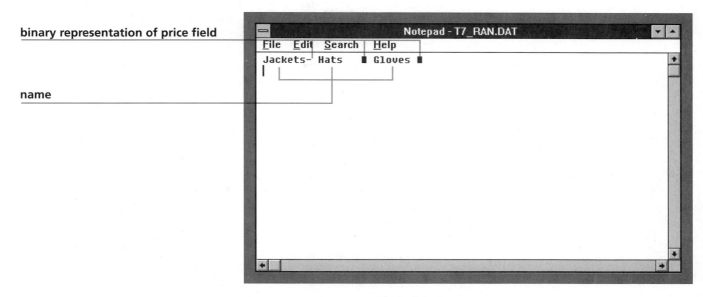

Figure 7-5: Random access file displayed in Notepad

Although the records are the same, notice that the random access file (Figure 7-5) looks different from the sequential access file (Figure 7-4). In the random access file, the three records appear on the same line with no commas separating the fields. The string field in the random access file does not contain quotation marks and the numbers in the price field display as strange-looking characters. The unusual characters appear because the numeric fields in a random access file are stored in a compressed format, called binary, which allows random access files to use less disk space than sequential access files when storing numbers. Figure 7-4 shows how the number 45 stored in a sequential file requires two storage locations—one for each digit. The same number stored in a random access file requires only one storage location. Since Notepad interprets all data it reads as text, the number 45 is interpreted as a single character (a dash). Many numbers are displayed only as small blocks because their binary codes are not associated with standard keyboard characters.

Unlike sequential access files, in random access files the number of characters contained in a field must be identical from record to record. When creating a random access file, the programmer first assigns a specific length, in bytes, to each field in the record. (You will learn how to assign the field length in the next section.) A **byte** is the amount of storage needed to hold one character; you can think of a byte as being equivalent to a character. In the random access file shown in Figure 7-5, the name field has a length of seven bytes (characters) and the price field has a length of two bytes.

If the data in a field is shorter than the length of the field, Visual Basic pads the unused space with blanks (spaces). In Figure 7-5, for example, the four-character string "Hats" is padded with three blanks before being stored in the seven-character name field. If, on the other hand, the data in the field is longer than the length of the field, Visual Basic crops (truncates) the data to fit the field. The eight-character string "Sweaters" would be cropped to a seven-character string ("Sweater") before being stored in the name field. Care must be taken to select the proper field length for string data. You don't want to have a string field so large that it wastes disk space, but you also don't want the field to be so small that it crops most of the strings.

Because the length of the fields in a random access file are identical from record to record, the length of each record in a random access file is also identical. That's why the records in a random access file are referred to as **fixed-length records**.

To summarize, sequential access files store variable-length records, whereas random access files store fixed-length records. The difference in the way the records are stored accounts for the difference in access time. Let's look at an illustration of this.

Example A in Figure 7-6 depicts five records stored in a sequential access file on a disk. Example B depicts the same five records in a random access file. (The <CR> in the sequential access file stands for carriage return. Recall that Visual Basic appends the carriage return character to the end of each record as the record is written to the sequential access file.) To make the random access file illustration easier to understand, numbers are shown in place of the binary characters.

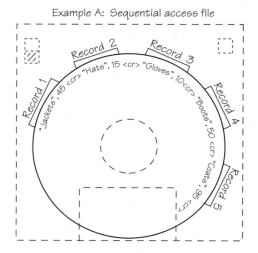

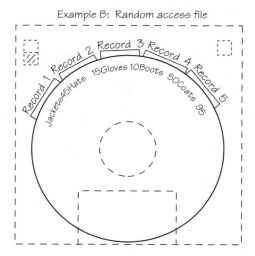

Figure 7-6: Examples of a sequential access and a random access file on disk

Notice that the length of each record in the sequential access file varies. The length of each record in the random access file, however, is nine bytes. Let's assume that you want the computer to read the fourth record in the sequential access file. Because the records in a sequential access file are of variable lengths, the fourth record might begin with the sixth character in the file, the 123rd character in the file, or the 179th character in the file. It all depends on the lengths of the first three records. Although the computer does not know the exact location of the fourth record in the file, it does know that the fourth record begins immediately after the third carriage return in the file. (You can verify that by looking at Example A in Figure 7-6.) So, to locate the fourth record, the computer starts at the beginning of the file and reads every character until it finds the third carriage return. The character immediately following the third carriage return is the beginning of the fourth record.

Now let's assume that you want the computer to read the fourth record in the random access file shown in Example B (in Figure 7-6). Recall that each record in the file is nine bytes (characters) long; so the fourth record in the file has to begin with the 28th character. (Characters one through nine are record 1, characters 10 through 18 are record 2, and characters 19 through 27 are record 3.) To read the fourth record in the file, the computer simply skips over the first 27 bytes (characters) in the file; it begins reading with the 28th character.

It may help to picture a file as a book and each record as a chapter in the book. Let's assume that you want to find Chapter 4 in a book that does not have a Table of Contents. If each chapter has a different length, similar to the records in a sequential access file, you would need to start at the beginning of the book and look at each page until you found the heading "Chapter 4." If, however, each chapter contains exactly the same number of pages, similar to the records in a random access file, you would know precisely where Chapter 4 begins and could turn to that page immediately. For example, if each chapter is 20 pages long, Chapter 4 would begin on page 61. (Pages 1 through 20 are Chapter 1, pages 21 through 40 are Chapter 2, and pages 41 through 60 are Chapter 3.)

Although this section discussed the difference in reading the records from both file types, the same concepts hold true for writing the records to the file. Because the records in a sequential access file are of variable length, the computer can't write the fourth record before it writes the first three records because it wouldn't know where to start writing. Therefore, the records in a sequential access file must be written to the file, in consecutive order, from the beginning of the file to the end of the file. The records in a random access file, however, can be written to the file in any order. Because the records in a random access file are all the same length, writing the fourth record before the first three is simple. If each record is 10 bytes long, the computer simply skips over the first 30 bytes in the file and begins writing the fourth record with the 31st byte.

In the next section you will learn how to assign the field lengths to the fields in a random access file.

The Type Statement

Before you can create a random access file, you need to define its **record structure**—the names, data types, and lengths of the fields in the record. You define the record structure with the Type statement. Figure 7-7 shows the syntax and an example of the Type statement.

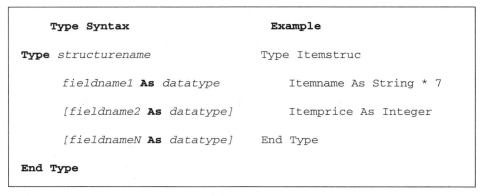

Figure 7-7: Syntax and an example of Type statement

The Type statement begins with the keyword Type followed by the name of the record structure; the statement ends with the keywords End Type. Between the Type and the End Type keywords, you place the name of each field in the record. The name of the record structure and the names of the fields must follow the same naming rules as for variables. (The rules for naming variables are listed in Figure 3-4 in Tutorial 3.) In Figure 7-7's example, the name of the record structure is Itemstruc and the names of the fields are Itemname and Itemprice.

Each field in the record structure must have a *datatype*, which defines the type of data the field will contain. When using the Type statement to define a record structure for a random access file, the *datatype* can be Integer, Long, Single, Double, Currency, or String. (If you are defining a record structure for a purpose other than a random access file, you can use other *datatype*s in the Type statement. To learn more about the Type statement, use the Help menu to search for its Help screen.) For all but the String *datatype*, the length of the field is fixed by the *datatype* you choose. If a field's *datatype* is Integer, for example, Visual Basic automatically assigns a length of two bytes to the field. Visual Basic assigns a length of four bytes to both Long and Single fields; Double and Currency fields are assigned a length of eight bytes. In the example shown in Figure 7-7, the Itemprice field is automatically set to two bytes because its *datatype* is Integer.

If a field's *datatype* is String, as is the Itemname field in Figure 7-7's example, you must specify the length of the field. You do so by appending both an asterisk (*) and a number, which represents the length of the field to the *datatype*. The *Itemname As String * 7* instruction in Figure 7-7, for example, tells Visual Basic to allocate seven bytes (characters) for the Itemname field.

The Type statement groups several related fields together into one unit—the record structure. The record structure itself actually becomes a data type, called a **user-defined data type**, which is separate and distinct from Visual Basic's standard data types. Figure 7-7's example groups together two fields, Itemname and Itemprice, into a record structure (a user-defined data type) named Itemstruc.

Once the user-defined data type (record structure) is created, you can declare a variable of that data type in your code, just as you can with Visual Basic's standard data types. For example, the **Dim** *Itemrec as Itemstruc* instruction creates an Itemstruc variable named Itemrec, similar to the way the *Dim Age as Integer* instruction creates an Integer variable named Age. The difference, however, is that the variable declared as a user-defined data type, called a

record variable, will itself contain one or more variables, called **field variables**. The *Dim Itemrec as Itemstruc* instruction, for example, creates a record variable named Itemrec and two field variables, Itemname and Itemprice. (Recall that Itemname and Itemprice are the names of the two fields in the Itemstruc user-defined data type.) When coding, you refer to the entire record variable by its name—in this case, Itemrec. To refer to the individual field variables, however, you must precede the field variable's name with the name of the record variable in which it is defined. You separate the record variable's name from the field variable's name with a period. For example, the names of the field variables within the Itemrec record variable are Itemrec.Itemname and Itemrec.Itemprice.

Before discussing random access files any further, let's look at the project that you will code in this lesson.

To view the t7_rand.mak project:

1 Launch Visual Basic and open the **t7_rand.mak** file, which is in either the tut7\ver2 or the tut7\ver3 directory on your Student Disk. The *Option Explicit* statement, which requires you to declare all variables, has already been entered in the general Declarations section of the form.

2 Save the form and the project as **t7a**. Click the **View Form button**, then maximize the form. The user interface appears on the screen, as shown in Figure 7-8.

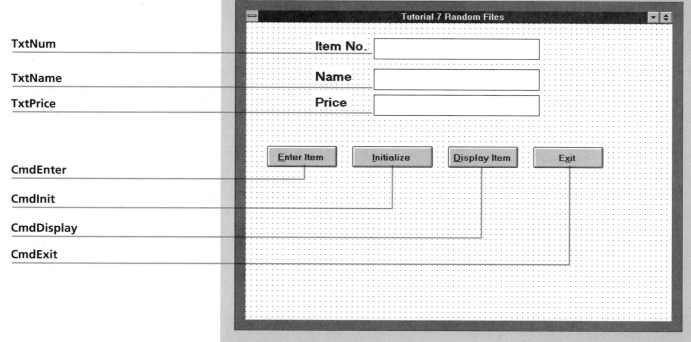

Figure 7-8: T7_rand user interface

3 After viewing the form, restore it to its standard size.

Using this application, a store owner can both save and display information about the items he or she sells. (You will learn about the Initialize button later on.) To save the item information, the user simply enters the item's number, name, and price into the appropriate Text boxes. The user then clicks the Enter Item button to save both the name and price in a random access file. To display the information about a specific item, the user first needs to enter the item's number in the Item No. Text box, then click the Display Item button. Visual Basic will skip to that item in the random access file and will display the item's name and its price in the Name and Price Text boxes, respectively. (To keep this application simple, the item numbers will be small integers that will correspond directly to the record numbers in a random access file. In other words, item number 1 will be record number one in the file, item number 2 will be record number 2, and so on. However, not all applications use small integers to identify the items, employees, and so on in a file. For example, a social security number is usually used to identify an employee.)

Let's begin coding this application.

Adding a Code Module to a Project

Our first step in coding this application is to enter the Type statement that defines the record structure for the item records. In this case the record structure will contain two fields: the item's name and price. (This is the information you want to save in the random access file.) You will name the record structure, Itemstruc, and the two fields, Itemname and Itemprice. (This is the same record structure shown in Figure 7-7's example.)

You enter the Type statement in the general Declarations section of a code module, which you have not yet seen. A **code module** (usually referred to simply as a module) is a separate file, added to your application, that contains no form and no objects—only code. An application can have more than one module, but this is rare. Items entered in a module are always **global**, which means they are available to every form and any other module in the entire application. User-defined constants, variables, procedures, and functions can all be global. You will get practice with two global constants and one global procedure when you create the Cole's Playhouse application. Then, in Lesson B, you will learn how to create multiform applications. The various forms in the application will draw upon the items entered in the code module.

When you declare a variable using a data type other than a standard one, Visual Basic searches the code module for a matching Type statement before creating the variable. (Recall that the Type statement simply defines the record structure; it does not actually create the record variable or the field variables.) Let's add a module to the project, and then enter the appropriate Type statement into it.

To add a code module to the current project, and then enter the Type statement:

1   Click **File**, then click **New Module** (or click the New Module icon 🖷). Visual Basic adds the Module1.bas file to the Project window, and the general Declarations section of the Module1.bas module appears. (The .bas extension stands for "Basic.")

2   Enter the instructions shown in Figure 7-9.

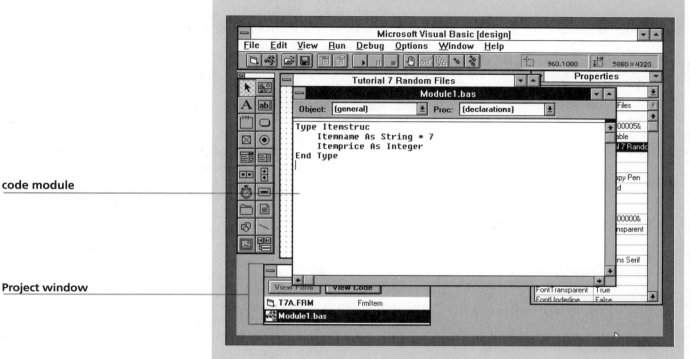

Figure 7-9: Type statement in code module and Project window

Each form and module in an application must be saved as a separate file. Because of this, an application can use forms and modules created for another application, often with few or no modifications. Now let's save the current module under a more descriptive name.

3   Click **File**, click **Save File As...**, then type **t7a** and press **[Enter]**. As the Project window shows, the module is now saved as t7a.bas.

4   Close the module's Code window.

Now that you have defined, coded, and saved the module, the form's Load event is the next procedure to code. The computer executes the Load event procedure whenever a form is first loaded. Because this will occur whenever the application is run, the Load event procedure will be the first procedure executed. Therefore, it should contain code to open the random access file that contains each item's name and price. Before writing this code, however, you will need to learn how to use the Open statement both to create a new random access file and to open an existing one.

Creating and Opening a Random Access File

As with sequential access files, the Open statement either creates a new random access file, if the file doesn't exist, or opens an existing random access file. The syntax of the Open statement used with random access files is **Open** *filename* [**For** *mode*] **As** #*filenumber* **Len** = *reclen*. Notice that the syntax is very similar to the one used for sequential access files. *Filename* is the name of the file you want to open and *filenumber* is the number assigned to the file. Unlike sequential access files, however, where the *mode* is Input, Output, or Append, the *mode* for random access files is always Random. Opening a file for Random allows you to both read and write to the file.

The Open statement for a random access file must include the record length (*reclen*) for each record in the file. *Reclen* must be a positive integer between 1 and 32767, inclusive. You calculate the record length by adding together the length of each field in the record structure. Because making that calculation by hand is time-consuming and prone to errors, it is much better to let Visual Basic calculate the record length for you. You do so by including the **Len** function in the Open instruction. The syntax of the Len function is **Len**(*variablename*), where *variablename* refers to the record variable's name. Assuming the record variable's name is Itemrec and the record length is 9 bytes, the two instructions *Open "a:\tut7\ver3\t7a.dat" for Random as #1 Len = 9* and *Open "a:\tut7\ver3\t7a.dat" for Random as #1 Len = Len(Itemrec)* are identical.

Using the Len function to calculate the record length also has another advantage: If the record length is modified in the Type statement, the Len function adjusts automatically to the new length.

In the current application, you will have Visual Basic open the random access file as soon as the application is run. You can do so by entering the Open statement in the form's Load event procedure. Recall from Tutorial 6 that a Load event occurs when the application is run and the form is loaded into the computer's memory. Visual Basic automatically executes the instructions contained in the Load event procedure's Code window when the Load event occurs.

tips

● ●

▶ Notice that Len is used in two ways in the Open statement. It's easy to confuse them. The Len keyword is a required part of the Open statement and is always to the left of the equal sign. It tells Visual Basic how much space to use on the disk for each record. The Len function, however, measures the length of the record variable as specified in the Type statement. As mentioned earlier, it is optional but its use is recommended. If used, it always appears to the right of the equal sign. In the Open Statement example, the Len function measures the size of the Itemrec variable; Visual Basic then uses that value as the length required in the syntax of the Open statement.

Coding the Form's Load Event Procedure

The first step in coding the form's Load event procedure is to declare the necessary variables. In this application the Load event needs one variable—a record variable—that the Len function will use to calculate the record length for the Open statement. You'll call the record variable Itemrec and declare it as a variable of the user-defined type, Itemstruc. (Recall that the name of the user-defined data type—the record structure—is Itemstruc.)

To code the form's Load event procedure:

1   Double-click the **form** to open its Code window. The Load event procedure appears. Maximize the Code window, press [**Tab**], then type **dim Itemrec as Itemstruc** and press [**Enter**].

Now enter the Open statement

2   Enter one of the following depending on your version of Visual Basic and the location of your Student Disk.

> Open "a:\tut7\ver2\t7a.dat" for random as #1 len=len(Itemrec)
> Open "b:\tut7\ver2\t7a.dat" for random as #1 len=len(Itemrec)
> Open "a:\tut7\ver3\t7a.dat" for random as #1 len=len(Itemrec)
> Open "b:\tut7\ver3\t7a.dat" for random as #1 len=len(Itemrec)
>
> While the random access file is open, the program can both read records from the file and write records to the file.
>
> **3** Close the Code window.

Remember that all open files should be closed before the application ends. Because it's so easy to forget to close the files, you should enter the Close instruction as soon after entering the Open instruction as possible. In this application you will have the Exit button close the t7a.dat file, and then end the application. Let's enter the appropriate code right now.

Closing a Random Access File

The Close statement closes both sequential access files and random access files. Recall that the syntax of the Close statement is **Close**(*filenumber*), where *filenumber* is the number used in the Open statement to open the file you now want to close. You will enter the Close statement in the Exit button's Click event procedure.

> **To enter the Close statement:**
>
> **1** Maximize the form, then double-click the **Exit button** to open its Code window. In the blank line immediately above the End statement, press [**Tab**], then type **close #1**.
>
> **2** Close the Code window and restore the form to its standard size.

The next control you will code is the Enter Item button, which, you remember, saves an item's name and price to a random access file. Before you can code this control, you will need to learn how to write a record (store data) to a random access file on disk.

Writing Records to a Random Access File

You use the **Put** statement to write a record to a random access file. (Recall that you use the Write # statement to write a record to a sequential access file.) The syntax of the Put statement is **Put #** *filenumber, [recordnumber], variablename*. *Filenumber* is the number used in the Open statement to open the file, *recordnumber* is the number of the record to be written, and *variablename* is the name of the record variable. Now let's see how to use the Put statement in the Enter Item button's Click event procedure.

Coding the Enter Item Button

The pseudocode for the Enter Item button is shown in Figure 7-10.

```
1.   Declare variables: Itemnum and Itemrec

2.   Assign item number to the Itemnum variable

3.   Assign the name and the price to the Itemrec variable

4.   Write the Itemrec record to the random access file

5.   Clear the Text boxes

6.   Set the focus to the TxtNum Text box
```

Figure 7-10: Pseudocode for the Enter Item button

To code the Enter Item button:

1 Double-click the **Enter Item button** to open its Code window. The CmdEnter control's Click event procedure appears.

This procedure requires two variables, which you will call Itemnum and Itemrec. Itemnum, an Integer variable, will store the item's number, which in this application corresponds to the record number. Itemrec, an Itemstruc variable, will store the record, which consists of an item's name and price. Both variables will be used in the Put statement to write the record to the file.

2 Press [**Tab**], type **dim Itemnum as integer, Itemrec as Itemstruc** and press [**Enter**].

You can now assign the appropriate values to the variables. First you will assign the item number, which the user entered in the TxtNum Text box, to the Itemnum variable.

3 Type **Itemnum = TxtNum.Text** and press [**Enter**].

Now you will assign the values in the other two Text boxes (TxtName and TxtPrice) to the Itemrec record variable. You do so by assigning each Text box value to a field variable in the record variable. In other words, you will assign the value in the TxtName control to the Itemrec.Itemname field variable; you will assign the value in the TxtPrice control to the Itemrec.Itemprice field variable.

4 Type **Itemrec.Itemname = TxtName.Text** and press [**Enter**]. Then type **Itemrec.Itemprice = TxtPrice.Text** and press [**Enter**].

According to the pseudocode, you can now write the record to the random access file. Recall that the syntax of the Put statement is **Put #** *filenumber, [recordnumber], variablename*. In this case the *filenumber* is 1, the *recordnumber* is the item number stored in the Itemnum variable, and the *variablename* is Itemrec.

5 Type **put #1, Itemnum, Itemrec** and press [**Enter**].

Remember to include the record variable's name, not the record structure's name or the names of the field variables, in the Put instruction. When Visual Basic writes the record variable to the file, it writes the information stored in each of the field variables. In this case, for example, Visual Basic will write the information stored in both the Itemrec.Itemname and Itemrec.Itemprice field variables to the file.

According to the pseudocode, all that remains is to clear the Text boxes and set the focus.

6   Enter the remaining code shown in Figure 7-11.

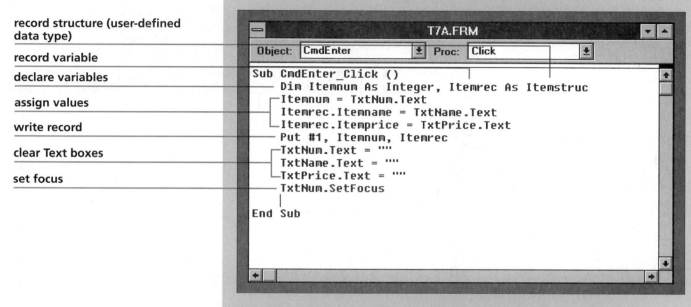

record structure (user-defined data type)
record variable
declare variables
assign values
write record
clear Text boxes
set focus

```
                                T7A.FRM
Object:  CmdEnter          ±    Proc:  Click              ±

Sub CmdEnter_Click ()
    Dim Itemnum As Integer, Itemrec As Itemstruc
    Itemnum = TxtNum.Text
    Itemrec.Itemname = TxtName.Text
    Itemrec.Itemprice = TxtPrice.Text
    Put #1, Itemnum, Itemrec
    TxtNum.Text = ""
    TxtName.Text = ""
    TxtPrice.Text = ""
    TxtNum.SetFocus

End Sub
```

Figure 7-11: Enter Item button Code window

7   Compare your code with Figure 7-11 and make any needed corrections before continuing to the next step.

8   Close the Code window.

tips

It's tempting (and often useful) to test an application with unusual, even absurd values. This example, however, is designed only to help you get the feel of how random access files work. If you enter an unusually large record number, Visual Basic will create a correspondingly large data file that can take up a great deal of space on your disk—and could possibly "crash" the program. Entering a non-positive record number or entering a string in the record number and/or price fields will also cause problems. For now, it's best to use the sample data provided.

Let's test the application to make sure the code you've entered is working correctly.

To test the application:

1   **Save and run** the application. Visual Basic executes the instructions in the form's Load event procedure. Because the t7a.dat file does not yet exist, the Load event instructions first create and then open the random access file. The user interface appears on the screen.

In a random access file, you can enter the items in any order. Let's enter item number 2 first.

2   Type **2** as the item number and press [Tab]. Type **Hats** as the item name and press [Tab]. Type **15** as the price, then click the **Enter Item button**.

Let's enter the fifth record next.

3   Type **5** as the item number and press [Tab]. Type **Coats** as the item name and press [Tab]. Type **95** as the price, then click the **Enter Item button**.

4   Click the **Exit button** to end the application.

tips

If [Alt][Tab] doesn't work, then click Visual Basic's Control menu box. Then click Switch To..., click Program Manager in the Task List, and click the Switch to button.

Let's look at the file you created by opening it in Notepad.

5   Press [Alt][Tab] to switch to Program Manager. Double-click the **Accessories icon** to open the Accessories group window, then double-click the **Notepad icon** to launch Notepad.

6   Click **File**, then click **Open....** Change the List Files of Type to All Files (*.*). Open the t7a.dat data file, which is in either the tut7\ver2 or the tut7\ver3 directory on your Student Disk. The t7a.dat data file appears. Your data file may contain some extra characters, as shown in Figure 7-12. (Don't be concerned if your screen does not look identical to Figure 7-12, or if your file does not contain any extra characters.)

extra characters (garbage)

record 2

extra characters (garbage)

record 5

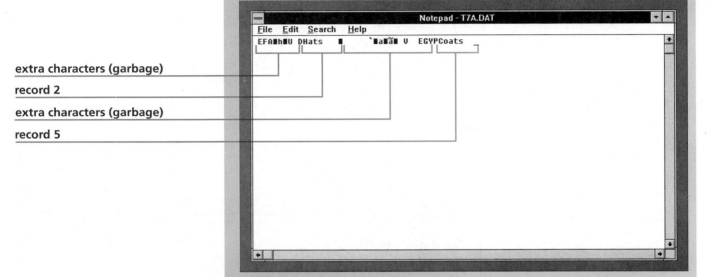

Figure 7-12: T7A.DAT random access file displayed in Notepad

You might find that a random access data file contains "garbage"—useless characters in places on the disk where records have not been written. Notice, for example, that the space reserved for record 1 in the t7a.dat file contains garbage. (Recall that you did not write any information to records 1, 3, and 4—only to records 2 and 5.) This is due to the way your computer's operating system saves and deletes files from a disk. When you save a file to a disk, the sectors that contain the file are marked as "in use." When you delete a file, the regions (sectors) on the disk that contain the file are marked as "available," but the file is not really erased from the disk. Those sectors will contain the remains of old files until you write over that information. When you don't write information to each record in a random access file, the space reserved for the unwritten records can contain anything. The solution to this problem is to initialize—in other words, to clear the disk space for the file. Let's do that next.

7   Click **File**, then click **Exit** to leave Notepad. (You do not need to save the file in Notepad.)

Initializing a Random Access File

You initialize a file by writing spaces to the string fields and a zero to the numeric fields. You should initialize a random access file *before* writing any records to it. If you initialize a file after records have been written to it, the good records will be overwritten with spaces and zeros. You may wish to initialize an existing data file so it can be reused for new data. If so, a confirmation message should appear that lets you confirm your intent.

Before you can initialize a data file, you need to estimate the maximum number of records the file will contain. (It doesn't hurt to overestimate.) Figure 7-13 shows the pseudocode to initialize a data file that will contain a maximum of 20 records.

```
1. Declare variables: Itemnum and Itemrec

2. Assign a zero to the price field in the Itemrec variable

3. Assign 7 spaces to the name field in the Itemrec variable

4. Repeat for Itemnum = 1 to 20 by 1

     Write the Itemrec record to the random access file

   End Repeat For
```

Figure 7-13: Pseudocode for the Initialize button

The code to initialize the t7a.dat has already been entered in the Initialize button. Let's look at that code right now.

To view the code in the Initialize button, then save and run the application:
1 Double-click the **Initialize button**. The Click event procedure appears as shown in Figure 7-14.

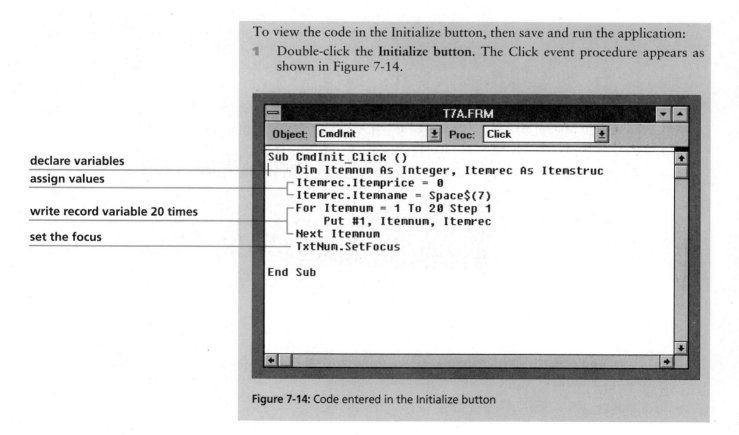

```
                                   T7A.FRM

Object: CmdInit          ±    Proc: Click              ±

Sub CmdInit_Click ()
    Dim Itemnum As Integer, Itemrec As Itemstruc
    Itemrec.Itemprice = 0
    Itemrec.Itemname = Space$(7)
    For Itemnum = 1 To 20 Step 1
        Put #1, Itemnum, Itemrec
    Next Itemnum
    TxtNum.SetFocus

End Sub
```

declare variables

assign values

write record variable 20 times

set the focus

Figure 7-14: Code entered in the Initialize button

The code begins by declaring two variables, Itemnum and Itemrec. Itemnum is an Integer variable and Itemrec is a record variable of the Itemstruc data type. Itemnum will store the item number and Itemrec will store the record—the item's name and price. After the variables are declared, the code assigns a zero to the Itemrec.Itemprice field variable and then uses the Space$ function to assign seven spaces to the Itemrec.Itemname field variable. The syntax of the Space$ function is **Space$**(*number*), where *number* is the number of spaces you want. A For...Next loop then initializes the data file by writing the record variable to the file, 20 times. The record variable, remember, contains seven spaces for the Itemname field and a zero for the Itemprice field. Finally, the SetFocus method sets the focus to the Item No. Text box.

2   Close the Code window.

Now, let's initialize the t7a.dat data file.

3   **Save and run** the application, then click the **Initialize button.** Visual Basic initializes the t7a.dat file.

Initializing a data file destroys all data in it. (Normally a warning message and an opportunity to cancel the operation should be presented.) Therefore, you will need to reenter records 2 and 5, as those records were overwritten by the initialization process. Let's do that now.

4   Type **2** as the item number and press [**Tab**]. Type **Hats** as the item name and press [**Tab**]. Type **15** as the price, then click the **Enter Item button.**

5   Type **5** as the item number and press [**Tab**]. Type **Coats** as the item name and press [**Tab**]. Type **95** as the price, then click the **Enter Item button.**

6   Click the **Exit button** to end the application.

7   If you want to verify that the file no longer contains "garbage," switch to Notepad and open the t7a.dat file. Any "garbage" that was visible in the file before initialization should now be gone.

8   When you're finished looking at the file, exit Notepad without saving the file.

Before you can code the last control, the Display Item button, you will need to learn how to read a record from a random access file.

Reading Records from a Random Access File

You use the Get statement to read a record from a random access file. (Recall that you use the Input # statement to read a record from a sequential access file.) The syntax of the Get statement is **Get #** *filenumber, [recordnumber], variablename. Filenumber* is the number used in the Open statement to open the file, *recordnumber* is the number of the record to be read, and *variablename* is the name of the record variable. Now let's see how to use the Get statement in the Display Item button's Click event procedure.

Coding the Display Item Button

To display the name and price of an existing item in the file, the user first needs to enter the item number in the Item No. Text box, then click the Display Item button. The pseudocode for the Display Item button is shown in Figure 7-15.

```
1. Declare variables: Itemnum and Itemrec

2. Assign the item number to the Itemnum variable

3. Read the record corresponding to the item number

4. Assign the name from the Itemrec variable to the Name

   Text box

5. Assign the price from the Itemrec variable to the

   Price Text box

6. Set the focus to the TxtNum Text box
```

Figure 7-15: Pseudocode for the Display Item button

Most of the code for this button has already been entered in the Code window for you; only three of the instructions are missing. Let's open the Code window and look at the existing code.

To view the code in the Display Item button's Code window:
1   Double-click the **Display Item button.** The CmdDisplay control's Click event procedure appears as shown in Figure 7-16.

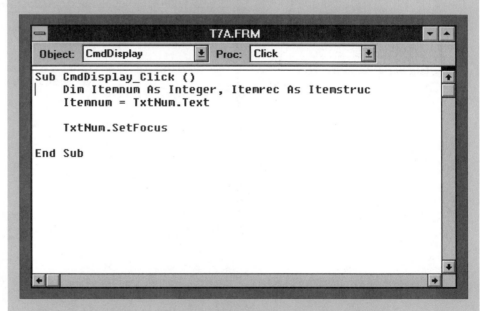

Figure 7-16: Partially completed Code window for the Display Item button

The code begins by declaring two variables: Itemnum and Itemrec. Itemnum, an Integer variable, will store the item number. Itemrec, an Itemstruc variable, will store the record. After the variables are declared, the code assigns the item number, which is entered in the TxtNum Text box, to the Itemnum variable.

According to the pseudocode, the next step is to read the record from the random access file. Recall that the syntax of the Get statement is **Get #** *filenumber, [recordnumber], variablename*. In this case the *filenumber* is 1, the *recordnumber* is the item number stored in the Itemnum variable, and the *variablename* is Itemrec.

2 In the blank line immediately below the *Itemnum = TxtNum.Text* assignment statement, type **get #1, Itemnum, Itemrec** and press [**Enter**].

This statement tells Visual Basic to read the record whose record number is stored in the Itemnum variable. As it reads the record, Visual Basic stores the first seven bytes of the record in the Itemrec.Itemname field variable and the last two bytes in the Itemrec.Itemprice field variable.

Now you need to display the contents of both field variables, Itemrec.Itemname and Itemrec.Itemprice, in the appropriate Text boxes.

3 In the line immediately below the Get statement, type **TxtName.Text = Itemrec.Itemname** and press [**Enter**]. Then type **TxtPrice.Text = Itemrec.Itemprice**. (Don't type the period after Itemrec.Itemprice.)

The instruction to set the focus is already entered in the Code window.

4 Compare your code with the code shown in Figure 7-17. Make any needed corrections before continuing to the next step.

read the record

assign field variable values to
Text boxes

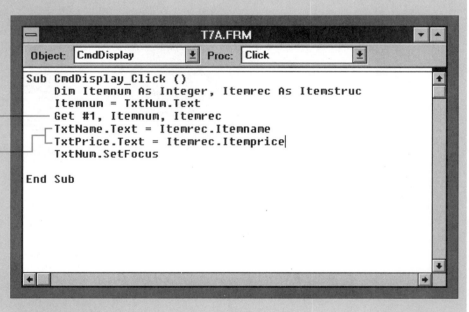

Figure 7-17: Completed Code window for the Display Item button

5 Close the Code window, then **save and run** the application.

Let's display the name and price of an existing item—item 5, for example.

6 Type 5 as the item number, then click the **Display Item button**. Item 5's name (Coats) and price (95) appear in the appropriate Text boxes.

Now let's display the name and price of an item that does not exist—item 1, for example.

7 Press [**Backspace**] to remove the 5 from the Item No. Text box, type **1** as the item number, then click the **Display Item button**. Nothing appears in the TxtName Text box, and a zero appears in the TxtPrice Text box. (Recall that you initialized the name field to spaces and the price field to zero.)

8 Click the **Exit button** to end the application. Visual Basic returns to the design screen.

You have now completed Lesson A. You can either take a break or complete the end-of-lesson questions and exercises.

S U M M A R Y

To determine sequential access vs. random access:

■ A sequential access file is similar to a cassette tape. Each song on a cassette tape is both stored and retrieved in consecutive order from beginning to end.

■ A random access file is similar to a CD. Each song on a CD can be played in any order by accessing its track (record) number.

To create a user-defined data type:

■ Enter the Type statement in the general Declarations section of a code module. Its syntax is:

> **Type** *structurename*
> > *fieldname*1 *As data type*
> > [*fieldname*2 *As data type*]
> > [*fieldname*N *As data type*]
>
> **End Type**

To add a code module to an application:

■ Click File, then click New Module. You can also click the New Module icon 🖼.

To create or open a random access file:

■ Use the Open statement. Its syntax is **Open** *filename* [**For** *mode*] **As #** *filenumber* **Len** = *reclen*.

■ *Filename* is the name of the file, including the drive letter and path, and must be enclosed in quotation marks. If the *filename* is stored in a variable or a property, you do not need quotation marks.

■ *Mode* is Random. Random mode opens the file for reading and writing.

■ *Filenumber* is an integer expression with a value between 1 and 255, inclusive.

■ *Reclen* is the length of each record in the file and must be an integer in the range of 1 through 32767, inclusive.

To determine the size of a record:

■ Use the Len function. Its syntax is **Len**(*variablename*).

To close a file:

■ Use the Close statement. Its syntax is **Close** *[# filenumber][, # filenumber]....* *Filenumber* is the number used in the Open statement to open the file. A Close statement with no arguments closes all open files.

To write a record to an open random access file:

■ Use the Put statement. Its syntax is **Put** # *filenumber, [recordnumber], variablename*. *Filenumber* is the number used in the Open statement to open the random access file. *Recordnumber* is the number of the record to write. *Variablename* is the name of the record variable.

To initialize a string to spaces:

■ Use the Space$ function. Its syntax is **Space$**(*number*), where *number* represents the number of spaces.

To read a record from an open random access file:

■ Use the Get statement. Its syntax is **Get** # *filenumber, [recordnumber], variablename*. *Filenumber* is the number used in the Open statement to open the random access file. *Recordnumber* is the number of the record to read. *Variablename* is the name of the record variable.

Q U E S T I O N S

1. You use the _____ statement to define the structure of a record.
   a. Declare
   b. Define
   c. Record
   d. Structure
   e. Type
2. Records in a random access file can be accessed _____.
   a. randomly
   b. sequentially
   c. either randomly or sequentially
3. The Type statement must be declared in the _____.
   a. event procedure of an object
   b. general Declarations section of a code module
   c. general Declarations section of a form
4. Which of the following will define a 15-character string field named City?
   a. City as String
   b. City as String(15)
   c. City as String X 15
   d. City as String by 15
   e. City as String * 15
5. If you store the string "Chicago" (without the quotes) in a 15-character field named City, what will Visual Basic actually store in the City field?
   a. The string "Chicago" (with the quotes).
   b. The string "Chicago" (without the quotes).

c. The string "Chicago" (with the quotes) followed by six blank spaces.

d. The string "Chicago" (without the quotes) followed by eight blank spaces.

e. Eight blank spaces followed by the string "Chicago" (without the quotes).

6. A _____ is equivalent to a character.
   a. bit
   b. byte
   c. integer
   d. number
   e. string

7. A field defined as Currency is stored in _____ bytes.
   a. 2
   b. 4
   c. 6
   d. 8
   e. 10

8. You create a random access file with the _____ statement.
   a. Create
   b. Declare
   c. Define
   d. Open
   e. Random

9. You open a random access file with the _____ statement.
   a. Create
   b. Declare
   c. Define
   d. Open
   e. Random

10. You use the _____ statement to write a record to a random access file.
    a. Define
    b. Get
    c. Put
    d. Record
    e. Write

11. You use the _____ statement to read a record from a random access file.
    a. Define
    b. Get
    c. Put
    d. Record
    e. Write

12. Which of the following Open statements are valid? (The name of the record variable is Employee. Each record is 100 bytes.) (Choose two.)
    a. Open a:\data.dat for random as #1 Len = Len(Employee)
    b. Open a:\data.dat for "random" as #1 Len = Len(Employee)
    c. Open "a:\data.dat" for random as #1 Len = Len(Employee)
    d. Open "a:\data.dat" for random Len = Len(Employee)
    e. Open "a:\data.dat" for random as #1 Len = 100

13. Which of the following will write the Employee record to a random access file?
    a. Put #1, Recnum, Lname, Fname
    b. Put Lname, Fname to #1
    c. Put Recnum, Lname, Fname to #1

    d. Put #1, Recnum, Employee

    e. Put Recnum, Employee to #1

14. Which of the following will close a random access file opened as file number 3?

    a. Close filenumber 3

    b. Close random #3

    c. Close file #3

    d. Close #3

    e. Close file 3

15. Which of the following will return the length of the Student record?

    a. Len(Student)

    b. Length(Student)

    c. Recordlength(Student)

    d. Student(Len)

    e. Student(Length)

16. Unless specified otherwise, an open random access file can be _____.

    a. read from only

    b. written to only

    c. either read from or written to

17. Which of the following will assign 10 spaces to a variable named Firstname?

    a. Firstname = Blank(10)

    b. Firstname = Blank$(10)

    c. Firstname = Space&(10)

    d. Firstname = Space$(10)

    e. Firstname = (10)Space$

Use the following information to answer Questions 18 through 25.

```
Type Custstruc
    Custname as String * 25
    Custphone as String * 12
    Custsalary as Currency
End Type
Dim Custrec as Custstruc
```

18. The name of the record structure is _____.

    a. Custname

    b. Custphone

    c. Custrec

    d. Custsalary

    e. Custstruc

19. The name of the record variable is _____.

    a. Custname

    b. Custphone

    c. Custrec

    d. Custsalary

    e. Custstruc

20. The names of the field variables are _____. (Choose three.)

    a. Custname

    b. Custphone

    c. Custrec

      d. Custsalary

      e. Custstruc

21. The length of the Custname field variable is _____.

      a. 8

      b. 12

      c. 25

      d. 45

      e. Can't tell from the information.

22. The length of the Custsalary field variable is _____.

      a. 8

      b. 12

      c. 25

      d. 45

      e. Can't tell from the information.

23. The length of the Custrec record is _____.

      a. 8

      b. 12

      c. 25

      d. 45

      e. Can't tell from the information.

24. When coding, you would refer to the Custphone field variable as _____.

      a. Custphone

      b. Custphone.Custrec

      c. Custphone.Custstruc

      d. Custrec.Custphone

      e. Custstruc.Custphone

25. When coding, you would refer to the record variable as _____.

      a. Custname

      b. Custphone

      c. Custrec

      d. Custsalary

      e. Custstruc

E X E R C I S E S

1. Write a Type statement that defines a record structure named Bookstruc. The record structure contains three fields: Booktitle, Bookauthor, Bookcost. Booktitle is a 20-character String field, Bookauthor is a 20-character String field, and Bookcost is a Currency field.

2. Write a Type statement that defines a record structure named Tapestruc. The record structure contains four fields: Tapename, Tapeartist, Tapesongs, and Tapelength. Tapename is a 25-character String field, Tapeartist is a 20-character String field, Tapesongs is an Integer field, and Tapelength is a 6-character String field.

3. Write a Dim statement that declares a Bookstruc variable named Bookrec.

4. Write a Dim statement that declares a Tapestruc variable named Taperec.

5. Write an Open statement that opens a random access file named "t7lae5.dat" on your Student Disk. Open the file as #1. The contents of the Bookrec record variable will be written to the file.

6. Write an Open statement that opens a random access file named "t7lae6.dat" on your Student Disk. Open the file as #1. The contents of the Taperec record variable will be written to the file.

7. Assume that the Recnum variable contains the number 5 and the random access file was opened as #1. Write a Put statement that will write the contents of the Bookrec record variable as the fifth record in the file.

8. Assume that the Recnum variable contains the number 2 and the random access file was opened as #1. Write a Put statement that will write the contents of the Taperec record variable as the second record in the file.

9. Assume that the Recnum variable contains the number 3 and the random access file was opened as #1. Write a Get statement that will read the third record in the file. The name of the record variable is Bookrec.

10. Assume that the Recnum variable contains the number 5 and the random access file was opened as #1. Write a Get statement that will read the fifth record in the file. The name of the record variable is Taperec.

11. Write the statement that will close the file opened as # 1.

Use the following record structure for Exercise 12.

> **Type Computerstruc**
> **Compname as String * 5**
> **Compcost as Currency**
> **End Type**

12. a. Write a Dim statement that declares a Computerstruc variable named Comprec.
    b. Write an Open statement that opens a random access file named "t7lae12.dat" on your Student Disk. Open the file as #1.
    c. Write the For...Next loop that will initialize the t7lbe12.dat file for 10 records.
    d. Write an assignment statement that will assign the name "IB-50" to the Compname field variable.
    e. Write an assignment statement that will assign the number 2400 to the Compcost field variable.
    f. Assuming that the Recnum variable contains the number 5, write the Put statement that will write the Comprec record as the fifth record in the random access file.
    g. Assuming that the Recnum variable contains the number 5, write the Get statement that will read the fifth record in the random access file.
    h. Write the assignment statements that will assign the value in the Compname field variable to the LblName control, and the value in the Compcost field variable to the LblCost control.
    i. Write the statement that will close the random access file.

Use the following record structure for Exercise 13.

> **Type Friendstruc**
> **Friendlast as String * 10**
> **Friendfirst as String * 10**
> **End Type**

13. a. Write a Dim statement that declares a Friendstruc variable named Friendrec.
    b. Write an Open statement that opens a random access file named "t7lae13.dat" on your Student Disk. Open the file as #1.
    c. Write the For...Next loop that will initialize the t7lbe13.dat file for five records.
    d. Write an assignment statement that will assign the value in the TxtFirst control to the Friendfirst field variable.
    e. Write an assignment statement that will assign the value in the TxtLast control to the Friendlast field variable.

f. Assuming that the Recnum variable contains the number 3, write the Put statement that will write the Friendrec record as the third record in the random access file.

g. Assuming that the Recnum variable contains the number 3, write the Get statement that will read the third record in the random access file.

h. Write the assignment statement that will assign the value in the Friendfirst field variable and the value in the Friendlast field variable to the LblName control. (Hint: You will need to use string concatenation, which you learned about in Tutorial 3.)

i. Write the statement that will close the random access file.

14. a. Write a Type statement that defines a record structure named Custstruc. The record structure contains three fields: Custname, Custphone, Custsales. Custname is a 25-character String field and Custphone is an 8-character String field. Custsales is a Currency field.

b. Write a Dim statement that declares a Custstruc variable named Custrec.

c. Write an Open statement that opens a random access file named "t7lae14.dat" on your Student Disk. Open the file as #1.

d. Write the For...Next loop that will initialize the t7lbe14.dat file for five records.

e. Write an assignment statement that will assign the value in the TxtName control to the Custname field variable.

f. Write an assignment statement that will assign the value in the TxtPhone control to the Custphone field variable.

g. Write an assignment statement that will assign the value in the TxtSales control to the Custsales field variable.

h. Assuming that the Recnum variable contains the number 3, write the Put statement that will write the Custrec record as the third record in the random access file.

i. Assuming that the Recnum variable contains the number 3, write the Get statement that will read the third record in the random access file.

j. Write the assignment statement that will assign the value in the Custname field variable to the TxtName control.

k. Write the assignment statement that will assign the value in the Custphone field variable to the TxtPhone control.

l. Write the assignment statement that will assign the value in the Custsales field variable to the TxtSales control.

m. Write the statement that will close the random access file.

15. Create the user interface shown in Figure 7-18

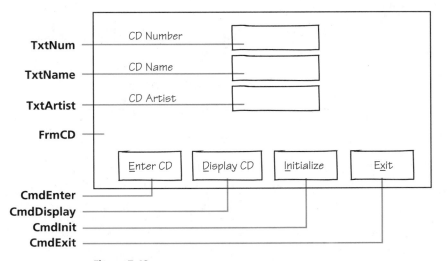

Figure 7-18

a. Save the form and the project as t7lae15.
b. Add a code module to the project. Define a record structure named Cdstruc in the code module. The record structure contains two fields: Cdname and Cdartist. Define both fields as 20-character String fields.
c. Save the code module as t7lae15.
d. In the form's Load event procedure, define a Cdstruc variable named Cdrec and open a file named t7lae15.dat. (The file is on your Student Disk.)
e. Code the Exit button so that it closes the data file and ends the application when clicked.
f. Code the Initialize button so that it initializes the t7lae15.dat random access file. The file will contain no more than five records. The pseudocode is shown in Figure 7-19.

```
1.  Declare variables: Cdnum and Cdrec

2.  Assign 20 spaces to the Cdname field variable

3.  Assign 20 spaces to the Cdartist field variable

4.  Repeat for Cdnum=1 to 5 by 1

            Write the record variable to the file

    End Repeat for

5.  Set the focus to the TxtNum Text box
```

Figure 7-19

g. Code the Enter CD button and the Display CD button according to the pseudocode shown in Figure 7-20.

```
Pseudocode for the Enter CD button:

1.  Declare variables: Cdnum and Cdrec

2.  Assign CD number to the Cdnum variable

3.  Assign the name and the artist to the Cdrec variable

4.  Write the Cdrec record to the random access file

5.  Clear the Text boxes

6.  Set the focus to the TxtNum Text box

Pseudocode for the Display CD button:

1.  Declare variables: Cdnum and Cdrec

2.  Assign the CD number to the Cdnum variable

3.  Read the record corresponding to the Cd number

4.  Assign the name from the Cdrec variable to the name Text box

5.  Assign the artist from the Cdrec variable to the artist Text box

6.  Set the focus to the TxtNum Text box
```

Figure 7-20

h. Save and run the application.
i. To test the application:
   1) Initialize the t7lae15.dat file.
   2) Use the Enter CD button to enter the following three records, shown as CD number, CD name, and artist name:
      4, Western Way, Mingo Colfax
      2, Country For All, Barbara Mender
      1, Line Dancing, Helen Starks
   3) Enter CD number 2 and click the Display CD button. The Country For All CD by Barbara Mender should appear in the form.
   4) Click the Exit button to end the application.
   5) Print the form and the code.

16. Create the user interface shown in Figure 7-21. Also, print the t71ae15.dat file in Notepad.

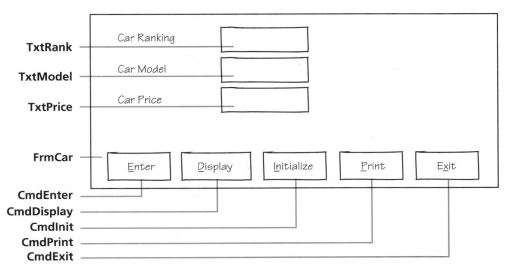

Figure 7-21

a. Save the form and the project as t7lae16.
b. Add a code module to the project. Define a record structure named Carstruc in the code module. The record structure contains two fields: Carmodel and Carprice. Carmodel is a 15-character String field and Carprice is a Currency field.
c. Save the code module as t7lae16.
d. In the form's Load event procedure, define a Carstruc variable named Carrec and open a file named t7lae16.dat.
e. Code the Exit button so that it ends the application and closes the data file when clicked.
f. Code the Initialize button so that it initializes the t7lae16 random access file. The file will contain no more than 10 records.
g. Code the Enter button so that it writes the car model and the car price to the random access file.
h. Code the Display button so that it displays the car model and the car price associated with the ranking number.
i. Code the Print button according to the pseudocode shown in Figure 7-22. (Hint: Recall that you need to use the Printer.EndDoc instruction to tell Visual Basic to print the document.)

```
1.  Declare variables: Carrank and Carrec

2.  Repeat for Carrank = 1 to 10 by 1

      Read the Carrec record from the random access file

      Print the Carrec record to the printer.(Separate into fields.

      Print each field on the same line)

    End Repeat For
```

Figure 7-22

    j. Save and run the application.
    k. To test the application:
        1) Initialize the t7lae16.dat file.
        2) Use the Enter button to enter the following three records, shown as ranking number and model:
            1, Firebird, 22000
            2, Camaro, 22500
            3, Stealth, 30000
        3) Enter ranking number 3 and click the Display button. Stealth should appear in the TxtModel Text box and 30000 should appear in the TxtPrice Text box.
        4) Click the Print button.
        5) Click the Exit button to end the application.
        6) Print the form and the code.

In this lesson you will learn how to:

■ **Include multiple forms in an application**

■ **Create a symbolic constant in a module**

■ **Create a sub procedure in a module**

■ **Refer to a control in another form**

■ **Show and hide a form**

Using Multiple Forms in the Cole's Playhouse Application

The Cole's Playhouse Application

As you'll recall, Cole's Playhouse runs plays performed by local talent. The theater holds only 48 seats. Tickets must be purchased in advance of the performance; no tickets are sold at the door. The manager, Max Phillips, wants an application that will keep track of the reserved seating for each play. Specifically, Mr. Phillips wants to record each patron's name and phone number.

Let's start by creating a prototype that contains all the essential features of the program. If Mr. Phillips is pleased with the overall look and feel of the application, we can add features that make it more reliable, user friendly, and powerful.

The Cole Playhouse application will contain three forms. The sketch of the user interface for each form is shown in Figure 7-23.

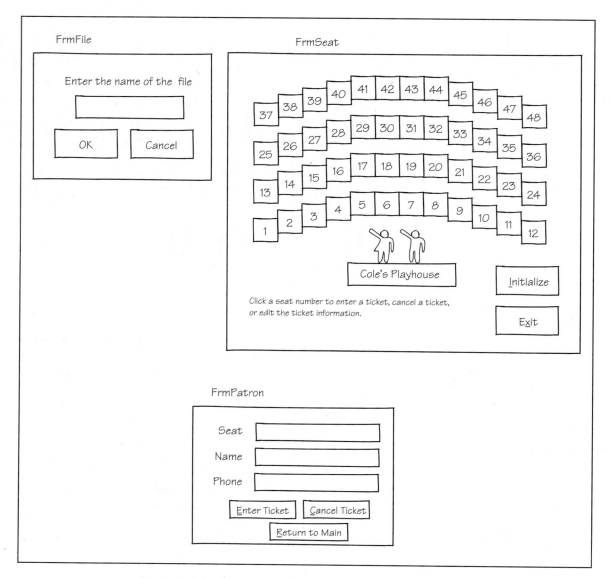

Figure 7-23: Sketch of three forms in the Cole's Playhouse application

You will code two of the three forms, FrmPatron and FrmSeat, in this lesson. You will code the FrmFile form in Lesson C. (If you are having trouble remembering the Cole's Playhouse application, you might want to run the COLE.EXE file from Program Manager before continuing with this lesson.) Let's begin by opening the partially completed Cole's Playhouse application on your Student Disk.

To open the partially completed Cole's Playhouse application:

1 Launch Visual Basic and open the **t7cole.mak** file, which is in either the tut7\ver2 or the tut7\ver3 directory on your Student Disk. The Option Explicit statement is already entered in the general Declarations section of the form.

Let's save the form and the project under a different name, so that the original files will remain intact.

2 Click **File**, then click **Save File As....** Type **t7bpatrn** in the Save File As dialog box and press [**Enter**].

3 Click **File**, then click **Save Project As....** Type **t7b** in the Save Project As dialog box and press [**Enter**].

The Project window shows that the project contains only one form—the FrmPatron form.

4 Click the **View Form button**. The FrmPatron form appears on the screen, as shown in Figure 7-24.

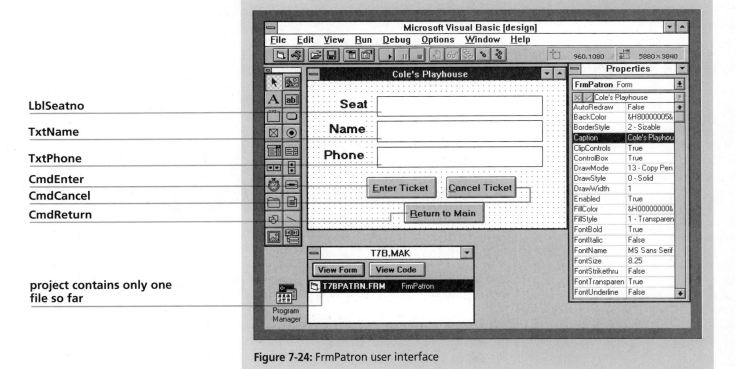

Figure 7-24: FrmPatron user interface

Using this form, the user will be able to enter the ticket information, cancel the ticket information, or return to the main screen—the FrmSeat form. Let's add the FrmSeat form to the current project.

Adding a Form to a Project

You can add a new form to the current project either by clicking the New Form icon (the first icon) in the toolbar or by clicking File, then clicking New Form. In this case, however, the FrmSeat form has already been created for you. You can add an existing form to the current project by clicking File, then clicking Add File.... Let's do that now.

To add an existing form to the current project:

1   Click **File**, then click **Add File....** The Add File dialog box appears.

The Drives box should display the drive containing your Student Disk. The Directories box should display either the tut7\ver2 directory or the tut7\ver3 directory.

2   Click **t7cole2.frm** in the File Name list box, then click the **OK button**. Visual Basic adds the t7cole2.frm form file to the current project. You can verify that by looking in the Project window.

Let's save the form under a different name, so the original t7cole2.frm file will remain intact.

3   Click **T7COLE2.FRM** in the Project window, click **File**, and then click **Save File As....** Type **t7bseat** in the Save File As dialog box and press **[Enter]**. Visual Basic records the new name of the form file, T7BSEAT.FRM, in the Project window.

An application can contain many forms. Each form must be saved with its own distinct filename.

Now save the t7b.mak project on your Student Disk. You should always save the project file whenever you make a change to the Project window.

4   Click the Save Project icon 🖫 in the toolbar. Visual Basic saves the project on your Student Disk.

5   T7BSEAT.FRM should be highlighted in the Project window, so click the **View Form button** and then maximize the form. The FrmSeat form appears on the screen, as shown in Figure 7-25.

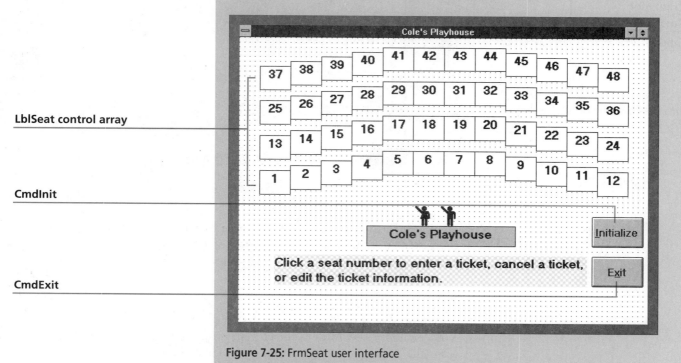

Figure 7-25: FrmSeat user interface

Forty-eight of the 50 Label controls in the FrmSeat form represent the 48 seats in the theater. Because each of those 48 controls will perform the same function, they were placed in a control array named LblSeat. Let's verify that.

To verify that the 48 Label controls belong to the LblSeat control array:

1   Click **seat number 1**, then press [F4] to display the Properties window. The LblSeat(0) label appears in the Object box in the Properties window. LblSeat is the name of the control array, and 0 is this Label control's index. The name is recorded in the Name property, and the index is recorded in the Index property. LblSeat(0) is the first control in the LblSeat control array.

2   Click **seat number 29**, then press [F4]. The LblSeat(28) label appears in the Object box in the Properties window. Notice that the value in the Index property is always one less than the seat number. In other words, the control with Index number 28 actually refers to seat number 29. This fact will become very important as you start coding this application.

3   Restore the form to its standard size.

When a project includes more than one form, you must tell Visual Basic which of the forms you want automatically displayed when the application is run. For now, the FrmSeat form will be the first screen that appears when the application is run. (Later, you'll add a third and final form that will allow the user to enter the name of the file that will hold the seating data. The file form will eventually become the first form the user sees.)

When the user wants to enter or cancel a ticket, he or she can simply click the appropriate seat number to display the FrmPatron form, which contains both the Enter Ticket and the Cancel Ticket buttons.

Specifying the Startup Form

When a multiform project is run, Visual Basic automatically loads and displays only one of the forms contained in the project. That form, called the **startup form,** can be any one of the forms in the project. You use the Options menu to specify which form you want Visual Basic to use as the startup form. In this case, the FrmSeat form should be the startup form.

To specify the startup form for the t7b.mak project:

1   Click **Options**, then click **Project....** The Project Options dialog box appears. See Figure 7-26

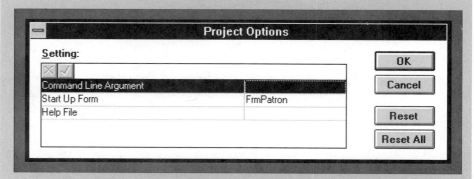

Figure 7-26: Project Options dialog box

FrmPatron appears as the startup form because it was the first form included in the t7b.mak project. You need to change the startup form to FrmSeat.

2   Click Start Up Form, then click the down arrow button in the Setting box. A list of form names included in this project appears.

3   Click **FrmSeat** in the list box. FrmSeat appears in the Start Up Form box.

4   Click the **OK button** to leave the Project Options dialog box. Visual Basic closes the dialog box.

When you run this multiform application, Visual Basic will automatically load and display the FrmSeat form on the screen. You can then use the Show method, which you will learn later in this lesson, to load and display the other forms in the project. You can now begin coding the Cole's Playhouse application. The TOE chart for this lesson is shown in Figure 7-27.

Task	Object	Event
FrmSeat form:		
Open the data file	Form	Load
Display reserved seats colored red		
Initialize the data file	Command button (Initialize)	Click
Get the seat number	48 Label controls (control array)	Click
Display FrmPatron form with patron information		
Close the data file	Command button (Exit)	Click
End the application		
FrmPatron form:		
Get name and phone number	2 Text boxes	None
Write the name and phone number to the file	Command button (Enter Ticket)	Click
Color the reserved seats red		
Remove the name and phone number from the file	Command button (Cancel Ticket)	Click
Color the cancelled seats white		
Return to the FrmSeat form	Command button (Return to Main)	Click

Figure 7-27: Initial TOE chart

Coding the Cole's Playhouse Application

Because this application will use a random access file, you will need to define the record structure for the records. Recall that you do so by entering the Type statement in a code module (often just called a module).

To add a code module to the project, and then define the record structure:

1 Click **File**, then click **New Module**. The Module1.bas filename appears in the Project window and in the title bar. The general Declarations section of the code module appears on the screen.

Each record in the random access file will contain a patron's name and his or her phone number. You will name the record structure (the user-defined data type), Patronstruc, and the fields, Patronname and Patronphone. Both fields will be strings. Patronname will be 20 characters long and Patronphone will be 8 characters long.

2 Enter the Type statement shown in Figure 7-28.

Figure 7-28: Type statement entered in code module

Let's save the code module using a more descriptive name.

3 The module1.bas code module should already be highlighted in the Project window. Click **File**, then click **Save File As....** Type **t7b** in the Save File As dialog box and press [**Enter**]. Visual Basic saves the code module as t7b.bas on your Student Disk. The T7B.BAS filename appears in the Project window.

4 Click the **Save Project** icon ▥.

Before closing the code module's Code window, you will learn how to create symbolic constants, which you will use in this application.

Symbolic Constants

In Tutorial 3 you learned about literal constants—specific values (like 3) that do not change while a program is running. Visual Basic also allows you to create symbolic constants. A **symbolic constant** is a memory location whose contents cannot be changed while the program is running. You create a symbolic constant with Visual Basic's **Const** statement. The syntax of the Const statement is **[Global] Const** *constantname = expression*, where *constantname* is the name of the symbolic constant and expression is the value you want assigned to it. Programmers usually enter the *constantname* using uppercase letters so the symbolic constants are easier to recognize in the code. The rules for naming a symbolic constant are the same as for variables.

Notice that the keyword, Global, is optional; including Global in the Const statement tells Visual Basic to create a **global constant,** which is a constant that can be referred to by every procedure in every form and module in the project. If you omit the Global keyword from the Const statement, the constant is available only to the form or procedure in which it is created.

Symbolic constants allow you to use meaningful words in place of values that are less clear. The symbolic constant PI, for example, is much more meaningful than 3.141593, the numeric value of pi. Once you create the symbolic constant, you can then use the constant's name, instead of its value, in the code.

The formula for the area of a circle, $A = \pi r^2$, points out the differences among literal constants, symbolic constants, and variables. Converted into Visual Basic code, the formula is: Area = PI * Radius ^ 2. Area and Radius are variables, PI is a symbolic constant and 2 is a literal constant. The ^ symbol is the exponentiation operator that tells Visual Basic to raise the variable Radius to the second power.

You will create two symbolic constants for this application: RED and WHITE. You will assign the color code for red (&HFF&) to a symbolic constant named RED and the color code for white (&HFFFFFF) to a symbolic constant named WHITE. Using the symbolic constants instead of the color codes will make your code much easier to enter and to understand. In this application, you will use the RED symbolic constant to change the BackColor property of the reserved seats to red and the WHITE symbolic constant to change the BackColor property of the available seats to white. (The seats, remember, are in the FrmSeat form.)

Let's take a moment and look at these strange color codes. What does &HFFFFFF mean? First, &H is Visual Basic's way of denoting that this is the beginning of a hexadecimal number. Hexadecimal is base-16 notation—a compact way of expressing numbers as the computer actually stores them in memory. Each hexadecimal digit represents one of the 16 values ranging from 0 to 15 (expressed by 0–9, A–F). The value &HFFFFFF is then nothing more than a number (16,777,215 to be exact).

How does Visual Basic translate that number into color? Each pair of digits in hexadecimal notation represents the amount of one of the primary colors that can be combined to create the final color. Each color's range is from 0 to 255 and is just a scale representing the amount of each color.

To enter the constant definitions:

1 Type the two constant definitions into the module, as shown in Figure 7-29.

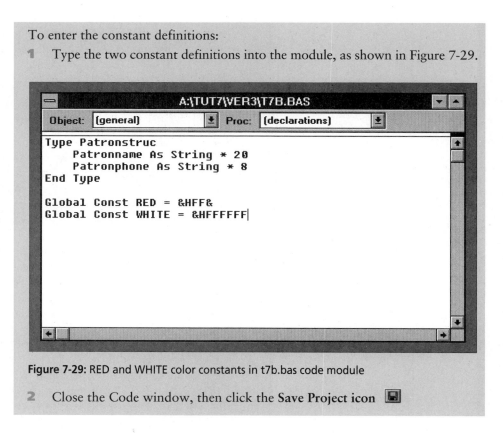

```
A:\TUT7\VER3\T7B.BAS

Object: [general]        Proc: [declarations]

Type Patronstruc
    Patronname As String * 20
    Patronphone As String * 8
End Type

Global Const RED = &HFF&
Global Const WHITE = &HFFFFFF|
```

Figure 7-29: RED and WHITE color constants in t7b.bas code module

2 Close the Code window, then click the **Save Project icon**

You will return to this module later to enter the initialization procedure. The procedure (called a user-defined **sub procedure**) will be called upon (**invoked**) from two forms. Remember from Lesson A that a module makes procedures, variables, and constants globally available to all forms in the project.

Coding the FrmSeat Form's Load Event Procedure

The pseudocode for the FrmSeat form's Load event procedure is shown in Figure 7-30.

```
1.  Declare variables: Seatnum and Patronrec

2.  Open the random access file

3.  Repeat for Seatnum = 1 to 48 by 1

            Read the record corresponding to the value in the Seatnum variable

            If the record contains a name then

                    change the BackColor property of the appropriate seat to red

                    (the appropriate seat's Index is one less than the value in the

                    Seatnum variable)

            End If

    End Repeat For
```

Figure 7-30: Pseudocode for the FrmSeat Load event procedure

According to the pseudocode, you must first declare the variables. This event procedure requires two variables: Seatnum and Patronrec. Seatnum will be an Integer variable that will store the seat number. Patronrec, a record variable, will store the patron's name and phone number. The Seatnum variable will be used by the For...Next loop. The Patronrec variable will be used by the Open statement.

After the necessary variables are declared, the random access file is opened. A For...Next loop is then used to read the 48 records in the file. If the record contains a patron's name, then the BackColor property of that seat is set to red.

To code the FrmSeat form's Load event procedure:

1 Double-click on **an empty area in the FrmSeat form.** The form's Load event procedure appears. The Code window's title bar should say T7BSEAT.FRM.

2 Maximize the Code window, press [**Tab**], then type **dim Seatnum as Integer, Patronrec as Patronstruc** and press [Enter].

You will now enter the instruction to open the random access file. The syntax of the Open statement for random access files, you may remember, is **Open** *filename* [**For** *mode*] **As #** *filenumber* **Len** = *reclen*.

3 Depending on your version of Visual Basic and the location of your Student Disk, type one of the following statements:

open "a:\tut7\ver2\t7b.dat" for random as # 1 len = len(Patronrec)

open "b:\tut7\ver2\t7b.dat" for random as # 1 len = len(Patronrec)

open "a:\tut7\ver3\t7b.dat" for random as # 1 len = len(Patronrec)

open "b:\tut7\ver3\t7b.dat" for random as # 1 len = len(Patronrec)

4 Press [**Enter**].

Keep in mind that this part of the code is only temporary. You will remove it when you code the File form in Lesson C. It's fine for now because it lets you test the application without having to enter a filename each time you run it.

You can now enter the For...Next loop.

5   Enter the instructions shown in Figure 7-31.

declare variables
open file
read record
color reserved seats red

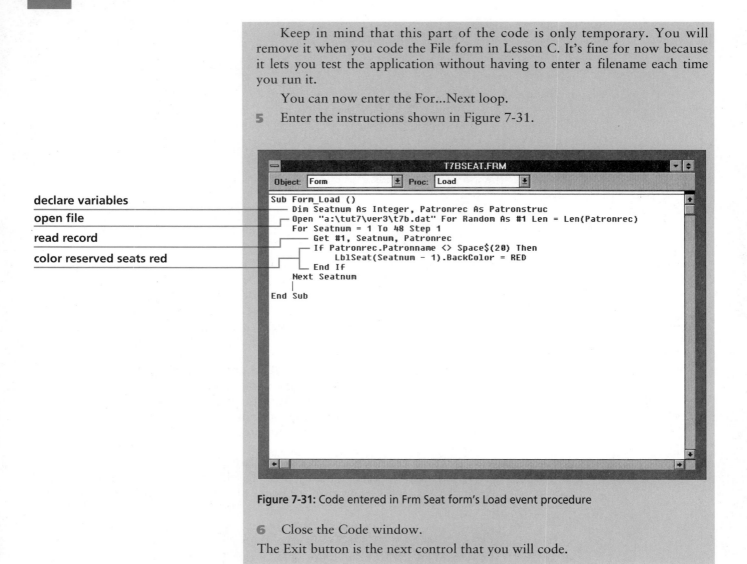

```
T7BSEAT.FRM
Object: Form          Proc: Load

Sub Form_Load ()
    Dim Seatnum As Integer, Patronrec As Patronstruc
    Open "a:\tut7\ver3\t7b.dat" For Random As #1 Len = Len(Patronrec)
    For Seatnum = 1 To 48 Step 1
        Get #1, Seatnum, Patronrec
        If Patronrec.Patronname <> Space$(20) Then
            LblSeat(Seatnum - 1).BackColor = RED
        End If
    Next Seatnum

End Sub
```

Figure 7-31: Code entered in Frm Seat form's Load event procedure

6   Close the Code window.

The Exit button is the next control that you will code.

Coding the Exit button

The Exit button should simply close the file and then end the application.

To code the Exit button:

1   Maximize the form, then double-click the **Exit button** to open its Code window. The Click event procedure appears. Press [**Tab**], type **close #1** and press [**Enter**], and then type **end** and press [**Enter**].

2   Close the Code window.

The Initialize button is next.

Coding the Initialize Button

Recall that Mr. Phillips told you that an Initialize button would be helpful as long as a warning message was present. The initialization procedure will need to be called upon (or invoked) from two places in the project. First, all new random access files should be initialized. This will remove any "garbage" left on the disk from previous files. This initialization of new files will be invoked from the FrmFile form you will develop in Lesson C. Second, the user should be able to invoke the initialization procedure from the FrmSeat form. That way, whenever a play closes, the user can clear the records to make room for reservations for the next play. The manager can also initialize practice files used to train new staff members.

User-Defined Sub Procedures

You are already familiar with procedures. Clicking a Command button, for example, causes an event procedure to occur, provided you have added the appropriate code. The Exit button you just coded is the most recent example. The initialization procedure for the Cole's Playhouse application must be invoked from two places in the program. In fact, it must be invoked from two different forms—the existing FrmSeat form and the FrmFile form you will code later in Lesson C. You could place the code for the initialization procedure in both forms, but that would be inefficient because several lines of code would be duplicated. A better approach is to place the initialization code in the code module (t7b.bas) and then have each form invoke it as needed. It can be invoked from the FrmFile form whenever a new file is created and from the FrmSeat form whenever the Initialize button is clicked. By placing it in the code module, you make it global—available to all forms—in the same way you previously made the symbolic constants, RED and WHITE, global. A procedure that you create that can be invoked from one or more places in your program is called a **user-defined sub procedure**, often just called a user-defined procedure. (A user-defined procedure does not have to be defined in a code module unless it must be available to more than one form. Often it will be **local**—available only to the form in which it is defined.)

A user-defined procedure can receive variables or constants that you send (**pass**) to it. These variables or constants are called **parameters.** You pass parameters when you want the procedure to process them in some way. For example, you might define and code a procedure that sorts a list of numbers. The parameters you pass would be the numbers themselves, and the procedure would then sort (and perhaps display) them. (You will learn how to pass parameters in Tutorial 9.)

You invoke a user-defined procedure with the **Call** statement. The syntax of the Call statement is: **Call** *procedurename* [(*parameterlist*)] The rules for naming a procedure are the same as those for naming variables and constants. The brackets indicate that the parameter list is optional and, if included, must be enclosed in parentheses. Parameters themselves must be separated by commas.

Some procedures do not require that variables or constants be passed to them. That will be the case in the initialization procedure you are about to define and code. It will work directly on the random access file and the BackColor property of the FrmSeat form's label array. Therefore, the call to it will not contain a parameter list.

Because the theater holds 48 seats, you will initialize 48 records. The pseudocode for the Initialize button is shown in Figure 7-32.

```
1.  Declare variables: Seatnum and Patronrec

2.  Assign 20 spaces to the Patronname field variable

3.  Assign 8 spaces to the Patronphone field variable

4.  Repeat for Seatnum = 1 to 48 by 1

            Write the record variable to the file

            Change BackColor property to white

    End Repeat For
```

Figure 7-32: Pseudocode for the Initialize button

Because the initialization procedure must be invoked from two places in the project, it should be defined in the t7b.bas module. That will make it global—available to all forms in the project.

To code the initialization procedure:

1 Restore the FrmSeat form, click **T7B.BAS** in the Project window, and then click the **View Code button** to display the t7b.bas module. The general Declarations section you entered earlier appears.

You define a user-defined procedure by selecting **New Procedure...** from the View menu in the menu bar.

2 Click **View**, then click **New Procedure...**. Type **Initialize** in the name box, then press [**Enter**]. A procedure window is opened so you can enter code. Notice the familiar *Sub* and *End Sub* keywords you've seen in all the event procedures you have coded. As with event procedures, your code will be entered between these two keywords. The empty set of parentheses indicates that no parameters will be passed.

3 Enter the instructions shown in Figure 7-33.

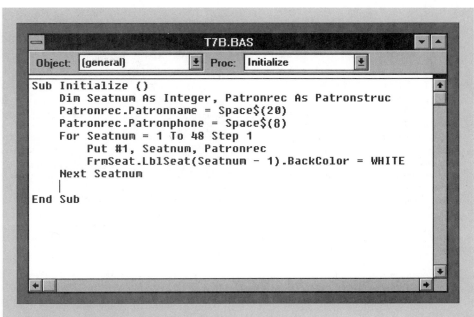

```
Sub Initialize ()
    Dim Seatnum As Integer, Patronrec As Patronstruc
    Patronrec.Patronname = Space$(20)
    Patronrec.Patronphone = Space$(8)
    For Seatnum = 1 To 48 Step 1
        Put #1, Seatnum, Patronrec
        FrmSeat.LblSeat(Seatnum - 1).BackColor = WHITE
    Next Seatnum
    
End Sub
```

Figure 7-33: Code entered in the Initialize sub procedure

The instructions begin by declaring two variables: Seatnum and Patronrec. The Seatnum variable will store the record number while the Patronrec variable, a record variable, will store the record itself. (Recall that the record contains two fields: Patronname and Patronphone.) The next two instructions use the Space$ function to assign spaces to the field variables contained in the record variable. A For...Next loop is used to write the record to the file 48 times and assign each seat a BackColor of white. One of the statements you just entered, **FrmSeat.LblSeat(Seatnum – 1).BackColor = WHITE**, deserves a closer look. Notice that the index of the LblSeat array is *one less* than the Seatnum variable that is used to write record numbers 1 through 48 to the file. Notice also that the name of the form (FrmSeat) is used as a prefix to the LblSeat control array. Since the procedure is defined outside the FrmSeat form, you must tell Visual Basic to which form you want the statement to apply. You'll learn more about this later in this tutorial.

Even though you have defined and coded the initialization procedure, it must be invoked from somewhere in the project. You can do that now by adding the Call statement to the Initialize button's Click event procedure in the FrmSeat form.

4   Close the t7b.bas module and **save** the project. Open and maximize the FrmSeat form. Double-click the **Initialize button** to open its code window.

    One line of code is all that's needed.

5   Press [**Tab**], then type **Call Initialize** and press [**Enter**].

    The Call statement tells Visual Basic to find and execute the Initialize procedure that you placed in the t7b.bas module in step 3.

The Initialize button is a useful, but potentially dangerous, feature because it can destroy valuable data. Clicking it causes Visual Basic to write over every record in the file. In Exercise 2 following Lesson C, you will create a message box that will allow the user to confirm his or her desire to initialize a file.

Let's test the Initialize button.

6   Close the Code window, restore the form to its standard size, then **save and run** the application. Because the t7b.dat file does not yet exist, Visual Basic creates and then opens a random access file named t7b.dat. The FrmSeat form appears on the screen. (Don't be concerned if some, or all, of the seats appear red; it simply means that your data file, which has not yet been initialized, contains some "garbage.")

7   Click the **Initialize button**. Visual Basic calls the Initialize sub procedure and initializes 48 records in the random access file. Note that any red seats turn white as soon as you click the Initialize button. Click the **Exit button**. Visual Basic closes the t7b.dat data file and ends the application.

Now let's code the 48 Label controls that represent the 48 seats.

Coding the LblSeat Control Array

The pseudocode for the LblSeat control array's Click event procedure is shown in Figure 7-34.

```
1.   Declare variables: Seatnum and Patronrec

2.   Assign the Index argument + 1 to the Seatnum variable

3.   Assign the Seatnum variable to the LblSeatnum control in the FrmPatron form

4.   If the seat's BackColor property is set to red then

           read the record corresponding to the value in the Seatnum variable

           assign the name and phone number from the record to the TxtName and

               TxtPhone controls in the FrmPatron form

     Else

           assign the null string to the TxtName and TxtPhone controls in the

               FrmPatron form

     End If

5.   Display the FrmPatron form

6.   Set the focus to the TxtName box in the FrmPatron form
```

Figure 7-34: Pseudocode for the LblSeat control array

This is the event that takes place whenever the user clicks on any of the 48 seats. The LblSeat control array will display the FrmPatron form on the screen, with the number of the chosen seat displayed in the LblSeatnum control. If the seat is reserved, the control array will also display the patron's name and phone number in the appropriate Text boxes in the FrmPatron form. If the seat is available, the name and phone number will be blank when the FrmPatron form appears. In the next section you will learn how to refer to a control in another form.

Referencing a Control in Another Form

When writing Visual Basic code for a form or one of its controls, you can refer to another control in the same form by using the control's name. For example, if the LblSeatnum control were in the same form as the LblSeat control array, you could refer to it as simply *LblSeatnum*. In this case, however, the LblSeatnum control is not in the same form as the control array—the LblSeatnum control is in the FrmPatron form and the control array is in the FrmSeat form. To refer to a control in another form, you simply precede the control's name with the name of the form in which it is contained. You separate the form name from the control's name with a period, like this: *Form.Control*. For example, to refer to the LblSeatnum control in the FrmPatron form, you will need to use *FrmPatron.LblSeatnum*; otherwise, Visual Basic will not be able to locate the control. To refer to the property of a control contained in another form, you use the following syntax: *Form.Control.Property*. Note that you already used this technique in the Initialize sub procedure. The *FrmSeat.LblSeat (Seatnum – 1).BackColor = WHITE* instruction was entered in the t7b.bas code module, but it affected the LblSeat control in the FrmSeat form.

To begin coding the LblSeat control array:

1 Maximize the FrmSeat form and double-click **any one of the Label controls in the LblSeat control array**. Recall that the controls in a control array use the same Code window, which you can open by double-clicking any of the controls in the array. The Code window for the LblSeat control array appears.

According to the pseudocode, your first step is to declare the variables. This event procedure will need two variables: Seatnum and Patronrec. Seatnum (an Integer variable) will store the seat number and Patronrec (a record variable) will store the record.

2 Maximize the Code window, press [Tab], then type **dim Seatnum as integer, Patronrec as Patronstruc** and press [Enter].

Now assign the appropriate seat number to the Seatnum variable. Recall that Visual Basic records, in the Index argument, the Index property of the control that is receiving the event. In this case, for example, if the user clicks seat number 1 (the LblSeat(0) control), Visual Basic records a zero in the Index argument; if the user clicks seat number 45 (the LblSeat(44) control), Visual Basic records the number 44 in the Index argument, and so on. Notice that the Indent argument will always be *one less* than the seat number. That means that you will need to add one to the Index argument in order to display the proper seat number in the FrmPatron form.

3   Type **Seatnum = Index + 1** and press [Enter].

Now assign the seat number to the LblSeatnum control in the FrmPatron form.

4   Type **FrmPatron.LblSeatnum.caption = Seatnum** and press [Enter].

According to the pseudocode, the next step is to see if the seat is reserved. In this application, the reserved seats will have a BackColor setting of red; the available seats will have a BackColor setting of white. If the BackColor setting is red, then you will need to read the patron's name and phone number from the random access file in order to display that information in the FrmPatron form. If the BackColor is not red, then the name and phone number should be blank when the FrmPatron form appears. You can use the If...Then...Else selection structure, which you learned in Tutorial 4, to compare the BackColor property to the global symbolic constant named RED.

5   Enter the selection structure shown in Figure 7-35.

enter this selection structure

```
T7BSEAT.FRM
Object: LblSeat()          Proc: Click

Sub LblSeat_Click (Index As Integer)
    Dim Seatnum As Integer, Patronrec As Patronstruc
    Seatnum = Index + 1
    FrmPatron.LblSeatnum.Caption = Seatnum
    If LblSeat(Index).BackColor = RED Then
        Get #1, Seatnum, Patronrec
        FrmPatron.TxtName.Text = Patronrec.Patronname
        FrmPatron.TxtPhone.Text = Patronrec.Patronphone
    Else
        FrmPatron.TxtName.Text = ""
        FrmPatron.TxtPhone.Text = ""
    End If

End Sub
```

Figure 7-35: Selection structure entered in LblSeat Click event procedure

According to the pseudocode, you still need to display the FrmPatron form on the screen and then set the focus to the TxtName control. You can use the Show method to display the form.

Using the Show Method

The syntax of the Show method is *Form*.**Show**, where *Form* is the name of the form you want to display or show. The **Show method** loads the form into the computer's memory, if necessary, then displays the form on the screen.

To finish coding the LblSeat control array, then test the application:

1 Align the blinking insertion point directly below the first character in the End If Statement. Type **FrmPatron.show** and press [**Enter**].

Now set the focus to the TxtName control in the FrmPatron form.

2 Type **FrmPatron.TxtName.setfocus** and press [**Enter**].

Let's see how the application works so far.

3 Close the Code window, then save **and run** the application. The FrmSeat form appears on the screen, with all of the seats colored white.

4 Click **seat number 2**. The FrmPatron form appears on the screen with the number 2 in the LblSeatnum control. The name and phone number Text boxes are empty because the ticket for this seat has not yet been purchased. The focus is in the TxtName control.

5 Click the **Exit button** in the FrmSeat form. Visual Basic closes the t7b.dat random access file and ends the application.

You have finished coding the FrmSeat form. You can minimize the form, as you won't be needing it for a while.

6 Click the **FrmSeat form's Minimize button**. A form icon with the Cole's Playhouse caption appears at the bottom of the screen. The t7bpatrn.frm form appears on the screen.

tips

. . . .

▶ If the t7bpatrn form does not appear on the screen, click **T7BPATRN.FRM** in the Project window, then click the View Form button.

▶ If you don't see the form's icon, it is possible that the Project window is covering it, or that there are too many applications currently minimized on the screen. It might be helpful to close the applications you are not using.

Coding the FrmPatron Form

The FrmPatron form allows the user to enter the ticket information, cancel the ticket information, and return to the main form—the FrmSeat form. Let's begin by coding the Enter Ticket button.

Coding the Enter Ticket Button

The pseudocode for the Enter Ticket button's Click event procedure is shown in Figure 7-36.

```
1.  Declare variables: Seatnum and Patronrec

2.  Assign the seat number to the Seatnum variable

3.  Assign the name and the phone number to the Patronrec variable

4.  Write the Patronrec record to the random access file

5.  Change the BackColor property of the seat to red

6.  Hide the FrmPatron form
```

Figure 7-36: Pseudocode for the Enter Ticket button

The first step is to declare the variables. This procedure will need two variables: Seatnum and Patronrec. Seatnum will store the seat number, which will also be the record number in the file. Patronrec, a record variable, will store the record—the name and phone number of the patron.

To code the Enter Ticket button:

1   Double-click the **Enter Ticket button** to open its Code window. In the Click event procedure, press [**Tab**], then type **dim Seatnum as integer, Patronrec as Patronstruc** and press [**Enter**].

The next step is to assign the appropriate values to the variables. First assign the seat number to the Seatnum variable. The seat number is in the Caption property of the LblSeatnum control.

2   Type **Seatnum = LblSeatnum.Caption** and press [**Enter**].

Now assign the name and phone number to the field variables in the Patronrec record variable. The name is in the TxtName control, and the phone number is in the TxtPhone control.

3   Type **Patronrec.Patronname = TxtName.Text** and press [**Enter**].

4   Type **Patronrec.Patronphone = TxtPhone.Text** and press [**Enter**].

After declaring the variables and assigning the appropriate values to them, you are ready to write the record to the random access file. Recall that you do that with the Put statement, whose syntax is **Put #** *filenumber,* *[recordnumber], variablename.*

5   Type **put #1, Seatnum, Patronrec** and press [**Enter**].

After a seat has been reserved, its BackColor property should be set to red. Recall that the value currently in the Seatnum variable is *one more* than the value in the seat's Index property. So, to refer to the appropriate seat in the LblSeat array, you will need to subtract 1 from the Seatnum variable. For example, if the Seatnum variable contains the number 2, you will want to set the BackColor property of the control named LblSeat(1) to red.

6   Type **FrmSeat.LblSeat(Seatnum – 1).BackColor = RED** and press [**Enter**].

The last step in the pseudocode is to hide the FrmPatron form, so the user can view the FrmSeat form again. You can use the Hide method to do so.

Using the Hide Method

You can use Visual Basic's **Hide method** to hide a form. A hidden form is removed from the screen, but it still remains in memory. The syntax of the Hide method is *Form*.**Hide**, where *Form* is the name of the form you want to hide. Let's use the Hide method to remove the FrmPatron form from the screen.

To finish coding the CmdEnter control (the Enter Ticket button), then test the application:

1   Type **FrmPatron.Hide** and press [**Enter**].

2   Compare your code with the code shown in Figure 7-37 and make any needed corrections before continuing to the next step.

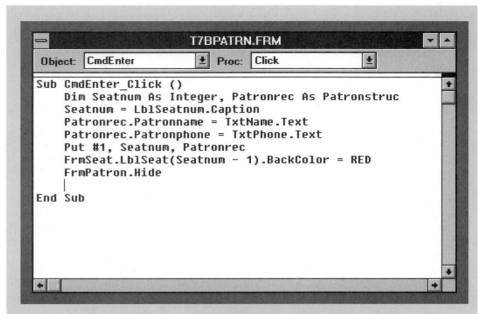

Figure 7-37: Code entered in the Enter Ticket button's Click event procedure

3 Close the Code window.

Now let's test the Enter Ticket button.

4 **Save and run** the application. Visual Basic opens the t7b.dat data file and the FrmSeat form appears on the screen. Click seat number 2. The FrmPatron form appears on the screen, with **seat number 2** in the LblSeatnum control.

5 Type **Khalid Patel** as the name, then press [**Tab**], and then type **444-4444** as the phone number. Click the **Enter Ticket button**. Visual Basic writes the name and phone number to the second record in the random access file. The FrmSeat form now appears on the screen with seat number 2 colored red.

You can also use the Enter Ticket button to edit an existing record.

6 Click **seat number 2**. The FrmPatron form appears on the screen. Notice that, in addition to the seat number, the patron's name and phone number also appear in the form.

7 Change the phone number to **444-4443**, then click the **Enter Ticket button**. The new information overwrites the existing record in the file.

8 Click the **Exit button** to end the application.

9 If you want, you can verify that the record was written to the file by switching to Notepad and opening the t7b.dat random access file. Don't save the file after exiting Notepad.

Let's code the Cancel Ticket button next.

Coding the Cancel Ticket Button

The Cancel Ticket button allows the user to remove a patron's name and phone number from the random access file. The pseudocode for the Cancel Ticket button's Click event procedure is shown in Figure 7-38.

```
1.   Declare variables: Seatnum and Patronrec

2.   Assign the seat number to the Seatnum variable

3.   Assign 20 spaces to the Patronname field variable

4.   Assign 8 spaces to the Patronphone field variable

5.   Write the Patronrec record to the random access file

6.   Change the BackColor property of the seat to white

7.   Hide the FrmPatron form
```

Figure 7-38: Pseudocode for the Cancel Ticket button

Notice that the pseudocode shown in Figure 7-38 is almost identical to the pseudocode shown in Figure 7-36. That means that the code for the Cancel Ticket button will be almost identical to the code for the Enter Ticket button. For that reason, you will copy the code from the Enter Ticket button to the Cancel Ticket button, and then make the necessary changes.

To code the Cancel Ticket button, then test the application:

1   Double-click the **Enter Ticket button.** The CmdEnter control's Click event procedure displays.

2   Highlight all of the instructions between the Sub statement and the End Sub statement. (Do not highlight either the Sub statement or the End Sub statement.) When the appropriate instructions are highlighted, press **[Ctrl][c]** to copy the instructions to the Windows Clipboard.

3   Click the **down arrow in the Code window's Object box,** scroll the list box, and then click **CmdCancel** in the drop-down list. The CmdCancel Click event procedure appears.

4   Press **[Ctrl][v]** to paste the instructions in the CmdCancel Click event procedure.

You will need to make three changes to the code in the Code window. When a ticket is cancelled, you will tell Visual Basic to write spaces over the existing name and phone number in the file. You can use the Space$ function, which you learned in Lesson A, to do that. (To cancel a record having a numeric field, you would write a zero over the existing data in that field.) You also need to change the BackColor property of the LblSeat control to white.

5   Enter the changes shown in Figure 7-39.

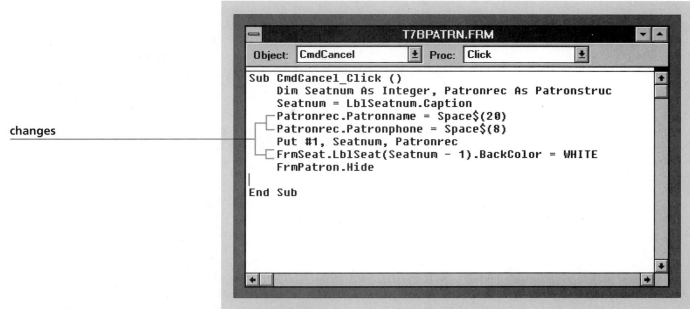

changes

```
                            T7BPATRN.FRM
Object: CmdCancel        ±   Proc: Click          ±

Sub CmdCancel_Click ()
    Dim Seatnum As Integer, Patronrec As Patronstruc
    Seatnum = LblSeatnum.Caption
   ┌Patronrec.Patronname = Space$(20)
   └Patronrec.Patronphone = Space$(8)
    Put #1, Seatnum, Patronrec
   ┌FrmSeat.LblSeat(Seatnum - 1).BackColor = WHITE
    FrmPatron.Hide

End Sub
```

Figure 7-39: Code entered in the Cancel Ticket button's Click event procedure

6   Close the Code window, then **save and run** the application. Notice that seat number 2 is colored red, which indicates that it is reserved.

7   Click **seat number 2**. Khalid Patel's record appears in the FrmPatron form. Click the **Cancel Ticket button**. Visual Basic replaces Khalid Patel's record with spaces. When the FrmSeat form appears again, seat number 2 is colored white.

8   Click the **Exit button** to end the application.

9   If you want, you can verify that the record was cancelled by switching to Notepad and opening the t7b.dat random access file. Don't save the file as you exit Notepad.

The last control you need to code in the FrmPatron form is the Return to Main button.

Coding the Return to Main Button

The Return to Main button allows the user to return to the FrmSeat form without either entering or cancelling a ticket. The user might need to use this button if he or she accidentally clicked the wrong seat, or he or she might simply be interested in the name and phone number of a patron. This button will simply hide the FrmPatron form.

To code the Return to Main button, then test the application:

1   Double-click the **Return to Main button**. The CmdReturn control's Click event procedure appears. Press **[Tab]**, then type **FrmPatron.hide** and press **[Enter]**.

2   Close the Code window, then **save and run** the application. The FrmSeat form appears on the screen. All of the seats are colored white because no seat has yet been reserved.

3   Click **seat number 33**. The FrmPatron form appears. Type **Sue Billings** as the name, press **[Tab]**, then type **111-1111** as the phone number. Click the **Enter Ticket button**. Visual Basic writes the record to the file, then hides the FrmPatron form. When the FrmSeat form reappears, seat number 33 is colored red.

Let's verify that you entered Sue Billings's information correctly.

4   Click **seat number 33**. The FrmPatron form appears with Sue Billings's information showing.

In some applications, it's convenient to be able to move a form to another part of the screen. For example, you might want to have Notepad visible alongside a form from your application so you can type and save notes pertaining to the development of your program. In the current application, you might want to move the form to determine if a seat currently covered by the FrmPatron form is reserved.

5   Place the mouse pointer on the FrmPatron form's title bar and drag the form to another part of the screen. When the FrmPatron form is where you want it, release the mouse button.

6   Click the **Return to Main button**. The FrmSeat form appears once again.

7   Click the **Exit button**. Visual Basic returns to the design screen.

You have now completed Lesson B. You can either take a break or complete the exercises and questions at the end of the lesson.

S U M M A R Y

To add a new form to an application:

■   Click File, then click New Form. You can also click the New Form icon 🗋.

To add an existing form to an application:

■   Click File, then click Add File.....

To specify the startup form:

■   Click Options, then click Project.... In the Project Options dialog box, click Start Up Form, then click the down arrow button in the Setting box. Click the name of the startup form, then click the OK button.

To create a symbolic constant:

■   Use the Const statement. Its syntax is [Global] Const *constantname* = *expression*.

To create a sub procedure in a module:

▨ Open a code module and select New Procedure... from the View menu.

To invoke a sub procedure:

▨ Use the Call statement. Its syntax is **Call** *procedurename* [(*parameter list*)].

To reference the property of a control in another form:

▨ Use the syntax *Form.Control.Property*.

To show a form:

▨ Use the Show method. Its syntax is *Form*.**Show**.

To remove a form from the screen, but leave the form in memory:

▨ Use the Hide method. Its syntax is *Form*.**Hide**.

Q U E S T I O N S

1. When a multiform project is run, Visual Basic automatically loads and displays the _____ form.
   a. beginning
   b. first
   c. initial
   d. loaded
   e. startup

2. You use Visual Basic's _____ menu to specify the startup form.
   a. Edit
   b. File
   c. Options
   d. Project
   e. Startup

3. You create a symbolic constant with the _____ statement.
   a. Const
   b. Constant
   c. Global
   d. Sym
   e. Symbolic

4. Which of the following will create a symbolic constant that can be used by every form or module in the application?
   a. Const PI = 3.141593
   b. Constant PI = 3.141593
   c. Global PI = 3.141593
   d. Global Const PI = 3.141593
   e. Symbolic Const PI = 3.141593

5. Which of the following will create a symbolic constant that can be used only in the form or event procedure in which it is defined?
   a. Const ONE = 1
   b. Constant ONE = 1
   c. Global ONE = 1
   d. Global Const ONE = 1
   e. Symbolic Const ONE = 1

6. Assume that you are coding an object in the FrmFriends form and you want to refer to the Text property of the TxtPhone Text box, which is also in the FrmFriends form. Which of the following could you enter into the Code window?
   a. FrmFriends.Text
   b. FrmFriends.Text.TxtPhone
   c. Text.TxtPhone
   d. TxtPhone.Text
   e. TxtPhone.Text.FrmFriends

7. Assume that you are coding an object in the FrmFriends form and you want to refer to the Text property of the TxtPhone Text box, which is in the FrmNumbers form. Which of the following could you enter into the Code window?
   a. FrmFriends.TxtPhone.Text
   b. FrmNumbers.TxtPhone.Text
   c. Text.TxtPhone
   d. TxtPhone.Text
   e. TxtPhone.Text.FrmNumbers

8. Which of the following methods will display a form?
   a. Access
   b. Display
   c. Form
   d. Show

9. Which of the following methods will remove a form from the screen, but keep it in memory?
   a. Blank
   b. Clear
   c. Erase
   d. Hide
   e. Remove

E X E R C I S E S

Note: In these exercises you will be asked to use various colors. The codes for these colors are:

Black	&H0&
Red	&HFF&
Green	&HFF00&
Yellow	&HFFFF&
Blue	&HFF0000
Magenta	&HFF00FF
Cyan	&HFFFF00
White	&HFFFFFF

1. Recall that you created a copyright screen in Tutorial 1. Now that you know how to manage a multiform project, you can include the copyright screen in your projects. In this exercise, you will add the copyright screen to the grade application created in Tutorial 5. The copyright screen is saved in a file named t1c.frm, which is in either the tut1\ver2 or the tut1\ver3 directory on your Student Disk. The grade application is saved in a file named t5c.frm, which is in either the tut5\ver2 or the tut5\ver3 directory on your Student Disk.

    a. Depending on your version of Visual Basic, use File Manager to copy the t1c.frm file and the t5c.frm file to either the tut7\ver2 or the tut7\ver3 directory.

    b. Launch Visual Basic, if necessary, and open a new project. Remove the Form1.frm file and the .VBX files.

    c. Add the t5c.frm file to the project. Save the form file as t7grade1.

    d. Add the t1c.frm file to the project. Save the form file as t7copy1.

    e. Save the project as t7lbe1.

    f. Make the FrmCopyright form the startup form.

    g. Remove the End statement from the copyright screen's Exit button. When the user clicks the Exit button, the FrmGrade form should appear and the FrmCopyright screen should be hidden.

    h. Save and run the application. Click the Exit button in the copyright screen. The FrmGrade form should appear. Click the Exit button in the grade application. The application should end.

    i. Print the code for the copyright screen only.

2. a. Create the user interface shown in Figure 7-40.

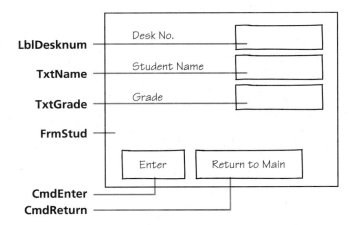

Figure 7-40

    b. Change the form's Name property to FrmStud. Save the form as t7stud2. Save the project as t7lbe2.

    c. Add a new form to the t7lbe2 project. Create the user interface shown in Figure 7-41.

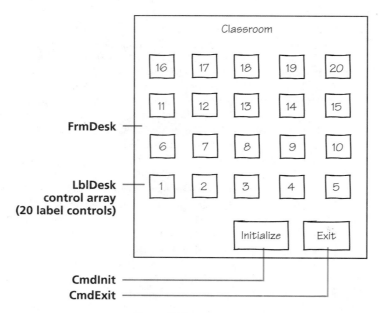

FrmDesk ⎯

LblDesk
control array
(20 label controls)

CmdInit ⎯⎯⎯⎯
CmdExit ⎯⎯⎯⎯

Figure 7-41

(Hint: Place the first label control on the form. Change its name property to LblDesk. Set any other properties. Copy the control to the clipboard. Then paste the control in the form 19 times.)

d. Change the form's name property to FrmDesk. Save the form as t7desk2. Save the project as t7lbe2.

e. The FrmDesk form should be the startup form.

f. Add a code module to the project. Define a record structure named Studstruc. The Studstruc contains two fields: Studname and Studgrade. Studname is a 20-character String field and grade is a 1-character String field.

g. Save the code module as t7lbe2.

h. Code the FrmDesk form's Load event procedure according to the pseudocode shown in Figure 7-42. Name the random access file t7lbe2.dat. The code for blue is &HFF0000.

```
1.   Declare variables: Desknum and Studrec

2.   Open the random access file

3.   Repeat for Desknum = 1 to 20 by 1

          Read the record corresponding to the value in the Desknum variable

          If the record contains a name then

               change the BackColor property of the appropriate desk to blue

               (the appropriate desk's Index is one less than the value in the

               Desknum variable)

          End If

     End Repeat For
```

Figure 7-42

i. Code the Initialize button in the FrmDesk form so that it initializes the t7lbe2.dat random access file for 20 records only. Don't forget to change the BackColor property to white (&HFFFFFF).

j. Code the Exit button so that it closes the data file and ends the application when clicked.

k. Code the LblDesk control array's Click event procedure according to the pseudocode shown in Figure 7-43.

```
1.  Declare variables: Desknum and Studrec

2.  Assign the Index argument + 1 to the Desknum variable

3.  Assign the Desknum variable to the LblDesknum control in the FrmStud form

4.  If the desk's BackColor property is set to blue then

            read the record corresponding to the value in the Desknum variable

            assign the name and grade from the record to the TxtName and

                  TxtGrade controls in the FrmStud form

      Else

            assign the null string to the TxtName and TxtGrade controls in the

                  FrmStud form

      End If

5.  Display the FrmStud form

6.  Set the focus to the TxtName box in the FrmStud form
```

Figure 7-43

l. Code the Return to Main button in the FrmStud form so that it hides the FrmStud form.

m. Code the Enter button so that it writes the record to the t7lbe2.dat random access file and hides the FrmStud form. Don't forget to set the BackColor property for the new record.

n. Save and run the application. Click the Initialize button to clear the file of "garbage."

o. Test the application by entering the following records, shown as desk number, student name, and grade:

     12, Mary Jane, A

     7, Fred Jones, C

     20, Ellen Berry, B

     These desks should be blue (&HFF0000).

p. Click desk number 20. Ellen Berry and a grade of B should appear in the FrmStud form. Click the Return to Main button.

q. Click the Exit button to end the application.

r. Print both forms and the code for both forms.

3.   a.   Create the user interface shown in Figure 7-44.

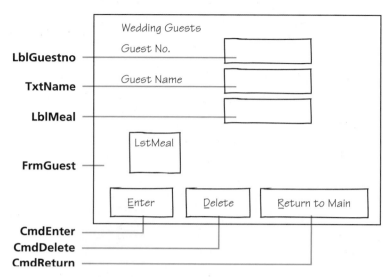

LblGuestno

TxtName

LblMeal

FrmGuest

CmdEnter
CmdDelete
CmdReturn

Figure 7-44

b.   Change the form's name property to FrmGuest. Save the form as t7guest3. Save the project as t7lbe3.

c.   Add the Frmwed.frm form file, which is in either the tut7\ver2 or the tut7\ver3 directory on your Student Disk, to the project. The form allows the user to keep track of the seating arrangement for a wedding party. The user interface is shown in Figure 7-45.

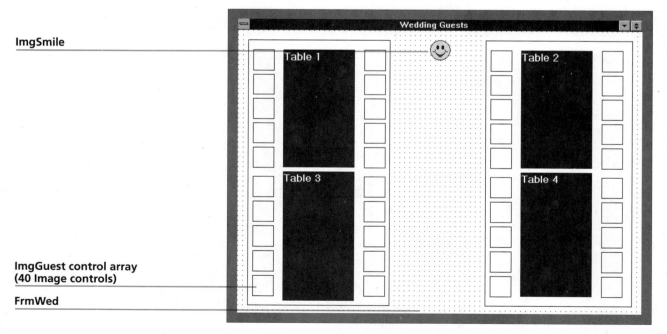

ImgSmile

**ImgGuest control array
(40 Image controls)**

FrmWed

Figure 7-45

d. Save the FrmWed form as t7wed3. Save the project again.

e. The FrmWed form should be the startup form.

f. Add a code module to the project. Define a record structure named Gueststruc. The Gueststruc contains two fields, Guestname, which is a 20-character String field and GuestMeal, a 10-character String field.

g. Save the code module as t7lbe3.

h. Code the form's Load event procedure according to the pseudocode shown in Figure 7-46.

Note the technique of "borrowing" the icon stored in ImgSmile to use in the appropriate seat. The Visible property of ImgSmile is set to False, so it cannot be seen when the application is run.

```
1.  Declare variables: Seatnum and Guestrec

2.  Open the random access file

3.  Repeat for Seatnum = 1 to 40 by 1

        Read the record corresponding to the value in the Seatnum variable

        If the record contains a name then

            set the appropriate seat's picture property to

            the picture property in the ImgSmile control

            (the appropriate seat's Index is one less than the value in

            the Seatnum variable)

        End If

    End Repeat for
```

Figure 7-46

i. Add an Initialize button to the FrmWed form and code it so that it initializes the t7lbe3.dat random access file for 40 records only. It should clear the Picture properties of all indexed images. Use the following statement: **ImgGuest(Seatnum − 1).Picture = LoadPicture()**.

j. Add an Exit button to the FrmWed form and code it so that it closes the file and ends the application when clicked.

k. Code the ImgGuest array's Click event procedure according to the pseudocode shown in Figure 7-47.

```
1.  Declare variables: Seatnum and Guestrec

2.  Assign the Index argument + 1 to the Seatnum variable

3.  Assign the Seatnum variable to the LblGuestnum control in the FrmGuest form

4.  If the Picture property contains an icon (see Hint below) then

            read the record corresponding to the value in the Seatnum variable

            assign the name from the record to the TxtName control in the FrmGuest
                form

            assign the meal from the record to the LblMeal control in the FrmGuest
                form

    Else

            assign the null string to the TxtName control in the FrmGuest form

            assign the null string to the LblMeal control in the FrmGuest form

    End If

5.  Display the FrmGuest form

6.  Set the focus to the TxtName box in the FrmGuest form


Hint: If an Image control does not contain an icon, its Picture property will be
0 (zero).
```

Figure 7-47

l. Code FrmGuest's Load event to use the AddItem method to add "Steak," "Fish," and "Vegetarian" to the LstMeal list box. Code the LstMeal List box's Click event to place the selected item into the caption of the LblMeal control. Use the following code: **LblMeal.Caption = LstMeal.List(LstMeal.ListIndex).** Recall that you worked with list boxes in Tutorial 6.

m. Code the Enter button so that it writes the record to the t7lbe3.dat random access file and assigns the Picture property of ImgSmile to the appropriate member of the ImgGuest array in the FrmWed form. It should also hide the FrmGuest form.

n. Code the Delete button so that it removes the guest's name from the file and eliminates the icon from the appropriate member of the ImgGuest array in the FrmWed form. It should hide the FrmGuest form.

o. Code the Return to Main button so that it hides the FrmGuest form.

p. Save and run the application. Click the Initialize button to clear the file of "garbage."

q. Test the application by entering the following guests anywhere you want:

Sue Shah   select Vegetarian from the List box

Ann Yonkers   select Fish from the List box

Ellen Alders   select Steak from the List box

These seats should have happy faces on them.

r. Click a seat with a smile. The guest's name and meal should appear in the FrmSeat form.

s. Click the Exit button to end the application. Rerun the application; the seats that had been assigned before should still have happy faces on them. Click the Exit button.

t. Print both forms and the code for both forms.

Exercises 4 and 5 are Discovery Exercises.

discovery ▶ 4.

a. Open the t7lbe1.mak project that you created in Exercise 1. Save the copyright screen as t7copy4. Save the grade application as t7grade4. Save the project as t7lbe4.

b. Use the Help screens to research the Timer control and the Timer event. Print both Help screens.

c. Add a Timer control to the copyright screen. Code the Timer control so that it displays the grade form if the user does not touch the keyboard or the mouse for 10 seconds.

d. Save and run the application. Wait for 10 seconds. The grade form should appear on its own.

e. Exit the application. Print the copyright screen form and its code.

discovery ▶ 5.

a. Open the t7lbe2.mak project that you created in Exercise 2.

b. Save the t7stud2.frm form as t7stud5.frm. Save the t7desk2.frm form as t7desk5.frm. Save the t7lbe2.bas code module as t7lbe5. Save the project as t7lbe5.

c. Change the code so that, in addition to changing the BackColor property of the LblDesk control to blue, the program also displays the student's grade in the LblDesk control. Remember that code can be found in both the CmdEnter's Click and FrmDesk's Load event procedures.

d. Now we must change the CmdInit Click event procedure to erase the grades and display the desk number. Remember, Desknum is Index + 1.

e. Save and run the application. Three grades, which correspond to the three records already in the file, should appear in the FrmDesk form.

f. Add the following record: 1, Steven Arito, F

g. Exit the application. Print the code for both forms.

h. Now change the code so that the color assigned to the BackColor property of a desk depends on the grade. This takes place in two locations, the FrmDesk's Load and CmdEnter's Click event procedures. The desks associated with grades of A should be magenta, grades of B should be red, grades of C should be yellow, grades of D should be green, and grades of F should be blue. Refer to the beginning of the exercises for the Color codes.

i. Because desks can be several colors, change the code that checks if the BackColor is blue so that it now checks if the BackColor is not white.

j. Save and run the application. Four grades, which correspond to the four records already in the file, should appear in the FrmDesk form. Each grade should be a different color.

k. Add the following record: 2, Darlene Burnham, D

l. Exit the application. Print the code for both forms.

Completing the Cole's Playhouse Application

The Cole's Playhouse Application

Recall that the Cole's Playhouse application will contain three forms. (The sketch of the user interface for each form is shown in Figure 7-23.) You coded two of the three forms, FrmPatron and FrmSeat, in Lesson B. You will code the FrmFile form in this lesson. The revised TOE chart for the Cole's Playhouse application, including all three forms, is shown in Figure 7-48. (You may want to compare Figure 7-48 with Figure 7-27.)

Task	Object	Event
FrmFile form:		
Open the data file		
Initialize the data file	Command button (OK)	Click
Display the FrmSeat form with reserved seats colored red		
Close the data file	Command button (Cancel)	Click
End the application		
FrmSeat form:		
Get the seat number	48 Label controls (control array)	Click
Display FrmPatron form with patron information		
Display the FrmFile form	Command button (Exit)	Click
Initialize the data file	Command button (Initialize)	Click
FrmPatron form:		
Get name and phone number	2 Text boxes	None
Write the name and phone number to the file	Command button (Enter Ticket)	Click
Color the reserved seats red		
Remove the name and phone number from the file	Command button (Cancel Ticket)	Click
Color the cancelled seats white		
Return to the FrmSeat form	Command button (Return to Main)	Click

Figure 7-48: Revised TOE chart

Let's begin by opening the t7b.mak project that you created in Lesson B.

To open the t7b.mak project:

1   Launch Visual Basic and open the **t7b.mak** file, which is in either the tut7\ver2 or the tut7\ver3 directory on your Student Disk.

    Now save the forms, the module, and the project under a different name.

2   The T7BPATRN.FRM file should be selected in the Project window, so you just need to click **File**, then click **Save File As...**. Type **t7cpatrn** in the Save File As dialog box and press **[Enter]**.

3   Click **T7BSEAT.FRM** in the Project window, click **File**, and then click **Save File As...**. Type **t7cseat** in the Save File As dialog box and press **[Enter]**.

4   Click **T7B.BAS** in the Project window, click **File**, and then click **Save File As...**. Type **t7c** in the Save File As dialog box and press **[Enter]**.

5   Click **File**, then click **Save Project As...**. Type **t7c** in the Save Project As dialog box and press **[Enter]**.

Cole's Playhouse will need to record each play's seating information in a separate file. The application you completed in Lesson B, however, saves the seating information in a file named t7b.dat; it doesn't allow the user to change the filename. You will fix that problem by adding the FrmFile form to the project. When the application is run, the FrmFile form will allow the user to enter either a new filename or an existing filename. Let's add the FrmFile form to the project. The form is named t7cole3.frm on your Student Disk.

To add the t7cole3.frm file to the current project:

1   Click **File**, then click **Add File...**. The t7cole3.frm file is in either the tut7\ver2 or the tut7\ver3 directory on your Student Disk. Click **t7cole3.frm** in the File Name list box, then click the **OK button**. The Option Explicit statement has already been entered into the general Declarations section of the form.

2   The t7cole3.frm file should be selected in the Project window. Click **File**, then click **Save File As...**. Type **t7cfile** and press **[Enter]**. Visual Basic saves the file under its new name.

3   Click the **Save Project icon** 🖫 to save the change you made to the Project window.

4   Click the **View Form button** to view the FrmFile form. The user interface appears on the screen, as shown in Figure 7-49.

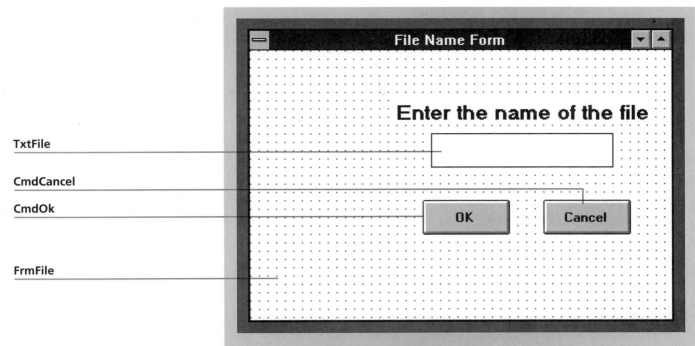

TxtFile

CmdCancel

CmdOk

FrmFile

Figure 7-49: FrmFile user interface

The FrmFile form allows the user to enter the name of the file he or she wants to open. The FrmFile form should be the first form the user sees, so you will need to change the startup form for this project.

5   Click **Options**, then click **Project....** The Project Options dialog box appears with FrmSeat in the Start Up Form box.

6   Click **Start Up Form**, then click the **down arrow button in the Setting box**. A list of form names included in this project appears.

7   Click **FrmFile** in the list box. FrmFile appears in the Start Up Form box.

8   Click the **OK button** to leave the Project Options dialog box. Visual Basic closes the dialog box.

9   **Save** the project.

Let's begin coding the FrmFile form. The Cancel button already contains the End instruction; you just need to code the OK button.

Coding the OK Button

The pseudocode for the OK button is shown in Figure 7-50.

```
1.  Declare variables: Seatnum, Patronrec, and Fname

2.  Assign Text property of TxtFile control to Fname variable

3.  If the filename in the Fname variable does not exist then

            open a new random access file

            initialize the file (call the Initialize procedure)

    Else

            open the existing random access file

            Repeat for Seatnum = 1 to 48 by 1

                Read the record corresponding to the value in the Seatnum variable

                If the record contains a name then

                    change the BackColor property of the seat to red

                    (the seat's Index is one less than the value in the Seatnum variable)

                Else

                    change the BackColor property of the seat to white

                    (the seat's Index is one less than the value in the Seatnum variable)

                End If

            End Repeat For

4.  Display the FrmSeat form

5.  Clear the TxtFile box

6.  Set the focus to the TxtFile box

7.  Hide the FrmFile form
```

Figure 7-50: Pseudocode for the OK button

When the user clicks the OK button, the program checks if the filename entered in the TxtFile Text box exists on the disk. If a file by that name already exists on the disk, the OK button opens the file and reads each record. As before, reserved seats are colored red. If the file does not exist, the OK button creates the random access file and initializes it for 48 records.

You will need to add only a few new instructions to the existing application. Most of the code has already been written in the forms you coded in Lesson B.

First you will declare the necessary variables. The OK button's Click event procedure will use three variables: Seatnum, Patronrec, and Fname. Seatnum will store the seat number, and Patronrec will store the record. Fname, short for "filename," will store the filename entered into the TxtFile Text box.

To begin coding the OK button:

1 Double-click the **OK button**. The CmdOk control's Click event procedure appears. Maximize the Code window, press [**Tab**], then type **dim Seatnum as integer, Patronrec as Patronstruc, Fname as string** and press [**Enter**].

Now assign the Text property of the TxtFile control to the Fname variable.

2 Type **Fname = TxtFile.Text** and press [**Enter**].

You now need to check if the filename already exists on the disk. You can use the Dir$ function to do so.

The Dir$ Function

You can use the Dir$ function to see if a filename exists on the disk. Its syntax is **Dir$**(*filespec*). If you use the Dir$ function with a filename as the *filespec*, the function either returns a copy of the filename (which means that the file exists) or returns an empty string (which means that the file does not exist). The instruction, *Dir$("a:\tut7\ver3\t7b.dat")*, for example, will return T7B.DAT if the t7b.dat file exists; it will return an empty string if the file does not exist.

You can also use a variable name as the *filespec*; in that case, however, you don't include the quotation marks around the *filespec*. For example, if the Fname variable contains the filename, the Dir$ function is correctly written as *Dir$(Fname)*. When the *filespec* does not have quotation marks around it, Visual Basic assumes that it is the name of either a variable or a control. Visual Basic then uses the contents of either the variable or the control as the filename. (The instruction, *Dir$("Fname")*, tells Visual Basic to look on the disk for a file named, literally, Fname.)

To continue coding the CmdOk control:

1 Type **if dir$(Fname) = " "** **then** and press [**Enter**]. Be sure you don't include any spaces between the quotation marks. If the Dir$ function returns an empty string, the file (whose name is stored in the Fname variable) does not exist and the If statement will evaluate as true. If, on the other hand, the Dir$ function does not return an empty string, the file does exist and the If statement will evaluate as false.

Let's code the true branch first. If the file doesn't exist, you need to use the Open statement to both create and then open it.

2   Press [**Tab**], then type **open Fname for random as #1 len = len(Patronrec)** and press [**Enter**]. When you use the name of a variable as the *filename* in the Open statement, notice that you don't enclose it in quotation marks, as you do when the *filename* is the actual name of the file.

You now need to initialize the file for the 48 records corresponding to the 48 seats in the theater. In Lesson B, you coded the user-defined Initialize procedure and placed it in the module you have since saved as t7c.bas. You also coded the FrmSeat form's Initialize button so that whenever the user clicks Initialize, the Call statement invokes the Initialize procedure. Now you will use a Call statement to invoke the Initialize procedure whenever the user creates a new file.

3   Type **Call Initialize** and press [**Enter**].

Now let's code the Else (false) branch of the If...Then...Else statement. Visual Basic will process the instructions in the Else branch only if the filename exists on the disk.

To continue coding the CmdOk control:

1   Press [**Backspace**], then type **else** and press [**Enter**]. (The Else instruction should be aligned with the If instruction.)

If the filename exists on the disk, you want Visual Basic to open the file.

2   Press [**Tab**], then type **open Fname for random as #1 len = len(Patronrec)** and press [**Enter**].

Now you want to read the records and change the BackColor property of the reserved seats to red and the BackColor property of the available seats to white. Recall that you already entered most of the code to do that in the FrmSeat form's Load event procedure. Let's copy those instructions to the CmdOk procedure and then make the necessary modifications.

Here you'll try a new way of switching between procedures in various forms or modules.

3   Press [**F2**] (or select **Procedures** from the Window menu). The View Procedures window appears. This dialog box lets you select a module or form and the procedure you want to view. See Figure 7-51.

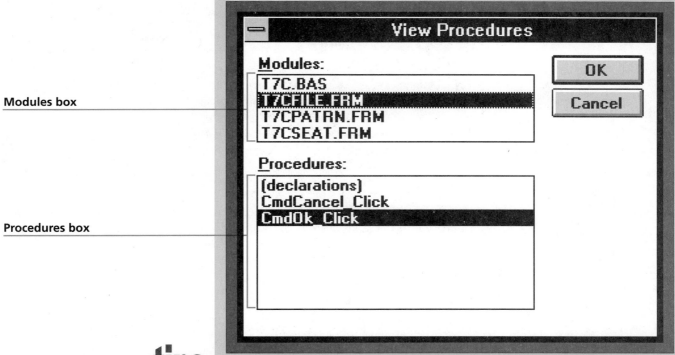

Figure 7-51: View Procedures dialog box

tips
· ·
▶ You cannot open the View Procedures dialog box unless a Code window is already open. If no Code window is open, you can double-click on any form or control to open its associated Code window and then press [F2] to open the View Procedures dialog box.

4 Click **T7CSEAT.FRM** in the Modules box, click **Form_Load** in the Procedures box, and then click the **OK button**. The FrmSeat form's Load event procedure appears.

5 Highlight the instructions shown in Figure 7-52.

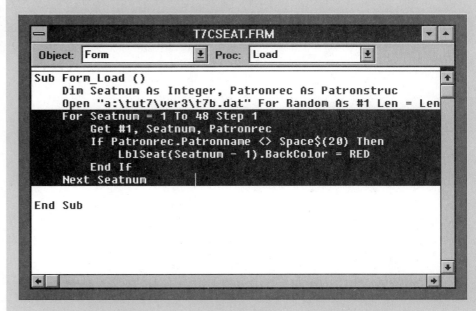

Figure 7-52: Highlighted instructions in the FrmSeat form's Load event procedure

6 Press [**Ctrl**][**c**] to copy the instructions to the Windows Clipboard, then close the T7CSEAT.FRM Code window only.

7 Return to the CmdOk Code window in the FrmFile form and paste the code from the Clipboard to the line just below the Open statement in the Else branch.

8 Highlight the six instructions below the Open statement in the Else branch, beginning with the For statement and ending with the Next Seatnum statement. Press [**Tab**] to indent the highlighted block of instructions.

9 Click in the **blank line immediately below the Next Seatnum instruction**. Align the blinking insertion point with the If and Else statements, then type **end if** and press [**Enter**].

You will need to make two changes to the code in the CmdOk Click event procedure. First, recall that the LblSeat control array is not in the same form with the OK button. That means you'll need to change the *LblSeat (Seatnum − 1).BackColor = RED* instruction to *FrmSeat.LblSeat(Seatnum − 1). BackColor = RED*.

To modify the code in the CmdOk control's Click event procedure:

1 Click to the **immediate left of the LblSeat(Seatnum − 1).BackColor = RED instruction**. Type **FrmSeat.**. (Be sure to include the period after FrmSeat.) The instruction should now say *FrmSeat.LblSeat(Seatnum − 1).BackColor = RED*.

You also need to add an Else branch to this selection structure. If the record does not contain a name, then the theater seat should be colored white.

2 Click to the **immediate right of the FrmSeat.LblSeat(Seatnum − 1).BackColor = RED instruction** and press [**Enter**]. Press [**Backspace**] to cancel the last indentation, then type **else** and press [**Enter**].

3 Press [**Tab**], then type **FrmSeat.LblSeat(Seatnum − 1).BackColor = WHITE**.

4 Click in **the line immediately below the End If instruction**.

According to the pseudocode, you now need to display the FrmSeat form on the screen, clear the TxtFile Text box, set the focus in the TxtFile Text box, and then hide the FrmFile form.

5 Enter the remaining instructions shown in Figure 7-53, then compare your code and correct any errors before continuing.

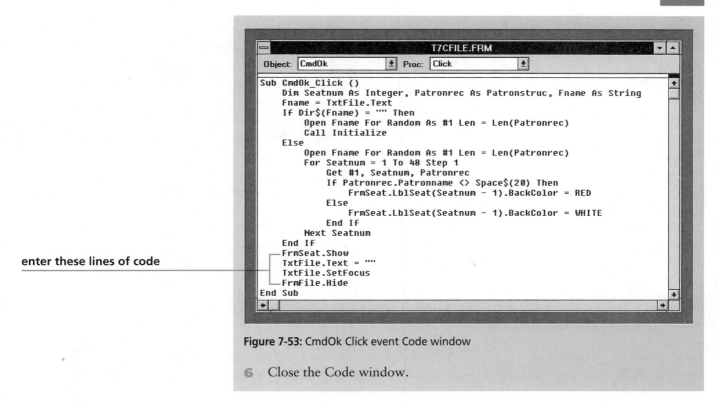

enter these lines of code

Figure 7-53: CmdOk Click event Code window

6   Close the Code window.

Now that the FrmFile form is used to open the desired file, the Form_Load procedure in the FrmSeat form is no longer necessary. Let's remove it.

To remove the unnecessary code from the FrmSeat form:

1   If necessary, display and maximize the FrmSeat form. Then double-click the **FrmSeat form**. (Be careful not to double-click any of the seat labels.) The Load event procedure for the FrmSeat form appears.

2   Highlight all of the instructions in the Form_Load Code window, including the Sub and End Sub instructions, then press [**Delete**]. The LblSeat Click event procedure appears.

3   Close the Code window.

According to the revised TOE chart shown in Figure 7-48, you need to make one more change to the FrmSeat form. Instead of ending the application, the Exit button should display the FrmFile form; then the user will be able to open the data file for another play.

4   Double-click the **Exit button**. The CmdExit_Click event procedure appears. It contains the *Close #1* statement and the *End* statement.

5   Delete only the *End* statement from the CmdExit Code window. Then type **FrmFile.show** in the line immediately below the Close statement and press [**Enter**].

6   Close the Code window and restore the form to its standard size.

Let's test the application.

To test the application:

1   **Save and run** the application. The FrmFile form, the startup form, appears on the screen first.

    First let's open an existing file—the t7b.dat file.

2   Type one of the following depending on your version of Visual Basic and the location of your Student Disk:

a:\tut7\ver2\t7b.dat	**a:\tut7\ver3\t7b.dat**
b:\tut7\ver2\t7b.dat	**b:\tut7\ver3\t7b.dat**

3   Click the **OK button**. Visual Basic opens the existing file and colors the one reserved seat red. Click the **Exit button**. The FrmFile form appears.

    Now let's open a new file.

4   Depending on your version of Visual Basic and the location of your Student Disk, type one of the following in the TxtFile Text box:

a:\tut7\ver2\t7c.dat	**a:\tut7\ver3\t7c.dat**
b:\tut7\ver2\t7c.dat	**b:\tut7\ver3\t7c.dat**

5   Click the **OK button**. Visual Basic first creates and then initializes the t7c.dat data file. Because all of the seats in the form are white, you know that none of them are yet reserved.

6   Experiment by entering data of your choosing into the application.

7   Experiment with the Initialize button. Any reserved (red) seats should turn white.

8   Click the **Exit button**. The FrmFile form appears. Click the **Cancel button**. The application ends and Visual Basic returns to the design screen.

You have now completed Lesson C and the Cole's Playhouse application prototype. In the exercises that follow, you will make important changes to the application to make it more user friendly.

You can either take a break or complete the questions and exercises at the end of the lesson.

S U M M A R Y

To test if a file exists:

■   Use the Dir$ function. Its format is **Dir$**(*filespec*). If you use the Dir$ function with a filename as the *filespec*, the function either returns a copy of the filename (which means that the file exists) or it returns an empty string (which means that the file does not exist). If *filespec* is the name of the file, the name must be enclosed in quotation marks—for example, Dir$("a:\tut7\ver3\t7b.dat"). If *filespec* is the name of a variable that contains the file's name, the name of the variable is not enclosed in quotation marks—for example, Dir$(Fname).

To switch between procedures in an open Code window:

■   Press [F2] to display the View Procedures dialog box.

Q U E S T I O N S

1. Assume you want to open the file whose name is entered in the Fname variable. Which of the following could you use in an If...Then...Else statement to test if the file exists?
   a. If Dir$("Fname") = True Then
   b. If Dir$("Fname") = Yes Then
   c. If Dir$("Fname") = "" Then
   d. If Dir$(Fname) = "" Then
   e. If Dir$(Fname) = True Then

2. Which of the following can you use in an If...Then...Else statement to test if the myfile.dat file exists?
   a. If Dir$(myfile.dat) = True Then
   b. If Dir$(myfile.dat) = Yes Then
   c. If Dir$("myfile.dat") = True Then
   d. If Dir$("myfile.dat") = " " Then
   e. If Dir$("myfile") = " " Then

3. If the friends.dat file exists, what will the following Dir$ function return?

   Dir$("friends.dat")

   a. FRIENDS.DAT
   b. the null string
   c. true
   d. yes

4. Use the _____ key to switch between procedures in an open Code window.
   a. [F1]
   b. [F2]
   c. [F3]
   d. [F4]
   e. [F5]

E X E R C I S E S

The manager of the Cole's Playhouse phoned to say that the prototype works well and he is anxious to discuss some revisions to it. Specifically, he would like you to do the following:

1. Create internal documentation for the Cole's Playhouse application.

2. Provide a warning message if the Initialize button is clicked.

3. Allow the user to open the file by pressing [Enter] immediately after typing the filename in the FrmFile form. He would also prefer that the Cancel button be labeled "Exit" and that the [Esc] key produce the same result as the Exit button.

4. Allow the user to select the OK button in the FrmFile form only when a filename is entered into the TxtFile control.

5. Allow the user to select the Enter Ticket button only when a name has been entered into the FrmPatron form.

6. Create a short user manual for new employees.

You will make these revisions in the following exercises.

1. Good software should have good documentation—both internal and external.
   a. Use the Help facility to look up the form of a remark. Search on either Rem, Remarks, or Comments. Study the Help screen. (Most programmers prefer to use the apostrophe when entering their internal documentation.)
   b. Open the Cole's Playhouse application (t7c.mak) and make comments (remarks) on lines of code that you feel would help you review the application when you return to it long after it's fresh in your mind. Also make comments that you feel would help other programmers understand the code.
   c. Save the application. Print the code.

2. Your clients like the Initialize button on the FrmSeat form. They can practice with the application and can reuse a file after a play is over. However, they are afraid of destroying valuable data. They want you to provide some type of warning message whenever the Initialize button is clicked.
   a. Open the Cole's Playhouse application (t7c.mak). Use the InputBox function to provide a warning message whenever the user clicks the Initialize button on the FrmSeat form. If the user answers "Y" to the InputBox function's prompt, then initialize the file; otherwise don't initialize the file. Use the MsgBox statement to confirm that the file has been initialized. The warning and confirmation should occur only when initialization takes place as a result of clicking the Initialize button. It need not occur when a new file is initialized from the FrmFile form.
   b. Save and run the application. Test the Initialize button by answering "N" to the InputBox function's prompt. Then test the Initialize button by answering "Y" to the InputBox function's prompt.
   c. Exit the application. Print the code.

3. Recall that, after you enter the filename in the TxtFile control of the FrmFile form, you need either to click the OK button or to press [Tab] and then [Enter]. It would be more convenient if you could simply press [Enter] after typing the filename. It would also be helpful if the user could press [Esc] to exit the application.
   a. Use the Help screens to research the Default and Cancel properties. These properties apply to Command buttons and can be set at design time or with code. Notice that only one Command button on a form can have its Cancel property set to True, and only one Command button on a form can have its Default property set to True. (Be careful that you do not confuse a Command button's Cancel property with its Caption property, whose value can be the word Cancel.)
   b. Open the Cole's Playhouse application (t7c.mak) and view the FrmFile form. Use the properties window to:
      1) Change the Caption of the Cancel button to Exit. Leave the button's name as CmdCancel.
      2) Set the Exit button's Cancel property to True.
      3) Set the OK button's Default property to True.
   c. Save and run the project. The OK button should have a darkened border, which indicates that it is the default button. Open the t7b.dat file by typing the filename and pressing [Enter].
   d. Return to the FrmFile form and exit the application by pressing [Esc].
   e. Print the form text for the FrmFile form only.

4. If the user neglects to enter a filename before clicking the OK button in the FrmFile form, Visual Basic will display an error message and the application will end abruptly. You could fix this problem by adding another If...Then...Else statement in the code for the OK button. The additional statement would check if the contents of the TxtFile control contained the null string. You could also enter an If...Then...Else statement in the Txtfile control's Change event procedure.

a. Use the Help screens to research the Change event procedure and the Enabled property.

b. Open the Cole's Playhouse application (t7c.mak) and view the FrmFile form. Set the OK button's Enabled property to False.

c. In the TxtFile control's Change event procedure, enter an If...Then...Else statement that will set the OK button's Enabled property to False if the Text property contains the null string; otherwise, it will set the Enabled property to True.

d. Save and run the application. The OK button should be grayed-out, which means that it is not available.

e. Type a filename into the TxtFile control. As soon as you type the first letter, the OK button should darken, indicating that it is available.

f. Remove the filename from the TxtFile control. When the entire Text box is empty, the OK button will be grayed-out again.

g. Exit the application. Print the code for the FrmFile form only.

5. Employees mentioned that if they inadvertently click the Enter Ticket button without entering any seat information, the seat will appear to be reserved when, in fact, the entry is blank. An empty phone field is fine, but a name should be required. One solution is to enter an If...Then...Else statement in the TxtName control's Change event procedure.

a. Use the Help screens to research the Change event procedure and the Enabled property.

b. Open the Cole's Playhouse application (t7c.mak) and view the FrmPatron form. Set the Enter Ticket button's Enabled property to False.

c. In the TxtFile control's Change event procedure, enter an If...Then...Else statement that will set the Enter Ticket button's Enabled property to False if the Text property contains the null string; otherwise, it will set the Enabled property to True.

d. Save and run the application. Open the t7b.dat file. Click an unreserved seat in the FrmSeat form. The Enter Ticket button should be grayed-out.

e. Type your name into the TxtName control. As soon as you type the first letter, the Enter Ticket button should darken.

f. Remove your name from the TxtName control. When the entire Text box is empty, the Enter Ticket button will be grayed-out again.

g. Click the Return to Main button. Exit the application. Print the code for the FrmPatron form only.

Exercises 6 and 7 are Discovery Exercises.

discovery ▶ 6. Mr. Phillips also expressed concerns about training employees to use the application. You have agreed to write a user manual to provide a reference for the different functions of your application.

Develop a user manual to be used by the employees of Cole's Playhouse. It should include step-by-step instructions for each function of the application. Use the word processor of your choice.

a. Start by creating an outline for the different sections of the manual. Be careful not to skip any of the functions of the program—retrieving data files, initializing data files, reserving seats, and so on.

b. Next, create the text for each section of your outline. Proofread and edit the text as necessary. To create a truly accurate manual, you must test it. Go through each of the sections while using the program. Keep in mind that the users will not have the working knowledge of the program that you have, so don't make any assumptions.

c. Are there still any ways to crash the program? If there are, be sure to add warnings explaining them in your manual. For example, what happens if * or ? is entered as a filename?

d. Once the manual is finished, print the final copy. Be sure to have a title page and a table of contents. For more complex applications, an index is important.

7. The following exercise involves the CD project you worked on in Lesson A.
    a. Open the t7lae15.mak project that you created in Lesson A's Exercise 15.
    b. Save the form, module, and project as t7lce7.
    c. Add the t7cole3.frm form to the project. Save the t7cole3.frm file as t7lce7a.
    d. The FrmFile form should be the startup form.
    e. Create a global procedure called Initialize. It will need to be in a .BAS module. Create code to initialize a file opened as #1. Remember, you set a maximum number of entries as 5 in Lesson A's exercise.
    f. Code the OK button in the FrmFile form so that it will create and initialize (use the global sub procedure) the file (whose name appears in the TxtFile Text box) if the file does not exist on the disk. If the file does exist, then the OK button should open it. Also have the OK button show the FrmCd form, clear the TxtFile Text box, set the focus to the TxtFile Text box, and then hide the FrmFile form.
    g. Code the CmdInit button to call the Initialize sub procedure, and set the focus to the TxtNum Text box.
    h. Remove the code from the FrmCd form's Load event procedure.
    i. Change the Exit button's code so that it closes the file and displays the FrmFile form.
    j. Save and run the application.
    k. To test the application:
        1) Open a file named t7lce7.dat. Be sure to include the appropriate drive letter and directory—for example, a:\tut7\ver3\t7lce7.dat.
        2) Use the Enter button to enter the following record, shown as CD number, CD name, and artist name: 3, Just Country, Sheeba McInter.
        3) Click the Exit button to close the data file and return to the FrmFile form.
        4) Click the Cancel button to end the application.
    l. Print both forms. Print the code for the forms and module.

D E B U G G I N G

Technique   As you learned in Tutorial 6, you can use Visual Basic's Debug window to help in debugging your code. The Debug window, which appears only when the application is in break mode, consists of the Immediate pane and the Watch pane. You learned about the Immediate pane in Tutorial 6's Debugging section. You will learn about the Watch pane in this Debugging section. The Watch pane, which is displayed below the Debug window's title bar, appears only when the application contains watch expressions—expressions whose values you want to monitor as the application runs. This Debugging section will also show you how to set a breakpoint and how to display an instant watch.

Debugging Example 1 — Setting a Breakpoint

On your Student Disk is a project named t7debug1.mak that is not working correctly. You will use a breakpoint and the Debug window to help you debug the project.

To test the t7debug1.mak project:

1 Launch Visual Basic (if necessary) and open the **t7debug1.mak** project, which is in either the tut7\ver2 or the tut7\ver3 directory on your Student Disk. Click the **View Form button** to view the form.

The two Command buttons have already been coded for you. The Exit button will exit the application. The Calc Average button will calculate and display the average of two numbers that are entered by the user. Let's run the application and calculate the average of the numbers 5 and 7.

2 Run, but don't save, the application. Click the **Calc Average button**, type 5 in the dialog box and press [**Enter**], then type 7 in the dialog box and press [**Enter**]. The average of the numbers 5 and 7 should be 6, but it is incorrectly displayed on the form as 4.

3 Click the **Exit button.** Visual Basic returns to the design screen.

Let's open the Calc Average button's Code window and debug its code.

To debug the Calc Average button's code:

1 Double-click the **Calc Average button** to open its Code window. The CmdCalc control's Click event procedure appears, as shown in Figure 7-54.

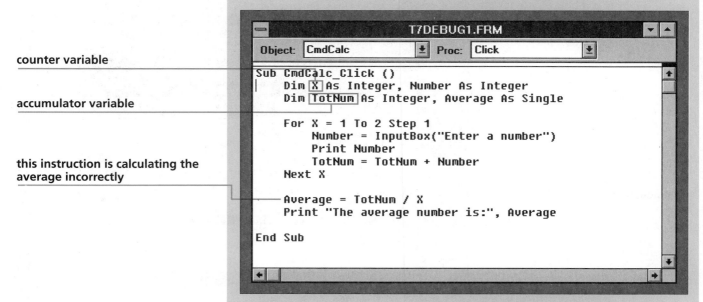

counter variable

accumulator variable

this instruction is calculating the average incorrectly

```
Sub CmdCalc_Click ()
    Dim X As Integer, Number As Integer
    Dim TotNum As Integer, Average As Single

    For X = 1 To 2 Step 1
        Number = InputBox("Enter a number")
        Print Number
        TotNum = TotNum + Number
    Next X

    Average = TotNum / X
    Print "The average number is:", Average

End Sub
```

Figure 7-54

The code declares four variables: X, Number, TotNum, and Average. The X variable, a counter variable, will be used by the For...Next loop to keep track of the number of items to request from the user—in this case, the application will request two numbers. The Number variable will store the user's response to the InputBox function's message. The TotNum variable will be used to accumulate the numbers entered by the user. The Average variable will store the average of the numbers.

The *Average* = *TotNum* / *X* instruction is calculating the average incorrectly. That means that either the TotNum variable or the X variable contains an incorrect value. To determine which variable—TotNum or X—is causing the problem, you will set a breakpoint at the *Average* = *TotNum* / *X* instruction. When Visual Basic encounters a breakpoint in the code as the application is running, Visual Basic puts the application in break mode, which temporarily halts program execution. Recall that when an application is in break mode, you can use the Debug window to debug your code. When this application is in break mode, for example, you will use the Debug window to view the values in the TotNum and the X variables to see which contains an incorrect value.

2   Click anywhere in the *Average* = *TotNum* / *X* instruction. The blinking insertion point should now be positioned somewhere in that instruction.

3   Click the **Breakpoint icon** ▣ (or click **Debug**, then click **Toggle Breakpoint**. You can also press [**F9**]). Visual Basic highlights the *Average* = *TotNum* / *X* instruction to indicate that it is a breakpoint.

When you run the application, Visual Basic will put the application in break mode immediately before processing the breakpoint instruction.

4   Close the Code window, then **run**, but don't save, the application. Click the **Calc Average button**, type **5** and press [**Enter**], then type **7** and press [**Enter**]. Before processing the *Average* = *TotNum* / *X* instruction, Visual Basic enters break mode. The screen appears as shown in Figure 7-55.

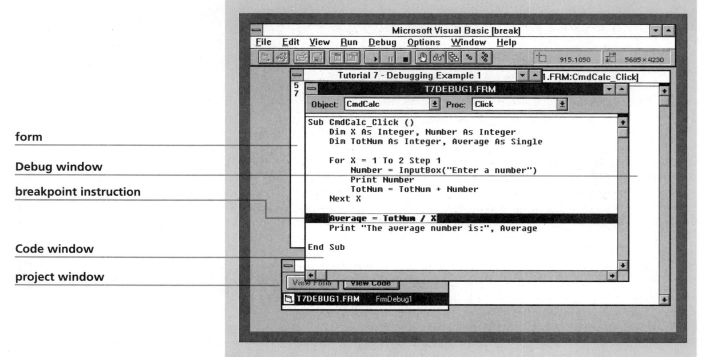

form

Debug window

breakpoint instruction

Code window

project window

Figure 7-55

Now that you are in break mode, you can use the Debug window to view the values in both the TotNum and the X variables.

5   Click **Window**, then click **Debug** (or press [**Ctrl**][**b**]).

First let's view the value in the TotNum variable. Because you entered the numbers 5 and 7, the value in TotNum should be 12.

6 In the Debug window's Immediate pane, type **print totnum** and press [**Enter**]. The number 12, which is the sum of 5 and 7, appears. The TotNum variable, therefore, contains the correct value.

Now let's look at the value in the X variable. Remember that you entered two numbers, so you want the value in X to be 2.

7 Type **print x** and press [**Enter**]. The Debug window shows that the X variable contains the number 3 instead of the number 2. The X variable, therefore, is causing the average to be calculated incorrectly. Now that you know which variable is causing the problem, you need to search the code to see how X gets its value. (It might be helpful to refer to Figure 7-55.)

The X variable is used as the counter variable in the For...Next loop. Recall that the For...Next loop stops when the value in its counter variable is greater than the *endvalue*. In this case, the For...Next loop ends when X reaches 3—one more than the *endvalue* of 2. So although two numbers are requested from the user, the value in X is 3 when the For...Next loop stops. To fix the code, you simply need to change the *Average = TotNum / X* instruction to *Average = TotNum / (X–1)*. Let's remove the breakpoint and fix the code.

8 Click the **Stop icon** ▪ in the toolbar to stop the application, then click the **Code window** to make it the active window. Click **Debug**, then click **Clear All Breakpoints**. Visual Basic removes the breakpoint.

9 Change the *Average = TotNum / X* instruction to *Average = TotNum / (X –1)*. Close the Code window, then **run**, but don't save, the application.

10 Click the **Calc Average button**, type 5 and press [**Enter**], then type 7 and press [**Enter**]. The correct average, 6, appears on the form. Click the **Exit button** to end the application. Visual Basic returns to the design screen.

In the next example, you will learn how to display an instant watch. (You do not need to save the t7debug1.frm form.)

Debugging Example 2 — Displaying an Instant Watch

On your Student Disk is a project named t7debug2.mak which is not working correctly. You will use a breakpoint and an instant watch to help you debug the project.

To test the t7debug2.mak project:

1 Open the **t7debug2.mak** project, which is in either the tut7\ver2 or the tut7\ver3 directory on your Student Disk. (You do not need to save the t7debug1.frm form.) Click the **View Form button** to view the form.

This application is the same one used in debugging example 1, except it contains a different bug (error). The Calc Average button, recall, calculates and displays the average of two numbers that are entered by the user. The Exit button closes the application.

2 **Run** the application. Click the **Calc Average button**, type 5 and press [**Enter**], then type 7 and press [**Enter**]. The average should be 6, but it is incorrectly displayed as 7.

3 Click the **Exit button**. Visual Basic returns to the design screen.

Let's open the Calc Average button's Code window and debug its code.

To debug the Calc Average button's code:

1   Double-click the **Calc Average button** to open its Code window. The CmdCalc control's Click event procedure appears, as shown in Figure 7-56.

counter variable

accumulator variable

this instruction is calculating the average incorrectly

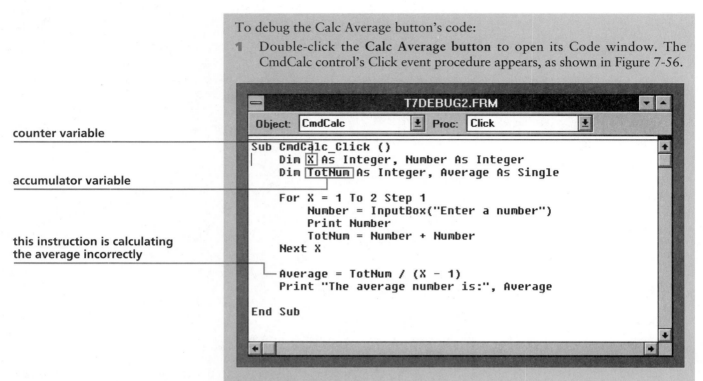

```
                    T7DEBUG2.FRM

Object: CmdCalc          ±  Proc: Click          ±

Sub CmdCalc_Click ()
    Dim X As Integer, Number As Integer
    Dim TotNum As Integer, Average As Single

    For X = 1 To 2 Step 1
        Number = InputBox("Enter a number")
        Print Number
        TotNum = Number + Number
    Next X

    Average = TotNum / (X - 1)
    Print "The average number is:", Average

End Sub
```

Figure 7-56

The Average = TotNum / (X – 1) instruction is calculating the average incorrectly. To determine the problem, you will set a breakpoint at the *Average = TotNum / (X – 1)* instruction. This time when the application enters break mode, you will use an instant watch—instead of the Debug window, as you did in debugging example 1—to display the value in the TotNum variable and in the *(X – 1)* expression.

2   Click anywhere in the *Average = TotNum / (X–1)* instruction. The blinking insertion point should now be positioned somewhere in that instruction.

3   Click the **Breakpoint icon** (or click **Debug**, then click **Toggle Breakpoint**; you can also press [F9]). Visual Basic highlights the *Average = TotNum / (X – 1)* instruction to indicate that it is a breakpoint.

4   Close the Code window, then **run** the application. Click the **Calc Average button**, type **5** and press **[Enter]**, then type **7** and press **[Enter]**. Before processing the *Average = TotNum / (X–1)* instruction, Visual Basic enters break mode. The Code window appears on the screen with the breakpoint highlighted.

Now that you are in break mode, you can use an instant watch to view the values in the *(X–1)* expression and in the TotNum variable.

5   Highlight the *(X–1)* expression, as shown in Figure 7-57.

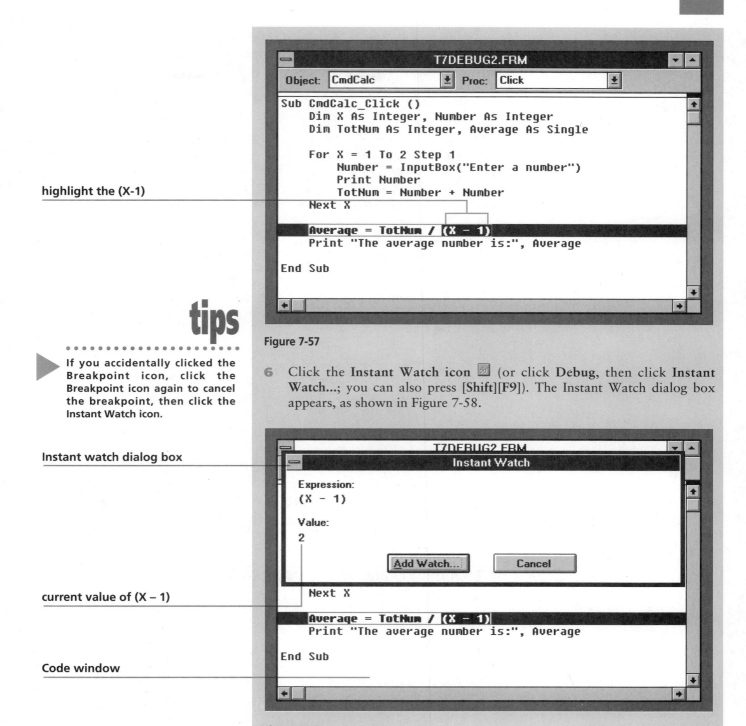

highlight the (X-1)

Figure 7-57

tips

• • • • • • • • • • • • • • • • • • •

If you accidentally clicked the Breakpoint icon, click the Breakpoint icon again to cancel the breakpoint, then click the Instant Watch icon.

6 Click the **Instant Watch icon** 🔲 (or click **Debug**, then click **Instant Watch...**; you can also press [Shift][F9]). The Instant Watch dialog box appears, as shown in Figure 7-58.

Instant watch dialog box

current value of (X – 1)

Code window

Figure 7-58

The Instant Watch dialog box shows that the current value of the expression *(X – 1)* is 2, which is correct. (Notice that using an instant watch is much quicker than displaying the Debug window and entering a Print statement.) Next let's look at the value in the TotNum variable.

7   Click the **Cancel button** to remove the Instant Watch dialog box. Highlight **TotNum** in the Dim statement (or in any statement in which it appears), then click the **Instant Watch icon** ▣. The Instant Watch dialog box appears and shows that the current value in TotNum is 14; you were expecting it to be 12 (the sum of the numbers 5 and 7).

Now that you know that the TotNum variable is causing the average to be calculated incorrectly, you need to search the code for the location where the TotNum variable gets its value.

8   Click the **Cancel button** to remove the Instant Watch dialog box, then click the **Stop icon** ▣ to stop the application.

9   Click the **Code window** to make it the active window.

The TotNum variable, which is an accumulator variable, gets its value from the *TotNum = Number + Number* instruction. (It might help to refer to Figure 7-57.) That instruction is incorrect. As you learned in Tutorial 6, the correct instruction for updating the TotNum variable, which is an accumulator variable, should be *TotNum = TotNum + Number*. Let's clear the breakpoint and fix the code.

To correct the code in the Calc Average button's Code window:

1   Click **Debug,** then click **Clear All Breakpoints.** Change the *TotNum = Number + Number* instruction to **TotNum = TotNum + Number.**

2   Close the Code window, then **run,** but don't save, the application.

3   Click the **Calc Average button.** Type 5 and press [**Enter**], then type 7 and press [**Enter**]. This time the correct average, 6, appears on the form.

4   Click the **Exit button** to end the application.

In the next example you will learn how to use the Debug window's Watch pane. (You do not need to save the t7debug2.frm form.)

Debugging Example 3 — Using the Watch Pane

On your Student Disk is a project named t7debug3.mak. You will use the Watch pane to verify the values in the variables and expressions as the application is running.

To test the t7debug3.mak project:

1   Open the **t7debug3.mak** project, which is in either the tut7\ver2 or the tut7\ver3 directory on your Student Disk. (You do not need to save the t7debug2.frm form.) Click the **View Form button** to view the form.

Let's look at the Display Total button's code.

2   Double-click the **Display Total button.** The CmdTotal control's Click event procedure appears as shown in Figure 7-59.

accumulator variable

exponentiation operator

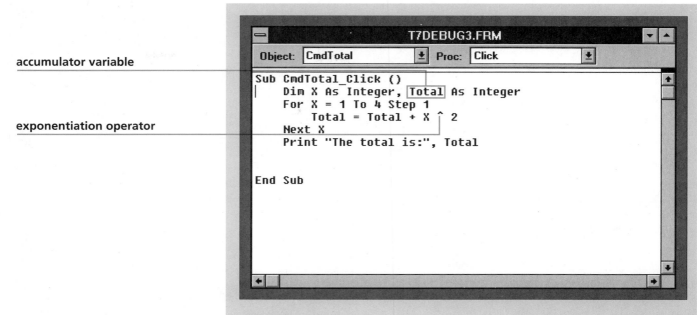

```
                        T7DEBUG3.FRM

Object:  CmdTotal          ▼   Proc:  Click          ▼

Sub CmdTotal_Click ()
    Dim X As Integer, Total As Integer
    For X = 1 To 4 Step 1
        Total = Total + X ^ 2
    Next X
    Print "The total is:", Total


End Sub
```

Figure 7-59

The code adds the squares of the numbers from 1 through 4—in other words, $1 * 1 + 2 * 2 + 3 * 3 + 4 * 4$. Let's run the application to see if it is working correctly.

3 Close the Code window, then **run**, but don't save, the application. Click the **Display Total button**. The application displays the number 30 as the total.

4 Click the **Exit button** to end the application.

Instead of manually computing the sum of the squares to see if 30 is correct, you can use the Debug window's Watch pane to view the values in the variables or expressions as the application is running. In this case you will view the values in X, $X ^ 2$, and Total. By doing so, you will be able to see how 30 was reached, which will allow you to verify that it is the correct answer.

To set up watch expressions:

1 Double-click the **Display Total button** to display its Click event procedure. Highlight X in the Dim statement (or in any statement in which it appears), then click **Debug**, and then click **Add Watch....** The Add Watch dialog box appears as shown in Figure 7-60.

watch expression

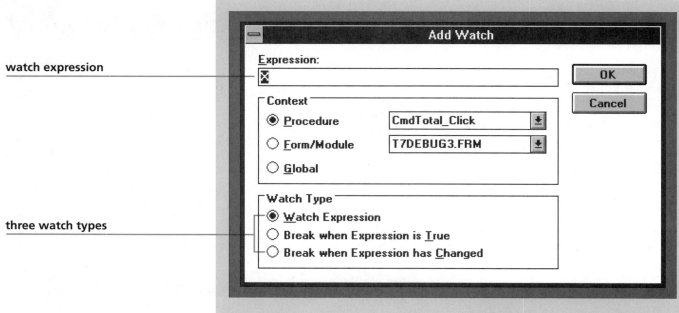

three watch types

Figure 7-60

Notice the three watch types.

2 Click the **OK button** to tell Visual Basic to watch the current expression—X.

3 Highlight **X ^ 2**, click **Debug**, then click **Add Watch...**, and then click the **OK button** to tell Visual Basic to watch the X^2 expression.

4 Highlight **Total** in the Dim statement (or in any statement in which it appears). Click **Debug**, then click **Add Watch...**. This time, click **Break when Expression has Changed**, and then click the **OK button**. This tells Visual Basic to put the application in break mode each time the value in Total changes.

5 Close the Code window.

You can verify the watch expressions by displaying the Watch dialog box. Let's do that before running the application.

6 Click **Debug**, then click **Edit Watch...**. The Watch dialog box appears, as shown in Figure 7-61.

tips

▶ **Be sure to click Break when Expression has changed, and not Break when Expression is True.**

Watch Expressions

Break when Expression has Changed

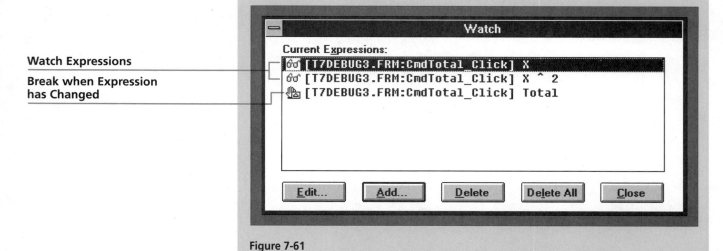

Figure 7-61

Notice the icons to the left of the expressions. The icons tell you which watch type is associated with the expression. The icon that looks like eye glasses represents the "Watch Expression" type; the other icon represents the "Break when Expression has Changed" type. Also notice that the Watch dialog box allows you to edit, add, and delete a watch expression. The Delete All button allows you to delete all of the watch expressions. The Close button simply closes the dialog box.

7   Click the **Close button** to close the Watch dialog box.

8   **Run,** but don't save, the application. Click the **Display Total button.** Visual Basic puts the application in break mode after processing the Total = Total + X ^ 2 instruction, which is the instruction that changes the value in the Total variable. (You should see a rectangle around the Next X instruction, which is the instruction after the Total = Total + X ^ 2 instruction.)

Let's switch to the Debug window and look in the Watch pane.

9   Click **Window,** then click **Debug.** The Watch pane shows the current value of X, X ^ 2, and Total. See Figure 7-62. (You may need to size the Debug Window.)

Values of watch expressions in Watch pane

Immediate pane

from debugging example 1 (to erase, highlight, and press the Delete key)

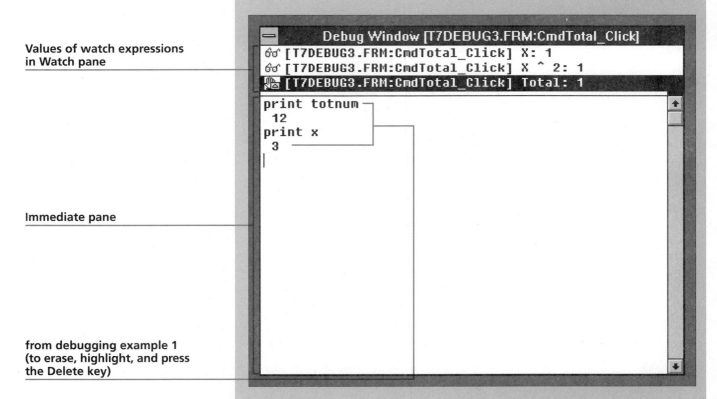

```
Debug Window [T7DEBUG3.FRM:CmdTotal_Click]
[T7DEBUG3.FRM:CmdTotal_Click] X: 1
[T7DEBUG3.FRM:CmdTotal_Click] X ^ 2: 1
[T7DEBUG3.FRM:CmdTotal_Click] Total: 1
print totnum
 12
print x
 3
```

Figure 7-62

To continue:

1   Click the **Run icon** ▣ (or press [F5]) to continue processing the application, then click the **Debug window.** Notice that the value of X is now 2, X ^ 2 is 4, and Total is 5 (the prior value of 1 plus 4 more).

2 Click the **Run icon** ▣ to continue processing the application, click **Window,** then click **Debug.** Notice that the value of X is now 3, $X \wedge 2$ is 9, and Total is 14 (the prior value of 5 plus 9 more).

3 Click the **Run icon** ▣ to continue processing the application, click **Window,** then click **Debug.** Notice that the value of X is now 4, $X \wedge 2$ is 16, and Total is 30 (the prior value of 14 plus 16 more).

4 Click the **Run icon** ▣ to continue processing. The correct sum, 30, appears on the form. Click the **Exit button.** Visual Basic returns to the design screen.

Let's remove the watch expressions. (In this case you are removing the watch expressions for practice only. Visual Basic automatically removes watch expressions and breakpoints when you either open another application or exit Visual Basic. Visual Basic does not save watch expressions or breakpoints when you save an application.)

5 Click **Debug,** then click **Edit Watch....** The Watch dialog box appears. Click the **Delete All** button, then click the **Close button.** You can now exit Visual Basic. You do not need to save the t7debug3.frm form.

TUTORIAL

8

Variable Arrays
The Personal Directory Application

case ▶ In this tutorial you will create a personal directory application. The personal directory will contain the names, phone numbers, and birthdays of your friends and relatives. The application will allow you to add information to the directory, delete information from the directory, display the phone number and birthday of a person in the directory, and display the name, phone number, and birthday of friends and relatives who were born in a specific month.

Previewing the Completed Application

As you've done in previous tutorials, you will preview the application before creating it.

To preview the completed application:

1 Launch Windows and make sure the Program Manager window is open and your Student Disk is in the appropriate drive. If necessary, click the Minimize on Use option on the Options menu to minimize the Program Manager on use.

2 Run one of the following .EXE files from the Program Manager. The file you run will depend on the location of your Student Disk and your version of Visual Basic.

a:\tut8\ver2\a2direct.exe

b:\tut8\ver2\b2direct.exe

a:\tut8\ver3\a3direct.exe

b:\tut8\ver3\b3direct.exe

The personal directory application's user interface appears on the screen. See Figure 8-1.

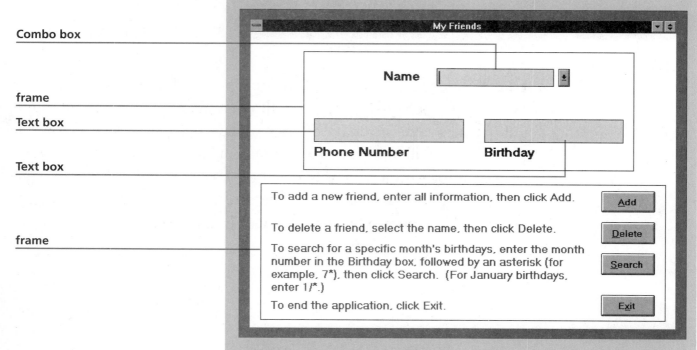

Figure 8-1: Personal directory user interface

This application on your Student Disk reads the names, phone numbers, and birthdays from a sequential access file and then stores that information in a variable array in the computer's memory. You will learn about variable arrays in Lesson A. In addition, the application stores the names of your friends and relatives in a Combo box. The Combo box control, which is covered in Lesson B, combines the features of a Text box and a List box in that it allows the user to either type an entry or select an item from a predefined list. Let's view the predefined list for the Combo box in this application.

3   Click the **down arrow button in the Combo box** to open its drop-down list. A drop-down list of names appears in alphabetical order.

When you click a name in the drop-down list, the application displays that person's phone number and birthday.

4   Click **Patel, Khalid** in the list. The drop-down list closes and the name "Patel, Khalid" (without the quotes) appears in the Combo box. Khalid's phone number and birthday appear in the appropriate Text boxes on the form.

You can also use the application to add a person to the directory.

5   Type **James, Amos** in the Combo box and press **[Tab]**, then type **333-4444** in the Phone Number Text box and press **[Tab]**, and then type **2/3/76** in the Birthday Text box and click the **Add button**. The Add button adds the name to the Combo box's drop-down list; it also adds the name, phone number, and birthday to the variable array.

Let's verify that the name was added to the Combo box's drop-down list.

6   Click the **down arrow button in the Combo box** to open the drop-down list. "James, Amos" (without the quotes) appears in the list.

The application also allows you to delete a person from the personal directory. Let's delete Amos James.

7   Click **James, Amos** in the drop-down list and then click the **Delete button**.

The Delete button removes the name from the drop-down list; it also removes the name, phone number, and birthday from the variable array.

Let's verify that the application removed the name from the Combo box's drop-down list.

8   Click the **down arrow button in the Combo box** to open the drop-down list. Notice that the deleted name—James, Amos—does not appear in the list.

9   Click the **down arrow button in the Combo box** to close the drop-down list.

You can also use the application to display the name, phone number, and birthday of friends and relatives born in a specific month. Let's try that now.

To display the information on friends and relatives born in a specific month:

1   Press **[Tab]** two times to move the blinking insertion point into the Birthday Text box.

To see who was born during the month of April, which is the fourth month in the year, you simply type the number 4 followed by an asterisk (*), like this: 4*. The 4 tells Visual Basic that the birthday must occur in month 4. The * tells Visual Basic that you don't care what characters follow the 4—in other words, you don't care what the day or the year is.

2   Type **4*** and click the **Search button**. The name, phone number, and birthday of Khalid Patel, the first friend or relative with an April birthday, appears in the form. The dialog box tells you to press Enter or click OK to continue.

3   Click the **OK button** to continue searching for April birthdays. The name, phone number, and birthday of the next person born in April, Tom Williams, appears in the form.

4   Click the **OK button** to continue searching for April birthdays. The "Search is complete" message appears, which means that no other friends or relatives listed in your personal directory were born in April.

5   Click the **OK button** to remove the "Search is complete" message.

6   You can now experiment with the personal directory application on your own, then click the **Exit button**. If you added or deleted a friend or relative from the personal directory, the Exit button updates the sequential access file accordingly. The personal directory application then ends.

You will now restore the t8b.dat sequential access data file, which is used by this application, to its original condition—the condition it was in before you added and deleted any records.

7   Launch File Manager. Use File Manager to copy the t8b.bak file to the t8b.dat file. Both files are on your Student Disk in either the tut8\ver2 or tut8\ver3 directory.

In Lesson A you will learn about variable arrays. The Combo box control is covered in Lesson B. You will begin coding the personal directory application in Lesson B and then complete it in Lesson C.

LESSON A
objectives

In this lesson you will learn how to:

- Create a one-dimensional variable array
- Search a variable array
- Compute the average of an array's contents
- Find the highest entry in an array
- Update the contents of an array
- Create a two-dimensional variable array

Variable Arrays

Variable Arrays

In addition to control arrays, which you learned how to create in Tutorial 5, Visual Basic also allows you to create variable arrays. A **variable array** is a group of variables that have the same name and data type and are related in some way. For example, each variable in the array may contain the name of a state, or each may contain an income tax rate, or each may contain an employee record (name, social security number, pay rate, and so on).

Unlike control arrays, you can't see variable arrays on the screen. It may help to picture a variable array as a group of tiny boxes inside the computer's memory. You can write information to the boxes and you can read information from the boxes; you just can't see the boxes.

Although variable arrays in Visual Basic can have as many as 60 dimensions, the most commonly used arrays in business applications are one-dimensional and two-dimensional. Figure 8-2 illustrates both a one-dimensional and a two-dimensional array. (Arrays having more than two dimensions, which are used in scientific and engineering applications, are beyond the scope of this book.)

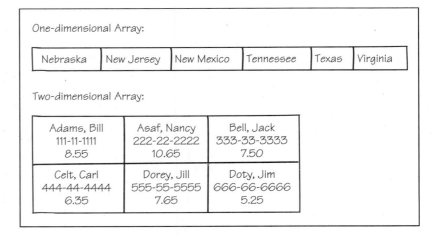

Figure 8-2: Illustrations of a one-dimensional and a two-dimensional array

As Figure 8-2 shows, a one-dimensional array is simply a row of variables. A two-dimensional array, on the other hand, resembles a table in that it has rows and columns.

Similar to the way Visual Basic assigns a unique number, called an index, to each of the controls in a control array, Visual Basic also assigns a unique number, called a **subscript**, to each of the variables in a variable array. You refer to each variable in the array by the array's name and the variable's subscript. The subscript is specified in a set of parentheses immediately following the name. For example, StateArray(5)—read "StateArray sub five"—refers to variable number 5 in a one-dimensional array named StateArray. EmpArray(2,3)—read "EmpArray sub two comma three"—refers to the variable located in row 2, column 3, of a two-dimensional array named EmpArray. Figure 8-3 illustrates this naming convention.

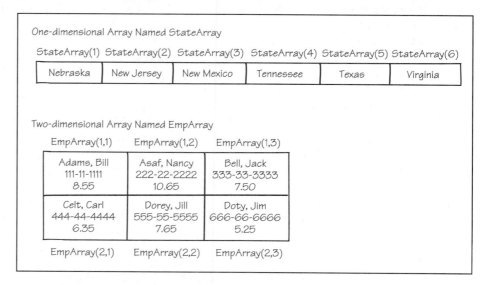

Figure 8-3: Names of the variables in one- and two-dimensional arrays

Advantages of Variable Arrays

Programmers use variable arrays to store related data in the internal memory of the computer. By doing so, a programmer can increase the efficiency of an application because data stored inside the computer can be both written and read much faster than data stored in a file on a disk. The following analogy may help illustrate this point: Think of the computer's internal memory as being comparable to your brain. Now let's assume that someone asks you to name the first U.S. president. Because that information is already stored in your brain, you can respond almost immediately with "George Washington." Similarly, the computer has almost immediate access to the information stored in internal memory—its brain.

Now imagine that someone asks you to name the eighth U.S. president. If that information is not stored in your brain, you will need to open a history book, find the page containing the listing of presidents, and then read the eighth name—a much more time-consuming process. Similarly, accessing information that is not stored in the computer's internal memory—rather, it is stored in a disk file—takes the computer much longer because it must wait for the disk drive to locate the needed information and then read that information into memory.

In addition to speedier access of information, another advantage of using a variable array is that data can be entered into an array once, usually at the beginning of the program, and can then be used by the application as many times as desired. For example, let's assume that you are creating a payroll program. In order to compute the net pay for an employee, his or her federal withholding tax must be calculated. By storing the federal withholding tax table in a variable array, at the beginning of the program, the application can use that stored information to calculate each employee's federal withholding tax.

Now that you know what variable arrays are and why they are used, you will learn how to create one. We will begin with one-dimensional arrays. Two-dimensional arrays are covered at the end of Lesson A.

Creating a One-Dimensional Variable Array

As with simple variables, you must declare a variable array before you can use it. (A **simple variable** is a variable that does not belong to an array.) You declare a variable array with the Dim statement, which is the same statement you use to declare a simple variable. The format of the Dim statement to declare a one-dimensional array is **Dim** *arrayname*(*lower subscript* **To** *upper subscript*) **As** *Datatype*. *Arrayname* is the name of the variable array; the name must follow the same rules as for simple variables. *Lower subscript* and *upper subscript* are numbers that define the lowest and the highest subscript, respectively, in the array. Although the subscripts can be numbers in the range of −32768 to 32767, inclusive, in most business applications, the *lower subscript* is set to either 0 (zero) or 1. (The applications in this book will use a *lower subscript* of 1.) *Datatype* is the data type of the variables in the array. (Recall that each of the variables in a variable array has the same data type.) The *Dim StateArray(1 to 5) as String* instruction, for example, declares a one-dimensional array named StateArray that contains five String variables. The name of the first String variable in the array is StateArray(1), the name of the second is StateArray(2), and so on. Figure 8-4 shows other examples of Dim statements that create one-dimensional variable arrays.

```
Dim MonthArray(1 to 12) as String      Creates an array of 12 String variables

Dim Square Array(1 to 5) as Integer    Creates an array of 5 Integer variables

Dim NumArray(1 to 10) as Single        Creates an array of 10 Single variables

Dim EmpArray(1 to 20) as EmpStruc      Creates an array of 20 EmpStruc variables
```

Figure 8-4: Examples of Dim statements

The Dim statement both creates and initializes the array variables in memory. Like simple variables, String and Variant array variables are initialized to the null string; Integer, Long, Single, Double, and Currency array variables are initialized to 0 (zero). Array variables also can be declared as a user-defined data type. (You learned about user-defined data types in Tutorial 7.) In those cases, the field variables that make up the data type are initialized in the same manner as simple variables.

After you declare an array, you can then store data in it.

Storing Data in a One-Dimensional Variable Array

You can enter data into a one-dimensional array in a variety of ways. The examples shown in Figure 8-5, for instance, can be used to enter data into the arrays created by the Dim statements in Figure 8-4.

```
Example 1                           Example 2

MonthArray(1) = "January"           For X = 1 to 5 Step 1

MonthArray(2) = "February"              SquareArray(X) = X * X

MonthArray(3) = "March"             Next X

MonthArray(4) = "April"

MonthArray(5) = "May"               Example 3

MonthArray(6) = "June"              For X = 1 to 10 Step 1

MonthArray(7) = "July"                  NumArray(X) = Val(InputBox("Enter a number"))

MonthArray(8) = "August"            Next X

MonthArray(9) = "September"

MonthArray(10) = "October"          Example 4

MonthArray(11) = "November"         Do While Not EOF(1)

MonthArray(12) = "December"             X = X + 1

                                        Input #1, EmpArray(X).Name, EmpArray(X).Salary

                                    Loop
```

Figure 8-5: Examples of entering data into an array

In the first example, the 12 assignment statements will enter the names of the 12 months into the MonthArray variable array. In the second example, a For...Next loop will fill the SquareArray array with the square of the numbers from one through five. In the third example, the Inputbox function within the For...Next loop will enter the user's responses into the NumArray array. In the fourth example, the Input # statement within the Do...While loop will read the data from a sequential access file and store it in the EmpArray variable array.

Now let's look at an application that uses a one-dimensional array.

The President Application

On your Student Disk is a file named T8_PRES.MAK, which contains the president application. The president application uses a one-dimensional variable array to store the names of the first 10 U.S. presidents.

To open the T8_PRES.MAK project:

1 Launch Visual Basic, if necessary. Open the **t8_pres.mak** file, which is in either the tut8\ver2 or the tut8\ver3 directory on your Student Disk.

2 **Save** the form and the project as **t8a1**.

3 Click the **View Form button**, then maximize the form. The user interface appears on the screen, as shown in Figure 8-6.

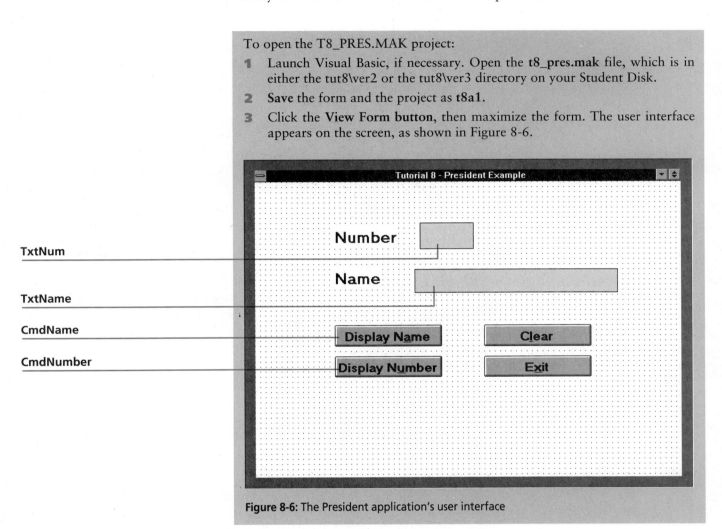

Figure 8-6: The President application's user interface

You can use this application to study for a test on U.S. presidents. When you run the application, it will store the names of the first 10 U.S. presidents in a variable array named PresArray. The name of the first president will be stored in PresArray(1), the name of the second president will be stored in PresArray(2), and so on. You can enter a number between 1 and 10 in the TxtNum Text box and then click the Display Name button to display the corresponding president's name. You can also enter the name of a president in the TxtName Text box and then click the Display Number button to display the president's number.

Most of the president application is already coded for you; only a few lines of code are missing. For example, the instruction to declare the PresArray variable array has not yet been entered. You will do that next.

Coding the President Application

The PresArray variable array will need to be available to more than one procedure in the form, so you will declare it as a form-level variable array. Form-level variables, you may remember, are declared in the general Declarations section of the form and are available to all procedures in the form.

> To declare a form-level variable array in the general Declarations section of the form:
>
> **1** Double-click the **form** to open its Code window. Click the **down arrow button in the Code window's Object box,** then click **(general)** in the drop-down list. (You will need to scroll the drop-down list.) The form's general Declarations section appears with the *Option Explicit* statement already entered in the Code window.
>
> The PresArray array will need to store 10 names, so you will declare it as a String array containing 10 variables.
>
> **2** Press the [**down arrow**] to position the blinking insertion point below the *Option Explicit* statement, then type **dim PresArray(1 to 10) as string** and press [**Enter**].

The form's Load event procedure is next.

The Form's Load Event Procedure

The form's Load event procedure will enter the names of the presidents into the PresArray variable array as soon as the form is loaded into memory. Let's look at the code already entered in the Load event procedure.

> To view the form's Load event procedure:
>
> **1** The Code window for the form's general Declarations section should be open, so you simply need to click the **down arrow button in the Code window's Object box** and then click **Form**. The form's Load event procedure appears, as shown in Figure 8-7.

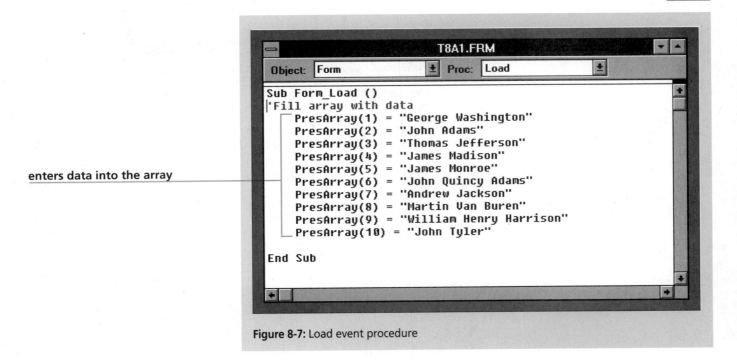

enters data into the array

Figure 8-7: Load event procedure

When the application is run and the form is loaded into memory, the 10 assignment statements shown in Figure 8-7 will enter the names of the first 10 U.S. presidents into the PresArray variable array.

The next procedure you will view is the Display Name button's Click event procedure.

The Display Name Button

When the user enters a number in the TxtNum Text box and then clicks the Display Name button, the name of the president that corresponds to the number will appear in the TxtName control. Let's open the Display Name button's Click event procedure and view its code.

To view the code in the CmdName control's Click event procedure:

1   The Code window for the form's Load event procedure should be open, so you simply need to click the **down arrow button in the Code window's Object box** and then click **CmdName** in the drop-down list. The CmdName control's Click event procedure appears, as shown in Figure 8-8.

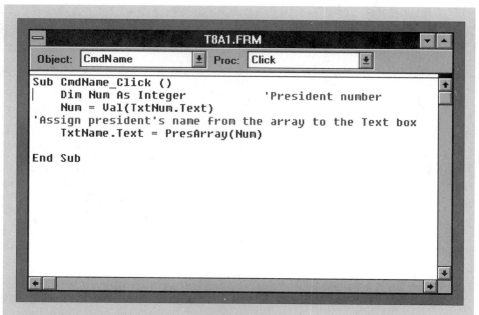

Figure 8-8: Display Name button's Click event procedure

The code first declares a local Integer variable named Num. It then assigns the numeric equivalent of the TxtNum control's Text property to the Num variable. The *TxtName.Text = PresArray(Num)* instruction assigns the contents of the PresArray variable, whose subscript is contained in the Num variable, to the Text property of the TxtName control. If, for example, the Num variable contains the number 1, the instruction assigns the contents of the PresArray(1) variable—George Washington—to the TxtName control.

2 Close the Code window.

Let's run the application to see how the Display Name button works.

3 Restore the form to its standard size, then **save** and **run** the application. The code contained in the form's general Declarations section creates and initializes, to null, a variable array named PresArray. The array contains 10 String variables; each variable is named PresArray and each has a unique subscript from 1 to 10. The form's Load event procedure then enters the names of the first 10 U.S. presidents into the array and the user interface appears on the screen. At this point the variable array in memory looks like Figure 8-9.

PresArray(1)	George Washington
PresArray(2)	John Adams
PresArray(3)	Thomas Jefferson
PresArray(4)	James Madison
PresArray(5)	James Monroe
PresArray(6)	John Quincy Adams
PresArray(7)	Andrew Jackson
PresArray(8)	Martin Van Buren
PresArray(9)	William Henry Harrison
PresArray(10)	John Tyler

Note: You can picture a one-dimensional array as either a row of variables or a column of variables, as shown in this figure.

Figure 8-9: Status of PresArray array in memory

As you learned in previous tutorials, you should test your application with both good data and bad data. Good data in this application is the numbers 1 through 10—the valid subscripts for the array; bad data is any number that is either less than 1 or greater than 10. Let's begin by entering a valid number—the number 5, for example—in the TxtNum box.

4 Type 5 in the TxtNum box and click the **Display Name button** (or press [Alt][a]). The *Num = Val(TxtNum.Text)* instruction assigns the numeric equivalent of your entry—a 5—to the Num variable. The *TxtName.Text = PresArray(Num)* statement then displays the contents of the PresArray(5) variable—James Monroe—in the TxtName control.

Now let's see what happens if you enter a number that is not within the lower subscript and the upper subscript of the array; in other words, the number is not within the range of 1 to 10, inclusive.

5 Click the **Clear button** (or press [Alt][l]) to remove the entries from both Text boxes, then type **12** in the TxtNum box and click the **Display Name button**. A dialog box containing the "Subscript out of range" error message appears. The message indicates that the subscript is not within the range of valid subscripts for this array.

6 Click the **OK button** to remove the error message. Visual Basic highlights the *TxtName.Text = PresArray(Num)* instruction. Recall that at this point the Num variable contains the number 12. Because the PresArray(12) variable does not exist, the *TxtName.Text = PresArray(Num)* instruction causes a "Subscript out of range" error.

Although the "Subscript out of range" message is meaningful to a programmer, most users will not know what to do when an application ends in this manner. Let's add some additional code to the Display Name button so that the application doesn't end abruptly if the user makes this type of error.

7 Close the Code window, restore the form to its standard size, then click the **Stop icon** ▪. Visual Basic returns to the design screen.

You can use a selection structure to prevent the application from ending abruptly with the "Subscript out of range" error message. The selection structure will verify that the Num variable contains a number that is within the range of the array subscripts—in this case, a number between 1 and 10, inclusive—before the *TxtName.Text = PresArray(Num)* instruction is processed. If the number is within the range of the array subscripts, then Visual Basic should process the *TxtName.Text = PresArray(Num)* instruction. If the number in the Num variable is not within the range of the array subscripts, however, Visual Basic should not process the *TxtName.Text = PresArray(Num)* instruction; rather, it should first display an error message alerting the user that he or she has entered an incorrect number and then return the user to the form. Before entering the selection structure, you will learn how to use the MsgBox statement to display the error message in a dialog box.

Using the MsgBox Statement

The MsgBox statement displays one of Visual Basic's predefined dialog boxes. The basic format of the MsgBox statement is MsgBox *msg*, where *msg* is the string expression you want to appear in the dialog box. You must enclose the string expression in quotation marks. The dialog box created by the MsgBox statement will automatically contain an OK Command button. (In addition to being a statement, MsgBox is also a function. You can use the MsgBox statement/function to specify both the number and type of Command buttons to display in the dialog box. You can also display an icon in the dialog box. You will learn about the MsgBox function in Tutorial 10.)

In this application you will use the following MsgBox statement to alert the user that he or she has entered an incorrect number: MsgBox *"The name of president " & Num & " is not available."* (Recall from Tutorial 3 that the ampersand—&—is the string concatenation operator.) This MsgBox statement tells Visual Basic to display the string "The name of president ", followed by the contents of the Num variable and the string " is not available.". For example, if the user enters the number 12 in the TxtNum Text box, the MsgBox instruction will display the following message (without the quotes) in a dialog box: "The name of president 12 is not available."

Now that you know how to use the MsgBox statement, you can enter the appropriate selection structure, which will prevent the application from ending abruptly with the "Subscript out of range" error message, in the Display Name button's Click event procedure.

Adding a Selection Structure to the Display Name Button

Recall that you want the selection structure to verify that the Num variable contains a valid number—a number that is within the range of the array subscripts—before processing the *TxtName.Text = PresArray(Num)* instruction. The valid subscripts for the PresArray array are numbers from 1 to 10, only. If the number entered by the user is in that range, then the selection structure should display the appropriate president's name. If the number entered by the user is not in that range, however, then the selection structure should display an error message alerting the user that the name of the president is not available. Figure 8-10 shows this logic in a flowchart.

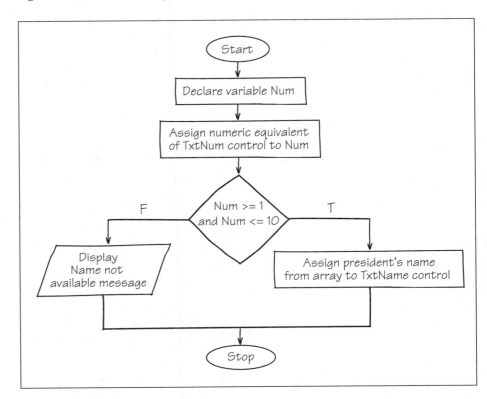

Figure 8-10: Flowchart for modified CmdName control's Click event procedure

Now let's open the Display Name button's Code window and add the selection structure to its Click event procedure.

To add a selection structure to the CmdName control's Click event procedure:

1   Double-click the **Display Name button,** then maximize the Code window. The CmdName control's Click event procedure appears. Change the code to match Figure 8-11.

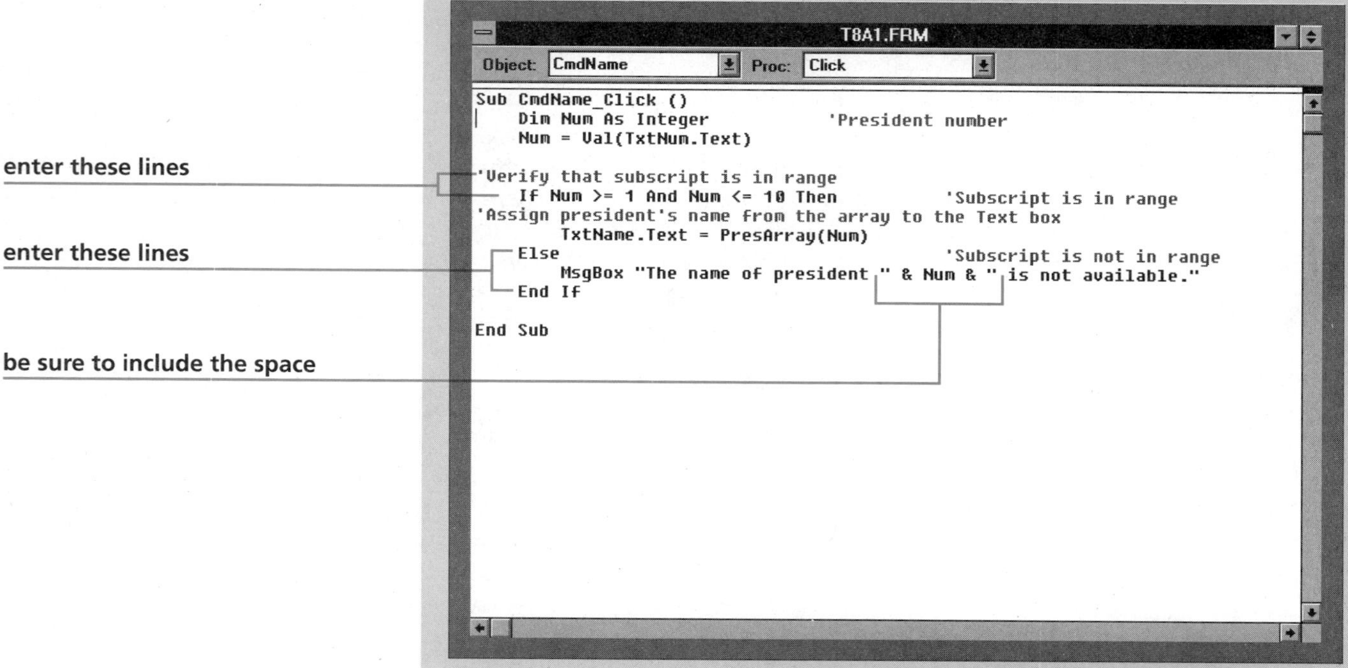
T8A1.FRM
Object: CmdName
Proc: Click
Sub CmdName_Click ()
Dim Num As Integer 'President number
Num = Val(TxtNum.Text)
'Verify that subscript is in range
If Num >= 1 And Num <= 10 Then 'Subscript is in range
'Assign president's name from the array to the Text box
TxtName.Text = PresArray(Num)
Else 'Subscript is not in range
MsgBox "The name of president " & Num & " is not available."
End If
End Sub
enter these lines
enter these lines
be sure to include the space

Figure 8-11: Selection structure added to CmdName control's Click event procedure

Now let's test the application again—first with good data and then with bad data.

2 Close the Code window, then **save and run** the application. Type **3** in the TxtNum box and click the **Display Name button.** "Thomas Jefferson" (without the quotes) appears in the Label control.

3 Click the **Clear button** to remove the entries from the Text boxes, then type **12** in the TxtNum box and click the **Display Name button.** The message—"The name of president 12 is not available."—appears in the MsgBox statement's dialog box, along with an OK button.

4 Click the **OK button** to remove the error message. Instead of the application ending abruptly, it returns the user to the form.

5 Click the **Exit button.** Visual Basic returns to the design screen.

Now let's look at the code in the Display Number button.

The Display Number Button

You can use the Display Number button to display the number of the president whose name is contained in the TxtName control. Figure 8-12 shows the flowchart for the Display Number button's Click event procedure.

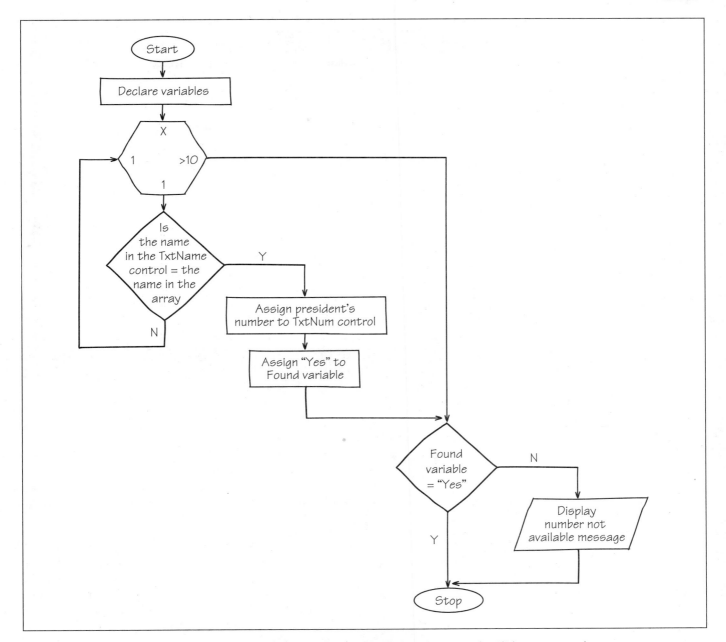

Figure 8-12: Flowchart for CmdNumber control's Click event procedure

Now let's view the code in the Display Number button.

To view the code in the CmdNumber control's Click event procedure:

1 Maximize the form. Double-click the **Display Number button,** then maximize the Code window. The CmdNumber control's Click event procedure appears as shown in Figure 8-13.

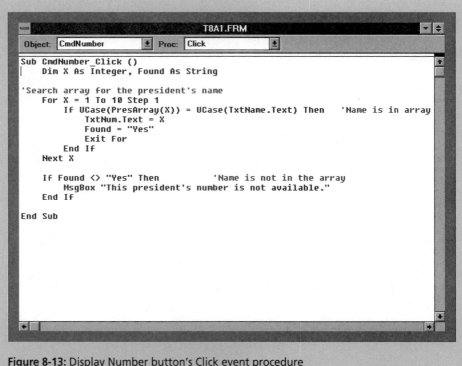

Figure 8-13: Display Number button's Click event procedure

The code begins by declaring an Integer variable named X and a String variable named Found. It then uses a For...Next loop to look at each of the 10 variables in the array, one at a time. Notice that the For...Next loop's *counter* variable, X, is also used as the array subscript.

The selection structure within the loop compares the uppercase name stored in each array variable with the uppercase name entered in the TxtName Text box. (Recall that the UCase function, which you learned in Tutorial 4, temporarily converts a string expression to uppercase.) If a name stored in the array matches the name contained in the Text box, then the selection structure performs three tasks. First it assigns the contents of the X variable to the TxtNum control; the number in the X variable, remember, represents the subscript of the array variable that contains the matching name. (If, for example, the name in the Text box matches the name in the PresArray(4) variable, then the number 4 will be assigned to and displayed in the TxtNum control.) Second, the selection structure sets the Found variable, which keeps track of whether a match was found, to "Yes." Setting the Found variable to "Yes" indicates that the name in the Text box matches a name in the array. Third, the selection structure processes the *Exit For* statement. The *Exit For* statement allows you to exit a For...Next loop before the loop reaches the *endvalue*. (Recall from Tutorial 5 that the *endvalue* tells the For...Next loop when to stop.) In this case, once the procedure finds a matching name in the array, there is no need to search the remaining array variables. After processing an *Exit For* statement, Visual Basic continues processing with the instruction following the *Next* clause. In this case, processing will continue with the second selection structure.

If, on the other hand, the name in the Text box does not match any of the names stored in the array, then the For...Next loop ends and processing continues with the second selection structure.

The second selection structure in the Code window compares the contents of the Found variable with the string "Yes". The Found variable will contain "Yes" only if the procedure finds a matching name in the array. If the Found variable does not contain "Yes", that means that the name is not in the array, so the MsgBox statement displays an appropriate error message. Let's run the application to see how the Display Number button works.

To test the Display Number button:

1 Close the Code window, restore the form to its standard size, then **save and run** the application.

First let's enter a name that we know is in the array.

2 Press [**Tab**] to move the insertion point into the TxtName control, then type **John Adams** and click the **Display Number button**. The Display Number button's Click event procedure searches each variable in the array, looking for the name John Adams. Because that name matches the name in the second variable in the array, a 2 appears in the TxtNum Text box. John Adams, therefore, was the second U.S. president.

Now let's enter a name that is not in the array.

3 Click the **Clear button** to remove the entries from the Text boxes. Press [**Tab**] to move the blinking insertion point into the TxtName control, then type **George Bush** and click the **Display Number button**. Because the name George Bush is not in the president array, the MsgBox statement displays the message, "This president's number is not available."

4 Click the **OK button** to remove the message, then click the **Exit button**. Visual Basic returns to the design screen.

If a 2 does not appear in the TxtNum Text box, you may have mistyped the president's name. Click the Clear button, then type John Adams in the TxtName Text box again and click the Display Number button. Be sure to spell the name correctly and include a space between John and Adams.

In the next example you will use an array to store the information contained in a sequential access file.

The Test Score Application

On your Student Disk is a file named T8_TSCOR.MAK, which uses a one-dimensional variable array to store the test scores earned by 20 students. The 20 test scores have already been entered into a sequential access file for you. Figure 8-14 shows the T8_TSCOR.DAT file displayed in Notepad.

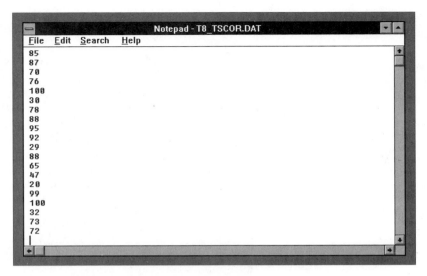

Figure 8-14: T8_TSCOR.DAT file displayed in Notepad

Let's open the T8_TSCOR.MAK project and view its code.

To view the code in the T8_TSCOR.MAK project:

1 Open the **t8_tscor.mak** file, which is in either the tut8\ver2 or the tut8\ver3 directory on your Student Disk.

2 **Save** the form and the project as **t8a2**.

3 Click the **View Form button**, then maximize the form. The user interface appears on the screen, as shown in Figure 8-15.

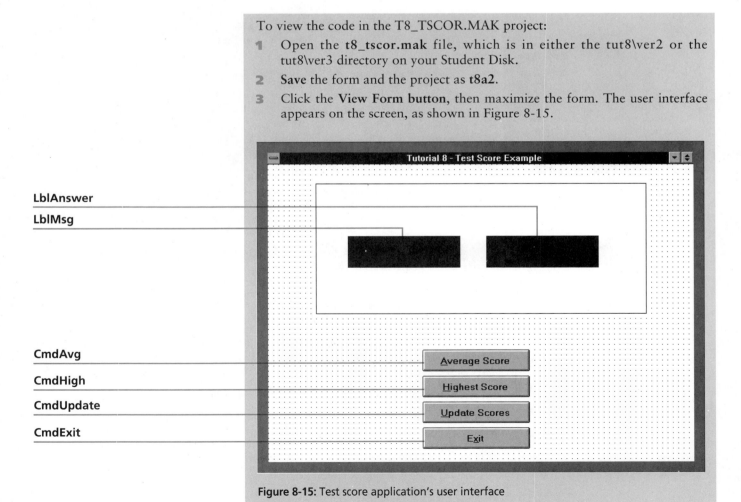

Figure 8-15: Test score application's user interface

An instructor can use this application to calculate and display the average score and the highest score earned by the 20 students. He or she can also use the application to increase each student's test score by a set amount. (Some instructors give additional points to each student to compensate for poorly written test questions.) Let's look at the code in this example. We'll begin with the form's general Declarations section.

To view the code for the test score example:

1   Double-click the **form** to open its Code window. Click the **down arrow button in the Code window's Object box,** then click (**general**) in the drop-down list. The form's general Declarations section appears.

The code begins with the *Option Explicit* statement. The *Dim TscoreArray(1 to 20) As Integer* instruction then declares a form-level array named TscoreArray, which contains 20 Integer variables. Now let's look at the code in the form's Load event procedure, where the array is filled with data.

2   Click the **down arrow button in the Code window's Object box,** then click **Form.** The form's Load event procedure appears, as shown in Figure 8-16. If necessary, change the drive letter to the drive containing your Student Disk.

if necessary, change the drive letter to the drive containing your Student Disk

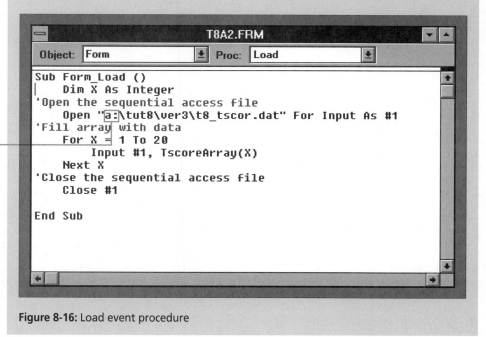

```
                          T8A2.FRM

Object:  Form                    Proc:  Load

Sub Form_Load ()
    Dim X As Integer
'Open the sequential access file
    Open "a:\tut8\ver3\t8_tscor.dat" For Input As #1
'Fill array with data
    For X = 1 To 20
        Input #1, TscoreArray(X)
    Next X
'Close the sequential access file
    Close #1

End Sub
```

Figure 8-16: Load event procedure

When the form is loaded into memory, the Open statement will open the sequential access file for input. (Recall that you learned about sequential access files in Tutorial 6.) The For...Next loop and the Input # statement will then read the 20 test scores from the file, one at a time, and store them in the 20 variables in the TscoreArray variable array. (As in the president example, notice that the For...Next loop's *counter* variable, X, is used as the array subscript.) When the For...Next loop has finished its processing, the sequential access file is closed.

The Average Score button is next.

The Average Score Button

An instructor can use the Average Score button to calculate and display the average test score earned by the 20 students. Figure 8-17 shows the flowchart for the Average Score button's Click event procedure.

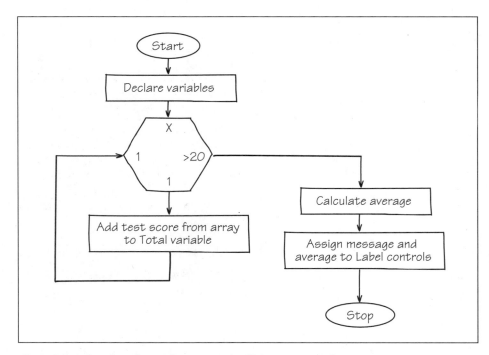

Figure 8-17: Flowchart for CmdAvg control's Click event procedure

Now let's view the code in the Average Score button.

To view the code in the Average Score button, then save and run the application:

1   The Code window should be open, so you simply need to click the **down arrow button in the Code window's Object box** and then click **CmdAvg** in the drop-down list. The Average Score button's Click event procedure appears, as shown in Figure 8-18.

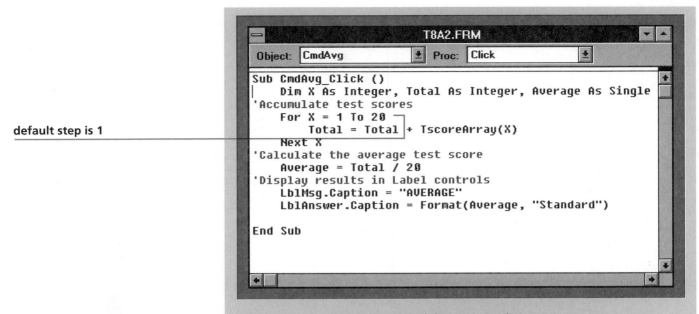

default step is 1

```
                        T8A2.FRM
Object: CmdAvg          ±   Proc: Click          ±
Sub CmdAvg_Click ()
    Dim X As Integer, Total As Integer, Average As Single
'Accumulate test scores
    For X = 1 To 20
        Total = Total + TscoreArray(X)
    Next X
'Calculate the average test score
    Average = Total / 20
'Display results in Label controls
    LblMsg.Caption = "AVERAGE"
    LblAnswer.Caption = Format(Average, "Standard")

End Sub
```

Figure 8-18: Average Score button's Click event procedure

The code declares three local variables: X, Total, and Average. The For...Next loop instructions add the 20 test scores from the array, one at a time, to the Total variable. (Recall that when you omit the *Step* in a For...Next loop, Visual Basic uses a default step of 1. In other words, *For X = 1 to 20* is equivalent to *For X = 1 to 20 Step 1*.) After the test scores are accumulated, the average score is calculated and then displayed in the appropriate Label controls. Let's see how the Average Score button works.

2   Close the Code window, restore the form to its standard size, then **save and run** the application. The form's general Declarations section creates the TscoreArray variable array. The form's Load event procedure then reads the scores from the sequential access file and enters them into the array. The user interface then appears on the screen.

3   Click the **Average Score button**. The Click event procedure accumulates the 20 scores. The procedure then calculates and displays the average—71.30.

4   Click the **Exit button**. Visual Basic returns to the design screen.

Now let's look at the Highest Score button.

The Highest Score Button

An instructor can use the Highest Score button to display the highest test score earned by the 20 students. Figure 8-19 shows the flowchart for the Highest Score button's Click event procedure.

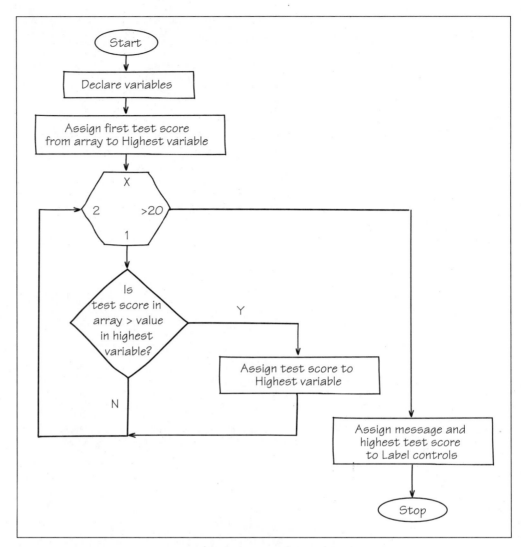

Figure 8-19: Flowchart for CmdHigh control's Click event procedure

Now let's view the code in the Highest Score button.

To view the code in the Highest Score button, then save and run the application:

1   Maximize the form, then double-click the **Highest Score button**. The Highest Score button's Click event procedure appears, as shown in Figure 8-20.

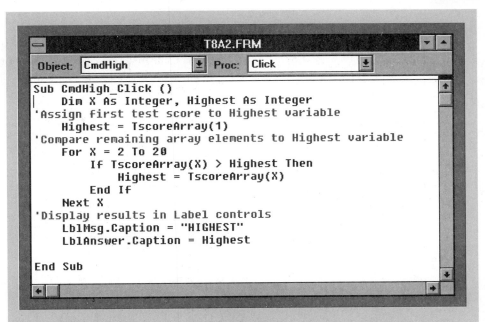

Figure 8-20: Highest Score button's Click event procedure

The code first declares two local Integer variables, X and Highest. It then assigns the contents of the first array variable's test score to the Highest variable. The For...Next loop compares the contents of each of the remaining variables in the array—the variables with subscripts of 2 through 20—to the contents of the Highest variable. If the test score contained in an array variable is greater than the test score contained in the Highest variable, then the array variable's test score is assigned to Highest. For example, if Highest contains the number 85 and the array variable contains the number 90, then the number 90 is assigned to Highest. The remaining variables in the array are then compared to the number 90, the current value of Highest. When the For...Next loop completes its processing, the Highest variable will contain the highest test score stored in the array; that score is then displayed in the appropriate Label control. Let's run the application to see how the Highest Score button works.

2   Close the Code window, restore the form to its standard size, then **save and run** the application. The user interface appears on the screen.

3   Click the **Highest Score button**. The Click event procedure searches the array for the highest test score and then displays that test score, 100, in the form.

4   Click the **Exit button**. Visual Basic returns to the design screen.

The last procedure you will view is the Click event procedure for the Update Scores button.

The Update Scores Button

An instructor can use the Update Scores button to update each student's score by a set amount. Figure 8-21 shows the flowchart for the Update Scores button's Click event procedure.

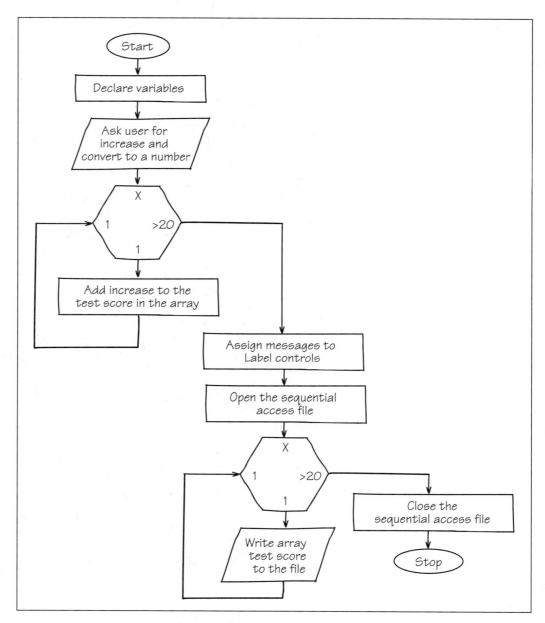

Figure 8-21: Flowchart for CmdUpdate control's Click event procedure

Now let's view the code in the Update Scores button.

To view the code in the Update Scores button, then save and run the application:

1   Maximize the form, double-click the **Update Scores button**, and then maximize the Code window. The CmdUpdate control's Click event procedure appears, as shown in Figure 8-22.

if necessary, change the drive letter to the drive containing your Student Disk

```
T8A2.FRM

Object: CmdUpdate          Proc: Click

Sub CmdUpdate_Click ()
    Dim X As Integer, Increase As Integer
'Prompt user for Increase
    Increase = Val(InputBox("Enter number of additional points"))
'Add Increase to each test score
    For X = 1 To 20
        TscoreArray(X) = TscoreArray(X) + Increase
    Next X

    LblAnswer.Caption = ""
    LblMsg.Caption = "UPDATED"
'Open sequential access file
    Open "a:\tut8\ver3\t8_tscor.dat" For Output As #1
'Write the updated test scores to the file
    For X = 1 To 20
        Write #1, TscoreArray(X)
    Next X
'Close the sequential access file
    Close #1

End Sub
```

Figure 8-22: Update Scores button's Click event procedure

This procedure declares two local Integer variables, X and Increase. The InputBox function prompts the user to enter the number of additional points and stores the numeric equivalent of the user's response in the Increase variable. The For...Next loop then adds the value in the Increase variable to each test score in the array. When the For...Next loop completes its processing, the updated scores are written from the array to the sequential access file on your Student Disk. Let's see how the Update Scores button works.

2   Close the Code window, restore the form to its standard size, then **save and run** the application.

Let's add four points to each student's test score.

3   Click the **Update Scores** button, type **4** in the InputBox dialog box, and press **[Enter]**. Visual Basic adds 4 to each score in the array and then writes the updated information to the sequential access file on your Student Disk. The word "UPDATED" appears in the LblMsg control on the form.

One way to prove that the Update Scores button increased the test scores by 4 is to click the Highest Score button. Recall that before you updated the test scores, the highest score was 100.

4   Click the **Highest Score button**. Notice that the highest score is now 104 instead of 100.

If you want to practice with the test score application, you can recreate the sequential access data file by switching to File Manager and copying the T8_TSCOR.BAK file to T8_TSCOR.DAT.

Now let's add a negative four points to each test score—in other words, let's subtract four points from the scores.

5 Click the **Update Scores** button, type **−4** (be sure to type the minus sign) in the InputBox dialog box, and press [**Enter**]. Visual Basic adds a negative 4 to each score in the array and then writes the updated information to the sequential access file on your Student Disk.

If you click the Highest Score button, the highest score should be 100 again.

6 Click the **Highest Score button**. As expected, the highest score is 100.

7 Click the **Exit button**. Visual Basic returns to the design screen.

The test score application works as long as the number of test scores is exactly 20. In the exercises at the end of Lesson A, you will modify the code so that the application will work for any number of test scores.

In the last example covered in this lesson, you will learn how to create and use a two-dimensional array.

The Classroom Application

On your Student Disk is a file named T8_CLASS.MAK, which uses a two-dimensional variable array to store the names of the eight students seated in a classroom. The names of the eight students have already been entered into a sequential access file for you. Figure 8-23 shows the T8_CLASS.DAT file displayed in Notepad.

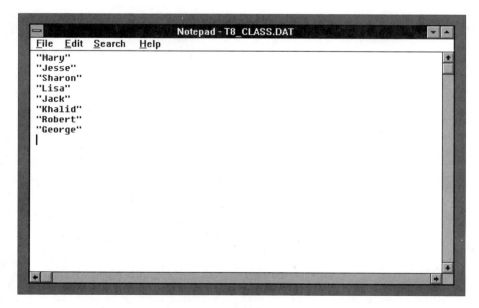

Figure 8-23: T8_CLASS.DAT file displayed in Notepad

Each seat in the classroom is identified by a row number and a column number, as shown in Figure 8-24.

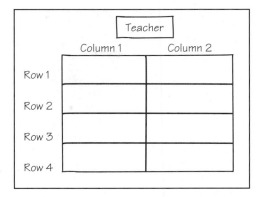

Figure 8-24: Illustration of classroom showing row number and column number

Most of the classroom application is already coded for you; only a few lines of code are missing. For example, the instruction to declare the ClassArray two-dimensional string array has not yet been entered. You will do that next.

To open the T8_CLASS.MAK project, then declare a two-dimensional array:

1 Open the **t8_class.mak** file, which is in either the tut8\ver2 or the tut8\ver3 directory on your Student Disk.

2 **Save** the form and the project as **t8a3**.

3 Click the **View Form button**, then maximize the form. The user interface appears on the screen, as shown in Figure 8-25.

TxtRow

TxtCol

LblName

CmdDisplay

CmdExit

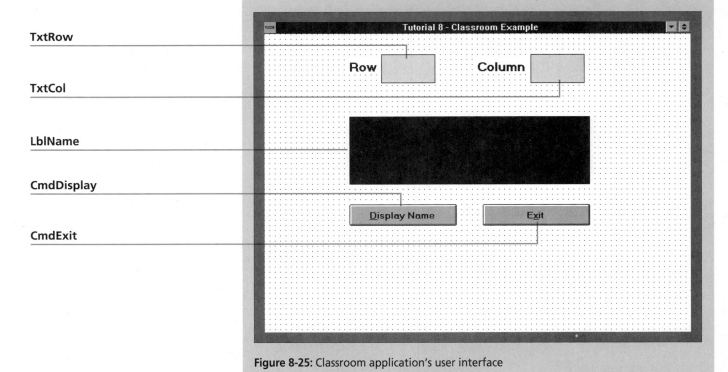

Figure 8-25: Classroom application's user interface

When the instructor enters both a row number and a column number and then clicks the Display Name button, he or she can display the name of the student sitting in that seat. Now let's declare the two-dimensional String array that will be used by this application.

4   Double-click the **form** to open its Code window. Press the **down arrow button in the Code window's Object box**, then click **(general)** in the drop-down list. The form's general Declarations section appears with the *Option Explicit* statement already entered in the Code window.

5   Press the **[down arrow]** to position the blinking insertion point in the blank line below the *Option Explicit* statement.

The format of the Dim statement to declare a two-dimensional array is **Dim** *arrayname(lower subscript* **To** *upper subscript, lower subscript* **To** *upper subscript)* **As** *Datatype*. The first set of subscripts represents the number of rows in the array; the second set represents the number of columns in the array. In this case the classroom has four rows and two columns, so the proper Dim statement is *Dim ClassArray(1 to 4, 1 to 2) As String*.

6   Type **dim ClassArray(1 to 4, 1 to 2) as string** and press **[Enter]**.

The next procedure you will view is the form's Load event procedure, where the array is filled with data. Figure 8-26 shows the flowchart for the Load event procedure.

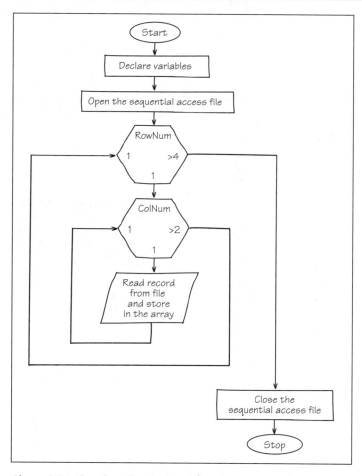

Figure 8-26: Flowchart for the form's Load event procedure

Now let's look at the corresponding code.

To view the form's Load event procedure:

1. The Code window should be open, so you simply need to press [F2] to open the View Procedures dialog box. Click **Form_Load** in the Procedures window, then click the **OK button**. The form's Load event procedure appears, as shown in Figure 8-27. If necessary, change the drive letter to the drive containing your Student Disk.

if necessary, change the drive letter to the drive containing your Student Disk

nested For...Next loops

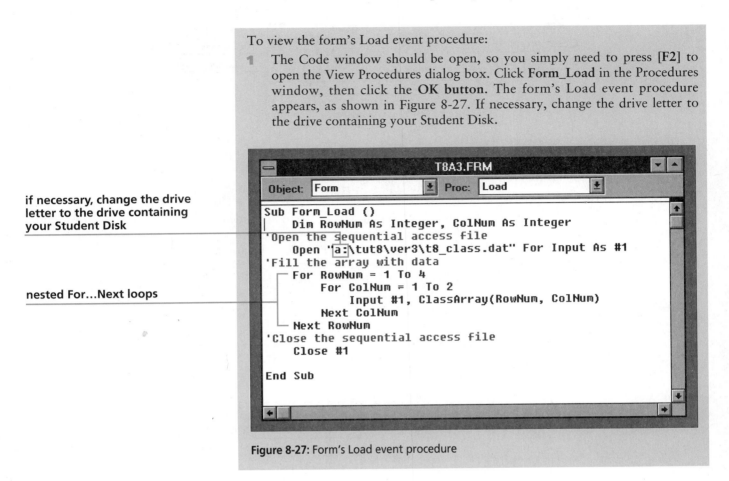

```
─                              T8A3.FRM                              ▼ ▲
Object: Form                    ±   Proc: Load                        ±
Sub Form_Load ()
    Dim RowNum As Integer, ColNum As Integer
'Open the sequential access file
    Open "a:\tut8\ver3\t8_class.dat" For Input As #1
'Fill the array with data
    For RowNum = 1 To 4
        For ColNum = 1 To 2
            Input #1, ClassArray(RowNum, ColNum)
        Next ColNum
    Next RowNum
'Close the sequential access file
    Close #1

End Sub
```

Figure 8-27: Form's Load event procedure

The code declares two local Integer variables, RowNum and ColNum. It then opens, for input, the sequential access file that contains the eight student names. The two For...Next loops read the names from the file and enter each name, row by row, into the appropriate variable in the array. (The For...Next loops are referred to as **nested loops** because the second loop is contained entirely within the first.) The first name in the sequential file (Mary) will be entered into ClassArray(1,1) and the second name (Jesse) will be entered into ClassArray(1,2). After entering data into the first row, the For...Next loops then enter data into the second row of the array; Sharon, the third name in the sequential file, will be entered into ClassArray(2,1) and Lisa, the fourth name in the file, will be entered into ClassArray(2,2). The For...Next loops will then fill the third row with data by entering the fifth name (Jack) into ClassArray(3,1) and the sixth name (Khalid) into ClassArray(3,2). Lastly, the For...Next loops will fill the fourth row with data by entering the seventh name (Robert) into ClassArray(4,1) and the eighth name (George) into ClassArray(4,2). Figure 8-28 illustrates the filled array in memory.

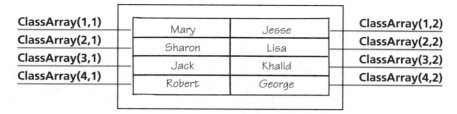

ClassArray(1,1)	Mary	Jesse	ClassArray(1,2)
ClassArray(2,1)	Sharon	Lisa	ClassArray(2,2)
ClassArray(3,1)	Jack	Khalid	ClassArray(3,2)
ClassArray(4,1)	Robert	George	ClassArray(4,2)

Figure 8-28: Status of ClassArray in memory

The Display Name button is next.

The Display Name Button

Recall that each seat in the classroom is identified by both a row number and a column number. To display the name of a student sitting in a specific seat, the instructor must first enter both the row and the column number and then click the Display Name button. Figure 8-29 shows the flowchart for the Display Name button's Click event procedure.

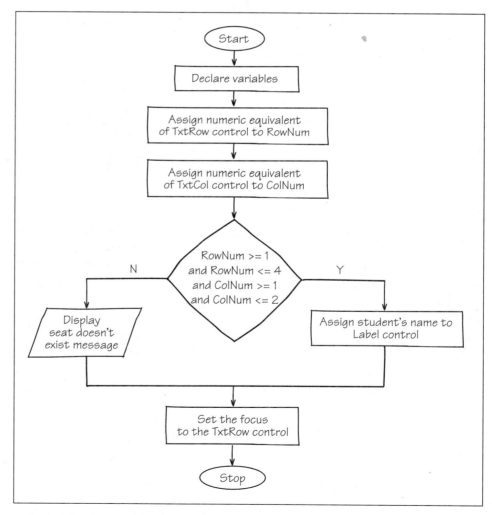

Figure 8-29: Flowchart for the CmdDisplay button's Click event procedure

Now let's look at the code in the Display Name button.

To view the code in the Display Name button, then save and run the application:

1 The Code window should be open, so press [F2] to open the View Procedures dialog box. Click **CmdDisplay_Click** in the Procedures window, click the **OK button**, and then maximize the Code window. The Display Name button's Click event procedure appears, as shown in Figure 8-30.

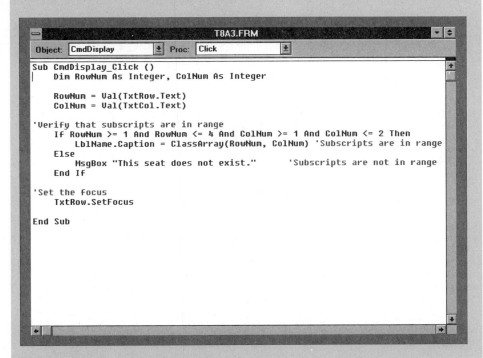

```
T8A3.FRM
Object: CmdDisplay          Proc: Click

Sub CmdDisplay_Click ()
    Dim RowNum As Integer, ColNum As Integer

    RowNum = Val(TxtRow.Text)
    ColNum = Val(TxtCol.Text)

'Verify that subscripts are in range
    If RowNum >= 1 And RowNum <= 4 And ColNum >= 1 And ColNum <= 2 Then
        LblName.Caption = ClassArray(RowNum, ColNum) 'Subscripts are in range
    Else
        MsgBox "This seat does not exist."          'Subscripts are not in range
    End If

'Set the focus
    TxtRow.SetFocus

End Sub
```

Figure 8-30: Display Name button's Click event procedure

The code declares two local Integer variables, RowNum and ColNum. It then assigns the numeric equivalent of the Text property of both Text boxes to the Integer variables. The RowNum variable will contain the row number of the seat in the array and the ColNum variable will contain the column number. Recall that the valid row numbers are 1 through 4, inclusive, and the valid column numbers are 1 and 2, only. If the numbers in both variables are valid, then the procedure displays the name of the student in the LblName control; otherwise, the MsgBox statement displays a message telling the user that the seat does not exist. The focus is then set to the TxtRow Text box.

Let's save and run the application to see how it works.

2 Close the Code window, restore the form to its standard size, then **save and run** the application.

First enter a seat that does exist—the seat in row 4, column 2.

3 Type **4** in the Row box and press **[Tab]**, then type **2** in the Column box and click the **Display Name button**. "George" (without the quotes) appears in the LblName control.

Now let's enter a seat that does not exist—the seat in row 6, column 2.

4 Press **[Backspace]** to remove the 4 from the Row box, then type **6** in the Row box and click the **Display Name button**. The MsgBox statement displays the message, "This seat does not exist.".

5 Click the **OK button** to remove the message, then click the **Exit button** to exit the application. Visual Basic returns to the design screen.

You have now completed Lesson A. You can either take a break or complete the end-of-lesson questions and exercises.

SUMMARY

To declare a one-dimensional variable array:

■ Use the Dim statement. Its syntax is:
Dim *arrayname*(*lower subscript* **To** *upper subscript*) **As** *Datatype*.

To display a message in one of Visual Basic's predefined dialog boxes:

■ Use the MsgBox statement. Its basic syntax is **MsgBox** *msg*. *Msg*, which must be enclosed in quotation marks, is the message you want displayed in the dialog box.

To declare a two-dimensional variable array:

■ Use the Dim statement. Its syntax is:
Dim *arrayname*(*lower subscript* **To** *upper subscript, lower subscript* **To** *upper subscript*) **As** *Datatype*.

QUESTIONS

1. A variable array is a group of variables that _____ . (Select three)
   a. are related in some way
   b. belong to a control array
   c. have the same data type
   d. have the same index
   e. have the same name

2. Variables in an array are identified by a unique _____ .
   a. data type
   b. index
   c. name
   d. order
   e. subscript

3. Stock(2) is read _____ .
   a. Stock 2
   b. Stock array 2
   c. Stock parenthesis 2
   d. Stock sub 2
   e. two sub Stock

4. Which of the following is NOT an advantage of a variable array?
   a. Data stored in an array can be accessed faster than data stored in a disk file.
   b. Data stored in an array needs to be entered only once.
   c. Variable arrays use many more variable names.
   d. Variable arrays allow the programmer to store information in internal memory.
   e. When using variable arrays, you will have fewer variable names to remember.

5. Which of the following Dim statements declares a one-dimensional variable array named ItemArray that consists of five variables, each of which can store the name of an item?
   a. Dim ItemArray(5 to 1) As String
   b. Dim as String ItemArray(1 to 5)
   c. Dim String as ItemArray(1 to 5)
   d. Dim Item as StringArray(1 to 5)
   e. Dim ItemArray(1 to 5) as String

6. Which of the following is NOT true about the Dim statement?
   a. You use the Dim statement to fill an array with data.
   b. You use the Dim statement to declare a variable array.
   c. The Dim statement initializes a String variable array to null.
   d. The Dim statement initializes a Currency variable array to zero.
   e. The Dim statement creates the storage locations in memory.

Use the following array, named StudentArray, to answer questions 7 through 9. The array was created with the following Dim statement: *Dim StudentArray(1 to 5) as String*.

Tom	Mary	Suman	Patrick	Sue

7. The instruction, *Printer.Print StudentArray(2)*, will print _____ .
   a. Tom
   b. Mary
   c. Suman
   d. Patrick
   e. Sue

8. The instruction, *StudentArray(4) = "Jan"*, will _____ .
   a. replace the name "Sue" with the name "Jan"
   b. replace the name "Patrick" with the name "Jan"
   c. replace the name "Jan" with the name "Patrick"
   d. concatenate the name "Jan" to the name "Patrick"
   e. have no effect on the array

9. The instruction, *StudentArray(1) = StudentArray(5)*, will _____ .
   a. replace the name "Sue" with the name "Tom"
   b. replace the name "Tom" with the name "Sue"
   c. concatenate the name "Sue" to the name "Tom"
   d. concatenate the name "Tom" to the name "Sue"
   e. have no effect on the array

Use the following array, named SalesArray, to answer questions 10 through 14. The array was created with the following Dim statement: *Dim SalesArray(1 to 5) as Currency.*

10000	12000	900	500	20000

10. The instruction, *SalesArray(4) = SalesArray(4) + 10*, will _____ .
    a. replace the 500 amount with 10
    b. replace the 500 amount with False
    c. replace the 500 amount with 510
    d. have no effect on the array
    e. result in an error message

11. The instruction, *SalesArray(4) = SalesArray(4-2)*, will _____ .
    a. replace the 500 amount with 12000
    b. replace the 500 amount with 498
    c. replace the 500 amount with False
    d. have no effect on the array
    e. result in an error message

12. The instruction, *Printer.Print SalesArray(1) + SalesArray(2)*, will print
    _____ .
    a. 22000
    b. 10000 + 12000
    c. SalesArray(1) + SalesArray(2)
    d. SalesArray(3)
    e. 900

13. Which of the following If clauses can be used to verify that the array subscript, called X, is valid?
    a. If SalesArray(X) >= 1 and SalesArray(X) < 5 then
    b. If SalesArray(X) >= 1 and SalesArray(X) <= 5 then
    c. If SalesArray(X) <= 1 and SalesArray(X) >= 5 then
    d. If X > 1 and X < 5 then
    e. If X >= 1 and X <= 5 then

14. Which of the following will correctly add 100 to each variable in the SalesArray array?
    a. For X = 1 to 5 Step 1
           X = X + 100
       Next X
    b. For X = 5 to 1 Step –1
           X = X + 100
       Next X
    c. For SalesArray(X) = 1 to 5 Step 1
           SalesArray(X) = SalesArray(X) + 100
       Next X
    d. For X = 1 to 5 Step 1
           SalesArray(X) = SalesArray(X) + 100
       Next X

Use the following array, named NumArray, to answer questions 15 through 17. The array was created with the following Dim statement: *Dim NumArray(1 to 4) as Integer*.

10	5	7	2

15. The average of the numbers in the NumArray array is _____ .
  a. 4
  b. 6
  c. 8
  d. 23.5
  e. 24

16. Which of the following will calculate and print the average of the NumArray variables? Assume that X, Totnum, and Avgnum are declared as Integer variables.
  a. For X = 1 to 4 Step 1
        NumArray(X) = Totnum + Totnum
    Next X
    Avgnum = Totnum / X
    Print Avgnum
  b. For X = 1 to 4 Step 1
        Totnum = Totnum + NumArray(X)
    Next X
    Avgnum = Totnum / X
    Print Avgnum
  c. For X = 1 to 4 Step 1
        NumArray(X) = NumArray(X) + Totnum
    Next X
    Avgnum = Totnum / X
    Print Avgnum
  d. For X = 1 to 4 Step 1
        Totnum = Totnum + NumArray(X)
    Next X
    Avgnum = Totnum / X – 1
    Print Avgnum
  e. For X = 1 to 4 Step 1
        Totnum = Totnum + NumArray(X)
    Next X
    Avgnum = Totnum / (X – 1)
    Print Avgnum

Only one of the five groups of code shown in Question 16 will print the average of the NumArray variables. What will the other groups of code print? Record your answers in questions 17 through 21. (Hint: If you store a number containing a decimal point in an Integer variable, Visual Basic rounds the number if the decimal portion is more than .5. Visual Basic truncates the decimal portion if it is .5 or less. For example, if you store the number 4.3 in an Integer variable, Visual Basic stores the number 4. If you store the number 4.7, however, Visual Basic stores the number 5.)

17. The code in question 16's answer "a" will print _____ .
  a. 0
  b. 3
  c. 4
  d. 5
  e. 6

18. The code in question 16's answer "b" will print _____ .
    a. 0
    b. 3
    c. 4
    d. 5
    e. 6

19. The code in question 16's answer "c" will print _____ .
    a. 0
    b. 3
    c. 4
    d. 5
    e. 6

20. The code in question 16's answer "d" will print _____ .
    a. 0
    b. 3
    c. 4
    d. 5
    e. 6

21. The code in question 16's answer "e" will print _____ .
    a. 0
    b. 3
    c. 4
    d. 5
    e. 6

22. You can use the _____ statement to display a message in one of Visual Basic's predefined dialog boxes.
    a. BoxDialog
    b. BoxMsg
    c. DialogBox
    d. MsgDialog
    e. MsgBox

23. Which of the following will display the message "Error" in a dialog box?
    a. BoxDialog "Error"
    b. BoxMsg "Error"
    c. DialogBox "Error"
    d. MsgDialog "Error"
    e. MsgBox "Error"

24. Which of the following Dim statements declares a two-dimensional String variable array named ItemArray that consists of three rows and four columns?
    a. Dim ItemArray(1 to 3, 1 to 4) As String
    b. Dim as String ItemArray(1 to 4, 1 to 3)
    c. Dim String as ItemArray(1 to 4, 1 to 3)
    d. Dim ItemArray as String(1 to 4, 1 to 3)
    e. Dim ItemArray(1 to 4, 1 to 3) as String

Use the following array, named NumArray, to answer questions 25 through 30. The array was created with the following Dim statement: *Dim NumArray(1 to 2, 1 to 3) as Integer*.

10	200	50
300	25	30

25. Which of the following Print statements will print the number 25 from the NumArray array?
   a. Print NumArray(1, 2)
   b. Print NumArray(2, 1)
   c. Print NumArray(2, 2)
   d. Print NumArray(1, 3)

26. Assume that a sequential access file contains the following numbers, in this order: 10, 200, 50, 300, 25, 30. Which of the following nested For...Next loops will fill the NumArray as shown above?

   a. For ColNum = 1 to 3 Step 1
         For RowNum = 1 to 2 Step 1
             Input #1, NumArray(RowNum, ColNum)
         Next RowNum
     Next ColNum

   b. For RowNum = 1 to 2 Step 1
         For ColNum = 1 to 3 Step 1
             Input #1, NumArray(RowNum, ColNum)
         Next ColNum
     Next RowNum

   c. For RowNum = 1 to 3 Step 1
         For ColNum = 1 to 2 Step 1
             Input #1, NumArray(RowNum, ColNum)
         Next ColNum
     Next RowNum

   d. For ColNum = 1 to 2 Step 1
         For RowNum = 1 to 3 Step 1
             Input #1, NumArray(RowNum, ColNum)
         Next RowNum
     Next ColNum

   Only one of the four groups of code shown in question 26 will fill the NumArray array as shown. What will the other groups of code do? Record your answers in questions 27 through 30.

27. Show what the NumArray array will look like in memory if you use the nested For...Next loops shown in question 26's answer "a."

The code shown in question 26's answer "a" will _____ .
   a. fill the array incorrectly
   b. result in the "Subscript out of range" message
   c. fill the array correctly

28. Show what the NumArray array will look like in memory if you use the nested For...Next loops shown in question 26's answer "b."

The code shown in question 26's answer "b" will _____ .
  a. fill the array incorrectly
  b. result in the "Subscript out of range" message
  c. fill the array correctly

29. Show what the NumArray array will look like in memory if you use the nested For...Next loops shown in question 26's answer "c."

The code shown in question 26's answer "c" will _____ .
  a. fill the array incorrectly
  b. result in the "Subscript out of range" message
  c. fill the array correctly

30. Show what the NumArray array will look like in memory if you use the nested For...Next loops shown in question 26's answer "d."

The code shown in question 26's answer "d" will _____ .
  a. fill the array incorrectly
  b. result in the "Subscript out of range" message
  c. fill the array correctly

E X E R C I S E S

Note: Unless specified otherwise, write your answers on a piece of paper.

1. Write the appropriate Dim statement to declare a one-dimensional variable array named StatesArray. The array should contain 50 variables, numbered 1 through 50. Each variable will store a string.

2. Write the appropriate Dim statement to declare a one-dimensional variable array named PopulationArray. The array should contain 10 variables, numbered 1 through 10. Each variable will store an integer.

3. a. Write the appropriate Dim statement to declare a variable array named MonthsArray. The array should contain six variables, numbered 1 through 6. Each variable will store a string.

   b. Write the assignment statements that will store the first six months of the year in the array.

   c. Draw the array. Include each variable's name and its contents in the drawing.

4. a. Write the appropriate Dim statement to declare a variable array named SalesArray. The array should contain four variables, numbered 1 through 4. Each variable will store a currency type number.

   b. Write the assignment statement that will assign the following four numbers to the array: 10000, 40000, 20000, 5000.

   c. Draw the array. Include each variable's name and its contents in the drawing.

5. a. Write the appropriate Dim statement to declare a one-dimensional variable array named CityArray. The array should contain five variables, numbered 1 through 5. Each variable will store a string.

   b. Write the code that will open a sequential access file named City.dat, which contains the names of five cities. The procedure should fill the array with the data contained in the file and then close the file.

6. a. Write the appropriate Dim statement to declare a one-dimensional variable array named ScoresArray. The array should contain 10 variables, numbered 1 through 10. Each variable will store an integer.

   b. Write a procedure that will open a sequential access file named Scores.dat, which contains 10 scores. The procedure should fill the array with the data contained in the file and then close the file.

7. Write the appropriate Dim statement to declare a two-dimensional variable array named ItemArray. The array should contain three rows and four columns. (Use a *lower subscript* of 1.) Each variable in the array will store a string.

8. Write the appropriate Dim statement to declare a variable array named SalesArray. The array should contain 10 rows and 20 columns. (Use a *lower subscript* of 1.) Each variable will store an integer.

9. a. Write the appropriate Dim statement to declare a two-dimensional variable array named EmployeeArray. The array should contain three rows and two columns. (Use a *lower subscript* of 1.) Each variable will store a string.

   b. Write the code that will open a sequential access file named Employ.dat, which contains employee names. The procedure should fill the array with the employee data, row by row, and then close the file.

   c. Now write the code that will open a sequential access file named Employ.dat, which contains employee names. This time have the procedure fill the array with the employee data, column by column, and then close the file.

10. Assume you have used the *Dim CityArray(1 to 10) as String* instruction to declare an array named CityArray. The array contains the names of 10 cities. When the user enters a number in the TxtNumber control on the form and then clicks the Display City button, he or she can display the name of the corresponding city. Write the Display City button's code according to the pseudocode shown in Figure 8-31.

```
1. Declare X as an Integer variable

2. Assign the Text property of the TxtNumber control to X

3. If X contains a valid number then

      Assign the appropriate array variable to the TxtCity control

   else

      Display a message indicating that the city number is not

      available

   end if
```

Figure 8-31

11. Assume you have used the *Dim CityArray(1 to 10) as String* instruction to declare an array named CityArray. The array contains the names of 10 cities. When the user enters the name of a city in the TxtCity control on the form and then clicks the Display Number button, he or she can display the number of the corresponding city. Write the Display Number button's code according to the pseudocode shown in Figure 8-32.

```
1. Declare X as an Integer variable, Found as a String variable

   2. Repeat For X = 1 to 10 by 1

         If a name in the array matches the name in the TxtCity

         control then

               Assign X to the TxtNum Text box

               Assign "Yes" to the Found variable

               Exit the loop

         End if

      End Repeat For

   3. If the Found variable does not contain "Yes" then

         Display an error message

      End If

      End If
```

Figure 8-32

12. Assume an application uses the *Dim SalesArray(1 to 10) as* Integer instruction to declare an array named SalesArray. The array contains 10 sales amounts. When the user clicks the Display Average button on the form, he or she can calculate and display the average sales. Write the code for the Display Average button. Format the average sales to currency and display it in the LblAverage control.

13. Assume an application uses the *Dim SalesArray(1 to 10) as Integer* instruction to declare an array named SalesArray. The array contains 10 sales amounts. When the user clicks the Display Highest button on the form, he or she can display the highest sales amount. Write the code for the Display Highest button. Format the highest sales amount to currency and display it in the LblHighest control.

14. Assume an application uses the *Dim SalesArray(1 to 10) as Integer* instruction to declare an array named SalesArray. The array contains 10 sales amounts. When the user clicks the Display Lowest button on the form, he or she can display the lowest sales amount. Write the code for the Display Lowest button. Format the lowest sales amount to currency and display it in the LblLowest control.

15. Assume an application uses the *Dim SalesArray(1 to 10) as Integer* instruction to declare an array named SalesArray. The array contains 10 sales amounts. When the user clicks the Update Sales button on the form, the Click event procedure will ask him or her for a number. The procedure will then add that number to each sales amount in the array. After the sales amounts are updated, the procedure will write the updated sales to a file named Sales15.dat. Write the code for the Update Sales button.

16. Assume an application uses the *Dim SnameArray(1 to 10, 1 to 2) as String* instruction to declare a two-dimensional array named SnameArray. The array contains the names of 20 salespeople. When the user enters the row number and the column number in the TxtRow and TxtCol controls, respectively, and then clicks the Display Name button on the form, the Click event procedure will display the corresponding sales person's name. Write the code for the Display Name button.

Exercises 17 through 22 are Discovery Exercises.

discovery ▶ 17. a. Open the T8A2 project, which is in either the tut8\ver2 or the tut8\ver3 directory on your Student Disk. Recall from Lesson A that this application will work only when the number of records in the data file is 20. Your task in this exercise is to modify the application's code so that it works for any number of records.
   b. Save the form and the project as T8LE17.
   c. Change the form's Load event procedure so that it uses the Do...While loop to read the records into the array. Be sure to count how many records are in the file. Call the counter variable RecCount.
   d. Find and then print the Help screen on the Redim statement.
   e. Use the Redim statement to resize the array to accommodate the number of records in the file.
   f. Modify the code so that all references to the number 20 are replaced with the RecCount variable. Be sure that RecCount is greater than zero before computing the average of the test scores.
   g. Save and run the application. Test the Average Score, Highest Score, and Update Scores buttons, then exit the application.
   h. Switch to Notepad and print the contents of the t8tests.dat file which is in either the tut8\ver2 or the tut8\ver3 directory on your Student Disk.
   i. Modify the form's Load event procedure so that it opens the t8tests.dat file instead of the t8_tscore.dat file.
   j. Save and run the application. Test the Average Score, Highest Score, and Update Scores buttons, then exit the application.
   k. Print the code. (You can re-create the T8TESTS.DAT file by switching to File Manager and copying the T8TESTS.BAK file to T8TESTS.DAT.)

discovery ▶ 18. Assume an application uses the *Dim SalesArray(1 to 10, 1 to 2) as Integer* instruction to declare a two-dimensional array named SalesArray. The array contains 20 sales amounts. When the user clicks the Display Average button in the form, he or she can display the average sales amount. Write the code for the Display Average button. Format the average sales amount to currency and display it in the LblAverage control.

discovery ▶ 19. Assume an application uses the *Dim SalesArray(1 to 10, 1 to 2) as Integer* instruction to declare a two-dimensional array named SalesArray. The array contains 20 sales amounts. When the user clicks the Display Highest button in the form, he or she can display the highest sales amount. Write the code for the Display Highest button. Format the highest sales amount to currency and display it in the LblHighest control.

discovery ▶ 20. Assume an application uses the *Dim SalesArray(1 to 10, 1 to 2) as Integer* instruction to declare a two-dimensional array named SalesArray. The array contains 20 sales amounts. When the user clicks the Update Sales button on the form, the Click event procedure will ask him or her for a number. The procedure will then add that number to each sales amount in the array. After the sales amounts are updated, the procedure will write the updated sales to a file named Sales19.dat. Write the code for the Update Sales button.

discovery ▶ 21. Assume an application uses the *Dim SalesArray(1 to 10, 1 to 2) as Integer* instruction to declare a two-dimensional array named SalesArray. The array contains 20 sales amounts. When the user clicks the Calculate Bonus button on the form, the Click event procedure should calculate and print each salesperson's bonus. Write the code for the Calculate Bonus button according to the pseudocode shown in Figure 8-33. (Hints: To calculate a bonus, you multiply the bonus percentage by the sales. Don't store the bonus in the array; simply print it.)

```
1. Declare variables

2. Prompt user for the bonus percentage (If salespeople are to receive
   a 5% bonus, the user should enter the number 5.)

3. Convert user response to its decimal equivalent (for example,
   convert 5 to .05.)

4. Repeat For row number = 1 to 10 by 1
        Repeat For column number = 1 to 2 by 1
           Calculate bonus
           print row number, column number, and bonus on the form
        End Repeat For column number
   End Repeat For row number
```

Figure 8-33

discovery ▶ 22. a. Create a user interface that contains one Text box and two Command buttons. Name the Text box TxtNum and remove the value in its Text property. Name one of the Command buttons CmdExit and change its Caption property to Exit. Name the other Command button CmdVerify and change its Caption property to Verify.
b. Save the form and the project as t8lae22.
c. Code the Exit button so that it exits the application when clicked.
d. Find and then print the Help screen on the MsgBox function/statement.
e. Code the Verify button so that it displays the message box shown in Figure 8-34 when the number entered in the TxtNum Text box is less than 100.

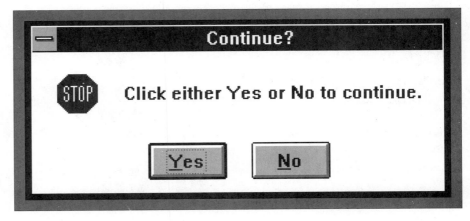

Figure 8-34

    f. If the user selects the Yes button, display the word "Yes" (without the quotes) in the TxtNum Text box. If the user selects the No button, display the word "No" (without the quotes) in the TxtNum Text box.

    g. Save and run the application. To test the application, enter the number 5 in the TxtNum Text box and click the Verify button. When the message box appears, click the Yes button. The word "Yes" should appear in the Text box.

    h. Test the application again by entering the number 5 in the TxtNum Text box and clicking the Verify button. This time, when the message box appears, click the No button. The word "No" should appear in the Text box.

    i. Exit the application. Print the form and the code.

List Boxes, Combo Boxes, and Array Processing

List Box and Combo Box Controls

Most Windows applications make extensive use of List boxes (which you learned about in Tutorial 6) and Combo boxes (which you will learn about in this lesson); both controls allow the user to enter data much more efficiently than can be done from the keyboard. For example, you can usually click an item in a List box or Combo box faster than you can type the item into a Text box. Also, because List boxes and Combo boxes display a set of predefined selections for the user, typing errors and invalid data errors are minimized. (An example of a typing error is entering Texsa instead of Texas. An example of an invalid data error is typing a letter when a number is expected.)

In the next sections, you will review the ListIndex property, which you learned about in Tutorial 6, and learn four additional properties of the List box and the Combo box: List, ListCount, NewIndex, and ItemData.

The ListIndex Property

The ListIndex property, whose format is *control*.**ListIndex**, stores the index of the item that is currently selected in the List box or Combo box. The index, you may remember, represents the position of the item in the control's list portion. The first item in the list has a ListIndex of 0 (zero), the second item has a ListIndex of 1, and so on. Let's assume, for example, that you enter the following five names into a List box named LstEmps: Amy, Beth, Carol, Dan, Edward. Figure 8-35 illustrates the LstEmps List box and its corresponding ListIndex values.

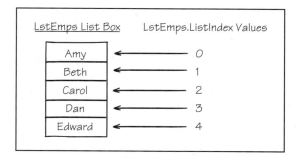

Figure 8-35: List box and ListIndex values

The Print LstEmps.ListIndex instruction will print 1 if Beth is selected in the List box; the instruction will print 4 if Edward is selected.

The List Property

You use the List property to access the individual values in the list portion of a List box or a Combo box. The format of the List property is *control*.**List**(*index*), where *control* is the name of the control and *index* is the index of the item that you want to access. *LstEmps.List(1)*, for example, refers to the second item listed in Figure 8-35's List box. (Recall that the index of the first item in the list is 0.) The instruction, *Print LstEmps.List(1)*, would, therefore, print "Beth" (without the quotes).

The ListCount Property

The ListCount property specifies the number of items in the list portion of a List box or a Combo box. The format of the ListCount property is *control*.**ListCount**. It is important to remember that the value in the ListCount property is always *one more* than the largest index value; that's because the first index value is 0. In the LstEmps List box shown in Figure 8-35, for example, the largest index value is 4; the ListCount value is, therefore, 5.

The NewIndex Property

The NewIndex property, whose format is *control*.**NewIndex**, specifies the index of the item most recently added to a List box or a Combo box. As you add an item to either of those controls with the AddItem method, Visual Basic inserts the item into the list portion either alphabetically (if the Sorted property is set to True) or at the end of the list (if the Sorted property is set to False). (Recall that you learned about the AddItem method and the Sorted property in Tutorial 6.) The NewIndex property tells you where in the list the new item was added. For example, assume that the LstEmps List box contains the five names shown in Figure 8-35. If the control's Sorted property is set to False and you add the name Betty to the list, Betty will be added at the end of the list and the NewIndex property will contain the number 5. If, on the other hand, the control's Sorted property is set to True and you add the name Betty to the list, Betty will be inserted after Beth and the NewIndex property will contain the number 2.

The ItemData Property Array

For each List box or Combo box that you create, Visual Basic automatically creates a corresponding array called the ItemData array. The ItemData array contains the same number of elements as the control's list—in other words, if the list contains five items, the ItemData array contains five items. Visual Basic assigns the Long data type to the ItemData array. (Recall from Tutorial 3 that the Long data type can store Integers in the range of –2,147,483,648 to 2,147,483,647.) You can use the ItemData array to associate a specific number with each item in the list—for example, you can assign an employee number to each of the employee names in the list, as illustrated in Figure 8-36.

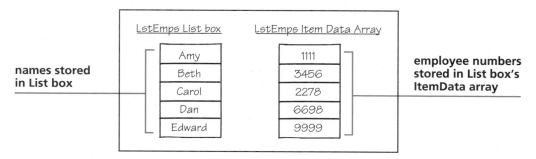

Figure 8-36: LstEmps List box and its ItemData array

You use the ItemData property to access the items in the ItemData array. The format of the ItemData property is *control*.**ItemData**(*index*), where *control* is the name of the List box or Combo box and *index* is the index of the item that you want to access. For example, *LstEmps.ItemData(1)* refers to position 1 in the ItemData array shown in Figure 8-36. The *Print LstEmps.ItemData(1)* instruction will, therefore, print the employee number 3456. Figure 8-37 recaps the ListIndex, List, ListCount, NewIndex, and ItemData properties.

Property	Use to:
ListIndex	Specify the index of the currently selected item
List	Access the individual items in the list
ListCount	Specify the number of items in the list
NewIndex	Specify the index of the item most recently added to the list
ItemData	Access the items in the ItemData array

Figure 8-37: Recap of List box and Combo box properties

Now let's look at how these properties are used in an application.

The Employee Example

On your Student Disk is an application that uses the ListIndex, ListCount, NewIndex, List, and ItemData properties. Let's open the file and view its code.

To open the T8_EMP.MAK file:
1   Launch Visual Basic, if necessary. Open the **t8_emp.mak** project, which is in either the tut8\ver2 or tut8\ver3 directory on your Student Disk.
2   **Save** the form and the project as **t8bemp.**
3   Click the **View Form button**, then maximize the form. The user interface appears on the screen, as shown in Figure 8-38.

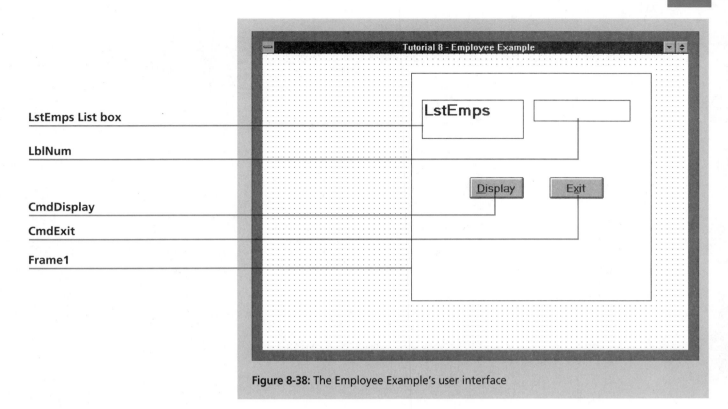

LstEmps List box

LblNum

CmdDisplay

CmdExit

Frame1

Figure 8-38: The Employee Example's user interface

This application contains a List box named LstEmps. When you run this application, the form's Load event procedure will enter the names of five employees into the List box and their corresponding employee numbers into the List box's ItemData array. Because the List box's Sorted property is set to False, Visual Basic will not sort the list items as they are entered into the list; rather, the items will appear in the order in which they are entered by the Load event procedure. After the List box and the ItemData array are filled with data, the user interface will appear on the screen. When you click an employee's name in the list, the List box's Click event procedure will display the employee's number on the form. When you click the Display button, its Click event procedure will display the contents of the List box and its corresponding ItemData array on the form. (The Display button will allow you to verify the contents of the ItemData array. It will also give you a chance to use the ListCount property.) Let's begin by looking at the code in the form's Load event procedure.

The Form's Load Event Procedure

When you run this application, the form's Load event procedure will enter the names of five employees into the List box and each employee's number into the List box's ItemData array.

To view the form's Load event procedure:

1   Double-click the **form**. The form's Load event procedure appears, as shown in Figure 8-39.

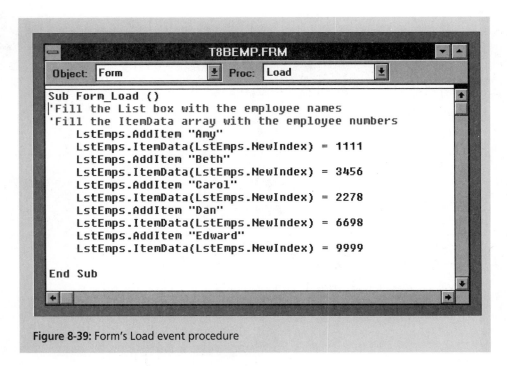

```
                            T8BEMP.FRM

Object:  Form           Proc:  Load

Sub Form_Load ()
'Fill the List box with the employee names
'Fill the ItemData array with the employee numbers
     LstEmps.AddItem "Amy"
     LstEmps.ItemData(LstEmps.NewIndex) = 1111
     LstEmps.AddItem "Beth"
     LstEmps.ItemData(LstEmps.NewIndex) = 3456
     LstEmps.AddItem "Carol"
     LstEmps.ItemData(LstEmps.NewIndex) = 2278
     LstEmps.AddItem "Dan"
     LstEmps.ItemData(LstEmps.NewIndex) = 6698
     LstEmps.AddItem "Edward"
     LstEmps.ItemData(LstEmps.NewIndex) = 9999

End Sub
```

Figure 8-39: Form's Load event procedure

The *LstEmps.AddItem "Amy"* instruction will add the name Amy to the List box. (Recall from Tutorial 6 that you use Visual Basic's AddItem method to specify the items you want displayed in a List box or a Combo box control. The syntax of the AddItem method is *Control*.**AddItem** *item*. *Item*, you may remember, is the string expression you want displayed in the control.) Because Amy is the first name inserted into the list, the List box's NewIndex property will contain a zero. (Recall that the NewIndex property contains the index of the item most recently added to the list and that the index of the first item in a list is 0.) Because *LstEmps.NewIndex* has a value of 0, the *LstEmps.ItemData (LstEmps.NewIndex) = 1111* instruction will enter the number 1111 into position zero of the List box's ItemData array.

After Amy's name and number have been added to the list and the ItemData array, respectively, the *LstEmps.AddItem "Beth"* instruction will add the name Beth as the second item in the list. The NewIndex property will contain a 1 (one) after Beth is added, so the *LstEmps.ItemData(LstEmps.NewIndex) = 3456* instruction will enter the number 3456 in position 1 of the ItemData array. The remaining code will enter each employee name into the List box and his or her employee number into the corresponding position of the ItemData array. Figure 8-40 illustrates the contents of the List box and its ItemData array when the Load event ends.

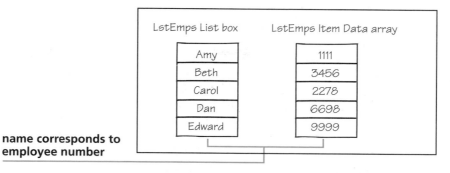

name corresponds to employee number

Figure 8-40: Contents of List box and ItemData array when Load procedure ends

Next let's look at the code in the List box's Click event procedure.

The List Box's Click Event Procedure

When you click an employee's name in the list, the List box's Click event procedure should display the employee's number in the LblNum control.

To view the code in the List box's Click event procedure:

1   The Code window should be open, so you simply need to press [F2] to display the View Procedures dialog box. Click **LstEmps_Click** in the Procedures section, then click the **OK button**. The List box's Click event procedure appears, as shown in Figure 8-41.

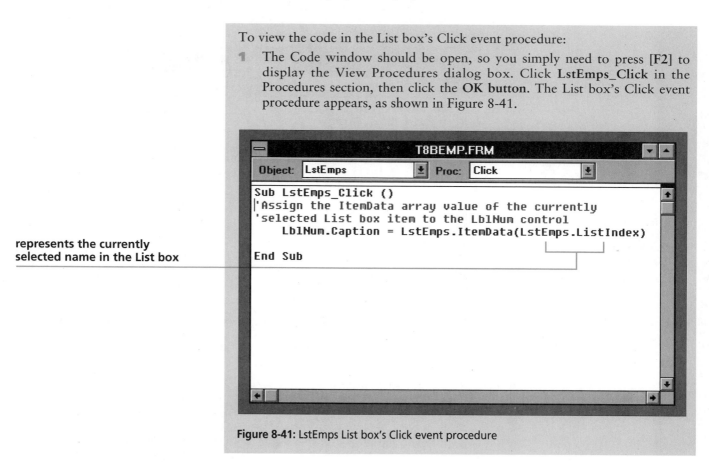

represents the currently selected name in the List box

Figure 8-41: LstEmps List box's Click event procedure

When you click an employee name in the List box, the *LblNum.Caption = LstEmps.ItemData(LstEmps.ListIndex)* instruction will display the corresponding employee number from the ItemData array. (Recall that the ListIndex property contains the index of the currently selected item in the list.) In other words, if you click "Beth" in the list, LstEmps.ListIndex will contain the number 1; the *LblNum.Caption = LstEmps.ItemData(LstEmps.ListIndex)* instruction will, therefore, assign the value in LstEmps.ItemData(1)—3456—to the LblNum control.

The last procedure you will view is the Display button's Click event procedure.

The Display Button's Click Event Procedure

The Display button will display the contents of the List box and its corresponding ItemData array on the form.

To view the Display button's Click event procedure:

1 The Code window should be open, so you simply need to press **[F2]** to display the View Procedures dialog box. Click **CmdDisplay_Click** in the Procedures section, then click the **OK button**. The Display button's Click event procedure appears, as shown in Figure 8-42.

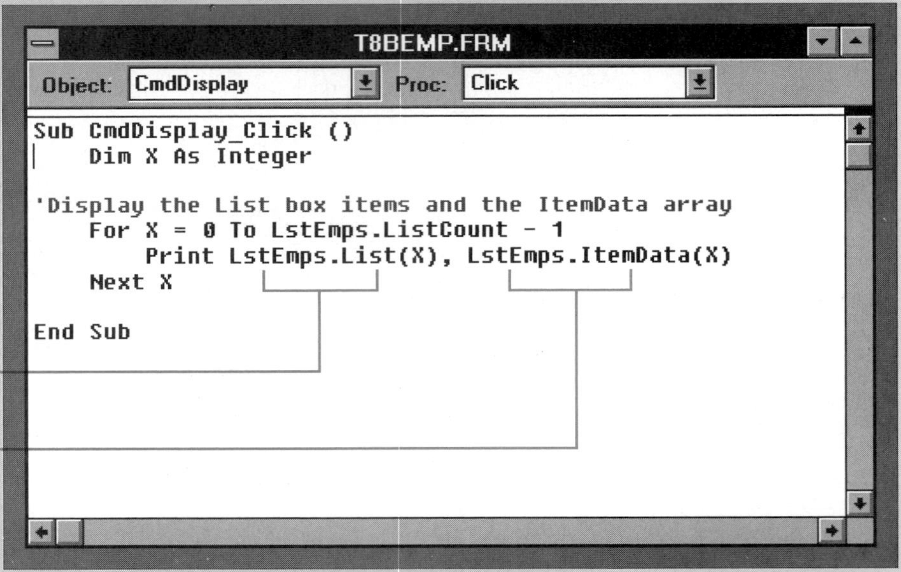

```
T8BEMP.FRM
Object: CmdDisplay          Proc: Click

Sub CmdDisplay_Click ()
    Dim X As Integer

'Display the List box items and the ItemData array
    For X = 0 To LstEmps.ListCount - 1
        Print LstEmps.List(X), LstEmps.ItemData(X)
    Next X

End Sub
```

name in List box

employee number in
ItemData array

Figure 8-42: Display button's Click event procedure

The code first declares an Integer variable named X. A For...Next loop is then used to display the contents of the List box—LstEmps.List(X)—and the contents of the ItemData array—LstEmps.ItemData(X)—on the form. Notice that the For...Next loop is initially set to 0, which is the index of the first item in the list. The loop's ending value is *LstEmps.ListCount – 1*, which is the index of the last item in the list. (Recall that the value in the ListCount property is always *one more* than the largest index. In other words, a List box having indexes of 0, 1, 2, 3, and 4 will have a ListCount value of 5.) Let's run this application to see how it works.

2   Close the Code window, restore the form to its standard size, then **save and run** the application. The form's Load event procedure fills the List box with the names of the five employees; it also fills the ItemData array with the corresponding employee numbers. You can verify that by clicking the Display button.

3   Click the **Display button.** The employee names and their corresponding numbers appear on the form, as shown in Figure 8-43.

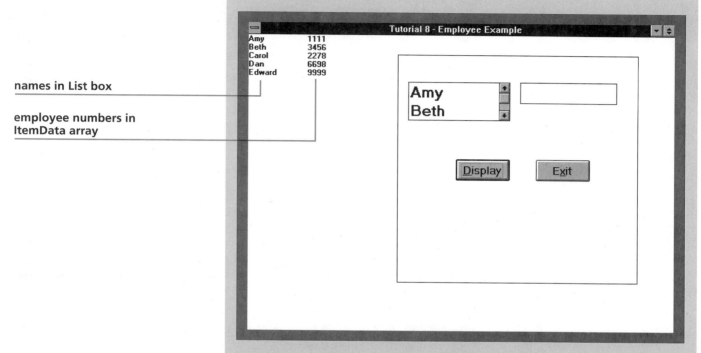

names in List box

employee numbers in
ItemData array

Figure 8-43: Employee names and numbers displayed on the form

4   Click **Beth** in the list. Because Beth is the second name in the list, Visual Basic displays the second employee number from the ItemData array, 3456, in the LblNum control.

5   Click the **Exit button** to end the application. Visual Basic returns to the design screen.

In the next section you will modify the employee example by setting the List box's Sorted property to True and adding another employee to the list.

Modifying the Employee Example

Let's see what happens to the List box and its ItemData array when you set the List box's Sorted property to True and then add another employee to the list.

To change the List box's Sorted property and then add an employee to the list:

1   Click the **LstEmps List box,** then double-click **Sorted** in the Properties list until the property says True.

2   Double-click the **form.** The form's Load event procedure appears.

Let's add Betty, who is employee number 1234, to the list of employees.

3   Maximize the Code window and enter the two lines of code shown in Figure 8-44.

enter these two lines of code

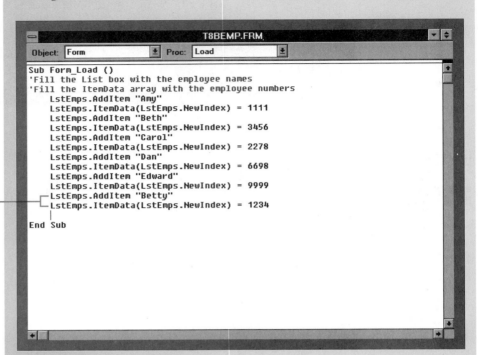

```
                                    T8BEMP.FRM
Object:  Form              Proc:  Load

Sub Form_Load ()
'Fill the List box with the employee names
'Fill the ItemData array with the employee numbers
     LstEmps.AddItem "Amy"
     LstEmps.ItemData(LstEmps.NewIndex) = 1111
     LstEmps.AddItem "Beth"
     LstEmps.ItemData(LstEmps.NewIndex) = 3456
     LstEmps.AddItem "Carol"
     LstEmps.ItemData(LstEmps.NewIndex) = 2278
     LstEmps.AddItem "Dan"
     LstEmps.ItemData(LstEmps.NewIndex) = 6698
     LstEmps.AddItem "Edward"
     LstEmps.ItemData(LstEmps.NewIndex) = 9999
     LstEmps.AddItem "Betty"
     LstEmps.ItemData(LstEmps.NewIndex) = 1234

End Sub
```

Figure 8-44: Modified Load event procedure

4   Close the Code window, **save and run** the application, then scroll the List box until you see Betty's name. The form's Load event procedure stores the first five names, which are already in alphabetical order, in positions 0 through 4 in the List box; the corresponding employee numbers are stored in positions 0 through 4 in the ItemData array. Because the List box's Sorted property is set to True, the *LstEmps.AddItem "Betty"* instruction inserts Betty's name after "Beth" in the list; the NewIndex property is set to 2. (Recall that the index of the first item in the list is 0.) The *LstEmps.ItemData(LstEmps.NewIndex) = 1234* instruction then stores Betty's number in position 2 of the ItemData array. The employee names and numbers that originally occupied positions 2, 3, and 4 in the list and in the ItemData array, respectively, are moved down to positions 3, 4, and 5. Figure 8-45 illustrates what happens to the List box and the ItemData array when Betty's name is inserted.

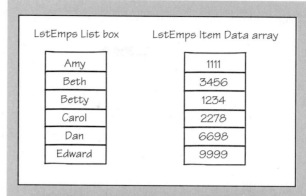

Figure 8-45: Contents of List box and its ItemData array after new name and number are added

5   Click the **Display button**. The contents of the List box and its ItemData array appear on the form. Notice that Betty's name and number are now included in the list and in the ItemData array, respectively.

6   Click **Betty** in the list. Betty's employee number, 1234, appears in the LblNum control.

7   On your own, click each of the other names in the List box and verify that their employee numbers appear correctly in the List box.

8   Click the **Exit button**. Visual Basic returns to the design screen.

Now that you know how to use the ListIndex, List, ListCount, NewIndex, and ItemData properties, you can create the personal directory application that you saw at the beginning of this tutorial.

The Personal Directory Application

Recall that your task in this tutorial is to create a personal directory application that will contain the names, phone numbers, and birthdays of your friends and relatives. (To make sure that you are familiar with the personal directory application, you may want to return to the beginning of this tutorial and run the appropriate .EXE file from Program Manager before continuing with this lesson.) The sketch of the user interface for this application is shown in Figure 8-46.

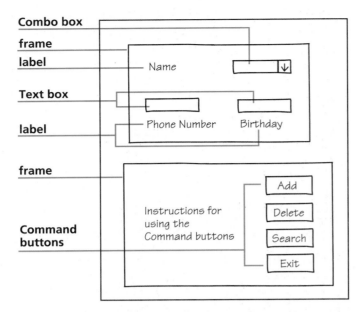

Figure 8-46: Sketch of the user interface for the personal directory application

According to the sketch, the application will contain various Label controls, Text boxes, Command buttons, Frame controls, and a Combo box. To save you time, your Student Disk contains a partially completed personal directory application. When you open the application you will notice that most of the user interface has already been created. You will finish creating the user interface in this lesson. You will also begin coding the application.

To open the partially completed application:

1   Open the **t8pdir.mak** project, which is in either the tut8\ver2 or tut8\ver3 directory on your Student Disk.

2   Save the form, the code module, and the project as **t8b**. (You will need to click T8PDIR.BAS in the Project window to save the code module.)

3   Click **T8B.FRM** in the Project window, click the **View Form button**, and then maximize the form. The user interface appears on the screen, as shown in Figure 8-47.

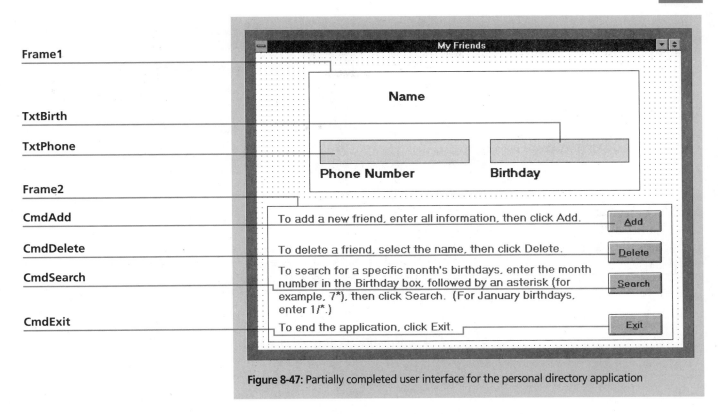

Frame1

TxtBirth

TxtPhone

Frame2

CmdAdd

CmdDelete

CmdSearch

CmdExit

Figure 8-47: Partially completed user interface for the personal directory application

One control is missing from the user interface—a Combo box. You will learn how to add that control in the next section.

Creating a Combo Box

A Combo box combines the features of a Text box and a List box in that it allows the user to either type an entry or select an item from a predefined list. In this case the Combo box will allow you to either type the name of a friend or relative in its Text box portion or select the name from its drop-down list.

To create a Combo box control:

1 Restore the form to its standard size, then double-click the **Combo box tool** in the Toolbox. A Combo box control appears on the form.

You will need to cut the Combo box from the form and then paste it into the Frame control at the top of the form.

2 The Combo box control should be selected. Press [Ctrl][x] to cut the Combo box from the form, then click the **Frame1 control at the top of the form** to select the Frame, and then press [Ctrl][v] to paste the Combo box into the Frame.

3 Set the following seven properties for the Combo box:

BackColor: **Pale yellow** (Skip this if you don't have a color monitor.)

FontSize: **12**

Left: **3000**

Name: **CboName** (The Cbo stands for Combo box.)

TabIndex: 0
Top: 480
Width: 3000

4 Double-click **Text** in the Properties list, press [**Delete**], then press [**Enter**] to delete the text shown in the Combo box.

5 Maximize the form. The Combo box appears, as shown in Figure 8-48.

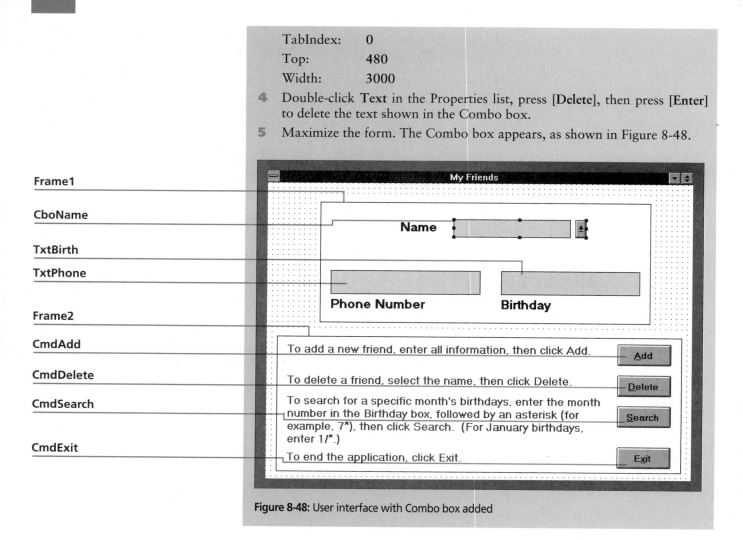

Frame1

CboName

TxtBirth

TxtPhone

Frame2

CmdAdd

CmdDelete

CmdSearch

CmdExit

Figure 8-48: User interface with Combo box added

Visual Basic offers three styles of Combo boxes. You tell Visual Basic which style you want by setting the Combo box's Style property. The default Combo box, Dropdown Combo, is the one currently on the screen. The Dropdown Combo style allows the user to make an entry in the Text box portion of the box. However, by clicking the down arrow button in the box, the user can also display a drop-down list of choices. Once the user makes a selection from the list, the drop-down list closes.

The second style of Combo box, the Simple Combo, is exactly the same as the Dropdown Combo except its drop-down list remains open at all times. Of the two styles, the Simple Combo is more convenient to use because the user doesn't have to click the down arrow button to display the list. However, the Dropdown Combo takes up less space on the form, and it is the preferred choice if many items must be displayed.

The third type of Combo box is the Dropdown List box. This style displays a list of choices when you click its down arrow button. Unlike the other two styles, this style of Combo box does not allow the user to type an entry into the Text box portion.

In deciding which of the three styles to use in this application, you rule out the Dropdown List box because you want to be able to type an entry into the Text box portion. You also rule out the Simple Combo box because, considering the number of friends and relatives that you have, that style would take up too much space on the form. The Dropdown Combo style is the best to use in this situation, so you will not need to change the Style property from its default value.

Just as with the List box, you use the AddItem method to specify the items to display in a Combo box; in this case you will display the names of your friends and relatives. The names, phone numbers, and birthdays of your friends and relatives have already been entered into a sequential access file for you. In a little while you will learn how to display those names in the Combo box.

Now let's begin coding the application.

Coding the Personal Directory Application

The TOE chart for the personal directory application is shown in Figure 8-49.

Task	Object	Event
Open sequential access data file	Form	Load
Enter names in Combo box		
Enter record location in ItemData array		
Enter record in array		
Display phone number and birthday of friend/relative	Combo box	Click
Get name from the user	Combo box	None
Get phone number from the user	Text box	None
Get birthday from user	Text box	None
Add a friend/relative to the personal directory	Command button (Add)	Click
Delete a friend/relative from the personal directory	Command button (Delete)	Click
Search the array for a birthday and display name and phone number	Command button (Search)	Click
Write the friend/relative records to the sequential access data file	Command button (Exit)	Click
End the application		

Figure 8-49: TOE chart for the personal directory application

On your Student Disk is a sequential access file named t8b.dat, which contains the names, phone numbers, and birthdays of five people. You will use this file in the personal directory application. Figure 8-50 shows the file displayed in Notepad.

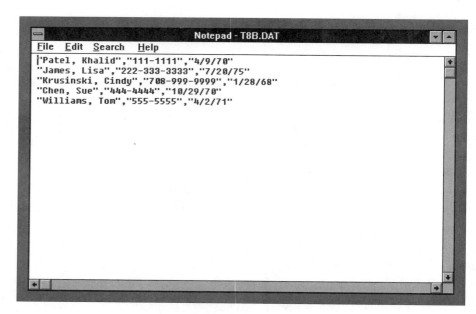

Figure 8-50: T8B. DAT file displayed in Notepad

In Tutorial 6 you learned that each line in a sequential access file represents a record and that records are composed of fields. Each record in the t8b.dat file, for example, contains three fields: name, phone number, and birthday. In this application, you will store the entire record—the three fields—in an array named DirArray. In order to store a record in an array, you need to create a record structure—a user-defined data type—for the record. (Recall that you also need to create a record structure for the records stored in a random access file.) As you learned in Tutorial 7, you create a record structure—a user-defined data type—by entering the Type statement in a code module. Let's enter the Type statement in the code module right now.

To enter the Type statement in the code module:

1 Restore the form to its standard size, click **T8B.BAS** in the Project window, then click the **View Code button.** The module's Code window appears.

The user-defined data type (the record structure) will contain three String fields: name, phone number, and birthday. You will name the user-defined data type DirStruc.

2 Enter the Type statement shown in Figure 8-51.

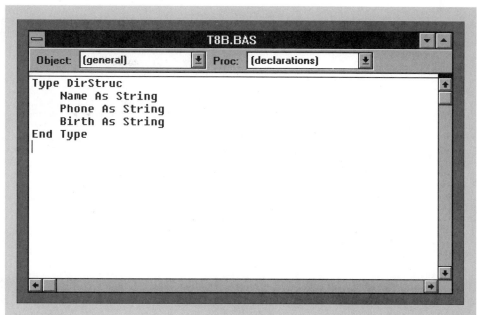

Figure 8-51: Type statement entered in code module

Notice that the Type statement shown in Figure 8-51 does not specify the length of the String fields, as did the Type statements in Tutorial 7. (Recall that you specify the length of a String field by appending both an asterisk and a number to the end of the field definition.) Unlike the records stored in a random access file, the records stored in a variable array do not have to be the same length.

3 Close the Code window.

After creating a user-defined data type, you can then declare a variable array of that type. You will declare the array in the form's general Declarations section because the array will be used by several procedures in the form.

To code the form's general Declarations section:

1 Double-click the **form**, then click the **down arrow button in the Code window's Object box**. Scroll the list box and then click **(general)** in the drop-down list. The form's general Declarations section appears with the *Option Explicit* statement already entered in the Code window.

You estimate that you will need to keep track of as many as 50 people. Let's declare a one-dimensional form-level array named DirArray that will store up to 50 records. The array will have a data type of DirStruc, which means that each variable in the array will contain three fields: name, phone number, and birthday.

2 Press the [**down arrow**] to position the blinking insertion point in the blank line below the *Option Explicit* statement, then type **dim DirArray(1 to 50) as DirStruc** and press [**Enter**].

The directory application will also need a variable in which it can keep track of the number of records stored in the array. You will use a form-level Integer variable named Numrec for that purpose.

3   Type **dim Numrec as integer**, press [Tab], then type **'Number of records in the array** and press [Enter].

If people are either added to the array or deleted from the array, the information in the sequential access file on your Student Disk will need to be updated to reflect the additions and deletions. You will use a form-level String variable named Updates to keep track of whether the file needs to be updated. (Be sure that you don't use Update as a variable name because it is a reserved word in Visual Basic; use Updates instead.)

4   Type **dim Updates as string**, press [Tab], then type **'Keeps track of file updates** and press [Enter].

5   Compare your code with Figure 8-52. Be sure to make any needed corrections before continuing.

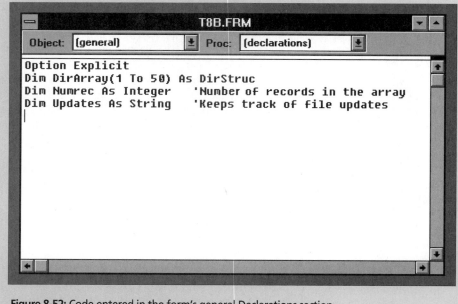

Figure 8-52: Code entered in the form's general Declarations section

6   Close the Code window.

Let's code the form's Load event procedure next.

Coding the Form's Load Event Procedure

The pseudocode for the form's Load event procedure is shown in Figure 8-53.

```
1. Open the sequential access file for input

2. Do while it is not the end of the file

        Add one to the number of records

        Read a record from the file and store it in the array

        Add the name from the array to the Combo box

        Add the record's array position to the ItemData array

    End the loop

3. Close the file
```

Figure 8-53: Pseudocode for the form's Load event procedure

When you run the application and the form is loaded into memory, the form's Load event procedure will open the sequential access file that contains the names, phone numbers, and birthdays of your friends and relatives. A Do...While loop will then check if the record pointer is at the end of the file. If the record pointer is at the end of the file, the file is closed and the Load event procedure ends. If, on the other hand, the record pointer is not at the end of the file, then the four instructions within the Do...While loop will be processed as follows: First the number of records in the array will be increased by 1, then the next record will be read from the file and stored in the array, then the name of the friend or relative will be added to the Combo box, and then the record's array location will be stored in the Combo box's ItemData array. The Do...While loop will repeat those instructions for each of the records in the sequential access file. When all of the records have been read and stored in the array, the Do...While loop will stop. At that point the sequential access file will be closed and the Load event procedure will end.

Now let's enter the corresponding code in the form's Load event procedure.

To code the form's Load event procedure:

1   Double-click the **form**. The form's Load event procedure appears.

First you need to open the t8b.dat sequential access file, which contains the names of your friends and relatives. That file is in either the tut8\ver2 or tut8\ver3 directory on your Student Disk.

2   Maximize the Code window, press [**Tab**], then type one of the following Open statements according to the location of your Student Disk and your version of Visual Basic:

open "a:\tut8\ver2\t8b.dat" for input as #1

open "b:\tut8\ver2\t8b.dat" for input as #1

open "a:\tut8\ver3\t8b.dat" for input as #1

open "b:\tut8\ver3\t8b.dat" for input as #1

3   Press [**Enter**].

Now you need to begin the Do...While loop. You want the loop to stop when all of the records in the sequential access file have been read—in other words, when the record pointer reaches the end of the file. As you learned in Tutorial 6, you can use the EOF function to test for the end of the file.

4   Type **do while not eof(1)** and press **[Enter]** to begin the loop.

If it's not the end of the file, then you need to add 1 to the Numrec variable, which keeps track of the number of records in the array. (Recall that Numrec is a form-level variable declared in the form's general Declarations section.)

5   Press **[Tab]**, then type **Numrec = Numrec + 1** and press **[Enter]**.

You will now use the Input # statement, which you learned about in Tutorial 6, to read a record from the sequential access file and store it in the array. The format of the Input # statement, you may remember, is **Input #** *filenumber, variablelist*. *Filenumber* is the number used in the Open statement to open the sequential access file and *variablelist* is one or more numeric or string variables, separated by a comma. In this case the *variablelist* will include the three field variables contained in the array. Recall that you refer to the individual field variables by preceding the field variable's name with the name of the record variable in which it is defined. You separate the record variable's name from the field variable's name with a period. Figure 8-54 illustrates the names of the record variables and the field variables in the DirArray variable array.

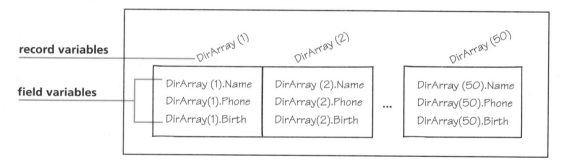

Figure 8-54: Record variables and field variables in the DirArray array

Notice that each record variable shown in Figure 8-54 has a subscript; that's because the record variables in this application belong to an array. The subscript indicates the position of the record variable in the DirArray array. In this application you can use the Numrec variable as the record variable's subscript; it will control into which array variable the next record will be read. For example, if Numrec contains the number 1, the record from the file will be input into DirArray(1). If Numrec contains the number 2, the record will be read into DirArray(2), and so on. Let's enter the Input # statement.

To continue coding the form's Load event procedure, then save and run the application:

1   Type **input #1, DirArray(Numrec).Name, DirArray(Numrec).Phone, DirArray(Numrec).Birth** and press **[Enter]**.

Now enter the name, which is stored in the DirArray array, into the Combo box.

2 Type **CboName.AddItem DirArray(Numrec).Name** and press **[Enter]**.

The next step is to enter the value stored in the Numrec variable, which represents the record's position in the DirArray array, into the Combo box's ItemData array. You can use the *CboName.ItemData(CboName.NewIndex) = Numrec* instruction to do so. (Recall that the NewIndex property specifies the index of the item most recently added to a Combo box. When a name is added to the Combo box, the value in Numrec will be entered into the corresponding position of the ItemData array.)

3 Type **CboName.ItemData(CboName.NewIndex) = Numrec** and press **[Enter]**.

You can now end the Do...While loop and close the sequential access file.

4 Press **[Backspace]**, type **loop** and press **[Enter]** to end the Do...While loop, and then type **close #1** and press **[Enter]** to close the sequential access file.

5 Enter the documentation shown in Figure 8-55. Also compare your code with the code shown in the figure and make any needed corrections before continuing to the next step. (You may need to scroll the Code window to see the rest of the Input # statement.)

the drive letter and version number will depend on the location of your Student Disk and your version of Visual Basic

scroll the window, if necessary, to view the rest of the Input instruction

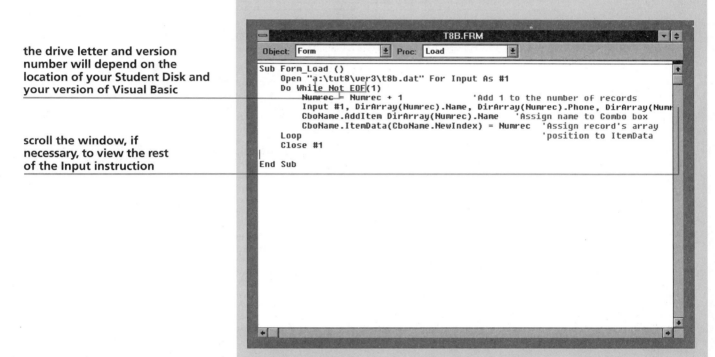

```
Sub Form_Load ()
    Open "a:\tut8\ver3\t8b.dat" For Input As #1
    Do While Not EOF(1)
        Numrec = Numrec + 1                    'Add 1 to the number of records
        Input #1, DirArray(Numrec).Name, DirArray(Numrec).Phone, DirArray(Numr
        CboName.AddItem DirArray(Numrec).Name    'Assign name to Combo box
        CboName.ItemData(CboName.NewIndex) = Numrec    'Assign record's array
    Loop                                           'position to ItemData
    Close #1

End Sub
```

Figure 8-55: Form's Load event procedure

Let's save and run the application to see how the Combo box works.

6 Close the Code window, then **save and run** the application. The Load event procedure reads the records from the sequential access file and enters each, one at a time, into the array. The procedure also enters the names into the Combo box and each name's DirArray array position into the ItemData array. Figure 8-56 illustrates the contents of the DirArray array, the list portion of the Combo box, and the ItemData array.

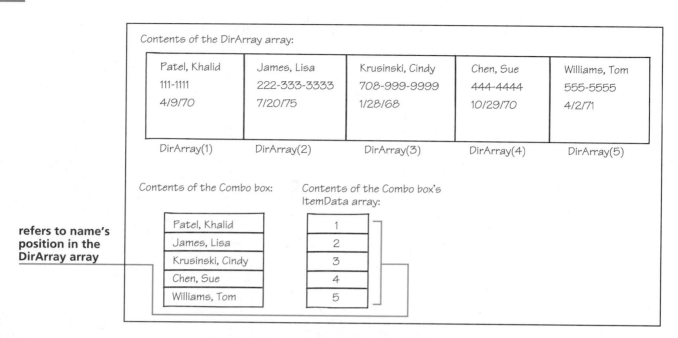

refers to name's position in the DirArray array

Figure 8-56: Contents of the DirArray array, the Combo box, and the Combo box's ItemData array

Let's open the Combo box and verify that the names were entered correctly.

7 Click the **down arrow button in the Combo box**. A drop-down list showing the five names from the file appears, as shown in Figure 8-57.

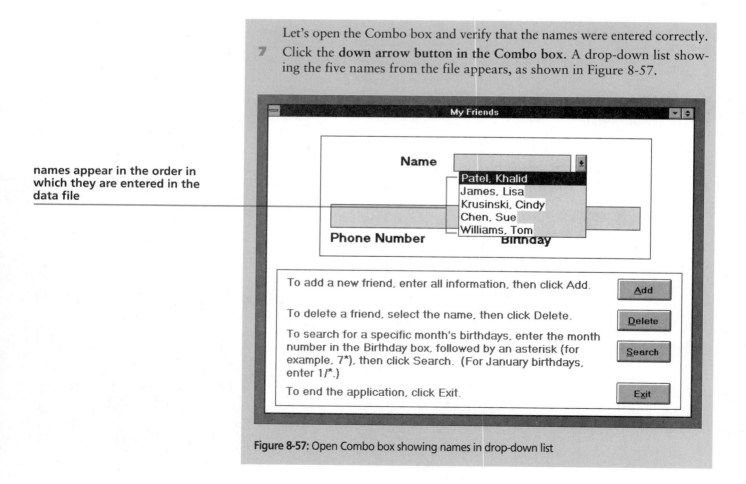

names appear in the order in which they are entered in the data file

Figure 8-57: Open Combo box showing names in drop-down list

The names appear in the order in which they were read from the sequential access file and stored in the array. It would be more convenient if the names appeared in the drop-down list in alphabetical order; then you could find a name more quickly. Let's stop the application and put the names in alphabetical order.

8   Click the **Exit button.** Visual Basic returns to the design screen.

You can put the names in alphabetical order by setting the Combo box's sorted property to True.

Sorting the Names in a Combo Box

Putting data in alphabetical or numerical order is called **sorting.** You can sort the strings contained in either a Combo box or a List box by setting the control's Sorted property. When set to the default value of False, the items in the list appear in the order in which they are entered into the list. When the Sorted property is set to True, the items are automatically sorted as they are entered into the list. Let's have Visual Basic sort the names contained in the Combo box's drop-down list.

To sort the names in the Combo box:

1   Click the **CboName Combo box** to select it, then double-click **Sorted** in the Properties list until the property says True.

2   **Save and run** the application.

3   Click the **down arrow button in the Combo box.** The names now appear in alphabetical order, as shown in Figure 8-58.

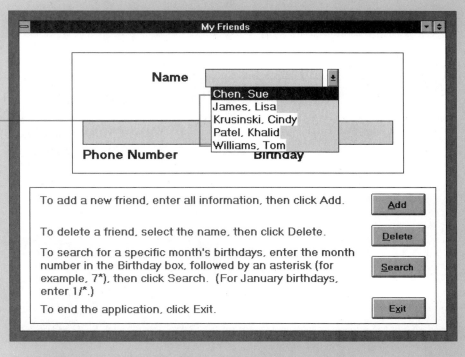

names are now in alphabetical order

Figure 8-58: Open Combo box showing sorted names

4 Click **James, Lisa.** "James, Lisa" (without the quotes) appears in the Text box portion of the Combo box. Visual Basic also records "James, Lisa" (without the quotes) in the Text property of the CboName control.

5 Click the **Exit button.** Visual Basic returns to the design screen.

In the next section you will code the Combo box so that it displays the phone number and birthday when you click a name in the drop-down list.

Coding the Combo Box

Recall that when you click a name in the CboName control's drop-down list, Visual Basic records the name in the control's Text property. You don't need to write any code for that to happen; Visual Basic handles it automatically. You do, however, need to write the code to tell the Combo box's Click event procedure to display the phone number and birthday that correspond to the selected name. The pseudocode for the CboName control's Click event procedure is shown in Figure 8-59.

```
1. Declare Selection variable

2. Assign the currently selected item's ItemData value to the Selection
   variable

3. Assign the currently selected item's phone number from the array to the
   TxtPhone Text box

4. Assign the currently selected item's birthday from the array to the
   TxtBirth Text box
```

Figure 8-59: Pseudocode for the Combo box's Click event procedure

The Combo box's Click event procedure will use the values in the control's ItemData array, which correspond to the location of each name in the DirArray array, to display the phone number and birthday in the appropriate controls on the form. Let's write the corresponding code in the CboName control's Click event procedure.

To code the Combo box's Click event procedure, then save and run the application:

1 Double-click the **Combo box.** The CboName control's Change event procedure appears. Click the **down arrow in the Code window's Proc box,** then click **Click** in the drop-down list. Maximize the Code window, then enter the code shown in Figure 8-60.

be sure you enter the code in the
Click event procedure

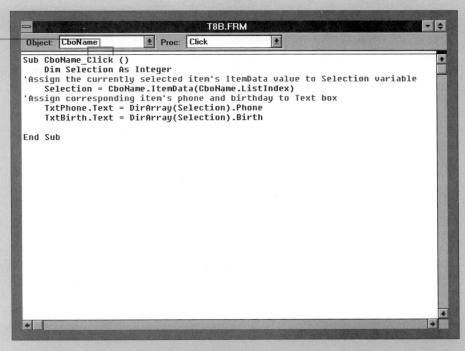

Figure 8-60: Combo box's Click event procedure

The code declares a local Integer variable named Selection. The *Selection = CboName.ItemData(CboName.ListIndex)* instruction assigns the value contained in the currently selected item's ItemData property to the Selection variable. (Recall that the ListIndex property stores the index of the currently selected item.) The value in the ItemData property, remember, tells Visual Basic where the record corresponding to the name is located in the DirArray array. For example, if a name's ItemData value is 3, its record is stored in DirArray(3).

The *TxtPhone.Text = DirArray(Selection).Phone* and *TxtBirth.Text = DirArray(Selection).Birth* instructions assign the phone number and birthday, which correspond to the name selected in the Combo box, to the appropriate Text boxes on the form.

Let's save and run the application to see how the Combo box's Click event procedure works.

2   Close the Code window, then **save and run** the application.

3   Click the **down arrow button in the Combo box,** then click **James, Lisa.** Lisa's name, phone number, and birthday appear on the screen, as shown in Figure 8-61.

Visual Basic automatically highlights the text in a Combo box when the control receives the focus

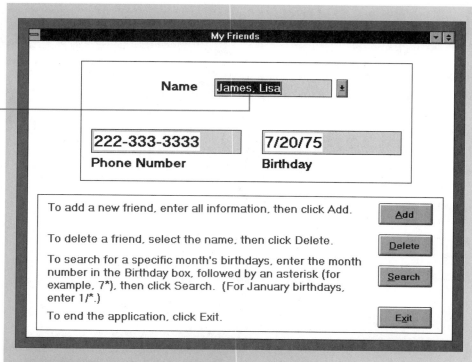

Figure 8-61: User interface showing Lisa James's information

Notice that the focus is in the Combo box, as indicated by the highlighted name. Visual Basic automatically highlights (or selects) the text in a Combo box when the control receives the focus. When you type a character into the Combo box or when you click another name from its drop-down list, the new entry will replace the highlighted (selected) text. You can also press either the Delete key or the Backspace key to remove the highlighted text. Let's see how this works.

4 Press [Delete] (or press [Backspace]) to remove the highlighted text from the Combo box. Notice that you only needed to press the Delete key (or the Backspace key) once to remove the selected text.

5 Click the **Exit button**. Visual Basic returns to the design screen.

You have now completed Lesson B. You will finish coding the personal directory application in Lesson C. You can now either take a break or complete the end-of-lesson questions and exercises.

SUMMARY

To combine the features of a Text box and a List box:

■ Use the Combo box control. The Combo box has three styles: Dropdown Combo, Simple Combo, and Dropdown List.

■ If you want the items in the Combo box to be sorted, set the Combo box's Sorted property to True.

To add an item to a Combo box:

■ Use the AddItem method. Its format is *Control*.**AddItem** *item*. *Control* is the name of the control, **AddItem** is the name of the method, and *item* is the string expression you want displayed in the control. Be sure to enclose the string expression in quotation marks.

To store a record in a variable array:

■ Use the Type statement to create a record structure—a user-defined data type. Enter the Type statement in a code module.
■ Use the user-defined data type to declare the array.

To exit a For...Next loop before the loop is finished processing:

■ Use the Exit For statement. Processing will continue with the instruction following the Next statement.

Q U E S T I O N S

1. The _____ property of a List box or Combo box stores the index of the item currently selected in the list.
   a. ItemData
   b. List
   c. ListCount
   d. ListIndex
   e. NewIndex

2. You use the _____ property to access the individual values in the list portion of a List box or Combo box.
   a. ItemData
   b. List
   c. ListCount
   d. ListIndex
   e. NewIndex

3. The _____ property specifies the number of items in the list portion of a Combo box or List box.
   a. ItemData
   b. List
   c. ListCount
   d. ListIndex
   e. NewIndex

4. The _____ property specifies the index of the item most recently added to a Combo box or List box.
   a. ItemData
   b. List
   c. ListCount
   d. ListIndex
   e. NewIndex

5. You use the _____ property to access the items in the ItemData array.
   a. ItemData
   b. List
   c. ListCount
   d. ListIndex
   e. NewIndex

Use the following information to answer questions 6 through 15:

Assume that the LstCity List box and its ItemData array, which stores the city's population, contain the following items, in the order shown:

ListCity List Box	ItemData Array
Glenview	10900
Boulder	35600
Watertown	5000
Amos	12000

6. LstCity.List(1) refers to _____ .
   a. Amos
   b. Boulder
   c. Glenview
   d. Watertown

7. Assume that you have clicked Glenview in the List box. Which of the following instructions will change Glenview's population to 20000? (Choose two answers.)
   a. LstCity.ItemData(0) = 20000
   b. LstCity.ItemData(0) = "20000"
   c. LstCity.ItemData(1) = 20000
   d. LstCity.ItemData(1) = "20000"
   e. LstCity.ItemData(LstCity.ListIndex) = 20000

8. If you click Watertown in the List box, the value in the LstCity.ListIndex will be _____ .
   a. 0
   b. 1
   c. 2
   d. 3
   e. 4

9. Which of the following instructions will display Boulder on the form?
   a. Print LstCity.List(0)
   b. Print LstCity.List(1)
   c. Print LstCity.ListIndex(0)
   d. Print LstCity.ListIndex(1)
   e. Print 544LstCity.Index(1)

10. The value of the LstCity control's ListCount property is _____ .
  a. 0
  b. 1
  c. 4
  d. 5
  e. 8

11. If you added the city of Carlton to the list, its NewIndex property would be

_____ .
  a. 0
  b. 1
  c. 4
  d. 5
  e. 6

12. Which of the following instructions will display the population of Watertown on the form?
  a. Print LstCity.ItemData(2)
  b. Print LstCity.ItemData(3)
  c. Print LstCity.ListIndex(2)
  d. Print LstCity.ListIndex(3)
  e. Print LstCity.Index(2)

13. Assuming that you have clicked the city of Amos in the List box, which of the following instructions will display the population of Amos on the form?
  a. Print LstCity.ItemData(LstCity.ListIndex)
  b. Print LstCity.ItemData(LstCity.NewIndex)
  c. Print LstCity.ListIndex(LstCity.ItemData)
  d. Print LstCity.ListIndex(LstCity.ListCount)
  e. Print LstCity.Index(LstCity.List)

14. If you set the LstCity control's Sorted property to True, what will happen to the List box and the ItemData array? Show the results in the chart below.

LstCity List Box   ItemData Array

15. Assuming that you have set the LstCity control's Sorted property to True, if you add the city of Carlton to the list, its NewIndex property would be

_____ .
  a. 0
  b. 1
  c. 2
  d. 5
  e. 6

16. The Combo box control combines the features of a _____ and a _____ . (Choose two answers.)

    a. Command button
    b. Frame control
    c. Label control
    d. List box
    e. Text box

17. You use this method to define the items in a Combo box.

    a. AddItem
    b. AddList
    c. ItemAdd
    d. ItemDefine
    e. ListAdd

18. Which of the following instructions will add the word COMPUTERS to a Combo box named CboItems?

    a. AddItem.CboItems COMPUTERS
    b. AddItem.CboItems "COMPUTERS"
    c. ItemAdd.CboItems "COMPUTERS"
    d. CboItems.AddItem "COMPUTERS"
    e. CboItems.ItemAdd "COMPUTERS"

19. Which of the following instructions will add the number 10 to the CboNums Combo box?

    a. AddItem.CboNums 10
    b. AddItem.CboNums "10"
    c. ItemAdd.CboNums "10"
    d. CboNums.AddItem "10"
    e. CboNums.ItemAdd "10"

20. This style of Combo box allows the user to make an entry in the Text box portion and also display a drop-down list when the down arrow button is clicked.

    a. Dropdown Combo
    b. Dropdown List
    c. Simple Combo
    d. Simple List

21. This style of Combo box displays the drop-down list at all times.

    a. Dropdown Combo
    b. Dropdown List
    c. Simple Combo
    d. Simple List

22. This is the only style of Combo box that does not allow the user to enter text into the box.

    a. Dropdown Combo
    b. Dropdown List
    c. Simple Combo
    d. Simple List

23. This property determines the style of the Combo box.

    a. BoxStyle
    b. ComboStyle
    c. ComboType
    d. Style
    e. Type

24. Putting names in alphabetical order and putting numbers in numerical order is called _____ .
   a. alphabetizing
   b. ordering
   c. positioning
   d. sorting
   e. styling

25. When set to True, the _____ property automatically sorts the items in a Combo box.
   a. Alphabet
   b. Order
   c. Position
   d. Sorted
   e. Style

26. When you click an item in a Combo box's drop-down list, Visual Basic automatically records the item in the control's _____ property.
   a. Caption
   b. Label
   c. Name
   d. Style
   e. Text

27. You can use the _____ statement to stop processing a For...Next loop.
   a. End
   b. Exit
   c. Exit For
   d. Stop
   e. Stop For

Use the following information to answer questions 28 through 30:
   a. You have entered the following Type statement in a code module:

      Type EmpStruc
            ID as String
            Name as String
      End Type

   b. You have entered the following Dim statement in the general Declarations section of the form: Dim EmpArray(1 to 15) as EmpStruc
   c. X, an Integer variable, is used to keep track of the array subscript.

28. You refer to the fifth ID in the array as _____ .
   a. EmpArray(5).ID
   b. EmpArray.ID(5)
   c. EmpStruc(5).ID
   d. EmpStruc.ID(5)

29. Which of the following can be used to enter the data from a sequential access file into the array? The first field in the file is the ID and the second field is the name.
   a. Input #1, EmpStruc(X).ID, EmpStruc(X).Name
   b. Input #1, EmpStruc.ID(X), EmpStruc.Name(X)
   c. Input #1, EmpArray(X).Name, EmpArray(X).ID
   d. Input #1, EmpArray.ID(X), EmpArray.Name(X)
   e. Input #1, EmpArray(X).ID, EmpArray(X).Name

30. Which of the following will add the ID from the array to a Combo box named
CboID?
a. CboID.AddItem EmpArray(X).ID
b. CboID.AddItem EmpArray.ID(X)
c. CboID.AddItem EmpStruc(X).ID
d. CboID.AddItem EmpStruc.ID(X)
e. CboID.AddItem(X) EmpStruc.ID

E X E R C I S E S

1. Create the user interface shown in Figure 8-62.

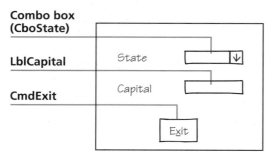

**Combo box
(CboState)**

LblCapital

CmdExit

State

Capital

Exit

Figure 8-62

a. Declare a user-defined data type that consists of two string fields: State and
Capital. Use the data type to declare a 50-element one-dimensional array.
b. Enter the 50 state names and their corresponding capitals into the one-dimensional array. The state names and their capitals are in the t8lbe1.dat file on your
Student Disk. The first field in the data file is the state name and the second field
is the capital.
c. Enter the 50 state names in the Combo box. The Combo box should be a
Dropdown List box style. Sort the names in the Combo box.
d. Code the Exit button so that it ends the application. Code the Combo box's
Click event procedure so that it displays the state's capital when you click the
state's name.
e. Save the form, code module, and project as t8lbe1.
f. Run the application. Test the application by clicking each state name in the
Combo box.
g. Exit the application. Print the form and the code for all modules.

2. Create the user interface shown in Figure 8-63.

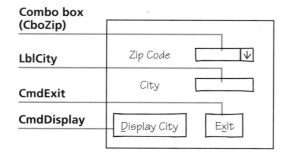

**Combo box
(CboZip)**

LblCity

CmdExit

CmdDisplay

Zip Code

City

Display City

Exit

Figure 8-63

a. Declare a user-defined data type that consists of two string fields: City and Zipcode. Use the data type to declare a 10-element one-dimensional array.

b. Enter the 10 cities and their corresponding zip codes into the one-dimensional array. The cities and their zip codes are in the t8city.dat file on your Student Disk. The first field in the data file is the city name and the second field is the zip code.

c. Enter the 10 cities in the Combo box. The Combo box should be a Dropdown List box style. Sort the cities in the Combo box.

d. Code the Exit button so that it ends the application. Code the Combo box's Click event procedure so that it displays the city's zip code when you click its name.

e. Save the form, code module, and project as t8lbe2.

f. Run the application. Test the application by clicking each city name in the Combo box.

g. Exit the application. Print the form and the code for all modules.

3. Create the user interface shown in Figure 8-64.

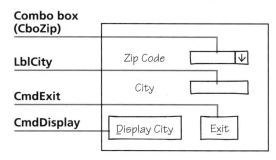

Figure 8-64

a. Declare a user-defined data type that consists of two string fields: City and Zipcode. Use the data type to declare a 10-element one-dimensional array.

b. Enter the 10 cities and their corresponding zip codes into the one-dimensional array. The cities and their zip codes are in the t8city.dat file on your Student Disk. The first field in the data file is the city name and the second field is the zip code.

c. Enter the 10 zip codes in the Combo box. The Combo box should be a Dropdown Combo box style. Sort the zip codes in the Combo box.

d. Code the Exit button so that it ends the application. Code the Display City button's Click event procedure so that it displays the name of the city corresponding to the zip code entered in the Combo box. If the zip code is not in the array, then display an error message.

e. Save the form, code module, and project as t8lbe3.

f. Run the application. Test the application by clicking a zip code in the Combo box and then clicking the Display City button. Then test the application by typing a zip code that you know is in the array and then clicking the Display City button. Last, test the application by typing a zip code that is not in the array and then clicking the Display City button.

g. Exit the application. Print the form and the code for all modules.

4. Create the user interface shown in Figure 8-65.

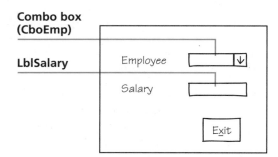

Figure 8-65

a. Declare a user-defined data type that consists of a string field named Employee and a Currency field named Salary. Use the data type to declare a 20-element one-dimensional array.

b. Enter the 20 employees and their corresponding salaries into the one-dimensional array. The employees and their salaries are in the t8emp.dat file on your Student Disk. The first field in the data file is the employee name and the second field is the salary.

c. Enter the names of the 20 employees in the Combo box. Enter the salaries in the Combo box's ItemData array. The Combo box should be a Dropdown Combo box style. Sort the employee names in the Combo box.

d. Code the Combo box's Click event procedure so that it displays the salary when you click the employee's name.

e. Code the Exit button so that it ends the application.

f. Save the form, code module, and project as t8lbe4.

g. Run the application. Test the application by clicking each name in the Combo box.

h. Exit the application. Print the form and the code for all modules. Then print the t8emp.dat file from Notepad.

Exercises 5 and 6 are Discovery Exercises.

discovery ▶ 5. Open the t8_grade.mak file, which is in either the tut8\ver2 or the tut8\ver3 directory on your Student Disk, then click the View Form button. You can use this application to display a student's grade. You simply enter the student's total points in the TxtPoints control and then click the Display Grade button. The grading scale is shown below.

Minimum Points	Maximum Points	Grade
0	299	F
300	349	D
350	399	C
400	449	B
450	500	A

a. Store the minimum points and the corresponding grade in a one-dimensional array. For example, in the first variable in the array, store the number 0 and the F grade.

b. Use a For...Next loop and a selection structure in the Display Grade button's Click event procedure to display the grade.

c. Save the form, the code module, and the project as t8lbe5.

d. Run the application. Test the application by entering the number 455 and clicking the Display Grade button; the grade should be an A. Then test the application by entering the number 210 and clicking the Display Grade button; the grade should be an F.

e. Exit the application. Print the form and the code for all modules.

discovery ▶ 6 Open the t8lbe5.mak application that you created in Exercise 5.

a. Add an InputBox statement to the form's Load event procedure. The InputBox statement should prompt the instructor for the total number of points that a student can earn in the course.

b. The form's Load event procedure contains the assignment statements that enter the data into the array. Modify the assignment statements according to the grading scale shown below. (For example, if the instructor enters the number 500 in response to the InputBox statement, the Load event should enter 450 (90% of 500) as the minimum number of points for an A. If the instructor enters the number 300, the Load event should enter 270 as the minimum number of points for an A.)

Minimum Points	Grade
Less than 60% of total points	F
60% of total points	D
70% of total points	C
80% of total points	B
90% of total of points	A

c. Save the form, the code module, and the project as t8lbe6.

d. Run the application. Test the application by entering the number 300 as the total number of points possible. Then enter 185 in the TxtPoints box and click the Display Grade button; the grade should be a D.

e. Exit the application. Then run the application again. This time enter 500 as the total number of points possible. Then enter 363 in the TxtPoints box and click the Display Grade button; the grade should be a C.

f. Exit the application. Print the form and the code for all modules.

LESSON C
objectives

In this lesson you will learn how to:

■ Add records to an array
■ Delete records from an array
■ Use the RemoveItem method
■ Use the SelStart method and the SelLength method

Completing the Personal Directory Application

Completing the Personal Directory Application

Before you can complete the personal directory application, you will need to open the t8b project that you created in Lesson B.

To continue coding the personal directory application:

1   Launch Visual Basic, if necessary, and open the **t8b.mak** project, which is in either the tut8\ver2 or tut8\ver3 directory on your Student Disk.
2   **Save** the form, the code module, and the project as **t8c**.
3   Click **T8C.FRM**, if necessary, in the Project window, click the **View Form button**, then maximize the form. The user interface appears on the screen.

Recall that you still need to code the Add button, the Delete button, the Search button, and the Exit button. Let's begin with the Add button, which is responsible for adding a person to the personal directory.

Coding the Add Button

To add a new person to the personal directory, you first enter his or her name in the Text box portion of the Combo box. When you do, Visual Basic records the name in the Combo box's Text property. You then enter the phone number and birthday in the appropriate Text boxes on the form and click the Add button. The pseudocode for the Add button's Click event procedure is shown in Figure 8-66.

```
1. Declare X variable and Found variable

2. Repeat For X = 1 to Numrec by 1

       If the uppercase name in the Combo box equals the uppercase name in the

       array then

               Display a "Duplicate Name" message

               Assign "Yes" to the Found variable

               Exit the For…Next loop

       End If

    End Repeat For

3. If Found <> "Yes" then

       Add one to the number of records

       Assign the name, phone number, and birthday to the array

       Assign the name from the array to the Combo box

       Assign the record number to the ItemData array

       Assign "Yes" to the Updates variable

    End if

4. Clear the Combo box and the Text boxes

5. Set the focus to the Combo box
```

Figure 8-66: Pseudocode for the Add button's Click event procedure

Before adding a name to the personal directory, the Add button's Click event procedure will compare the name in the Combo box's Text property with each name in the array. If the name in the Combo box matches a name in the array, then the procedure will display a message alerting the user that the name is already in the directory. If, however, the name in the Combo box does not match any of the names in the array, then the name, phone number, and birthday will be entered into the variable array. The name will also be added to the Combo box's drop-down list and its location in the DirArray array will be added to the ItemData array.

The code for the Add button is already entered in its Click event procedure; you will need to make only one modification to the code. Let's do that now.

To modify the code in the Add button's Click event procedure:

1 Double-click the **Add button**, then maximize the Code window. The CmdAdd control's Click event procedure appears.

You will need to remove the *Exit Sub* statement and its documentation, which are located below the *Sub CmdAdd_Click ()* instruction.

2 Highlight the *Exit Sub* statement and the documentation that follows in that line, press [Backspace] to remove the highlighted area, then press [Backspace] again to remove the blank line. The Code window should appear as shown in Figure 8-67.

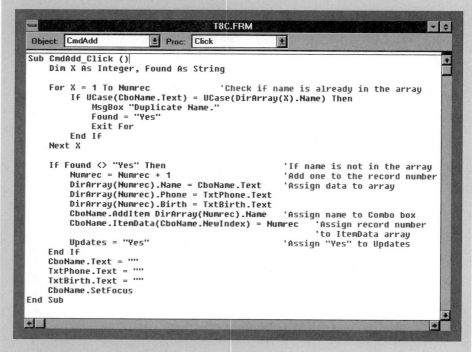

```
                               T8C.FRM
 Object:  CmdAdd          ±   Proc:  Click            ±
Sub CmdAdd_Click ()|
    Dim X As Integer, Found As String

    For X = 1 To Numrec              'Check if name is already in the array
        If UCase(CboName.Text) = UCase(DirArray(X).Name) Then
            MsgBox "Duplicate Name."
            Found = "Yes"
            Exit For
        End If
    Next X

    If Found <> "Yes" Then                    'If name is not in the array
        Numrec = Numrec + 1                   'Add one to the record number
        DirArray(Numrec).Name = CboName.Text  'Assign data to array
        DirArray(Numrec).Phone = TxtPhone.Text
        DirArray(Numrec).Birth = TxtBirth.Text
        CboName.AddItem DirArray(Numrec).Name     'Assign name to Combo box
        CboName.ItemData(CboName.NewIndex) = Numrec    'Assign record number
                                                        'to ItemData array
        Updates = "Yes"                       'Assign "Yes" to Updates
    End If
    CboName.Text = ""
    TxtPhone.Text = ""
    TxtBirth.Text = ""
    CboName.SetFocus
End Sub
```

Figure 8-67: CmdAdd control's Click event procedure

The Add button's Click event procedure declares a local Integer variable named X and a local string variable named Found. A For...Next loop and a selection structure then compare the uppercase name contained in the Combo box with the uppercase name stored in each array variable. (Recall that the UCase function, which you learned in Tutorial 4, temporarily converts a string expression to uppercase letters.) If the name in the Combo box matches a name in the array, then three tasks are performed: First a "Duplicate Name." message is displayed on the screen to alert the user that the name he or she entered in the Combo box is already in the directory. Second, the Found variable is set to "Yes" to indicate that a name matching the one in the Combo box was found in the directory. Third, the *Exit For* instruction exits the For...Next loop immediately; processing continues with the instruction following the *Next X* instruction.

After the For...Next loop is processed, another selection structure compares the value in the Found variable with the string "Yes". If the Found variable does not contain "Yes," it means that the name in the Combo box does not match any of the names in the directory. In that case, the number of records is increased by one; the name, phone number, and birthday are entered into the DirArray array; the name is added to the Combo box's drop-down list; and the location of the name in the DirArray array is stored in the Combo box's ItemData array. The Updates variable is then set to "Yes." Recall that the Updates variable is a form-level variable that records whether the sequential access file needs to be updated. When you add a new record to the directory, the sequential access file will need to be updated to include the new record. The instructions after the *End If* statement are then processed.

If, on the other hand, the Found variable does contain the string "Yes", which means that a name matching the one in the Combo box was found in the directory, then the procedure does not process the instructions within the selection structure; rather, processing skips to the instruction after the *End If* statement.

The instructions after the *End If* statement clear the Text property of the Combo box and the Text boxes and also set the focus to the Combo box. Let's test the Add button to see how it works.

tips

▶ If the "Duplicate Name." message did not appear, you may have misspelled the name. Simply repeat step 2.

To test the Add button:

1   Close the Code window, restore the form to its standard size, then **save and run** the application.

First let's try to add a name that is already in the directory.

2   Type **James, Lisa** (be sure to include the space between the comma and the letter L) and click the **Add button**. The Click event procedure searches the array for a name that matches the one in the Combo box. Because Lisa James's name is already in the file, the "Duplicate Name." message appears in the MsgBox statement's dialog box.

3   Click the **OK button** to remove the message. The focus moves to the Combo box.

Now let's add a new person to the directory.

4   Type **Lee, Jack** in the Combo box and press [**Tab**], type **888-8888** in the Phone Number Text box and press [**Tab**], and then type **12/20/48** in the Birthday Text box and click the **Add button**. The Add button's Click event procedure searches the array for a matching name. Because Jack Lee's name is not in the array, the procedure increases the number of records by 1. It then enters Jack's name, phone number, and birthday into the DirArray array. It also adds Jack's name to the Combo box and his location in the DirArray array to the ItemData array. It also sets the value in the Updates variable to "Yes" to indicate that the sequential access file needs to be updated to include Jack Lee's record.

5   Click the **down arrow button in the Combo box**. Notice that "Lee, Jack" (without the quotes) appears, in alphabetical order, in the drop-down list.

Let's display Jack Lee's phone number and birthday.

6   Click **Lee, Jack** in the drop-down list. The Combo box's Click event procedure locates Jack Lee's name in the array and displays his phone number and birthday on the form.

7   Click the **Exit button**. Visual Basic returns to the design screen.

It is important to note that, at this point, the Combo box includes Jack Lee's name and the DirArray array includes his record, but Jack's information is not yet saved in the sequential access file on your Student Disk. Because the information in both the Combo box and the DirArray array resides in the computer's internal memory, which is temporary, Jack Lee's information will be lost if you end the application or if the computer loses power. To make Jack's information permanent, you need to save it to the sequential access file on your Student Disk. You will write the instructions to update the sequential access file later on in this lesson. First, however, you will code the Delete button.

The Delete Button

You want to be able to delete a person from the directory by clicking his or her name in the Combo box's drop-down list and then clicking the Delete button. The pseudocode for the Delete button's Click event procedure is shown in Figure 8-68.

```
1. Declare Selection variable

2. Assign currently selected item's ItemData value to the Selection variable

3. Clear the record from the array by assigning null values

4. Remove the name from the Combo box

5. Assign "Yes" to Updates variable

6. Clear the Combo box and the Text boxes

7. Set the focus to the Combo box
```

Figure 8-68: Pseudocode for the Delete button's Click event procedure

When you click a name in the Combo box and then click the Delete button, the button's Click event procedure will clear the record, whose name matches the one selected in the Combo box, from the DirArray array and will remove the selected name from the Combo box. The Click event procedure will also assign the string "Yes" to the Updates variable to indicate that the sequential access file will need to be updated. The Text properties of the Text boxes and the Combo box will then be cleared and the focus set. Before viewing the code in the Delete button's Code window, you will learn about the RemoveItem method.

The RemoveItem Method

You can use the RemoveItem method to remove an item from a Combo box or a List box. The format of the RemoveItem method is *control*.**RemoveItem** *index*. *Control* is the name of the Combo box or List box, **RemoveItem** is the name of the method, and *index* is an integer that represents the position of the item in the list. The first item in the list has an index of 0 (zero), the second item has an index of 1, and so on. To remove the third item from a Combo box named CboName, for example, you would use the following RemoveItem instruction: *CboName.RemoveItem 2*.

But how do you tell Visual Basic to remove the currently selected item from a Combo box, as you need to do in the Delete button's Click event procedure? The answer is simple: You use the ListIndex property. The ListIndex property, recall, contains the index of the currently selected item in a List box or a Combo box. The following instruction, therefore, will tell Visual Basic to remove the currently selected item from the CboName control's drop-down list: *CboName.RemoveItem CboName.ListIndex*.

The code for the Delete button has already been entered into its Click event procedure; you will need to make only one modification to it. Let's view the code and make the modification.

To modify the code in the Delete button's Click event procedure, then save and run the application:

1 Maximize the form, double-click the **Delete button**, then maximize the Code window. The CmdDelete control's Click event procedure appears.

2 Highlight the *Exit Sub* statement, which is located below the *Sub CmdDelete_Click ()* statement, and the documentation that follows in that line, then press [**Backspace**] two times. The Code window should appear as shown in Figure 8-69.

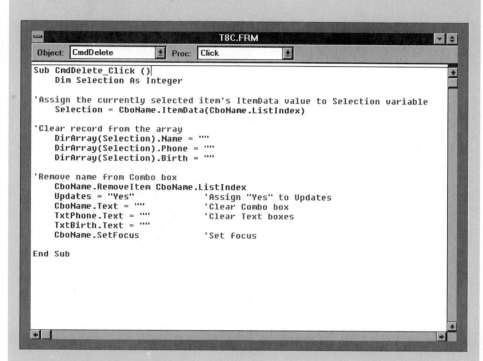

```
T8C.FRM

Object: CmdDelete          Proc: Click

Sub CmdDelete_Click ()
    Dim Selection As Integer

'Assign the currently selected item's ItemData value to Selection variable
    Selection = CboName.ItemData(CboName.ListIndex)

'Clear record from the array
    DirArray(Selection).Name = ""
    DirArray(Selection).Phone = ""
    DirArray(Selection).Birth = ""

'Remove name from Combo box
    CboName.RemoveItem CboName.ListIndex
    Updates = "Yes"                'Assign "Yes" to Updates
    CboName.Text = ""              'Clear Combo box
    TxtPhone.Text = ""             'Clear Text boxes
    TxtBirth.Text = ""
    CboName.SetFocus               'Set focus

End Sub
```

Figure 8-69: CmdDelete control's Click event procedure

The code declares an Integer variable named Selection. The *Selection = CboName.ItemData(CboName.ListIndex)* instruction assigns the value stored in the currently selected item's ItemData property to the Selection variable. (Recall that the ItemData property array contains the location of each name in the DirArray array.) The *DirArray(Selection).Name = " "*, *DirArray(Selection).Phone = " "*, and *DirArray(Selection).Birth = " "* instructions clear the record, which corresponds to the name selected in the Combo box, from the DirArray array. The *CboName.RemoveItem CboName.ListIndex* instruction removes the selected name from the Combo box's drop-down list. The Updates variable is then set to "Yes," which indicates that the sequential access file will need to be updated. Last, the Combo box and the Text boxes are cleared and the focus is set.

3 Close the Code window, then restore the form to its standard size.

Now let's test the Delete button to see how it works.

4 **Save and run** the application. Click the **down arrow button in the Combo box,** click **Chen, Sue** in the list, then click the **Delete button.**

Now let's prove that Sue Chen's name was removed from the Combo box.

5   Click the **down arrow button in the Combo box**. Notice that Sue Chen's name does not appear in the drop-down list.

6   Click the **down arrow button in the Combo box** to close the list.

Now let's prove that Sue Chen's name was removed from the DirArray array. You can do so by simply adding Sue Chen's information to the personal directory. Recall that the Add button's Click event procedure searches the array for a name matching the one entered in the Combo box. If the procedure finds a matching name in the array, then it will not allow the record to be entered in the personal directory. Only when the procedure does not find a matching name in the array does it allow the record to be entered.

7   Type **Chen, Sue** in the Name Combo box and press [**Tab**]. Type **444-4444** in the Phone Number Text box and press [**Tab**]. Type **10/29/70** in the Birthday Text box and click the **Add button**. Because Sue Chen's name is not in the array, the Add button enters her record in the personal directory and her name in the Combo box.

Let's prove that Sue Chen's name was added to the Combo box.

8   Click the **down arrow button in the Combo box**. Notice that Sue Chen's name appears in the list. Click the **down arrow button in the Combo box** to close the list.

Now let's prove that Sue Chen's name was added to the DirArray array. If her name is in the array, the "Duplicate Name." message will appear in a dialog box when you try to add her information to the personal directory.

9   Type **Chen, Sue** in the Combo box, then click the **Add button**. The "Duplicate Name." message appears.

10 Click the **OK button** to remove the message, then click the **Exit button**. Visual Basic return to the design screen.

The next procedure you will view is the Exit button's Click event procedure.

Coding the Exit Button's Click Event Procedure

When you exit the application, the Exit button's Click event procedure will need to check whether the Updates variable contains the word "Yes." If it does, then the procedure should write the array records to the sequential access file on your Student Disk. Only the records whose names appear in the Combo box, however, should be written to the file. The pseudocode for the Exit button's Click event procedure is shown in Figure 8-70.

```
1. Declare X variable and Rec variable

2. If the Updates variable contains "Yes" then

        Open the sequential access file for output

        Repeat For X = 0 to CboName.ListCount -1 by 1

                Write the array records to the file

        End Repeat For

        Close the file

    End If
```

Figure 8-70: Pseudocode for the Exit button's Click event procedure

The code for the Exit button is already entered in its Click event procedure; you just need to make a minor modification to it.

To modify the code in the Exit button's Click event procedure, then save and run the application:

1 Maximize the form, double-click the **Exit button**, then maximize the Code window.

2 Highlight the *End* statement, which appears below the *Sub CmdExit_Click ()* statement, and the documentation that follows on that line. Press [**Backspace**] two times. The Code window should appear as shown in Figure 8-71. If necessary, change the drive letter to the drive containing your Student Disk.

if necessary, change the drive letter to the drive containing your Student Disk

```
                                    T8C.FRM
Object: CmdExit          Proc: Click

Sub CmdExit_Click ()

    Dim X As Integer, Rec As Integer

    If Updates = "Yes" Then              'The sequential file needs updating
        Open "a:\tut8\ver3\t8b.dat" For Output As #1
'Write the record corresponding to each name in the Combo box to the file
        For X = 0 To CboName.ListCount - 1
            Rec = CboName.ItemData(X)    'Assign record number to Rec variable
            Write #1, DirArray(Rec).Name, DirArray(Rec).Phone, DirArray(Rec).E
        Next X

        Close #1                         'Close the sequential file
    End If

End Sub
```

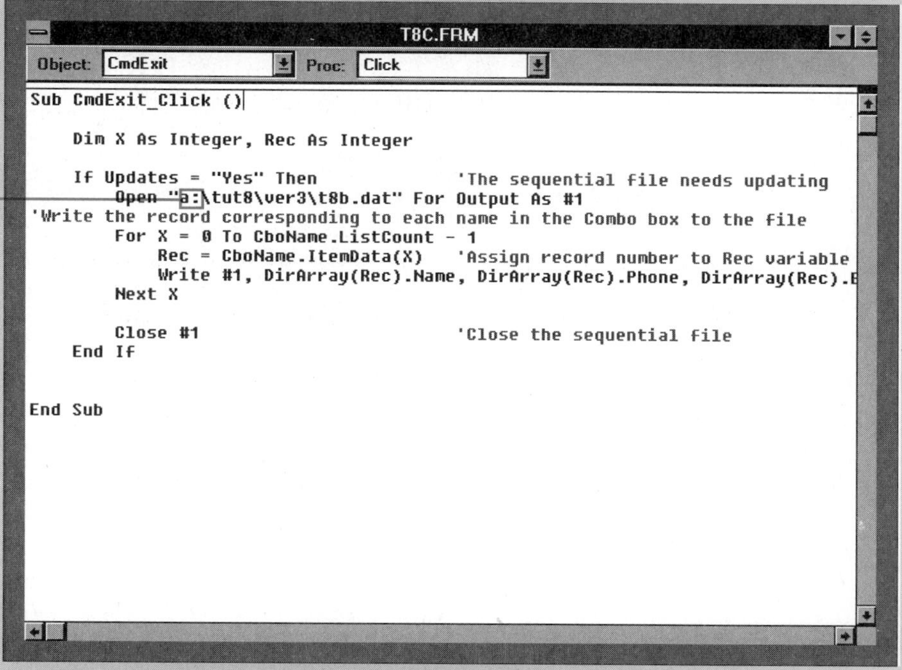

Figure 8-71: Cmd Exit control's Click event procedure

The code declares two Integer variables, X and Rec. (Rec stands for "record.") The selection structure compares the contents of the Updates variable to the string "Yes". If the Updates variable contains "Yes", then the sequential access file is opened for output. The For...Next loop is used to refer to each name in the list portion of the Combo box. The *Rec = CboName.ItemData(X)* instruction within the loop assigns each name's record number, which is contained in the ItemData array, to the Rec variable. The Write # instruction then writes the corresponding record to the sequential access file.

Let's test the Exit button to see how it works.

3   Close the Code window, restore the form to its standard size, then **save and run** the application.

First let's add a record.

4   Type **Lee, Jack** in the Name Text box and press [**Tab**]. Type **888-8888** in the Phone Number Text box and press [**Tab**]. Type **12/20/48** in the Birthday Text box, then click the **Add button**.

Now let's delete a record.

5   Click the **down arrow button in the Combo box**, then click **James, Lisa** in the drop-down list, and then click the **Delete button**. The Delete button's Click event procedure removes Lisa James's name from the Combo box. The procedure then assigns "Yes" to the Updates variable, clears the Combo box and the Text boxes, and then sets the focus.

Let's verify both that Jack Lee's name was added to and that Lisa James's name was removed from the Combo box.

6   Click the **down arrow button in the Combo box**. Notice that Jack Lee's name appears in the drop-down list; Lisa James's name does not.

7   Click the **Exit button**. The Exit button's Click event procedure first compares the contents of the Updates variable to the word "Yes". In this case the Updates variable does contain "Yes", so the procedure writes the records whose names appear in the Combo box to the sequential access file on your Student Disk. Visual Basic then returns to the design screen. (If you want to verify which records were written to the sequential access file, open the t8b.dat file in Notepad, then exit Notepad without saving the file.)

The last procedure you will code is the Search button's Click event procedure, which allows you to search the directory for friends and relatives born in a specific month. Before coding that procedure, you will learn about the Like operator.

The Like Operator

You can use the Like operator to compare two string expressions. The format of the Like operator is *string expression* **Like** *pattern*, where *pattern* is also a string expression. The difference between *string expression* and *pattern* is that *pattern* can contain special characters, called wildcard characters, but *string expression* cannot. (You'll learn about wildcard characters near the end of this lesson.) If the *string expression* matches the *pattern*, then the string comparison is true; otherwise, the string comparison is false. Keep in mind that the string comparisons made by the Like operator are case-sensitive, which means that an

uppercase letter is not equivalent to a lowercase letter—in other words, *"JAN"
Like "JAN"* is true, but *"JAN" Like "jan"* is false. Figure 8-72 shows other
examples of the Like operator. (When you compare the contents of string variables, it's best to use the UCase function.)

Expression:	Result:
"Alaska" Like "ALASKA"	False
California Like "Calif"	False
"ILLINOIS" Like "ILLINOIS"	True
UCase(State) Like "FLORIDA"	True if State variable contains Florida (entered in uppercase lowercase or any case combination); otherwise False

Figure 8-72: Examples of the Like operator

As already mentioned, the *pattern* can contain wildcard characters. One of
the wildcard characters is the asterisk (*). Similar to a wildcard in a game of
poker, you can use the asterisk to represent anything you want. *UCase(State)
Like "T*"*, for example, tells Visual Basic to compare the first character of the
string expression with the letter T; you don't care how many letters follow the
T in the *string expression*, nor do you care what those letters are. The
comparison will result in true if the State variable contains either "Texas" or
"Tennessee"; otherwise it will result in false. Figure 8-73 shows other examples
of the Like operator. (If you want to learn more about the Like operator, use
the Help menu to view the Help screen on the Like topic.)

Expression:	Result:
"Alaska" Like "A*"	True
"C*" Like "California"	False (only the pattern can contain a wildcard character)
"Arizona" Like "Ark*"	False
UCase(State) Like "I*"	True if State contains a word that begins with the letter I (entered in uppercase, lowercase, or any case combination).
UCase(State) Like "TEX"	True if the State variable contains a word that begins with the three letters TEX (entered in uppercase, lowercase, or any case combination).

Figure 8-73: Examples of the Like operator using the asterisk (*) wildcard

Now let's use the Like operator to search for the birthdays occurring in a specific month.

The Search Button

You want to be able to use the Search button to search the directory for the birthdays occurring in a specific month. The pseudocode for the Search button's Click event procedure is shown in Figure 8-74.

```
1. Declare X variable and Birthday variable

2. Assign Txt Birth.Text to Birthday variable

3. Repeat For X = 1 to Numrec

        If the birthday in the array is like the contents of the Birthday

        variable then

                Display the name, phone number, and birthday

                Display the "Press Enter or click OK to continue." message

        End If

    End Repeat For

4. Display the "Search is complete." message

5. Set the focus to the Combo box
```

Figure 8-74: Pseudocode for the Search button's Click event procedure

To search for the birthdays occurring in a specific month, you type the month's number followed by an * (asterisk) in the TxtBirth Text box; the month's number and the asterisk will serve as the *pattern* for the Like operator. The procedure will search the array for birthdays matching the *pattern*. When a match is found, the procedure will display that person's name, phone number, and birthday in the appropriate controls on the form.

The Search button's code is already entered in its Click event procedure. You need to make only one modification to it.

To view the code in the Search button:

1 Maximize the form, double-click the **Search button**, then maximize the Code window. The CmdSearch button's Click event procedure appears.

2 Highlight the *Exit Sub* instruction, which is below the *Sub CmdSearch_Click ()* statement, and the documentation on that line. Press [**Backspace**] two times. The Code window should look like Figure 8-75.

```
T8C.FRM
Object: CmdSearch          Proc: Click

Sub CmdSearch_Click ()

    Dim X As Integer, Birthday As String
    Birthday = TxtBirth.Text          'Assign birthday pattern to Birthday

'Search array for birthdays matching the birthday pattern
    For X = 1 To Numrec
        If DirArray(X).Birth Like Birthday Then  'If birthday matches pattern
            CboName.Text = DirArray(X).Name       'Assign data to controls
            TxtPhone.Text = DirArray(X).Phone
            TxtBirth.Text = DirArray(X).Birth
            MsgBox "Press Enter or click OK to continue."  'Display continue
        End If                                             'message
    Next X

    MsgBox "Search is complete."
    CboName.SetFocus

End Sub
```

Figure 8-75: CmdSearch control's Click event procedure

The code declares two local variables, X and Birthday. It then assigns the *pattern,* which is entered by the user into the TxtBirth Text box, to the Birthday variable. A For...Next loop then searches the entire array, looking for birthdays that match the *pattern* in the Birthday variable. When a match is found, that person's name, phone number, and birthday are displayed on the form. The MsgBox statement, which displays a dialog box that contains the "Press Enter or click OK to continue." message, temporarily halts the program so that you can read the information on the screen. After the For...Next loop searches the entire array, a MsgBox statement displays the "Search is complete." message. The focus is then set to the Combo box. Let's save and run the application to see how the Search button works.

3   Close the Code window, restore the form to its standard size, then **save and run** the application.

4   Press [**Tab**] two times to position the blinking insertion point in the TxtBirth Text box.

Let's search for the people born in April—the fourth month of the year.

5   Type 4* in the TxtBirth Text box and click the **Search button**. The Click event procedure stores the 4* (the *pattern*) in the Birthday variable. It then compares each of the birthdays in the array with the contents of the Birthday variable. The information about Khalid Patel, the first friend or relative in the array whose birthday is in April, appears on the form. The MsgBox statement's dialog box tells you to press Enter or click OK to continue.

6   Click the **OK button** to continue. The name, phone number, and birthday of the next friend born in April, Tom Williams, appears. The MsgBox statement tells you to press Enter or click OK to continue.

tips

....

▶ If you can't see the name, phone number, or birthday, simply drag the dialog box to another location on the screen.

7 Click the **OK button** to continue. The MsgBox statement displays the "Search is complete." message. Click the **OK button** to remove the "Search is complete." message. The Search button's Click event procedure ends.

Notice that the text in the Combo box is highlighted. As mentioned in Lesson B, Visual Basic automatically highlights (selects) the text in a Combo box when the control receives the focus. Let's enter another person into the directory.

8 Type **Milton, Tom** in the Combo box. Visual Basic replaces the highlighted (selected) text with "Milton, Tom" (without the quotes).

Now let's see what Visual Basic does when a Text box receives the focus.

9 Press **[Tab]** to move the insertion point into the TxtPhone Text box. When a Text box receives the focus, Visual Basic does not automatically highlight its contents. To enter a new phone number, you would first need to remove the existing number—a time-consuming task. In the next section, you will learn how to tell Visual Basic to automatically highlight the text in a Text box when the control receives the focus.

10 Press **[Tab]** to move the insertion point into the TxtBirth Text box. Here again, you would first need to remove the existing birthday before you can enter a new one.

You won't enter Tom Milton's record at this time.

11 Click the **Exit button** to end the application. Visual Basic returns to the design screen.

You could improve the directory application by having Visual Basic automatically highlight the contents of the TxtPhone and TxtBirth Text boxes when those controls receive the focus. You will learn how to do that in the next section.

The SelStart and SelLength Properties

You will need to use both the SelStart and the SelLength properties to highlight (select) the text in a Text box. The SelStart property tells Visual Basic where in the Text box to position the blinking insertion pointæin other words, where to start the text selection; the SelLength property tells Visual Basic how many characters to select.

The format of the SelStart property is *control*.**SelStart** = *index*. *Control* is the name of the Text box or Combo box in which the characters are to be selected and *index* is a number that indicates the position of the insertion point. The first position in the box is position 0, the second is position 1, and so on. The instruction, *TxtPhone.SelStart = 0*, for example, will place the blinking insertion point in position 0æthe first position in the Text box.

After positioning the blinking insertion point in its proper place, you can use the SelLength property to select (highlight) the text in the control. The format of the SelLength property is *control*.**SelLength** = *length*, where *control* is the name of the Text box or Combo box in which the text is to be selected and *length* is the number of characters to select. The *TxtPhone.SelLength = 5* instruction, for example, will select five characters, beginning with the character to the immediate right of the blinking insertion point.

But how do you select all of the text in a Text box when you don't know precisely how many characters it contains? In those cases, you can use the Len function to determine the number of characters for you. You used the Len function in Tutorial 7 to compute the length of a variable; you can also use the Len function to compute the length of a Text box's Text property. The *Len(TxtPhone.Text)* instruction, for example, returns the number of characters contained in the TxtPhone control. To select the number of characters contained in the TxtPhone Text box, you would use the *TxtPhone.SelLength = Len(TxtPhone.Text)* instruction.

You will enter both the instruction to set the SelStart property and the instruction to set the SelLength property in the GotFocus event procedure for the TxtPhone Text box and for the TxtBirth Text box. (The GotFocus event occurs when a control receives the focus.) Let's do that now.

To code the GotFocus event procedure for the two Text boxes:

1   Double-click the **TxtPhone Text box**. The control's Change event procedure appears.

2   Click the **down arrow button in the Proc box**, then click **GotFocus** in the drop-down list. The Code window for the GotFocus event procedure appears.

First you will set the SelStart property to zero, which will position the blinking insertion point at the beginning of the text in the TxtPhone Text box.

3   Press **[Tab]**, type **TxtPhone.SelStart = 0** and press **[Tab]**, then type **'Position insertion point** and press **[Enter]**.

You will now set the SelLength property to the length of the text in the Text box.

4   Type **TxtPhone.SelLength = Len(TxtPhone.Text)** and press **[Tab]**, then type **'Select text** and press **[Enter]**.

5   Compare your code with the code shown in Figure 8-76. Make any necessary corrections before continuing with the next step.

be sure you entered the code in the GotFocus procedure

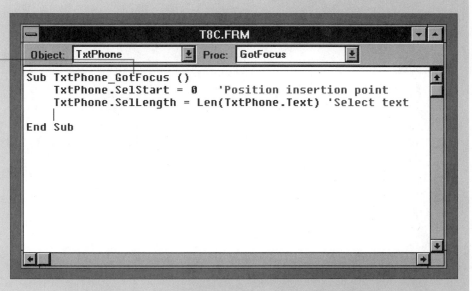

```
Sub TxtPhone_GotFocus ()
    TxtPhone.SelStart = 0    'Position insertion point
    TxtPhone.SelLength = Len(TxtPhone.Text) 'Select text

End Sub
```

Figure 8-76: TxtPhone control's GotFocus procedure

6   Click the **down arrow in the Code window's Object box,** then click **TxtBirth** in the drop-down list. The Change event procedure appears.

7   Click the **down arrow in the Code window's Proc box,** and then click **GotFocus** in the drop-down list. The GotFocus event procedure appears.

8   Enter the code shown in Figure 8-77.

be sure you entered the code in the GotFocus procedure

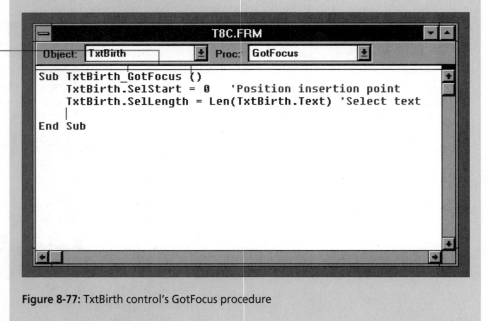

```
                        T8C.FRM
Object:  TxtBirth          ±   Proc:  GotFocus          ±
Sub TxtBirth_GotFocus ()
    TxtBirth.SelStart = 0    'Position insertion point
    TxtBirth.SelLength = Len(TxtBirth.Text) 'Select text

End Sub
```

Figure 8-77: TxtBirth control's GotFocus procedure

9   Close the Code window.

Now let's save and run the application to see how the GotFocus event procedure works.

To test the GotFocus event procedure for both Text boxes:

1   **Save and run** the application.

2   Click the **down arrow button in the Combo box,** then click **Lee, Jack** in the drop-down list. Jack Lee's name, phone number, and birthday appear on the screen.

    Now let's add a new record to the directory.

3   Type **Smith, Mary** in the Combo box, then press **[Tab]**. Visual Basic selects (highlights) the text in the TxtPhone Text box, as shown in Figure 8-78.

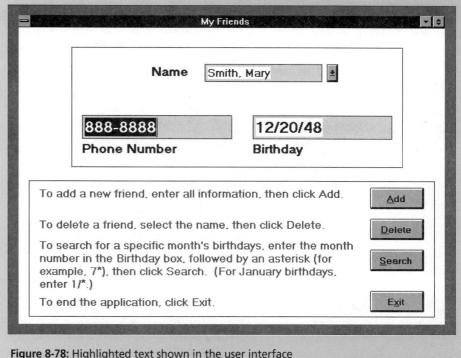

Figure 8-78: Highlighted text shown in the user interface

4   Type **999-9999** in the TxtPhone Text box. Visual Basic replaces the selected text with the new phone number.

5   Press [**Tab**]. Visual Basic highlights the text in the TxtBirth Text box.

6   Type **8/6/60** in the TxtBirth Text box. Visual Basic replaces the selected text with the new birthday.

7   Click the **Add button**, then click the **Exit button**. Visual Basic returns to the design screen.

Before leaving Lesson C, you will restore the t8b.dat file to its original condition—the condition it was in at the beginning of this tutorial, before you entered or deleted records.

To restore the t8b.dat file to its original condition:

1   Use File Manager to copy the t8b.bak file to the t8b.dat file. Both files are on your Student Disk in either the tut8\ver2 or the tut8\ver3 directory.

You have now completed Lesson C and the personal directory application. You can either take a break or complete the exercises and questions at the end of the lesson.

S U M M A R Y

To remove an item from a List box or a Combo box:

■ Use the RemoveItem method. Its format is *Control*.**RemoveItem** *index*. *Control* is the name of the List box or Combo box, **RemoveItem** is the name of the method, and *index* is an integer that represents the position of the item in the list. The first item in the list has an index of 0 (zero).

To refer to the index of the currently selected item in a List box or a Combo box:

■ Use the ListIndex property.

To compare two string expressions:

■ Use the Like operator. Its format is *string expression* **Like** *pattern*. The *pattern* can contain wildcard characters, such as the asterisk (*).

To position the blinking insertion point in a Text box or a Combo box:

■ Use the SelStart property. Its format is *control*.**SelStart** *index*. *Control* is the name of either the Text box or the Combo box in which the characters are to be selected. *Index* is a number that indicates the position of the insertion point. The first position is position 0 (zero).

To select the characters in a Text box or a Combo box:

■ Use the SelLength property. Its format is *control*.**SelLength** *length*. *Control* is the name of either the Text box or the Combo box in which the characters are to be selected. *Length* is the number of characters to select. The SelLength property selects the characters beginning at the location of the insertion point.

To process code when a control receives the focus:

■ Enter the code in the control's GotFocus event procedure.

Q U E S T I O N S

1. Use the _____ method to remove an item from a Combo box's drop-down list.
   a. DeleteItem
   b. EraseItem
   c. ItemErase
   d. ItemRemove
   e. RemoveItem

2. Which of the following will remove the first item from a Combo box named CboName?
   a. CboName.DeleteItem 0
   b. CboName.EraseItem 1
   c. CboName.ItemErase 0
   d. CboName.ItemRemove 1
   e. CboName.RemoveItem 0

3. When you click an item in a Combo box's drop-down list, Visual Basic records the index of that item in the _____ property.
   a. Index
   b. IndexList
   c. List
   d. ListIndex
   e. ListNumber

4. Which of the following will remove the currently selected item from a Combo box named CboName?
   a. CboName.DeleteItem CboName.Index
   b. CboName.EraseItem CboName.IndexList
   c. CboName.ItemErase CboName.List
   d. CboName.ItemRemove CboName.ListNumber
   e. CboName.RemoveItem CboName.ListIndex

5. You can use this operator to compare two string expressions.
   a. Comp
   b. Compare
   c. Like
   d. Match
   e. Pair

6. Which of the following comparisons are true? (Choose two.)
   a. "TEXAS" Like "T*"
   b. "TEXAS" Like "t*"
   c. "Texas" Like "T"
   d. "Texas" Like "T*"
   e. "T*" Like "TEXAS"

7. If the City variable contains "Atlanta," which of the following comparisons are true? (Choose two.)
   a. City Like "ATL*"
   b. City Like "At*"
   c. City Like "At"
   d. "City" Like "A*"
   e. UCase(City) Like "ATLANTA"

8. If the Birthday variable contains 7/20/50, which of the following comparisons are true? (Choose two.)
   a. Birthday Like "7*"
   b. Birthday Like "7/20"
   c. Birthday Like "7/20*"
   d. "Birthday" Like "7/20/50"
   e. Birthday Like "*/20/50"

9. You can use the _____ property to position the blinking insertion point in either a Text box or a Combo box.
   a. BeginSel
   b. BeginText
   c. Position
   d. SelLength
   e. SelStart

10. You can use the _____ property to select (highlight) the text in either a Text box or a Combo box.
    a. Highlight
    b. Select
    c. SelText
    d. SelLength
    e. SelStart

11. Which of the following will position the blinking insertion point in the first position of a Combo box named CboName?
    a. CboName.BeginSel = 0
    b. CboName.BeginText = 1
    c. CboName.SelLength = 0
    d. CboName.SelStart = 0
    e. CboName.SelStart = 1

12. Assume that the blinking insertion point is in the first position of a Combo box named CboName. Which of the following will highlight all of the characters in the Combo box?
    a. CboName.BeginSel = Len(CboName.Text)
    b. CboName.BeginText = Len(CboName.Text)
    c. CboName.SelLength = Len(CboName.Text)
    d. CboName.SelStart = Len(CboName.Text)
    e. CboName.SelText = Len(CboName.Text)

13. This event occurs when a control receives the focus.
    a. Focus
    b. GotFocus
    c. ReceiveFocus
    d. SelectFocus
    e. ViewFocus

E X E R C I S E S

1. a. Use File Manager to copy the Song.bak sequential access file, which is located in either the tut8\ver2 or the tut8\ver3 directory on your Student Disk, to t8lce1.dat.
   b. Open the t8lce1.dat file in Notepad. Print the file.
   c. Launch Visual Basic, if necessary. Create the user interface shown in Figure 8-79.

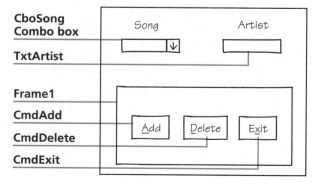

Figure 8-79

d. The Combo box should be a Dropdown Combo. Set its Sorted property to True.

e. Create a user-defined data type named SongStruc that contains two fields, Song and Artist.

f. Save the form, module, and project as t8lce1.

g. Declare a SongStruc array named SongArray that can contain as many as 10 records.

h. Code the form's Load event procedure so that it adds each record from the t8lce1.dat file to the SongArray array. The procedure should also add each song's name to the Combo box and add each song's array position to the ItemData array.

i. Code the Combo box so that it displays the artist when the user clicks a song in the list.

j. Code the Add button's Click event procedure so that it adds the song and the artist to the array. It should also add the song to the Combo box and the song's array position to the ItemData array. Don't allow duplicate songs to be added to the array or to the Combo box.

k. Code the Delete button's Click event procedure so that it clears, from the SongArray array, the record corresponding to the song selected in the Combo box. The procedure should also remove the song from the Combo box.

l. Code the Exit button so that it saves the array records to the t8lce1.dat sequential access file on your Student Disk before ending the application. Don't save the records that were cleared from the array by the Delete button.

m. Code the TxtArtist's control so that the existing text is highlighted when the control receives the focus.

n. Save and run the application. Test the application as follows:

(1) Click a song in the Combo box; the name of its artist should appear in the Artist box.

(2) Enter "Persons" (without the quotes) in the Song Combo box, then enter "Barb Streis" (without the quotes) in the Artist Text box. Click the Add button. The button's Click event procedure should add the record to the array, the song's name to the Combo box, and the song's array location to the ItemData array.

(3) Click "Blue Rain" in the Combo box, then click the Delete button. The button's Click event procedure should clear the record from the array and remove the name from the Combo box.

(4) Click the Exit button. The button's Click event procedure should write the array records to the t8lce1.dat sequential access file on your Student Disk, then end the application.

o. Print the form and the code. Also print the t8lce1.dat file in Notepad.

2. a. Use File Manager to copy the Song.bak sequential access file, which is located in either the tut8\ver2 or the tut8\ver3 directory on your Student Disk, to t8lce2.dat.

b. Open the t8lce2.dat file in Notepad. Print the file.

c. Launch Visual Basic, if necessary. Create the user interface shown in Figure 8-80.

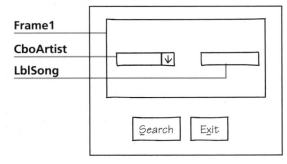

Figure 8-80

d. The Combo box should be a Dropdown List, which does not allow the user to enter information in the Text portion. Set the Combo box's Sorted property to True.

e. Create a user-defined data type named SongStruc that contains two fields, Song and Artist.

f. Save the form, module, and project as t8lce2.

g. Declare a SongStruc array named SongArray that can contain as many as 10 records.

h. Code the form's Load event procedure so that it adds the following four artists to the Combo box.

> Paul Jones
> Maria Casey
> Rolling Rocks
> Strawberries

The Load event should also read the records from the t8lce2.dat sequential access file and store each in the SongArray array.

i. Code the Search button's Click event procedure so that it searches the array for the artist whose name is selected in the Combo box. If the artist's name is in the array, display the corresponding song or songs (one at a time) in the LblSong control.

j. Code the Exit button so that it ends the application.

k. Save and run the application. To test the application, click Rolling Rocks in the Combo box, then click the Search button. The Search button should display this group's songs, one at a time, in the LblSong control.

l. Print the form and the code.

Exercises 3 through 5 are Discovery Exercises.

discovery ▶ 3.
a. Use File Manager to copy the t8b.bak sequential access file, which is located in either the tut8\ver2 or the tut8\ver3 directory on your Student Disk, to t8lce3.dat.

b. Open the t8lce3.dat file in Notepad. Print the file.

c. Launch Visual Basic, if necessary. Load the t8c.mak project that you created in Lesson C.

d. Save the form, the module, and the project as t8lce3.

e. Change the code in both the Load event procedure and the Exit button's Click event procedure so that the procedures open the t8lce3.dat file instead of the t8b.dat file.

f. Change the Dim statement in the general Declarations section from *Dim DirArray(1 to 50) as DirStruc* to *Dim DirArray(1 to 8) as DirStruc*.

The *Dim DirArray(1 to 8) as DirStruc* instruction will allow the DirArray array to store up to eight records only. Currently, if the user clicks the Add button to enter the ninth record into the array, the application will "crash" (that is, it will end unexpectedly).

g. Change the code in the Add button's Click event procedure so that it will not allow the user to enter more than eight records in the DirArray array. Display an appropriate error message if the user tries to add more than eight records.

h. Save and run the application. To test the application, enter the following records:

Schmidt, Paul	711-11-7711	2/4/65
Bender, Jan	991-00-0002	5/6/87
Rice, Rich	334-55-6789	12/30/75
Zorch, Pat	123-45-3211	11/2/60

When you click the Add button to enter Pat Zorch's record, which will be the ninth record, an error message should be displayed. The record should not be added to the file, and the name should not be entered into the Combo box.

i. Exit the application, then print the code. Also print the t8lce3.dat file in Notepad.

discovery ▶ 4.

   a. Use File Manager to copy the t8b.bak sequential access file, which is located in either the tut8\ver2 or the tut8\ver3 directory on your Student Disk, to t8lce4.dat.

   b. Open the t8lce4.dat file in Notepad. Print the file.

   c. Launch Visual Basic, if necessary. Load the t8lce3 project that you created in Lesson C's Exercise 3. (If you did not complete Exercise 3, then load the t8c project that you created in Lesson C.)

   d. Save the form, the module, and the project as t8lce4.

   e. Change the code in both the Load event procedure and the Exit button's Click event procedure so that the procedures open the t8lce4.dat file.

   f. Modify the Delete button's Click event procedure so that it displays a "Do you want to delete <name>" message (without the quotes) in a dialog box when a record is deleted. (For example, if the user deletes Sue Chen, the message should say "Do you want to delete Chen, Sue?" (without the quotes). Use the MsgBox function (not the MsgBox statement) to display the Yes and No Command buttons. If the user clicks Yes, then delete the record; otherwise, don't delete the record.

   g. To delete a person from the directory, you click his or her name in the Combo box and then click the Delete button. Currently, the application will "crash" (that is, it will end unexpectedly) when the user clicks the Delete button if he or she types the person's name in the Combo box (instead of clicking the name in the list) or if he or she doesn't enter a name in the Combo box. To prove this, run the application, type **Chen, Sue** in the Combo box, then click the Delete button. Visual Basic displays the "Invalid property array index" message. Press [F1] to display a Help screen on this error message. Close the Help screen, then click the OK button to remove the error message. Visual Basic highlights the *CboName.ItemData(CboName.ListIndex)* instruction.

   h. Stop the application. Based on the error message and its Help screen, correct the code in the Delete button's Click event procedure so that the code does not "crash" if the user types the name in the Combo box (instead of clicking it in the list) or neglects to enter a name. Rather, use the MsgBox statement to display a message telling the user that he or she must click a name in the list in order to delete a name.

   i. Save and run the application. To test the application:

     (1) Click the Delete button without selecting a name from the Combo box. A message telling you to select a name to delete should appear. You should then be returned to the form.

     (2) Type **Chen, Sue** in the Combo box, then click the Delete button. A message telling you to select a name to delete should appear. You should then be returned to the form.

     (3) Click Chen, Sue in the Combo box's list, then click the Delete button. A message asking you if you want to delete Sue Chen's record should appear. Click the No button to return to the form without deleting Sue Chen's record.

     (4) Click Chen, Sue in the Combo box's list, then click the Delete button. A message asking you if you want to delete Sue Chen's record should appear. Click the Yes button to delete Sue Chen's record.

   j. Exit the application, then print the code.

discovery ▶ 5.

   a. Use File Manager to copy the t8b.bak sequential access file, which is located in either the tut8\ver2 or the tut8\ver3 directory on your Student Disk, to t8lce5.dat.

   b. Open the t8lce5.dat file in Notepad. Print the file.

   c. Launch Visual Basic, if necessary. Load the t8lce4 project that you created in Lesson C's Exercise 4. (If you did not complete Exercise 4, then load the t8lce3 project that you created in Exercise 3. If you did not complete Exercise 3, then load the t8c project that you created in Lesson C.)

   d. Save the form, the module, and the project as t8lce5.

   e. Change the code in both the Load event procedure and the Exit button's Click event procedure so that the procedures open the t8lce5.dat file.

f. Change the Add button's Caption property to Add/Edit. Modify the Add/Edit button's code to allow the user to make changes to the person's name, phone number, and birthday. In other words, if the user clicks an existing name in the Combo box's list and then makes changes to the name, phone number, or birthday, the new information should replace the existing information in the array when the Add/Edit button is clicked. If the user changes the name, the name should be changed in the Combo box's list also. [For example, assume that Sue Chen's record is stored in DirArray(4). If the user clicks Chen, Sue in the Combo box's list and then changes her name, phone number, or birthday, the new information should replace the existing information in DirArray(4) when the Add/Edit button is clicked. If the user changes the name (for example, changes Chen, Sue to Chen, Susan), the new name (Chen, Susan) should replace the existing name (Chen, Sue) in the Combo box.]

g. Save and run the application. To test the application:
   (1) Enter Phillips, John in the Name Combo box. Enter 222-2987 in the Phone Number box. Click the Add/Edit button. The record should be added to the personal directory.
   (2) Click Chen, Sue in the Combo box's list. Change her name to Chen, Susan. Click the Add/Edit button. The new name should be entered in the array and in the Combo box.
   (3) Click Phillips, John in the Combo box's list. Enter 1/5/85 in the Birthday box, then click the Add/Edit button. The birthday should be included in the array.
   (4) Click Chen, Susan in the Combo box's list. Her phone number (444-4444) and birthday (10/29/70) should appear in the appropriate controls on the form.
   (5) Click Phillips, John in the Combo box's list. His phone number (222-2987) and birthday (1/5/85) should appear in the appropriate controls on the form.

h. Exit the application, then print the form and the code. Also print the t8lce5.dat file in Notepad.

D E B U G G I N G

Technique   As you already know, when an error occurs in an application's code, Visual Basic displays a dialog box containing an appropriate error message. While the dialog box is on the screen, you can press the F1 key to display a Help screen that explains the error message. The Help screen will list the types of errors that generate the error message.

Your Student Disk contains a file that you can use to practice this tutorial's debugging technique.

To debug the T8_DEBUG.MAK project:

1 Launch Visual Basic, if necessary, and open the **t8_debug.mak** project which is in either the tut8\ver2 or the tut8\ver3 directory on your Student Disk.

2 Click the **View Form button**. The user interface, which contains a List box and a Command button, appears on the screen.

3 Save the form and the project as **t8dbgd**.

4 **Run** the application. Visual Basic displays a dialog box that contains the "Property 'NewIndx' not found" message.

5   Press [F1] to display a Help screen that explains the error message. The Help screen for the "Property ' item ' not found" error, which is Error number 422, appears.

According to the Help screen, either your code includes a property that is not defined for a control or you misspelled the name of a property.

6   Close the Help screen, then click the **OK button** to remove the error message. Visual Basic returns to the Code window. The period between LstName and NewIndx is highlighted.

In this case, the property is misspelled; it should be NewIndex.

7   Change NewIndx to **NewIndex** in the Code window.

Now let's save and run the application again.

To continue debugging the application:

1   **Save and run** the application. The "Variable not defined" message appears in a dialog box on the screen.

2   Press [F1] to display a Help screen for this error. The "Variable not defined" Help screen appears.

According to the Help screen, your code contains a variable that was not defined.

3   Close the Help screen, then click the **OK button** to remove the error message. Visual Basic highlights LstNames in the Code window.

Judging from the name and its use in the code, LstNames should be the name of the List box in the user interface. You can use the Code window's Object box to verify the names of the controls on the form.

4   Click the **down arrow button in the Code window's Object box**. The drop-down list shows that the name of the List box is LstName, not LstNames.

5   Click the **down arrow button in the Code window's Object box** to close the list.

6   Change LstNames to **LstName** in the Code window.

7   Close the Code window, then **save and run** the application. Click the Exit **button**. Visual Basic returns to the design screen.

tips

● ● ● ● ● ● ● ● ● ● ● ● ● ● ● ● ● ● ●

▶ **Notice that Visual Basic also displays the "Variable not found" error message when your code refers to a control whose name Visual Basic does not recognize. When Visual Basic does not recognize a name, it assumes that the name belongs to a variable.**

TUTORIAL

9

Sorting, Menus, and Passing Parameters

The Gifts Express Application

case ▶ The telemarketers at Gifts Express make long distance calls to customers all over the United States. Because of the different time zones, it is essential that the telemarketer knows the state that he or she is calling, so he or she doesn't call too early or too late. The manager of Gifts Express, Ms. Susan Li, has asked you to create an application that will display a list of area codes along with the corresponding states. Ms. Li would like to display the list in area code order and in state order. She also wants to be able to print the list on the printer.

Previewing the Completed Application

Let's begin by previewing the completed Gifts Express application.

To preview the completed application:

1   Launch Windows and make sure the Program Manager window is open and your Student Disk is in the appropriate drive. If necessary, click the Minimize on Use option on the Options menu to minimize the Program Manager on use. **Run** the **GIFTS.EXE** file, which is in either the tut9\ver2 or the tut9\ver3 directory on your Student Disk. The Gifts Express application's user interface appears on the screen. See Figure 9-1.

Menu control

Text box

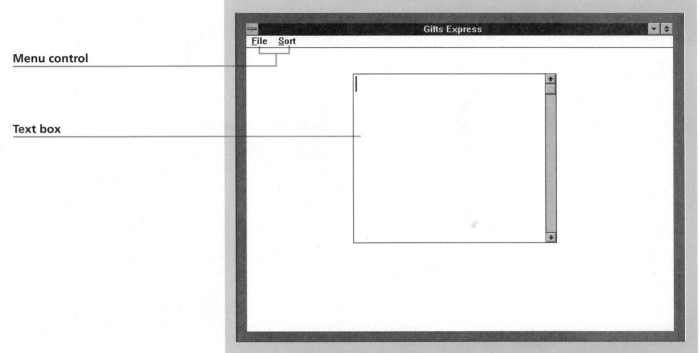

Figure 9-1: Gifts Express user interface

This application contains a new control, a Menu control, which you will learn about in Lesson B. The application allows you to display a list of area codes and their corresponding states in either area code order or state order. Let's display the list in area code order.

2   Click **Sort** in the menu bar, then click **Area Code**. A list of area codes and states appears in the Text box on the form, as shown in Figure 9-2. Notice that the list is ordered by area code. (The data file used in this application contains only 25 area codes and states.)

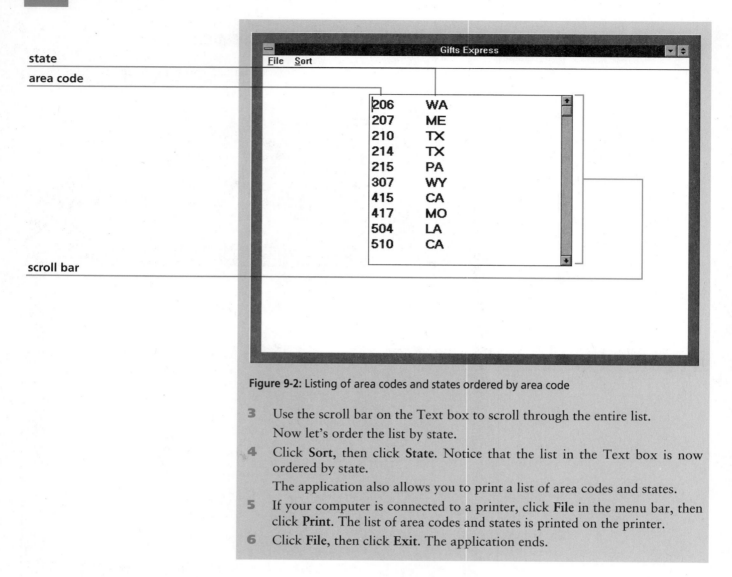

state

area code

scroll bar

Gifts Express

File   Sort

206	WA
207	ME
210	TX
214	TX
215	PA
307	WY
415	CA
417	MO
504	LA
510	CA

Figure 9-2: Listing of area codes and states ordered by area code

3 Use the scroll bar on the Text box to scroll through the entire list.

Now let's order the list by state.

4 Click **Sort**, then click **State**. Notice that the list in the Text box is now ordered by state.

The application also allows you to print a list of area codes and states.

5 If your computer is connected to a printer, click **File** in the menu bar, then click **Print**. The list of area codes and states is printed on the printer.

6 Click **File**, then click **Exit**. The application ends.

In this tutorial you will learn how to sort data, create a menu, and pass parameters to a user-defined sub procedure.

LESSON A
o b j e c t i v e s

In this lesson you will learn how to:

■ Use a List box or a Combo box to sort strings

■ Write a bubble sort

■ Write a Shell sort

Sorting Data

Sorting Data

Sorting data—that is, arranging it in either alphabetical or numerical order—is a common task performed by a program. When data is displayed in a sorted order, it allows a user to quickly find the information for which he or she is searching In Tutorial 8's personal directory application, for example, you sorted the Combo box entries into alphabetical order so that the user could easily locate a specific entry.

You can sort both numeric and string data in either ascending (from smallest to largest) or descending (from largest to smallest) order, as illustrated in Figure 9-3.

Sorted Numerical Data		Sorted String Data	
Ascending Order	*Descending Order*	*Ascending Order*	*Descending Order*
1	5	A	E
2	4	B	D
3	3	C	C
4	2	D	B
5	1	E	A

Figure 9-3: Illustration of numeric and alphabetic data in ascending and descending order

In this lesson you will learn several ways to sort data; which method you use will depend on both the type and the amount of data you are sorting. We'll begin with a quick and easy method that you can use to sort string data.

Sorting Method #1—Sorting Strings Using a List/Combo Box

You can use either a List box or a Combo box to sort a list of strings. Before learning this sorting method, take a few minutes to review some of the properties of both controls. Figure 9-4 summarizes the properties that you will use in this sorting method. (The ListIndex property was covered in Tutorial 6. The other four properties were covered in Tutorial 8.)

Property	Use to:
ListIndex	Specify the index of the currently selected item
List	Access the individual items in the list
ListCount	Specify the number of items in the list
NewIndex	Specify the index of the item most recently added to the list
ItemData	Access the items in the ItemData array

Figure 9-4: Summary of List box and Combo box properties

In the next two sections, you will see two examples that use a List box to sort the string data contained in a sequential access data file. The first example will show you how to sort a file that contains one string field, and the second example will show you how to sort a file that contains more than one field. Although both examples use a List box, you could also use a Combo box instead.

The Pet Example

In this first example you will use a List box to sort the contents of a sequential access file named t9pet.dat. Figure 9-5 shows the t9pet.dat file displayed in Notepad.

each record contains one String field

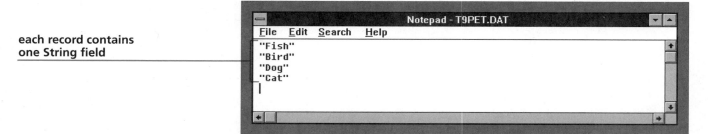

Figure 9-5: T9PET.DAT file displayed in Notepad

Notice that each record in the file has only one field—a string field that contains a type of pet—and that the pet types are not in any specific order. To sort the file, you will first read the strings (pet types) into a List box whose Sorted property is set to True, and then write the sorted contents of the List box to another sequential access file named t9pet.srt. (The .srt in the filename is short for "sorted." You can also write the sorted data to the original t9pet.dat sequential access file. We will use a different file, however, so that the original file remains intact.) After the sort is completed, the t9pet.dat file will contain the unsorted data and the t9pet.srt file will contain the alphabetically sorted data. Let's look at the application that you will use to sort the pet types.

To view the code in the Pet example application:

1 Launch Visual Basic and open the **t9pet.mak** file, which is in either the tut9\ver2 or the tut9\ver3 directory on your Student Disk. Click the **View Form button**. The user interface appears on the screen, as shown in Figure 9-6.

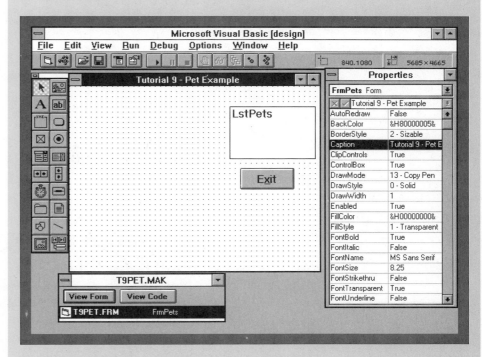

Figure 9-6: Screen showing the Pets Example's user interface

First let's look at the form's Load event procedure, where the pet types from the t9pet.dat file are added to the List box.

2 Double-click the **form** to open its Code window, then maximize the Code window. The form's Load event procedure appears, as shown in Figure 9-7. If necessary, change the drive letter in the Open Statement to the drive containing your Student Disk.

When the application is run and the form is loaded into memory, the Load event procedure will declare a String variable named Pet and will open the t9pet.dat sequential access file for input. The Do...While loop will then read each string (pet type) from the file and add it to the List box. Because the List box's Sorted property is set to True, Visual Basic will automatically sort the pet types in ascending alphabetical order as they are added to the list. When all of the strings have been read and added to the List box, the sequential access file will be closed. At this point the List box will contain the pet types in alphabetical order.

if necessary, change the drive letter to the drive containing your Student Disk

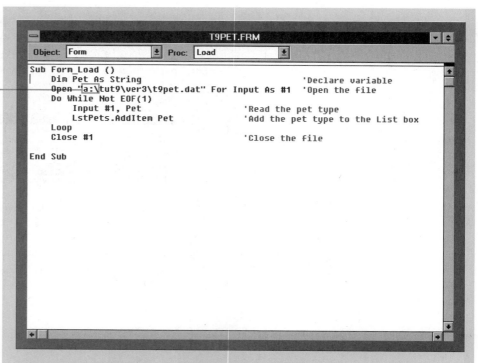

```
                                    T9PET.FRM
Object: Form            ±   Proc: Load            ±

Sub Form_Load ()
    Dim Pet As String                            'Declare variable
    Open "a:\tut9\ver3\t9pet.dat" For Input As #1  'Open the file
    Do While Not EOF(1)
        Input #1, Pet                   'Read the pet type
        LstPets.AddItem Pet             'Add the pet type to the List box
    Loop
    Close #1                            'Close the file

End Sub
```

Figure 9-7: Code window showing the form's Load event procedure

Now let's look at the Exit button's Click event procedure, where the sorted contents of the List box are written to the t9pet.srt file.

3 Press [F2] to open the View Procedures dialog box. Click **CmdExit_Click** in the Procedures box, then click the **OK button**. The Exit button's Click event procedure appears, as shown in Figure 9-8. If necessary, change the drive letter in the Open statement to the drive containing your Student Disk.

if necessary, change the drive letter to the drive containing your Student Disk

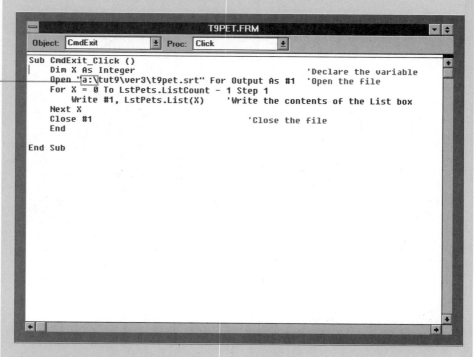

```
                                    T9PET.FRM
Object: CmdExit         ±   Proc: Click           ±

Sub CmdExit_Click ()
    Dim X As Integer                             'Declare the variable
    Open "a:\tut9\ver3\t9pet.srt" For Output As #1   'Open the file
    For X = 0 To LstPets.ListCount - 1 Step 1
        Write #1, LstPets.List(X)     'Write the contents of the List box
    Next X
    Close #1                            'Close the file
    End

End Sub
```

Figure 9-8: Code window showing the Exit button's Click event procedure

When you click the Exit button, its Click event procedure will declare an Integer variable named X and will open the t9pet.srt sequential access file for output. The For...Next loop will then write the sorted contents of the List box to the t9pet.srt file on your Student Disk. (Recall that the first item in a List box has a List property value of 0 and that the value in the ListCount property is always one more than the largest List value.) The List box, remember, contains the alphabetized pet types. The t9pet.srt file will then be closed. Let's run the application to see how it works.

4   Close the Code window, then **run**, but don't save, the application. The form's Load event procedure reads the pet types from the t9pet.dat sequential access file and enters each into the LstPets List box. (Because you are loading the List box from a file on your Student Disk, it may take a little while for the form to appear.) Because the List box's Sorted property is set to True, Visual Basic sorts the pet types as they are entered into the list. (The List box contains Bird, Cat, Dog, and Fish.) The Load event procedure then closes the t9pet.dat file.

5   Click the **Exit button**. The Click event procedure opens the t9pet.srt file for output, writes the sorted List box items to the file, and then closes the file. The application then ends and Visual Basic returns to the design screen.

6   Switch to Program Manager, then open the Accessories group and launch Notepad. Open the **t9pet.srt** file, which is in either the tut9\ver2 or the tut9\ver3 directory on your Student Disk. (You will need to change the List Files of Type box to All Files (*.*).) Figure 9-9 shows the t9pet.srt displayed in Notepad. Notice that the pet types are arranged in alphabetical order.

pet types are now in alphabetical order

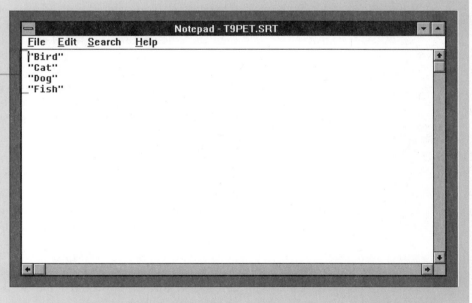

Figure 9-9: The T9PET.SRT file displayed in Notepad

7   Minimize Notepad, then switch back to Visual Basic.

8   Click **File** in Visual Basic's menu bar, then click **New Project**. If you are asked if you want to save the changes to the form or the project, click the **No button**.

To summarize, a simple way of sorting a list of strings is to enter the strings in a List box whose Sorted property is set to True and then write the sorted contents of the List box to a file. In the next example you will learn how to use a List box to sort a file that contains more than one field.

The Product Example

In this example you will again use a List box to sort the data contained in a sequential access file. This time, however, each record in the file contains more than one field. Figure 9-10 shows the file, named t9prod.dat, displayed in Notepad.

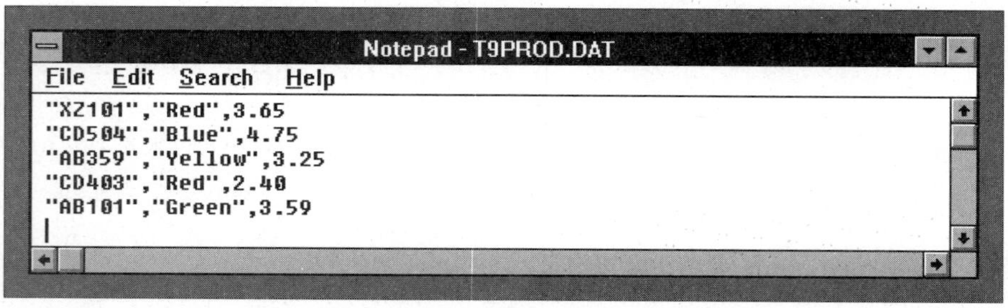

```
─                    Notepad - T9PROD.DAT              ▼ ▲
File  Edit  Search  Help
"XZ101","Red",3.65                                           ↑
"CD504","Blue",4.75
"AB359","Yellow",3.25
"CD403","Red",2.40
"AB101","Green",3.59
|                                                            ↓
←                                                          →
```

Figure 9-10: The T9PROD.DAT file displayed in Notepad

Each record in the file contains two String fields and one Currency field. The first String field is the product's ID, the second String field is the product's color, and the Currency field is the product's price. To sort the file, you first need to determine the **sort key**, which is the field on which you want to sort. If, for example, you want the records in product ID order, then the product ID field is the sort key. If, on the other hand, you want the records in color order, then the color field is the sort key. To order the records by price, you would need to use a different sorting method because you can enter only strings in a List box or Combo box control. (In Discovery Exercise 8 at the end of Lesson A, you will research both the Str$ and the Format$ functions, which you can use to tell Visual Basic to treat a number as though it were a string.) In the product application, you will have the sort key be the ID field, so the records will be sorted in product ID order.

After you determine the sort key, the next step is to enter each of the records into an array, which we'll refer to as the record array. As you do so, you also enter the record's sort key into a List box, whose Sorted property is set to True, and the record's array location into the List box's ItemData array. (Recall that you learned about the ItemData array in Tutorial 8.) When all of the records have been entered, you use the values in the ItemData array to write the contents of the record array to a file, in alphabetical order by the sort key. Let's see how this method works.

On your Student Disk is an application named T9PROD.MAK, which you can use to sort the t9prod.dat file by the product ID. Let's open that project and view its code.

To view the code in the Product example application:

1 Open the **t9prod.mak** project, which is in either the tut9\ver2 or the tut9\ver3 directory on your Student Disk. Click the **View Form button**. The user interface appears, as shown in Figure 9-11.

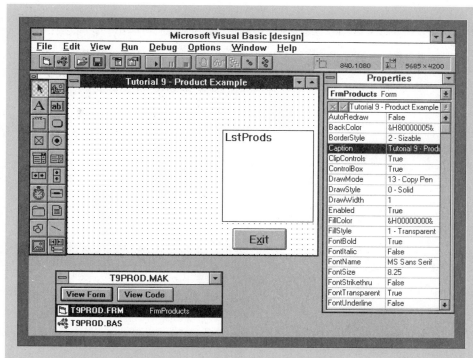

Figure 9-11: Screen showing the Product Example's user interface

In order to store records in an array, you first need to define the record structure. Recall that you use the Type statement to do so and that the Type statement is entered into a code module. Let's look at the code in this application's code module.

2   Click **T9PROD.BAS** in the Project window, then click the **View Code button**. The Code window for the code module appears, as shown in Figure 9-12.

declares a user-defined data type (record structure)

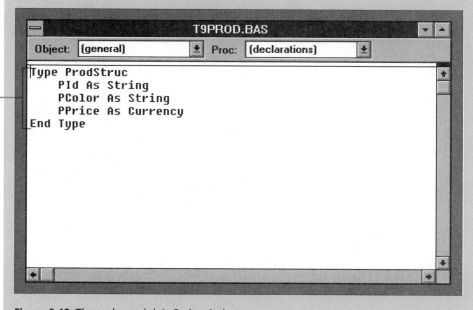

Figure 9-12: The code module's Code window

The Type statement in the code module declares a user-defined data type (record structure) called ProdStruc, which consists of a product's ID, color, and price.

3   Close the Code window.

Now that the data type (record structure) is defined, you can declare an array of that type. The array will be used to store the five records contained in the t9prod.dat data file. Because more than one procedure will need to access the data in the array, the array will be declared as a form-level array in the form's general Declarations section. Let's look at that code next.

4   Double-click the **form** to open its Code window. Press [**F2**] to display the View Procedures dialog box, click (**declarations**), and then click the **OK button**. The form's general Declarations section appears, as shown in Figure 9-13.

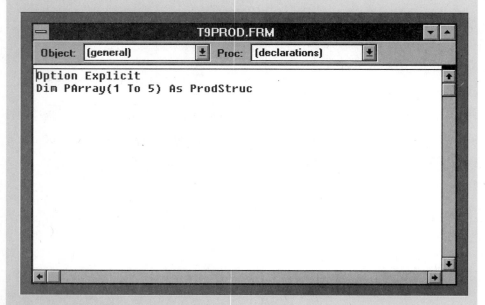

Figure 9-13: Code window showing the form's general Declarations selection

The Code window contains the *Option Explicit* statement, which, remember, tells Visual Basic to warn you if you use the name of an undeclared variable in your code. The Dim statement then declares a five-element array named PArray. The array is declared as a ProdStruc data type, which means that each record in the array will contain a product ID, color, and price. Now that the array is defined, you can fill it with data, which you will do in the form's Load event procedure.

5   Press [**F2**] to open the View Procedures dialog box, click **Form_Load**, and then click the **OK button**. Maximize the Code window. The form's Load event procedure appears, as shown in Figure 9-14. If necessary, change the drive letter in the Open statement to the drive containing your Student Disk.

if necessary, change the drive letter to the drive containing your Student Disk

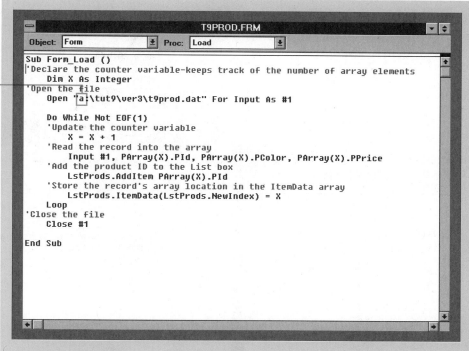

```
T9PROD.FRM
Object: Form          Proc: Load

Sub Form_Load ()
'Declare the counter variable-keeps track of the number of array elements
    Dim X As Integer
'Open the file
    Open "a:\tut9\ver3\t9prod.dat" For Input As #1

    Do While Not EOF(1)
     'Update the counter variable
        X = X + 1
     'Read the record into the array
        Input #1, PArray(X).PId, PArray(X).PColor, PArray(X).PPrice
     'Add the product ID to the List box
        LstProds.AddItem PArray(X).PId
     'Store the record's array location in the ItemData array
        LstProds.ItemData(LstProds.NewIndex) = X
    Loop
'Close the file
    Close #1

End Sub
```

Figure 9-14: Code window showing the form's Load event procedure

The form's Load event procedure first declares an Integer variable named X. The X variable will be used to count the number of records in the file. The procedure then opens the t9prod.dat sequential access file for input. For each record in the file, the procedure adds 1 to the X variable before reading the record from the t9prod.dat file. As the record is read, it is stored in the PArray array at the location specified in the X variable. In other words, when X contains the number 1, the record is stored in the first array location—PArray(1). Likewise, when X contains the number 2, the record is stored in the second array location—PArray(2), and so on. The value in the X variable, therefore, represents the position of the record in the PArray array.

The Load event procedure also adds each product ID to the List box. (Recall that the ID field is the sort key. Also recall that the List box's Sorted property is set to True, so the IDs will be sorted as they are entered into the list.) As each product ID is inserted into the list, its position in the PArray array—which is indicated by the value in the X variable—is stored in the corresponding element of the ItemData array. For example, AB101 is the fifth product ID in the t9prod.dat file, so it will be stored in the fifth position of the PArray—in other words, PArray(5). When the AB101 product ID is added to the List box, however, it will be sorted, alphabetically, as the first item in the list. As a result, the number 5, which is AB101's position in the PArray, will be stored in the first position of the ItemData array. Before the Load event procedure ends, it closes the t9prod.dat file.

Now let's look at the Exit button's Click event procedure, where the records are written to the t9prod.srt file in alphabetical order by the sort key.

6   Press [F2] to display the View Procedures dialog box, click **CmdExit_Click**, then click the **OK button**. The Exit button's Click event procedure appears, as shown in Figure 9-15. If necessary, change the drive letter in the Open statement to the drive containing your Student Disk.

if necessary, change the drive letter to the drive containing your Student Disk

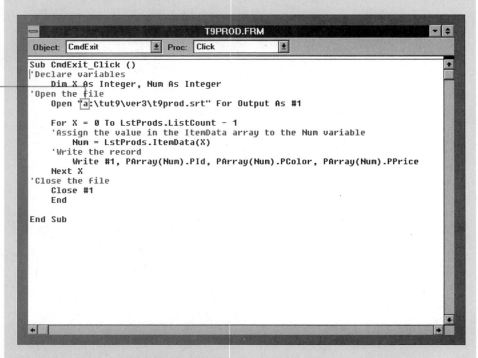

```
                              T9PROD.FRM
Object:  CmdExit          ±    Proc:  Click           ±

Sub CmdExit_Click ()
'Declare variables
    Dim X As Integer, Num As Integer
'Open the file
    Open "a:\tut9\ver3\t9prod.srt" For Output As #1

    For X = 0 To LstProds.ListCount - 1
    'Assign the value in the ItemData array to the Num variable
        Num = LstProds.ItemData(X)
    'Write the record
        Write #1, PArray(Num).PId, PArray(Num).PColor, PArray(Num).PPrice
    Next X
'Close the file
    Close #1
    End

End Sub
```

Figure 9-15: Code window showing the Exit button's Click event procedure

The code declares two Integer variables, X and Num. It then opens the t9prod.srt sequential access file for output. (Here again, you will write the sorted records to a different file so that the original t9prod.dat file remains intact.) The For...Next loop will write the records to the t9prod.srt file in the order specified by the values in the ItemData array. (Recall that the values in the ItemData array represent each record's position in the PArray array.) For example, if the ItemData array contains the numbers 5, 3, 4, 2, 1, then the For...Next loop will write the record contained in PArray(5) first, then the record contained in PArray(3), then the record contained in PArray(4), and so on. Before the Exit button's Click event procedure ends, it closes the t9prod.srt file.

7   Close the Code window.

Let's run the application to see how it works.

To test the t9prod.mak application:

1   **Run**, but don't save, the application. The form's Load event procedure reads the records from the t9prod.dat file and stores them in the PArray array. It also adds the product IDs to the List box, sorting the product IDs as it enters them into the list, and stores each record's array position in the corresponding position of the List box's ItemData array. The file is then closed. Figure 9-16 illustrates the PArray array, the List box, and the ItemData array after the form's Load event procedure ends.

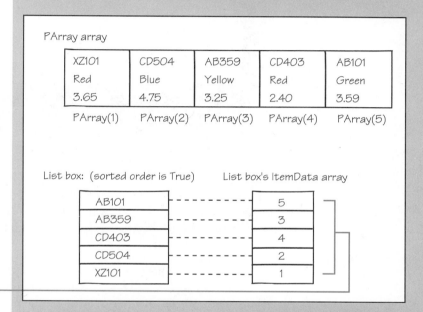

stores record's position in PArray array

Figure 9-16: The PArray array, List box, and ItemData array after the Load procedure ends

2   Click the **Exit button**. The Click event procedure opens the t9prod.srt file for output. The For...Next loop then uses the values in the ItemData array to write the records, in ascending alphabetical order by the product ID, to the t9prod.srt file. Following the contents of the ItemData array shown in Figure 9-16, for example, record 5 is written first, followed by record 3, record 4, record 2, and finally record 1. The file is then closed.

Let's see if the records were written correctly to the t9prod.srt file.

3   Switch to Notepad, open the **t9prod.srt** file, and view its contents. (Be sure to open the t9prod.srt file, not the t9prod.dat file.) Figure 9-17 shows the file displayed in Notepad.

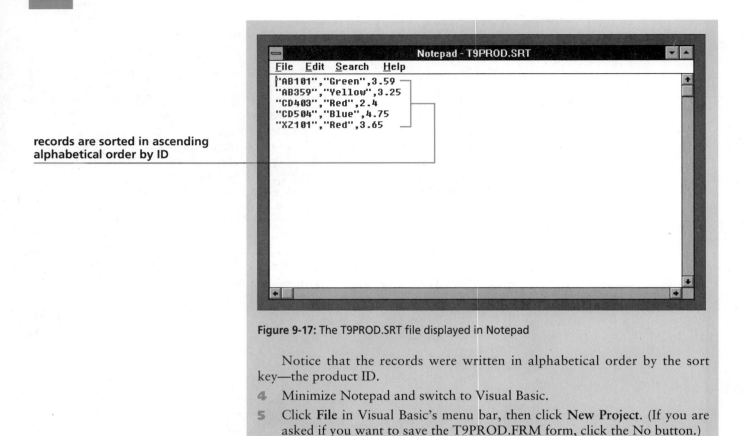

records are sorted in ascending
alphabetical order by ID

Figure 9-17: The T9PROD.SRT file displayed in Notepad

Notice that the records were written in alphabetical order by the sort key—the product ID.

4   Minimize Notepad and switch to Visual Basic.

5   Click **File** in Visual Basic's menu bar, then click **New Project**. (If you are asked if you want to save the T9PROD.FRM form, click the No button.)

Although the List box and the Combo box provide a quick way to sort data, they have one very important limitation: Because both controls can contain only strings, neither control can be used to sort numeric data. Fortunately, programmers have worked many long and tedious hours creating algorithms that can be used to sort both numeric and string data. (An **algorithm** is a step-by-step solution to a problem.) Two of the most popular of these sort algorithms are the bubble sort and the Shell sort. Let's look at the bubble sort first.

Sorting Method #2—The Bubble Sort

The bubble sort provides a quick and easy way to sort the items in an array, as long as the number of items is relatively small—for example, less than 50. You can use the algorithm to sort either string or numeric data.

The bubble sort algorithm works by comparing adjacent array elements and interchanging (swapping) the ones that are out of order. The algorithm continues comparing and swapping until the data in the array is sorted. To illustrate the logic of a bubble sort, let's sort, on paper, the numbers 9, 8, and 7 in ascending order. Figure 9-18 shows the data before, during, and after the bubble sort.

Original Data	9 8 7		
	Comparison	**Swap**	**Result**
Pass 1:	⌐ 9 8 7	Yes	8 9 7
	⌐ 8 9 7	Yes	8 7 9
Pass 2:	⌐ 8 7 9	Yes	7 8 9
	⌐ 7 8 9	No	7 8 9
Pass 3:	⌐ 7 8 9	No	7 8 9
	⌐ 7 8 9	No	7 8 9

Figure 9-18: Data before, during, and after the bubble sort

The bubble sort algorithm begins by comparing the first value in the list with the second value. If the first value is less than or equal to the second value, then no swap is made. If, on the other hand, the first value is greater than the second value, then both values are interchanged. In this case the first value (9) is greater than the second (8), so the values are swapped, as shown in Figure 9-18's Result column.

After comparing the first value in the list with the second, the algorithm then compares the second value with the third. In this case 9 is greater than 7, so the two values are swapped, as shown in Figure 9-18.

At this point the algorithm has completed its first time through the entire list of values—referred to as a **pass**. Notice that, at the end of the first pass, the largest value (9) is at the end of the list. The bubble sort gets its name from the fact that as the larger values drop to the end of the list, the smaller values rise, like bubbles, to the beginning. Now let's see what the algorithm does on its second pass through the data.

The bubble sort algorithm begins the second pass by comparing the first value in the list with the second value. In this case, 8 is greater than 7, so the two values are interchanged, as shown in Figure 9-18. Then the second value is compared with the third; in this case 8 is not greater than 9, so no swap is made. Notice that at the end of the second pass, the data is sorted. The bubble sort algorithm will, however, make one more pass on the data to verify that it is sorted.

In the third pass, the first value is compared with the second value; 7 is not greater than 8, so no swap is made. The second value is then compared with the third value; 8 is not greater than 9, so no swap is made. Notice that no swaps were made during the entire pass. This indicates that the data is sorted, so the sort algorithm stops.

Now let's look at the code for the bubble sort algorithm. The code is already entered in a file on your Student Disk.

To view the code for the bubble sort algorithm:

1   Open the **t9bub.mak** file, which is in either the tut9\ver2 or the tut9\ver3 directory on your Student Disk.

2   Save the form and the project as **t9buba**.

3   Click the **View Form button**. The user interface appears on the screen, as shown in Figure 9-19.

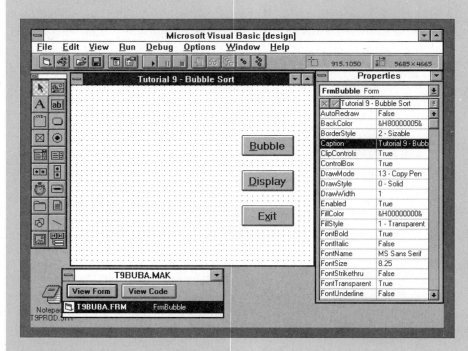

Figure 9-19: Screen showing the Bubble Sort example's user interface

This application will read, into an array, the numbers contained in a sequential access file named t9bub.dat. The Bubble button will use the bubble sort to sort the numbers into ascending numerical order. The Display button will display the contents of the array on the form, and the Exit button will end the application. (This application will not save the sorted contents of the array to a file.)

First let's look at the form's general Declarations section, which declares the array that will contain the numbers to be sorted.

4   Double-click the **form**. Press [**F2**] to open the View Procedures dialog box, click (**declarations**), then click the **OK button**. The form's general Declarations section appears, as shown in Figure 9-20.

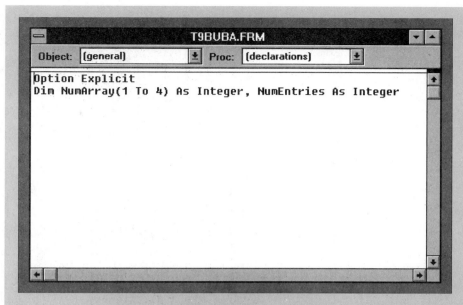

Figure 9-20: Code window showing the form's general Declarations section

The Dim statement appearing below the Option Explicit statement declares an Integer array named NumArray that can store as many as four numbers. The Dim statement also declares the NumEntries variable, which will store the number of entries in the array. Next, let's look at the form's Load event procedure, where the array is filled with data.

5   Press [F2] to open the View Procedures dialog box, click **Form_Load**, then click the **OK button**. The form's Load event procedure appears, as shown in Figure 9-21. If necessary, change the drive letter in the Open statement to the drive containing your Student Disk.

if necessary, change the drive letter to the drive containing your Student Disk

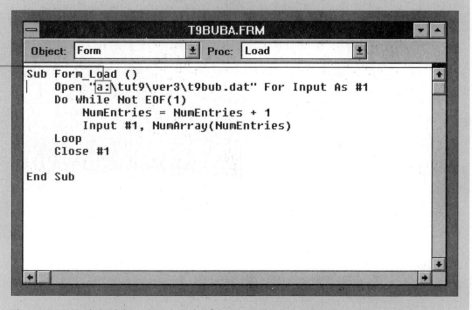

Figure 9-21: Code window showing the form's Load event procedure

The Load event procedure opens the t9bub.dat sequential access data file for input. The t9bub.dat file contains the numbers 3, 6, 2, and 5. (You can verify that, if you want, by switching to Notepad and opening the t9bub.dat file.) The Do...While loop adds 1 to the NumEntries variable before reading a number into the NumArray array. When the Do...While loop ends, the NumArray array contains the four numbers and the NumEntries variable contains the number 4. The Load event procedure then closes the t9bub.dat file.

Next let's look at the Display button's code, which will display the contents of the array on the form.

6 Press [F2] to open the View Procedures dialog box, click **CmdDisplay_Click**, then click the **OK button**. The CmdDisplay control's Click event procedure appears, as shown in Figure 9-22.

clears text from the form

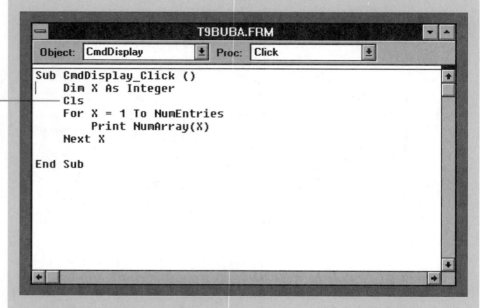

Figure 9-22: Code window showing the Display button's Click event procedure

After declaring an Integer variable named X, the code uses the *Cls* method to clear any text displayed on the form by the Print method. A For...Next loop and the Print method are then used to display the contents of the NumArray array on the form.

Last, let's look at the CmdBubble control's Click event procedure, which contains the code for the bubble sort.

7 Press [F2] to open the View Procedures dialog box. Click **CmdBubble_Click**, then click the **OK button**. Maximize the Code window. The CmdBubble control's Click event procedure appears, as shown in Figure 9-23.

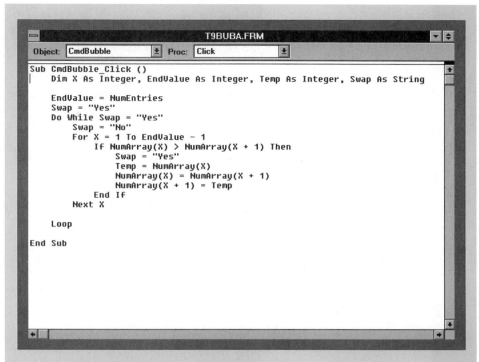

```
                        T9BUBA.FRM
Object: CmdBubble            ±    Proc: Click              ±

Sub CmdBubble_Click ()
    Dim X As Integer, EndValue As Integer, Temp As Integer, Swap As String

    EndValue = NumEntries
    Swap = "Yes"
    Do While Swap = "Yes"
        Swap = "No"
        For X = 1 To EndValue - 1
            If NumArray(X) > NumArray(X + 1) Then
                Swap = "Yes"
                Temp = NumArray(X)
                NumArray(X) = NumArray(X + 1)
                NumArray(X + 1) = Temp
            End If
        Next X

    Loop

End Sub
```

Figure 9-23: Code window showing the Bubble button's Click event procedure

The code declares three Integer variables—X, EndValue, and Temp—and one String variable named Swap. (In some versions of Basic, Swap is a reserved word; however it is not a reserved word in Visual Basic.) Both the X and the EndValue variables control the processing of the For...Next loop. The Temp variable is necessary to store the contents of an array element temporarily so that a swap can be made. The Swap variable will keep track of whether a swap was made during a pass of the array. (Remember that the algorithm will stop when no swaps have been made for an entire pass.)

After the necessary variables are declared, the EndValue variable will be assigned the value currently in the NumEntries variable. (Recall that the NumEntries variable is a form-level variable that stores the number of array elements.) The Swap variable is then initialized to "Yes." The Do...While loop, which is responsible for making the passes over the array data, will repeat its instructions as long as the Swap variable contains the string "Yes." The "Yes" indicates that a swap was made and, therefore, the Do...While loop needs to be processed again. Let's look at the instructions within the Do...While loop a little more closely.

The first instruction within the Do...While loop sets the Swap variable to "No". When entering the loop, the algorithm assumes that no swaps will be necessary—in other words, it assumes that the array is already in sorted order. The For...Next loop is then used to make the necessary passes through the array. The selection structure within the For...Next loop will compare the values in the adjacent elements of the array. If the NumArray(X) value is greater than the NumArray(X+1) value, then the Swap variable is set to "Yes", indicating that a swap is necessary, and the value in NumArray(X) is swapped with the value in NumArray(X+1). To accomplish the swap, the NumArray(X) value is first stored in the Temp variable. The NumArray(X+1) value is then assigned to the NumArray(X) element. [If you did not store the NumArray(X) value in Temp, the NumArray(X+1) value would write over the value in NumArray(X) and value in NumArray(X) would be lost.] At this point the value in NumArray(X) is the same as the value in NumArray(X+1). To complete the swap, the value in the Temp variable is assigned to the NumArray(X+1) element. Figure 9-24 illustrates the swap.

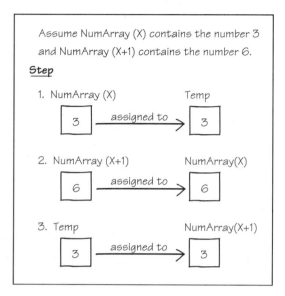

Figure 9-24: Illustration of three steps necessary to accomplish the swap

After the For...Next loop completes the first pass through the array, the Do...While loop again checks the value in the Swap variable. If the value is "Yes", then the instructions within the loop are processed again. If, on the other hand, the value in Swap is not "Yes", it means that the array is sorted, so the bubble sort algorithm ends. Let's run the application to see how it works.

To test the application:

1   Close the Code window, then **save and run** the application. The form's Load event procedure opens the t9bub.dat sequential access file and reads its contents—the numbers 3, 6, 2, and 5—into the NumArray array. It also adds 1 to the NumEntries variable—which keeps track of the number of array elements—for each number read. The t9bub.dat file is then closed.

First let's display the array on the form so that you can verify its contents.

2   Click the **Display button**. The unsorted contents of the NumArray array (3, 6, 2, and 5) appear on the form. Notice that the numbers appear in the order in which they were entered into the array.

Now let's sort the numbers in the array.

3   Click the **Bubble button**. The CmdBubble control's Click event sorts the data in the array, as shown in Figure 9-25.

```
Original Array Data        3 6 2 5

              Comparison      Swap        Result

Pass 1:       ⌐⌐
              3 6 2 5         No          3 6 2 5
                ⌐⌐
              3 6 2 5         Yes         3 2 6 5
                  ⌐⌐
              3 2 6 5         Yes         3 2 5 6

Pass 2:       ⌐⌐
              3 2 5 6         Yes         2 3 5 6
                ⌐⌐
              2 3 5 6         No          2 3 5 6
                  ⌐⌐
              2 3 5 6         No          2 3 5 6

Pass 3:       ⌐⌐
              2 3 5 6         No          2 3 5 6
                ⌐⌐
              2 3 5 6         No          2 3 5 6
                  ⌐⌐
              2 3 5 6         No          2 3 5 6
```

Figure 9-25: Results of the bubble sort

Now display the array again.

4   Click the **Display button.** The contents of the NumArray array appear on the form. Notice that the numbers in the array are now sorted in ascending numerical order—2, 3, 5, and 6.

5   Click the **Exit button.** The application ends, and Visual Basic returns to the design screen.

Although the bubble sort you just learned is quick and easy, it is somewhat inefficient because it makes more comparisons than are necessary. For example, look closely at Pass 1's third comparison in Figure 9-25. Notice that it compares and then swaps the last two elements of the array—the 6 and the 5. At the end of the first pass, the last two elements of the array are in their proper order. Notice, however, that the third comparison in both Pass 2 and Pass 3 also compare those two numbers with each other; both are unnecessary comparisons. You can improve the efficiency of the bubble sort algorithm by adding some additional code to direct the algorithm to compare adjacent items from the beginning of the array only to the point where the last swap was made, instead of from the beginning of the array through the end of the array. Everything after the point where the last swap was made is already in order, so the algorithm doesn't need to compare those elements.

To modify the bubble sort code, then save and run the application:

1   Double-click the **Bubble button**. The CmdBubble control's Click event procedure appears.

2   Maximize the Code window, then add the additional Dim statement and the two lines of code shown in Figure 9-26.

enter these three lines of code

```
T9BUBA.FRM

Object: CmdBubble          Proc: Click

Sub CmdBubble_Click ()
    Dim X As Integer, EndValue As Integer, Temp As Integer, Swap As String
    Dim LastSwap As Integer

    EndValue = NumEntries
    Swap = "Yes"
    Do While Swap = "Yes"
        Swap = "No"
        For X = 1 To EndValue - 1
            If NumArray(X) > NumArray(X + 1) Then
                Swap = "Yes"
                Temp = NumArray(X)
                NumArray(X) = NumArray(X + 1)
                NumArray(X + 1) = Temp
                LastSwap = X
            End If
        Next X
        EndValue = LastSwap
    Loop

End Sub
```

Figure 9-26: Code window showing the modified code in the Bubble button's Click event procedure

When a swap occurs, the position of the array element that was swapped will be recorded in the Integer variable named LastSwap. Each time the For...Next loop completes a pass through the array, the value in LastSwap will be assigned to the EndValue variable. The EndValue variable is used to tell the For...Next loop the array location at which to stop comparing.

3   Close the Code window, then **save** and **run** the application. The form's Load event procedure opens the t9bub.dat file and enters the unsorted numbers into the NumArray array.

4   Click the **Display button**. The unsorted numbers (3, 6, 2, and 5) appear on the form.

5   Click the **Bubble button**. The CmdBubble control's Click event procedure sorts the data in the array, as shown in Figure 9-27

```
Original Array Data         3 6 2 5

                     Comparison      Swap        Result

Pass 1:
                        ⌐⌐
                       3 6 2 5         No         3 6 2 5
                          ⌐⌐
                       3 6 2 5         Yes        3 2 6 5
                            ⌐⌐
                       3 2 6 5         Yes        3 2 5 6

Pass 2:
                        ⌐⌐
                       3 2 5 6         Yes        2 3 5 6
                          ⌐⌐
                       2 3 5 6         No         2 3 5 6
```

Figure 9-27: Results of the modified bubble sort

If you compare both Figure 9-25 and Figure 9-27, you will notice that, with the addition of the few lines of code, the modified bubble sort requires fewer steps to sort the data.

6   Click the **Display button**. The sorted data (2, 3, 5, and 6) are displayed on the form.

7   Click the **Exit button**. The application ends and Visual Basic returns to the design screen.

8   Click **File**, then click **New Project**. Visual Basic removes the t9bub.mak project from the screen. A new project appears.

As mentioned earlier, the bubble sort is useful for sorting a small amount of data. In cases where you need to sort large amounts of data, you should use the Shell sort instead.

Sorting Method #3—The Shell Sort

The Shell sort, which is named after its creator Donald Shell and is a variation of the bubble sort, provides a fast and efficient way of sorting a large amount of data. Instead of comparing adjacent items in an array and swapping them one position at a time, the Shell sort compares and swaps nonadjacent items. Because the items are swapped a greater distance, the Shell sort sorts data faster than the bubble sort does. (In Lesson C's Exercise 3, you will run an application that times both sorts.) Figure 9-28 illustrates the logic of a Shell sort to sort eight numbers.

```
Original Array Data: 8 7 3 5 1 4 2 6
                    Comparison        Swap      Result
Pass 1: Gap = 4
Compare 1        8735 1426           Yes       1735 8426
Compare 2        1735 8426           Yes       1435 8726
Compare 3        1435 8726           Yes       1425 8736
Compare 4        1425 8736           No        1425 8736
Pass 2: Gap = 2
Compare 1        14 25 87 36         No        14 25 87 36
Compare 2        14 25 87 36         No        14 25 87 36
Compare 3        14 25 87 36         No        14 25 87 36
Compare 4        14 25 87 36         No        14 25 87 36
Compare 5        14 25 87 36         Yes       14 25 37 86
Compare 6        14 25 37 86         Yes       14 25 36 87
Pass 3: Gap = 2
Compare 1        14 25 36 87         No        14 25 36 87
Compare 2        14 25 36 87         No        14 25 36 87
Compare 3        14 25 36 87         No        14 25 36 87
Compare 4        14 25 36 87         No        14 25 36 87
Pass 4: Gap = 1
Compare 1        1 4 2 5 3 6 8 7     No        1 4 2 5 3 6 8 7
Compare 2        1 4 2 5 3 6 8 7     Yes       1 2 4 5 3 6 8 7
Compare 3        1 2 4 5 3 6 8 7     No        1 2 4 5 3 6 8 7
Compare 4        1 2 4 5 3 6 8 7     Yes       1 2 4 3 5 6 8 7
Compare 5        1 2 4 3 5 6 8 7     No        1 2 4 3 5 6 8 7
Compare 6        1 2 4 3 5 6 8 7     No        1 2 4 3 5 6 8 7
Compare 7        1 2 4 3 5 6 8 7     Yes       1 2 4 3 5 6 7 8
Pass 5: Gap = 1
Compare 1        1 2 4 3 5 6 7 8     No        1 2 4 3 5 6 7 8
Compare 2        1 2 4 3 5 6 7 8     No        1 2 4 3 5 6 7 8
Compare 3        1 2 4 3 5 6 7 8     Yes       1 2 3 4 5 6 7 8
Compare 4        1 2 3 4 5 6 7 8     No        1 2 3 4 5 6 7 8
Compare 5        1 2 3 4 5 6 7 8     No        1 2 3 4 5 6 7 8
Compare 6        1 2 3 4 5 6 7 8     No        1 2 3 4 5 6 7 8
Pass 6: Gap = 1
Compare 1        1 2 3 4 5 6 7 8     No        1 2 3 4 5 6 7 8
Compare 2        1 2 3 4 5 6 7 8     No        1 2 3 4 5 6 7 8
```

Figure 9-28: Data before, during, and after the Shell sort

Let's follow the first pass shown in Figure 9-28. The Shell sort begins by splitting the array into two sections. In this case, because the array contains eight elements, four numbers constitute the first section and the remaining four numbers constitute the second section. The distance between the first values in both sections is called the **gap**. In Figure 9-28, for example, the first value in section 1 is in position 1 and the first value in section 2 is in position 5, so the gap is 4—5 minus 1.

After splitting the array in half, the algorithm compares the first value in section 1 with the first value in section 2. If section 1's value is greater than section 2's value, then the values are swapped. In Pass 1's first comparison, for instance, the 8 (section 1's value) and the 1 (section 2's value) are swapped because 8 is greater than 1. The Shell sort algorithm then compares the second value in section 1 with the second value in section 2. (Notice that the distance between those two numbers is 4—the value of the gap.) Because 7 is greater than 4, both values are swapped. The sort algorithm then compares the third value in section 1 with the third value in section 2. The number 3 is greater than the number 2, so a swap is made. The algorithm then compares the fourth value in section 1 with the fourth value in section 2. In this case, 5 is not greater than 6, so the values are not swapped.

Before making the second pass, the algorithm divides the gap in half. In this case, for example, the gap in Pass 2 is 2 (the original gap of 4 divided by 2). The algorithm will use a gap of 2 until a full pass is made with no swaps; as Figure 9-28 shows, this occurs in Pass 3. Once a gap produces no swaps, it is again halved—in this case, the gap is now 1, which is half of 2. At this point the algorithm works similar to the bubble sort in that it compares adjacent items. As Figure 9-28 shows, Pass 4 makes seven comparisons using a gap of 1. Because Pass 4 produces some swaps, a fifth pass is needed. Here again, because a swap occurs during the fifth pass, a sixth pass is needed. Notice that the sixth pass makes no swaps, which indicates that the array is sorted. The Shell sort algorithm stops at this point. Now let's look at the code for the Shell sort.

On your Student Disk is a file named T9SHELL.MAK, which contains the code for a Shell sort. Let's open that file and look at the code.

To view the code in the T9SHELL.MAK project:

1 Open the **t9shell.mak** project, which is in either the tut9\ver2 or the tut9\ver3 directory on your Student Disk. Click the **View Form button** to view the form. The user interface appears, as shown in Figure 9-29.

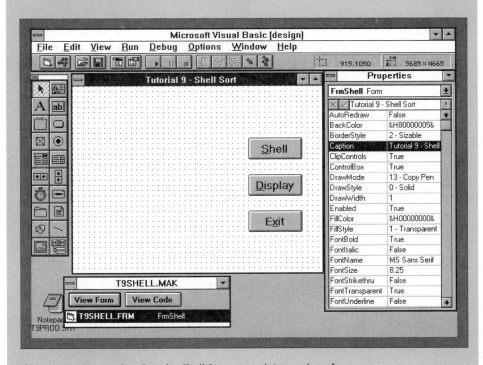

Figure 9-29: Screen showing the Shell Sort example's user interface

This application will read, into an array, the numbers contained in a sequential access file named t9shell.dat. The Shell button will use the Shell sort to sort the numbers into ascending numerical order. The Display button will display the contents of the array on the form, and the Exit button will end the application. (This application will not save the sorted contents of the array to a file.)

First let's look at the form's general Declarations section, which declares the array that will contain the numbers to be sorted.

2   Double-click the **form** to open its Code window. Press **[F2]** to open the View Procedures dialog box, click **(declarations)** in the Procedures box, then click the **OK button**. The form's general Declarations section appears, as shown in Figure 9-30.

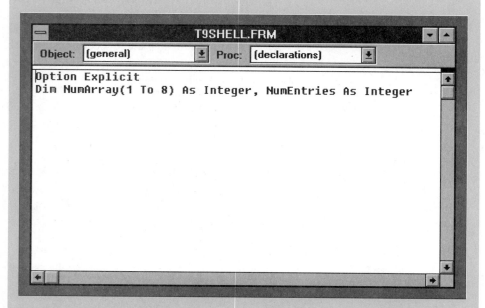

```
─                        T9SHELL.FRM                      ▼ ▲
Object: (general)            ±    Proc: (declarations)       ±
Option Explicit
Dim NumArray(1 To 8) As Integer, NumEntries As Integer
```

Figure 9-30: Code window showing the form's general Declarations section

The code declares an eight-element Integer array named NumArray and an Integer variable named NumEntries. The NumEntries variable will contain the number of entries in the array. Now let's look at the form's Load event procedure, where the array is filled with data.

3   Press **[F2]** to open the View Procedures dialog box, click **Form_Load**, and then click the **OK button**. The form's Load event procedure appears, as shown in Figure 9-31. If necessary, change the drive letter in the Open statement to the drive containing your Student Disk.

if necessary, change the drive letter to the drive containing your Student Disk

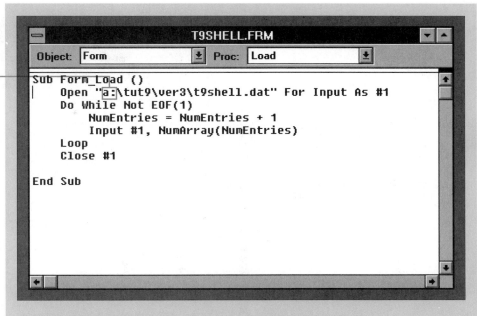

```
T9SHELL.FRM
Object:  Form                  Proc:  Load

Sub Form_Load ()
    Open "a:\tut9\ver3\t9shell.dat" For Input As #1
    Do While Not EOF(1)
        NumEntries = NumEntries + 1
        Input #1, NumArray(NumEntries)
    Loop
    Close #1

End Sub
```

Figure 9-31: Code window showing the form's Load event procedure

The Load event procedure opens a sequential access file named t9shell.dat for input. The t9shell.dat file contains the numbers 8, 7, 3, 5, 1, 4, 2, and 6. (You can verify that, if you want, by opening the file in Notepad.) The Do...While loop adds 1 to the NumEntries variable before reading a number into the NumArray array. (Recall that NumEntries is a form-level variable that keeps track of the number of array elements.) The data file is then closed.

4   If you want, you can look at the code in the Display button's Click event procedure, which is identical to the code shown in Figure 9-22.

Next let's look at the Shell button's Click event procedure, which contains the code for the Shell sort.

5   Press **[F2]** to open the View Procedures dialog box, click **CmdShell_Click**, and then click the **OK button**. Maximize the Code window. The CmdShell control's Click event procedure appears, as shown in Figure 9-32.

```
┌─────────────────────────────────────────────────────────────────────┐
│ ─                              T9SHELL.FRM                      ▼ ▲▼  │
│ Object: [CmdShell          ▼]  Proc: [Click                ▼]          │
│ ┌───────────────────────────────────────────────────────────────┐ ▲ │
│ │ Sub CmdShell_Click ()                                         │   │
│ │     Dim Gap As Integer, EndValue As Integer, X As Integer     │   │
│ │     Dim Temp As Integer, LastSwap As Integer, Swap As String  │   │
│ │                                                                │   │
│ │     Gap = NumEntries \ 2                                       │   │
│ │  ┌─ Do While Gap >= 1                                          │   │
│ │  │      EndValue = NumEntries                                  │   │
│ │  │      Swap = "Yes"                                           │   │
│ │  │   ┌─ Do While Swap = "Yes"                                  │   │
│ │  │   │      Swap = "No"                                        │   │
│ │  │   │      For X = 1 To EndValue - Gap                        │   │
│ │  │   │          If NumArray(X) > NumArray(X + Gap) Then        │   │
│ │  │   │              Swap = "Yes"                               │   │
│ │  │   │              LastSwap = X                               │   │
│ │  │   │              Temp = NumArray(X)                         │   │
│ │  │   │              NumArray(X) = NumArray(X + Gap)            │   │
│ │  │   │              NumArray(X + Gap) = Temp                   │   │
│ │  │   │          End If                                         │   │
│ │  │   │      Next X                                             │   │
│ │  │   │      EndValue = LastSwap                                │   │
│ │  │   └─ Loop                                                   │   │
│ │  │      Gap = Gap \ 2                                          │   │
│ │  └─ Loop                                                       │   │
│ │                                                                │   │
│ │ End Sub                                                        │ ▼ │
│ └───────────────────────────────────────────────────────────────┘   │
│ ◄ ▓▓▓▓▓                                                          ► ▼ │
└─────────────────────────────────────────────────────────────────────┘
```

nested Do...While loops

Figure 9-32: Code window showing the Shell button's Click event procedure

The Shell sort's code uses five Integer variables (Gap, EndValue, X, Temp, LastSwap) and one String variable (Swap). The Gap variable will keep track of the gap. The X and the Endvalue variables will control the For...Next loop. The Temp variable will store, temporarily, the data in the NumArray(X) element before it is swapped with the NumArray(X+Gap) element. The LastSwap variable will keep track of the location of the last swap. The string variable, Swap, will keep track of whether a swap was made during the current pass.

After the necessary variables are declared, the *Gap = NumEntries \ 2* instruction will calculate the first gap. Recall from Tutorial 2 that the backslash (\) represents integer division. (The slash (/), on the other hand, represents regular division.) Integer division returns only the integer portion of the quotient—for example, the expression 7\2 results in 3. (The expression 7/2, on the other hand, results in 3.5.)

After calculating the first gap, a Do...While loop verifies that the Gap variable contains a number that is greater than or equal to 1. If the number in Gap is not greater than or equal to 1 (in other words, if it's less than 1), then the Do...While loop ends. (The distance between two numbers—the gap—can't be less than 1.) If, on the other hand, the value in Gap is greater than or equal to 1, the value in NumEntries, which represents the number of entries in the array, is assigned to the Endvalue variable, and the word "Yes" is assigned to the Swap variable. (Recall that the Swap variable keeps track of whether a swap was made.) Another Do...While loop then tests if the Swap variable contains the word "Yes". If it does, the Do...While loop assigns "No" to the Swap variable. (As in the bubble sort, the Shell sort algorithm assumes that the array is, initially, in sorted order, so no swaps will need to be made.) A For...Next loop then compares two elements of the array: NumArray(X) and NumArray(X+Gap). [Recall that the bubble sort algorithm compares NumArray(X) and NumArray(X+1).] If the NumArray(X) variable contains a number that is greater than the number in NumArray(X+Gap), then the following happens:

(1.) The Swap variable is set to "Yes", which indicates that a swap is necessary.

(2.) The value in X, which stores the position of the array variable being swapped, is assigned to the LastSwap variable.

(3.) The value in NumArray(X) is swapped with the value in NumArray(X+Gap). To accomplish the swap, first the value in NumArray(X) is assigned to the Temp variable. Then the value in NumArray(X+Gap) is assigned to NumArray(X) and, last, the value in Temp is assigned to NumArray(X+Gap). This is illustrated in Figure 9-33.

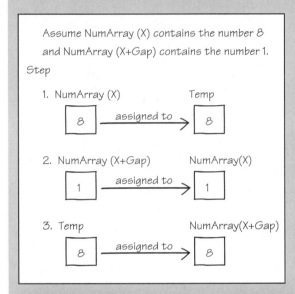

Figure 9-33: Illustration of three steps necessary to accomplish the swap

After the For...Next loop has completed a pass through the array, the value in the LastSwap variable, which indicates where the last swap occurred, is assigned to the EndValue variable. (As with the bubble sort, this line of code allows the algorithm to perform more efficiently by ending the comparisons at the location of the last swap. Remember that everything after that location is already in sorted order.) The inner loop (the *Do While Swap = "Yes"* loop) then checks the value in the Swap variable. If Swap contains "Yes", then the inner loop instructions are processed again. If Swap does not contain "Yes", then the gap is halved (*Gap = Gap \ 2*) and the outer loop (the *Do While Gap > = 1*) checks the value in the Gap variable. If Gap is greater than or equal to 1, then the outer loop instructions are processed again. If, however, Gap is not greater than or equal to 1, then the loop stops and the *End Sub* instruction is processed. Let's run the application to see how the Shell sort works.

6   Close the Code window, then **run** the application. (If you are asked if you want to save the application, click the No button.) The form's Load event procedure opens the t9shell.dat sequential access file and enters the eight numbers into the NumArray array. The NumEntries variable is increased by 1 for each number entered into the array. The t9shell.dat file is then closed.

First display the unsorted contents of the array.

7   Click the **Display button**. The unsorted contents of the array (8, 7, 3, 5, 1, 4, 2, and 6) appear on the form.

Now use the Shell sort to sort the array.

8   Click the **Shell button**. The CmdShell control's Click event procedure sorts the contents of the array (the eight numbers) in ascending numerical order.

Let's display the contents of the array to prove that the numbers are sorted.

9   Click the **Display button**. The contents of the array, now sorted in ascending numerical order (1, 2, 3, 4, 5, 6, 7, and 8), appear on the screen.

10 Click the **Exit button**. The application ends and Visual Basic returns to the design screen. Click **File**, then click **New Project**. If you are asked if you want to save the file, click the No button.

You have now completed Lesson A. You can either take a break or complete the end-of-lesson questions and exercises.

SUMMARY

To summarize the sorting methods covered in this lesson:

■   Sorting method #1—use a List box or a Combo box to sort strings.
■   Sorting method #2—use the bubble sort to sort a relatively small amount of either string or numeric data (for example, fewer than 50 items).
■   Sorting method #3—use the Shell sort to sort a large amount of either string or numeric data.

To use sorting method #1 to sort records containing one field:

■   Read the data to be sorted into a List box or a Combo box whose Sorted property is set to True.
■   Write the sorted data from the List or Combo box to a file.

To use sorting method #1 to sort records containing more than one field:

■   Determine the sort key, which is the field on which you want to sort.
■   Read the records into an array (referred to as the record array). As you read the records, enter the record's sort key into either a List box or a Combo box and enter the record's array location into the List or Combo box's ItemData array.
■   Use the values in the ItemData array to write the contents of the record array to a file, in alphabetical order by the sort key.

QUESTIONS

1. Sorting data means to arrange it in _____ order.
    a. alphabetical
    b. numerical
    c. alphabetical or numerical

2. Data sorted from the largest value to the smallest value is sorted in
   _____ order.
   a. alphabetical
   b. ascending
   c. descending
   d. numerical
   e. descending and numerical

3. This property of a List box or Combo box specifies the index of the currently
   selected item.
   a. ItemData
   b. List
   c. ListCount
   d. ListIndex
   e. NewIndex

4. This property of a List box or Combo box allows you to access the individual items
   in the list.
   a. ItemData
   b. List
   c. ListCount
   d. ListIndex
   e. NewIndex

5. This property of a List box or Combo box specifies the number of items in the list.
   a. ItemData
   b. List
   c. ListCount
   d. ListIndex
   e. NewIndex

6. This property of a List box or Combo box specifies the index of the item most
   recently added to the list.
   a. ItemData
   b. List
   c. ListCount
   d. ListIndex
   e. NewIndex

7. This property of a List box or Combo box allows you to access the items in the
   ItemData array.
   a. ItemData
   b. List
   c. ListCount
   d. ListIndex
   e. NewIndex

8. A List box or a Combo box can be used to sort _____ .
   a. numbers
   b. strings
   c. numbers and strings

9. To sort the data in a List box or a Combo box, the control's Sorted property must
   be set to _____ .
   a. False
   b. On
   c. Sort
   d. True
   e. Yes

10. The field on which you want to sort is called the _____ .
    a. ID field
    b. sort ID
    c. sort key
    d. sort order

11. The _____ algorithm works by comparing adjacent array elements and swapping the ones that are out of order.
    a. bubble sort
    b. Combo box
    c. List box
    d. Shell sort

12. The _____ algorithm works by comparing nonadjacent array elements and swapping the ones that are out of order.
    a. bubble sort
    b. Combo box
    c. List box
    d. Shell sort

13. The distance between the elements being compared in a Shell sort is called the
    _____ .
    a. difference
    b. gap
    c. interval
    d. span

E X E R C I S E S

1. In this exercise you will use a List box (sorting method #1) to sort the 10 names contained in a sequential access file named t9names.dat, which is in either the tut9\ver2 or the tut9\ver3 directory on your Student Disk.
   a. Launch Notepad. Open the t9names.dat file and print its contents.
   b. Launch Visual Basic and create the user interface shown in Figure 9-34.

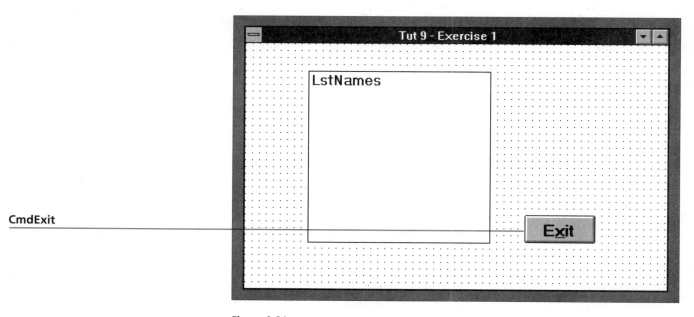

Figure 9-34

c. Set the LstNames control's Sorted property to True.

d. Save the form and the project as t9lae1.

e. Code the form's Load event procedure so that it fills the List box with the names contained in the t9names.dat file.

f. Code the Exit button's Click event procedure so that it writes the sorted contents of the List box to a sequential access file named t9lae1.srt. The Exit button should then end the application.

g. Save and run the application, then click the Exit button.

h. Switch to Notepad. Print the contents of the t9lae1.srt file. Close Notepad.

i. Switch to Visual Basic. Print the form and the code.

2. In this exercise you will use a List box (sorting method #1) to sort the 10 records contained in a sequential access file named t9owners.dat, which is in either the tut9\ver2 or the tut9\ver3 directory on your Student Disk.

a. Launch Notepad. Open the t9owners.dat file and print its contents.

b. Launch Visual Basic and create the user interface shown in Figure 9-35.

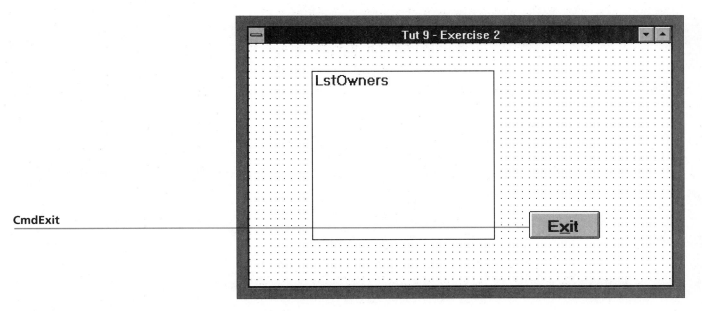

Figure 9-35

c. Set the LstOwners control's Sorted property to True.

d. Add a code module to the project. Declare a user-defined data type (record structure) named OwnerStruc, which consists of an owner's name, a license plate number, the car type, and the price. The price field should be declared as Single, and the other three fields should be declared as String.

e. Save the form, the code module, and the project as t9lae2.

f. The form's general Declarations section should include the *Option Explicit* statement and a Dim statement that declares a 10-element Ownerstruc array named OwnerArray.

g. Code the form's Load event procedure so that it fills the OwnerArray array with the records contained in the t9owners.dat file. The Load event should also fill the List box with the owner names and fill the List box's ItemData array with the position of each owner name in the OwnerArray array.

h. Code the Exit button's Click event procedure so that it uses the ItemData array to write the sorted records to a sequential access file named t9lae2.srt. The Exit button should then end the application.

i. Save and run the application, then click the Exit button.

j. Switch to Notepad. Print the contents of the t9lae2.srt file. Close Notepad.

k. Switch to Visual Basic. Print the form and the code.

3. In this exercise you will use the bubble sort (sorting method #2) to sort the 10 numbers contained in a sequential access file named t9nums.dat, which is in either the tut9\ver2 or the tut9\ver3 directory on your Student Disk.

a. Launch Notepad. Open the t9nums.dat file and print its contents.

b. Launch Visual Basic and create the user interface shown in Figure 9-36.

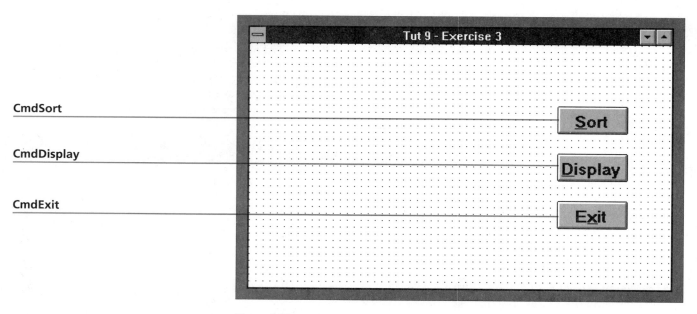

CmdSort

CmdDisplay

CmdExit

Figure 9-36

c. Save the form and the project as t9lae3.

d. The form's general Declarations section should include the *Option Explicit* statement, a Dim statement that declares a 10-element Currency array named SalesArray, and a Dim statement that declares an Integer variable named NumEntries that will keep track of how many entries are in the array.

e. Code the form's Load event procedure so that it fills the SalesArray array with the numbers contained in the t9nums.dat file. The Load event should also count the number of numbers in the t9nums.dat file and then close the file.

f. Code the Display button's Click event procedure so that it displays the contents of the SalesArray array on the form.

g. Code the Sort button's Click event procedure so that it uses the bubble sort to sort the numbers in the SalesArray array. (Hint: Here's an easy way to copy code from one project to another. Use the Add File... option on Visual Basic's File menu to add the t9buba.frm form, which you completed in Lesson A, to the current t9lae3 project. Copy the bubble sort code from the Bubble button to the Clipboard, then paste the code from the Clipboard into the Sort button. You can then use the Remove File option from Visual Basic's File menu to remove the t9buba.frm form from the current project. Last, make the necessary changes to the code in the Sort button.)

h. Code the Exit button's Click event procedure so that it writes the contents of the SalesArray array to a sequential access file named t9lae3.srt. The Exit button should then end the application.

i. Save and run the application.

j. Click the Display button. The unsorted contents of the SalesArray array should appear on the form.

k. Click the Sort button, then click the Display button. The sorted contents of the SalesArray array should appear on the form.

l. Click the Exit button.

m. Switch to Notepad. Print the contents of the t9lae3.srt file. Close Notepad.

n. Switch to Visual Basic. Print the form and the code.

4. In this exercise you will use the bubble sort (sorting method #2) to sort the 10 names contained in a sequential access file named t9names.dat, which is in either the tut9\ver2 or the tut9\ver3 directory on your Student Disk.

a. Launch Notepad. Open the t9names.dat file and print its contents.

b. Launch Visual Basic and create the user interface shown in Figure 9-37.

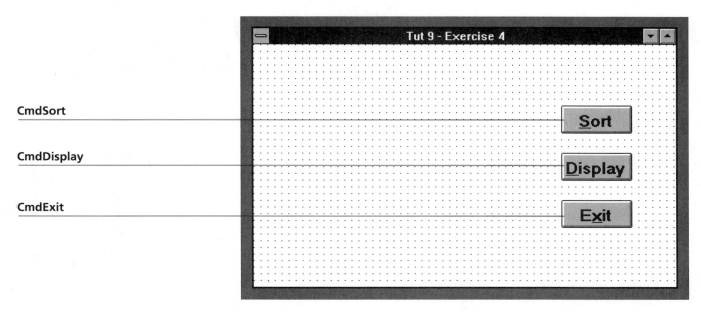

Figure 9-37

c. Save the form and the project as t9lae4.

d. The form's general Declarations section should include the *Option Explicit* statement, a Dim statement that declares a 10-element String array named NamesArray, and a Dim statement that declares an Integer variable named NumEntries that will keep track of how many entries are in the array.

e. Code the form's Load event procedure so that it fills the NamesArray array with the 10 names contained in the t9names.dat file.

f. Code the Display button's Click event procedure so that it displays the contents of the NamesArray array on the form.

g. Code the Sort button's Click event procedure so that it uses the bubble sort to sort the names in the NamesArray array. (Hint: Here's an easy way to copy code from one project to another. Use the Add File... option on Visual Basic's File menu to add the t9buba.frm form, which you completed in Lesson A, to the current t9lae4 project. Copy the bubble sort code from the Bubble button to the Clipboard, then paste the code from the Clipboard into the Sort button. You can then use the Remove File option from Visual Basic's File menu to remove the t9buba.frm form from the current project. Last, make the necessary changes to the code in the Sort button. Be sure to change the Temp variable to String.)

h. Code the Exit button's Click event procedure so that it writes the contents of the NamesArray array to a sequential access file named t9lae4.srt. The Exit button should then end the application.

i. Save and run the application.

j. Click the Display button. The unsorted contents of the NamesArray array should appear on the form.

k. Click the Sort button, then click the Display button. The sorted contents of the NamesArray array should appear on the form.

l. Click the Exit button.

m. Switch to Notepad. Print the contents of the t9lae4.srt file. Close Notepad.

n. Switch to Visual Basic. Print the form and the code.

5. In this exercise you will use the Shell sort (sorting method #3) to sort the 10 numbers contained in a sequential access file named t9nums.dat, which is in either the tut9\ver2 or the tut9\ver3 directory on your Student Disk.

a. Launch Notepad. Open the t9nums.dat file and print its contents.

b. Launch Visual Basic and create the user interface shown in Figure 9-38.

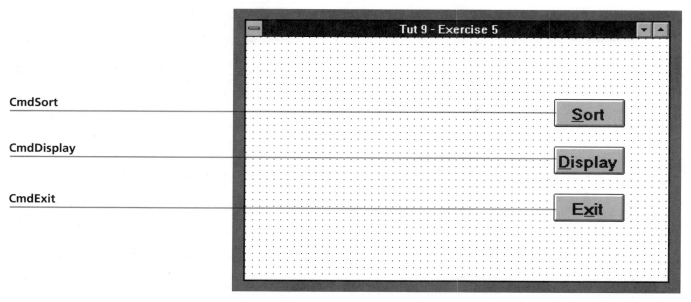

CmdSort

CmdDisplay

CmdExit

Figure 9-38

c. Save the form and the project as t9lae5.

d. The form's general Declarations section should include the *Option Explicit* statement, a Dim statement that declares a 10-element Currency array named SalesArray, and a Dim statement that declares an Integer variable named NumEntries that will keep track of how many entries are in the array.

e. Code the form's Load event procedure so that it fills the SalesArray array with the numbers contained in the t9nums.dat file. The Load event should also count the number of numbers in the t9nums.dat file.

f. Code the Display button's Click event procedure so that it displays the contents of the SalesArray array on the form.

g. Code the Sort button's Click event procedure so that it uses the Shell sort to sort the numbers in the SalesArray array. (Hint: Here's an easy way to copy code from one project to another. Use the Add File... option on Visual Basic's File menu to add the t9shell.frm form, which you completed in Lesson A, to the current t9lae5 project. Copy the Shell sort code from the Shell button to the Clipboard, then paste the code from the Clipboard into the Sort button. You can then use the Remove File option from Visual Basic's File menu to remove the t9shell.frm form from the current project. Last, make the necessary changes to the code in the Sort button.)

h. Code the Exit button's Click event procedure so that it writes the contents of the SalesArray array to a sequential access file named t9lae5.srt. The Exit button should then end the application.

i. Save and run the application.

j. Click the Display button. The unsorted contents of the SalesArray array should appear on the form.

k. Click the Sort button, then click the Display button. The sorted contents of the SalesArray array should appear on the form.

l. Click the Exit button.

m. Switch to Notepad. Print the contents of the t9lae5.srt file. Close Notepad.

n. Switch to Visual Basic. Print the form and the code.

6. In this exercise you will use the Shell sort (sorting method #3) to sort the 10 names contained in a sequential access file named t9names.dat, which is in either the tut9\ver2 or the tut9\ver3 directory on your Student Disk.

a. Launch Notepad. Open the t9names.dat file and print its contents.

b. Launch Visual Basic and create the user interface shown in Figure 9-39.

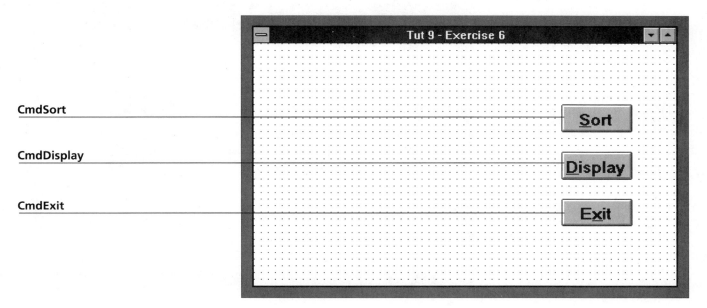

Figure 9-39

c. Save the form and the project as t9lae6.

d. The form's general Declarations section should include the *Option Explicit* statement, a Dim statement that declares a 10-element String array named NamesArray, and a Dim statement that declares an Integer variable named NumEntries that will keep track of how many entries are in the array.

e. Code the form's Load event procedure so that it fills the NamesArray array with the 10 names contained in the t9names.dat file.

f. Code the Display button's Click event procedure so that it displays the contents of the NamesArray array on the form.

g. Code the Sort button's Click event procedure so that it uses the Shell sort to sort the names in the NamesArray array. (Here's an easy way to copy code from one project to another: Use the Add File... option on Visual Basic's File menu to add the t9shell.frm form, which you completed in Lesson A, to the current t9lae6 project. Copy the Shell sort code from the Shell button to the Clipboard, then paste the code from the Clipboard into the Sort button. You can then use the Remove File option from Visual Basic's File menu to remove the t9shell.frm form from the current project. Last, make the necessary changes to the code in the Sort button.)

h. Code the Exit button's Click event procedure so that it writes the contents of the NamesArray array to a sequential access file named t9lae6.srt. The Exit button should then end the application.

    i. Save and run the application.

    j. Click the Display button. The unsorted contents of the NamesArray array should appear on the form.

    k. Click the Sort button, then click the Display button. The sorted contents of the NamesArray array should appear on the form.

    l. Click the Exit button.

    m. Switch to Notepad. Print the contents of the t9lae6.srt file. Close Notepad.

    n. Switch to Visual Basic. Print the form and the code.

Exercises 7 through 13 are Discovery Exercises.

discovery ▶   **7.** In this exercise you will use a List box (sorting method #1) to sort five numbers.

    a. Launch Visual Basic and create the user interface shown in Figure 9-40.

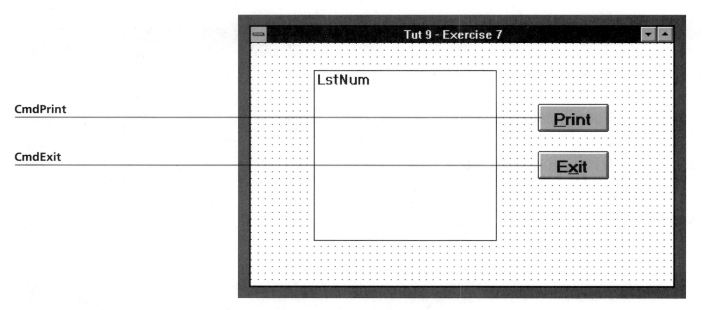

Figure 9-40

    b. Set the LstNum control's Sorted property to True. Size the List box so that the five numbers will show.

    c. Save the form and the project as t9lae7.

    d. Use the AddItem method in the form's Load event procedure to fill the List box with the following numbers: 300, 250, 100, 150, 800. Be sure to enclose each number in quotation marks, which will make it a string.

    e. Code the Print button's Click event procedure so that it prints the form on the printer when clicked.

    f. Code the Exit button's Click event procedure so that it ends the application.

    g. Save and run the application. Click the Print button. (Be sure the five numbers appear in the List box on the printout.) Click the Exit button to end the application.

    h. Open the form's Load event procedure. Change the last number in the AddItem method from 800 to 1000.

    i. Save and run the application. Click the Print button. (Be sure the five numbers appear in the List box on the printout.) Click the Exit button to end the application.

    j. Notice that the List box in the first printout (from step g) sorts the entries in the following order: 100, 150, 250, 300, 800. Notice that the List box in the second printout (from step i) sorts the numbers in the following order, which is not correct: 100, 1000, 150, 250, 300. Why was the data in the second printout sorted incorrectly? Write your answer on a piece of paper. How can you fix this problem? Write your answer on a piece of paper.

k. Fix the problem according to your answer to step j. Save and run the application. Click the Print button. (Be sure the five numbers appear in the List box on the printout.) Click the Exit button to end the application.

l. Print the form and the code.

discovery ▶ 8. In this exercise you will use a List box (sorting method #1) to sort the numbers contained in a sequential access file.

a. Launch Notepad. Open the t9nums.dat file and print its contents; then open the t9nums2.dat file and print its contents.

b. Launch Visual Basic and create the user interface shown in Figure 9-41.

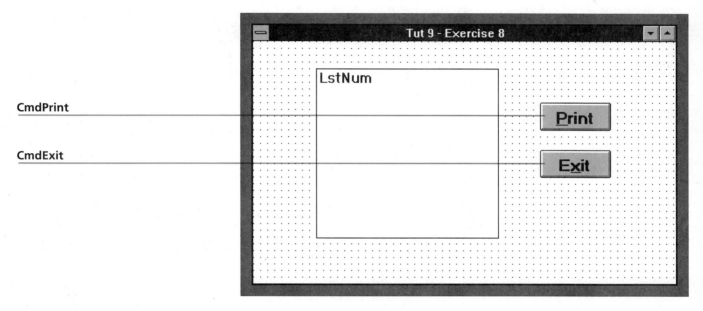

Figure 9-41

c. Save the form and the project as t9lae8.

d. Set the LstNum control's Sorted property to True. Size the List box so that as many as 10 numbers will show.

e. Use Visual Basic's Help screens to research the Str$ function.

f. Using your knowledge of the Str$ function, code the form's Load event procedure so that it fills the List box with the 10 numbers, treated as strings, that are contained in the t9nums.dat file.

g. Code the Print button's Click event procedure so that it prints the form.

h. Code the Exit button's Click event procedure so that it ends the application.

i. Save and run the application. Click the Print button. (Be sure the 10 numbers appear in the List box on the printout.) Click the Exit button to end the application.

j. Modify the form's Load event procedure so that it opens the t9nums2.dat file.

k. Save and run the application. Click the Print button. Explain on paper why the numbers sort incorrectly.

l. Click the Exit button, then print the form and the code.

m. Research the Format$ function. Modify the form's Load event procedure so that it uses the Format$ function instead of the Str$ function. Format the List box entries so that each entry is three characters long. In other words, instead of adding "50" to the List box, the Format$ function will add "050."

n. Save and run the application. Click the Print button. (Be sure the 10 numbers appear in the List box on the printout. The numbers should be sorted correctly.) Click the Exit button to end the application, then print the code.

discovery ▶ 9. In this exercise you will use a bubble sort (sorting method #2) to sort the 10 records contained in a sequential access file named t9owners.dat, which is in either the tut9\ver2 or the tut9\ver3 directory on your Student Disk.

a. Launch Notepad. Open the t9owners.dat file and print its contents.

b. Launch Visual Basic and create the user interface shown in Figure 9-42.

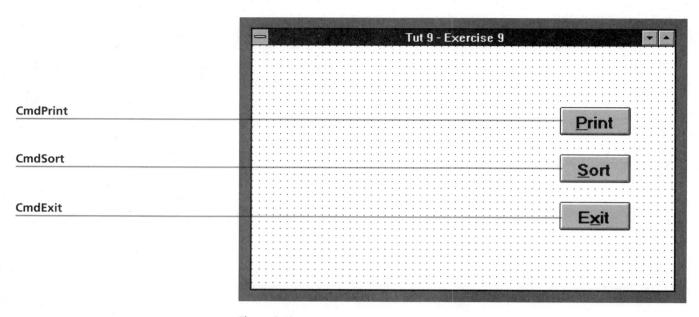

CmdPrint

CmdSort

CmdExit

Figure 9-42

c. Add a code module to the project. Declare a user-defined data type (record structure) named Ownerstruc, which consists of an owner's name, a license plate number, the car type, and the price. The price field should be declared as Single, and the other three fields should be declared as String.

d. Save the form, the code module, and the project as t9lae9.

e. The form's general Declarations section should include the *Option Explicit* statement, a Dim statement that declares a 10-element Ownerstruc array named OwnerArray, and a Dim statement that declares an Integer variable named NumEntries, which will store the number of entries in the array.

f. Code the form's Load event procedure so that it fills the OwnerArray array with the records contained in the t9owners.dat file.

g. Code the Sort button's Click event procedure so that it uses a bubble sort to sort the records in the OwnerArray array. The sort key should be the price field. (Hint: Consider declaring an Ownerstruc variable named Temp, which will temporarily store the contents of the array element so that a swap can be made.)

h. Code the Print button's Click event procedure so that it prints the contents of the array on the printer.

i. Code the Exit button's Click event procedure so that it writes the contents of the array to a sequential access file named t9lae9.srt. The Exit button should then end the application.

j. Save and run the application. Click the Print button. The contents of the OwnerArray array, unsorted, are printed on the printer.

k. Click the Sort button, then click the Print button. The contents of the OwnerArray array, sorted by price, are printed on the printer.

l. Click the Exit button to first write the sorted array to the t9lae9.srt file and then end the application.

m. Print the form and the code.

n. Launch Notepad. Open the t9lae9.srt file and print its contents. Close Notepad.

discovery ▶ 10. In this exercise you will use a Shell sort (sorting method #3) to sort the 10 records contained in a sequential access file named t9owners.dat, which is in either the tut9\ver2 or the tut9\ver3 directory on your Student Disk.

a. Launch Notepad. Open the t9owners.dat file and print its contents.

b. Launch Visual Basic and create the user interface shown in Figure 9-43.

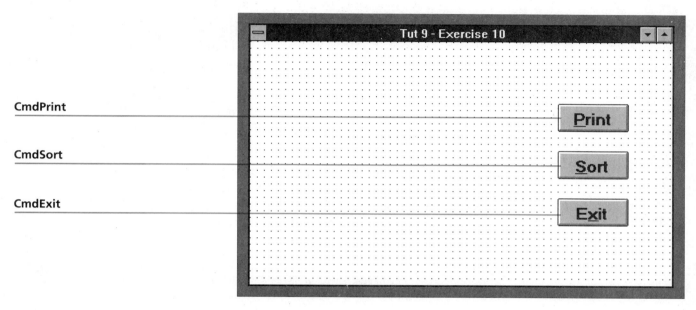

CmdPrint

CmdSort

CmdExit

Figure 9-43

c. Add a code module to the project. Declare a user-defined data type (record structure) named Ownerstruc, which consists of an owner's name, a license plate number, the car type, and the price. The price field should be declared as Single, and the other three fields should be declared as String.

d. Save the form, the code module, and the project as t9lae10.

e. The form's general Declarations section should include the *Option Explicit* statement, a Dim statement that declares a 10-element Ownerstruc array named OwnerArray, and a Dim statement that declares an Integer variable named NumEntries, which will store the number of entries in the array.

f. Code the form's Load event procedure so that it fills the OwnerArray array with the records contained in the t9owners.dat file.

g. Code the Sort button's Click event procedure so that it uses a Shell sort to sort the records in the OwnerArray array. The sort key should be the price field. (Hint: Consider declaring an Ownerstruc variable named Temp, which will temporarily store the contents of the array element so that a swap can be made.)

h. Code the Print button's Click event procedure so that it prints the contents of the array on the printer.

i. Code the Exit button's Click event procedure so that it writes the contents of the array to a sequential access file named t9lae10.srt. The Exit button should then end the application.

j. Save and run the application. Click the Print button. The contents of the OwnerArray array, unsorted, are printed on the printer.

k. Click the Sort button, then click the Print button. The contents of the OwnerArray array, sorted by price, are printed on the printer.

l. Click the Exit button to first write the sorted array to the t9lae10.srt file and then end the application.

m. Print the form and the code.

n. Launch Notepad. Open the t9le10.srt file and print its contents. Close Notepad.

discovery ▶ 11. a. Open the t9lae1.mak project that you created in Exercise 1.

b. Save the form and the project as t9lae11.

c. Modify the Exit button's code so that it writes, in descending order, the sorted contents of the List box. Write the data to a sequential access file named t9lae11.srt.

d. Save and run the application, then click the Exit button.

e. Print the code. Also print the t9lae11.srt file in Notepad.

discovery ▶ 12. a. Open the t9lae3.mak project that you created in Exercise 3.

b. Save the form and the project as t9lae12.

c. Modify the Sort button's code so that it uses the bubble sort to sort the numbers in the SalesArray array in descending order.

d. Modify the Exit button's code so that it writes the contents of the SalesArray array, which is sorted in descending order, to a sequential access file named t9lae12.srt.

e. Save and run the application. Click the Sort button, then click the Exit button.

f. Print the code. Also print the t9lae12.srt file in Notepad.

discovery ▶ 13. a. Open the t9lae6.mak project that you created in Exercise 6.

b. Save the form and the project as t9lae13.

c. Modify the Sort button's code so that it uses the Shell sort to sort the names in the NamesArray array in descending order.

d. Modify the Exit button's code so that it writes the contents of the NamesArray array, which is sorted in descending order, to a sequential access file named t9lae13.srt.

e. Save and run the application. Click the Sort button, then click the Exit button.

f. Print the code. Also print the t9lae13.srt file in Notepad.

Menus

The Gifts Express Application

Recall that the telemarketers at Gifts Express call long distance to customers all over the United States. Because of the different time zones, it is essential for the telemarketers to know the state to which the call is going, so they don't call too early or too late. In this lesson you will create an application that will allow the Gifts Express personnel to both display and print a list of area codes and states in either area code order or state order.

On your Student Disk is a partially completed application for Gifts Express. Let's begin by opening the partially completed application.

To open the partially-completed Gifts Express application:

1   Launch Visual Basic and open the **t9gifts.mak** file, which is in either the tut9\ver2 or the tut9\ver3 directory on your Student Disk. Click the **View Form button**, then maximize the form. Only one Text box, named TxtList, appears on the form, as shown in Figure 9-44.

TxtList

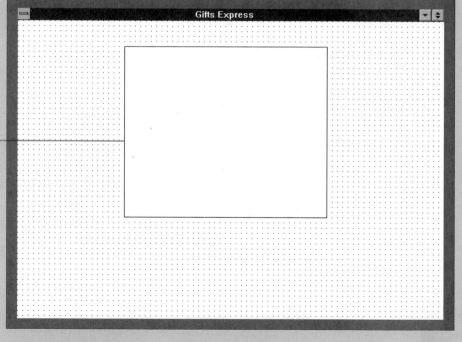

Figure 9-44: Partially completed user interface for Gifts Express application

2   Restore the form to its standard size, then **save** the form and the project as **t9b**.

In addition to the many controls that you have learned about in previous tutorials, another common element found in most Windows applications is a menu. You will create a menu for the Gifts Express application. The menu will allow the user to sort and display the area codes and states in either area code order or state order. The menu will also allow the user to print the area codes and states on the printer and exit the application.

Creating a Menu

In Visual Basic, you create a menu in the Menu Design Window, which you have not yet seen. The menus you create can contain the following elements: menu titles, menu items, submenu titles, and submenu items. Figure 9-45 identifies the location of these elements in a Visual Basic form.

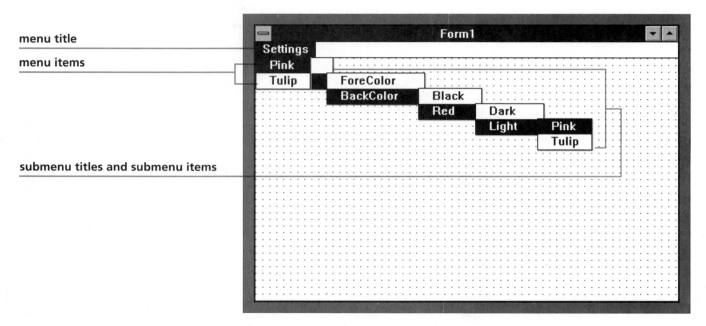

Figure 9-45: Menu elements

As Figure 9-45 shows, menu titles appear in the menu bar at the top of the form. When you click a menu title, its corresponding menu opens and displays a list of options, called menu items. These menu items can be commands (such as Open or Exit), separator bars, or submenu titles. As in all Windows-based applications, clicking a command in a menu executes the command, and clicking a submenu title opens an additional menu of options. The purpose of a separator bar is to group related menu items together; you can't click a separator bar.

Although you can create up to four levels of submenus, it's best to use only one level in your application. Too many layers of submenus can be confusing.

Let's start the menu design process now.

To display the Menu Design Window:

1 Click the **Menu Design Window icon** 🔳 in the toolbar (or click **Window**, then click **Menu Design**; you can also press **[Ctrl][M]**). The Menu Design Window appears on the screen. See Figure 9-46.

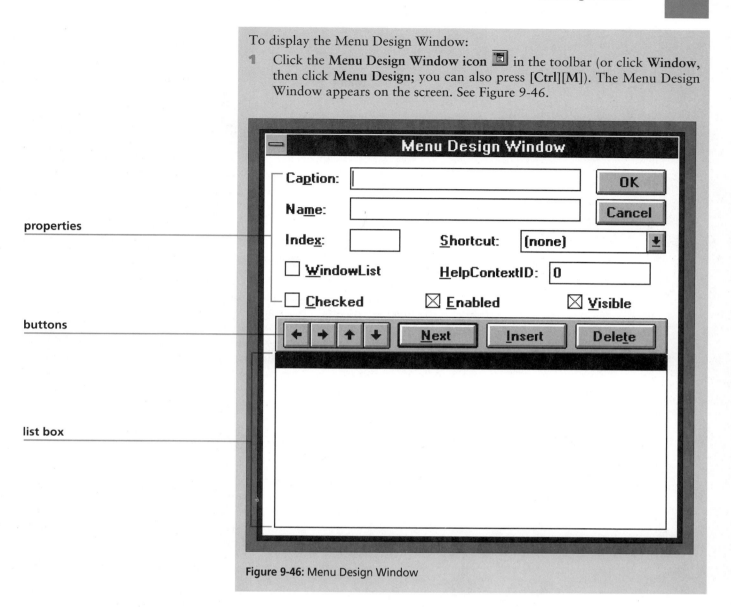

properties

buttons

list box

Figure 9-46: Menu Design Window

The top portion of the Menu Design Window contains the properties associated with Menu controls. (You will use the Checked, Enabled, and Visible properties in the Discovery Exercises at the end of Lesson B.) At the bottom of the Menu Design Window is a list box that displays the Menu controls as you are creating them. Visual Basic treats each entry in the list box as a separate Menu control, so each entry can have its own properties and its own Visual Basic code.

Immediately above the list box are seven buttons. Figure 9-47 explains the purpose of each button.

Button	Purpose
left arrow and right arrow	Change the indentation level of the Menu controls
up arrow and down arrow	Move a Menu control to another location in the list box
Next	Creates a new Menu control or moves highlight to the next Menu control in the list
Insert	Inserts a new Menu control between two existing controls
Delete	Deletes the highlighted Menu control

Figure 9-47: The Menu Design Window's buttons

As you know by now, the applications you create in Visual Basic should follow, as much as possible, the standard conventions used in other Windows programs. For example, the File menu is normally the left-most menu title in the menu bar. The File menu customarily contains options for opening files, printing files, and exiting the application. In this project, the File menu will have a Print option and an Exit option only. You will also include another menu title, called Sort, in the menu bar. The Sort menu will have two options: Area Code and State.

Like Command buttons, the menu controls can have access keys. Recall from Tutorial 2 that an access key allows the user to select an object using the Alt key in combination with a letter. (For example, you can use [Alt][F] to open Visual Basic's File menu. The letter "F" is the File menu's access key.) You can assign an access key to any control that has a Caption property. You create an access key for a control by including an ampersand (&) in the control's caption. You enter the ampersand to the immediate left of the character you want to designate as the access key. Let's begin by creating the File menu. As is customary in Windows applications, the letter "F" will be the access key for the File menu.

tips

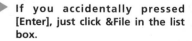

If you accidentally pressed the Enter key instead of the Tab key, click &File in the list box, then position the mouse pointer inside the Name box (located below the Caption box) and click inside the Name box.

If you accidentally pressed [Enter], just click &File in the list box.

If you accidentally clicked the down arrow button above the list box, simply click the up arrow button, then click the Next button.

To enter Menu controls in the Menu Design Window:

1 Type **&File** in the Caption box, then press [**Tab**]. &File appears in the Caption box and in the list box, and the insertion point moves into the Name box.

You must complete the Caption property and the Name property for each Menu control in the list box. The Caption property controls the text appearing in the Menu control, and the Name property gives the Menu control a name to which you can refer when writing Visual Basic code.

2 Type **MnuFile** in the Name box, but don't press [Enter] yet. You use Mnu in the name to remind you that File is a Menu control.

3 Click the **Next button** to enter the next Menu control. The highlight moves down one line in the list box.

You want Print to be the first item on the File menu. The Print option will print the area codes and their corresponding states. The letter P is customarily the access key for the Print option in Windows menus.

4   Type **&Print** in the Caption box, press [**Tab**], then type **MnuFilePrint** in the Name box. (You choose this name to help you remember that Print is a menu item on the File menu.) &Print appears as a Menu control in the list box.

Let's see what the menu looks like so far.

5   Click the **OK button** to leave the Menu Design Window. Visual Basic displays the menu in the form, as shown in Figure 9-48.

two menu titles

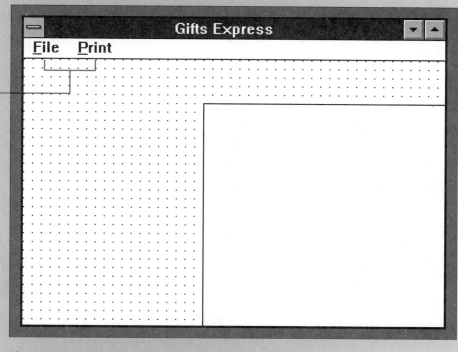

Figure 9-48: Menu in the form

Notice that Print appears as a separate menu title in the menu bar. You actually want Print to be a menu item on the File menu, not a separate menu title. Let's fix this problem next.

Creating Menu Items

You control the placement of menu titles, menu items, submenu titles, and submenu items by indenting the entries in the list box of the Menu Design Window. As you just saw, entries appearing flush left in the list box are displayed as menu titles on the menu bar. If you want a control to be an option (that is, an item) on a menu, you must indent the entry once in the list box. Entries indented even further in the list box become submenu titles, and items indented below submenu titles become options (submenu items) on that submenu. Figure 9-49 illustrates the placement of menu titles, menu items, submenu titles, and submenu items in the list box.

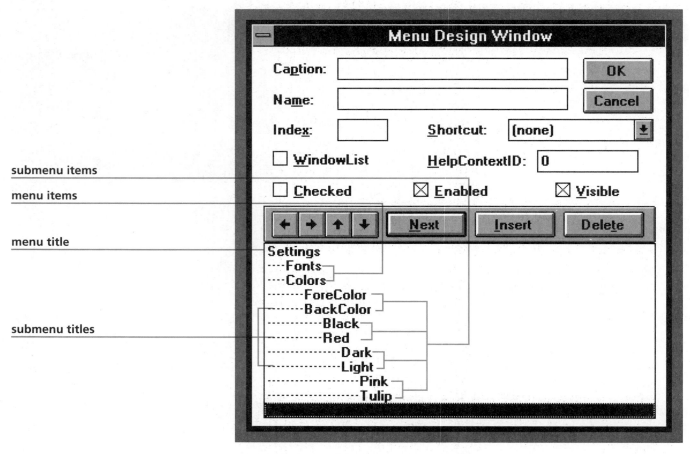

Figure 9-49: Menu elements in the list box

submenu items

menu items

menu title

submenu titles

You will now open the Menu Design Window and designate Print as a menu item on the File menu.

If you indented the &Print option too far in the list box, simply click the left arrow button above the list box until the option is indented correctly.

To designate a control as a menu item:

1 Click the **Menu Design Window icon** 🔳 in the toolbar. The Menu Design Window opens.

2 Click **&Print** in the list box, then click the **right arrow button above the list box** to indent &Print. Four dots (....) appear before &Print in the list box. Visual Basic will now display Print as a menu item on the File menu, instead of as a separate menu title on the menu bar. See Figure 9-50.

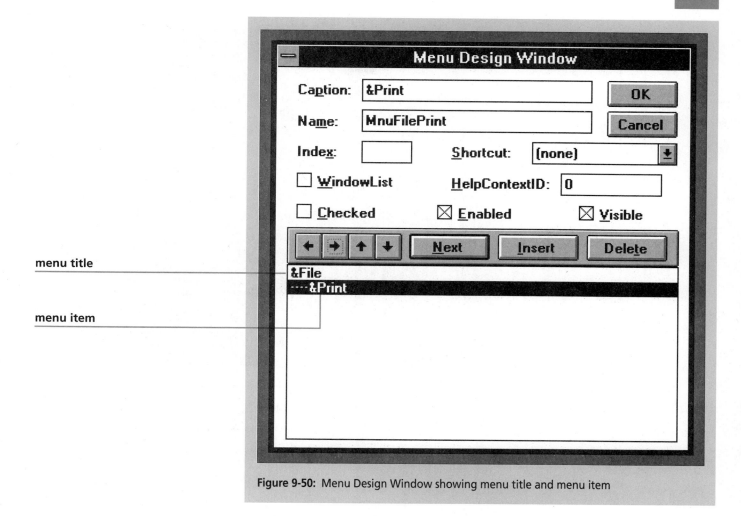

menu title

menu item

Figure 9-50: Menu Design Window showing menu title and menu item

You also want to include an Exit option in the File menu. The Exit option will allow the user to quit the application. Because the Exit option will perform a task that is entirely different from the task performed by the Print option, you decide to use a horizontal line, called a **separator bar,** to separate the two menu items.

Creating a Separator Bar

Using a separator bar to divide menu items into logical groups is another Windows convention. In Visual Basic, you create a separator bar by placing one hyphen (-) in the Caption box of a Menu control. Let's add a separator bar to this menu and then complete the File menu.

If you accidentally clicked the down arrow button above the list box, simply click the up arrow button, then click the Next button.

To enter a separator bar in the File menu:

1   Click the **Next button** to enter a new Menu control. The highlight moves to the next line (the line immediately below the Print option) in the list box. Visual Basic assumes that this new entry will be another menu item, so it indents the entry for you.

2   Type - (a hyphen) in the Caption box, press [**Tab**], then type **Hyphen1** in the Name box. (Be sure you don't include a space between Hyphen and 1.) When the application is run, the File menu will display a separator bar between the Print option and the Exit option.

As you already know, you can add another control to the list box by clicking the Next button. You can also press [Enter].

3   Press [**Enter**] to add a new control. The highlight moves down one line in the list box.

The letter X is the standard access key for the Exit option in Windows applications.

4   Type **E&xit** in the Caption box, press [**Tab**], then type **MnuFileExit** in the Name box. Visual Basic adds the E&xit option to the File menu.

Let's view the menu before adding any more controls to it.

5   Click the **OK button** to leave the Menu Design Window. The form appears on the screen. File is now the only menu title on the menu bar.

6   Click **File in the form's menu bar** to open the File menu. The File menu opens and displays its list of menu items, as shown in Figure 9-51.

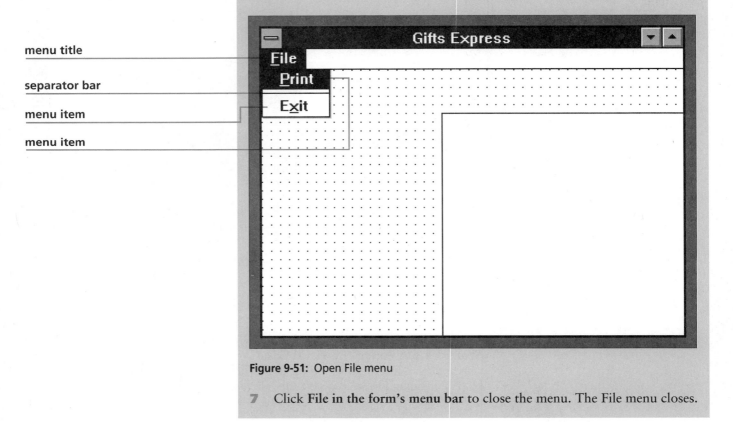

menu title

separator bar

menu item

menu item

Figure 9-51: Open File menu

7   Click **File in the form's menu bar** to close the menu. The File menu closes.

In addition to access keys, Visual Basic also allows you to assign shortcut keys to the menu items. Let's look at where shortcut keys appear in the menus. You can do so by opening Visual Basic's File menu.

To open the Visual Basic File menu:

1   Press [**Alt**][**f**]. (Hold down the Alt key as you type the letter f.) The Visual Basic File menu opens, as shown in Figure 9-52.

underlined letter F is the access key

underlined letter P is the access key

shortcut key

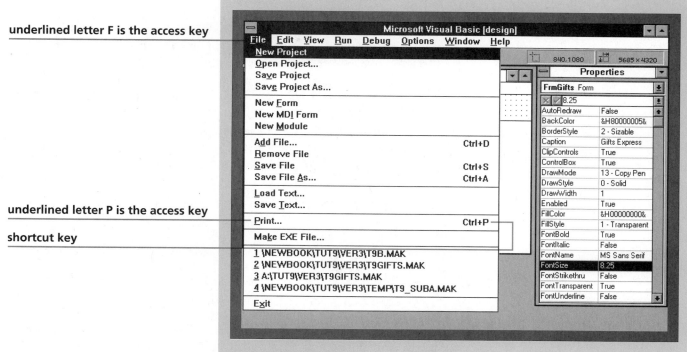

Figure 9-52: Open Visual Basic File menu

Notice that some of the menu items in Visual Basic's File menu have shortcut keys. **Shortcut keys,** which are displayed to the right of the menu item, allow you to select a menu item without opening the menu. For example, pressing the Ctrl key as you type the letter P will select the Print option even if the File menu is not open.

2   Click **File in Visual Basic's menu bar** to close the Visual Basic File menu. The File menu closes.

Let's assign a shortcut key to the Print option in the area code application.

tips

If you accidentally clicked the down arrow button above the list box instead of the down arrow button in the Shortcut combo box, simply click the up arrow button above the list box, then click the down arrow button in the Shortcut combo box.

To assign a shortcut key to the Print option:

1   Click the **Menu Design icon** 🖼, then click **....&Print** in the list box.

In most Windows applications, [Ctrl][P] is the shortcut key assigned to the Print menu item. You will use this Windows standard in this application.

2   Locate the Shortcut combo box on the screen and then click the **down arrow button in the Shortcut combo box.** A list of shortcut keys appears.

3   Scroll the list of shortcut keys until Ctrl+P appears, then click **Ctrl+P.** Ctrl+P appears in the Shortcut combo box and to the right of the ....Print option in the Menu Design Window's list box. Now you will be able to print the area codes and state abbreviations by pressing [Ctrl][P].

Now let's complete the menu by adding the Sort menu title and two menu items, Area Code and State.

To complete the menu:

1   Click the **Next button** three times. The highlight moves to the line immediately below the Exit option in the list box. Visual Basic assumes that this new entry will be another menu item, so it indents the entry for you.

You want Sort to be a separate menu title on the menu bar, not an item on the File menu, so you will need to remove the indentation so that Sort appears flush left in the list box.

2   Click the **left arrow button above the list box**. Visual Basic removes the four dots from the entry in the list box.

3   Click inside the Caption box. The insertion point appears in the Caption box.

4   Type **&Sort** in the Caption box, press **[Tab]**, type **MnuSort** in the Name box, and then press **[Enter]**. &Sort is now flush left in the list box, so it will appear as a menu title on the menu bar.

In the Sort menu, you want to display two options: Area Code and State. The access keys for these two options will be A and S, respectively. The shortcut keys will be Ctrl+A and Ctrl+S, respectively.

5   Type **&Area Code** in the Caption box, press **[Tab]**, then type **MnuSortArea** in the Name box, but don't press **[Enter]** yet. The option should be a menu item on the Sort menu, not a menu title on the menu bar, so you will need to indent the item in the list box.

6   Click the **right arrow button above the list box** to indent the &Area Code option.

7   Click the **down arrow button in the Shortcut combo box**, then click **Ctrl+A**. Ctrl+A appears in the Shortcut combo box and to the right of the ....&Area Code option in the Menu Design Window's list box.

8   Click the **Next button**, type **&State** in the Caption box, press **[Tab]**, then type **MnuSortState** in the Name box. Click the **down arrow button in the Shortcut combo box**. Scroll the list of shortcut keys until Ctrl+S appears, then click **Ctrl+S**. Ctrl+S appears in the Shortcut combo box and to the right of the ....&State option in the Menu Design Window's list box.

The Menu Design Window should now look like Figure 9-53.

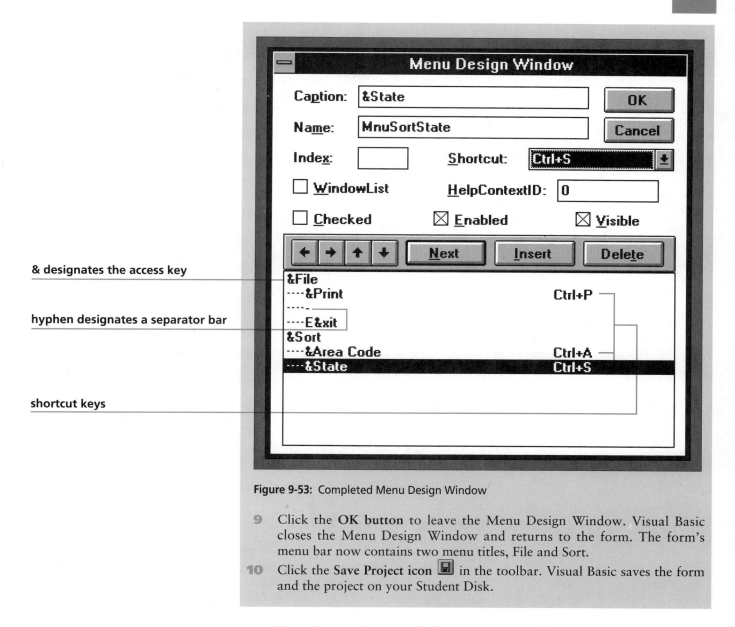

& designates the access key

hyphen designates a separator bar

shortcut keys

Figure 9-53: Completed Menu Design Window

9   Click the **OK button** to leave the Menu Design Window. Visual Basic closes the Menu Design Window and returns to the form. The form's menu bar now contains two menu titles, File and Sort.

10   Click the **Save Project icon** in the toolbar. Visual Basic saves the form and the project on your Student Disk.

Now that you've created the menu, you can begin coding the application. The TOE chart is shown in Figure 9-54.

Task	Object	Event
Read area codes and states from file	Form	Load
Enter area codes and states into arrays		
Sort area codes and states by area code	Sort menu - Area Code option	Click
Sort area codes and states by state	Sort menu - State option	Click
Print area codes and states	File menu - Print option	Click
End the application	File menu - Exit option	Click

Figure 9-54: TOE chart for the Gifts Express application

We'll begin by coding the general Declarations section of the form.

Coding the Form's General Declarations Section

This application will use one form-level variable and two form-level arrays. The variable, named NumEntries, will store the number of array entries. One of the arrays, named AreaArray, will store the area codes; the other array, named StateArray, will store the two-letter state abbreviation for the state that corresponds to the area code. The two arrays used in this application are referred to as **parallel arrays** because they have corresponding elements. In other words, the area code in AreaArray(1) corresponds to the state abbreviation in StateArray(1), the area code in AreaArray(2) corresponds to the state abbreviation in StateArray(2), and so on. Let's code the form's general Declarations section now.

To code the form's general Declarations section:

1   Double-click the **form** to open its Code window. Click the **down arrow in the Code window's Object box,** then click (**general**) in the drop-down list. The form's general Declarations section appears with the *Option Explicit* statement already entered.

2   Maximize the Code window, then enter the two Dim statements shown in Figure 9-55.

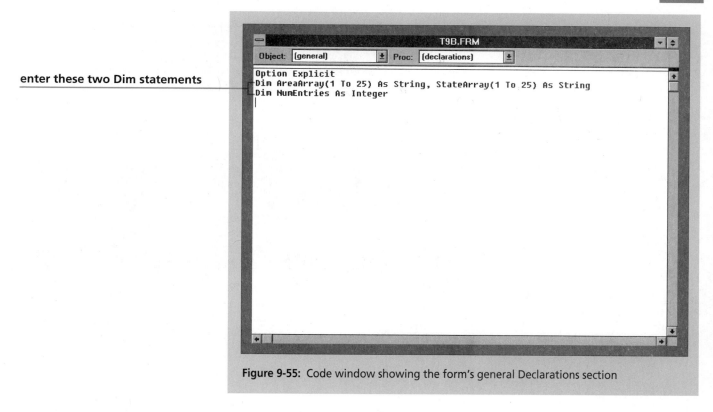

enter these two Dim statements

```
T9B.FRM
Object: [general]        Proc: [declarations]

Option Explicit
Dim AreaArray(1 To 25) As String, StateArray(1 To 25) As String
Dim NumEntries As Integer
```

Figure 9-55: Code window showing the form's general Declarations section

Next let's code the form's Load event procedure, where the arrays will be filled with data.

Coding the Form's Load Event Procedure

The pseudocode for the form's Load event procedure is shown in Figure 9-56.

```
1.   Open the t9gifts.dat sequential access file for input

2.   Repeat while it's not the end of the file

          Add 1 to the NumEntries variable

          Read the area code into the AreaArray array and read the state abbreviation

          into the StateArray array

     End repeat

3.   Close the file
```

Figure 9-56: Pseudocode for the form's Load event procedure

The records for the Gifts Express application are stored in the t9gifts.dat sequential access data file on your Student Disk. Each record consists of an area code and the two-letter abbreviation of its corresponding state. The Load event will read the area codes and the state abbreviations into their respective arrays: The area codes will be stored in the AreaArray array, and the state abbreviations will be stored in the StateArray array. As each record is read, the counter variable, NumEntries, will be increased by 1. When the form's Load event procedure is finished, NumEntries will contain the number of elements in each array.

To code the form's Load event procedure:

1   Click the **down arrow in the Code window's Object box**, then click **Form** in the drop-down list. The form's Load event procedure appears.

2   Enter the code shown in Figure 9-57. If necessary, change the drive letter to the drive containing your Student Disk.

if necessary, change the drive letter to the drive containing your Student Disk

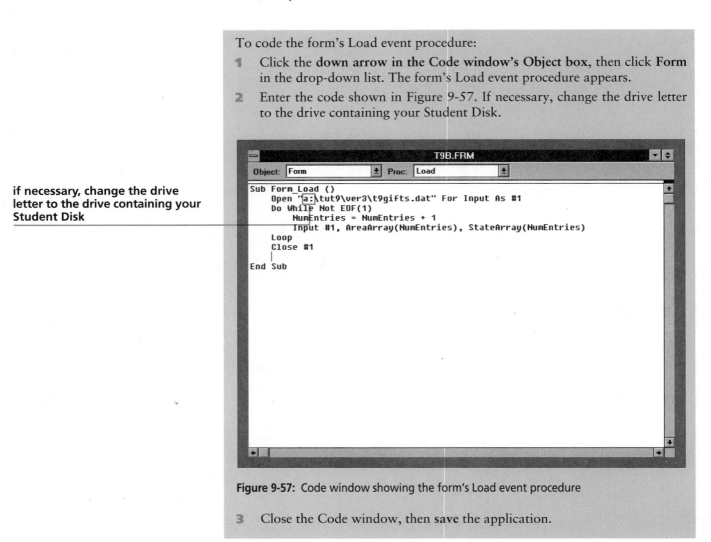

```
                              T9B.FRM
Object: Form              Proc: Load

Sub Form_Load ()
     Open "a:\tut9\ver3\t9gifts.dat" For Input As #1
     Do While Not EOF(1)
         NumEntries = NumEntries + 1
         Input #1, AreaArray(NumEntries), StateArray(NumEntries)
     Loop
     Close #1

End Sub
```

Figure 9-57: Code window showing the form's Load event procedure

3   Close the Code window, then save the application.

Now you can begin coding the items on the menus. You will code the File menu in this lesson and the Sort menu in Lesson C. You'll begin with the File menu's Exit option.

Coding Menu Items

The first menu item you will code is the Exit option on the File menu. When the user clicks this option, the application should end.

To code the Exit option, then save and run the application:

1 Click **File in the form's menu bar** to open the File menu. (Be sure to open the form's File menu, not Visual Basic's File menu.) The form's File menu opens.

You open a Menu control's Code window by clicking the control, not double-clicking as you do with other controls.

2 Click **Exit** to open the MnuFileExit Code window. The Code window opens and displays the Click event procedure, which is the only event procedure a Menu control recognizes.

3 Press [**Tab**], type **end** and press [**Enter**].

4 Close the Code window.

Let's see if the Exit option works correctly.

5 **Save and run** the application. Click **File** (or press [**Alt**][**F**]) to open the File menu. The File menu opens. Type **x** (the Exit option's access key) to end the application. Visual Basic returns to the design screen.

tips

••••••••••••••••••

If you accidentally chose Exit from Visual Basic's File menu, launch Visual Basic and open the t9b.mak project. Click File in the form's menu bar, then click Exit to open the MnuFileExit Code window.

The next menu option you will code is the File menu's Print option.

Coding the File Menu's Print Option

The pseudocode for the Print option is shown in Figure 9-58.

```
1.   Declare an Integer variable named X

2.   Print "Area Code" and "State" as column headings

3.   Repeat for 1 to NumEntries by 1

          Print the area code from the AreaArray array and print the

          state abbreviation from the StateArray array

     End repeat

4.   Tell printer to print the document
```

Figure 9-58: Pseudocode for the File menu's Print option

This option will print the contents of both the AreaArray and the StateArray arrays on the printer.

To code the Print option, then save and run the application:

1 Click **File in the form's menu bar** to open the File menu. (Be sure to open the form's File menu, not Visual Basic's File menu.) The form's File menu opens.

2 Click **Print** to open the MnuFilePrint Code window. The Code window opens and displays the Click event procedure.

3   Enter the code shown in Figure 9-59.

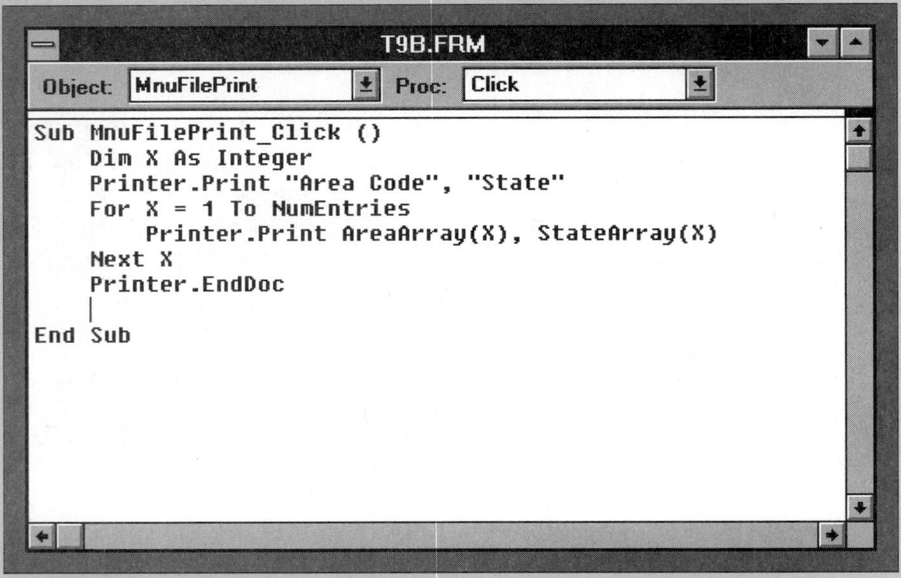

```
T9B.FRM
Object:  MnuFilePrint          Proc:  Click

Sub MnuFilePrint_Click ()
    Dim X As Integer
    Printer.Print "Area Code", "State"
    For X = 1 To NumEntries
        Printer.Print AreaArray(X), StateArray(X)
    Next X
    Printer.EndDoc
    |
End Sub
```

Figure 9-59: Code window showing the code for the File menu's Print option

The procedure declares an Integer variable named X that will control the processing of the For...Next loop. The column headings "Area Code" and "State" are printed before the For...Next loop prints the area codes and states in two columns on the printout. The *EndDoc* instruction, you may recall, tells the printer to print the document.

4   Close the Code window.

Let's test the Print option to see if it works correctly.

5   **Save and run** the application. If your computer is connected to a printer, then click **File** (or press [**Alt**][**F**]) to open the File menu, and then click **Print** (or press **p**) to print the contents of the two arrays. The printout should resemble Figure 9-60.

```
Area Code                                        State

504                                              LA
806                                              TX
918                                              OK
206                                              WA
215                                              PA
417                                              MO
814                                              PA
701                                              ND
704                                              NC
915                                              TX
817                                              TX
719                                              CO
207                                              ME
307                                              WY
615                                              TN
606                                              KY
602                                              AZ
907                                              AK
914                                              NY
919                                              NC
210                                              TX
510                                              CA
415                                              CA
214                                              TX
912                                              GA
```

Figure 9-60: Printout from the File menu's Print option

The printout shows the area codes and states in the order in which they appear in the t9gifts.dat sequential access file.

6 Click **File**, then click **Exit** to exit the application. Visual Basic returns to the design screen.

7 Click **File in the Visual Basic menu bar**, then click **New Project**. If you are asked if you want to save the form or the project, click the Yes button.

You have now completed Lesson B. You can either take a break or complete the end-of-lesson questions and exercises. You will complete the Gifts Express application in Lesson C.

S U M M A R Y

To create a Menu control:

- Click the Menu Design Window icon in the toolbar 🗔 (or click Window, then click Menu Design; you can also press [Ctrl][M]).
- Complete the Caption property and the Name property for each Menu control. Complete other properties as necessary. Click the OK button to leave the Menu Design Window.

To create a separator bar in a menu:

- Type - (one hyphen) in the Caption property of the Menu control. Also type a name in the Name property of the Menu control.

To assign a shortcut key to a Menu control:

- Open the Menu Design Window, then click the appropriate menu control in the list box. Click the down arrow button in the Shortcut combo box, then click the desired shortcut key in the drop-down list. Click the OK button to leave the Menu Design Window.

To assign an access key to a Menu control:

- Open the Menu Design Window, then click the appropriate menu control in the list box. In the Caption property of the control, type an ampersand (&) to the immediate left of the letter you want to designate as the access key.

To open the Code window for a Menu control:

- Click the Menu control to open its Code window.

Q U E S T I O N S

1. You must complete these properties for each Menu control. (Choose two answers.)
   a. Caption
   b. Menu
   c. Name
   d. Shortcut
   e. Text

2. Which of the following is the only event to which a Menu control can react?
   a. Change
   b. Click
   c. Double-click
   d. Load
   e. Show

3. Entries that are flush left in the list box of the Menu Design Window will appear as _____ .
   a. menu items
   b. menu titles
   c. submenu items
   d. submenu titles

4. The horizontal line in a menu is called a(n) _____ .
   a. dashed line
   b. hyphen line
   c. item separator
   d. menu bar
   e. separator bar

5. You create the horizontal line in a menu by typing a(n) _____ in the Caption property of a Menu control.
   a. asterisk
   b. dash
   c. hyphen
   d. underscore

6. The underlined letter in a menu title, menu item, submenu title, or submenu item is called a(n) _____ key.
   a. access
   b. dash
   c. menu
   d. open
   e. shortcut

7. A _____ key allows you to access a menu item without opening the menu.
   a. access
   b. dash
   c. menu item
   d. open
   e. shortcut

8. You create an access key for a control by entering a(n) _____ to the immediate left of the appropriate character in the Caption property.
   a. ampersand (&)
   b. asterisk (*)
   c. dash (−)
   d. plus sign (+)
   e. underscore (_)

E X E R C I S E S

1. a. Create the user interface shown in Figure 9-61.

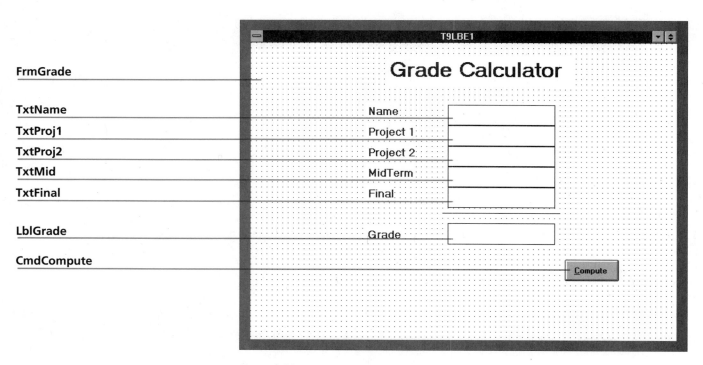

Figure 9-61

You can use this application to compute a student's letter grade; you just need to enter his or her project and test scores, and then click the Compute button. The application will also allow you to print the form.

b. Save the form and the project as t9lbe1.

c. Code the Compute button's Click event procedure so that it sums the project and test scores and then assigns the appropriate grade according to the following chart:

Total Points	Grade
270 – 300	A
240 – 269	B
210 – 239	C
180 – 209	D
Less than 180	F

d. Add a File menu to the application. The File menu should contain a Print option and an Exit option. Include a separator bar between both options. Assign access keys to the menu and its options. Assign Ctrl+P as the shortcut key for the Print option.

e. Code the Print option so that it prints the form. Code the Exit option so that it exits the application.

f. Save and run the application. Test the application by entering the following data: Jill Strait, 50, 45, 75, 80. Click the Compute button. Open the File menu and click Print, then open the File menu and click Exit.

g. Print the code.

2.   a. Create the user interface shown in Figure 9-62. The car model Option buttons should be a control array. The package type Option buttons should also be a control array. Set the ImgLogo control's Picture property to VB\icons\industry\cars.ico.

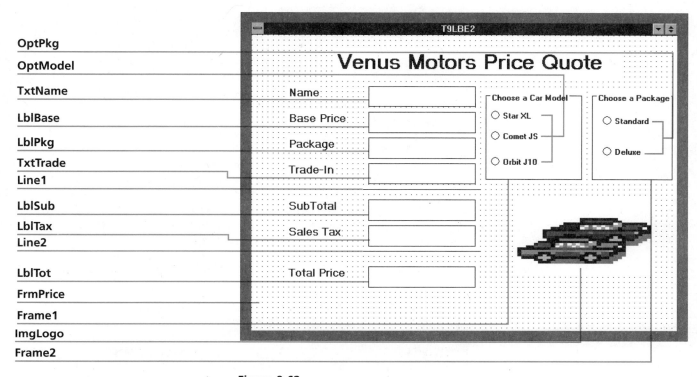

OptPkg

OptModel

TxtName

LblBase

LblPkg

TxtTrade
Line1

LblSub

LblTax
Line2

LblTot

FrmPrice

Frame1

ImgLogo

Frame2

Figure 9-62

You can use this application to calculate the total price of a car for a customer; you just need to furnish the customer's name, the car model, the package type, and the value of any trade-in.

   b. Save the form and the project as t9lbe2.

   c. Code the car model Option button array so that it displays the appropriate base price in the LblBase control. The base prices are as follows:

Car Model	Base Price
Star XL	10500
Orbit J10	15500
Comet JS	21000

   d. Code the package Option button array so that it displays the appropriate package price in the LblPkg control. The Standard package costs $2000, and the Deluxe package costs $3000.

   e. Add a File menu to the application. The File menu should contain a Clear option, a Print option, and an Exit option. Include a separator bar between each option. Assign access keys to the menu and its options.

   f. The Print option should have two submenu options, With Logo and No Logo. Code the With Logo option so that it prints the form. Code the No Logo option so that it hides the ImgLogo control, prints the form, and then displays the ImgLogo control. (Recall that you hide/display a control by setting its Visible property.)

   g. Code the Clear option so that it removes the data from the Name and Trade-In Text boxes. It should also remove the data from the Subtotal, Sales Tax, and Total Price Label controls.

   h. Code the Exit option so that it exits the application.

i. Add a Compute menu to the application. The Compute menu should contain a Rate – 5% option and a Rate – 7% option. Assign access keys to the menu and its options.

j. Code the Rate – 5% option so that it calculates and displays the subtotal, the sales tax, and the total price. To calculate the subtotal, add the base price to the package price, then subtract the trade-in value. Display the subtotal in the LblSub control. To calculate the sales tax, multiply the subtotal by .05. Display the sales tax in the LblTax control. To calculate the Total Price, add the subtotal to the sales tax. Display the total price in the LblTot control.

k. Code the Rate – 7% option so that it calculates and displays the subtotal, the sales tax, and the total price. Use the same calculations shown in step j above, except use a 7% sales tax rate.

l. Save and run the application. Test the application as follows:
    (1) Enter Darlene Zimmer as the name and 2000 as the trade-in value. Click Comet JS and Deluxe.
    (2) Open the Compute menu and click Rate - 7%.
    (3) Open the File menu and click Print, then click No Logo.
    (4) Open the File menu and click Clear.
    (5) Enter Dana Chou as the name and 1500 as the trade-in value. Click Orbit J10 and Standard.
    (6) Open the Compute menu and click Rate - 5%.
    (7) Open the File menu and click Print, then click With Logo.
    (8) Open the File menu and click Exit.

m. Print the code.

3. a. Create the user-interface shown in Figure 9-63. Set the ImgLogo1 control's Picture property to VB\icons\industry\rocket.ico.

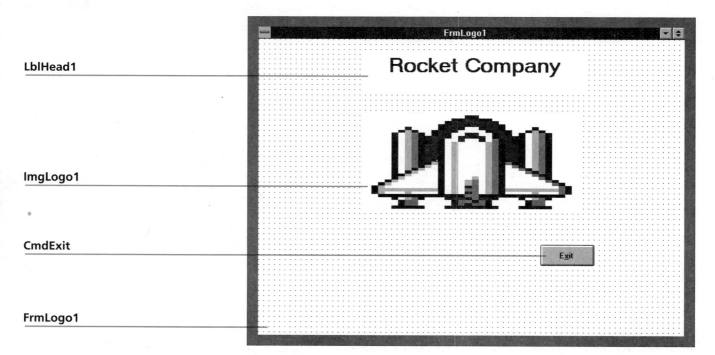

Figure 9-63

b. Save the form as t9logo1.frm. Save the project as t9lbe3.
c. Add another form to the t9lbe3 project. Create the user-interface shown in Figure 9-64. Set the ImgLogo2 control's Picture property to VB\icons\industry\bicycle.ico.

LblHead2

ImgLogo2

CmdExit

FrmLogo2

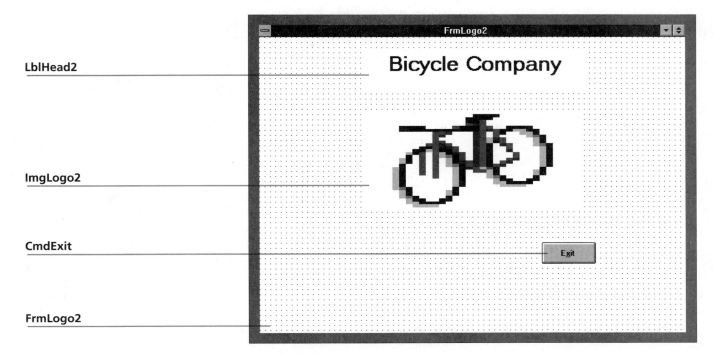

Figure 9-64

d. Save the form as t9logo2.frm. Save the project as t9lbe3.
You can use this application to switch between the two forms included in the project.
e. Code the Exit button in both forms so that each exits the application.
f. Add a File menu to each form. Each File menu should contain two options, Print and Switch Screen. Include a separator bar between both options. Assign access keys to the menu and its options. Assign Ctrl+P as the shortcut key for the Print option.
g. Code the Print option so that it prints the form.
h. Code the Switch Screen option so that it shows the hidden screen and hides the current one.
i. Verify that the Startup form is the FrmLogo1 form. Save and run the application. Test the application as follows:
   (1) Open the File menu and click Switch Screen, then open the File menu and click Print.
   (2) Open the File menu and click Switch Screen, then press [Ctrl][p] to print the screen.
   (3) Click the Exit button to exit the application.
j. Print the code.

Exercises 4 and 5 are Discovery Exercises.

discovery ▶ 4. a. Open a new project. Add the t9logo1.frm that you created in Lesson B's Exercise 3.

b. Save the form and the project as t9lbe4.

c. Click the LblHead1 control to select it. Press [Ctrl][c] to copy the control to the Windows Clipboard, then press [Ctrl][v] to paste the control onto the form. When Visual Basic asks if you want to create a control array, click the No button.

d. Change the new Label control's Name property to LblHead2. Change its Caption to Bicycle Company. Change its Visible property to False. Drag the LblHead2 control directly on top of the LblHead1 control.

e. Click the ImgLogo1 control to select it. Press [Ctrl][c] to copy the control to the Windows Clipboard, then press [Ctrl][v] to paste the control onto the form. When Visual Basic asks if you want to create a control array, click the No button.

f. Change the new Image control's Name property to ImgLogo2. Change its Picture property to vb\icons\industry\bicycle.ico. Change its Visible property to False. Drag the ImgLogo2 control directly on top of the ImgLogo1 control.

You will use this application to switch between the two different headings and two different icons included in the project.

g. Delete the Switch Screen option and the separator bar from the File menu.

h. Add a Display menu to the application. The Display menu should have two options, Rocket and Bicycle. Assign access keys to the menu and its options. Assign Ctrl+R as the shortcut key for the Rocket option and Ctrl+B as the short-cut key for the Bicycle option.

i. Use the Help screens to research the Checked property and the Enabled property, as they pertain to Menu controls.

j. Open the Menu Design Window. Click Rocket in the list. Check the Checked box to turn it on. Check the Enabled box to turn it off.

k. Code the Bicycle option's Click event procedure so that it hides both the LblHead1 and ImgLogo1 controls and displays both the LblHead2 and ImgLogo2 controls. (Recall that you hide and display controls by setting the Visible property.) The procedure should also turn the Bicycle option's Checked property on and its Enabled property off, and turn the Rocket option's Checked property off and its Enabled property on.

l. Code the Rocket option's Click event procedure so that it hides both the LblHead2 and ImgLogo2 controls and displays both the LblHead1 and ImgLogo1 controls. The procedure should also turn the Rocket option's Checked property on and its Enabled property off, and turn the Bicycle option's Checked property off and its Enabled property on.

m. Save and run the application. The Rocket Company heading and the Rocket logo should appear. Test the application as follows:

(1) Open the Display menu. The Rocket option should be dimmed and checked. The Bicycle option should be unchecked and not dimmed.

(2) Click Bicycle in the menu. The Bicycle Company heading and the bicycle logo should appear.

(3) Open the Display menu again. The Bicycle option should be dimmed and checked. The Rocket option should be unchecked and not dimmed.

(4) Click Rocket in the menu. The Rocket Company heading and rocket logo should appear.

(5) Click the Exit button.

n. Print the code.

discovery ▶ 5. a. Create the user interface shown in Figure 9-65. The LblNum controls should be a control array.

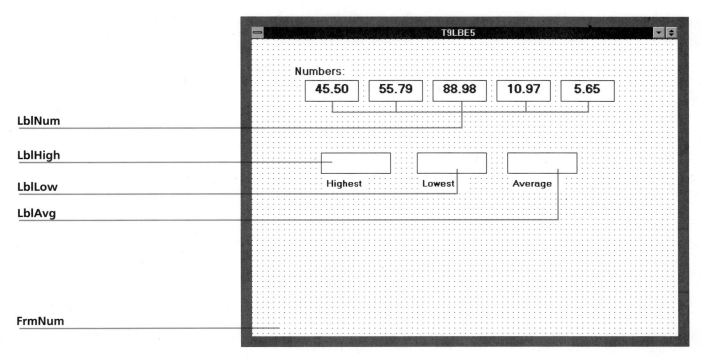

LblNum

LblHigh

LblLow

LblAvg

FrmNum

Figure 9-65

b. Save the form and the project as t9lbe5.

You can use this application to calculate the highest, lowest, and average number in a control array.

c. Add a File menu to the application. The File menu should contain a Print option and an Exit option. Include a separator bar between all options. Assign access keys to the menu and its options. Assign Ctrl+P as the shortcut key for the Print option.

d. Code the Print option so that it prints the form. Code the Exit option so that it ends the application.

e. Add a Calculate menu to the application. The Calculate menu should have four options: Highest Number, Lowest Number, Average Number, and Clear. Assign access keys to the menu and its options.

f. Use the Help screens to research the Enabled property, as it pertains to Menu controls.

g. Code the Highest Number option so that it first displays the Highest Number in the LblHigh control and then disables the Highest Number option in the menu.

h. Code the Lowest Number option so that it first displays the Lowest Number in the LblLow control and then disables the Lowest Number option in the menu.

i. Code the Average Number option so that it first displays the Average Number in the LblAvg control and then disables the Average Number option in the menu.

j. Code the Clear option so that it enables the Highest Number, Lowest Number, and Average Number options in the menu. It should also clear the LblHigh, LblLow, and LblAvg controls.

k. Save and run the application. Test the application as follows:

(1) Open the Calculate menu and click Highest Number.

(2) Open the File menu and click Print.

(3) Open the Calculate menu and click Lowest Number.

(4) Open the File menu and click Print.

(5) Open the Calculate menu and click Average Number.

(6) Open the File menu and click Print.

(7) Open the Calculate menu and click Clear.

(8) Open the Calculate menu and click Average Number.

(9) Open the File menu and click Print.

(10) Open the File menu and click Exit.

l. Print the code.

In this lesson you will learn how to:

- Pass parameters to a sub procedure
- Define the Newline character
- Use the MultiLine property and the ScrollBar property of a Text box

Sub Procedures

Completing the Gifts Express Application

Recall that you still need to code the Sort menu in the Gifts Express application. To do so, you will need to open the T9B.MAK project that you created in Lesson B.

> To continue coding the Gifts Express Application:
>
> 1 Launch Visual Basic (if necessary) and open the **t9b.mak** project, which is in either the tut9\ver2 or tut9\ver3 directory on your Student Disk. Click the **View form button** in the Project window to view the form.
>
> 2 **Save** the form and the project as **t9c**.

Now let's code the Sort menu.

Coding the Sort Menu

Recall that the Sort menu contains two options, Area Code and State. The Area Code option should sort the contents of both arrays (AreaArray and StateArray) by area code and then display the results in the Text box on the form. The State option, on the other hand, should sort the contents of both arrays by state and then display the results in the Text box on the form. You will use a Shell sort to sort the array elements in the required order. Instead of entering the Shell sort's code in the Code windows for both menu options, you will enter the code in a user-defined sub procedure, which you will call ShellSort, and then call (or invoke) the ShellSort procedure from both menu options. You will create another sub procedure, which you will call DisplayData, that will display the contents of both arrays in the Text box. The DisplayData procedure will also be called from both menu options. Before creating the ShellSort and DisplayData sub procedures, you will first enter the code to call (or invoke) the procedures in the Area Code and the State menu options.

To code the Sort menu options:

1 Click **Sort** in the form's menu bar to open the Sort menu. The form's Sort menu opens.

2 Click **Area Code** to open the MnuSortArea Code window. The Code window opens and displays the MnuSortArea_Click procedure.

As you learned in Tutorial 7, you invoke a user-defined procedure with the Call statement, whose syntax is **Call** *procedurename* [(*parameterlist*)]. A user-defined procedure, you may remember, can receive variables or constants that you send (pass) to it. These variables or constants are called parameters. You pass parameters when you want the procedure to process them in some way. In this case, you will pass the AreaArray array and the StateArray array to both procedures (ShellSort and DisplayData). (The parameters in the Call statement are referred to as the **sending parameters** because they are the parameters that are being sent to the sub procedure.) The ShellSort procedure will sort the contents of both arrays. The DisplayData procedure will display the contents of both arrays in the Text box on the form. To pass an entire array to a procedure, you must furnish the array's name followed by an empty set of parentheses.

3 Enter the code shown in Figure 9-66. Be sure to include the proper number of parentheses. (Notice that although you haven't yet created the two procedures, you can still enter the appropriate Call statements.)

be sure you enter the code in the MnuSortArea_Click procedure

area code array is listed first; state array is listed second

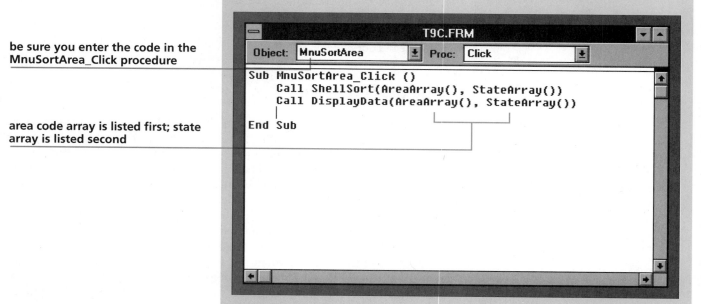

Figure 9-66: Code window for the Sort menu's Area Code option

In both Call statements, notice that the AreaArray array appears first in the parameter list and the StateArray array appears second. That point will become more important when you create the two sub procedures.

4 Click the **down arrow in the Code window's Object box,** then click **MnuSortState** in the drop-down list. The MnuSortState_Click procedure appears.

5 Enter the code shown in Figure 9-67.

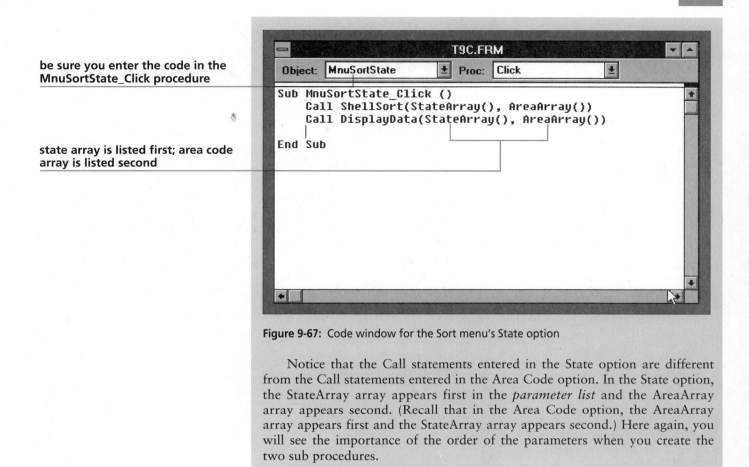

be sure you enter the code in the MnuSortState_Click procedure

state array is listed first; area code array is listed second

```
                        T9C.FRM
Object:  MnuSortState      ±  Proc:  Click        ±
Sub MnuSortState_Click ()
    Call ShellSort(StateArray(), AreaArray())
    Call DisplayData(StateArray(), AreaArray())

End Sub
```

Figure 9-67: Code window for the Sort menu's State option

Notice that the Call statements entered in the State option are different from the Call statements entered in the Area Code option. In the State option, the StateArray array appears first in the *parameter list* and the AreaArray array appears second. (Recall that in the Area Code option, the AreaArray array appears first and the StateArray array appears second.) Here again, you will see the importance of the order of the parameters when you create the two sub procedures.

6   Close the Code window.

Now that the menu options are coded, you will create the two sub procedures. You'll begin with the ShellSort procedure, which will sort the data contained in both arrays (AreaArray and StateArray).

Creating the ShellSort User-Defined Sub Procedure

In Tutorial 7 you learned how to create a user-defined sub procedure. Recall that a user-defined sub procedure is a procedure that you create that can be invoked from one or more places in your program. If the procedure needs to be available to more than one form in the project, referred to as a global user-defined procedure, recall that you define the procedure in a code module. If, on the other hand, the procedure needs to be available only to the current form, you define the procedure in the form in which it is needed. Such procedures are referred to as **form-level** procedures. They are available only to the form in which they are defined and to other procedures in that form. In this case you will create two form-level procedures—ShellSort and DisplayData. Let's begin with the ShellSort procedure, which will sort the contents of the two arrays.

To create the form-level ShellSort procedure:

1 Double-click the **form** to open its Code window. Click **View**, then click **New Procedure....** The New Procedure dialog box appears with the Sub option button selected.

2 Type **ShellSort** in the Name Text box, then click the **OK button**. Visual Basic creates the Code window for this new procedure. Notice that the Code window contains the familiar Sub and End Sub statements.

Recall that the menu options that call this procedure pass it two parameters, the AreaArray array and the StateArray array. (Recall that these are referred to as the sending parameters.) When you pass parameters to a procedure, the procedure needs to know both the data type and the number of parameters being passed. You give the procedure that information by placing parameters of the same data type and number within the set of parentheses in the Sub statement. The parameters in the Sub statement are referred to as the **receiving parameters**. In this application, the menu options will be passing two string arrays, so we will need to list two string arrays in the ShellSort procedure's parameter list. We'll call the arrays Array1 and Array2.

3 Click inside the parentheses in the Sub statement, then enter the two parameters shown in Figure 9-68.

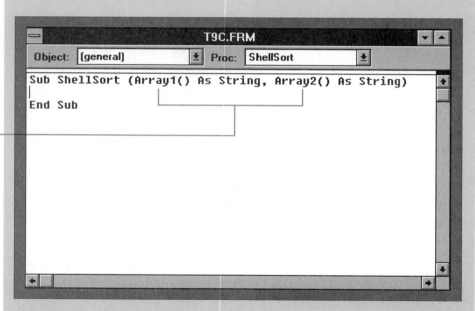

enter these two parameters; be sure to enter the proper number of parentheses

```
T9C.FRM
Object:  (general)          Proc:  ShellSort

Sub ShellSort (Array1() As String, Array2() As String)

End Sub
```

Figure 9-68: The ShellSort procedure's Code window

So that you don't have to type the Shell sort code, the code is already entered into a text file for you on your Student Disk. You simply need to load the contents of the file into the Code window.

4 First **save** the project. You are saving at this point so that if an error occurs while you are trying to load the text file, you will be able to open the project and try loading the text again.

5 Position the blinking insertion point immediately below the "S" in Sub, as shown in Figure 9-68. Click **File in Visual Basic's menu bar**, then click **Load Text....** The Load Text dialog box appears.

If you mistakenly chose the Replace button instead of the Merge button, then open the t9c.mak project again without saving the current one. Double-click the form, press [F2], click ShellSort, then repeat steps 5 and 6.

6 Click **shell.txt** in the filename box, then click the **Merge button**. The Merge button tells Visual Basic to merge (combine) the contents of the shell.txt file with the existing contents of the Code window.

7 Maximize the Code window, then scroll until the beginning of the code is visible. The Code window appears, as shown in Figure 9-69.

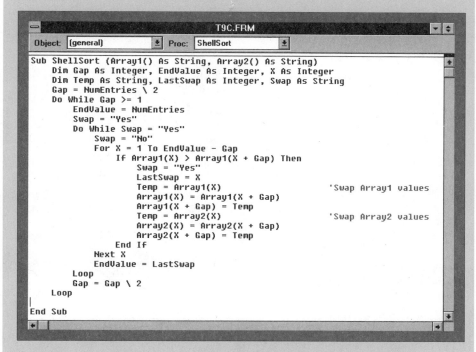

```
Sub ShellSort (Array1() As String, Array2() As String)
    Dim Gap As Integer, EndValue As Integer, X As Integer
    Dim Temp As String, LastSwap As Integer, Swap As String
    Gap = NumEntries \ 2
    Do While Gap >= 1
        EndValue = NumEntries
        Swap = "Yes"
        Do While Swap = "Yes"
            Swap = "No"
            For X = 1 To EndValue - Gap
                If Array1(X) > Array1(X + Gap) Then
                    Swap = "Yes"
                    LastSwap = X
                    Temp = Array1(X)                'Swap Array1 values
                    Array1(X) = Array1(X + Gap)
                    Array1(X + Gap) = Temp
                    Temp = Array2(X)                'Swap Array2 values
                    Array2(X) = Array2(X + Gap)
                    Array2(X + Gap) = Temp
                End If
            Next X
            EndValue = LastSwap
        Loop
        Gap = Gap \ 2
    Loop
End Sub
```

Figure 9-69: The ShellSort code within the ShellSort procedure's Code window

Recall that the Call statement entered in the Area Code menu option says *Call ShellSort(AreaArray(), StateArray())*, whereas the Call statement entered in the State menu option says *Call ShellSort(StateArray(), AreaArray())*. When the ShellSort procedure is called from the Area Code menu option, the AreaArray array, which is listed first in the parameter list, will be passed to the procedure as Array1 and the StateArray array, which is listed second in the parameter list, will be passed to the procedure as Array2. When the ShellSort procedure is called from the State menu option, on the other hand, the StateArray array, which is listed first in the parameter list, will be passed to the procedure as Array1 and the AreaArray array, which is listed second in the parameter list, will be passed to the procedure as Array2. Because the ShellSort procedure sorts the arrays by the values in Array1, both arrays will be sorted by area code when the procedure is called from the Area Code menu option, but they will be sorted by state when called from the State menu option.

8 Close the ShellSort procedure's Code window.

Now let's write the DisplayData procedure, which will display the contents of both arrays in the Text box.

Creating the DisplayData User-Defined Procedure

The DisplayData procedure should display the contents of both arrays in two columns in the Text box on the form. When called by the Area Code menu option, the procedure should display the area code in the first column and the state abbreviation in the second column. When called by the State option, the procedure should display the state abbreviation in the first column and the area code in the second column.

To create the form-level DisplayData procedure, then save and run the application:

1 Double-click the **form** to open its Code window. Click **View**, then click **New Procedure...**. The New Procedure dialog box appears with the Sub option button selected.

2 Type **DisplayData** in the Name Text box, then click the **OK button**. Visual Basic creates the Code window for this new procedure.

3 Maximize the Code window, then enter the code shown in Figure 9-70. Be sure to include the Array1 and Array2 parameters in the Sub statement.

be sure to enter the two parameters and to use the proper number of parentheses

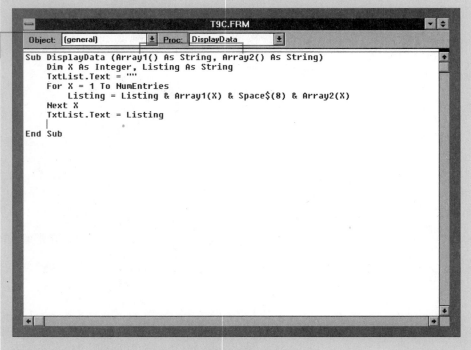

```
Sub DisplayData (Array1() As String, Array2() As String)
    Dim X As Integer, Listing As String
    TxtList.Text = ""
    For X = 1 To NumEntries
        Listing = Listing & Array1(X) & Space$(8) & Array2(X)
    Next X
    TxtList.Text = Listing

End Sub
```

Figure 9-70: The DisplayData procedure's Code window

The code declares an Integer variable named X and a String variable named Listing. The *TxtList.Text* = " " instruction removes the current contents of the Text box, if any. The *Listing = Listing & Array1(X) & Space$(8) & Array2(X)* tells Visual Basic to concatenate the current contents of the Listing variable with the value in the first array, eight spaces, and the value in the second array. The concatenated value is then assigned to the Listing

tips
· ·

▶ If Visual Basic displays the "Reference to undefined Function or array" message, click the OK button to remove the error message box. Verify that you have entered both Array1( ) as String and Array2( ) as String between the parentheses in both the ShellSort procedure's Sub statement and the DisplayData procedure's Sub statement.

variable. After the For...Next loop completes its processing, the *TxtList.Text = Listing* instruction assigns the contents of the Listing variable to the TxtList Text box. As a result, the list of area codes and states will display in the Text box.

4   Close the Code window, then **save and run** the application.

First let's sort the area codes and states in area code order.

5   Click **Sort**, then click **Area Code**. The MnuSortArea_Click procedure first calls the ShellSort procedure, passing it the AreaArray and StateArray arrays. The ShellSort procedure sorts the arrays by area code. When the ShellSort procedure ends, the program returns to the MnuSortArea_Click procedure, which then calls the DisplayData procedure, again passing the AreaArray and StateArray arrays. The DisplayData procedure displays the area code and the state abbreviation in the Text box, as shown in Figure 9-71.

data appears incorrectly on one line in the Text box

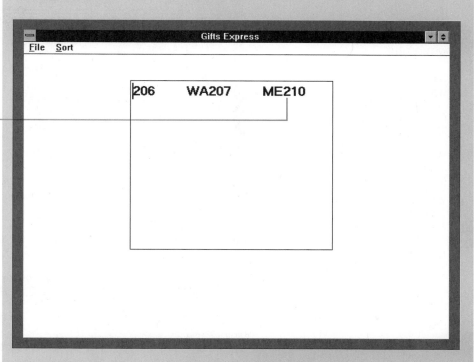

Figure 9-71: Area codes and states listed in the Text box

Notice that the area codes and state abbreviations appear on one line in the Text box, instead of on separate lines. To tell Visual Basic to begin text on a new line, you need to include a special character, called the newline character, in your Visual Basic code.

6   Click **File**, then click **Exit**. Visual Basic returns to the design screen.

The Newline Character

The **newline character**, which is *Chr(13)* & *Chr(10)*, instructs Visual Basic to issue a carriage return followed by a line feed. (The combination of the carriage return followed by a line feed will advance the insertion point to the next line in the Text box.) Whenever you want Visual Basic to start a new line, simply type the newline character at that location in your code. In this case, you want Visual Basic to advance to a new line after displaying each area code and state abbreviation.

To include the newline character in your code:

1 Double-click the **form** to open its Code window. Press **[F2]** to open the View Procedures dialog box, click **DisplayData,** then click the **OK button.** The DisplayData procedure's Code window appears.

2 Maximize the Code window, then add the additional code shown in Figure 9-72.

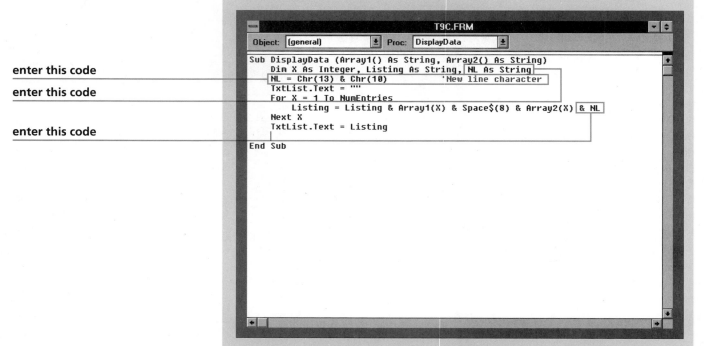

enter this code

enter this code

enter this code

Figure 9-72: DisplayData procedure's Code window showing additional code for the newline character

The additional code declares a String variable named NL, which stands for "new line." It then assigns the newline character, *Chr(13) & Chr(10),* to the NL variable. The NL variable is then concatenated to the assignment statement within the For...Next loop.

3 Close the Code window.

In addition to using the newline character in your code, you will also need to set the Text box's MultiLine property to True and its ScrollBars property to 2-Vertical.

The MultiLine Property and the ScrollBars Property

The MultiLine property controls whether a Text box can accept and display multiple lines of text. The default value is False, which means that only one line is allowed in the Text box. When set to True, the MultiLine property allows a Text box to accept and display more than one line of text. Visual Basic automatically wraps the text in a multiline box if the text extends beyond the size of the box.

The ScrollBars property specifies whether a Text box has no scroll bars (the default), horizontal scroll bars, vertical scroll bars, or both horizontal and vertical scroll bars. In this application, you will place a vertical scroll bar on the Text box so that you can scroll the list of area codes and states.

To set the Text box's MultiLine and ScrollBars properties, then save and run the application:

1 Click the **TxtList Text box** to select that control, then double-click **MultiLine** in the Properties list until the property says True.

2 Double-click **ScrollBars** in the Properties list until the property says 2-Vertical. (You will need to double-click two times.)

Now let's save and run the application again.

3 **Save and run** the application. Click **Sort,** then click **Area Code.** The list of area codes and state abbreviations, in area code order, appears as shown in Figure 9-73.

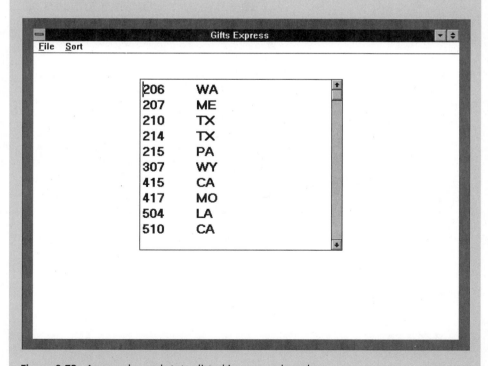

Figure 9-73: Area codes and states listed in area code order

Use the Text box's vertical scroll bar to scroll the list.

4   Click **Sort**, then click **State**. The list of area codes and state abbreviations, in state order, appears as shown in Figure 9-74.

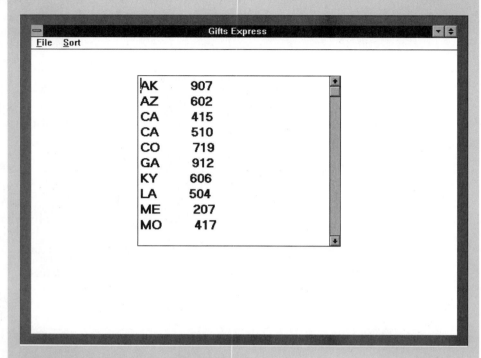

Figure 9-74: States and area codes listed in state order

6   If your computer is connected to a printer, click **File**, then click **Print**. The list of area codes and state abbreviations, in state order, prints on the printer.

7   Click **File**, then click **Exit**. The application ends and Visual Basic returns to the design screen.

8   Click **File**, then click **New Project**. If you are asked if you want to save the form or the project, click the Yes button.

You have now completed Lesson C and the Gifts Express application. You can either take a break or complete the questions and exercises at the end of the lesson.

S U M M A R Y

To call a sub procedure:

■   Use the Call statement. Its syntax is Call *procedurename* [(*parameterlist*)]. The parameters in the Call statement are referred to as the sending parameters.

■   To pass an entire array to a procedure, place the array name followed by a set of empty parentheses within the *parameterlist*.

■   The parameters in the Call statement must match in number and data type the parameters listed in the sub procedure's Sub statement.

To create a form-level user-defined sub procedure:

◾ Open any Code window. Click View, then click New Procedure.... Enter the name of the sub procedure in the Name Text box, then click the OK button.

To have a sub procedure receive parameters:

◾ Place the receiving parameters within the set of parentheses in the procedure's Sub statement.
◾ To receive an entire array, place the array name followed by an empty set of parentheses within the set of parentheses in the procedure's Sub statement.
◾ The parameters in the sub procedure's Sub statement must match in number and data type the parameters listed in the Call statement that invokes the procedure.

To use the newline character:

◾ Enter *Chr(13)* & *Chr(10)* in the code.

To allow a Text box to accept and display more than one line of text:

◾ Set the Text box's MultiLine property to True.

To control whether a Text box contains scroll bars:

◾ Set the Text box's ScrollBars property to either 0-None (the default), 1-Horizontal, 2-Vertical, or 3-Both.
◾ For a Text box with a setting of 1-Horizontal, 2-Vertical, or 3-Both, you must set the MultiLine property to True.

Q U E S T I O N S

1. Which of the following will call a procedure named PrintName, passing it no parameters?
   a. Call PrintName
   b. Call (PrintName)
   c. CallSub PrintName
   d. Invoke PrintName
   e. Sub PrintName

2. Which of the following will call a procedure named PrintName, passing it one parameter—a String variable named EmpName?
   a. Call PrintName (EmpName)
   b. Call (PrintName) EmpName as String
   c. CallSub PrintName (EmpName)
   d. Invoke PrintName (EmpName as String)
   e. Sub PrintName (EmpName)

3 Which of the following will call a procedure named PrintName, passing it one parameter—a String array named EmpNames?
   a. Call PrintName (EmpNames as String)
   b. Call PrintName (EmpNames())
   c. CallSub PrintName (EmpNames)
   d. Invoke PrintName (EmpName() as String)
   e. Sub PrintName (EmpName())

4. If you invoke a sub procedure using the statement *Call DisplayName (Friend)*, which of the following is a correct Sub statement for the DisplayName procedure? (Friend is a String variable.)
    a. Sub DisplayName ()
    b. Sub DisplayName(Call MyFriend)
    c. Sub DisplayName MyFriend
    d. Sub DisplayName MyFriend as String
    e. Sub DisplayName (MyFriend as String)

5. If you invoke a sub procedure using the statement *Call UpdateAge (Friend, Age)*, which of the following is a correct Sub statement for the UpdateAge procedure? (Friend is a String variable and Age is an Integer variable.)
    a. Sub UpdateAge ()
    b. Sub UpdateAge(MyAge as Integer, MyFriend as String)
    c. Sub (UpdateAge) MyFriend as String, MyAge as Integer
    d. Sub UpdateAge (MyFriend as String, MyAge as String)
    e. Sub UpdateAge (MyFriend as String, MyAge as Integer)

6. If you invoke a sub procedure using the statement *Call UpdateAge (Friends(), Ages())*, which of the following is a correct Sub statement for the UpdateAge procedure? (Friends() is a String variable, and Ages() is an Integer array.)
    a. Sub UpdateAge ()
    b. Sub UpdateAge(MyAge() as Integer, MyFriend() as String)
    c. Sub UpdateAge (MyFriend() as String, MyAge() as Integer)
    d. Sub UpdateAge (MyFriend as String, MyAge as String)
    e. Sub UpdateAge (MyFriend as String, MyAge as Integer)

7. The parameters listed in the Call statement are referred to as the _____ parameters.
    a. calling
    b. receiving
    c. sending
    d. sub

8. The parameters listed in the Sub statement of a procedure are referred to as the _____ parameters.
    a. calling
    b. receiving
    c. sending
    d. sub

9. Which of the following is the newline character?
    a. Chr(10)
    b. Chr(13)
    c. Chr(10) & Chr(13)
    d. Chr(13) & Chr(10)

10. When set to True, the _____ property allows a Text box to accept and display more than one line of text.
    a. DisplayMultiple
    b. MultiLine
    c. MultiText
    d. Text

11. This property controls whether a Text box displays scroll bars.
    a. Bars
    b. Scroll
    c. ScrollBars
    d. VerticalBars

12. For a Text box to display scroll bars, this property must be set to True.
   a. Bars
   b. MultiLine
   c. MultiText
   d. Scroll
   e. ScrollBars

E X E R C I S E S

1. In this exercise you will create an application that will open a sequential access file and load its contents into a 10-element array. The application will allow you to sort the file using either a bubble sort or a Shell sort. It will also allow you to print the form.

   a. Create the user interface shown in Figure 9-75.

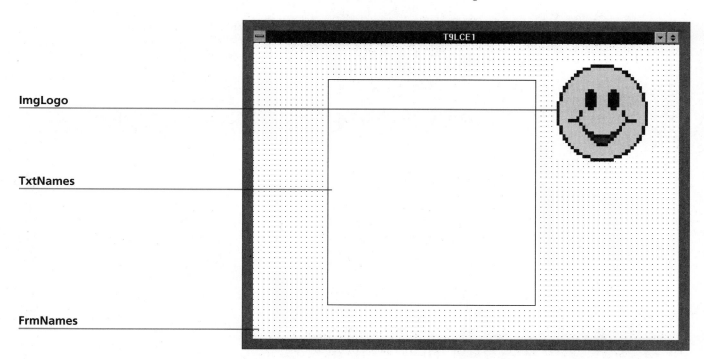

ImgLogo

TxtNames

FrmNames

Figure 9-75

   b. Set the Image control's Picture property to vb\icons\misc\face03.ico. Set the Text box's MultiLine property to True and its ScrollBars property to 2-Vertical. Save the form and the project as t9lce1.

   c. Add a File menu to the application. The File menu should contain a Print option and an Exit option. Include a separator bar between each option. Assign access keys to the menu and its options. Assign Ctrl+P as the shortcut key for the Print option.

   d. Code the form's Load event procedure so that it opens a sequential access file named t9names.dat, which is located in either the tut9\ver2 or the tut9\ver3 directory on your Student Disk. Code the Print option so that it prints the form. Code the Exit option so that it exits the application.

e. Add a Display menu to the application. The Display menu should contain a Bubble Sort option and a Shell Sort option. Assign access keys to the Display menu (D) and its options (B and S). Assign Ctrl+B as the shortcut key for the Bubble Sort option and assign Ctrl+S as the shortcut key for the Shell Sort option.

f. Code the Bubble Sort option so that it uses a bubble sort to sort the names contained in the array. The option should display the names in the Text box on the form.

g. Code the Shell Sort option so that it uses a Shell sort to sort the names in the array. The option should display the names in the Text box on the form.

h. Save and run the application. Test the application as follows:
   (1) Open the Display menu and click Bubble Sort, then open the File menu and click Print.
   (2) Open the File menu and click Exit.
   (3) Run the application again. This time open the Display menu and click Shell Sort, then press [Ctrl][p] to print the form.
   (4) Open the File menu and click Exit.

i. Print the code.

2. In this exercise you will create an application for Hoppers Hat Shoppe. The application will print two notes. One note will inform the customer that a hat has been special-ordered and the other note will inform the customer that the special-order hat is ready for pickup.

a. Create the user interface shown in Figure 9-76.

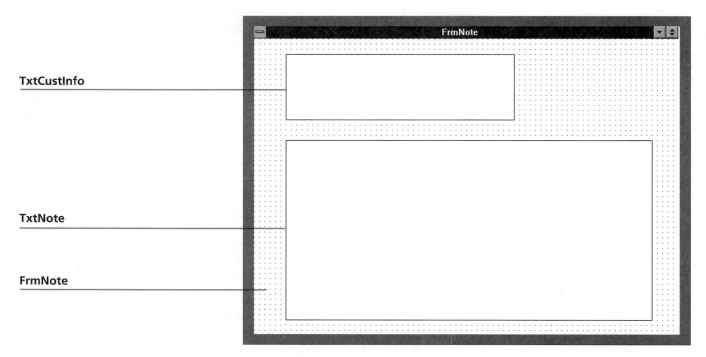

Figure 9-76

b. Set the MultiLine property of both Text boxes to True. Set their FontSize property to 12.

c. Name the form FrmNote. Save the form as t9note. Save the project as t9lce2.

d. Create a File menu and a Notes menu. The File menu should contain a Print option, a separator bar, and an Exit option. The Notes menu should contain an Order option, an Arrival option, and a Clear option.

e. Code the Print option so that it prints the FrmNote form. Code the Exit option so that it ends the application.

f. The Order option should display the following note in the appropriate Text box:

Dear Customer:

Thank you for your recent order. This is to inform you that we have special-ordered your hat. It should arrive at the store in about two weeks.

(Hint: Assign each sentence to a String variable. Then use string concatenation to concatenate each sentence with the newline character.)

g. The Arrival option should display the following note in the appropriate Text box:

Dear Customer:

Your special-order hat has arrived at the store. You may pick it up at your convenience. Thank you for shopping at Hopper's Hat Shoppe.

h. The Clear option should remove the text from the Text boxes.

i. Save and run the application.

j. Print the order note for the following customer. (Enter the customer information into the TxtCustInfo control. Press the Enter key at the end of each line.)

Janice Wong

123 Main Street

Westmont, Ill. 60159

k. Print the arrival note for the following customer:

Tammy Coleman

555 West Street

Westmont, Ill. 60159

l. Exit the application. Print the form and the code.

Exercise 3 is a Discovery Exercise.

discovery ▶ **3.** As mentioned in Lesson A, the bubble sort is an efficient way of sorting a small number of items—say, less than 50. If you have a lot of data to sort, however, the Shell sort is much more efficient than the bubble sort. In this exercise you will compare the processing times for both sorts. You will see that as the number of items increases, the difference between processing times will increase dramatically.

a. Open the t9time.mak project, which is in either the tut9\ver2 or the tut9\ver3 directory on your Student Disk, then click the View Form button.

b. Open the Help screen on the Rnd function. If your computer is connected to a printer, print the Help screen. Notice the purpose of the Rnd function. Also notice the formula for generating random integers.

c. Open the Help screen on the Randomize statement. If your computer is connected to a printer, print the Help screen. Notice the purpose of the Randomize statement.

d. Open the Help screen on the Int function. If your computer is connected to a printer, print the Help screen. Notice the purpose of the Int function.

e. Open the Help screen on the Time$ function. If your computer is connected to a printer, print the Help screen. Notice the purpose of the function. Close the Help screens.

f. Double-click the form, then press [F2] to open the View Procedures dialog box. The following procedures contain code: (declarations), Display (a user-defined procedure), CmdBubble_Click, CmdExit_Click, CmdShell_Click, CmdShow_Click, Form_Load. If your computer is connected to a printer, print the application's code. Study the code in each of the procedures.

g. Open the Code window for the form's general Declarations section. Notice that the code declares two Integer arrays (Num1Array and Num2Array) and an Integer variable (NumItems). The arrays can hold up to 500 integers. The NumItems variable will store the total number of items in each array.

h. Open the form's Load event procedure. Notice that the procedure assigns the number 10 to the NumItems variable. The procedure also uses the Int function and the Rnd function to assign 10 random integers, between 1 and 100, to both arrays.

i. Open the CmdShow_Click procedure. Notice that it displays the first 10 integers from both arrays.

j. Open the CmdBubble_Click procedure. The procedure uses the bubble sort to sort the items in the Num1Array. Before the bubble sort begins, the current time is assigned to the StartTime variable. When the bubble sort is completed, the current time is assigned to the StopTime variable. The StartTime and StopTime variables are then printed on the form. A call is then made to the Display user-defined procedure, which displays the Num1Array array on the form.

k. Open the CmdShell_Click procedure. The procedure uses the Shell sort to sort the items in the Num2Array. Before the Shell sort begins, the current time is assigned to the StartTime variable. When the Shell sort is completed, the current time is assigned to the StopTime variable. The StartTime and StopTime variables are then printed on the form. A call is then made to the Display user-defined procedure, which displays the Num2Array array on the form.

l. Open the Display procedure's Code window. This user-defined procedure accepts the Integer array that is passed to it by either the CmdBubble_Click procedure or the CmdShell_Click procedure. It then uses a For...Next loop to display the contents of the passed array on the form.

m. Close the Code window, then run, but don't save the application.

n. Click the Show Arrays button. The 10 random integers stored in both arrays appear on the form.

o. Click the Bubble button. The start and stop times appear on the form, followed by the contents of the Num1Array array, which is now sorted. Notice that with only 10 items in the array, the bubble sort takes very little time.

p. Click the Shell button. The start and stop times appear on the form, followed by the contents of the Num2Array array, which is now sorted. Here again, with only 10 items in the array, the Shell sort takes about the same amount of time as the bubble sort.

q. Click the Exit button to end the application. Now let's compare the processing times needed to sort 500 integers.

r. Open the form's Load event procedure. Change the NumItems = 10 instruction to *NumItems = 500*. Close the Code window.

s. Run, but don't save, the application.

t. Click the Bubble button. The start and stop times appear on the form, followed by the first numbers stored in the Num1Array array, which is now sorted. Notice that the bubble sort takes much longer to sort 500 items than it does to sort 10 items. Let's see how the bubble sort's time compares to the Shell sort's time.

u. Click the Shell button. The start and stop times appear on the form, followed by the first 10 numbers stored in the Num2Array array, which is now sorted. Notice that the Shell sort sorted the 500 numbers much more quickly than the bubble sort did.

v. Click the Exit button to end the application.

w. Open the form's general Declarations section. Change both Dim statements to allow the arrays to store up to 1000 integers.

x. Open the form's Load event procedure. Change the NumItems = 500 instruction to *NumItems = 1000*. Close the Code window.

y. Run, but don't save, the application. Click the Bubble button. (Be patient—it will take a little time to sort.) Write the start and stop times on a piece of paper. Click the Shell button. Write the start and stop times on a piece of paper. Click the Exit button.

z. Click File, then click New Project. When you are asked if you want to save the form, click the No button.

D E B U G G I N G

Technique Visual Basic's Edit menu provides two options that you can use to edit the code in an application quickly. These options are Find... and Replace....

Your Student Disk contains a file that you can use to practice this tutorial's debugging technique.

To debug the T9_DEBUG.MAK project:

1 Launch Visual Basic, if necessary, and open the **t9_debug.mak** project which is in either the tut9\ver2 or the tut9\ver3 directory on your Student Disk.

2 Click the **View Form button**. The user interface—which contains a List box, a Label control, a File menu, and a Display menu—appears on the screen.

You can use this application to display the names of the salespeople located in either Nebraska or New Mexico.

3 Save the form and the project as **t9dbgd**.

4 **Run** the application. Visual Basic displays a dialog box that contains the "Variable not defined" message. As you learned in Tutorial 8's Debugging section, you can press [F1] to learn more about the error message. In this case, however, the message is self-explanatory—the code contains a variable whose name Visual Basic does not recognize.

5 Click the **OK button** to remove the message. The MnuDisplayNebraska_Click procedure appears, as shown in Figure 9-77.

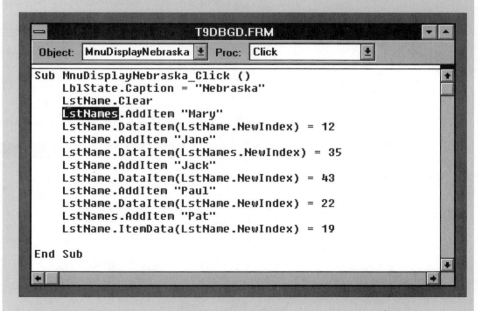

Figure 9-77: LstNames highlighted in Code window

LstNames is highlighted in the Code window because that is the name that Visual Basic does not recognize. You can use the Code window's Object box to verify the names of the controls in the application.

6 Press the **down arrow in the Code window's Object box.** The Object box's drop-down list appears. According to the list, the name of the List box is LstName, not LstNames.

7 Press the **down arrow in the Code window's Object box.** The drop-down list closes.

Notice that the incorrect name, LstNames, appears in several places in the Code window. Instead of searching on your own for each incorrect name and then replacing each individually, you can use Visual Basic's Edit menu to do the searching and replacing for you.

To tell Visual Basic to search for every occurrence of LstNames and replace it with LstName:

1 Click **Edit** to open Visual Basic's Edit menu. The Edit menu opens.

Notice that the Edit menu contains a Find... and a Replace... option. You use the Find... option to simply search for text. You use the Replace... option to search for text and then replace it with other text. In this case you will use the Replace... option because you want to search for LstNames and replace it with LstName.

2 Click **Replace....** The Replace dialog box appears, as shown in Figure 9-78.

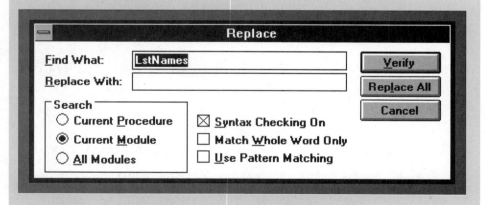

Figure 9-78: Replace dialog box

The Replace dialog box contains a Find What: Text box and a Replace With: Text box. You enter the search text—the text you want to search for—in the Find What: box and you enter the replacement text—the new text—in the Replace With: box. In this case, because LstNames was highlighted in the

Code window, it automatically appears in the Find What: Text box. LstNames is the text for which you want to search, so you do not need to change this entry. You do need to enter LstName—the replacement text—in the Replace With: Text box.

3　Press [Tab] to move the focus to the Replace With: Text box, then type **LstName** in the Replace With: Text box.

Notice the three option buttons (Current Procedure, Current Module, All Modules) in the Replace dialog box. (See Figure 9-78.) If you select the Current Procedure option, Visual Basic will search for the search text in the current procedure only. If you select the Current Module option, Visual Basic will search for the search text in the current module only; the current module includes the procedures in the current form and its controls. If you select the All Modules option, Visual Basic will search the entire application—every procedure in every form, control, and module included in the application.

In this case, you will select the Current Module option, which will search all of the procedures in the current form and its controls.

4　If necessary, click the **Current Module Option button**. A dot should appear in the Option button.

The Replace dialog box (see Figure 9-78) also contains three Check boxes (Syntax Checking On, Match Whole Word Only, Use Pattern Matching). If you check the Syntax Checking On Check box, Visual Basic will verify the syntax of the replacement text after making the replacement. If the Match Whole Word Only Check box is checked, Visual Basic will search for the full word by itself, not as part of another word. If the Use Pattern Matching Check box is checked, you can use Visual Basic's pattern matching characters in the Find What: text box. (To learn more about the pattern matching characters, use the Help menu to display a Help screen on "pattern matching.")

In this case only the Syntax Checking On box needs to be checked.

5　If necessary, click the **Syntax Checking On Check box**. An X should be displayed in the box.

The Replace dialog box also has three Command buttons (Verify, Replace All, Cancel). If you click the Verify Command button, Visual Basic will ask you to confirm (verify) the replacement of each occurrence of the search text before the replacement is made. The Replace All button tells Visual Basic to replace all occurrences of the search text without asking for confirmation each time. The Cancel button closes the dialog box; no search or replacement is made.

In this case, let's verify each replacement.

6　Click the **Verify button**. Visual Basic highlights the first occurrence of the search text, which is found in the MnuDisplayNebraska Click event procedure. A dialog box that asks if you want to replace the selected text appears, as shown in Figure 9-79.

tips

▶ If you can't see the highlighted occurrence of LstNames, place the mouse pointer on the dialog box's title bar and drag the dialog box out of the way.

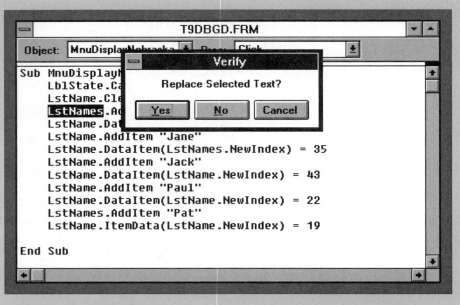

```
                              T9DBGD.FRM
Object:  MnuDisplayNebraska            Proc   Click

Sub MnuDisplayN                    Verify
    LblState.Ca
    LstName.Cle           Replace Selected Text?
    LstNames.Ad
    LstName.Dat              Yes      No      Cancel
    LstName.AddItem "Jane"
    LstName.DataItem(LstNames.NewIndex) = 35
    LstName.AddItem "Jack"
    LstName.DataItem(LstName.NewIndex) = 43
    LstName.AddItem "Paul"
    LstName.DataItem(LstName.NewIndex) = 22
    LstNames.AddItem "Pat"
    LstName.ItemData(LstName.NewIndex) = 19

End Sub
```

Figure 9-79: Verify dialog box

7 Click the **Yes button**. Visual Basic highlights the next occurrence of LstNames, which is also in the MnuDisplayNebraska Click event procedure.

8 Click the **Yes button** two times to replace every occurrence of LstNames in the MnuDisplayNebraska Click event procedure. Notice that the search continues in the MnuDisplayNewmex Click event procedure.

9 Click the **Yes button** until the "Search complete" message appears, then click the **OK button**.

10 Close the Code window.

Now that you've replaced the occurrences of LstNames with LstName, let's save and run the application to see if it is working correctly.

To test the application again:

1 **Save and run** the application. The "Property 'DataItem' not found" message appears in a dialog box. Click the **OK** button to remove the message.

Visual Basic highlights the period between LstName and DataItem.

The property should be ItemData, not DataItem. Let's use the Edit menu to replace the incorrect property name with the correct one.

2 Highlight **DataItem** in the Code window. (Be sure you don't highlight the period or the left parenthesis.) Click **Edit**, then click **Replace....** The Replace dialog box appears.

3 Press [**Tab**] to move the focus to the Replace With: box, then type **ItemData**.

This time, you will use the Replace All button, which will replace all occurrences of DataItem with ItemData without asking you for confirmation.

4   Click the **Replace All button**. When the "Search complete" message appears, click the **OK button**.

5   Close the Code window, then **save and run** the application.

6   Click **Display**, then click **Nebraska**. A list of Nebraska salespeople appears in the List box. Click **Display**, then click **New Mexico**. A list of New Mexico salespeople appears in the List box.

7   Click **File**, then click **Exit**. Visual Basic returns to the design screen.

TUTORIAL

10

Data Validation, Error Trapping, and Drag and Drop

The Mingo Sales Application

case ▶ Mingo Sales, an Indiana firm specializing in audio equipment sales, employs salespeople in three northern states (Michigan, Minnesota, and Wisconsin) and three southern states (Alabama, Georgia, and Florida). The manager of the company, Mr. James Colfax, has hired you to create an application that the home office can use to display the names of the salespeople in each of those states. Then, if a customer calls the home office, the call can be routed to a salesperson in the area.

Previewing the Completed Application

Let's begin by previewing the completed application.

To preview the completed application:

1. Launch Windows and make sure the Program Manager window is open and your Student Disk is in the appropriate drive. If necessary, click the Minimize on Use option on the Options menu to minimize the Program Manager on use. **Run** the **MINGO.EXE** file, which is in either the tut10\ver2 or the tut10\ver3 directory on your Student Disk. The application's user interface appears on the screen. See Figure 10-1.

Figure 10-1: Mingo Sales user interface

This form uses the drag-and-drop feature of Visual Basic, which you will learn about in Lesson C.

2. Drag the North icon to the Region box, then release the mouse button. An Open dialog box is displayed, as shown in Figure 10-2. (Your drive, directory, and file information may be different from what is shown in Figure 10-2.)

Directory List box

File List box

Drive List box

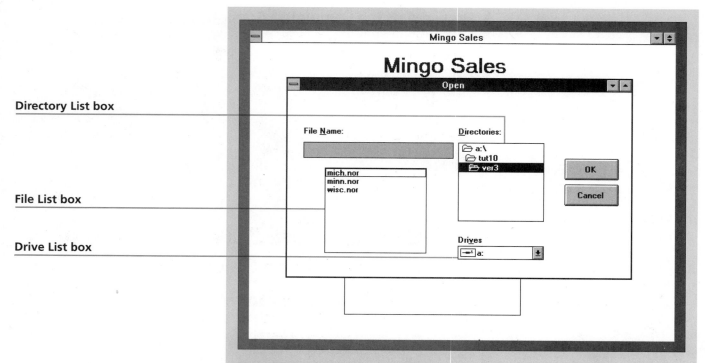

Figure 10-2: Open dialog box user interface

The Open dialog box form contains three new controls—a Drive List box, a Directory List box, and a File List box. You will learn about these controls in Lesson B.

The Open dialog box form allows you to open a file by selecting the drive, directory, and filename from List boxes, instead of typing the information. For example, let's open the minn.nor file, which is located in either the tut10\ver2 or the tut10\ver3 directory on your Student Disk. The minn.nor file contains the names of the salespeople located in Minnesota.

3   Click **minn.nor** in the File List box, then click the **OK button**. The application hides the Open dialog box form and displays the original user interface, where a list of the Minnesota salespeople appears in the List box, as shown in Figure 10-3.

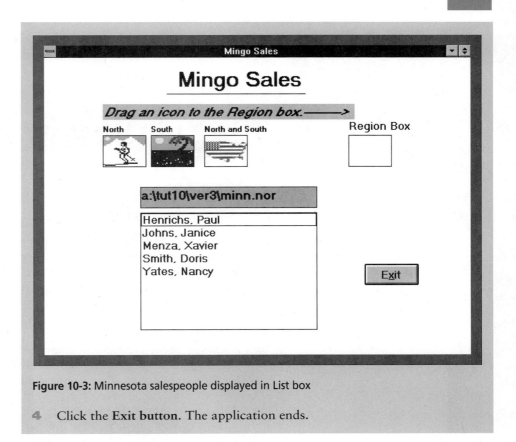

Figure 10-3: Minnesota salespeople displayed in List box

4 Click the **Exit button.** The application ends.

In Lesson A you will learn about validating the data that the user enters from the keyboard—a process called data validation. In Lesson B you will learn how to use the Drive, Directory, and File List box controls; you will also learn about error trapping. The drag-and-drop feature of Visual Basic will be covered in Lesson C.

In this lesson you will learn how to:

- Complete a Data Validation chart
- Use the IsNumeric function
- Make a Command button the default button
- Use the Left$, Right$, and Mid$ functions
- Verify a check digit (in Lesson A's Exercise 7)

Data Validation

Data Validation

As mentioned in previous tutorials, even though an interface may be simple and easy to use, human beings will, at times, make mistakes when entering the necessary data. For example, a user may enter a letter where only numbers are acceptable, or he or she may enter the letter "M" where only "Y" and "N" are allowed. Fortunately, in an object-oriented/event-driven language, such as Visual Basic, you can prevent many data entry errors by using List boxes, Combo boxes, Check boxes, and Option buttons to display the valid input data for the user. Unfortunately, however, the data required by an application cannot always be predetermined. In those cases, the user will need to enter the data from the keyboard, which can result in invalid entries.

Invalid data can cause an application either to give incorrect results or to "crash" (that is, end unexpectedly)—both are serious problems that must be avoided. To prevent these two disasters from happening, a programmer should verify, as much as possible, that the data a user supplies to an application is valid—a process referred to as **data validation**. Programmers usually perform one or more of the data validation checks shown in Figure 10-4 on the data entered by the user.

Data Validation Checks

- Type check

- Length check

- Range check

- Code check

- Check digit check

Figure 10-4: Data validation checks

The **type check** examines the input data to see if it is the correct type. For example, if the application expects the user to enter a number, the type check would verify that the user did, in fact, enter either a number or a string that can be converted to a number.

The **length check** verifies that the user entered the required number of characters. In an application that requires the entry of a five-character part number, for example, the length check would verify that the user entered exactly five characters.

The **range check** verifies that the input data falls within a specific range. If, for example, a company pays its employees an hourly rate of $7 to $10, inclusive, the range check would confirm that each employee's hourly rate falls within that range of numbers.

The **code check**, which is a special type of range check, verifies that the input data matches a predetermined list of values. In a personnel application, for example, the code check would verify that the sex of an employee is either "F" for female or "M" for male.

The **check digit check**, which is used for applications such as credit card processing, verifies the assignment of a special digit to an identification number. The special digit helps guard against transpositions when a long series of numbers must be entered. Although many different schemes have been developed for assigning the special digit, most involve performing an arithmetic operation on the digits of the identification number. The result of the arithmetic operation is then added as an extra digit to the end of the number. In an application that requires the user to enter the identification number, the check digit check would verify that the extra digit is correct. (You will learn how to use the check digit check in Lesson A's Exercise 7.)

In this lesson, you will use the Data Validation chart shown in Figure 10-5 to summarize which input items should be validated and which data validation checks should be performed on those items.

Data Validation Chart

DATA	TYPE CHECK	LENGTH CHECK	RANGE CHECK	CODE CHECK	CHECK DIGIT

Figure 10-5: Data Validation Chart

Before looking at the first example involving data validation, you will learn about the IsNumeric function. (The IsNumeric function was discussed briefly in Tutorial 5's Debugging Section.)

The IsNumeric Function

You can use the IsNumeric function, whose format is **IsNumeric**(*expression*), to verify that an *expression* either is numeric or can be converted to a number. If the *expression* is numeric, or if it can be converted to a number, then the IsNumeric function returns the Boolean value True. (You learned about Boolean values in Tutorial 2.) If the *expression* is not numeric, or if it cannot be converted to a number, then the function returns the Boolean value False. The IsNumeric function recognizes the characters shown in Figure 10-6 as either being numeric or capable of being converted to a number.

Character	Examples
the numeric digits 0 through 9	7508
a comma	2,450
a decimal point	10.96
a leading plus or minus sign	+34, -4.67
a trailing plus or minus sign	56.78+, 3450-
parentheses	(45.67)

Note: The leading and trailing plus signs indicate a positive number. The leading and trailing minus signs and the parentheses indicate a negative number.

Figure 10-6: Characters recognized by the IsNumeric function as being numeric

Figure 10-7 shows some examples of the IsNumeric function and their resulting evaluations.

Contents of TxtNum Control	Evaluation of IsNumeric(TxtNum.Text)
57	True
1,234.57	True
-5	True
(45.67)	True
3.87-	True
$125	False (contains a dollar sign)
5%	False (contains a percent sign)
12A	False (contains a letter)

Figure 10-7: Examples of the IsNumeric function

Now let's look at the first example of data validation.

Data Validation Example 1

The T10_EX1.MAK project on your Student Disk contains the first example of data validation. Let's open that project now.

To open the T10_EX1.MAK project:

1 Launch Visual Basic, if necessary. Open the **t10_ex1.mak** file which is in either the tut10\ver2 or tut10\ver3 directory on your Student Disk.

2 **Save** the form and the project as **t10a1**.

3 Click the **View Form button**, then maximize the form. The user interface appears on the screen, as shown in Figure 10-8.

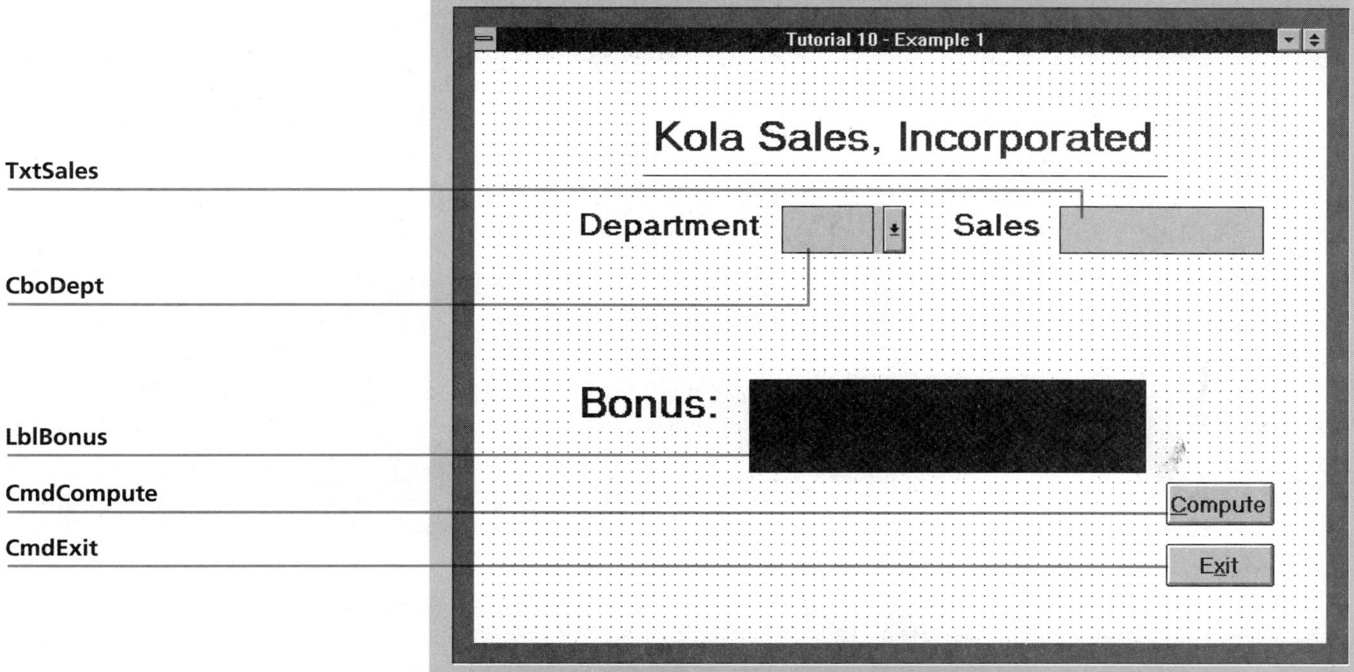

TxtSales

CboDept

LblBonus

CmdCompute

CmdExit

Figure 10-8: User interface for data validation Example 1

You can use this application to calculate a salesperson's bonus; you simply enter the department and the sales, then click the Compute button. Notice that the application uses a Combo box for the department entry and a Text box for the sales entry. The Combo box is a Dropdown Combo style, which means that the user can either enter the department in the text portion of the control or select the department from the control's drop-down list.

The valid departments at Kola Sales, Incorporated are A, B, C, D, and E only. Departments A, B, and C receive a 5% commission on their sales, and departments D and E receive an 8% commission. The sales amount, which must be greater than zero, can contain numbers, the comma, and a decimal point. Figure 10-9 shows the Data Validation chart for this application.

DATA	TYPE CHECK	LENGTH CHECK	RANGE CHECK	CODE CHECK	CHECK DIGIT
Department	string	1	N/A	A, B, C, D, E	N/A
Sales	numbers, comma, period	N/A	> 0	N/A	N/A

Figure 10-9: Data Validation chart for Kola Sales application

Notice that the first column of the chart lists the two items of data that are, or can be, entered by the user: department and sales. In the remaining columns of the chart are the different validation checks that should be performed on each item of input data. If a validation check is not applicable to a data item, it is marked N/A ("not applicable").

Let's open the View Procedures dialog box and look at the procedures that have already been coded for you.

To view the code in the Kola Sales application:

1 Double-click the **form** to open its code window, then press **[F2]** to open the View Procedures dialog box. The View Procedures dialog box appears, as shown in Figure 10-10.

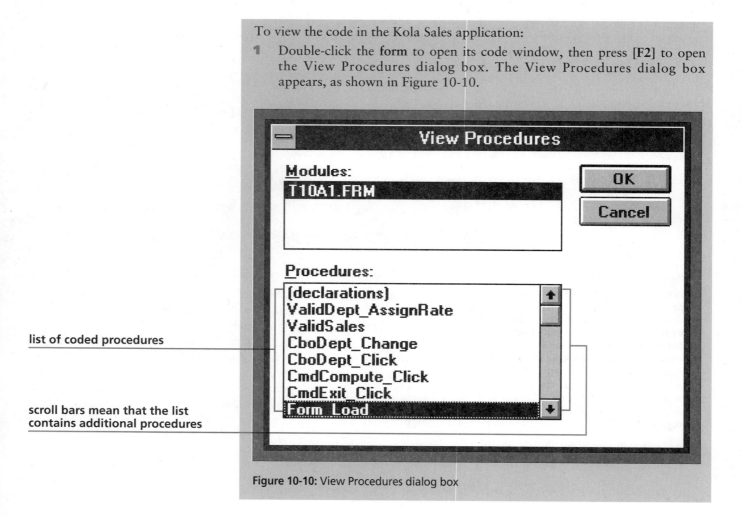

list of coded procedures

scroll bars mean that the list contains additional procedures

Figure 10-10: View Procedures dialog box

2 On your own, verify that the (declarations) section contains the *Option Explicit* statement only and that the CmdExit_Click event procedure contains the *End* statement.

Now let's look at the code in the form's Load event procedure.

3 If necessary, press [F2] to open the View Procedures dialog box, click **Form_Load** in the Procedures box, then click the **OK button**. The form's Load event procedure appears.

The Code window contains five AddItem instructions, which add the valid departments (A, B, C, D, and E) to the Combo box when the form is loaded into memory. The *CboDept.ListIndex = 0* instruction then selects the first item in the Combo box.

The next procedure you will view is the CboDept_Click procedure, which occurs when the user clicks a department in the Combo box's drop-down list.

4 Press [F2] to open the View Procedures dialog box, click **CboDept_Click** in the Procedures box, then click the **OK button**. The CboDept_Click procedure appears.

The procedure contains one instruction, *LblBonus.Caption = " "*. This instruction tells Visual Basic to remove the contents of the LblBonus control when the user clicks a department in the Combo box's list. Recall that not all departments receive the same bonus rate; so, when a user selects a department from the list, the bonus currently in the LblBonus control may be incorrect and should be recalculated.

Now let's look at the CboDept_Change procedure, which occurs when the user types the department into the text portion of the Combo box.

5 Press [F2] to open the View Procedures dialog box, click **CboDept_Change** in the Procedures box, then click the **OK button**. The CboDept_Change procedure appears.

The procedure contains two instructions: *CboDept.Text = UCase(CboDept.Text)* and *LblBonus.Caption = " "*. The first instruction changes the user's keyboard entry to uppercase. The second instruction removes the current bonus from the LblBonus control when the department has changed. Here again, if the user changes the department, the bonus will need to be recalculated.

Now let's look at the TxtSales_Change procedure, which occurs when the user changes the sales amount entered in the TxtSales control.

6 Press [F2] to open the View Procedures dialog box. Scroll the Procedures box until you see TxtSales_Change, click **TxtSales_Change** in the Procedures box, and then click the **OK button**. The TxtSales_Change procedure appears.

The procedure contains one instruction, *LblBonus.Caption = " "*, which tells Visual Basic to remove the current bonus from the LblBonus control when the sales amount changes; if the user changes the sales amount, the bonus will need to be recalculated.

Now let's look at the TxtSales_GotFocus procedure. This time you will use the Page Down (or PgDn) key to view the next procedure.

7 Press [**Page Down**] (or [**PgDn**]). The TxtSales_GotFocus procedure appears.

The procedure contains two instructions: *TxtSales.SelStart = 0* and *TxtSales.SelLength = Len(TxtSales.Text)*. Recall from Tutorial 8 that you need to use both the SelStart and the SelLength properties to highlight (select) the existing text in a Text box. The SelStart property tells Visual Basic where in the Text box to position the blinking insertion point—in other words, where to start the text selection. The SelLength property tells Visual Basic how many characters to select. In this case, the *TxtSales.SelStart = 0* instruction tells Visual Basic to start selecting at the beginning of the entry. The *TxtSales.SelLength = Len(TxtSales.Text)* instruction tells Visual Basic to select all of the existing text. These two instructions will select (highlight) the existing text when the TxtSales Text box receives the focus.

The next procedure you will view is the CmdCompute_Click procedure. Before doing so, however, study its flowchart, shown in Figure 10-11.

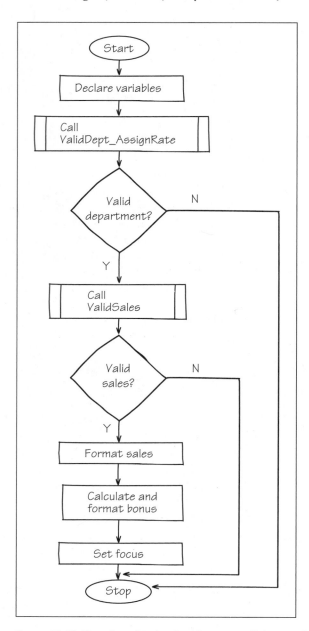

Figure 10-11: Flowchart for the CmdCompute_Click procedure

According to the flowchart, the procedure will first declare the necessary variables. It will then call the ValidDept_AssignRate procedure. Notice the symbol—a rectangle with side borders—used for calling a procedure. The symbol is called the **subroutine box** or the **sub procedure box**. The ValidDept_AssignRate procedure, which is a user-defined procedure whose code you have not yet viewed, is responsible for validating the department and assigning the correct bonus rate. If the ValidDept_AssignRate procedure determines that the department is not valid, then the CmdCompute_Click procedure will end, without computing the bonus. If, on the other hand, the ValidDept_AssignRate procedure determines that the department is valid, the CmdCompute_Click procedure will call the ValidSales procedure. The ValidSales procedure, which is a user-defined procedure, is responsible for validating the sales entry. If the ValidSales procedure determines that the sales entry is not valid, then the CmdCompute_Click procedure will end without computing the bonus. If, on the other hand, the ValidSales procedure determines that the sales entry is valid, the CmdCompute_Click procedure will format the sales entry, calculate and format the bonus, and set the focus before the procedure ends. Notice that the sales entry is formatted and the bonus is calculated and formatted only when both the department and sales entries are valid.

Now let's look at the code in the CmdCompute_Click procedure.

To view the code in the Compute button's Click event procedure:

1   The Code window should be open, so simply press **[F2]** to open the View Procedures dialog box. Click **CmdCompute_Click** in the Procedures box, click the **OK button**, and then maximize the Code window. The Compute button's Click event procedure appears, as shown in Figure 10-12.

passing procedure

receiving procedure

nested selection structure

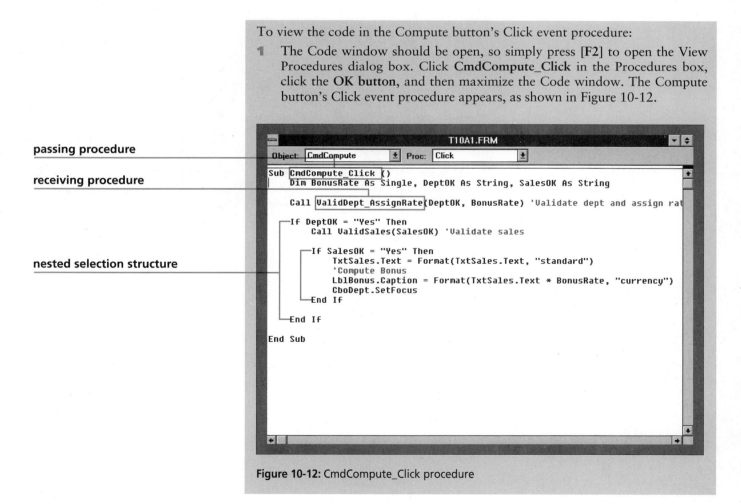

Figure 10-12: CmdCompute_Click procedure

```
Sub CmdCompute_Click ()
    Dim BonusRate As Single, DeptOK As String, SalesOK As String

    Call ValidDept_AssignRate(DeptOK, BonusRate) 'Validate dept and assign rat

    If DeptOK = "Yes" Then
        Call ValidSales(SalesOK) 'Validate sales

        If SalesOK = "Yes" Then
            TxtSales.Text = Format(TxtSales.Text, "standard")
            'Compute Bonus
            LblBonus.Caption = Format(TxtSales.Text * BonusRate, "currency")
            CboDept.SetFocus
        End If

    End If

End Sub
```

The procedure declares a local Single variable named BonusRate and two local String variables named DeptOK and SalesOK. The CmdCompute_Click procedure will use these variables to communicate with both the ValidDept_AssignRate and ValidSales procedures. (You could also use form-level variables to communicate with the various procedures in a form. Form level variables, you may remember from Tutorial 3, are available to all procedures in the form. Using local variables that are passed to the various procedures allows you to restrict the variables to only the procedures that need them.)

After declaring the necessary variables, the CmdCompute_Click procedure calls the ValidDept_AssignRate procedure. The CmdCompute_Click procedure passes two of its local variables, DeptOK and BonusRate, to the ValidDept_AssignRate procedure. Both variables are **passed by reference**, which means that their actual addresses in memory are passed to the ValidDept_AssignRate procedure. When variables are passed by reference, their contents can be changed by the receiving procedure—in this case, by the ValidDept_AssignRate procedure. (The procedure that receives the variables is called the **receiving procedure**. The procedure that passes the variables is called **the passing procedure**.) Variables can also be **passed by value**, which means that only the value of the variable is passed, not its actual address in memory. Lesson A's Exercise 9 will show you the difference between passing by value and passing by reference.

When the *Call ValidDept_AssignRate(DeptOK, BonusRate)* statement is processed, the program will leave the CmdCompute_Click procedure, temporarily, in order to process the instructions in the ValidDept_AssignRate procedure. When the ValidDept_AssignRate procedure ends, the program will return to the CmdCompute_Click procedure, to the line below the Call statement—the *If DeptOK = "Yes" Then* instruction.

Before looking at the Click event's code any further, let's view the code in the ValidDept_AssignRate user-defined procedure.

2   Press [F2] to open the View Procedures dialog box. Click **ValidDept_AssignRate** in the Procedures box, then click the **OK button**. The procedure appears as shown in Figure 10-13.

receiving variables

procedure assumes department
is valid

valid department

invalid department

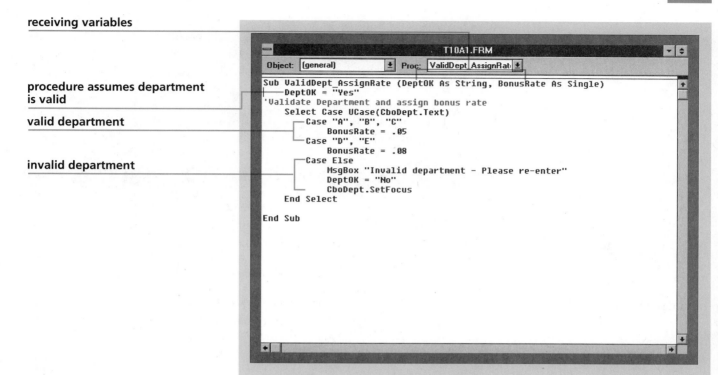

```
                                    T10A1.FRM
Object:  [general]          ±   Proc:  ValidDept AssignRat ±
Sub ValidDept_AssignRate (DeptOK As String, BonusRate As Single)
    DeptOK = "Yes"
'Validate Department and assign bonus rate
    Select Case UCase(CboDept.Text)
        Case "A", "B", "C"
            BonusRate = .05
        Case "D", "E"
            BonusRate = .08
        Case Else
            MsgBox "Invalid department - Please re-enter"
            DeptOK = "No"
            CboDept.SetFocus
    End Select

End Sub
```

Figure 10-13: ValidDept_AssignRate procedure

Recall that you declare the receiving variables within the Sub statement's parentheses. The ValidDept_AssignRate procedure declares two receiving variables, DeptOK as String and BonusRate as Single. Although, in this example, the receiving variables have the same name as the passing variables, the names of both the receiving variables and the passing variables do not have to be the same. The receiving parameters, however, must be the same type as the passing parameters, and they must be listed in the same order as the passing parameters. In other words, if the passing procedure passes a String variable first and a Single variable second, then the receiving procedure must receive a String variable first and a Single variable second. In this case, because the CmdCompute_Click procedure passed the DeptOK variable (a String variable) first and the BonusRate variable (a Single variable) second, the receiving procedure receives the String variable first and the Single variable second.

After declaring the receiving variables, the procedure assigns "Yes" to the DeptOK variable; unless determined otherwise, the procedure assumes that the department entry is valid. The procedure then uses the Case structure, which you learned in Tutorial 5, to validate the department entry and assign the appropriate bonus rate. (Recall that the Data Validation chart shown in Figure 10-9 indicates that the department must be a one-character string, either A, B, C, D, or E.)

If the department entry is valid, the appropriate rate is assigned to the BonusRate variable, and the ValidDept_AssignRate procedure ends; otherwise, a message is displayed alerting the user that the department entry is not valid, "No" is assigned to the DeptOK variable, the focus is set to the Department Combo box, and the ValidDept_AssignRate procedure ends. When the ValidDept_AssignRate procedure ends, the program returns to the CmdCompute_Click procedure, to the line below the *Call ValidDept_AssignRate (DeptOK, BonusRate)* instruction. Let's return to the CmdCompute_Click procedure and look at the code that follows the Call statement.

3   Press [F2] to open the View Procedures dialog box. Click **CmdCompute_Click** in the Procedures box, then click the **OK button**. The CmdCompute_Click procedure appears, as shown in Figure 10-14.

program returns to this statement

nested selection structure

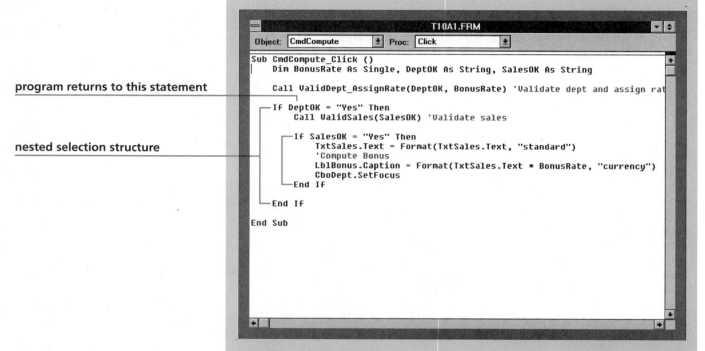

```
T10A1.FRM
Object:  CmdCompute          Proc:  Click

Sub CmdCompute_Click ()
    Dim BonusRate As Single, DeptOK As String, SalesOK As String

    Call ValidDept_AssignRate(DeptOK, BonusRate) 'Validate dept and assign rat

    If DeptOK = "Yes" Then
        Call ValidSales(SalesOK) 'Validate sales

        If SalesOK = "Yes" Then
            TxtSales.Text = Format(TxtSales.Text, "standard")
            'Compute Bonus
            LblBonus.Caption = Format(TxtSales.Text * BonusRate, "currency")
            CboDept.SetFocus
        End If

    End If

End Sub
```

Figure 10-14: CmdCompute_Click procedure

When the program returns to the CmdCompute_Click procedure, it returns to the line below the Call statement—the *If DeptOK = "Yes" Then* instruction. That instruction compares the contents of the DeptOK variable to the string "Yes". Recall that the Call statement passed the DeptOK variable to the ValidDept_AssignRate procedure, which assigned either "Yes" or "No" to it. If the DeptOK variable does not contain "Yes", it means that the department entry is not valid. In that case, the CmdCompute_Click procedure ends and the user is returned to the form, where a new department can be entered. If, on the other hand, the DeptOK variable contains "Yes", it means that the department entry is valid. In that case, the CmdCompute_Click procedure processes the next instruction—*Call ValidSales(SalesOK)*, which is responsible for validating the sales entry. The *Call ValidSales(SalesOK)* instruction passes, by reference, the local String variable named SalesOK. Let's look at the code in the ValidSales user-defined procedure.

4   Press [F2] to open the View Procedures dialog box. Click **ValidSales** in the Procedures box, then click the **OK button**. The procedure appears, as shown in Figure 10-15.

receiving variable

procedure assumes sales entry is valid

nested selection structure

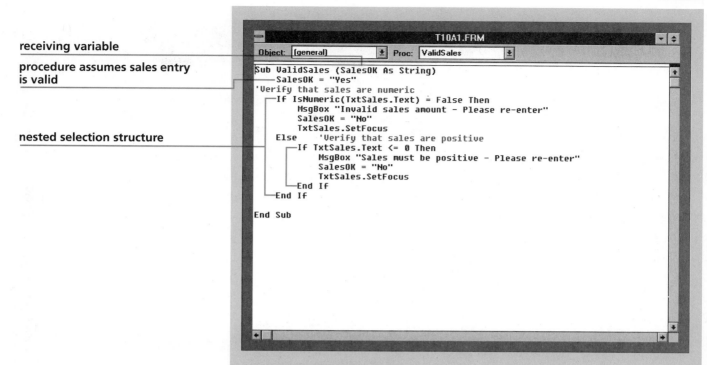

```
                        T10A1.FRM
Object: [general]          Proc: ValidSales

Sub ValidSales (SalesOK As String)
    SalesOK = "Yes"
'Verify that sales are numeric
    If IsNumeric(TxtSales.Text) = False Then
        MsgBox "Invalid sales amount - Please re-enter"
        SalesOK = "No"
        TxtSales.SetFocus
    Else    'Verify that sales are positive
        If TxtSales.Text <= 0 Then
            MsgBox "Sales must be positive - Please re-enter"
            SalesOK = "No"
            TxtSales.SetFocus
        End If
    End If

End Sub
```

Figure 10-15: ValidSales procedure

The ValidSales procedure declares one receiving variable, SalesOK As String. The procedure then assigns "Yes" to the SalesOK variable; unless determined otherwise, the procedure assumes that the sales entry is valid.

The ValidSales procedure uses a nested selection structure to validate the sales entry. (Recall that the Data Validation chart shown in Figure 10-9 indicates that the sales entry must be numeric and must be greater than 0.) The first selection structure uses the IsNumeric function to verify that the sales entry either is a number or can be converted to a number. (Recall that the IsNumeric function results in a Boolean value—either True or False.) If the entry is not numeric—which means that either it is not a number or it can't be converted to a number—then an appropriate message is displayed, "No" is assigned to the SalesOK variable, the focus is set to the Sales Text box, and the ValidSales procedure ends. If, on the other hand, the sales entry is numeric, then the second selection structure is processed.

The second selection structure compares the sales entry to the number 0. If the entry is less than or equal to 0, then an appropriate message is displayed, "No" is assigned to the SalesOK variable, the focus is set to the Sales Text box, and the ValidSales procedure ends. If, on the other hand, the sales entry is not less than or equal to 0 (that is, it is greater than 0), then the ValidSales procedure ends.

When the ValidSales procedure ends, the program returns to the CmdCompute_Click procedure, to the line below the Call statement. Let's open the CmdCompute_Click procedure to finish viewing its code.

5   Press **[F2]** to open the View Procedures dialog box. Click **CmdCompute_Click** in the Procedures box, then click the **OK button**. The CmdCompute_Click procedure appears, as shown in Figure 10-16.

program returns to this statement

nested selection structure

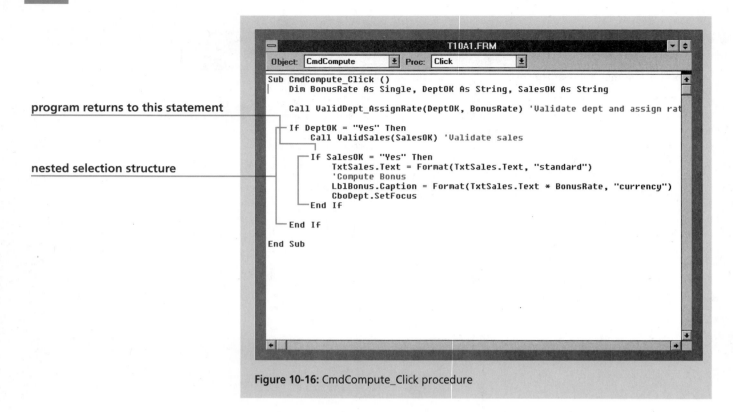

```
                                    T10A1.FRM

Object:  CmdCompute        ±   Proc:  Click              ±

Sub CmdCompute_Click ()
    Dim BonusRate As Single, DeptOK As String, SalesOK As String

    Call ValidDept_AssignRate(DeptOK, BonusRate) 'Validate dept and assign rat

  If DeptOK = "Yes" Then
      Call ValidSales(SalesOK) 'Validate sales

    If SalesOK = "Yes" Then
        TxtSales.Text = Format(TxtSales.Text, "standard")
        'Compute Bonus
        LblBonus.Caption = Format(TxtSales.Text * BonusRate, "currency")
        CboDept.SetFocus
    End If

  End If

End Sub
```

Figure 10-16: CmdCompute_Click procedure

When control returns from the ValidSales procedure to the CmdCompute_Click procedure, it returns to the *If SalesOK = "Yes" Then* instruction. Recall that the Call statement passed the SalesOK variable to the ValidSales procedure, which assigned either "Yes" or "No" to it. If the SalesOK variable contains "Yes", it means that the sales entry is valid. In that case, the sales entry is formatted; the bonus is calculated, formatted, and assigned to the LblBonus control; and the focus is set to the Department Combo box, ready to calculate the next bonus. If the SalesOK variable does not contain "Yes", then the CmdCompute_Click procedure ends and the user is returned to the form, where he or she can re-enter the sales amount. (Notice that the bonus is calculated only when both the department and sales entries are valid.)

Now let's run the application to see how it works:

To test the application:

1   Close the Code window, restore the form to its standard size, then **save and run** the application.

    First let's enter an incorrect department and a correct sales amount.

2   Type **h** in the Department Combo box, then press [**Tab**]. (Recall that the CboDept_ Change procedure uses the UCase function to convert the entry to uppercase.) Type **100** in the Sales Text box, then press [**Tab**]. The focus is on the Compute button. Press [**Enter**] (or click the **Compute button**). Because the department entry is not valid, a message box prompting you to re-enter the department appears.

3   Press [**Enter**] (or click the **OK button**) to remove the message box. The focus appears in the Department Combo box.

Now let's enter a correct department, but an incorrect sales amount—one that cannot be converted to a number.

4   Click the **Combo box's down arrow button** to open the Combo box, click **A**, then click in the Sales Text box. Type **5a** in the Sales Text box, then click the **Compute button**. Because the sales entry cannot be converted to a number, a message box prompting you to re-enter the sales amount appears.

5   Click the **OK button** to remove the message box. The focus appears in the Sales Text box.

Now let's enter a sales amount that is not greater than 0.

6   Type **–5** in the Sales Text box, then click the **Compute button**. Because the sales entry is not greater than 0, a message box prompting you to re-enter the sales amount appears.

7   Click the **OK button** to remove the message box. The focus appears in the Sales Text box.

Now let's enter a correct sales amount and a correct department.

8   Type **1,500.75** in the Sales Text box. Open the Combo box and click **D**, then click the **Compute button**. The correct bonus, $120.06, appears in the LblBonus control, and the focus is in the Department Combo box.

9   Click the **Exit button**. Visual Basic returns to the design screen.

You can make this application easier to use by making the Compute button the default button, which you will do in the next section.

Making a Command Button the Default Button

As you've learned in previous tutorials, you can choose a Command button by pressing the Enter key when the button has the focus. If you make a Command button the default button, however, you can choose it by pressing the Enter key when the button does not have the focus.

The Default property, which is applicable to Command buttons only, determines which Command button is the default button. When you create a Command button, its Default property is initially set to False, which means that it is not the default button. If you want a Command button to be the default button, you must set its Default property to True. Because only one Command button on a form can be the default button, setting a Command button's Default property to True sets the Default property of every other Command button in the form to False.

To make the Compute button the default button, then save and run the application:

1   Click the **down arrow in the Properties window's Object box** (located below the Properties window's title bar), then click **CmdCompute CommandButton** in the drop-down list to select the Compute button. The Object box should say CmdCompute CommandButton.

2   Double-click **Default** in the Properties list until the property says True.

3   **Save and run** the application. The user interface appears on the screen. Notice the darkened border around the Compute button, which indicates that it is the default button.

Let's enter a department and a sales amount, then use the Enter key to choose the Compute button.

4   Open the Combo box and click **B** (or press the [**down arrow**] on the keyboard). Click in the Sales Text box, then type **2000** and press [**Enter**]. The Enter key chooses the Compute button, which displays the bonus, $100.00, in the LblBonus control.

5   Experiment on your own by entering different departments and sales amounts, then click the **Exit button.** Visual Basic returns to the design screen.

Before viewing the second data validation example, you will learn about the Left$ and Right$ functions.

The Left$ and Right$ Functions

Functions, you may remember, always return a value. The Left$ and Right$ functions, for example, return one or more characters from a string. Figure 10-17 lists the format and the purpose of both functions, as well as some examples of each.

Function Format	Purpose
Left$ *(stringexpression, n)*	Returns the leftmost *n* characters of the *stringexpression.*
Right$ *(stringexpression, n)*	Returns the rightmost *n* characters of the *stringexpression.*

Examples: Assume that the ProgName variable contains "Visual Basic" (without the quotes).

Function	Resulting String
Left$("January", 3)	Jan
Right$("January", 2)	ry
Left$(ProgName, 6)	Visual
Right$(ProgName, 5)	Basic

Figure 10-17: Format, purpose, and examples of the Left$ and Right$ functions

In the first two examples, the Left$ and Right$ functions are used to return one or more characters from the *stringexpression* "January". In the first example, the Left$ function returns the leftmost three characters in the *stringexpression*—Jan. In the second example, the Right$ function returns the rightmost two characters in the *stringexpression*—ry.

In the last two examples shown in Figure 10-17, a string variable is used as the *stringexpression*. When the *stringexpression* is a string variable, the Left$ and Right$ functions use the contents of the variable, not the variable name itself. In other words, the leftmost six characters in the string contained in the ProgName variable are "Visual"; the rightmost five characters in the string are "Basic."

You will use both the Left$ and Right$ functions in the second data validation example.

Data Validation Example 2

The T10_EX2.MAK project on your Student Disk contains the second example of data validation. Let's open that project now.

To view the T10_EX2.MAK project:

1   Open the **t10_ex2.mak** file, which is in either the tut10\ver2 or tut10\ver3 directory on your Student Disk.

2   **Save** the form and the project as **t10a2.**

3   Click the **View Form button,** then maximize the form. The user interface appears on the screen, as shown in Figure 10-18.

ImgSnow

ImgEarth

TxtID

LblSize

ImgDesign

Frame1

CmdDisplay

CmdExit

ImgSun

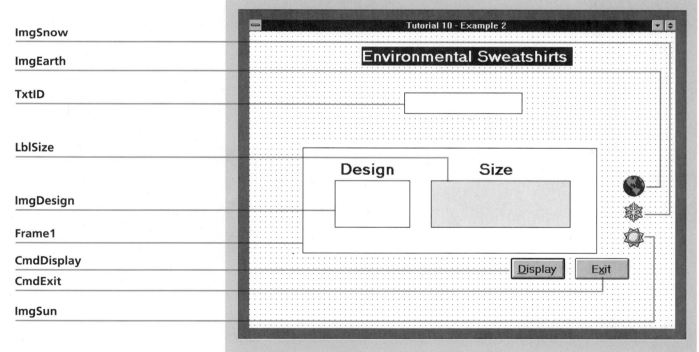

Figure 10-18: User interface for data validation Example 2

The Environmental Sweatshirts application contains a Text box, a Frame control, four Image controls, a Label control, and two Command buttons. You can use the application to display a sweatshirt's design and its size based on the ID entered in the TxtID control.

A sweatshirt's ID consists of five characters: The first three characters—which can be 100, 200, or 300—indicate the type of design; the last two characters—which can be XS, SM, MD, LG, or XL—indicate the size. Design 100 is a picture of the earth, design 200 is a picture of a snowflake, and design 300 is a picture of the sun. XS stands for "extra small," SM for "small," MD for "medium," LG for "large," and XL for "extra large." Figure 10-19 shows the Data Validation chart for this application.

DATA	TYPE CHECK	LENGTH CHECK	RANGE CHECK	CODE CHECK	CHECK DIGIT
ID	string	5	N/A	First 3 characters: 100, 200, or 300; last 2 characters: XS, SM, MD, LG, XL	N/A

Figure 10-19: Data Validation chart for Environmental Sweatshirts application

The Environmental Sweatshirts application has already been coded for you. Let's view the code.

To view the code in the t10a2 application:
1   Double-click the **form** to open its Code window, then press [**F2**] to open the View Procedures dialog box. The View Procedures dialog box appears, as shown in Figure 10-20.

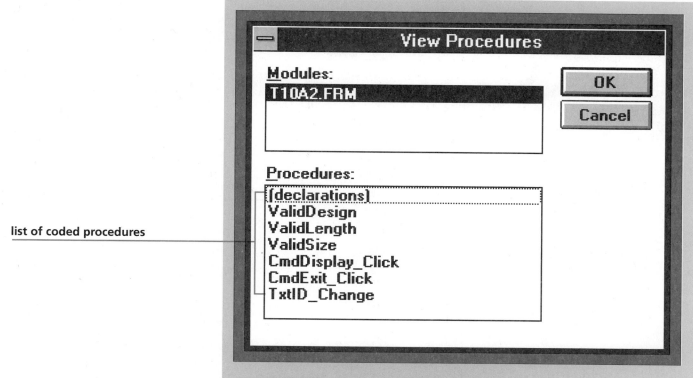

list of coded procedures

Figure 10-20: View Procedures dialog box

2   On your own, verify that the (declarations) section contains the *Option Explicit* statement only and that the CmdExit_Click procedure contains the *End* statement.

Now let's look at the TxtID_Change procedure, which occurs when the user changes the ID in the TxtID control.

3   If necessary, press **[F2]** to open the View Procedures dialog box. Click **TxtID_Change** in the Procedures box, then click the **OK button**. The TxtID_Change procedure contains the *ImgDesign.Picture = LoadPicture()* instruction and the *LblSize.Caption = " "* instruction.

The two instructions in the TxtID_Change procedure tell Visual Basic to clear the Picture property of the ImgDesign control and the Caption property of the LblSize control, respectively, when a change is made to the contents of the TxtID control. (You use the LoadPicture function, you may remember, to load a picture into an Image control. If you don't furnish a picture's name in the parentheses following the LoadPicture function's name, the function clears the existing picture from the Image control.)

Before looking at the CmdDisplay_Click procedure, study its flowchart, which is shown in Figure 10-21.

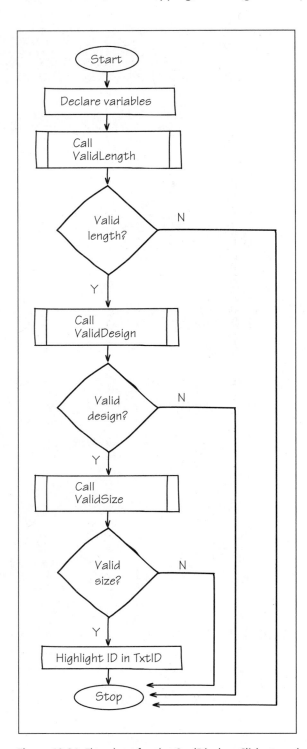

Figure 10-21: Flowchart for the CmdDisplay_Click procedure

According to the flowchart, when the user clicks the Display button, the CmdDisplay_Click procedure will first declare the variables and then call the ValidLength procedure, which will validate the length of the ID entry. If the length is not valid, then the CmdDisplay_Click procedure will end; otherwise the CmdDisplay_Click procedure will call the ValidDesign procedure.

The ValidDesign procedure will verify that the ID's first three characters, which represent the design, are valid. If the design is not valid, then the CmdDisplay_Click procedure will end; otherwise, the CmdDisplay_Click procedure will call the ValidSize procedure.

The ValidSize procedure will verify that the ID's last two characters, which represent the size, are valid. If the size is not valid, then the CmdDisplay_Click procedure will end; otherwise the CmdDisplay_Click procedure will highlight the ID in the TxtID control before the procedure ends. Now let's look at the code in the CmdDisplay_Click procedure.

To view the code in the CmdDisplay_Click procedure:

1   The Code window should be open, so you just need to press [F2] to open the View Procedures dialog box. Click **CmdDisplay_Click** in the Procedures box, click the **OK button**, and then maximize the Code window. The CmdDisplay_Click procedure appears, as shown in Figure 10-22.

nested selection structure

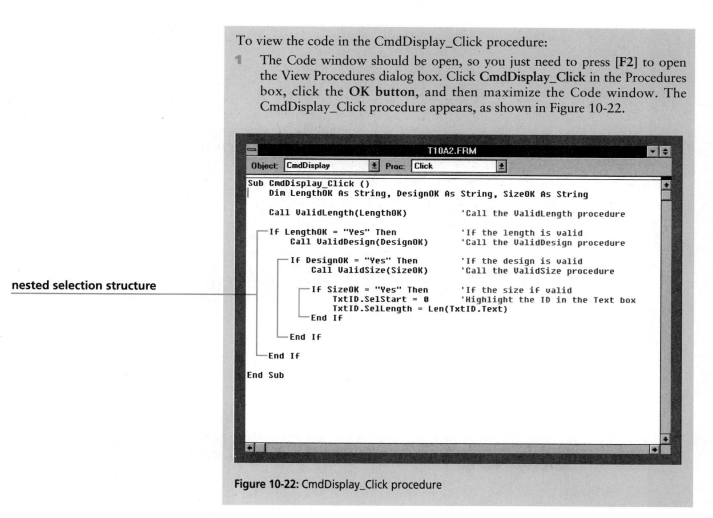

Figure 10-22: CmdDisplay_Click procedure

The procedure declares three local String variables—LengthOK, DesignOK, SizeOK. The CmdDisplay_Click procedure will use these variables to communicate with the ValidLength, ValidDesign, and ValidSize procedures.

After declaring the necessary variables, the CmdDisplay_Click procedure calls the ValidLength procedure and passes the LengthOK local variable to it. When the *Call ValidLength(LengthOK)* statement is processed, the program leaves the CmdDisplay_Click procedure, temporarily, in order to process the instructions in the ValidLength procedure. When the ValidLength procedure ends, the program returns to the CmdDisplay_Click procedure, to the line below the Call statement—the *If LengthOK = "Yes" Then* instruction. If the LengthOK variable does not contain "Yes", which indicates that the length is not valid, the

CmdDisplay_Click procedure ends and the user is returned to the form, where he or she can re-enter the ID.

If, on the other hand, the LengthOK variable contains "Yes," which indicates that the length is valid, then the CmdDisplay_Click procedure calls the ValidDesign procedure and passes the DesignOK variable to it. When the *Call ValidDesign(DesignOK)* statement is processed, the program leaves the CmdDisplay_Click procedure, temporarily, in order to process the instructions in the ValidDesign procedure. When the ValidDesign procedure ends, the program returns to the CmdDisplay_Click procedure, to the line below the Call statement—the *If DesignOK = "Yes" Then* instruction. If the DesignOK variable does not contain "Yes", which indicates that the design is not valid, then the CmdDisplay_Click procedure ends and the user is returned to the form, where he or she can re-enter the ID.

If, on the other hand, the DesignOK variable contains "Yes," which indicates that the design is valid, then the CmdDisplay_Click procedure calls the ValidSize procedure and passes the SizeOK variable to it. When the *Call ValidSize(SizeOK)* statement is processed, the program leaves the CmdDisplay_Click procedure, temporarily, in order to process the instructions in the ValidSize procedure. When the ValidSize procedure ends, the program returns to the CmdDisplay_Click procedure, to the line below the Call statement—the *If SizeOK = "Yes" Then* instruction. If the SizeOK variable contains "Yes", which indicates that the size is valid, then the CmdDisplay_Click procedure uses the SelStart and the SelLength properties to highlight the text in the TxtID control; otherwise, the CmdDisplay_Click procedure ends and the user is returned to the form, where he or she can re-enter the ID. Figure 10-23 illustrates the concept of the multiple calls in a procedure.

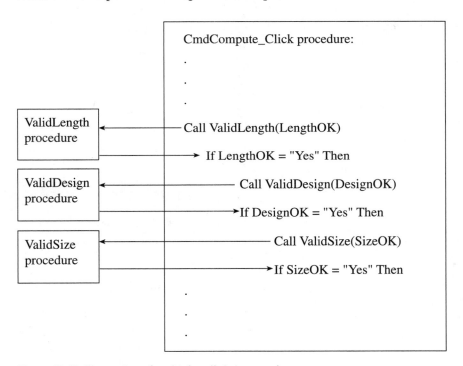

Figure 10-23: Illustration of multiple calls in a procedure

Now let's view the three user-defined procedures: ValidLength, ValidDesign, and ValidSize.

To view the three user-defined procedures:

1 The Code window should be open, so you just need to press [F2] to open the View Procedures dialog box. Click **ValidLength** in the Procedures box, then click the **OK button**. The ValidLength procedure appears, as shown in Figure 10-24.

receiving variable

valid length

invalid length

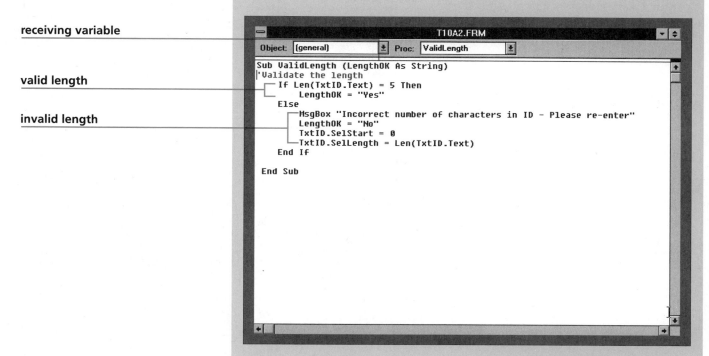

```
                              T10A2.FRM
Object: [general]          ±  Proc: ValidLength      ±
Sub ValidLength (LengthOK As String)
'Validate the length
    If Len(TxtID.Text) = 5 Then
         LengthOK = "Yes"
    Else
        MsgBox "Incorrect number of characters in ID - Please re-enter"
        LengthOK = "No"
        TxtID.SelStart = 0
        TxtID.SelLength = Len(TxtID.Text)
    End If

End Sub
```

Figure 10-24: ValidLength procedure

To agree with the Call statement in the CmdDisplay_Click procedure, the ValidLength procedure declares one receiving variable—a String variable named LengthOK. The Len function is then used to determine the length of the ID. If the ID's length is equal to 5, the procedure assigns "Yes" to the LengthOK variable and the ValidLength procedure ends; otherwise, an appropriate message is displayed, "No" is assigned to the LengthOK variable, and the text in the TxtID control is highlighted before the ValidLength procedure ends. Recall that when the ValidLength procedure ends, the program returns to the line below the *Call ValidLength(LengthOK)* statement in the CmdDisplay_Click procedure.

Now let's look at the ValidDesign user-defined procedure.

2 Press [F2] to open the View Procedures dialog box. Click **ValidDesign** in the Procedures box, then click the **OK button**. The ValidDesign procedure appears, as shown in Figure 10-25.

receiving variable

local variable

procedure assumes data entry is valid

valid design

invalid design

these instructions highlight the first three characters of the ID

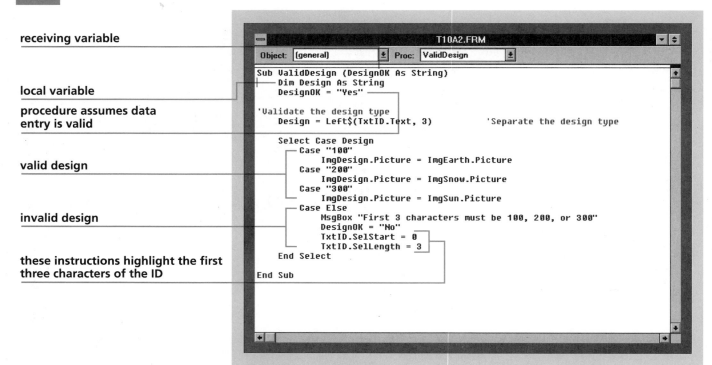

```
                              T10A2.FRM

Object: (general)              Proc: ValidDesign

Sub ValidDesign (DesignOK As String)
    Dim Design As String
    DesignOK = "Yes"

    'Validate the design type
    Design = Left$(TxtID.Text, 3)                  'Separate the design type

    Select Case Design
        Case "100"
            ImgDesign.Picture = ImgEarth.Picture
        Case "200"
            ImgDesign.Picture = ImgSnow.Picture
        Case "300"
            ImgDesign.Picture = ImgSun.Picture
        Case Else
            MsgBox "First 3 characters must be 100, 200, or 300"
            DesignOK = "No"
            TxtID.SelStart = 0
            TxtID.SelLength = 3
    End Select

End Sub
```

Figure 10-25: ValidDesign procedure

The ValidDesign procedure declares one receiving variable—a String variable named DesignOK—and one local variable named Design. The procedure assigns "Yes" to the DesignOK variable; unless determined otherwise, the procedure assumes that the design entry is valid.

The next instruction, *Design = Left$(TxtID.Text, 3)*, assigns the ID's leftmost three characters to the Design variable. (Recall that the first three characters in the ID represent the design. Also recall that the Data Validation chart shown in Figure 10-19 indicates that the valid designs are 100, 200, and 300 only.)

The Case structure uses the Design variable to validate the design. If the Design variable contains a valid design, the procedure displays the appropriate icon (earth, snowflake, sun) in the ImgDesign control and the ValidDesign procedure ends. (Notice that, instead of loading the icon files from the disk each time you want to display a picture in the ImgDesign control, the pictures are copied from the ImgEarth, ImgSnow, and ImgSun controls that are already on the form.) If, on the other hand, the design is not valid, an appropriate message is displayed, "No" is assigned to the DesignOK variable, the first three characters of the ID are highlighted in the TxtID control, and the ValidDesign procedure ends. Recall that when the ValidDesign procedure ends, the program returns to the line below the *Call ValidDesign(DesignOK)* statement in the CmdDisplay_Click procedure.

Now let's look at the ValidSize user-defined procedure.

3 Press **[F2]** to open the View Procedures dialog box. Click **ValidSize** in the Procedures box, then click the **OK button**. The ValidSize procedure appears, as shown in Figure 10-26.

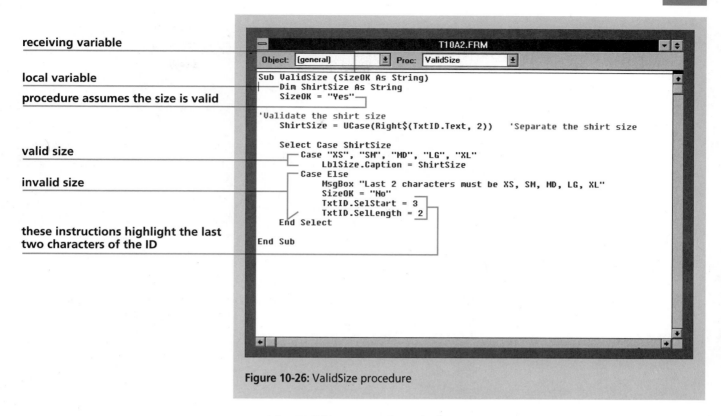

receiving variable

local variable

procedure assumes the size is valid

valid size

invalid size

these instructions highlight the last two characters of the ID

```
                           T10A2.FRM
Object: [general]        ±   Proc: ValidSize       ±

Sub ValidSize (SizeOK As String)
    Dim ShirtSize As String
    SizeOK = "Yes"

'Validate the shirt size
    ShirtSize = UCase(Right$(TxtID.Text, 2))     'Separate the shirt size

    Select Case ShirtSize
      Case "XS", "SM", "MD", "LG", "XL"
          LblSize.Caption = ShirtSize
      Case Else
          MsgBox "Last 2 characters must be XS, SM, MD, LG, XL"
          SizeOK = "No"
          TxtID.SelStart = 3
          TxtID.SelLength = 2
    End Select

End Sub
```

Figure 10-26: ValidSize procedure

The ValidSize procedure declares one receiving variable—a String variable named SizeOK—and one local variable named ShirtSize. (Be careful that you don't use Size as a variable name. Size is a reserved word in Visual Basic.) The procedure assigns "Yes" to the SizeOK variable; unless determined otherwise, the procedure assumes that the size is valid.

The next instruction, *ShirtSize = UCase(Right$(TxtID.Text, 2))*, assigns the rightmost two characters of the ID in uppercase to the ShirtSize variable. (Recall that the last two characters in the ID represent the size. Also recall that the Data Validation chart shown in Figure 10-19 indicates that the valid sizes are XS, SM, MD, LG, and XL only.)

The Case structure uses the ShirtSize variable to validate the size. If the ShirtSize variable contains a valid size, the procedure displays the size in the LblSize control and the ValidSize procedure ends. If, on the other hand, the size is not valid, an appropriate message is displayed, "No" is assigned to the SizeOK variable, the last two characters of the ID are highlighted in the TxtID control, and the ValidSize procedure ends. Recall that when the ValidSize procedure ends, the program returns to the line below the *Call ValidSize(SizeOK)* statement in the CmdDisplay_Click procedure.

Now let's run the application to see how it works.

To test the application:

1   Close the Code window, restore the form to its standard size, then **save and run** the application. Notice that the earth icon, snowflake icon, and sun icon do not appear on the form. That's because their Visible properties are set to False.

    First let's enter an ID that has an incorrect number of characters.

2 Type **5sm** as the ID. Notice that the Display button has a darkened border, which indicates that it is the default Command button. To select the Display button, press [**Enter**]. The message informs you that you have entered an incorrect number of characters and it prompts you to re-enter the ID. Press [**Enter**] to remove the message.

3 On your own, try entering each of the following IDs:

500ss (a message regarding an error in the first three characters is displayed)

100ss (a message regarding an error in the last two characters is displayed)

100md (the earth icon and the letters MD are displayed in the form)

4 Click the **Exit button** to end the application.

Before looking at Example 3, you will learn about the Mid$ function.

The Mid$ Function

The Mid$ function, whose format is **Mid$**(*stringexpression, start[,n]*), returns *n* characters from a *stringexpression*, beginning with the *start* character. Figure 10-27 shows the format, purpose, and examples of the Mid$ function.

Function Format	Purpose
Mid$ *(stringexpression, start[,n])*	Returns *n* characters of the *stringexpression* beginning at position *start*. (If *n* is omitted, the function returns all characters from the *start* position through the end of the *stringexpression*.)

Examples: Assume that the ProgName variable contains "Visual Basic" (without the quotes).

Function	Resulting String
Mid$("January", 2, 1)	a
Mid$("January", 4, 2)	ua
Mid$(ProgName, 8, 1)	B

Figure 10-27: Format, purpose, and examples of the Mid$ function

In the first two examples, the Mid$ function is used to return one or more characters from the *stringexpression* "January". The first example, *Mid$("January", 2, 1)*, returns one character, beginning with the second character, in the *stringexpression*—the letter a. In the second example, the Mid$ function returns two characters, beginning with the fourth character, in the *stringexpression*—the letters ua.

In the last two examples shown in Figure 10-27, the ProgName variable is used as the *stringexpression*. As the examples show, the one character, beginning with the eighth character in the string contained in the ProgName variable, is the letter B. The five characters, beginning with the eighth character in the string, are Basic.

You will use the Mid$ function in the third example of data validation.

Data Validation Example 3

The T10_EX3.MAK project on your Student Disk contains the third data validation example. Let's open that project now.

To view the T10_EX3.MAK application:

1 Open the **t10_ex3.mak** project, which is in either tut10\ver2 or the tut10\ver3 directory on your Student Disk.

2 Save the form and the project as **t10a3**.

3 Click the **View Form button**, then maximize the form. The user interface appears, as shown in Figure 10-28.

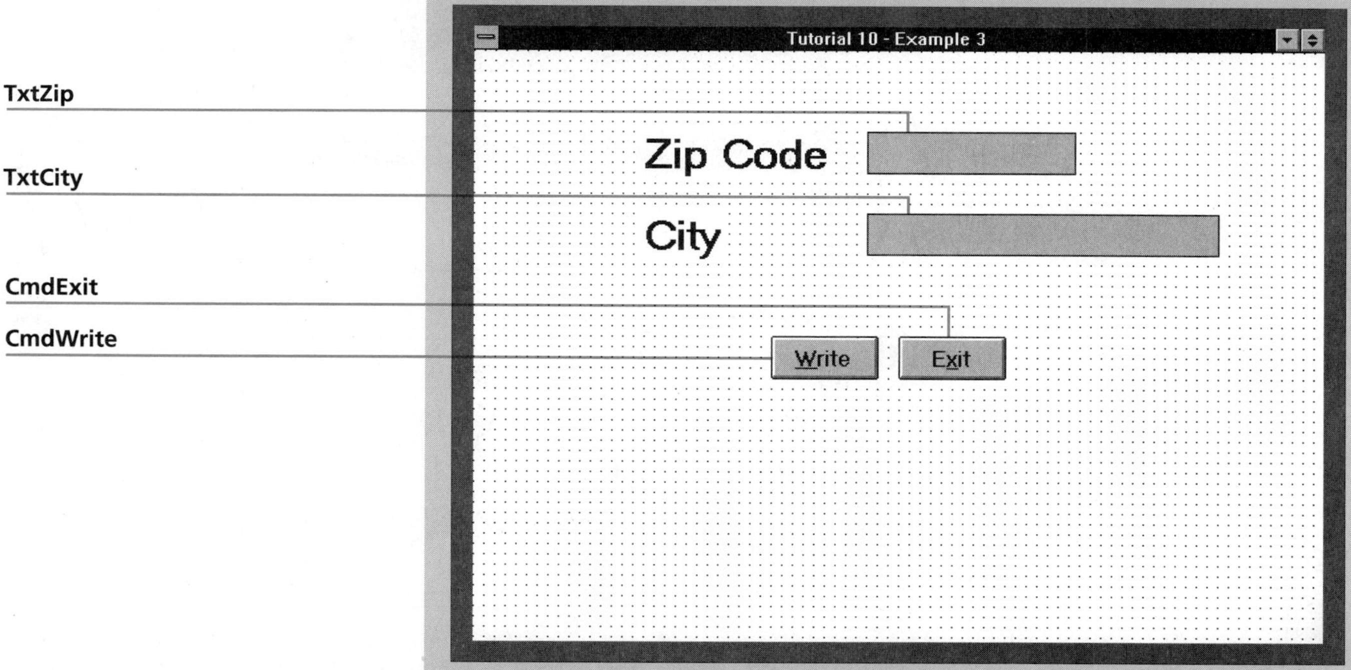

Figure 10-28: User interface for data validation Example 3

This application will validate the Zip codes and city names entered by the user before they are written to a sequential access file on your Student Disk. A Zip code must be five characters in length and can consist of the numbers 0 through 9 only; no commas or decimal points are allowed. The city name must be at least 1 character, but can't be longer than 20 characters. Figure 10-29 shows the Data Validation chart for this application.

DATA	TYPE CHECK	LENGTH CHECK	RANGE CHECK	CODE CHECK	CHECK DIGIT
Zip code	numbers only	5	N/A	N/A	N/A
City	string	>=1 and <=20	N/A	N/A	N/A

Figure 10-29: Data Validation chart for the Zip code application

The Zip code application has already been coded for you. Let's look at the coded procedures.

To view the code in the Zip code application:

1 Double-click the **form**, then press [**F2**] to open the View Procedures dialog box. The View Procedures dialog box appears, as shown in Figure 10-30.

list of coded procedures

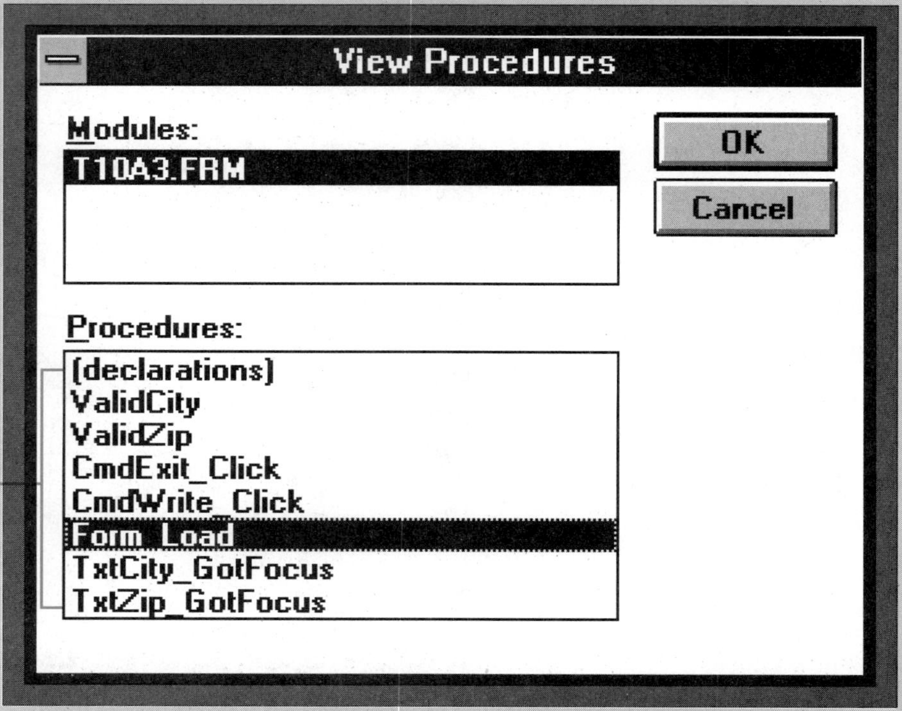

Figure 10-30: View Procedures dialog box

2 On your own, verify that the (declarations) section contains the *Option Explicit* statement and that the CmdExit_Click procedure contains the *Close #1* and *End* statements. Also verify that the TxtCity_GotFocus procedure and the TxtZip_GotFocus procedure contain the SelStart and SelLength instructions, which will select the existing text when the controls receive the focus.

Now let's view the code in the form's Load event procedure.

3   If necessary, press [F2] to open the View Procedures dialog box. Click **Form_Load** in the Procedures box, then click the **OK button**. The Form_Load procedure, which contains the Open statement that will open the t10_ex3.dat file for append, appears.

4   If necessary, change the drive letter in the Open statement to the drive containing your Student Disk.

Before viewing the code in the CmdWrite_Click procedure, study its flow-chart, which is shown in Figure 10-31.

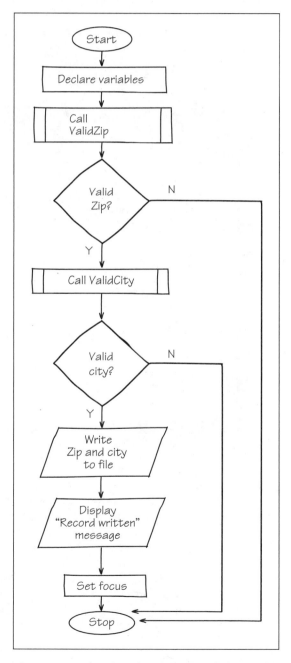

Figure 10-31: Flowchart for CmdWrite_Click procedure

After declaring the necessary variables, the CmdWrite_Click procedure will call the ValidZip procedure, which will validate the Zip code. If the Zip code is valid, then the CmdWrite_Click procedure will call the ValidCity procedure; otherwise, the CmdWrite_Click procedure will end.

If the Zip code is valid, the ValidCity procedure will validate the city entry. If the city entry is valid, the CmdWrite_Click procedure will write the Zip code and the city to the t10_ex3.dat file, display a "Record written" message, and set the focus before the CmdWrite_Click procedure ends; otherwise, the CmdWrite_Click procedure will simply end.

Now let's look at the code in the CmdWrite_Click procedure.

To view the code in the CmdWrite_Click procedure:

1   The Code window should be open, so you just need to press [F2] to open the View Procedures dialog box. Click **CmdWrite_Click** in the Procedures box, click the **OK button**, and then maximize the Code window. The CmdWrite_Click procedure appears, as shown in Figure 10-32.

nested selection structure

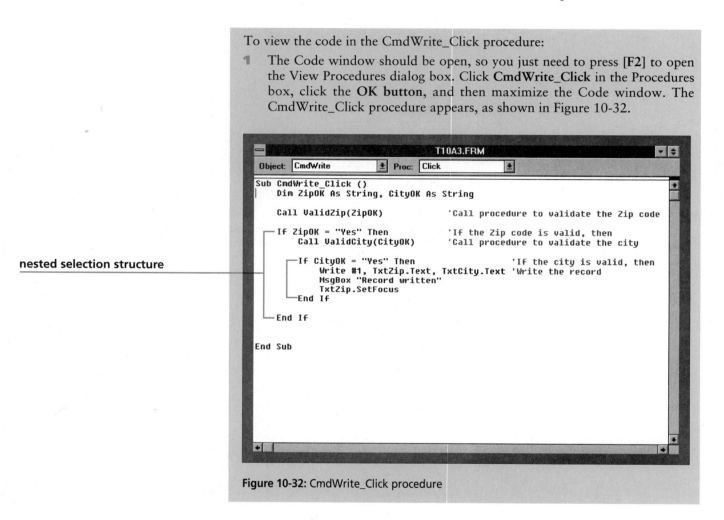

```
Sub CmdWrite_Click ()
    Dim ZipOK As String, CityOK As String

    Call ValidZip(ZipOK)                      'Call procedure to validate the Zip code

    If ZipOK = "Yes" Then                     'If the Zip code is valid, then
        Call ValidCity(CityOK)                'Call procedure to validate the city

        If CityOK = "Yes" Then                        'If the city is valid, then
            Write #1, TxtZip.Text, TxtCity.Text 'Write the record
            MsgBox "Record written"
            TxtZip.SetFocus
        End If
    End If


End Sub
```

Figure 10-32: CmdWrite_Click procedure

After declaring two local String variables, ZipOK and CityOK, the procedure calls the ValidZip procedure and passes the ZipOK local variable to it. When the *Call ValidZip(ZipOK)* statement is processed, the program leaves the CmdWrite_Click procedure, temporarily, in order to process the instructions in the ValidZip procedure. When the ValidZip procedure ends, the program returns to the *If ZipOK = "Yes" Then* instruction in the CmdWrite_Click procedure. If the ZipOK variable does not contain "Yes", which indicates that the Zip code is not valid, the CmdWrite_Click procedure ends and the user is returned to the form, where he or she can re-enter the Zip code.

If, on the other hand, the ZipOK variable contains "Yes," which indicates that the Zip code is valid, then the CmdWrite_Click procedure calls the ValidCity procedure and passes the CityOK variable to it. When the *Call ValidCity(CityOK)* statement is processed, the program leaves the CmdWrite_Click procedure, temporarily, in order to process the instructions in the ValidCity procedure. When the ValidCity procedure ends, the program returns to the *If CityOK = "Yes" Then* instruction in the CmdWrite_Click procedure. If the CityOK variable contains "Yes", which indicates that the city is valid, the CmdWrite_Click procedure writes the Zip code and the city to the t10_ex3.dat sequential access file, displays a "Record written" message, and sets the focus to the TxtZip control before the CmdWrite_Click procedure ends; otherwise, the CmdWrite_Click procedure ends and returns the user to the form, where he or she can re-enter the city's name.

Now let's view the ValidZip user-defined procedure.

To view the ValidZip user-defined procedure:

1   The Code window should be open, so you just need to press [F2] to display the View Procedures dialog box. Click **ValidZip** in the Procedures box, then click the **OK button**. The ValidZip procedure appears, as shown in Figure 10-33.

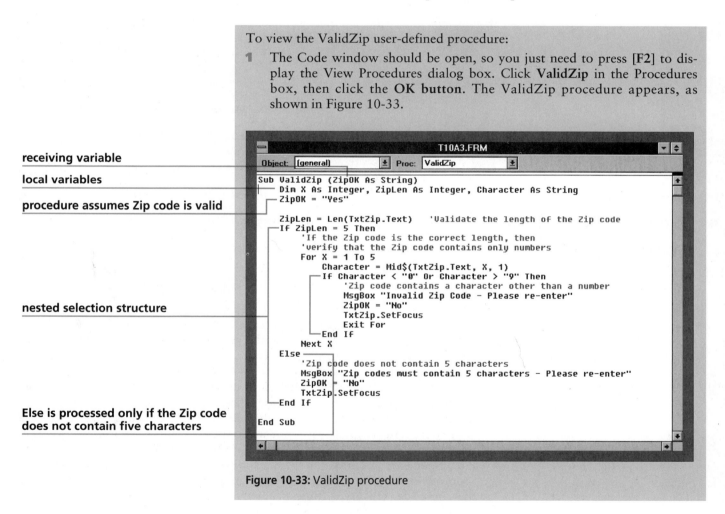

receiving variable

local variables

procedure assumes Zip code is valid

nested selection structure

Else is processed only if the Zip code does not contain five characters

Figure 10-33: ValidZip procedure

The ValidZip procedure declares one receiving variable—a String variable named ZipOK. The procedure also declares two local Integer variables (X and ZipLen) and one local String variable (Character). After declaring the variables, the procedure assigns "Yes" to the ZipOK variable; unless determined otherwise, the procedure assumes that the Zip code is valid. The procedure then assigns the length of the Zip code entry to the ZipLen variable. If the Zip code does not contain exactly five characters, then the Else instructions are processed; those instructions display an appropriate message, assign "No" to the ZipOK variable, and set the focus to the TxtZip control before the ValidZip procedure ends. If, on the other hand, the Zip code entry does contain exactly five characters, then the For...Next loop instructions are processed before the ValidZip procedure ends. Let's take a closer look at the instructions within the For...Next loop.

The *For X = 1 to 5* instruction will initialize the counter variable, X, to 1. Each time the loop is processed, the value in X will be increased by 1. The loop will stop when the value in X is greater than 5—in this case, when the value is 6. Each time through the loop, the *Character = Mid$(TxtZip.Text, X, 1)* instruction will assign one character from the Zip code to the Character variable. Figure 10-34 illustrates how each of the five characters are assigned, individually, to the Character variable.

Assume that the Text property of the TxtZip control contains 60753. The chart below shows the value in the X variable, the value of the Mid$(TxtZip.Text,X,1) function, and the value in the Character variable each time the For...Next loop is processed.

	X	**Mid$(TxtZip.Text, X, 1)**	**Character**
First time For...Next loop is processed	1	Mid$(TxtZip.Text, 1, 1)	6
Second time For...Next loop is processed	2	Mid$(TxtZip.Text, 2, 1)	0
Third time For...Next loop is processed	3	Mid$(TxtZip.Text, 3, 1)	7
Fourth time For...Next loop is processed	4	Mid$(TxtZip.Text, 4, 1)	5
Fifth time For...Next loop is processed	5	Mid$(TxtZip.Text, 5, 1)	3

Figure 10-34: Illustration of how the For...Next loop processes the Mid$ function

Each time the *Character = Mid$(TxtZip.Text, X, 1)* instruction assigns a character to the Character variable, the procedure must verify that the character is a number. You can't use the IsNumeric function here because, you may recall, the IsNumeric function treats characters other than numbers as numeric—for example, a comma and a period are treated as numeric. Instead of the IsNumeric function, notice that the procedure uses a selection structure to verify that the character is a number. If the character is less than "0" or if it is greater than "9", then it's not a number; so an appropriate message is displayed, "No" is assigned to the ZipOK variable, the focus is set, the For...Next loop is exited, and the ValidZip procedure ends. (Notice that the code will exit the For...Next loop when an incorrect character is encountered in the Zip code. Once you find an incorrect character, there is no reason to validate the remaining characters because the Zip code is already invalid.)

If, on the other hand, the character in the Character variable is a number, then the For...Next loop continues processing until each of the five characters has been validated. After completing the validation task, the ValidZip procedure will end. When the ValidZip procedure ends, the program returns to the line below the *Call ValidZip(ZipOK)* statement in the CmdWrite_Click procedure.

Now let's look at the ValidCity procedure.

To view the ValidCity procedure:

1   The Code window should be open, so you just need to press [F2] to open the View Procedures dialog box. Click **ValidCity** in the Procedures box, then click the **OK button**. The ValidCity procedure appears, as shown in Figure 10-35.

receiving variable

local variable

procedure assumes city is valid

invalid city

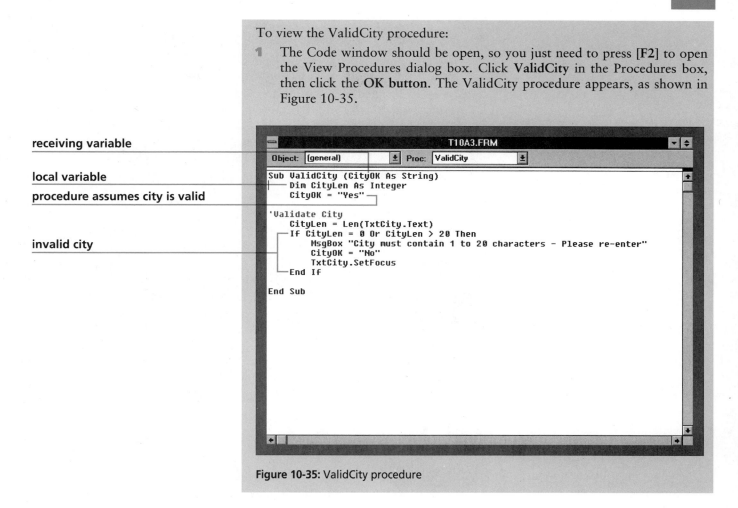

Figure 10-35: ValidCity procedure

The ValidCity procedure declares one receiving variable—a String variable named CityOK—and one local Integer variable named CityLen. After declaring the variables, the procedure assigns "Yes" to the CityOK variable; unless determined otherwise, the procedure assumes that the city entry is valid. The procedure then assigns the length of the city entry to the CityLen variable. If the length of the city entry is equal to 0, which means that the user did not enter a city into the City Text box, or if the length is greater than 20, then an appropriate message is displayed, "No" is assigned to the CityOK variable, and the focus is set before the ValidCity procedure ends. If, on the other hand, the length of the city is between 1 and 20 characters, inclusive, then the ValidCity procedure simply ends. When the ValidCity procedure ends, the program returns to the line below the *Call ValidCity(CityOK)* statement in the CmdWrite_Click procedure.

Now let's run the application to see how it works.

To test the application:

1   Close the Code window, restore the form to its standard size, then **save and run** the application.

First let's enter a Zip code that does not have five characters.

2   Type **6013** as the Zip code, then click the **Write button**. A message appears and informs you that the Zip code must contain five characters;

you will need to re-enter the Zip code. Click the **OK button** to remove the message.

Now let's type a Zip code that contains a letter.

3   Type **6013a**, then press **[Alt][w]** to choose the Write button. A message appears and informs you that the Zip code is invalid; you will need to re-enter it. Press **[Enter]** to remove the message.

Now let's enter a correct Zip code, but an incorrect city entry.

4   Type **60999** as the Zip code, then click the **Write button**. A message appears and informs you that the city entry must contain from 1 to 20 characters; you will need to re-enter the city. Click the **OK button** to remove the message. The focus is in the TxtCity control.

5   Type **Glenview** in the TxtCity control, then click the **Write button**. The "Record written" message appears. Click the **OK button** to remove the message.

6   On your own, try entering a Zip code that is longer than five characters. Also try entering a city that is longer than 20 characters.

7   Click the **Exit button**. Visual Basic returns to the design screen.

You have now completed Lesson A. You can either take a break or complete the questions and exercises at the end of the lesson.

S U M M A R Y

To validate the input data:

■   Use one or more of the following data validation checks:
- ■   The type check examines the input data to see if it's the correct type.
- ■   The length check verifies that the input data contains the correct number of characters.
- ■   The range check verifies that the input data falls within a specific range.
- ■   The code check verifies that the input data matches a predetermined list of values.
- ■   The check digit check verifies the assignment of a special digit to an identification number.

To verify that an *expression* either is a number or can be converted to a number:

■   Use the IsNumeric function. Its format is **IsNumeric**(*expression*). Refer to Figure 10-6 for the characters that the IsNumeric function treats as numeric.

To make a Command button the default button:

■   Set the Command button's Default property to True. Only one Command button on a form can be the default button.

To extract one or more characters from a string:

■   Use the Left$, Right$, or Mid$ functions.
■   The Left$ function returns the leftmost *n* characters from the *stringexpression*. The format of the Left$ function is **Left$**(*stringexpression, n*).

■ The Right$ function returns the rightmost *n* characters from the *stringexpression*. The format of the Right$ function is **Right$**(*stringexpression, n*).

■ The Mid$ function returns *n* characters of the *stringexpression* beginning at position *start*. The format of the Mid$ function is **Mid$**(*stringexpression, start[,n]*).

QUESTIONS

1. If the application expects the user to enter a number, a programmer would use the _____ check to verify that the user entered either a number or a string that can be converted to a number.
   a. check digit
   b. code
   c. length
   d. range
   e. type

2. If the input data must be either "X" or "Y," a programmer would use the _____ check to verify that the user entered either an "X" or a "Y" only.
   a. check digit
   b. code
   c. length
   d. range
   e. type

3. Assume that an application requires the user to enter an employee's name in a Text box. The Text box must be completed, but the entry cannot exceed 25 characters. In this application, a programmer would use the _____ check to validate the employee's name.
   a. check digit
   b. code
   c. length
   d. range
   e. type

4. Assume that an application requires the user to enter a bonus rate. The bonus rate must be either 2%, 3%, or 5%. In this application, a programmer would use the _____ check to validate the bonus rate.
   a. check digit
   b. code
   c. length
   d. range
   e. type

5. Assume that an application requires the user to enter the number of hours an employee worked in a week. The number of hours can't be negative, and it can't exceed 50. In this application, a programmer would use the _____ check to validate the hours worked.
   a. check digit
   b. code
   c. length
   d. range
   e. type

6. A programmer would use the _____ check to verify the assignment of a special digit added to the end of an identification number.
    a. check digit
    b. code
    c. length
    d. range
    e. type

7. You can use the _____ function to verify that an expression either is a number or can be converted to a number.
    a. IsNum
    b. IsNumb
    c. IsNumber
    d. IsNumeric
    e. IsNumerical

8. You can use either of these functions to extract one or more characters from the left side of a string. (Choose two answers.)
    a. IsNumeric
    b. Left$
    c. Mid$
    d. Right$
    e. Xtract$

9. You can use either of these functions to extract one or more characters from the right side of a string. (Choose two answers.)
    a. IsNumeric
    b. Left$
    c. Mid$
    d. Right$
    e. Xtract$

10. The _____ function allows you to extract *n* characters from a *stringexpression*, beginning with the *start* character.
    a. IsNumeric
    b. Left$
    c. Mid$
    d. Right$
    e. Xtract$

11. To make a Command button the default button, set its _____ property to True.
    a. Caption
    b. Command
    c. Default
    d. Enter
    e. Focus

12. Assume that the CmdDisplay_Click procedure declares a local String variable named JobclassOK and a Single variable named HrlyRate. The CmdDisplay_Click procedure uses the following Call statement to call the ValidJobclass procedure: *Call ValidJobclass(HrlyRate, JobclassOK)*. Which of the following could be used by the ValidJobclass procedure to receive the variables? (Choose two answers.)
   a. Sub ValidJobclass (X as String, Y as Single)
   b. Sub ValidJobclass (HrlyRate as Single, JobclassOK as String)
   c. Sub ValidJobclass (JobclassOK as String, HrlyRate as Single)
   d. Sub ValidJobclass (X as Single, Y as String)

13. The *Left$(EmpName, 3)* instruction is equivalent to which of the following?
   a. Mid$(EmpName, 3, 1)
   b. Mid$(EmpName, 1, 3)
   c. Mid$(EmpName, 3, 0)
   d. Mid$(EmpName, 0, 3)
   e. Mid$(EmpName, 3, 3)

14. Assuming the EmpName variable contains the name "John Jeffries" (without the quotes), the *Right$(EmpName, 3)* instruction is equivalent to which of the following?
   a. Mid$(EmpName, 3, 10)
   b. Mid$(EmpName, 10, 3)
   c. Mid$(EmpName, 3, 11)
   d. Mid$(EmpName, 11, 3)
   e. Mid$(EmpName, 3, 3)

EXERCISES

1. Evaluate the following as either True or False. If the evaluation is False, write the reason why it is False:

Value in TxtNum Control	Evaluation of IsNumeric(TxtNum.Text)	
1,300.57		
1,234.a		
−10		
8%		
(36)		
2−		
$125		

2. Evaluate the following:

Function	Resulting String
Left$("Mary Jones", 4)	
Right$("Sam Smith", 2)	
Mid$("Bobby Day", 1, 1)	
Mid$("Jack Li", 3, 2)	

3. Assuming that the StateName variable contains "California" (without the quotes), evaluate the following:

Function	Resulting String
Mid$(StateName, 8, 1)	_____
Left$(StateName, 6)	_____
Right$(StateName, 5)	_____
Mid$(StateName, 3, 5)	_____

4. Each salesperson at BobCat Motors is assigned a number, which consists of three characters. The first two characters are the salesperson's initials, and the last character is either a 1 or a 2. A 1 indicates that the salesperson sells new cars, and a 2 indicates that the salesperson sells used cars.

a. Create the user interface shown in Figure 10-36.

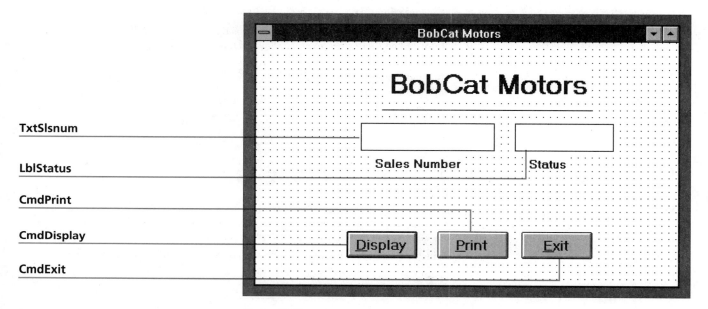

Figure 10-36

b. Make the Display button the default Command button.

c. Save the form and the project as t10lae4.

d. Code the Exit button so that it ends the application. Code the Print button so that it prints the form.

e. Code the Display button according to the flowchart shown in Figure 10-37.

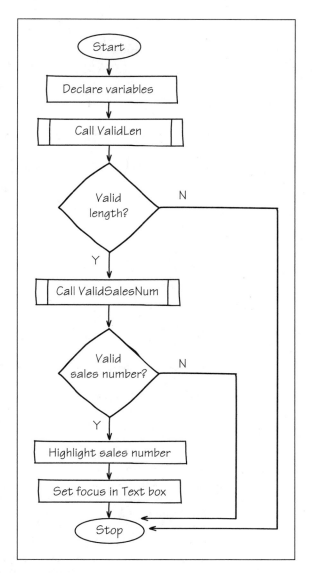

Figure 10-37

You will use the Data Validation chart shown in Figure 10-38 to code the sub procedures.

DATA	TYPE CHECK	LENGTH CHECK	RANGE CHECK	CODE CHECK	CHECK DIGIT
Sales number	string	3	First two characters must be A–Z, or a–z	Last two characters must be 1 or 2	N/A

Figure 10-38

f. Create a sub procedure named ValidLen. (Recall that you can create a procedure by opening a Code window and then selecting New Procedure... from the View menu.) The ValidLen procedure should perform a length check on the salesperson's number. Refer to the Data Validation chart shown in Figure 10-38. Use the MsgBox statement to display an appropriate error message if the length is incorrect.

g. Create a sub procedure named ValidSalesNum, which will perform a type, range, and code check on the salesperson's number. Refer to the Data Validation chart shown in Figure 10-38. Use the MsgBox statement to display an appropriate error message if the sales number is incorrect. If the sales number is correct and the last character is a 1, display the message New Cars in the LblStatus control; otherwise display the message Used Cars.

h. Save and run the application.

i. Enter number JH45 and press [Enter]. An appropriate error message should appear. Write the message down on a piece of paper.

j. Enter number L22 and press [Enter]. An appropriate error message should appear. Write the message down on a piece of paper.

k. Enter number PH5 and press [Enter]. An appropriate error message should appear. Write the message down on a piece of paper.

l. Enter number JB1 and press [Enter]. A message indicating that the salesperson sells new cars should appear in the Label control. Click the Print button.

m. Enter number BJ2 and press [Enter]. A message indicating that the salesperson sells used cars should appear in the Label control. Click the Print button.

n. Click the Exit button, then print the code.

5. Each employee at Acme Wares is assigned an employee number, which consists of four characters. If the employee is salaried, the second digit in the employee number is a 1—for example, employee number 1167 would indicate a salaried employee. If the employee is hourly, the second digit in the number is a 2—for example, employee number 1267 would indicate an hourly employee.

a. Create the user interface shown in Figure 10-39.

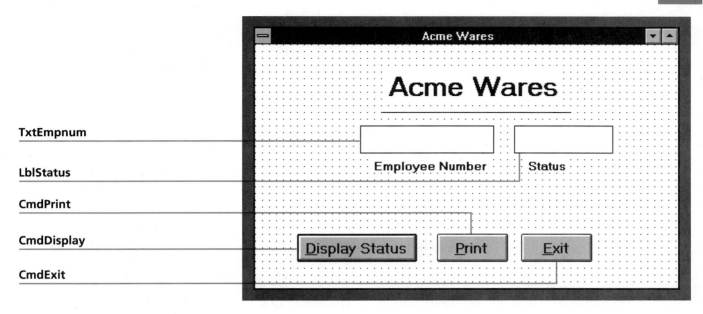

TxtEmpnum

LblStatus

CmdPrint

CmdDisplay

CmdExit

Figure 10-39

b. Make the Display Status button the default Command button.

c. Save the form and the project as t10lae5.

d. Code the Exit button so that it ends the application. Code the Print button so that it prints the form.

e. Draw a flowchart for the Display Status button. The button's Click event procedure will need to call three user-defined procedures: ValidLen, ValidType, ValidCode.

f. Code the CmdDisplay_Click procedure according to your flowchart.

You will use the Data Validation chart shown in Figure 10-40 to code the sub procedures.

DATA	TYPE CHECK	LENGTH CHECK	RANGE CHECK	CODE CHECK	CHECK DIGIT
Employee number	numbers only	4	N/A	Second digit must be a 1 or a 2	N/A

Figure 10-40

g. Create a sub procedure named ValidLen. (Recall that you can create a procedure by opening a Code window and then selecting New Procedure... from the View menu.) The ValidLen procedure should perform a length check on the employee number. Refer to the Data Validation chart shown in Figure 10-40. Use the MsgBox statement to display an error message if the length is incorrect.

h. Create a sub procedure named ValidType, which will perform a type check on the employee number. Refer to the Data Validation chart shown in Figure 10-40. Use the MsgBox statement to display an error message if the type is incorrect.

i. Create a sub procedure named ValidCode, which will perform a code check on the second digit of the employee number. Refer to the Data Validation chart shown in Figure 10-40. Use the MsgBox statement to display an error message if the code is incorrect. If the employee number is correct and the second digit is a 1, display the message Salaried in the LblStatus control; otherwise display Hourly.

j. Save and run the application.

k. Enter employee number 2345 and press [Enter]. An appropriate error message should appear. Write the message down on a piece of paper.

l. Enter employee number 214a and press [Enter]. An appropriate error message should appear. Write the message down on a piece of paper.

m. Enter employee number 21 and press [Enter]. An appropriate error message should appear. Write the message down on a piece of paper.

n. Enter employee number 3256 and press [Enter]. A message indicating that the employee is hourly should appear in the Label control. Click the Print button.

o. Enter employee number 3123 and press [Enter]. A message indicating that the employee is salaried should appear in the Label control. Click the Print button.

p. Click the Exit button, then print the code.

6. In this exercise you will create an application that will calculate gross pay, given the number of hours worked and the rate of pay. The number of hours worked can be from 0 to 50 hours, inclusive. The rate of pay can be from $7 to $10.50, inclusive. Employees working over 40 hours should get time and one-half on the hours over 40.

a. Create the user interface shown in Figure 10-41. Assign the vb\icons\misc\misc20.ico file to the Image1 control and assign the vb\icons\misc\misc22.ico file to the Image2 control.

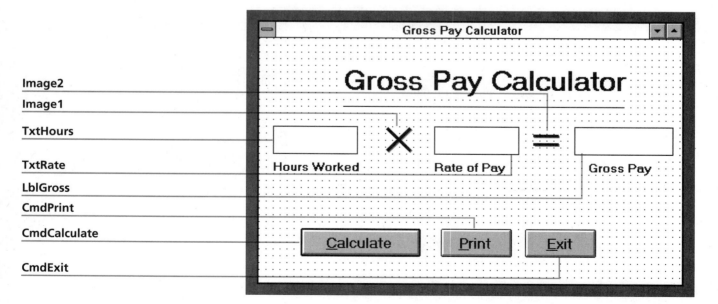

Figure 10-41

b. Make the Calculate button the default Command button.

c. Save the form and the project as t10lae6.

d. Code the Exit button so that it ends the application. Code the Print button so that it prints the form.

e. Draw a flowchart for the Calculate button. The button's Click event procedure will need to call two user-defined procedures: ValidHours and ValidRate.

f. Code the CmdCalculate_Click procedure according to your flowchart.

g. Complete the Data Validation chart shown in Figure 10-42.

DATA	TYPE CHECK	LENGTH CHECK	RANGE CHECK	CODE CHECK	CHECK DIGIT
Hours					
Pay rate					

Figure 10-42

h. Create a sub procedure named ValidHours. (Recall that you can create a procedure by opening a Code window and then selecting New Procedure... from the View menu.) Code the ValidHours procedure according to your Data Validation chart. Use the MsgBox statement to display an appropriate error message if the hours are not valid.

i. Create a sub procedure named ValidRate. Code the ValidRate procedure according to your Data Validation chart. Use the MsgBox statement to display an appropriate message if the rate is not valid.

j. Save and run the application.

k. Enter 51 as the hours worked, then press [Enter]. An appropriate error message should appear. Write the message down on a piece of paper.

l. Enter 4a as the hours worked, then press [Enter]. An appropriate error message should appear. Write the message down on a piece of paper.

m. Enter 10 as the hours worked, enter 5 as the rate of pay, and then press [Enter]. An appropriate error message should appear. Write the message down on a piece of paper.

n. Enter 10 as the hours worked, then enter 10 as the rate of pay, and then press [Enter]. The gross pay should appear in the Label control. Click the Print button.

o. Enter 45 as the hours worked, then enter 8 as the rate of pay, and then press [Enter]. The gross pay should appear in the Label control. Click the Print button.

p. Click the Exit button, then print the code.

Exercises 7 through 9 are Discovery Exercises.

discovery ▶ 7. As mentioned in Lesson A, the check digit check is used to verify the assignment of a special digit to the end of an identification number. Many methods for creating the check digit have been developed. One simple method is to multiply every other number in the ID by 2, then add the products to the remaining numbers to get the total. You then take the last digit in the total and add it to the end of the number, as illustrated in Figure 10-43.

Check Digit Algorithm

Original Number: 1357

Step 1:   Multiply every other number by 2:   1   3   5   7

                                                                         *2   *2

              Result ————————————————————▶ 1   6   5   14

Step 2:   Sum the numbers   1 +   6 +   5   +   14 = 26

Step 3:   Take the last digit in the sum and

              append it to the orginal number: 1   3   5   7   6

New Number: 13576

Figure 10-43

a. Based on the check digit algorithm shown in Figure 10-43, calculate the check digits for the following numbers, then write the number with the check digit. The first example has already been completed for you.

Number	Number with Check Digit
1357	13576
4273	_____
3907	_____
4621	_____

b. Open the t10_ex7.mak project, which is in either the tut10\ver2 or tut10\ver3 directory on your Student Disk.

c. Save the form and the project as t10lae7, then click the View Form button to display the user interface.

A sales clerk can use this application to verify a customer's five-digit account number. Most of the application has been coded for you. You will need to code only one procedure—the ValidCheckDigit procedure.

d. If your computer is connected to a printer, print the application's code; otherwise, open the View Procedures dialog box and view the coded procedures in the form.

e. Code the ValidCheckDigit procedure according to the flowchart shown in Figure 10-44.

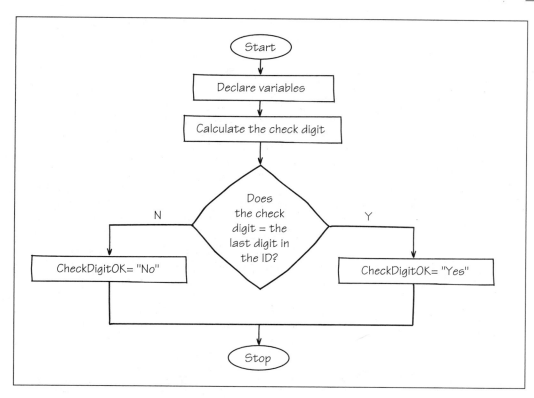

Figure 10-44

f. Save and run the application. Type 13579 in the ID Text box and press [Enter]. The "Incorrect ID" message should appear in the Label control. Click the Print button.

g. Now type 13576 in the ID Text box and press [Enter]. The "Correct ID" message should appear in the Label control. Click the Print button.

h. Verify the check digits for the remaining numbers shown in Step 7-a.

i. Print the code.

discovery ▶ 8. a. Create the user interface shown in Figure 10-45.

TxtName

CmdAdd

CmdPrint

CmdExit

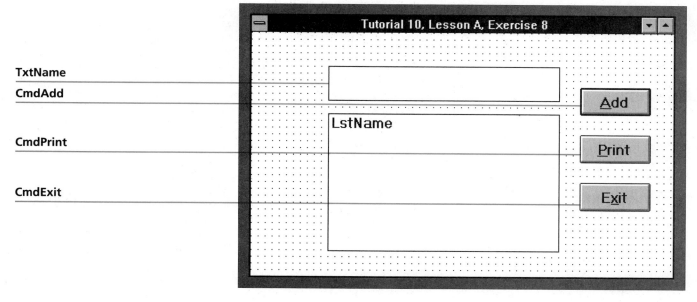

Figure 10-45

    b. Save the form and the project as t10lae8.

    c. Make the Add button the default Command button.

    d. Set the List box's Sorted property to True. Set its FontSize property to 12. Make the List box large enough to display five items.

    e. Code the Exit button so that it ends the application. Code the Print button so that it prints the form.

This application should allow you to enter a person's name, in first and last name order, into the TxtName Text box. When you choose the Add button, its Click event procedure should add the person's name to the List box and then clear the name from the TxtName Text box. When adding the name to the List box, add it in last name and first name order; the last name and first name should be separated by a comma and a space. In other words, if you enter John Dillon into the TxtName Text box and then choose the Add button, the Add button should add the name "Dillon, John" (without the quotes) to the List box, and then remove the name from the Text box.

    f. Code the Add button according to the above description of the application.

    g. Save and run the application. Enter the following names. (Be sure to choose the Add button after entering each name.)

John Dillon

Mary Sanders

Sue Reuss

Paul Jones

<enter your name>

    h. After entering the names, click the Print button. (Be sure that the five names appear in the printout.)

    i. Click the Exit button, then print the code.

discovery ▶ 9. In this exercise you will see the difference between passing arguments by reference and by value.

    a. Open the t10_ex9.mak project, which is in either the tut10\ver2 or tut10\ver3 directory on your Student Disk. Click the View Form button to view the user interface, which contains a Label control and three Command buttons (Display, Print, and Exit).

    b. Print the existing code.

Notice that the CmdDisplay_Click procedure declares a local Integer variable named Number, to which it assigns the number 10. The procedure then calls the DoubleNumber user-defined procedure and passes it the Number variable. After processing the instructions in the DoubleNumber procedure, the program returns to the CmdDisplay_Click procedure, where the value in the Number variable is displayed in the LblNumber control. Notice that the DoubleNumber procedure receives an Integer variable named X. (Recall that the name of the receiving variable does not have to match the name of the passing variable.) The DoubleNumber procedure is receiving the variable by reference. That means that although the receiving variable's name is different from the passing variable's name, they both refer to the same location in the computer's memory. Passing a variable by reference gives the receiving procedure access to the variable in memory.

Let's see what it means to pass by reference.

    c. To see what it means to pass by reference, run (but don't save) the application. Click the Display button. The CmdDisplay_Click procedure calls the DoubleNumber procedure, passing it the Number variable, which contains the number 10. The DoubleNumber procedure multiplies the contents of the number variable—10—times 2, giving 20. The value in the Number variable is now 20. When control returns to the CmdDisplay_Click procedure, the number 20 is assigned to the LblNumber control on the form.

    d. Click the Print button, then click the Exit button.

Now let's see what it means to pass by value.

e. Open the DoubleNumber procedure. Change the sub statement to
Sub DoubleNumber (ByVal Number as Integer).
The ByVal keyword tells Visual Basic that the Number variable should be passed by value, and not by reference. That means that only the contents of the variable—in this case, the number 10—are passed. In other words, the DoubleNumber procedure is not given access to the Number variable in memory. Now let's see what effect that will have on the application.

f. To see what it means to pass by value, run (but don't save) the application. Click the Display button. The CmdDisplay_Click procedure calls the DoubleNumber procedure, passing it the contents of the Number variable—in other words, passing it the number 10. The DoubleNumber procedure multiplies 10 times 2, giving 20. The calculation has no effect on the contents of the Number variable because the DoubleNumber procedure does not have access to that variable in memory. When control returns to the CmdDisplay_Click procedure. The value in the Number variable is still 10, as the LblNumber control shows.

g. Click the Print button, then click the Exit button.

LESSON B

objectives

In this lesson you will learn how to:

- Synchronize the Drive, Directory, and File List box controls
- Use the Err, Error$, and MsgBox functions
- Use the On Error, Resume, and Error statements

Drive, Directory, and File List Boxes and Error Trapping

Creating an Open Dialog Box

In most applications that use files, you will want to give the user the ability to select the appropriate drive, directory, and filename from List boxes. Visual Basic has three controls for that purpose: the Drive List box, the Directory List box, and the File List box. Let's create an application that you can use to open a file by selecting the drive, directory, and filename from List boxes. Your Student Disk contains a partially completed Open dialog box application.

To begin completing the Open dialog box application:

1. Launch Visual Basic, if necessary, and open the **T10B_1.MAK** project, which is in either the tut10\ver2 or tut10\ver3 directory on your Student Disk.

2. **Save** the form and the project as **t10open**.

3. Click the **View Form button**, then maximize the form. The user interface appears on the screen, as shown in Figure 10-46. (The general Declarations section already contains the *Option Explicit* statement.)

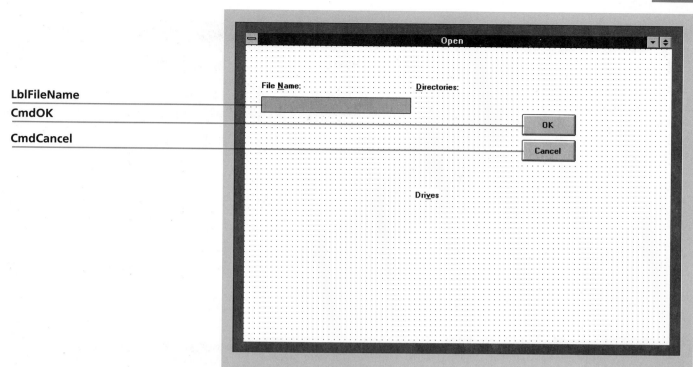

LblFileName

CmdOK

CmdCancel

Figure 10-46: Partially completed Open dialog box application

First, let's include a Drive List box on the form. The Drive List box will allow the user to select the drive from a drop-down list of drives.

4 Restore the form to its standard size, then double-click the **Drive List box tool** 🖭. A Drive List box control named Drive1 appears on the form. Set the following properties for the Drive1 control:

Left: **3840** Top: **3600** Width: **1935**

Next let's add a Directory List box to the form. The Directory List box will display the directories located on the drive that is selected in the Drive List box.

5 Double-click the **Directory List box tool** 🖭. A Directory List box control named Dir1 appears on the form. Set the following properties for the Dir1 control:

Height: **1830** Left: **3840** Top: **1200** Width: **1935**

Now let's put a File List box on the form. The File List box will list the filenames located in the current directory—the one selected in the Directory List box.

6 Double-click the **File List box tool** 🖭. A File List box control named File1 appears on the form. Set the following properties for the File1 control:

Height: **1980** Left: **840** Top: **1800** Width: **2295**

7 Maximize the form. The user interface appears, as shown in Figure 10-47. (The drive, directory, and filenames displayed in the List boxes will depend on the location of your version of Visual Basic; your screen may differ from the one shown in Figure 10-47.)

Dir1 List box

LblFileName

File List box

Drive1 List box

CmdCancel

CmdOK

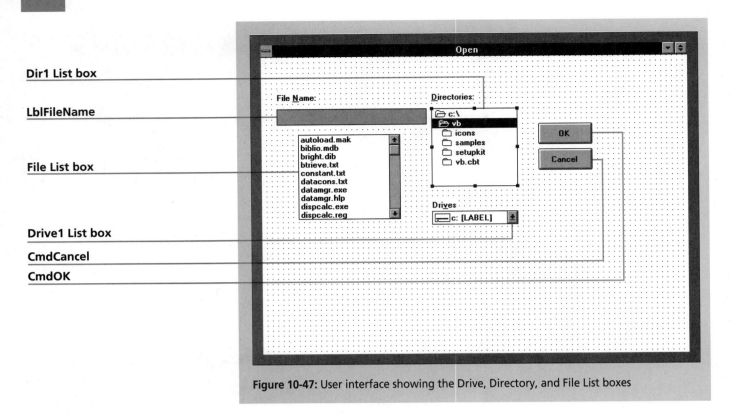

Figure 10-47: User interface showing the Drive, Directory, and File List boxes

Now that the three controls are on the form, the next step is to set their TabIndex properties. Recall that the TabIndex property determines the order in which a control receives the focus when the user is tabbing. In this application, you want the File List box to receive the focus first, followed by the Directory List box, the Drive List box, the OK button, and the Cancel button.

To set the TabIndex properties, then save and run the application:

1 Restore the form to its standard size, then set each control's TabIndex property as follows:

Control Name	TabIndex Property
File1	0
Dir1	1
Drive1	2
CmdOK	3
CmdCancel	4

2 **Save and run** the application. The focus—a dotted rectangle around the first filename—appears in the File List box. Press the [**Tab**] key five times to verify that the focus moves correctly.

3 Click the **down arrow button in the Drive List box**. A drop-down list of drives, which are valid for your system, opens.

4 Click a **different drive in the list**. The new drive letter appears in the Drive List box, but the contents of the Directory List box and the File List box do not change.

In the next section you will learn about the four properties that you will use to connect the Drive List box, Directory List box, File List box, and LblFileName control.

Properties of Drive, Directory, and File List Boxes

In order to synchronize the Drive List box, the Directory List box, the File List box, and the LblFileName control, you will need to learn four new properties: Drive, Path, Filename, and Pattern. The Drive property, which is applicable to the Drive List box only, stores the currently selected drive. When you click a drive in the Drive List box's drop-down list, the letter of the selected drive is stored in the control's Drive property. For example, if you click a: in the drop-down list, a: is stored in the Drive property.

The Path property, which is applicable to the Directory and File List boxes only, stores the current path as a string. The **path** is the designation of the location of files or directories on your disk. For example, "a:\tut8\ver3" is the path to the \ver3 subdirectory in the \tut8 directory on drive a:; "c:\vb\icons" is the path to the \icons subdirectory in the \vb directory on drive c:. When you click a directory in the Directory List box, or when you click a filename in the File List box, the path is stored in the control's Path property.

The FileName property is applicable to the File List box only. When you click a filename in the File List box, the filename is stored in the File List box's FileName property. If no filename is selected in the File List box, then the FileName property stores the null string ("").

The Pattern property is applicable to the File List box only; it stores a string that determines which filenames are displayed in the File List box at run time. The string (or pattern) can contain any characters that are valid for a filename, including the * and ? wildcard characters. (You learned about the * wildcard character in Tutorial 8. Recall that the * stands for one or more characters. The ? wildcard, on the other hand, stands for only one character.) The default Pattern property setting is "*.*", which means that the File List box will display all of the filenames contained in the current directory. If you want the File List box to display only files with the .dat extension, you would set the Pattern property to "*.dat". To display the Bud80.wk1 through Bud89.wk1 files, you would set the Pattern property to "Bud8?.wk1". You can also include multiple patterns in the Pattern property, as long as you separate each pattern with a semicolon (;). For example, to display files with the .txt and the .dat extension, you would set the Pattern property to "*.txt";"*.dat".

Figure 10-48 summarizes the Drive, Path, FileName, and Pattern properties.

Property	Purpose	Applicable to
Drive	Stores the currently selected drive	Drive List box
Path	Stores the current path	Directory and File List boxes
FileName	Stores the currently selected filename	File List box
Pattern	Stores a string that determines which filenames are displayed in the File List box	File List box

Figure 10-48: Summary of the Drive, Path, FileName, and Pattern properties

Now that you know the purpose of the four properties, you can use them to synchronize the three List boxes and the Label control in the Open dialog box application.

Synchronizing the Drive, Directory, and File List Boxes and the Label Control

To synchronize the three List boxes and the Label control, you first connect the Drive List box to the Directory List box, then connect the Directory List box to the File List box, and then connect the File List box to the Label control, as illustrated in Figure 10-49.

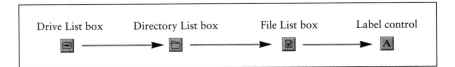

Drive List box   Directory List box   File List box   Label control

Figure 10-49: Illustration of connection between the List boxes and the Label control

When the user selects a new drive from the Drive List box, the contents of the Directory List box should change to show the directories contained on the currently selected drive. When the contents of the Directory List box changes, the contents of the File List box should change to show the filenames contained in the currently selected directory. If the user selects a filename from the File List box, the LblFileName control should change to display the currently selected file. You can synchronize the four controls by coding the Change event procedure of the Drive List box, the Change event procedure of the Directory List box, and the Click event procedure of the File List box.

To synchronize the List boxes and the Label control, then save and run the application:

1   Double-click the **Drive List box**. The Drive1_Change procedure, which occurs when the user selects a drive in the Drive List box, appears.

When a user selects a new drive from the Drive List box, the directories listed in the Directory List box should change to display the directories on the new drive. To synchronize the two List boxes in this manner, you simply assign the Drive List box's Drive property to the Directory List box's Path property. Recall that the Drive property stores the currently selected drive and the Path property stores the currently selected path.

2   Press [Tab], then type **Dir1.Path = Drive1.Drive** and press [Enter]. This instruction will change the contents of the Directory List box to reflect the directories contained on the currently selected drive.

When the contents of the Directory List box change, the contents of the File List box will need to change; the File List box should show the names of the files in the currently selected directory. To synchronize the Directory List box and the File List box in this manner, you simply assign the Directory List box's Path property to the File List box's Path property.

3   Click the **down arrow in the Code window's Object box**, then click **Dir1** in the drop-down list. The Dir1_Change procedure appears. Press [Tab], then type **File1.Path = Dir1.Path** and press [Enter]. This instruction will change the contents of the File List box to reflect the filenames contained in the currently selected directory.

Now that the List boxes are synchronized, you can connect the LblFileName control to the File1 List box. When the user clicks a filename in the File1 List box, you want both the path and name of the currently selected file to appear in the LblFileName control. Therefore, you will need to place the appropriate instruction in the File1 control's Click event procedure.

4   Click the **down arrow in the Code window's Object box**, then click **File1** in the drop-down list. The File1_Click procedure appears.

Recall that when the user clicks a filename in the File List box, the file's name is stored in the control's FileName property and its path is stored in the control's Path property. To display both the path and the filename in the LblFileName control, you will need to concatenate the path to the filename.

5   Press [Tab], then type **LblFileName.Caption = File1.Path & File1.FileName** and press [Enter]. When the user selects a filename from the File list box, this instruction will display the concatenated path and filename in the Label control.

Let's see how the application works so far.

6   Close the Code window, then **save and run** the application. Be sure your Student Disk is in drive A: (or drive B:). Click the **down arrow in the Drive List box**, then click the **drive containing your Student Disk**.

First let's select a file from the root directory on your Student Disk.

7   Depending on the location of your Student Disk, double-click either **a:** or **b:** in the Directory List box, then click **file10.txt** in the File List box. A:\file10.txt (or b:\file10.txt) appears in the LblFileName control, as shown in Figure 10-50.

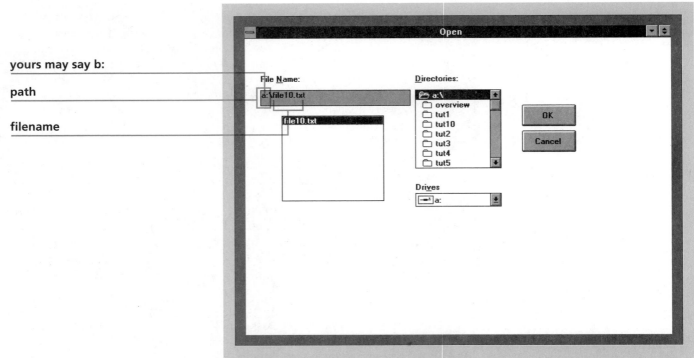

yours may say b:

path

filename

Figure 10-50: Filename (located in root directory) displayed in Label control

Now let's select a file from a subdirectory on your Student Disk.

8 Double-click **tut10** in the Directory List box. Depending on your version of Visual Basic, double-click either **ver2** or **ver3** in the Directory List box, then click **file10.txt** in the File Name List box. A:\tut10\ver3file10.txt (yours may say b: and/or ver2) appears in the LblFileName control, as shown in Figure 10-51.

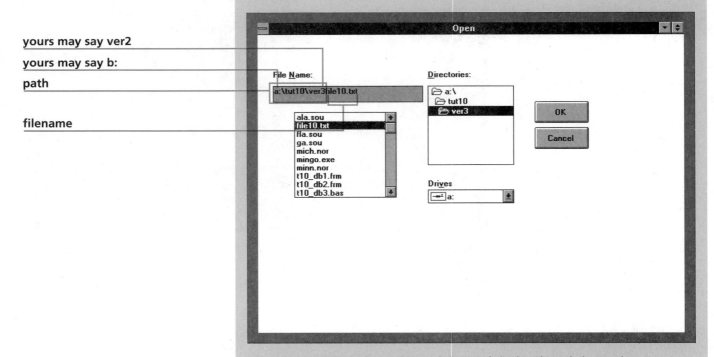

yours may say ver2

yours may say b:

path

filename

Figure 10-51: Filename (located in a subdirectory) displayed in Label control

Now compare the contents of the LblFileName control shown in Figure 10-50 with its contents shown in Figure 10-51. Notice that when you select a file located in the root directory (Figure 10-50), the path recorded in the Path property includes the backslash (\) that separates the path (a:\) from the filename (file10.txt). When you select a file located in a subdirectory (Figure 10-51), however, the path recorded in the Path property does not include the backslash that separates the path (a:\tut10\ver3) from the filename (file10.txt). Without the backslash separator, the computer will not know where the path ends and the filename begins. Let's stop the application and correct this problem.

9 Click the **Cancel button**. Visual Basic returns to the design screen.

You can correct the problem of the missing backslash separator by including a selection structure in the File1_Click procedure. The selection structure will use the Right$ function, which you learned in Lesson A, to examine the last character in the path. (Recall that the path is stored in the File List box's Path property.) If the last character is a \, then the *LblFileName.Caption = File1.Path & File1.FileName* instruction, which is currently in the File1_Click event procedure, will be processed; otherwise, the *LblFileName.Caption = File1.Path & "\" & File1.FileName* instruction, which concatenates a "\" to the path and the filename, will be processed.

To modify the File1_Click event procedure, then save and run the application:

1 Double-click the **File1 List box**, then maximize the Code window. Change the File1_Click procedure as shown in Figure 10-52.

will display a file in the root directory

will display a file in a subdirectory

```
                              T10OPEN.FRM
Object: File1              ▼   Proc: Click              ▼

Sub File1_Click ()
    If Right$(File1.Path, 1) = "\" Then
        LblFileName.Caption = File1.Path & File1.FileName
    Else            'Concatenate backslash to path and filename
        LblFileName.Caption = File1.Path & "\" & File1.FileName
    End If

End Sub
```

Figure 10-52: Modified code in the File1 Click event procedure

2 Close the Code window, then **save and run** the application. In the Drive List box, click **the drive containing your Student Disk**. Either the tut10\ver2 or the tut10\ver3 directory should be open. Click **file10.txt** in the File Name List box. A:\tut10\ver3\file10.txt (yours may say b: and/or ver2) appears in the LblFileName control. Notice that a backslash separator now appears between the path and the filename.

3 Click the **Cancel button**. Visual Basic returns to the design screen.

Figure 10-53 summarizes the instructions needed to synchronize the List boxes and the Label control.

Drive List box Change procedure   **Directory List box Change procedure**

```
Dir1.Path = Drive1.Drive                      File1.Path = Dir1.Path
```

File List box Click procedure

```
If Right$(File1.Path, 1) = "\" Then

    LblFileName.Caption = File1.Path & File1.FileName

Else

    LblFileName.Caption = File1.Path & "\" & File1.FileName

End If
```

Figure 10-53: Instructions needed to synchronize the List boxes and the Label control

You have now finished connecting the List boxes and the LblFileName control. In the next section you will learn about error trapping, which you will include in the Open dialog box application.

Error Trapping

In Lesson A you learned how to prevent the user's entry errors from crashing the application. Unfortunately, errors other than entry errors can make an application crash. Forgetting to put a disk in the drive, trying to save a file to a disk that is full, and forgetting to turn the printer on are some examples of non-entry errors that can occur while an application is running.

If a run-time error occurs, Visual Basic will usually display an error message on the screen, then the application will "crash." You can prevent the application from crashing by including code that both intercepts the error and instructs the application on how to handle the error without crashing. The process of intercepting and handling a run-time error is called **error trapping**. The set of instructions that tells the application how to handle the error is called the **error-handling routine**, or **error handler**.

When an error occurs, the error handling routine can either try to remedy the problem (for example, tell the user to turn the printer on) or, if the problem can't be remedied (for example, the disk drive is not working), allow the user to exit the application in a user-friendly manner. Before learning how to trap errors and create an error-handling routine, let's look at the types of errors that Visual Basic allows you to trap.

To view a listing of trappable errors:

1 Click **Help**, then click **Contents**. When the Visual Basic Help screen appears, click **Trappable Errors**, then maximize the Trappable Errors Help screen. The Help screen appears, as shown in Figure 10-54.

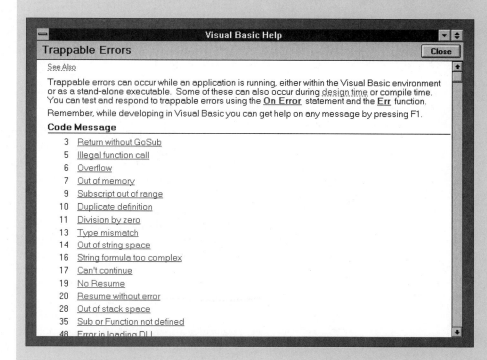

Figure 10-54: Trappable Errors Help screen

Notice that each error is identified by a code and a message (its name).

2 Scroll the Help screen until error codes 68 through 71 appear.

In the current application, you will trap error 68 (Device unavailable) and error 71 (Disk not ready).

3 Click **Device unavailable** (error 68) in the Help screen. A Help screen pertaining to error code 68 appears. Notice that the error occurs when a device either is not online or doesn't exist.

4 Use the Control menu box to close the "Device unavailable" Help screen.

5 Click **Disk not ready** (error 71) in the Help screen. A Help screen pertaining to error code 71 appears. Notice that the error occurs when there is no disk in the drive or when the drive door is open.

6 Use the control menu box to close the "Disk not ready" Help screen.

7 Scroll through the remaining error codes, then close any open Help screens.

In the next section you will learn about two functions (Err and Error$) and two statements (On Error and Resume). You will also learn how to use the MsgBox function. (Recall that you learned about the MsgBox statement in Tutorial 8). You will use these functions and statements to include error trapping in the Open dialog box application.

The Err Function and the Error$ Function

When an error occurs, Visual Basic assigns the error's code to the Err function; it assigns the error's message to the Error$ function. For example, if the application attempts to divide an expression by zero, Visual Basic assigns the number 11 (the error code corresponding to a "Division by zero" error) to the Err function and it assigns the string "Division by zero" (without the quotes) to the Error$ function.

The On Error Statement

The On Error statement turns the error trapping process on. The syntax of the On Error statement is **On Error GoTo** *linelabel*, where *linelabel* is a label that identifies the position of the procedure's error handler—the set of instructions that will prevent the application from "crashing" due to an error.

For the proper error trapping to occur, the On Error statement must be processed before the error occurs. Therefore, it is recommended that you place the On Error statement at the beginning of the procedure in which the errors you want to trap may occur. The On Error statement alerts Visual Basic to watch for any run-time errors in the code listed below the On Error statement. If an error occurs, the On Error statement will send program control to the error-handling routine to determine how to handle the error. How the error is handled will depend on the type of error that occurred. Recall that the type of error is stored in both the Err and Error$ functions; the Err function stores the error's code, and the Error$ function stores the error's name.

A procedure that includes error trapping will usually follow the structure shown in Figure 10-55.

error handler

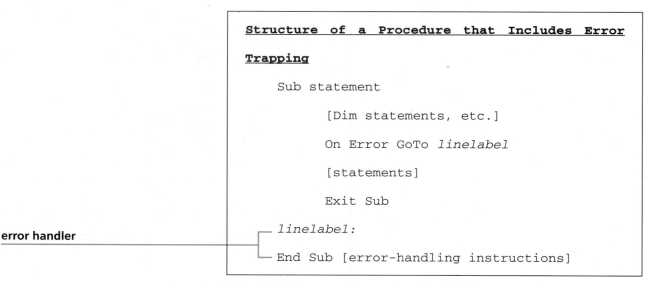

```
Structure of a Procedure that Includes Error
Trapping

    Sub statement

        [Dim statements, etc.]

        On Error GoTo linelabel

        [statements]

        Exit Sub

    linelabel:

    End Sub [error-handling instructions]
```

Figure 10-55: Structure of a procedure that includes error trapping

Notice the *Exit Sub* statement, which is placed ahead of the error handler in the code. The *Exit Sub* statement prevents the error-handling routine from being processed when no error has occurred. Also notice that *linelabel* located immediately above the error-handling instructions has a colon at the end, but *linelabel* used in the On Error statement does not.

The Resume Statement

You use the Resume statement, whose syntax is **Resume [Next | *linelabel*]**, to resume program execution after the error-handling routine is finished. (The | character in the syntax means either/or. In other words, you can choose either Next or *linelabel*, but not both.) Resume, by itself, causes program execution to resume with the statement that caused the error. For example, let's assume that, when attempting to process a print instruction, an application determines that the printer is not online. When the On Error statement traps this error, it sends program control to the error handler. The error handler instructions can prompt the user to turn the printer on, wait until he or she does, and then use the Resume statement to resume program execution with the print instruction that caused the error.

The *Resume Next* instruction, on the other hand, causes program execution to resume with the statement immediately following the one that caused the error. If, for example, an instruction causes an "Internal error" (error code 51), the error handler instructions can prompt the user to copy the error message down on paper, wait for the user to do so, and then use the Resume Next statement to resume program execution with the instruction immediately following the one that caused the error.

You use Resume *linelabel* in cases where the application cannot resume execution either with the instruction that caused the error or with the one immediately below that instruction. Resume *linelabel* allows the error handler to resume program execution at *linelabel*, which is a label that identifies an instruction located somewhere in the procedure.

Figure 10-56 summarizes the Err and Error$ functions and the On Error and Resume statements.

Function	Purpose
Err	Stores the error's code.
Error$	Stores the error's message.
Statement	**Purpose**
On Error	Turns the error trapping process on. Its syntax is **On Error GoTo** *linelabel*.
Resume	Allows the error handler to resume program execution either with the statement that caused the error, with the statement immediately following the one that caused the error, or with another statement in the program. Its syntax is **Resume** [**Next**	*linelabel*].

Figure 10-56: Summary of the Err and Error$ functions and the On Error and Resume statements

Before including these functions and statements in the current application, you will learn about the MsgBox function.

Using the MsgBox Function

Like the MsgBox statement, which you learned about in Tutorial 8, the MsgBox function displays one of Visual Basic's predefined dialog boxes and waits for the user to choose a button. Unlike the MsgBox statement, however, the MsgBox function returns a value that indicates which button the user chose. When a run-time error occurs in an application, you can use the MsgBox function to communicate interactively with the user. For example, you can use the MsgBox function to prompt the user to turn the printer on, and then have him or her click the OK button to let the application know when the printer is turned on.

The syntax of the MsgBox function is **MsgBox**(*msg*[,[*type*][,*title*]]) where *msg* is the string expression you want to appear in the dialog box. *Type* is an optional numeric expression that specifies the number and types of buttons to display, the icon style to use, the identity of the default button, and the modality. *Title* is a string expression displayed in the title bar of the dialog box. To learn more about this function, let's display its Help screen.

To view the Help screen on the MsgBox function/statement:

1   Click **Help**, then click **Search for Help On...** (**Search...** in version 2). Type **ms** in the Text box. Visual Basic highlights the MsgBox topic in the List box. Click the **Show Topics button**, then click the **Go To button**. The Help screen appears.

Let's look more closely at the *type*. According to the Help screen, the *type* "is the sum of values specifying the number and type of buttons to display, the icon style to use, the identity of the default button, and the modality." Let's see how this works.

2   Scroll the Help screen as shown in Figure 10-57.

number and types of buttons

icon style

default button

modality (not shown)

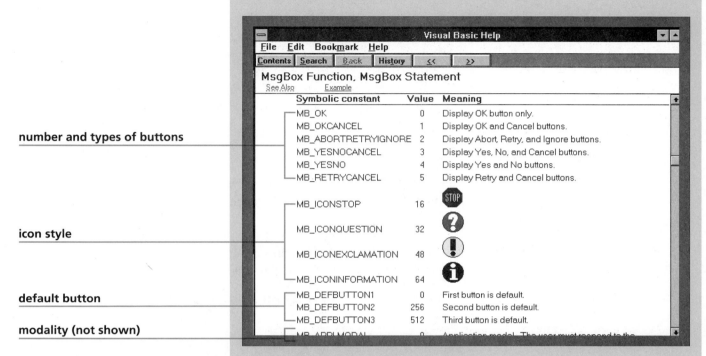

Figure 10-57: MsgBox Function, MsgBox Statement Help screen

Listed below the *type* definition are four groups of numbers. The first group, which consists of the numbers 0 through 5, controls the number and types of buttons displayed in the dialog box. The second group of numbers— 16, 32, 48, and 64—controls the style of the icon displayed in the dialog box. (The second group actually contains another number, 0, which means that no icons will appear in the dialog box.) The third group of numbers—0, 256, and 512—identifies the default button. (The default button is the button that is chosen automatically when the user presses the Enter key.) The fourth group of numbers—0 and 4096—controls the dialog box's modality, which can be either application modal or system modal. **Application modal**, the default modality, means that the user must respond to the message in the dialog box before he or she can continue working in the current application. **System modal** means that all applications are suspended until the user responds to the message in the dialog box. The *type* is the sum of one of the numbers from each group. (Remember, the second group also contains a 0, which means that no icon is displayed in the dialog box.)

The default value for *type* is 0, which means that the dialog box will display an OK button only; it will not contain an icon. The OK button will be the default button and the dialog box will be application modal. Now let's say that you want the dialog box to display Yes and No buttons along with the question mark icon. Additionally, you want the No button to be the default button, and you want the dialog box to be application modal. To display a dialog box matching that description, you would need to enter the number 292 as the *type*. Figure 10-58 shows how the 292 was calculated. (Remember, the *type* is the sum of one of the numbers from each group.)

Dialog box should include:	Value
Yes and No buttons	4
Question mark icon	32
Second button is the default	256
Application modal	<u>0</u>
	292

Figure 10-58: Calculation of *type* in MsgBox function

Now here's one for you to try: Let's say that you want the Abort, Retry, and Ignore buttons, with the stop sign icon, the second button as the default, and system modal. What *type* would you enter? You should get a *type* of 4370 (2 + 16 + 256 + 4096).

Now let's continue viewing the MsgBox function's Help screen.

To continue viewing the Help screen:

1 Scroll the Help screen as shown in Figure 10-59.

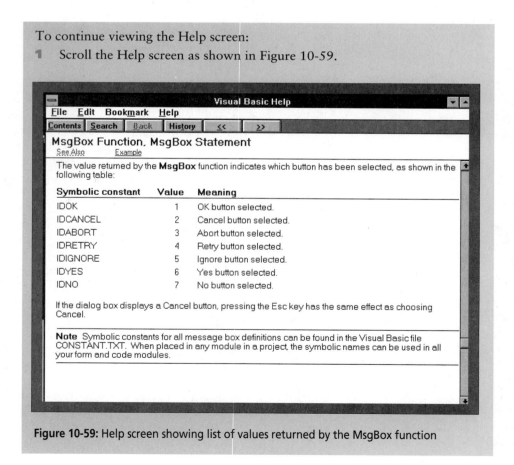

Figure 10-59: Help screen showing list of values returned by the MsgBox function

The Help screen lists the values returned by the MsgBox function. The returned value indicates which button the user selected in the dialog box. For example, if the Yes button was selected, the MsgBox function returns the number 6.

2   Close the Help screen. Visual Basic returns to the design screen.

Now that you know the purpose of the Err and Error$ functions, the On Error and Resume statements, and the MsgBox function, you can include error trapping in the Open dialog box application.

Including Error Trapping in the Open Dialog Box Application

Recall that the Open dialog box application allows the user to select a drive from the Drive List box on the form. If the drive the user selects is not available, or if a disk is not in the drive, or if the drive door is open, then the application will crash. You can prevent the application from crashing when any of these errors occur by trapping error code 68 (Device unavailable) and error code 71 (Disk not ready). Because changing the drive in the Drive1 control is the action that could cause these errors to occur, you will include the error trapping code in the Drive1_Change procedure.

To include error trapping in the Drive1_Change procedure:

1   Double-click the **Drive1 List box**, then maximize the Code window. The Drive1_Change procedure appears. Press [**Enter**] to insert a blank line below the *Sub* statement, then press the [**Up arrow**] on the keyboard to position the blinking insertion point above the *Dir1.Path = Drive1.Drive* instruction.

If an error occurs in this procedure, you will use the MsgBox function to both display a message to the user and wait for a response. You will record the message in a String variable named Message, and you will record the user's response in an Integer variable named Answer. (Recall that the MsgBox function returns a number that indicates which button the user selected.)

2   Type **dim Message as string, Answer as integer** and press [**Enter**].

You will now create constants for the two errors that the procedure will trap.

3   Type **Const DEVICE_UNAVAILABLE = 68, DISK_NOT_READY = 71** and press [**Enter**]. Recall that it is standard practice to capitalize the constants so they are easier to recognize in the code. By creating constants to represent the errors, you will be able to quickly identify which errors the procedure will trap.

Let's also create constants for the buttons that will be displayed in the MsgBox function's dialog box. By creating constants to represent the buttons, you will be able to quickly identify which buttons the MsgBox function will display.

4   Type **Const OK_BUTTON = 0, YES_NO_BUTTONS = 4** and press [**Enter**].

Let's also create constants for the icons that will be displayed in the MsgBox function's dialog box.

5   Type **Const STOPSIGN = 16, EXCLAMATION = 48** and press [**Enter**].

Last, let's create a constant for the user's Yes response. Recall that when the user clicks the Yes button, the MsgBox function returns the number 6. (Refer to Figure 10-59.)

6   Type **Const YES = 6** and press [**Enter**].

You can now enter the On Error statement, which must be entered before the error you are trapping can occur. Recall that the syntax of the On Error statement is **On Error GoTo** *linelabel*, where *linelabel* is the location of the error handler in the procedure. You will use the *linelabel*, ErrHandler.

7   Type **on error goto ErrHandler**. (Don't type the period.)

Recall that you need to enter an *Exit Sub* statement immediately before the error handler code. (Refer to Figure 10-55 for the structure of a procedure that contains error trapping.) The *Exit Sub* statement prevents the error-handling routine from being processed when no error has occurred.

8   Click in the **line below the** *Dir1.Path = Drive1.Drive* **instruction**, then type **exit sub** and press [**Enter**] two times. Compare your code with the code shown in Figure 10-60. Make any necessary corrections before continuing.

location of error-handling routine

prevents error-handling routine from being processed when no error has occurred

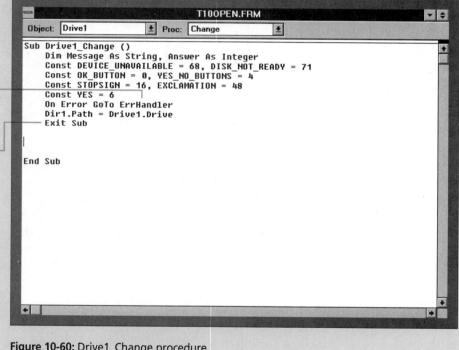

Figure 10-60: Drive1_Change procedure

You will enter the error-handling routine next. First you need to enter the *linelabel* that identifies the location of the error handler.

To enter the error handler code:

1. Type **ErrHandler:** and press [**Enter**]. Be sure to type the colon (:) after the word ErrHandler.

   You can use the Case structure to determine the error code, which Visual Basic stores in the Err function, and then take the appropriate action.

2. Press [**Tab**], then type **select case Err** and press [**Enter**].

   First list the two errors that you are trying to trap.

3. Press [**Tab**], then type **case DEVICE_UNAVAILABLE, DISK_NOT_READY** and press [**Enter**].

   If either of these errors occurs, you will use the MsgBox function to display a message that alerts the user to check the disk. The message will also ask the user if he or she wants to try the disk drive again.

4. Press [**Tab**], then type **Message = "Please check the disk. Try again?"** and press [**Enter**].

5. Type **Answer = msgbox(Message, YES_NO_BUTTONS + EXCLAMATION, "")** and press [**Enter**]. This MsgBox function will display Yes and No buttons, an exclamation point icon, and an empty title bar.

   If the user clicks the Yes button, he or she wants the application to try the disk drive again, so you will want the application to resume with the statement that caused the error—the *Dir1.Path = Drive1.Drive* instruction.

6. Type **If Answer = YES Then** and press [**Enter**].

7. Press [**Tab**], then type **Resume** and press [**Enter**].

   If the user clicks the No button, then you want to resume with the *Exit Sub* statement, which is located immediately below the *Dir1.Path = Drive1.Drive* instruction—the instruction that caused the error.

8. Press [**Backspace**] to cancel one indentation, then type **else** and press [**Enter**].

9. Press [**Tab**], then type **Resume Next** and press [**Enter**].

10. Press [**Backspace**] to cancel the indentation, then type **End If** and press [**Enter**].

In most applications, you cannot always determine every type of error that may occur. You should, therefore, include instructions in the error handler to handle any unexpected errors. In this application, for example, you will include a *Case Else* section to handle errors other than the "Device unavailable" or the "Disk not ready" errors. The *Case Else* instructions will display the unexpected error's message in a dialog box and request that the user copy the message down on paper so that it can be given to the programmer for resolution. After the user copies the message, the *Case Else* instructions will return the user to the form.

To continue coding the error handling routine:

1   Enter the code, including the documentation, shown in Figure 10-61.

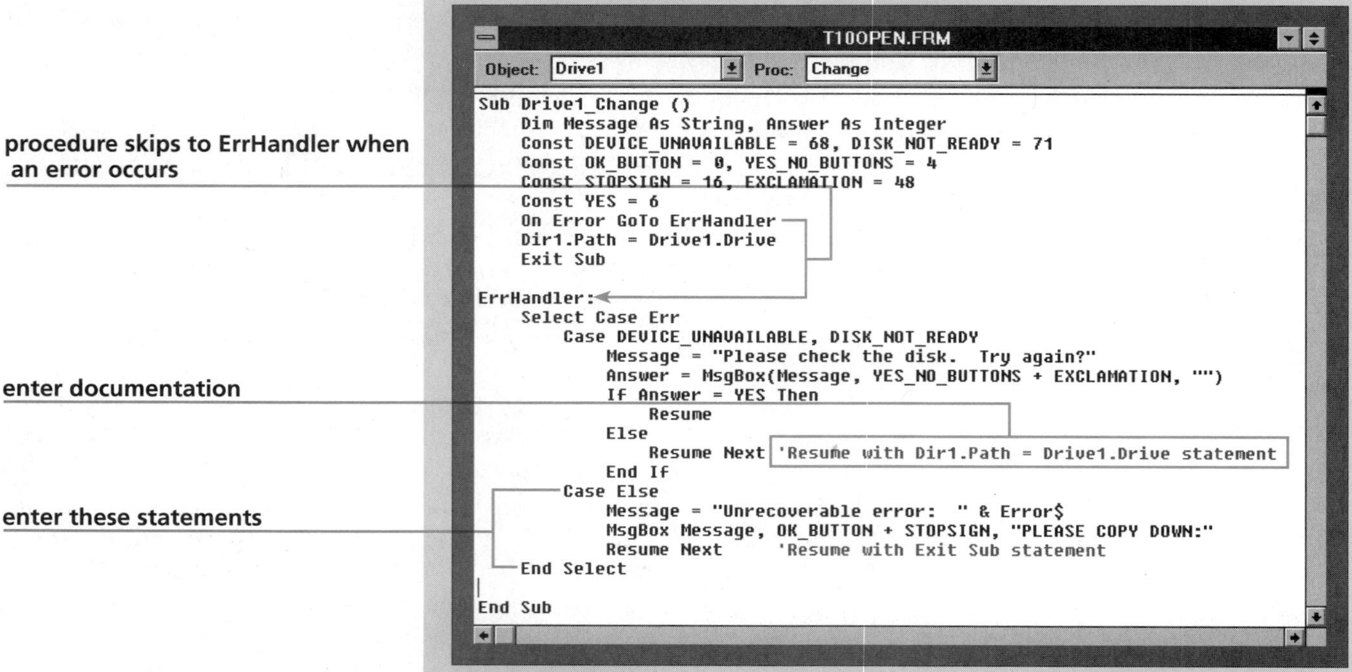

procedure skips to ErrHandler when an error occurs

enter documentation

enter these statements

```
                          T10OPEN.FRM
Object: Drive1          ±   Proc: Change          ±

Sub Drive1_Change ()
    Dim Message As String, Answer As Integer
    Const DEVICE_UNAVAILABLE = 68, DISK_NOT_READY = 71
    Const OK_BUTTON = 0, YES_NO_BUTTONS = 4
    Const STOPSIGN = 16, EXCLAMATION = 48
    Const YES = 6
    On Error GoTo ErrHandler
    Dir1.Path = Drive1.Drive
    Exit Sub

ErrHandler:
    Select Case Err
        Case DEVICE_UNAVAILABLE, DISK_NOT_READY
            Message = "Please check the disk.  Try again?"
            Answer = MsgBox(Message, YES_NO_BUTTONS + EXCLAMATION, "")
            If Answer = YES Then
                Resume
            Else
                Resume Next   'Resume with Dir1.Path = Drive1.Drive statement
            End If
        Case Else
            Message = "Unrecoverable error:  " & Error$
            MsgBox Message, OK_BUTTON + STOPSIGN, "PLEASE COPY DOWN:"
            Resume Next     'Resume with Exit Sub statement
    End Select

End Sub
```

Figure 10-61: Drive1_Change procedure containing error-trapping code

2   Compare your code with the code shown in Figure 10-61. Make any necessary corrections before continuing.

Now let's try the application.

3   Close the Code window, then **save** and **run** the application.

4   Remove your Student Disk from the drive. Click the **down arrow button in the Drive List box**, then click the **drive that usually contains your Student Disk**. The dialog box shown in Figure 10-62 appears.

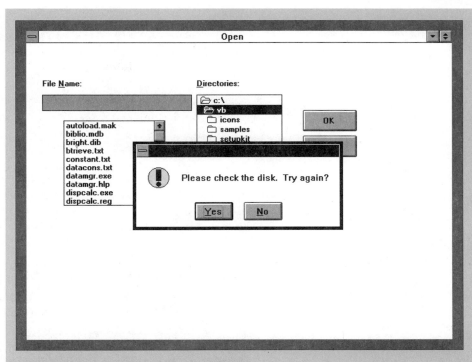

Figure 10-62: Message displayed in MsgBox function's dialog box

5   Click the **No button** to remove the message. The screen appears, as shown as Figure 10-63.

incorrect drive

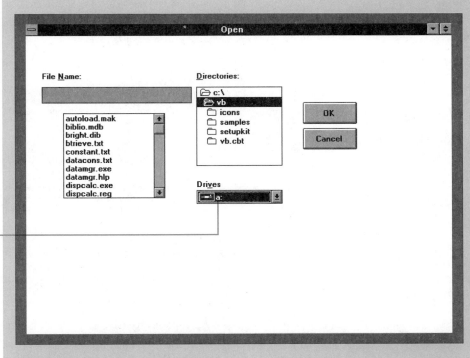

Figure 10-63: User interface showing error in Drive List box

Notice that the Drive List box shows, incorrectly, the letter of the drive that you were not able to access. The Directory and File List boxes, however, still display the directories and filenames located on the hard drive (or the network drive). The hard drive (or network drive) was the drive that was current before the error occurred. To fix this problem, you will need to modify the code in the Drive1_Change procedure.

6 Put your Student Disk in the appropriate drive, then click the **Cancel button**. Visual Basic returns to the design screen.

If an error occurs when the application is reading the drive, and the user does not want to try reading the drive again, the Drive List box should display the same drive as the one shown in the Directory List box. Let's modify the code in the Drive1_Change procedure.

To modify the code in the Drive1_Change procedure:

1 Double-click the **Drive List box**, then maximize the Code window. The Drive1_Change procedure appears.

2 Enter the one line of code shown in Figure 10-64.

enter this instruction

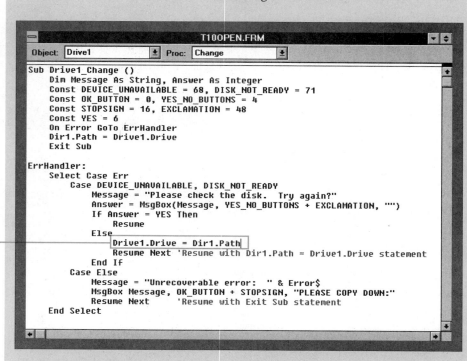

```
                          T10OPEN.FRM
Object: Drive1              ±  Proc: Change            ±

Sub Drive1_Change ()
    Dim Message As String, Answer As Integer
    Const DEVICE_UNAVAILABLE = 68, DISK_NOT_READY = 71
    Const OK_BUTTON = 0, YES_NO_BUTTONS = 4
    Const STOPSIGN = 16, EXCLAMATION = 48
    Const YES = 6
    On Error GoTo ErrHandler
    Dir1.Path = Drive1.Drive
    Exit Sub

ErrHandler:
    Select Case Err
        Case DEVICE_UNAVAILABLE, DISK_NOT_READY
            Message = "Please check the disk.  Try again?"
            Answer = MsgBox(Message, YES_NO_BUTTONS + EXCLAMATION, "")
            If Answer = YES Then
                Resume
            Else
                Drive1.Drive = Dir1.Path
                Resume Next 'Resume with Dir1.Path = Drive1.Drive statement
            End If
        Case Else
            Message = "Unrecoverable error:  " & Error$
            MsgBox Message, OK_BUTTON + STOPSIGN, "PLEASE COPY DOWN:"
            Resume Next      'Resume with Exit Sub statement
    End Select
```

Figure 10-64: Modified Drive1_Change procedure

This instruction tells the Change procedure to assign the Directory List box's Path property to the Drive List box's Drive property.

3 Close the Code window, then **save and run** the application. Take your Student Disk out of the drive, click the **down arrow button in the Drive List box**, then click the **drive that usually contains your Student Disk**. When the dialog box appears, click the **No button**. The Drive List box

now reflects the correct drive—the one that was current before the error occurred.

Now let's test the Yes button in the dialog box.

4 With your Student Disk still out of the drive, click the **down arrow button in the Drive List box**, then click the **drive that usually contains your Student Disk.** When the dialog box appears, put your Student Disk in the appropriate drive, then click the **Yes button.** The Drive, Directory, and File List boxes now display the drive, directory, and filenames pertaining to your Student Disk.

5 Click the **Cancel button** to end the application.

You still need to test the *Case Else* section of the error handler. Recall that that section handles any unexpected errors. In order to test the *Case Else* instructions, you will need to learn how to simulate an error.

The Error Statement

You can use the Error statement to simulate the occurrence of any error. The syntax of the Error statement is **Error** *errorcode*, where *errorcode* is one of Visual Basic's error codes. (You can also define your own error code. See the Error statement's Help screen.) To test the instructions in the *Case Else* section of the error handler, you will simulate a code 57 (Device I/O error) error.

To simulate the occurrence of an error:

1 Double-click the **Drive List box**, then maximize the Code window. The Drive1_Change procedure appears.

2 Enter the one line of code shown in Figure 10-65.

enter this line of code to generate an error 57

```
                          T100OPEN.FRM
Object: Drive1             Proc: Change

Sub Drive1_Change ()
    Dim Message As String, Answer As Integer
    Const DEVICE_UNAVAILABLE = 68, DISK_NOT_READY = 71
    Const OK_BUTTON = 0, YES_NO_BUTTONS = 4
    Const STOPSIGN = 16, EXCLAMATION = 48
    Const YES = 6
    On Error GoTo ErrHandler
    error 57
    Dir1.Path = Drive1.Drive
    Exit Sub

ErrHandler:
    Select Case Err
        Case DEVICE_UNAVAILABLE, DISK_NOT_READY
            Message = "Please check the disk.  Try again?"
            Answer = MsgBox(Message, YES_NO_BUTTONS + EXCLAMATION, "")
            If Answer = YES Then
                Resume
            Else
                Drive1.Drive = Dir1.Path
                Resume Next 'Resume with Dir1.Path = Drive1.Drive statement
            End If
        Case Else
            Message = "Unrecoverable error:  " & Error$
            MsgBox Message, OK_BUTTON + STOPSIGN, "PLEASE COPY DOWN:"
            Resume Next      'Resume with Exit Sub statement
    End Select
```

Figure 10-65: Error statement in the Drive1_Change procedure

3   Close the Code window, then **save and run** the application. Click the **down arrow button in the Drives box**, then click the **letter corresponding to the location of your Student Disk**. The screen should look like Figure 10-66.

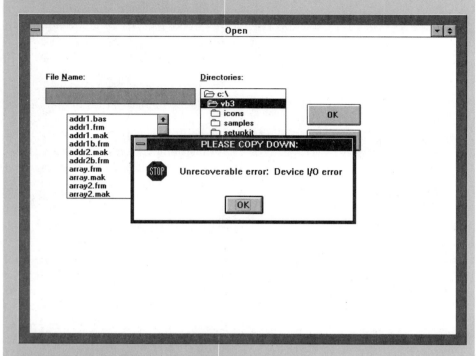

Figure 10-66: MsgBox statement's dialog box

4   Click the **OK button** to remove the error message. Instead of the application ending abruptly, it returns the user to the form, where he or she can click the Cancel button to exit the application.

5   Click the **Cancel button**. Visual Basic returns to the design screen.

Before ending Lesson B, you will remove the *Error 57* instruction from the Code window.

6   Double-click the **Drive List box**. The Drive1_Change procedure appears. Remove the *Error 57* instruction, then close the Code window and **save** the application.

You have now completed Lesson B. In Lesson C, you will complete the Open dialog box application. For now, however, you can either take a break or complete the questions and exercises at the end of the lesson.

S U M M A R Y

To allow the user to select a drive, directory, and filename from a List box:

■   Use the Drive List box tool, the Directory List box tool, and the File List box tool.

To synchronize the Drive, Directory, and File List boxes:

■ Code the Change procedure of both the Drive List box and the Directory List box. For example, assuming that the Drive List box is named Drive1, the Directory List box is named Dir1, and the File List box is named File1, you would enter the *Dir1.Path = Drive1.Drive* instruction in the Drive1_Change procedure and the *File1.Path = Dir1.Path* instruction in the Dir1_Change procedure.

To display the path and name of the file that is currently selected in the File List box:

■ Code the File List box's Click event procedure. Be sure to include a selection structure that will check if the last character in the path is a \. If it's not, you will need to concatenate the \ between the path and the filename.

To determine an error's name and error code:

■ Use the Err function to determine the error code. Use the Error$ to determine the error's name.

To turn error trapping on:

■ Use the On Error statement. Its syntax is **On Error GoTo** *linelabel*, where *linelabel* is a label that identifies the location of the error-handling routine (error handler) in the procedure.

To resume program execution after an error has occurred:

■ Use the Resume statement. Its syntax is **Resume [Next |** *linelabel***]**. (The | character means either/or; you can select either Next or *linelabel*, but not both.)
■ Resume, by itself, causes program execution to resume with the statement that caused the error. Resume Next causes program execution to resume with the statement immediately following the one that caused the error. Resume *linelabel* causes program execution to resume with the statement identified by *linelabel*.

To add error trapping to a procedure:

■ Follow the structure below:
    Sub statement
        [Dim statements, etc.]
        On Error GoTo *linelabel*
        [statements]
        Exit Sub

    linelabel:
        [error-handling instructions]
    End Sub

To display a dialog box that returns the user's response:

■ Use the MsgBox function. Its syntax is **MsgBox(***msg***[,[***type***][,***title***]])**. *Msg* is the string expression you want to appear in the dialog box. *Type* is an optional numeric expression that specifies the number and types of buttons to display, the icon style to use, the identity of the default button, and the modality. *Title* is a string expression displayed in the title bar of the dialog box.

To simulate a run-time error:

■   Use the Error statement. Its syntax is **Error** *errorcode*, where *errorcode* is either a Visual Basic error code or a user-defined error code.

Q U E S T I O N S

1. This List box control allows the user to select the drive from a drop-down list.
    a. Directory
    b. Disk
    c. Drive
    d. File
    e. Path

2. This List box control allows the user to select the directory from a list.
    a. Directory
    b. Disk
    c. Drive
    d. File
    e. Path

3. This List box control allows the user to select a filename from a list.
    a. Directory
    b. Disk
    c. Drive
    d. File
    e. Path

4. This property determines the order in which a control receives the focus when the user is tabbing.
    a. Control
    b. Focus
    c. Order
    d. TabControl
    e. TabIndex

5. This property, which is applicable to the Drive List box only, stores the currently selected drive.
    a. CurDrive
    b. CurrentDrive
    c. Drive
    d. Path
    e. SelectDrive

6. This property, which is applicable to the Directory and File List boxes only, stores the current path as a string.
    a. CurPath
    b. CurrentPath
    c. DrivePath
    d. Path
    e. SelectPath

7. This property, which is applicable to the File List box only, stores the name of the currently selected file.
    a. CurFile
    b. CurrentFile
    c. File
    d. FileName
    e. SelectFile

8. This property, which is applicable to the File List box only, stores a string that determines which filenames are displayed in the File List box.
    a. CurFile
    b. CurPath
    c. FileName
    d. FilePattern
    e. Pattern

9. Which of the following patterns will display all files with the .bat extension only?
    a. "*.bat"
    b. "?.bat"
    c. "*.*"
    d. "?.?"
    e. "bat.*"

10. Which of the following patterns will display all files with the .exe and the .com extension?
    a. "*.*"
    b. "*.exe;*.com"
    c. "*.exe","*.com"
    d. "*.exe";"*.com"

11. Which of the following instructions will change the contents of the Dir1 Directory List box to reflect the directories contained on the currently selected drive?
    a. Drive1.Drive = Dir1.Path
    b. Dir1.Path = Drive1.Drive
    c. Dir1.Drive = Drive1.Path
    d. Drive1.Path = Dir1.Drive

12. Which of the following instructions will change the contents of the File1 List box to reflect the filenames contained in the currently selected directory?
    a. File1.Path = Dir1.Path
    b. Dir1.Path = File.Path
    c. File1.Drive = Drive1.Path
    d. Drive1.Path = File1.Filename

13. When an error occurs, its numeric error code is stored in the _____ function.
    a. Err
    b. ErrCode
    c. Error
    d. Error$
    e. NumErr

14. When an error occurs, its name is stored in the _____ function.
   a. Err
   b ErrCode
   c. Error
   d. Error$
   e. NumErr

15. This statement turns error trapping on.
   a. Begin Err
   b. Err On
   c. Error On
   d. On Error
   e. Trap On

16. This instruction will resume program execution with the statement that created the error.
   a. Err Resume
   b. Resume
   c. Resume Again
   d. Resume Next

17. This instruction will resume program execution with the statement immediately following the one that created the error.
   a. Err Resume
   b. Resume
   c. Resume Again
   d. Resume Next

18. The *type* information in the MsgBox function controls all but which one of the following?
   a. Number and type of buttons displayed
   b. Default button
   c. String displayed in the title bar
   d. Icon style
   e. Modality of the dialog box

19. You can use the _____ statement to simulate the occurrence of an error.
   a. Err
   b. ErrCode
   c. Error
   d. Error$
   e. NumErr

E X E R C I S E S

1. a. Open the t10b_nam project, which is in either the tut10\ver2 or tut10\ver3 directory on your Student Disk.
   b. Save the form and the project as t10lbe1. Click the View Form button. The user interface appears, as shown in Figure 10-67.

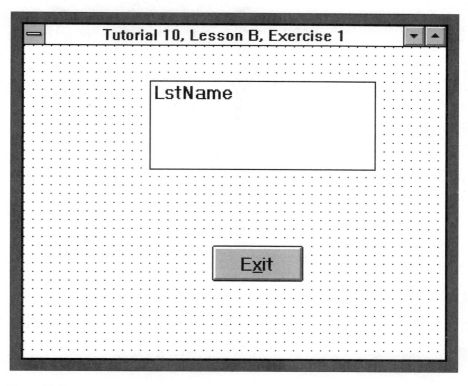

Figure 10-67

This application is supposed to write the sorted contents of the List box to a file on your Student Disk.

    c. Open the Exit button's Click event procedure. Notice that the Open statement says *Open "a:\tut22\t10lbe1.dat" for output as #1.* If necessary, change the drive to the drive containing your Student Disk.

    d. Print the existing code.

    e. Save and run the application, then click the Write button. Visual Basic displays an error message in a dialog box. Write down the error message on a piece of paper.

    f. Include error trapping in the Exit button. Display appropriate error messages. Be sure to include a section in the error handler that will trap any unexpected errors.

    g. Use the Error statement to include an unexpected error in the code. Run the application to see if the error handler handles the unexpected error correctly, then stop the application and print the code.

    h. Remove the Error statement from the code, then save and run the application to see if the error handler handles the expected error correctly. Stop the application and print the code.

2. a. Open the t10b_pay project, which is in either the tut10\ver2 or tut10\ver3 directory on your Student Disk.

    b. Save the form and the project as t10lbe2. Click the View Form button, then maximize the form. The user interface appears, as shown in Figure 10-68.

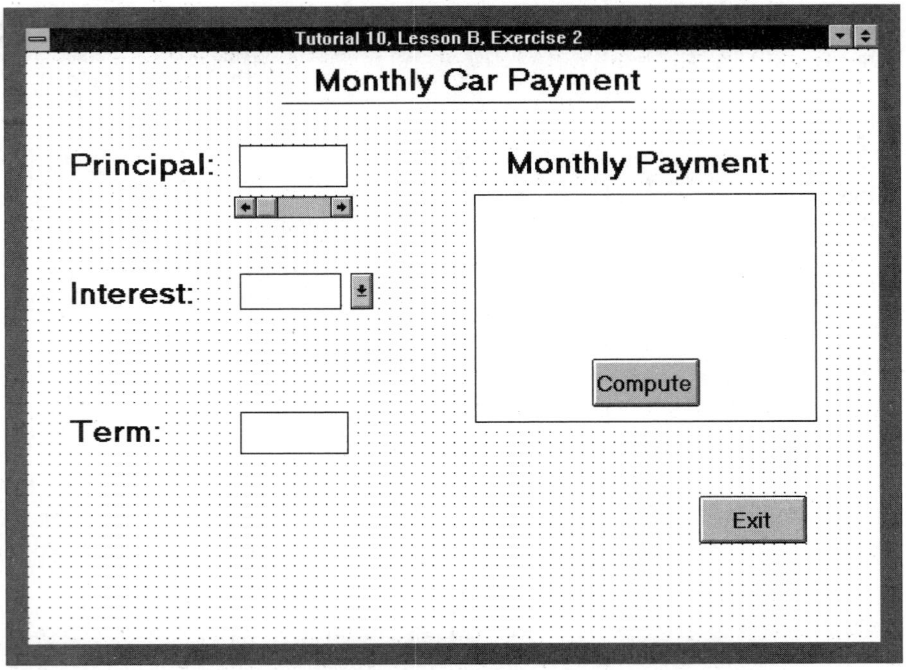

Figure 10-68

You can use this application to calculate the monthly payment on a loan.

c. Print the existing code.

You can determine the expected errors in an application by simply running the application and using it improperly—in other words, in a manner that the programmer did not intend. In steps d, e, and f, for example, you will see what happens if the user doesn't enter an interest rate or a term. You will also see what happens if the user enters a string as the term.

d. Run the application, then click the Compute button. Visual Basic displays an error message in a dialog box. Write down the error message on a piece of paper, then stop the application.

e. Run the application, click 0.07 in the Interest Combo box, then click the Compute button. Visual Basic displays an error message in a dialog box. Write down the error message on a piece of paper, then stop the application.

f. Run the application. Click 0.07 in the Interest Combo box, then click in the Term Text box and type the letter a. Click the Compute button. Visual Basic displays an error message in a dialog box. Write down the error message on a piece of paper, then stop the application.

g. Include error trapping in the Compute button. (Don't use the data validation techniques that you learned in Lesson A.) Display appropriate error messages. Be sure to include a section in the error handler that will trap any unexpected errors. Save and run the application. Test the error handler by performing steps d, e, and f.

h. Use the Error statement to include an unexpected error in the code. Run the application to see if the error handler handles the unexpected error correctly, then stop the application and print the code.

i. Remove the Error statement from the code, then save the application.

LESSON C
objectives

In this lesson you will learn how to:

■ Include the Open dialog box in an application

■ Use Visual Basic's drag-and-drop feature

Drag-and-Drop

The Mingo Sales Application

Recall that Mr. James Colfax, manager of Mingo Sales, wants an application that the home office can use to display the names of its sales force. The company has salespeople located in six states: Michigan, Minnesota, Wisconsin, Alabama, Florida, and Georgia. The names of the salespeople are saved in six sequential access files; each state has its own file of names—for example, the names of the Alabama salespeople are saved in a file named ALA.SOU, and the names of the Michigan salespeople are saved in a file named MICH.NOR. The .SOU and .NOR extensions in the filename indicate whether the state is in the north or the south, the two regions in which Mingo Sales sells. Let's begin coding the application.

To begin coding the Mingo Sales application:

1 Launch Visual Basic, if necessary, and open the **T10C_1.MAK** project, which is in either the tut10\ver2 or tut10\ver3 directory on your Student Disk.

2 **Save** the form and the project as **t10sales**. Click the View Form button, then maximize the form. The user interface appears on the screen, as shown in Figure 10-69.

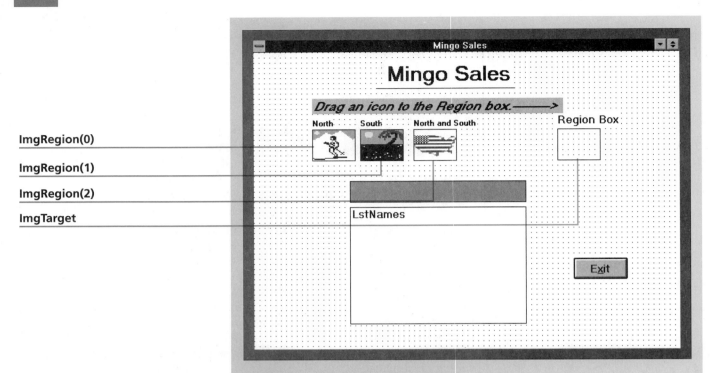

ImgRegion(0)

ImgRegion(1)

ImgRegion(2)

ImgTarget

Figure 10-69: Mingo Sales user interface

The user interface contains four Image controls. The three Image controls that contain icons belong to a control array whose name is ImgRegion. That means that the first Image control's name is ImgRegion(0), the second control's name is ImgRegion(1), and the third control's name is ImgRegion(2). The Image control that does not contain an icon is named ImgTarget.

Notice that the user interface prompts the user to drag an icon to the Region box; when the user does, you want the Open dialog box that you created in Lesson B to appear. The icon the user drags to the Region box will control which filenames are displayed in the File1 List box that is located in the Open dialog box form (the FrmOpen form)—in other words, the icon will control the File1 control's Pattern property. The skier icon will display filenames with the .NOR extension, the island icon will display filenames with the .SOU extension, and the map of the United States will display all the files on the disk. The Open dialog box will allow the user to select the file he or she wants from the list.

3 Restore the form to its standard size.

Let's add the Open dialog box form (the FrmOpen form) that you created in Lesson B to the Mingo Sales application.

4 Click **File**, then click **Add File...**. Click **t10open.frm** in the File List box and click the **OK button**. (The t10open.frm file is in either the tut10\ver2 or tut10\ver3 directory on your Student Disk.)

5 If necessary, click **T10OPEN.FRM** in the Project window. Save the t10open.frm form as **t10open2**, then click the **Save Project icon** 🖫.

Recall that when you have more than one form in a project, you must specify the startup form. (You learned about multiform projects in

Tutorial 7.) The startup form in this project should be the FrmSales form. Let's verify that the FrmSales form is the startup form.

6 Click **Options**, then click **Project....** The Project Options dialog box appears and displays FrmSales in the Start Up Form box. Click the **OK button** to close the Project Options dialog box.

The FrmOpen form and the FrmSales form will need to communicate with each other. Specifically, the FrmOpen form will need to know which file pattern the user selected in the FrmSales form. The file pattern, remember, is controlled by the icon that the user drags to the Region box. The FrmSales form, on the other hand, will need to know which file the user selected in the File1 List box on the FrmOpen form; the selected file is the one that the FrmSales form will open. One way of having both forms communicate with each other is to create global variables. Global variables, you may remember from Tutorial 7, are available to every form and module in the entire application.

In this application you will create two global variables, SelectedFile and FilePattern. The SelectedFile will store the name, including the path, of the file selected in the File List box on the FrmOpen form. The FilePattern variable will store a string that represents which files to display in the File List box on the FrmOpen form. Recall that you declare global variables in a code module.

To continue coding the application:

1 Click **File**, then click **New Module** (or click the New Module icon). Visual Basic adds the Module1.bas file to the Project window, and the general Declarations section of the Module1.bas module appears.

2 Click **File**, then click **Save File As....** Save the module as **t10open2**.

3 Type **global SelectedFile as string, FilePattern as string** and press **[Enter]**, then close the code module. Click the **Save Project icon** .

Next you will code the OK button and the Cancel button in the Open dialog box form.

4 Click **T10OPEN2.FRM** in the Project window, then click the **View Form button**. Maximize the form, then double-click the **OK button**. The CmdOK_Click procedure appears.

When the user clicks the OK button in the Open dialog box form, the name of the selected file, which is stored in the LblFileName control on the form, should be assigned to the SelectedFile variable. Because the SelectedFile variable is global, both the FrmOpen and FrmSales forms will have access to its contents.

5 Press **[Tab]**, then type **SelectedFile = LblFileName.Caption** and press **[Enter]**.

The next step is to hide the FrmOpen form; after the user selects the filename and clicks the OK button, the Open dialog box is not needed.

6 Type **hide** and press **[Enter]**.

Now let's code the Cancel button, which currently contains the *End* statement.

7 Press **[F2]** to open the View Procedures dialog box. Click **CmdCancel_Click** in the Procedures box, then click the **OK button**. The CmdCancel_Click procedure appears.

First you will remove the *End* statement from the procedure.

8   Remove the *End* statement from the CmdCancel_Click procedure.

If the user clicks the Cancel button in the form, it means that he or she doesn't want to open a file; in that case, the SelectedFile variable should contain the null string ("").

9   Type **SelectedFile = " "** and press [**Enter**], then type **hide** and press [**Enter**].

Now that you have finished coding the FrmOpen form, you will size it and change its WindowState property from 2-Maximized to 0-Normal.

To complete the FrmOpen form:

1   Close the Code window and restore the form to its standard size. Size the Open dialog box form, as shown in Figure 10-70.

size the form

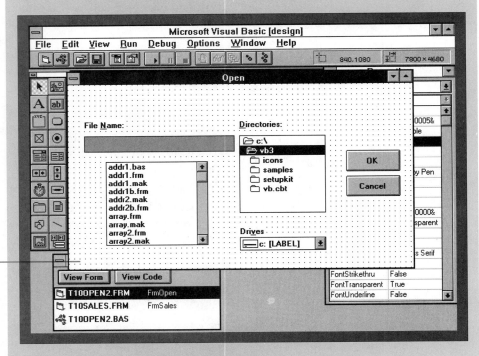

Figure 10-70: Open dialog box sized in user interface

2   Click the **form** to select it. Double-click **WindowState** in the Properties list until the property says 0-Normal.

3   Double-click the **FrmOpen form's control menu box** to close the FrmOpen form. (Don't close Visual Basic.) The FrmSales form should appear on the screen.

tips

If the FrmSales form does not appear, click T10SALES.FRM in the Project window and then click the View Form button.

Before you can code the FrmSales form, you will need to learn about Visual Basic's drag-and-drop feature.

Visual Basic's Drag-and-Drop Feature

Recall that when you are creating a user interface during design time, you can drag controls on the form and drop them in the desired location. Visual Basic's drag-and-drop feature extends this ability to the user during run time by allowing the user to drag objects on the form and then drop them in either the same or a different form. The term **drag** refers to the process of holding down the left mouse button as you move the mouse; the term **drop** refers to releasing the mouse button in order to end a drag operation.

In the next sections you will learn about two properties (DragMode and DragIcon) and one event (DragDrop). You will use both properties and the event to include the drag-and-drop feature in the current application.

The DragMode Property

The ability to drag a control during run time is determined by the value in the control's DragMode property. When the DragMode property is set to 1-Automatic, you can drag the control by positioning the mouse pointer on the control and then pressing the left mouse button down as you move the mouse. In this application you want to allow the user to drag the three icons that are contained in the three ImgRegion controls.

To enable dragging of the ImgRegion Image controls:

1   The FrmSales form should be on the screen. Click the **ImgRegion(0) control**, [Ctrl]-click the **ImgRegion(1) control**, and then [Ctrl]-click the **ImgRegion(2) control**. (Recall that [Ctrl]-click means to hold down the Control key as you click.) The three ImgRegion controls should be selected.

2   Double-click **DragMode** in the Properties window until the property says 1-Automatic.

3   **Save and run** the application. Practice dragging and dropping the **skier icon** anywhere on the form. Notice that the mouse pointer drags a rectangle when you drag the object. (When you drop the icon, it will still be in its original location.)

4   Click the **Exit button**. Visual Basic returns to the design screen.

The mouse pointer would look more meaningful to the user if, during a drag-and-drop operation, the pointer were the same shape as the icon you are dragging. You can control the icon that Visual Basic displays when an object is dragged by setting the control's DragIcon property.

The DragIcon Property

The DragIcon property determines the icon to be displayed when you are dragging a control. In this application, you will set each ImgRegion control's DragIcon property to the same setting as its Picture property.

To set the DragIcon property of the ImgRegion controls:

1   Click the **ImgRegion(0) control** (the skier), then click **DragIcon** in the Properties list. Notice that the DragIcon property says (none). Set the DragIcon property to **\vb\icons\misc\misc43.ico.** (Be sure to verify the location of the icon files with your instructor.) The DragIcon property should now say (icon).

2   Click the **ImgRegion(1) control** (the island), then click **DragIcon** in the Properties list. Set the DragIcon property to **\vb\icons\misc\misc42.ico.**

3   Click the **ImgRegion(2) control** (the U.S. icon), then click **DragIcon** in the Properties list. Set the DragIcon property to **\vb\icons\flags\ctrusa.ico.**

4   **Save and run** the application. Practice dragging and dropping the icons on the form. Notice that the mouse pointer turns into the appropriate icon during the drag operation.

5   Click the **Exit button.**

Now that the icons can be dragged and dropped, the next step is to tell the ImgTarget control how it should respond when the user drops an icon into it. You will do so by coding the ImgTarget's DragDrop event.

The DragDrop Event

When you drag a control over an object and release the mouse button, the object's DragDrop event occurs. The control being dragged is referred to as the **source,** and the object on which it is dropped is referred to as the **target.** Let's view the ImgTarget control's DragDrop event.

To view the ImgTarget control's DragDrop event:

1   Maximize the form, then double-click the **ImgTarget control** (the Region box), and then maximize the Code window. The ImgTarget control's DragDrop event procedure appears, as shown in Figure 10-71. (Some of the code has already been entered into the Code window for you.)

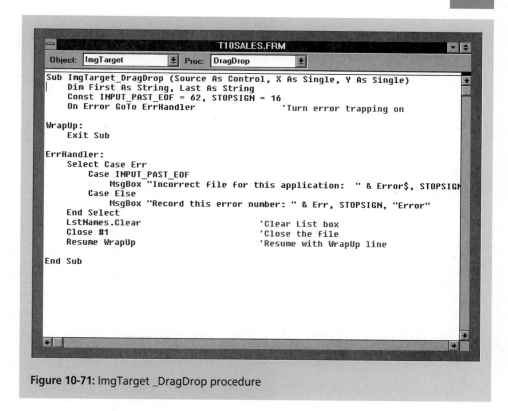

Figure 10-71: ImgTarget _DragDrop procedure

The DragDrop event displays three arguments within the set of parentheses: Source As Control, X As Single, and Y As Single. (These arguments are supplied, automatically, by the DragDrop event. You don't have to enter them yourself.) The Source argument refers to the control being dragged. You can use this argument to refer to the properties and methods of that control—for example, Source.Visible would refer to the Visible property of the control that is being dragged and Source.Index would refer to its Index property. The X and Y arguments in the DragDrop event procedure refer to the horizontal and vertical position of the mouse pointer within the target object.

Before adding any more code to the ImgTarget control, let's look at its flowchart, which is shown in Figure 10-72.

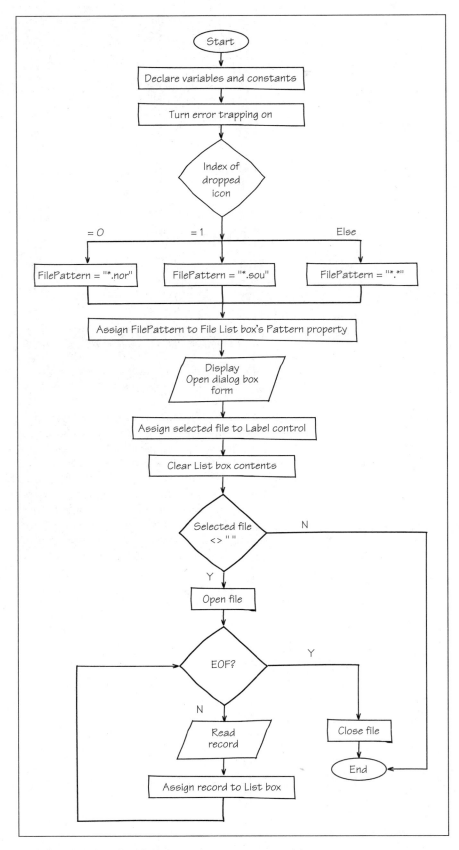

Figure 10-72: Flowchart for ImgTarget_DragDrop procedure

According to the flowchart, the DragDrop event will declare the necessary variables and constants and then turn on error trapping. It will then use a Case structure to determine which icon was dragged to the Region box. You can determine that by looking at the Index property of the icon that was dropped into the Region box. The Case structure will assign the appropriate file pattern to the FilePattern variable. Recall that the FilePattern variable is a global variable that will control which files are displayed in the File1 List box on the FrmOpen form.

After the Case structure assigns the appropriate file pattern to the FilePattern variable, the FilePattern is assigned to the File1 List box's Pattern property in the FrmOpen form. The Open dialog box form (the FrmOpen form) is then displayed on the screen.

After the user closes the FrmOpen form by clicking either the OK or the Cancel buttons, the FrmSales form will appear on the screen. The name of the selected file will be assigned to the LblFile control on the FrmSales form and the List box's contents will be cleared. A selection structure will then be used to determine if the user selected a filename in the FrmOpen form. If the SelectedFile variable contains the null string (""), it means that the user did not select a filename from the FrmOpen form, so the DragDrop procedure ends. If, on the other hand, the SelectedFile variable does not contain the null string—instead, it contains a filename—then the file is opened and a Do...While loop is used to both read each salesperson's name and add it to the List box. When the names of all of the salespeople have been read, the file is closed and the DragDrop procedure ends. Now let's finish coding the DragDrop procedure. The code that declares the variables and constants has already been entered, and so has the On Error statement, so you will begin with the Case structure.

To finish coding the ImgTarget's DragDrop event procedure:

1 Enter the Case statement shown in Figure 10-73.

enter all of these statements

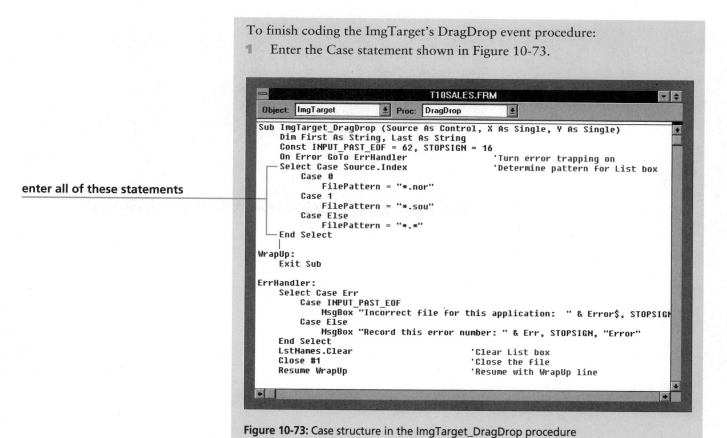

```
Sub ImgTarget_DragDrop (Source As Control, X As Single, Y As Single)
    Dim First As String, Last As String
    Const INPUT_PAST_EOF = 62, STOPSIGN = 16
    On Error GoTo ErrHandler                    'Turn error trapping on
    Select Case Source.Index                    'Determine pattern for List box
        Case 0
            FilePattern = "*.nor"
        Case 1
            FilePattern = "*.sou"
        Case Else
            FilePattern = "*.*"
    End Select

WrapUp:
    Exit Sub

ErrHandler:
    Select Case Err
        Case INPUT_PAST_EOF
            MsgBox "Incorrect file for this application: " & Error$, STOPSIGN
        Case Else
            MsgBox "Record this error number: " & Err, STOPSIGN, "Error"
    End Select
    LstNames.Clear              'Clear List box
    Close #1                    'Close the file
    Resume WrapUp               'Resume with WrapUp line
```

Figure 10-73: Case structure in the ImgTarget_DragDrop procedure

The Case structure will assign the appropriate file pattern to the FilePattern variable. Now let's assign the value in the FilePattern variable to the File1 List box's Pattern property. Recall that the File1 control is in the FrmOpen form, not in the current form—the FrmSales form. As you learned in Tutorial 7, when you want to refer to a control in another form, you must preface the control's name with the name of the form in which it is located.

2   In the line below the *End Select* instruction, type **FrmOpen.File1.Pattern = FilePattern** and press **[Enter]**. This instruction will assign the contents of the FilePattern variable to the File List box's Pattern property.

The next step is to display the FrmOpen form. You can use the Show method to do so. The basic syntax of the Show method, which you learned about in Tutorial 7, is *Form*.**Show**. The Show method also allows you to designate whether the form will be modeless or modal. **Modeless** means that the window does not require the user to take any action before the focus can switch to another form or dialog box. The Code window is an example of a modeless window. **Modal**, on the other hand, means that the window does require the user to take some action before the focus can switch to another form or dialog box. The syntax of the Show method that designates whether the form will be modeless or modal is *Form*.**Show** *style*, where *style* is either 0 (zero) for modeless or 1 (one) for modal. In this application, you want the FrmOpen form to be modal, because you want the user to select either the OK or the Cancel button before the application can return to the FrmSales form.

3   Type **FrmOpen.Show 1** and press **[Enter]**. This instruction will display the Open dialog box form in a modal style.

Now let's assign the value in the SelectedFile variable to the LblFile control, which is located in the FrmSales form (the current form).

4   Type **LblFile.Caption = SelectedFile** and press **[Enter]**.

Now let's clear the contents of the List box. You can use the Clear method to do so.

5   Type **LstNames.Clear** and press **[Enter]**.

Next you will enter the selection structure that will determine if the user selected a filename in the FrmOpen form.

6   Type the selection structure and the documentation shown in Figure 10-74.

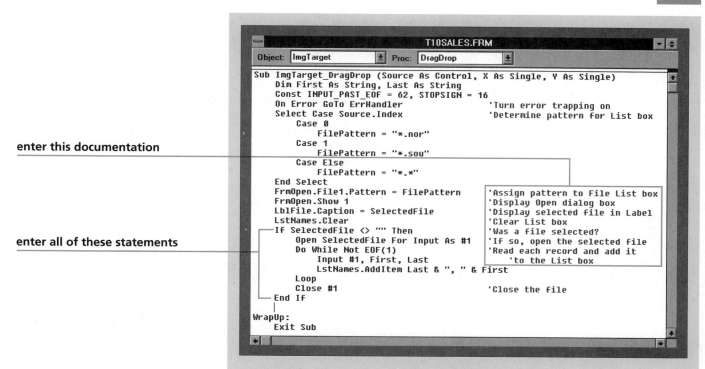

enter this documentation

enter all of these statements

Figure 10-74: Completed ImgTarget_DragDrop procedure

7   Compare your code with the code shown in Figure 10-74. Make any necessary corrections before continuing.

8   Close the Code window, restore the form to its standard size, then **save and run** the application. Drag the **island icon** to the Region box, then drop it in the box. When the Open dialog box form appears, click the drive containing your Student Disk. Depending on your version of Visual Basic, open either the **tut10\ver2** or the **tut10\ver3** directory on your Student Disk. Click **ala.sou** in the File List box, then click the **OK button**. The FrmSales form appears with the names of the Alabama salespeople listed in the List box.

9   Practice displaying the names of other salespeople by selecting one of the following files: fla.sou, ga.sou, mich.nor, minn.nor, wisc.nor. Then, to test the error handler, try selecting a file other than one with a .sou or a .nor extension.

10 Click the **Exit button**.

You have now completed Lesson C and the Mingo Sales application. You can either take a break or complete the questions and exercises at the end of the lesson.

S U M M A R Y

To allow a user to drag a control using the mouse:

■ Set the control's DragMode property to 1-Automatic.

To display an icon when dragging a control:

■ Assign an icon file to the control's DragIcon property.

To have an object respond to the completion of a drag-and-drop operation:

■ Code the object's DragDrop event.

Q U E S T I O N S

1. Using this feature, the user can drag controls during run time and then drop them in another location on either the same or a different form.
    a. copy-and-move
    b. drag-and-drop
    c. drop-and-drag
    d. push-and-pull

2. The term _____ refers to the process of holding down the left mouse button as you move the mouse.
    a. copy
    b. drag
    c. drop
    d. push
    e. shove

3. The term _____ refers to releasing the mouse button after you have dragged a control to its destination.
    a. detach
    b. drag
    c. drop
    d. move
    e. pull

4. The ability to drag a control during run time is determined by the value in the control's _____ property.
    a. Drag
    b. DragDrop
    c. DragIcon
    d. DragMode
    e. DragStatus

5. The _____ property determines the icon that is displayed when you drag a control.
    a. Drag
    b. DragDrop
    c. DragIcon
    d. DragMode
    e. DragPicture

6. The _____ event occurs when a drag-and-drop operation is completed.
   a. Drag
   b. DragDrop
   c. DragIcon
   d. DragMode
   e. DragPicture

7. The control that is being dragged is referred to as the _____ .
   a. draggee
   b. dragger
   c. source
   d. target

8. In a drag-and-drop operation, the destination object is referred to as the _____ .
   a. droppee
   b. dropper
   c. source
   d. target

E X E R C I S E S

1. a. Create the user interface shown in Figure 10-75. Set the ImgOperator(0)'s Picture property to vb\icons\misc\misc20.ico. Set the ImgOperator(1)'s Picture property to vb\icons\misc\misc21.ico. Set the ImgTarget control's Stretch property to true. (Verify the location of the icon files with your instructor.)

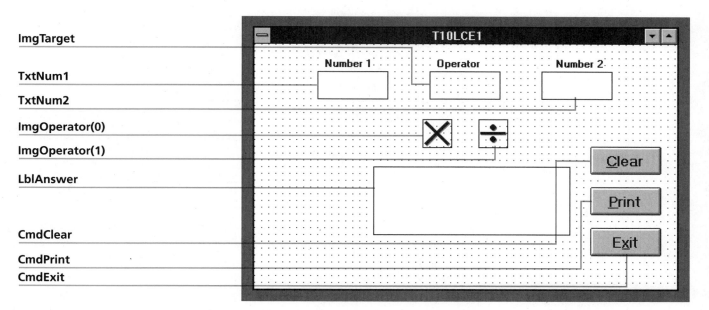

ImgTarget
TxtNum1
TxtNum2
ImgOperator(0)
ImgOperator(1)
LblAnswer
CmdClear
CmdPrint
CmdExit

Figure 10-75

b. Save the form and the project as t10lce1.

You can use this application to practice multiplication and division. After entering two numbers, you then drag one of the ImgOperator controls to the ImgTarget control. When you drop the ImgOperator control into the ImgTarget control, the ImgTarget control's DragDrop event will perform the necessary calculation.

c. Change the DragMode property of the ImgOperator control array to 1-Automatic. Set the DragIcon property of the ImgOperator(0) control to vb\icons\misc\misc20. Set the DragIcon property of the ImgOperator(1) control to vb\icons\misc\misc21. (Verify the location of the icon files with your instructor.)

d. Code the Clear button so that it clears the Text boxes, the Label control, and the ImgTarget control. (You can use the LoadPicture () function to clear an Image control.)

e. Code the Print button so that it prints the form.

f. Code the Exit button so that it ends the application.

g. Code the ImgTarget control's DragDrop event according to the flowchart shown in Figure 10-76.

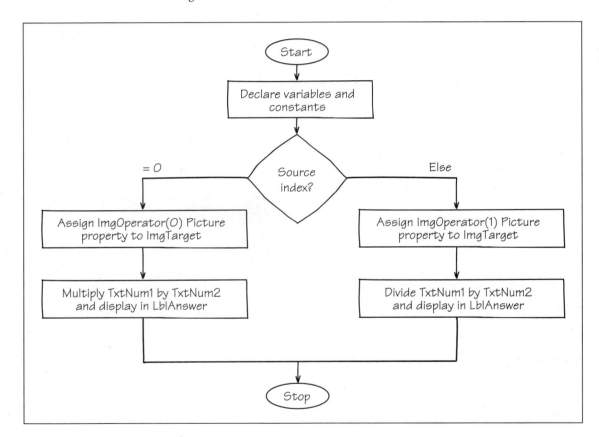

Figure 10-76

h. Include error trapping in the DragDrop event. One error you should trap is the Division by Zero error, which is error code 11. (For example, if the user enters the number 0 in the TxtNum2 Text box, the application will crash if the user selects the division operator.)

i. Save and run the application. Enter 10 in the TxtNum1 box, then enter 2 in the TxtNum2 box. Drag the multiplication operator to the ImgTarget control. The number 20 should appear in the Label control. Click the Print button.

j. Click the Clear button. Enter 20 in the TxtNum1 box, then enter 5 in the TxtNum2 box. Drag the division operator to the ImgTarget control. The number 4 should appear in the Label control. Click the Print button.

k. Click the Clear button. Enter 100 in the TxtNum1 box, then enter 0 in the TxtNum2 control. Drag the division operator to the ImgTarget control. The error message that you included in the error handler should appear. Remove the error message. Click the Exit button.

l. Print the form and the code.

Exercise 2 is a Discovery Exercise.

discovery ▶ 2. a. Create the user interface shown in Figure 10-77. Set the Picture property of the ImgFlag control array as follows. (Verify the location of the icon files with your instructor.)

Control	Icon File
ImgFlag(0)	VB\icons\flags\FlgCan.ico
ImgFlag(1)	VB\icons\flags\FlgFran.ico
ImgFlag(2)	VB\icons\flags\FlgJapan.ico
ImgFlag(3)	VB\icons\flags\FlgMex.ico

Set the ImgFlag control array's Stretch property to true.

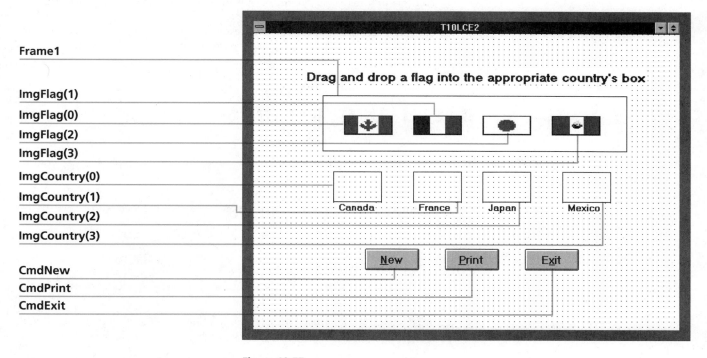

Figure 10-77

b. Save the form and the project as t10lce2.

You can use this application to study the flags used by different countries. The user interface contains two Image control arrays, ImgFlag and ImgCountry. The ImgFlag control array contains the flag icons. When you drag an icon to its appropriate location in the ImgCountry array, the icon should disappear from the ImgFlag array and appear in its correct position in the ImgCountry array. For example, if you drag Japan's icon to the ImgCountry control located above the Japan label, the flag should disappear from the ImgFlag(2) control and appear in the ImgCountry(2) control.

c. Change the DragMode property of the ImgFlag control array to 1-Automatic. Set the DragIcon property of each ImgFlag array control appropriately.

d. Code the New button so that it clears the flag icons from the ImgCountry controls and uses the LoadPicture function to re-display them in the ImgFlag controls. This will allow you to practice matching the flags with their countries again.

e. Code the Print button so that it prints the form.

f. Code the Exit button so that it ends the application.

g. Code the ImgTarget control's DragDrop event accordingly.

h. Save and run the application. Drag each flag to its appropriate position.

i. Click the Exit button. When you return to the design screen, drag the ImgFlag controls to different locations, so that they are not immediately above their corresponding countries.

j. Save and run the application. Drag each flag to its appropriate position, then click the Print button. Click the Clear button, then click the Exit button.

k. Print the code.

D E B U G G I N G

Technique　In this tutorial, you will use the debugger to step through an application as you are debugging it.

Your Student Disk contains a file that you can use to practice with Visual Basic's debugger.

To debug the T10DEBUG.MAK project:

1　Launch Notepad. Open the **t10debug.dat** file and print its contents. Then close Notepad.

2　Launch Visual Basic, if necessary, and open the **t10debug.mak** project, which is in either the tut10\ver2 or tut10\ver3 directory on your Student Disk.

3　Click the **View Form button**. The user interface appears on the screen.

4　Double-Click the **form** to open its Code window. Press [F2] to open the View Procedures dialog box, click **CmdCalc_Click**, then click the **OK button**. If necessary, change the drive letter in the Open statement to the drive that contains your Student Disk. Close the Code window.

5　Save the form and the project as **t10dbgd**.

6　Print the code.

7 **Run** the application. Click the **Calc Statistics button**. Write the error message down on a piece of paper, then click the **OK button** to remove the error message.

Notice that, although the data file is incorrect, the statistical information still appears in the user interface, which will be misleading to the user. If the data file is incorrect, the application should not show any statistical information on the form. Let's stop the application and see why this error occurs and how you can fix it.

8 Click the **Exit button** to end the application.

9 Double-click the **form** to open its Code window. Press **[F2]** to open the View Procedures dialog box, click **CmdCalc_Click**, then click the **OK button**.

10 Set a breakpoint in the Do While Not EOF(1) instruction, then close the Code window.

11 **Run**, but don't save, the application. Click the **Calc Statistics button**. Maximize the Code window, then keep pressing the **[F8]** key until you locate the source of the problem—the reason why the statistics display on the form when the data file is incorrect.

12 Stop the application, remove the breakpoint, then correct the problem.

13 **Save and run** the application. Click the **Calc Statistics button**, then click the **OK button** to remove the error message. The user interface should not show any statistical information.

14 Print the code.

APPENDIX

A

Binary Search

In Tutorial 8 you learned how to search an array for data. Lesson A's examples, for instance, showed you how to search for both the highest and the lowest number contained in an array. Tutorial 8's personal directory application showed you how to search an array for both the name of a friend or relative and a birthday that matched a specific pattern. All of the searches performed in Tutorial 8 were serial searches. In a serial search, the program begins the search with the first array element. The program then continues searching, element by element, until either a match is found or the end of the array is encountered. A serial search is useful when the amount of data that must be searched is small. If you have a large amount of data, however, the serial search is extremely inefficient. In those cases, you should use a binary search.

In order for a binary search to work, the data in the array must be arranged in either alphabetical or numerical order. In other words, if you are searching for a last name, then the last names in the array must be in alphabetical order. If you are searching for a Zip code, then the Zip codes must be in numerical order.

Instead of beginning the search with the first array element, the binary search algorithm begins the search in the middle of the array, as shown in Figure 1.

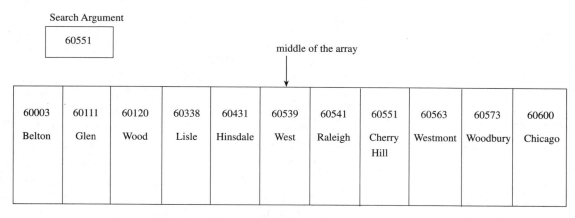

Figure 1: Beginning of binary search

If the search argument—the data for which you are searching—is equal to the value in the middle of the array, then the search ends. If, on the other hand, the search argument is greater than the value in the array, the search continues in the upper half of the array; otherwise, it continues in the lower half of the array. In Figure 1, the search argument (60551) is greater than the array value (60539), so the search would continue in the upper half of the array.

When continuing the search, the upper half of the array is halved again, as shown in Figure 2.

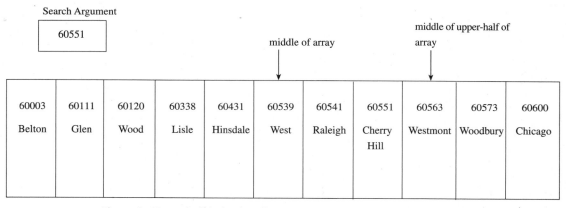

Figure 2: Upper half halved again

Here again, if the search argument is greater than the value in the array, the search continues in the array elements above the current one; otherwise, it continues in the array elements below the current one. In Figure 2, the search argument (60551) is less than the array value (60563), so the search would continue in the elements located between the middle of the array and the current element. The binary search algorithm continues to halve the remaining array elements until it either finds a match or determines that no match exists.

Let's look at an application that uses a binary search.

To view an application that uses a binary search:

1   Launch Visual Basic, if necessary. Open the **ZIP.MAK**, which is in either the tutappen\ver2 or the tutappen\ver3 directory on your Student Disk. Click the **View Form** button. The user interface appears on the screen.

In this application, the user will only need to enter the Zip code. When the user presses the Enter key, the application will complete the city entry automatically.

2   On your own, view the code that has already been entered in this application.

3   **Run**, but don't save the application. Type **60338** as the Zip code, then press [**Enter**]. Lisle appears in the Label control on the form. Click **File**, then click **Print** to print the form.

4   Type **40444** as the Zip code. The message "Unrecognized Zip code" appears in the Label control on the form. Click **File**, then click **Print** to print the form.

5   Click **File**, then click **Exit** to exit the application.

APPENDIX

B

Using Visual Basic to Access a Database

Database Concepts and Terminology

Recall that you learned how to create data files in both Tutorial 6 and Tutorial 7. In Tutorial 6 you created a sequential access data file for the Chicago UFO club; in Tutorial 7 you created a random access data file for Cole's Playhouse. A data file, you may remember, is organized into fields and records. A field, also called a data element, is a single item of information about a person, place, or thing—for example, a social security number, a city, or a price. A record is a group of related fields that contain all of the necessary data about a specific person, place, or thing. Recall that each record in Tutorial 6's data file contained two fields: Age and Response. Each record in Tutorial 7's data file also contained two fields: Name and Phone Number. Data files that contain records relating to a specific topic or purpose are called **databases.** The records in Tutorial 6's data file form the UFO Club's respondents' database; the records in Tutorial 7's data file form the Cole's Playhouse patrons' database.

Most businesses store information about their employees, invoices, and inventory in databases. But you don't have to be a business to make use of a database. Many people use one to keep track of their medical records, their tape collections, and even their golf scores.

Many software packages exist for creating databases. Some of the most popular are Btrieve®, dBASE®, Microsoft Access™, Microsoft FoxPro®, and Paradox®. These database packages not only create the databases, but allow you to manipulate them as well. Using Visual Basic, you can access the data stored in these databases, even though they were not created in Visual Basic. This allows a company to use Visual Basic to create a standard user interface that employees can use to access database information stored in a variety of formats. Instead of learning each database package's user interface, the employee only needs to know one user interface. Which format the database is in will be transparent to the user.

In this appendix you will learn how to use Visual Basic to create, access, and manipulate a Microsoft Access database. You will also learn how to use Visual Basic to access and manipulate a dBASE IV database. You will only be able to complete this appendix if you have access to Visual Basic 3.0.

Creating a Microsoft Access Database

Both Visual Basic and Access are Microsoft products. In fact, the same database engine that powers Microsoft Access is also found in Microsoft Visual Basic Version 3; that means you can use Visual Basic to create databases that have the same format as Microsoft Access databases. Let's use Visual Basic to create a database that will keep track of the college courses you have taken. The database will consist of four fields: course number, course title, credit hours, and grade.

To use Visual Basic to create a Microsoft Access database:

1 Launch Visual Basic. Make sure the Visual Basic Student Disk is in the appropriate disk drive. Click **Window** in the Visual Basic menu bar, then click **Data Manager.** The Data Manager screen, which shows three menu choices (File, Window, and Help), appears.

You want to create a new database file.

2 Click **File** in the Data Manager menu bar, click **New Database**, then click **Access 1.1.** The New Database dialog box appears.

First you need to give the database a name and save it on your Student Disk.

3 Click the **down arrow button in the Drives list box**, then click the **drive letter corresponding to the location of your Student Disk.** Double-click **tutappen** in the Directories list box to open that folder, then double-click **ver3** to open that folder. Type **school** in the File Name box, then click the **OK button.** When the file is saved on your Student Disk, Visual Basic will append the .mdb extension to the filename, which indicates that the file is a Microsoft Access database.

A Microsoft Access database is composed of one or more tables. Each table is a collection of fields related to a single topic of information. In our case we need only one table, which we will call Courses; the Courses table will contain four fields.

tips

∙ ∙ ∙ ∙ ∙ ∙ ∙ ∙ ∙ ∙ ∙ ∙ ∙ ∙ ∙ ∙

▶ **A database can contain more than one table. For example, a CD (compact disc) database could be composed of an artist table that contains the CD's number, the CD's name, and the artist's name. Another table in the same database—the song table—would then contain the CD's number, each song's name, and each song's track number (its location on the CD).**

4   Click the **New button**. The Create New Table dialog box appears. Type **Courses**, then click the **OK button**.

Once the table is created, you need to add fields to it. The Courses table will consist of four fields: Number, Title, Hours, Grade.

5   Click the **Add button** in the Fields section. The Add Field dialog box appears. Type **Number** as the name of the field. Click the **down arrow button in the Field Type box**, scroll the list box and then click **Text**. Click in the Field Size box, type 8, then click the **OK button**.

6   Use the Add button to add the remaining three fields as shown below. (You will not need to define the field size for the Hours field because Integer fields have a default size of 8.)

Field Name	Field Type	Field Size
Title	Text	20
Hours	Integer	
Grade	Text	1

The next step is to add an index to the database. An index gives you several advantages: It allows you to order records by a key field. In this case, for example, creating an index on the Number field will order the records by course number. Creating an index on the Grade field, on the other hand, will order the records by grade. Creating an index also speeds up the process of finding records in the indexed field. In addition, you can use an index to tell the database to allow only unique values in a field.

A table does not have to have an index. If it does, it can have one or more. (Not every field in a table needs to be indexed. In fact, creating too many indexes can slow down database processing. Only create indexes for fields on which you want either to order records or to search.) When you create the application that will access the current database, you will want the records displayed in course number order; you will also want to search the course number field for a specific course number. Therefore, you will add one index to the Courses table; the index will be on the Number field.

To add an index to the Courses table:

1   Click the **Add button in the Indexes section**. The Add Index dialog box appears.

You will need to give the index a name, which is usually the same name as the field to which the index relates, and then select the field that you want to index.

2   Type **Number** in the Index Name box, then click **Number** in the Fields in Table list.

You can order the records in ascending (Asc) or descending (Dec) order. (Notice that you can also remove an index.) Let's order the records in ascending order.

3   Click the **Add (Asc) button**. +Number appears in the Fields in Index box.

Notice the two Check boxes, Require Unique Index Values and Primary Index, at the bottom of the dialog box. You will make the Number field the primary index. The primary index is the field whose values uniquely identify each record. In this case, the Number field uniquely identifies each record because no two courses will have the same course number.

4   Click **Primary Index**. (You do not need to select Require Unique Index Values for the primary index. Because the values in the primary index have to be unique, Visual Basic displays an error message, automatically, if you attempt to enter a duplicate value in the primary index field.) Your screen should look like Figure B-1.

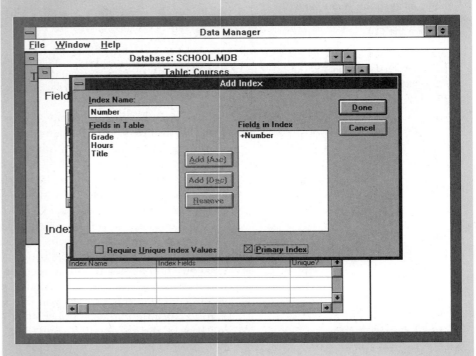

Figure B-1: Add Index dialog box

tips

If you accidentally clicked the control menu box for the Tables screen, click File, click Open Database, click Access, and then click school.mdb (which is located in the tutappen\ver3 directory on your Student Disk.) Click the OK button to display the Tables screen.

5   Click the **Done button**.

The Indexes section should say Number below Index Name, +Number below Index Fields, Unique below Unique?, and Primary below Primary?. (You'll need to scroll to see Primary.) Notice that the Number index is specified as Unique, even though you did not choose the Require Unique Index Values option when creating the index.

6   Click the **Table: Courses control menu box**, then click **Close** to close the dialog box. The Data Manager returns to the Tables screen.

Notice that the Tables screen has four buttons: New, Open, Design, and Delete. The New button, as you just learned, allows you to create a new table. The Open button allows you to access and manipulate the records in a database. You use the Design button to change the design of an existing table. You use the Delete button to delete an existing table. Let's use the Open button to add three records to the database.

To add records to the database:

1   Click the **Open button.** The screen appears as shown in Figure B-2.

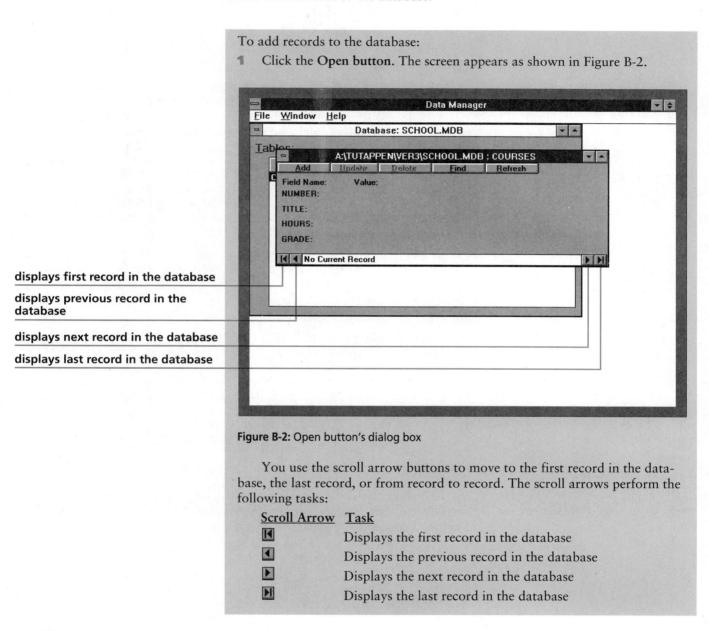

displays first record in the database

displays previous record in the database

displays next record in the database

displays last record in the database

Figure B-2: Open button's dialog box

You use the scroll arrow buttons to move to the first record in the database, the last record, or from record to record. The scroll arrows perform the following tasks:

Scroll Arrow	Task
⏮	Displays the first record in the database
◀	Displays the previous record in the database
▶	Displays the next record in the database
⏭	Displays the last record in the database

The five buttons perform the following tasks:

Button	Task
Add	Adds a new, blank record to the end of the database
Update	Saves changes to an existing record in the database
Delete	Deletes the current record from the database
Find	Searches the database for a record that matches a search expression
Refresh	Reopens the database

Let's add three records to the database.

2   Click the **Add button.** The Data Manager adds a new, blank record to the end of the database. Type **CIS100** in the NUMBER box and press [**Tab**]. Type **Intro to Computers** in the TITLE box and press [**Tab**]. Type **3** in the HOURS box and press [**Tab**]. Type **A** in the GRADE box.

3   Click the **Add button** to save the current record and add another blank record to the end of the database. Enter the following record: **CIS131, Intro to Databases, 3, B.**

4   Click the **Add button** to save the current record and add another blank record to the end of the database. Enter the following record: **CIS110, Intro to Programming, 3, A.**

In this case, you want to save the current record but you don't want to add another record. You can save the current record without adding another one by pressing one of the scroll arrows in the dialog box. You can also click the Update button.

5   Click either of the **right scroll arrow buttons** or either of the **left scroll arrow buttons.** Either button will allow you to save the current record. Click the **Yes button** when you are asked if you want to save the new record.

6   Practice with the scroll arrow buttons. Notice how they allow you to move to the first record in the database, the last record, and from record to record.

7   Double-click the **Data Manager's control menu box** to close the Data Manager. Visual Basic returns to the design screen.

Although the Data Manager allows you to access and manipulate the records in a database, its user interface cannot be altered. If you want to give the user a customized user interface with which he or she can access and manipulate database records, you will need to create a Visual Basic application. You will do so in the next section.

The School Application

Your Student Disk contains a partially completed Visual Basic application that will allow you to access and manipulate the school.mdb Microsoft Access database.

To open the partially completed application:

1 Open the **appenb.mak** project, which is in the tutappen\ver3 directory on your Student Disk. Save the form and the project as **school**. Click the **View Form button**, then maximize the form. The user interface appears on the screen.

Applications that can access and manipulate the data stored in databases are referred to as **data-aware applications**. You can use Visual Basic's Data control to make the school application a data-aware application.

The Data Control

Visual Basic's Data control allows you to access the data stored in any of the following database formats: Microsoft Access, FoxPro Version 2.0, FoxPro Version 2.5, dBASE III®, dBASE IV®, Paradox, and Btrieve. (The Professional Edition of Visual Basic Version 3 also allows you to access ODBC databases including Microsoft, SQL Server, and Oracle®.) Let's add a Data control to the School application. Adding the data control is the first step in making an application data-aware; it will allow the application to access the database.

To make the application data-aware, then save and run the application:

1 Restore the form to its standard size, then double-click the **Data control** . The Data1 control appears on the form. Set the Data1 control's properties as follows:

Property	Value	Property	Value
Height	375	Top	5040
Left	360	Width	8895

2 Maximize the form. The screen appears as shown in Figure B-3.

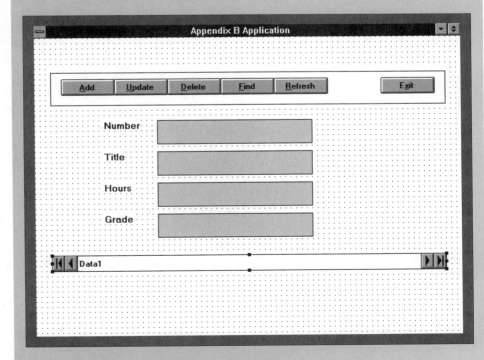

Figure B-3: Data control displayed in the user interface

The next step is to set the Data control's DatabaseName property, which tells Visual Basic the name of the database to connect to the Data control. You will connect the Data control to the Microsoft Access database that you created earlier in this appendix. Recall that the name of that database is school.mdb.

3   Restore the form to its standard size. The Data1 control should be selected. Click **DatabaseName** in the Properties window, then click **...** in the Settings box. If necessary, change the Drives list box to the drive containing your Student Disk. Click **school.mdb**, which is located in the tutappen\ver3 directory on your Student Disk, then click the **OK button**.

Now you need to set the Data control's RecordSource property, which tells Visual Basic which table in the database to use when accessing the records.

4   Click **RecordSource** in the Properties window. Click the **down arrow button** in the Settings box, then click **Courses** in the drop-down list.

Notice that the method for accessing a Microsoft Access database is quite simple. You first add the Data control to the form, then set its DatabaseName and RecordSource properties. (If you need to access a database other than a Microsoft Access database, you will also need to set the Data control's Connect property. You will learn about the Connect property when you access the dBASE IV database later in this appendix.)

Now that the Data control is on the form and its DatabaseName and RecordSource properties have been set, you can connect the four Text boxes to it. Connecting a control to the Data control is called **binding**, and the connected controls are referred to as **data-aware controls** or **bound controls**. (The following controls can be bound to a Data control: Check box, Image, Label, Picture box, and Text box.) By binding the Text boxes to the Data control, the Text boxes will display the data from the database specified in the Data control's DatabaseName property.

You bind a Text box to the Data control by setting the Text box's DataSource and DataField properties. In the DataSource property you enter the name of the Data control to which the Text box is to be bound. In this application, the four Text boxes should be bound to the Data1 control. You can set the DataSource property for all four Text boxes at the same time.

5   Maximize the form. Click the **TxtNumber Text box**, [Ctrl]-click the **TxtTitle Text box**, [Ctrl]-click the **TxtHours Text box**, and [Ctrl]-click the **TxtGrade Text box**. Press [F4] to display the Properties window. Click **DataSource** in the Properties window, click the **down arrow button** in the Settings box, then click **Data1**. Click the **form** to cancel the selection of the four Text boxes.

Now you need to set each Text box's DataField property, which tells Visual Basic the name of the database field whose contents you want displayed in the Text box. For example, in the TxtNumber Text box, you want to display the contents of the Number field from the database.

6   Click the **TxtNumber Text box** to select that control. Press [F4] to display the Properties window. Click **DataField** in the Properties window, click the **down arrow button** in the Settings box, then click **Number**.

7 Set the DataField properties for the remaining three Text boxes as follows:

Text Box	DataField
TxtTitle	Title
TxtHours	Hours
TxtGrade	Grade

Now let's save and run the application to see how it works so far.

8 Restore the form to its standard size, then **save and run** the application. Use the scroll arrow buttons to view the three records in the database. Because you defined the Number field as the primary key when you created the school.mdb database, the records display in course number order. Click the **Exit button** to end the application.

In the next section you will code the Add button so that it allows you to add a record to the database.

Coding the Add Button

You use a Data control's Recordset property, which refers to the set of records included in the database, and the AddNew method to add a blank record to the end of the database. The syntax of the command that adds a record to the record set is *datacontrol*.**Recordset.AddNew**.

To code the Add button, then save and run the application:

1 Double-click the **Add button** to open its Code window. The CmdAdd_Click event procedure appears. Press [**Tab**], then type **Data1.recordset.addnew** and press [**Enter**].

When the user clicks the Add button, the focus should appear in the TxtNumber control, ready for the user to enter the new record's course number.

2 Type **TxtNumber.setfocus** and press [**Enter**], then close the Code window. Let's test the Add button.

3 **Save and run** the application. Click the **Add button.** Enter the following record: **ACCOU111, Intro to Accounting, 3, C.**

To save the current record and then add another record, you would click the Add button. To save the current record without adding another record, you would click one of the scroll arrow buttons. (After the Update button is coded, you will be able to use it to also save the current record without adding a new record.)

4 Click the **leftmost scroll arrow button** to save the current record without adding another record. Visual Basic saves the current record and then displays the first record in the database—the record with course number CIS100. Now click the **rightmost scroll arrow button.** Visual Basic displays the last record in the database—the record with course number ACCOU111.

Notice that the new record, ACCOU111, does not appear in the correct position, alphabetically. The ACCOU111 record appears at the end of the database instead of at the beginning of the database. As mentioned earlier, when you add a new record to the database, it is added to the end of the database. You can reorder the records, which will put the records in their correct order, by refreshing the database. **Refreshing** refers to the process of opening or reopening a database. You will code the Refresh button in the next section.

5   Click the **Exit button** to end the application.

Coding the Refresh Button

You use a Data control's Refresh method to open a closed database or reopen an open database. When you either open or reopen a database, Visual Basic reorders the records by the primary key. If you have added one or more records, or if you are using a multiuser database, it is a good practice to refresh the database periodically to make sure that the recordset contains the latest information from the database, and the recordset is in the proper order. The syntax of the Refresh method is *datacontrol*.**Refresh**.

To code the Refresh button:

1   Maximize the form, then double-click the **Refresh button** to open its Code window. The CmdRefresh_Click procedure appears. Press [**Tab**], then type **Data1.refresh** and press [**Enter**].

2   Close the Code window, restore the form to its standard size, then **save and run** the application. When you run the application, it automatically opens the school database and the records are put in their proper order. That's why the ACCOU111 record displays first.

Let's add another record to the database.

3   Click the **Add button**, then add the following record: **BIOL110, Intro to Biology, 3, B.** Click the **leftmost scroll arrow button** to save the current record and display the first record in the database. Now scroll through the records, one at a time. Notice that the BIOL110 record does not appear in the correct alphabetic order; it appears at the end of the database.

4   Click the **Refresh button.** Visual Basic reopens the school database. In doing so, the records are automatically reordered. The first record in the database, **ACCOU111**, appears on the screen. Scroll through the records, one at a time. You will notice that the records are in their proper order. Click the **Exit button** to end the application.

The next button you will code is the Delete button, which will allow you to delete the current record from the database.

Coding the Delete Button

You use the Recordset property and the Delete method to remove the current record—the record displayed currently on the screen—from a database. The syntax of the command to delete a record is *datacontrol*.**Recordset.Delete**. Although this command removes the current record from the recordset, it does not erase the record from the screen until you move to another record. You can use the MoveNext method to move to another record so that the current record is erased from the screen. The syntax of the MoveNext method is *datacontrol*.**Recordset**.**MoveNext**.

Most of the code for the Delete button has already been entered in its Click event procedure. You will need to enter only two more lines of code: *Data1.Recordset.Delete* and *Data1.Recordset.MoveNext*.

To finish coding the Delete button:

1   Double-click the **Delete button** to open its Code window. Maximize the Code window, then enter the two lines of code shown in Figure B-4.

enter these two lines of code

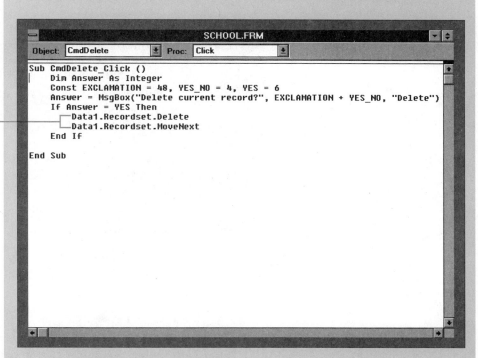

```
                            SCHOOL.FRM
Object: CmdDelete          Proc: Click

Sub CmdDelete_Click ()
    Dim Answer As Integer
    Const EXCLAMATION = 48, YES_NO = 4, YES = 6
    Answer = MsgBox("Delete current record?", EXCLAMATION + YES_NO, "Delete")
    If Answer = YES Then
        Data1.Recordset.Delete
        Data1.Recordset.MoveNext
    End If

End Sub
```

Figure B-4: The Delete button's Code window

When the user clicks the Delete button, the MsgBox function, which you learned about in Tutorial 10, prompts the user to confirm the deletion. The MsgBox function's dialog box contains both a Yes and a No button. If the user clicks the Yes button, the current record is deleted. If the user clicks the No button, the deletion is cancelled.

2   Close the Code window, then **save and run** the application. Use the scroll bar to display the second record (the BIOL110 record), then click the **Delete button**. When the Delete dialog box appears, click the **Yes button**. The *Data1.Recordset.Delete* instruction, which you entered into the Delete button's Code window, removes the record from the database. The *Data1.Recordset.MoveNext* instruction then moves to the next record in the database.

3   Scroll through the records to prove that the deleted record is no longer in the database, then click the **Exit button** to end the application.

The next button you will code is the Update button, which will allow the user to save any changes he or she makes to an existing record.

Coding the Update Button

When you make a change to an existing record, the change is saved automatically when you move to another record in the database. This application, however, includes an Update button, which allows the user to save the change without moving to another record. You can use the Recordset property and the Update method to save changes made to an existing record in the database. The syntax of the command to save changes made to a record is *datacontrol*.**Recordset.Update**.

To code the Update button, then save and run the application:

1   Double-click the **Update button** to open its Code window. In the CmdUpdate_Click procedure, press [**Tab**], then type **Data1.recordset.update** and press [**Enter**].

2   Close the code window, then **save and run** the application. Display the CIS100 record. Change the grade to **B**, then click the **Update button**. The change to the record is now saved in the database. Click the **Exit button** to end the application.

The last button you will view is the Find button, which allows you to search the Number field for a specific course number.

Coding the Find Button

The code for the Find button has already been entered into its Click event procedure for you. Let's look at that code right now.

To view the code in the Find button:

1   Double-click the **Find button** to open its Code window, then maximize the Code window. The Click event procedure appears as shown in Figure B-5.

notice the double and single quotes

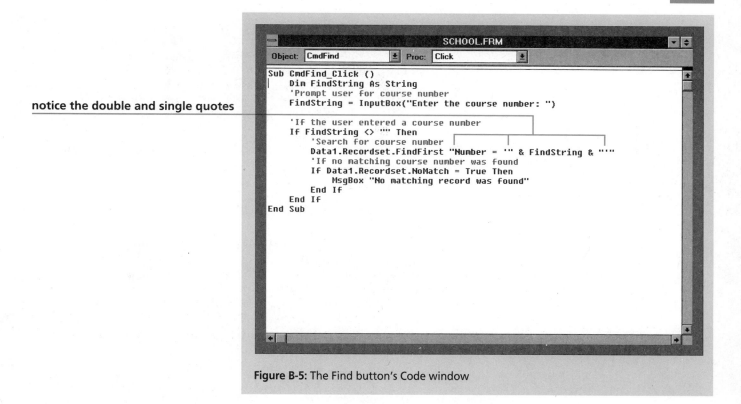

```
SCHOOL.FRM
Object: CmdFind          Proc: Click

Sub CmdFind_Click ()
    Dim FindString As String
    'Prompt user for course number
    FindString = InputBox("Enter the course number: ")

    'If the user entered a course number
    If FindString <> "" Then
        'Search for course number
        Data1.Recordset.FindFirst "Number = '" & FindString & "'"
        'If no matching course number was found
        If Data1.Recordset.NoMatch = True Then
            MsgBox "No matching record was found"
        End If
    End If
End Sub
```

Figure B-5: The Find button's Code window

The Click event procedure begins by declaring a local String variable named FindString. It then uses the InputBox function to prompt the user to enter the course number of the record that he or she wants to find. The user's response is assigned to the FindString variable. If the FindString variable does not contain the null string (""), which means that the user entered a course number in the InputBox function's dialog box, then the *Data1.Recordset.FindFirst "Number = '"* & *FindString* & *"'"* instruction tells Visual Basic to search the Number field for the course number stored in the FindString variable. This command uses the Recordset property and the FindFirst method to locate the desired record. Notice the syntax of the command is *datacontrol*.**Recordset.FindFirst** *searchstring*. Also notice the use of the double and single quotation marks to concatenate the field name—Number—with the String variable. The single quotation marks are necessary because the contents of the string variable must be enclosed in quotation marks within the *searchstring*.

The *If Data1.Recordset.NoMatch = True Then* instruction uses the Recordset and NoMatch properties to determine if a matching record was found. If the NoMatch property contains the Boolean value True, then a message indicating that no matching record was found is displayed. Let's test the application.

To test the application:

1   Close the Code window, then **run** the application. Click the **Find button.** Type **cis110** and click the **OK button.** The CIS110 record displays. (Notice that the *searchstring* is not case sensitive.) Click the **Exit button** to end the application.

In the last section in this appendix, you will use the same application to connect to a dBASE IV database.

Connecting to a dBASE IV Database

The procedure to connect to an external database, a database other than a Microsoft Access database, is the same as the procedure to connect to a Microsoft Access database, with one exception. When connecting to an external database, you must set the Data control's Connect property. The Connect property specifies the type of database and, in some cases, the database password. You will connect to an external database created with the dBASE IV software package. The database, which is named school.dbf, is in the tutappen\ver3 directory on your Student Disk.

To connect the school application to a dBASE IV database:

1   Open the **appenb2.mak** project, which is in the tutappen\ver3 directory on your Student Disk. Save the form and the project as **school2.** Click the **View Form button,** then maximize the form.

2   Click the **Data1 control,** click [**F4**], then click **Connect** in the Properties window. The Connect setting for a dBASE IV database is dbase IV;. Type **dbase IV;** in the Connect property and press [**Enter**]. (Be sure to type the semicolon at the end.) The DatabaseName setting for a dBASE IV database is **drive:\path**—in this case either a: \tutappen\ver3 or b: \tutappen\ver3.

3   Click **DatabaseName** in the Properties window. Depending on the location of your Student Disk, type either **a:\tutappen\ver3** or **b:\tutappen\ver3** and press [**Enter**]. The name of the database is school.

4   Click **RecordSource** in the Properties window. Click the **down arrow button** in the Settings box, then click **SCHOOL** in the drop-down list.

5   Click the **TxtNumber Text box,** [Ctrl]-click the **TxtTitle Text box,** [Ctrl]-click the **TxtHours Text box,** and [Ctrl]-click the **TxtGrade Text box.** Press [**F4**] to display the Properties window, click **DataSource** in the Properties window, click the **down arrow button** in the Settings box, then click **Data1.** Click the **form** to cancel the selection of the four Text boxes.

6   Set the DataField properties for the four Text boxes as follows:

Text Box	DataField
TxtNumber	Number
TxtTitle	Title
TxtHours	Hours
TxtGrade	Grade

7   Restore the form to its standard size, then **save and run** the application. All of the buttons have already been coded. The code is identical to the school application that accessed the Access database.

8   Click the **Exit button** to end the application, then exit Visual Basic.

Glossary

accumulator — a variable or a control that is used to accumulate, or sum, a group of numbers. (5, 6)

algorithm — a step-by-step solution to a problem. (9)

Append — one of three sequential access file modes. You open a file for Append when you want to add information to an existing file. (If the file doesn't exist, Visual Basic creates it.) (6)

Application modal — describes a window in which the user must respond to a message before he or she can continue working in the current application. (10)

argument — a piece of information passed to a procedure or function; also called a parameter. (5)

assembler — a program that converts assembly language instructions into machine code—the 0s and 1s the computer can understand. (O)

assembly language — a computer programming language that uses mnemonics in place of machine code (0s and 1s) in the program. (O)

automatic counter loop — the For...Next loop; it repeats a block of statements a specified number of times. (5)

binary — the compressed format used to store numbers in a random access file. (7)

boolean — the True and False values named after the English mathematician George Boole. (2)

byte — the amount of storage needed to hold one character; you can think of a byte as being equivalent to a character. (7)

check digit check — the data validation check that is used for applications such as credit card processing; it verifies the assignment of a special digit to an identification number. (10)

code — program instructions. (1)

code check — the data validation check that verifies that the input data matches a predetermined list of values; it is a special type of range check. (10)

compiler — a program that translates the entire high-level language program into machine code before running the program. (O)

concatenates — links together. (2)

concatenating — connecting (or linking) strings together. (3)

concatenation operator — the ampersand (&); used to concatenate strings. (3)

condition — the part of the If...Then...Else structure that specifies the decision you are making. The condition should be phrased so that it results in either a true (yes) or a false (no) answer only. (4)

constant — a value that does not change while the program is running. (3)

control — a graphical object (such as a button, box, or scroll bar) that you place on a form. (1)

control array — a group of controls of the same type that have the same name and share the same set of event procedures. (5)

counters — variables or controls used for counting something. (5, 6)

data element — a single item of information about a person, place, or thing (for example, a social security number, a city, or a price); also called a field. (6)

data file — a collection of related records. (6)

data validation — the process of verifying that the data a user supplies to an application is valid. (10)

decision structure — the programming structure used to make a decision or comparison and, based on the result of that decision or comparison, to select one of two paths; also called the selection structure. (4)

design time — occurs when you are designing your application. (1)

direct access files — random access files. (7)

documentation — a printout of the form, the properties of the objects included in the form (called the form text), and the code. This information will help you understand and maintain the application in the future. (1)

drag — the process of holding down the left mouse button as you move the mouse in a drag-and-drop operation. (10)

drop — releasing the mouse button in order to end a drag operation. (10)

error handler — the set of instructions that tell an application how to handle an error; also called an error-handling routine. (10)

error-handling routine — the set of instructions that tell an application how to handle an error; also called an error handler. (10)

error trapping — the process of intercepting and handling a run-time error. (10)

event — an action, such as a click, a double-click, or a scroll. (1)

event procedure — the program instructions that tell an object how to respond to an event. (1)

expression — any combination of variables, constants, functions, operators, and properties. (5)

extended selection structure — the Case structure. (5)

field — a single item of information about a person, place, or thing (for example, a social security number, a city, or a price); also called a data element. (6)

field variable — a variable within a record variable. (7)

fixed-length records — the records in a random access file. (7)

floating-point number — a number that is expressed as a multiple of some power of 10. (3)

flowlines — the lines connecting the symbols in a flowchart. (3)

focus — indicated by either a highlighted caption or border, it means that the control is ready to receive input from you. (2)

font — the general shape of the characters in the text. (1)

form-level variable — a variable declared in a form's general Declarations section. (3)

form-level procedure — a procedure that is available only to the form in which it is defined and to other procedures in that form. (9)

Form window — the window in which you design the user interface for your application. (1)

function — a predefined procedure that performs a specific task. Unlike a method, a function results in a value. (2)

gap — the distance between the values to be compared in a Shell sort. (9)

global constant — a constant that can be referred to by every procedure in every form and module in the project. (7)

global variable — a variable declared in the general Declarations section of a code module. (3)

GUI — graphical user interface. (O)

high-level language — a computer programming language that uses instructions that more closely resemble the English language. (O)

incrementing — adding a number to the value stored in a counter or an accumulator; also called updating. (6)

index — the unique number assigned to each of the controls in a control array. (5)

initializing — assigning a beginning value to a variable or the property of a control. (3, 6)

Input — one of three sequential access file modes. You open a file for Input when you want to read its contents. (6)

input/output symbol — the flowchart symbol (a parallelogram) that is used to represent input tasks (such as getting information from the user) and output tasks (such as displaying information). (3)

integer — a whole number, which means a number without any decimal places. (3)

internal documentation — the explanatory messages that programmers enter into the Code window. (2)

interpreter — a program that translates high-level language instructions into machine code, line by line, as the program is running. (O)

keyword — a word that has a specific meaning in a programming language. (5)

length check — the data validation check that verifies that the user entered the required number of characters. (10)

local variable — a variable declared in an event procedure; its use is limited to only the procedure in which it is declared. (3)

looping — the repetition structure. (5)

machine code — instructions written in 0s and 1s; also called machine language. (O)

machine language — instructions written in 0s and 1s; also called machine code. (O)

menu bar — displays the commands you can use to build your application. (1)

menu items — the options listed in a menu. (9)

method — a predefined Visual Basic procedure. (2)

mnemonics — the alphabetic abbreviations used in assembly languages; mnemonics serve as memory aids for instructions. (O)

Modal — describes a window that requires the user to take some action before the focus can switch to another form or dialog box. (10)

Modeless — describes a window that does not require the user to take any action before the focus can switch to another form or dialog box. The Code window is an example of a modeless window. (10)

nested loop — a loop that is contained entirely within another loop. (8)

newline character — Chr(13) & Chr(10); this character instructs Visual Basic to issue a carriage return followed by a line feed. (9)

null string — a zero-length string; it is a set of quotation marks with nothing between them, like this: "". (2)

Object box — the box that is located immediately below the Properties window's title bar; it displays the name of the selected object. (1)

object-oriented/event-driven language — a programming language in which the emphasis of a program is on the *objects* included in the user interface (such as scroll bars and buttons) and the *events* that occur on those objects (such as scrolling and clicking). Visual Basic, SmallTalk, and C++ are popular object-oriented/event-driven languages. (O)

Output — one of three sequential access file modes. You open a file for Output when you want to create a new sequential access file and then write data to it. (If the file already exists, Visual Basic erases its contents before writing the new information.) (6)

parallel arrays — arrays whose controls are related by their position in the arrays (in other words, by their index). (5, 9)

parameter — a piece of information passed to a procedure or function; also called an argument. (5)

pass — one complete time through an array that is being sorted. (9)

passed by reference — the actual memory address of an argument (parameter) is passed to the receiving procedure. (10)

passed by value — only the value of the argument (parameter) is passed to the receiving procedure, not its actual address in memory. (10)

path — the designation of the location of files or directories on a disk. (10)

point — 1/72 of an inch; the size of a font is measured in points. (1)

posttest loop — a loop that evaluates (tests) the *condition* after processing the instructions within the loop; the Do...Until loop is a posttest loop. (6)

pretest loop — a loop that evaluates (tests) the *condition* before processing any of the instructions within the loop; the Do...While loop and the For...Next loop are pretest loops. (6)

procedure-oriented language — a programming language in which the emphasis of the program is on *how* to accomplish a task. The programmer determines and controls the order in which the computer should process the instructions. COBOL, BASIC, Pascal, and C are popular procedure-oriented languages. (O)

process symbol — the flowchart symbol (a rectangle) used to represent tasks such as declaring variables, clearing information from the screen, assigning values to variables and to the properties of controls, setting the focus, and for calculations. (3)

program — the directions given to a computer. (O)

program code — the Visual Basic program instructions that tell the objects how to respond when scrolled, clicked, and so on. (2)

program file — a file that contains the instructions that create the user interface and tell the objects how to respond to events. (6)

programmer — a person who writes computer programs. (O)

programming language — the means by which a programmer communicates with a computer. (O)

properties — the set of characteristics associated with each Visual Basic object that control the object's appearance and behavior. (1)

Properties list — the two columns located in the Properties window. The left column displays all the properties associated with the selected object and the right column displays the current value, or setting, of each of those properties. (1)

Properties window — the window that contains the Object box, the Settings box, and the Properties list. (1)

pseudocode — the English-like statements that programmers use to help them plan the steps that an object will need to take in order to perform its assigned task. (2)

range check — the data validation check that verifies that the input data falls within a specific range. (10)

receiving parameter — a parameter in a Sub statement. (9)

receiving procedure — a procedure that receives one or more parameters. (10)

record — a group of related fields that contain all of the necessary data about a specific person, place, or thing. (6)

record number — the unique number assigned to each record in a random access file; the record number indicates the record's position in the file. (7)

record structure — the names, data types, and lengths of the fields in the record; a user-defined data type. (7)

record variable — a variable declared as a user-defined data type. (7)

scope — indicates which procedures in the application can use a variable. (3)

selection structure — the programming structure used to make a decision or comparison and, based on the result of that decision or comparison, to select one of two paths; also called the decision structure. (4)

sending parameter — a parameter in the Call statement; this type of parameter is sent to a sub procedure. (9)

sending procedure — a procedure that sends one or more parameters. (10)

separator bar — the horizontal line used to separate menu items. (9)

sequential processing — one of three programming structures; also referred to as the sequence structure. In sequential processing, the instructions are processed, one after another, in the order in which they are entered in the Code window. (1)

sequence structure — one of three programming structures; also referred to as sequential processing. In the sequence structure, the instructions are processed, one after another, in the order in which they are entered in the Code window. (1)

Settings box — the box that is located immediately above the Properties list; it shows the current setting, or value, of the selected property. (1)

shortcut keys — the keys, displayed to the right of a menu item, that allow you to select a menu item without opening the menu. (9)

simple variable — a variable that does not belong to an array. (8)

sorting — arranging information in either alphabetical or numerical order. (6, 8, 9)

sort key — the field on which you want to sort. (9)

source — the control being dragged in a drag-and-drop operation. (10)

start/stop oval — the flowchart symbol that identifies the beginning and ending of the flowchart. (3)

startup form — the form that Visual Basic loads automatically when a project is run. (7)

string — a group of characters enclosed in quotation marks. (2)

sub procedure — a block of code that performs a specific task; also called a subroutine. (1)

subroutine — a block of code that performs a specific task; also called a sub procedure. (1)

subroutine box — the flowchart symbol (a rectangle with side borders) that represents a call to a sub procedure. (10)

subscript — the unique number assigned to each of the variables in a variable array. (8)

symbolic constant — a memory location whose contents cannot be changed while the program is running; created with Visual Basic's Const statement. (3, 7)

syntax — the rules of a language. (1)

system modal — describes a window in which all applications are suspended until the user responds to a message. (10)

target — the object on which a control is dropped in a drag-and-drop operation. (10)

toolbar — the icons located below the menu bar; the icons provide quick access to the most commonly used menu commands. (1)

Toolbox — contains the set of tools you use when designing a Visual Basic application. (1)

Truth Table — a table that indicates how Visual Basic evaluates the logical operators in an expression. (4)

twip — 1/1440 of an inch; the location of an object in a form is measured in twips from the edges of the form. (1)

type check — the data validation check that verifies that the input data is the correct type. (10)

undeclared variable — a variable whose name does not appear in a Dim statement. (3)

updating — adding a number to the value stored in a counter or an accumulator; also called incrementing. (6)

user-defined data type — a data type created by the user that is separate and distinct from Visual Basic's standard data types; a record structure. (7)

user interface — what you see and interact with when running a Windows application. (1)

Val function — the function that converts a character string into a numeric value. (2)

variable — a memory location inside the computer whose contents can change as the program is running. (3)

variable array — a group of variables that have the same name and data type and are related in some way. (8)

variable-length records — the records in a sequential access file. (7)

Index

C

D

E

H

W

Z

Microsoft Software License
Microsoft® Visual Basic® Programming System for Windows™
Visual Basic 2.0 Primer Edition

READ THIS FIRST. Your use of the Microsoft software (the "SOFTWARE") is governed by the legal agreement below.

BY OPENING THE SEALED DISKETTE PACKAGE YOU ARE AGREEING TO BE BOUND BY THE TERMS AND CONDITIONS SET BELOW. IF YOU DO NOT AGREE WITH SUCH TERMS AND CONDITIONS, YOU SHOULD RETURN THE UNOPENED DISKETTE PACKAGE TOGETHER WITH THE BOOK TO THE PLACE YOU OBTAINED THEM FOR A REFUND.

1. GRANT OF LICENSE. Microsoft grants to you the right to use one copy of the enclosed SOFTWARE on a single terminal connected to a single computer (i.e. with a single CPU). You must not network the SOFTWARE or otherwise use it on more than one computer or computer terminal at the same time.

2. COPYRIGHT. The SOFTWARE is owned by Microsoft or its suppliers and is protected by United States copyright laws and international treaty provisions. Therefore, you must treat the SOFTWARE like any other copyrighted material (e.g. a BOOK or musical recording) except that you may either (a) make a copy of the SOFTWARE solely for backup or archival purposes, or (b) transfer the SOFTWARE to a single hard disk provided you keep the original solely for backup or archival purposes. You may not copy the written materials.

3. OTHER RESTRICTIONS. You may not rent or lease the SOFTWARE, but you may transfer the SOFTWARE and written materials on a permanent basis provided you retain no copies and the recipient agrees to the terms of this Agreement. You may not reverse engineer, decompile, or disassemble the SOFTWARE.

DISCLAIMER OF WARRANTY AND LIMITED WARRANTY

THE SOFTWARE AND ACCOMPANYING WRITTEN MATERIALS (INCLUDING INSTRUCTIONS FOR USE) ARE PROVIDED "AS IS" WITHOUT WARRANTY OF ANY KIND. FURTHER, MICROSOFT DOES NOT WARRANT, GUARANTEE, OR MAKE ANY REPRESENTATIONS REGARDING THE USE, OR THE RESULTS OF USE, OR THE SOFTWARE OR WRITTEN MATERIALS IN TERMS OF CORRECTNESS, ACCURACY, RELIABILITY, CORRECTNESS, OR OTHERWISE. THE ENTIRE RISK AS TO THE RESULTS AND PERFORMANCE OF THE SOFTWARE IS ASSUMED BY YOU. IF THE SOFTWARE OR WRITTEN MATERIALS ARE DEFECTIVE, YOU, AND NOT MICROSOFT OR ITS DEALERS, DISTRIBUTORS, AGENTS, OR EMPLOYEES, ASSUME THE ENTIRE COST OF ALL NECESSARY SERVICING, REPAIR, OR CORRECTION.

Microsoft warrants to the original LICENSEE that (a) the disk on which the SOFTWARE is recorded is free from defects in materials and workmanship under normal use and service for a period of ninety (90) days from the date of delivery as evidenced by a copy of the receipt. Further, Microsoft hereby limits the duration of any implied warranty(ies) on the disk to the respective periods stated above. Some states do not allow limitations on duration of an implied warranty, so the above limitation may not apply to you.

Microsoft's entire liability and your exclusive remedy as to the disk shall be at Microsoft's option, either (a) return of the purchase price or (b) replacement of the disk that does not meet Microsoft's Limited Warranty which is returned to Course Technology, Inc. with a copy of the receipt. If failure of the disk has resulted from accident, abuse, or misapplication, Microsoft shall have no responsibility to replace the disk or refund the purchase price. Any replacement disk will be warranted for the remainder of the original warranty period or thirty (30) days, whichever is longer.

NO OTHER WARRANTIES. MICROSOFT DISCLAIMS ALL OTHER WARRANTIES, EITHER EXPRESS OR IMPLIED, INCLUDING BUT NOT LIMITED TO IMPLIED WARRANTIES OF MERCHANTABILITY AND FITNESS FOR A PARTICULAR PURPOSE, WITH RESPECT TO THE SOFTWARE AND ANY ACCOMPANYING HARDWARE. THIS LIMITED WARRANTY GIVES YOU SPECIFIC LEGAL RIGHTS. YOU MAY HAVE OTHERS, WHICH VARY FROM STATE TO STATE.

NO LIABILITIES FOR CONSEQUENTIAL DAMAGES. IN NO EVENT SHALL MICROSOFT OR ITS SUPPLIERS BE LIABLE FOR ANY DAMAGES WHATSOEVER (INCLUDING WITHOUT LIMITATION DAMAGES FOR LOSS OF BUSINESS PROFITS, BUSINESS INTERRUPTION, LOSS OF BUSINESS INFORMATION, OR OTHER PECUNIARY LOSS) ARISING OUT OF THE USE OR INABILITY TO USE THIS MICROSOFT PRODUCT EVEN IF MICROSOFT HAS BEEN ADVISED OF THE POSSIBILITY OF SUCH DAMAGES. BECAUSE SOME STATES DO NOT ALLOW THE EXCLUSION OR LIMITATION OF LIABILITY FOR CONSEQUENTIAL OR INCIDENTAL DAMAGES, THE ABOVE LIMITATION MAY NOT APPLY TO YOU.

U.S. GOVERNMENT RESTRICTED RIGHTS

The software and any associated Microsoft documentation is provided with RESTRICTED RIGHTS. Use, duplication, or disclosure by the Government is subject to restrictions as set forth in subparagraph (c)(1)(ii) of the Rights in Technical Data and Computer Software clause at DFARS 252.227-7013 or subparagraphs (c)(1) and (2) of 48 CFR 52.227-19, as applicable. Contractor/manufacturer is Microsoft Corporation/One Microsoft Way/Redmond, WA 98052-6399.

This Agreement is governed by the laws of the State of Washington.

This program was reproduced by Course Technology, Inc. under a special arrangement with Microsoft Corporation. For this reason, Course Technology, Inc. is responsible for the product warranty and for support. If your diskette is defective, please return it to Course Technology, Inc., which will arrange for its replacement. PLEASE DO NOT RETURN IT TO MICROSOFT CORPORATION. Any product support will be provided, if at all, by Course Technology, Inc. PLEASE DO NOT CONTACT MICROSOFT CORPORATION FOR PRODUCT SUPPORT. End users of this Microsoft program shall not be considered "registered owners" of a Microsoft product and therefore shall not be eligible for upgrades, promotions, or other benefits available to "registered owners" of Microsoft products.